'In this superb biography of J. M. W. Turner,
Bailey explores the evolution of Britain's
greatest artist from an accomplished technician
… into a visionary genius'
Independent

'Excellent'
Mail on Sunday

'An enthralling and meticulously researched
biography that displays Bailey's talent
for bringing the past vividly to life'
Publishers Weekly

'A splendid book'
Time Out

'A cracking good biography'
Financial Times

'A thorough, careful biography … Bailey
gradually illuminates the artist's character'
Kirkus Reviews

About the author

Anthony Bailey was born in Portsmouth, Hampshire, in 1933. During the Second World War he was evacuated by ship across the Atlantic and spent four years in Dayton, Ohio. After military service with the West African Frontier Force and a history degree from Oxford University, he lived for fifteen years in the United States. For many years he was a writer for *The New Yorker* magazine. His many pieces of reporting, short stories, poems and criticism have appeared in that magazine and in the *New Republic* in the USA and in the *Observer*, *Sunday Times*, *Spectator*, and *New Statesman* in Britain. He is the author of twenty-three books, which include novels, memoirs and biographies. Now living on Mersea Island, on the North Sea coast of East Anglia, he is married, with four daughters and nine grandchildren.

Standing
in the Sun

By the same author

FICTION
Making Progress
The Mother Tongue
Major André

NON-FICTION
The Inside Passage
Through the Great City
The Thousand Dollar Yacht
The Light in Holland
In the Village
A Concise History of the Low Countries
Rembrandt's House
Acts of Union
Along the Edge of the Forest
Spring Jaunts
The Outer Banks
A Walk Through Wales
The Coast of Summer
Responses to Rembrandt
A View of Delft: Vermeer Then & Now
John Constable: A Kingdom of His Own
Velázquez and The Surrender of Breda

AUTOBIOGRAPHY
America, Lost & Found
England, First & Last

Standing in the Sun

A LIFE OF J. M. W. TURNER

Anthony Bailey

Tate Publishing

This edition first published 2013
by order of the Tate Trustees
by Tate Publishing, a division of Tate Enterprises Ltd,
Millbank, London SW1P 4RG
www.tate.org.uk/publishing

First published 1997 by Sinclair-Stevenson, London

A catalogue record for this book is available from the British Library

ISBN 978 1 84976 192 5

Distributed in the United States and Canada by ABRAMS, New York
Library of Congress Control Number applied for

Designed by Esterson Associates, London
Reproduction by D.L. Interactive Ltd
Printed in Spain by Grafos S.A., Barcelona

Cover: details from Turner's *Self-Portrait* c.1799

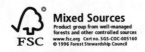

To the memory of
Cowper Goldsmith Bailey
and Phyllis Maud Bailey

Contents

List of Illustrations xii
Preface xv
Chronology xx
Map xxii
1 Mere Beginnings 1
2 Up and Coming 17
3 Rising Star 42
4 Fair Winds and Foul 63
5 Aladdin's Cave 76
6 Golden Apples, Silver Thames 89
7 Boxing Harry 106
8 The Bite of the Print 121
9 Deep Puzzles 143
10 Crossing the Brook 165
11 Sir George Thinks Otherwise 188
12 Dear Fawkes 205
13 The Squire of Sandycombe 224
14 Southern Light 244
15 Figures on the Shore 268
16 Varnishing Days 286
17 Liberty Hall 305
18 Home and Away 323
19 The Rigours of Winter 348
20 Chelsea Harbour 367
21 World's End 392
22 Turner's Gift 404
Appendix 419
Notes 421
Bibliography 454
Index 461

List of Illustrations

Between pp.216 and 217
All photographs of the works illustrated are copyright of the owners, unless otherwise stated.

George Dance Jr (1741–1825), *Portrait of J. M. W. Turner*, dated 4 August 1792, pencil and watercolour on paper, oval 21.6 × 16 cm. Private collection. Photo: courtesy Sotheby's Picture Library, London

J. M. W. Turner (1775–1851), *Self-Portrait*, c. 1799, oil on canvas, 74.3 × 58.4 cm. Tate

Charles Turner (1773–1857), *'A Sweet Temper': Portrait of J. M. W. Turner*, c. 1795, graphite on paper, 18.4 × 11.6 cm. The Trustees of the British Museum

J. M. W. Turner, *Study of the Head of a Woman wearing a Ruched Cap, Looking Down* (probably Mary Turner, Turner's mother), from *'Marford Mill' sketchbook*, c.1794, graphite on paper, 15.2 × 9.9 cm. Tate

John Linnell (1792–1882), *Portrait Study of J. M. W. Turner's Father, with a Sketch of Turner's Eyes, Made during a Lecture*, 1812, graphite on paper, 18.7 × 22.5 cm. Tate

John Wykeham Archer (1808–1864), *26 Maiden Lane (Birthplace of J. M. W. Turner) and Entrance to Hand Court*, 1852, watercolour on paper 35.5 × 22.2 cm. The Trustees of the British Museum

47 Queen Anne Street. An engraved illustration from the *Art-Journal*, c. 1852

'Road Leading to the Fort', from the book *Picture of Margate and its Vicinity, by W.C. Oulton, Esq., illustrated with a map and twenty views engraved by J. J. Shury, from Drawings by Captain G. Varlo, R.M.*, London, 1820. Margate Local History Museum, Margate. Photo: courtesy Anthony Lee

After William Havell (1782–1857), *Sandycombe Lodge, Twickenham, Villa of J. M. W. Turner*, engraved by W.B. Cooke, published 1814, engraving on paper. Tate

Francis Hawkesworth Fawkes (1797–1871), *Caricature of J. M. W. Turner*, c. 1818, ink and graphite on paper, 31.8 × 26. Indianapolis Museum of Art

S. W. Parrott (1830–after 1891), *Turner on Varnishing Day*, c. 1840, oil on canvas 25.1 × 22.9 cm. The Collection of the Guild of St George, Sheffield. (This picture is generally dated to 1846 but Ian Warrell has noted that it appears to record Turner at work on the first of his square canvases, *Bacchus and Ariadne*, exhibited at the Royal Academy in 1840). Photo: The Bridgeman Art Library

John Wykeham Archer, *Turner's House at Chelsea*, 1852, watercolour on paper, 37.5 × 27.3 cm. The Trustees of the British Museum

After Count Alfred D'Orsay (1801–1852), *Portrait of J. M. W. Turner ('The Fallacy of Hope')*, engraved by J. Hogarth, published 1851, lithograph on paper, 32.8 × 22.5 cm. Tate

Turner's death mask (attributed to Thomas Woolner), 1851, plaster cast, 25.4 cm high. National Portrait Gallery, London

Preface

Turner's friend and colleague C. R. Leslie remembered him thus:

> Turner was short and stout, and had a sturdy, sailor-like walk.
> There was, in fact, nothing elegant in his appearance. He might
> be taken for the captain of a river steamboat at a first glance; but a
> second would find far more in his face than belongs to any ordinary
> mind. There was that peculiar keenness of expression in his eye that
> is only seen in men of constant habits of observation.[1]

Like many keen observers, Turner was not keen on being observed.
Friends found it hard to penetrate his domestic existence. Women
were sometimes on hand but not introduced. He assumed names
that were not his own. Like an animal, he adopted a defensive
posture part of the time. He was absorbed by painting, and by
making drawing after drawing as raw material for painting; but he
also made frequent appearances at the Royal Academy, often to serve
dutifully, sometimes – it seemed – to perform flamboyantly. After
periods secure in his studio, he emerged to spend days in the country
homes of a few good patrons or to go on an afternoon's excursion
with his fellow painters. He was churlish one moment, helpful
the next. Some people found him tight-fisted, others extremely (if
taciturnly) generous. He was both lonely and gregarious, private and
vainglorious. He was a confused speaker, a muddled writer, and an
artist – sometimes touchingly precise, sometimes blazingly free –
who could with a grunt and a gesture suggest to a colleague what
was wrong with his work and how to put it right. His contradictions
have puzzled many, but they endear him to me. He was and is a
challenge.

Biographers have bounced off Turner. Books about him abound,
but the most successful tend to be specialist studies like Cecilia
Powell's *Turner in the South* and David Hill's *Turner on the Thames*.

Nevertheless a comprehensive up-to-date biography of Turner has seemed to me worth tackling. I have felt grateful for the labours of Thornbury, Finberg and Lindsay, his main biographers to date, yet I remain greatly dissatisfied by their books. In the last few decades there has been a fine growth of Turner scholarship, visible in the periodicals *Turner Studies* and *Turner Society News*, by special exhibitions at the Tate Gallery and in works by, among others, Andrew Wilton, Eric Shanes, Selby Whittingham and John Gage. Gage's collection of Turner's correspondence is a tool earlier biographers had to do without.

One feeling prompted by Walter Thornbury's biography is that he presents much of the material in the wrong place; another is that some of the material has been pirated, and some is untrue. Thornbury's book was first published in two volumes in 1862 and reissued in a revised second edition in one volume in 1877. (I have relied mostly on the 1877 version, though where necessary I have given references to the first.) Thornbury, a London journalist, recognized Turner as a good story. He had access to many people who had known Turner well, he had Ruskin's encouragement, and he produced a hodgepodge of a book full of excellent anecdotes and improbable suggestions. It was, as Robert Leslie (son of C. R. Leslie) pointed out, 'a sort of hashed-up life of Brown, Jones, and Robinson, with badly done bits of Turner floating about in it'.[2] A major problem in using Thornbury has been in deciding what is accurate and what is not. I have been considerably helped by access to a copy of the first edition, at the time the property of Professor Francis Haskell, which earlier belonged to Turner's friend (and executor) George Jones. (This has now been given by Professor Haskell to the Tate Gallery.) Jones collected responses to Thornbury by other friends and colleagues, for example John Pye, Hugh Munro and David Roberts, and inserted some of their remarks at the appropriate places in the work; he also made his own marginal notes. So these denials and dissents and expressions of outrage have been valuable. Where they were missing, I have generally given Thornbury the benefit of the doubt, though remaining aware of his habit of taking a small fact and then elaborating it, the result being three-quarters invention.

The rewards (and the problems) of A. J. Finberg's heroic chronicle biography of 1939 (revised second edition 1961) are different. For Turner's painting career, his life as an Academician and the reactions of his contemporaries to his work, Finberg's book is still first rate, though some of the details can now be quibbled with. However, the laborious chronological method tends to leave the reader groping for the major themes – something Thornbury had intended to express in his own book, as shown by his chapter titles, but had failed to deliver. Moreover, Finberg shied away from Turner as a human being with human appetites, and got some crucial biographical facts wrong. (For an academic work, his book is also very sparse with references and notes.) But, as Lawrence Gowing noted, there were benefits in the disadvantages: 'Finberg's inclination was philosophical. For enjoyment he would retire to bed with a volume of Hegel, and he appreciated an intellectual grandeur in Turner that is commonly overlooked.'[3]

Gratitude and exasperation remain the keynotes of one's response to the most recent critical biography, now thirty years old, by Jack Lindsay. Lindsay has much of interest to say about Turner's poetry and Turner's readings in such poets as James Thomson and Mark Akenside. His reflections on Turner's inner life are sometimes full of insight and sometimes simplistic, expressed in modish psychoanalytic language. Of other biographies: Bernard Falk's 1938 *Turner the Painter: His Hidden Life* combines a tabloid style, a prurient approach and much speculation with some nuggets of private history derived from Turner family documents. Cosmo Monkhouse's deliberately modest brief life of 1879 distils various sources and both uses and corrects Thornbury; it remains valuable. The great Turner biographer *manqué* was, of course, John Ruskin. Instead the world got the five volumes of *Modern Painters*, in which Turner was the inspiration for a massive reverie on art, a splendid if somewhat indigestible soup with well-done bits of Turner floating in it.

I have attempted to look at almost all of Turner's sketchbooks and many of his watercolours and paintings. I have tried to see at first hand the primary documents to do with his life and those close to him: records of birth, marriage, property ownership and death, in rate books and parish registers and family papers. I have found a few facts that seem hitherto to have gone unnoticed – for example, regarding the date of the death of Turner's little sister – and have, I think, put together some known, previously disparate facts to shed new light here and there. At one point, when looking into the location of Cowley Hall, the home of a Turner host (and Thornbury informant) Thomas Rose, I became aware that well ahead of me in Turner detective work was Selby Whittingham, and I have been consequently grateful for his researches into the nooks and crannies of the Turner, Marshall and Danby families, and into Turner's various wills and testaments. My aim has been to produce a work of synthesis, one which pulls together material old and new, which juxtaposes facts in a way that creates a better-rounded portrait of the man. It is a project of collaboration, as it were, with the work of my many predecessors and of contemporary scholars, not trying to repeat everything they have said but winnowing and rearranging the many details to make a truthful and evocative picture. I hope the Turner who emerges is a little more living, at one with the elements but with his feet on the ground.

This is the biography of an artist rather than a work of art history. In writing about Turner's pictures, I have tried to bear in mind what Turner said in response to Ruskin's writings: 'He knows a great deal more about my pictures than I do. He puts things into my head, and points out meanings in them I never intended.'[4] And there are other voices one should listen to. Among them are those of Claude Debussy, who called Turner 'the finest creator of mystery in the whole of art',[5] and Walter Sickert, who hailed Turner's 'inexhaustible toughness'.[6]

I am indebted for much advice, help and encouragement. Among the many people I am grateful to are Fred Bachrach, Margot Bailey, David Bromwich, David Blaney Brown, Bernard Carter, Ann Chumbley, William Clarke, Lord Egremont, Gillian Forrester, Carolyn Hammond, Francis Haskell, Luke Herrmann, Nicholas Horton-Fawkes, Ralph Hyde, Samuel Hynes, Peter James, Evelyn Joll, Anne Lyles, Alison McCann, Pieter van der Merwe, Cecilia Powell, Judith Severne, Rosalind Turner, Ian Warrell, Selby Whittingham, Edward Yardley and Robert Yardley.

I have been assisted by the staffs of the archives and local history libraries at Canterbury, Chiswick, Margate, Chichester (West Sussex), Camden and Westminster (Victoria and Marylebone branches), the staffs of the London Library, Cambridge University Library, Guildhall and St Paul's Cathedral Libraries and the Study

Room of the Turner Collection at the Clore Gallery. And I thank the Masters and Fellows of Magdalene College, Cambridge, for their hospitality.

Illustrations for a book about an artist – especially one as prolific as Turner – pose a dilemma if the book is to be affordable. There are many books in print – for instance, Andrew Wilton's *Turner in his Time* – that provide fine coverage of Turner's work. I have tried to furnish here pictures that have a biographical relevance.

Author's Note for the 2013 edition

I am delighted that Tate Publishing is bringing out this new edition of *Standing in the Sun*, especially as Tate Britain is the home of the Turner Bequest, and houses the world's largest collection of Turner's work. The text has been freshly typeset but is otherwise unchanged from the 1997 edition except for a very few minor corrections. As before, illustrations have been selected for their biographical interest. However, for readers wishing to look at the artworks referred to, images of all the Turner paintings, watercolours and sketches in the Tate collection, along with many others in museums around the world, can be found on the 'Turner' pages of the Tate website (see www.tate.org.uk).

Chronology

1775	Baptised 14 May, St Paul's, Covent Garden. Parents living at 21 Maiden Lane
1783	Death of his sister Mary Ann
1785	To schools in Brentford and Margate
1787	First signed and dated drawings
1789	Admitted to RA Schools
1790	First watercolour exhibited at RA
1791	Travels in West Country
1792	Travels in West Country and Wales
1794	Working at Dr Monro's
1796	First oil exhibited at RA
1797	Tour of North of England
1798–9	Sarah Danby becomes his mistress
1799	Elected ARA. Moves from Maiden Lane to 64 Harley St
1800	His mother admitted to Bedlam
1801	19 Sept. Baptism of his daughter Evelina
1802	Elected RA. Visit to France and Switzerland
1804	Death of his mother. Opens his own gallery
1805–6	On the Thames at Isleworth
1806–11	On the Thames at Hammersmith
1807	Publication of *Liber Studiorum* part 1. Elected Professor of Perspective, RA
1808–24	Many visits to Walter Fawkes and family at Farnley Hall, near Leeds, Yorkshire
1811	First professorial lectures. Birth of his daughter Georgiana
1811 & 1813	Tours of the West Country
1813	Twickenham House finished
1815–16	Trips to North of England

1817	Trip to Belgium, Rhineland and Holland. Evelina married
1819	First visit to Italy. Fawkes's collection exhibited in London
1820–21	At work on his new house and gallery in Queen Anne St
1821	Trip to France
1824	First journey to the Meuse and Mosel. Tours of eastern and southeastern England
1825	Trip to Holland. Death of Walter Fawkes
1825–37	Many visits to Petworth House, Sussex
1828	Last perspective lectures at RA
1828–29	Second visit to Italy
1829	Death of his father
1829 & 1832	Tours for 'Rivers of France' project
1830	Tour of English Midlands
1831	Trip to Scotland
1833	European journey, to and from Venice
1834	Sees Houses of Parliament on fire
1830s	Frequently in Margate with Mrs Booth
1837	Death of Lord Egremont. Turner resigns as Professor of Perspective
1839	*The Fighting Temeraire*. Second Meuse and Mosel tour
1840	Meets John Ruskin. Trip to Venice
1841–44	Annual trips to Switzerland
1843	Death of Georgiana
1845	Last trip abroad, to northern France. Acting President of RA
1845–50	Continues to visit Kent coast
1846	Moves to Chelsea; 'Mr Booth'
1850	Last exhibits at RA
1851	19 December: death in Chelsea

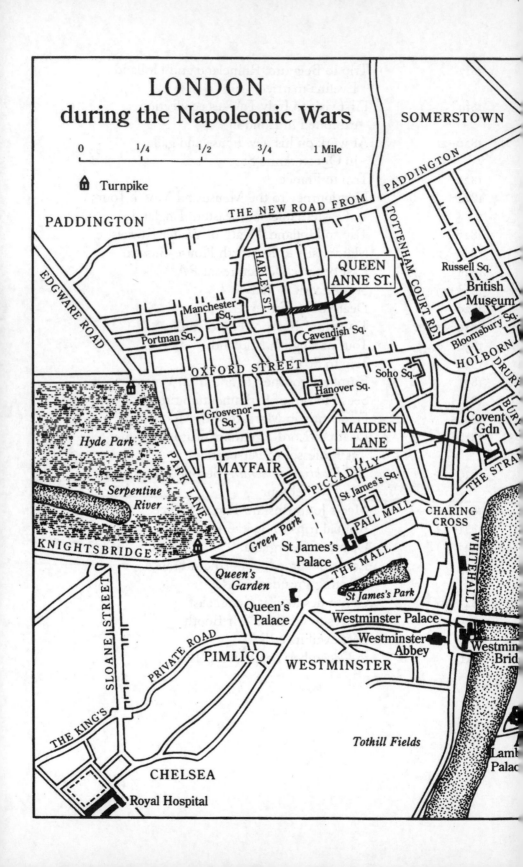

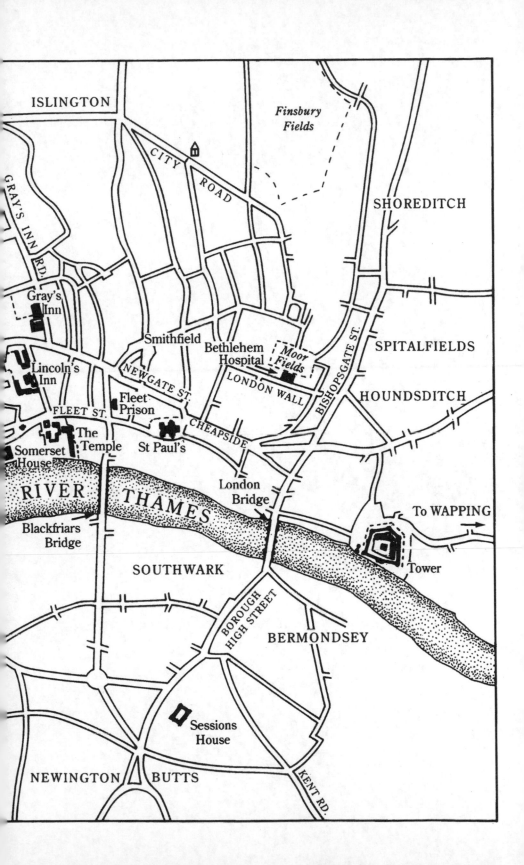

1: Mere Beginnings

From high above, the river winding through the city looked like a shining snake sliding under three bridges. The spring sun struck the tiles and slates of a hundred thousand damp rooftops and shimmered on the lead of spires, steeples, domes and belfries. Pigeons and seagulls circled in the hazy air, and a few spiralled down towards a large rectangular space among the buildings crowded on the north side of the river – a paved piazza where market stalls and barrows stood empty. Because it was Sunday, the only clamour came from the bells pealing in the broad-roofed church that stood at the west side of the Piazza: St Paul's, Covent Garden, London. On the path leading through the churchyard, a man and a woman carrying a well-swaddled baby walked towards the main door.

Sometimes, talking in later days about his origins, Turner bemused people by claiming that he was born in the country rather than the city. During a tour of the west of England in the 1810s, he went sailing on the St German's river with the journalist Cyrus Redding, and the names of various West Country artists were bandied about. Turner told Redding: 'You may add my name to the list. I am a Devonshire man.' And when Redding asked from what part of that county, Turner replied, 'From Barnstaple.'[1] Others heard him say that he hailed from Kent; one man to whom he made this claim believed that Turner did so simply out of fondness for the Medway valley. Some years on, his affection for Kent's Thanet coast, and particularly for Deal and Margate, was strongly expressed. Then, too, in later life he enjoyed mystifying the curious about his age. Andrew Wilson, a Scots painter, got the impression from Turner that, like Wilson himself, he was born in 1769, the year when Napoleon and the Duke of Wellington had been born. Causing confusion seemed to amuse Turner. It is perhaps not surprising that when he died in December

1851 his executors let him be buried in a coffin inscribed 'Aged 79', though he was most probably seventy-six. His death certificate gave his age as eighty-one, which would put his birth in 1770.

Turner's age remains slightly uncertain because when he was christened in St Paul's, Covent Garden, on that morning of 14 May 1775, the current practice in that parish was not to write a birthdate in the register. We depend on Turner himself, twenty-one years later, to affirm that the year was indeed 1775. In 1796 he exhibited a watercolour he had done of the interior of Westminster Abbey and used a floor-paving tombstone to flaunt his own name: 'William Turner, Natus 1775'.[2] In a codicil he signed on 20 August 1832 to a will made the year before, he gave the residue of his investments in Government Funds to the Royal Academy, subject to it holding a dinner for its members 'every year on the 23rd of April (my birthday)'.[3] So destiny – or the artist – chose the day which was Shakespeare's birthday and – for complete patriotic identification – St George's Day, the holy day of the patron saint of England.

In Inigo Jones's great barn of a church in Covent Garden on 14 May 1775 the presumably still infant boy was held over the font and christened Joseph Mallord William Turner by the Rector, James Tattersall. However, when it came to entering the child's three Christian names in the baptism register, the Reverend Tattersall wrote – misspelling the unusual second name – 'Joseph Mallad William, son of William Turner by Mary his wife'.[4] The future artist's difficulties with spelling and syntax seem to have a precursor here. But no other child in the register for that year had the honour of three Christian names. Although they were names common in his mother's family, it was as if his parents were declaring, rather than merely hoping as parents will, 'Our child is going to be somebody.'

It was in this same 140-year-old church that William Turner, bachelor aged twenty-eight, and Mary Marshall, spinster aged thirty-four, had been married twenty-one months before. The celebrant at the ceremony on 29 August 1773 was the curate, Ezekiel Rance; their witnesses were Ellis and Martha Price. Both parties to the marriage claimed to be 'of this parish', and had been living in it for at least four weeks. William Turner was indeed a Devon man – which may have inspired his son to claim the same tie. William Turner's father had been a saddler in the Devon village of South Molton, ten miles from the coastal town of Barnstaple, and William was born in South Molton on 29 June 1745. He was twenty when his father died and left him, the second son, his best white dress coat and – like his six siblings – the sum of one guinea when he reached the age of twenty-one. William's brother John, also a saddler, achieved the locally influential position of governor of the Barnstaple workhouse; another brother, Jonathan, was a baker. William became a barber and perruquier or wig-dresser, and at some point made his way to the metropolis, where he met and wooed Mary Marshall. He was described by one who knew him as a shortish man with 'small blue eyes, parrot nose, projecting chin, and a fresh complexion'. He 'talked fast ... [with] a peculiar transatlantic twang ... and a smile was always on his countenance'.[5]

Six years older than her West Country lover, Mary Marshall had perhaps reached an age when she could no longer wait for a better match. There is a suggestion that, although she too came from a background of artisans and small tradesmen, the Marshalls had grander ideas of themselves than the Turners. Her father, also a William, was a 'salesman' of Islington, a village then just north of the city of London. One brother, Joseph Mallord William Marshall, became a butcher in Brentford, a village eight miles west of Maiden Lane. (Mallord was the surname of her maternal grandfather, an Islington butcher.) An elder sister of Mary's married a curate, the Reverend Henry Harpur, which indicates that the family had some social ambitions.[6]

For the time being Covent Garden was the centre of young William's world. The hairdresser and his wife set up home at 21 Maiden Lane, a narrow three-storey brick house in a tight little street not far from the Piazza. William Turner senior's name first appears in the Poor Rate Collector's Books of St Paul's parish for the period from Lady Day (25 March) 1774 to Lady Day 1775. It appears again in the following year, 1775–6, with the rateable value, based on annual rent, of £30, and rates of £2. But then 'William Turner' disappears from the St Paul's books, not to reappear for twenty years, and then in relation to 26 Maiden Lane, a property more or less opposite, on the north side of the street. However, it seems likely that unless the family moved to Devon for a while after 1776, partly validating the artist's later claim, they went on living in the Covent Garden neighbourhood; the barber may have been a tenant or subtenant rather than leaseholder, and his landlord paid the rates. (In the rate books, some entries record 'Paid for tenants' without mentioning the tenants' names.) The Turners may well have been at number 21, and then number 26, as other evidence will imply, for longer than the rate books indicate.

Covent Garden was no longer the district of high fashion it had been 140 years before. The porticoed buildings of the Piazza, designed by Inigo Jones for his patron the Earl of Bedford, were intended to attract 'persons of great distinction', and three earls were among the first residents. In the thirteenth century the monks of Westminster Abbey had an orchard here, the convent garden. In the seventeenth century the area was gradually developed and the fields around St Martin's church built over. An informal market flourished for a time before the Earl of Bedford received a royal charter in 1671 to hold one. By the latter part of the eighteenth century it was 'the greatest market in England for herbs, fruits, and flowers'.[7] Carts and wagons poured in from the countryside in the small hours and unloaded at the sheds and stalls in the Piazza. By dawn light it was a boisterous scene, with the dealers crying their wares. By 7 a.m., most of the fruit and vegetables had been sold, though much litter remained.

The market had an impact on the social tone, for the neighbourhood changed. The elegant people moved west, and tradesmen, lodging-house keepers and artists moved in. Among the artists who lived in or near the Piazza were John Hoskins, the Fleming Remigius van Leemput, Samuel Cooper, Francis Clein, Sir Peter Lely, Sir Godfrey Kneller, Sir James Thornhill, his son-in-law William Hogarth, Samuel Scott and Richard Wilson. Covent Garden's raffish reputation grew with the opening of theatres, gaming houses and low taverns evocatively called 'night-cellars'. These caused an influx of 'notorious characters', so the local tradesmen said. They appealed to Westminster Sessions in 1730 about 'frequent outcries in the night, fighting, robberies, and all sorts of debaucheries ... all night long'.[8] Sir John Fielding, who succeeded his novelist half-brother Henry as Bow Street magistrate in 1780, complained of all the 'brothels and irregular houses' in the area. Although, thanks to high corn prices, the worst of the cheap gin drinking age was past, Sir John thought enforcement of licensing laws too lax, and he condemned those, selling spirits from chandlers' shops, 'who are permitted to vend … this liquid fire by which men drink their hell beforehand'.[9]

The increasing number of dubious lodging houses and 'bagnios' added to Covent Garden's notoriety. At some bagnios a customer could obtain a room and a meal and use the 'sweating and bathing facilities'; at some he could get more. One writer in 1776 pro claimed Covent Garden 'the great square of Venus, and its purlieus are crowded with the votaries of this goddess … The jelly-houses are now become the resort of abandoned rakes and shameless prostitutes. These and the taverns afford an ample supply of provisions for the flesh; while others abound for the consummation of the desires which are thus excited.'[10]

Crime, of course, was a by-product of these conditions: Exeter Street, Change Court, Eagle Court and Little Catherine Street were 'infamous', according to Sir John. Some alleys and rookeries off Long Acre and St Martin's Lane were particularly dangerous for pedestrians, but James Boswell had his handkerchief picked out of his pocket while walking down the Strand, the broad former riverfront street that bounded Covent Garden to the south. In the Strand was the Spread Eagle, a hostelry much favoured by young men after the theatre, whose landlord once remarked that 'his was a very uncommon set of customers, for what with hangings, drownings, and sudden deaths, he had a change every six months'.[11] However, towards the end of the century night-crime was reduced by the new oil-burning parish lamps, set up in all Westminster streets.

Although Turner grew up in what would now be called a red-light district, plenty of ordinary life and business went on. Many inns and chop-houses served respectable clients. The Turk's Head, where the Reverend James Woodforde (in town from his Norfolk parish) supped and slept, stood in the Strand opposite Catherine Street, just to the west of Somerset House, and 'was kept by one Mrs Smith, a widow, and a good motherly kind of woman'.[12] Printsellers and bookdealers favoured this part of town. Tom Davies kept a bookshop at 8 Russell Street, where on 16 May 1763 Boswell first met Dr Samuel Johnson. John Raphael Smith, engraver, miniature-painter and printdealer, was in King Street. Among the district's merchants were several jewellers and publishers. A number of perruquiers, making or refurbishing wigs, worked in Henrietta and Tavistock Streets. Apart from William Turner in Maiden Lane, a

John Turner (no relation) had a hair dressing business in nearby Exeter Street. The rate books reveal the presence of several other Turners in the area.

Maiden Lane, the scene of Turner's infancy and of part at least of his childhood and youth, was lined with mostly three-storey houses with cellars beneath. The street was formed from an old pathway through the convent garden, and in winter its narrowness made it hard for the sun to penetrate to the lower floors. When first laid out in 1631, the Lane was a cul-de-sac at its east end, but a foot passage through to Southampton Street was created in the mid-eighteenth century, and this was widened to the width of the rest of the Lane a hundred years later. Like most streets in the neighbourhood it had artistic associations. Andrew Marvell had lodged there in 1677 and Voltaire in 1727–8, the latter at the White Peruke, a lodging house kept by an old French barber and wig maker. John Ireland, watchmaker and biographer of Hogarth, lived in Maiden Lane from 1769 to 1780. Judging by rateable values it was a middling sort of street, though one Maiden Lane ratepayer was excused having to pay the rates in 1784, 'being very poor'.

At the time of Turner's birth, number 21 had recently been separated from the larger premises of number 20 next door. At number 20 was an auction room that had been used by the Free Society of Artists for their annual exhibitions in 1765 and 1766, and from 1769 to 1773 by the Incorporated Society of Artists for an academy of painting, drawing and modelling. Artists who attended classes here included George Romney, Francis Wheatley, Henry Walton, Ozias Humphrey, and Joseph Farington, who was to have a part in Turner's story. In the basement beneath this room was a tavern called the Cider Cellar. Here theatregoers could drink and listen to music and singing before or after the play, while rubbing shoulders with such habitués as the silversmith J. Brasbridge, who liked going there to talk politics, and the classics don Richard Porson. Porson, the son of a Norfolk weaver, became professor of Greek at Cambridge but continued to live in London at the Temple and spend his often dishevelled nights in Covent Garden.

How much noise from the likes of Porson and company came through the party wall from the Cider Cellar, we can only guess. The Turners probably had their eating quarters in their own cellar, under the barber shop, and rooms for sleeping above. Here, or across the road at number 26, a small boy would have shuttled mostly between the two main theatres of below-stairs and ground floor: the kitchen fire and table, tended by his mother, and the barber's chair, served by his father. To us the trade of hairdresser may seem humble enough, but to a small child it would have been fascinating: jugs of hot water brought up from the kitchen range, soapsuds and froth and steam, the swish of the straight-edged razor being stropped on leather and the gleam of the blade, the strong smell of ungents, bay rum, cologne. And then there was all the paraphernalia of hot tongs, curling papers, braiding pins and crimping irons for the dressing of wigs, and the clouds of white powder.

The wigs were splendidly various: the old perukes and periwigs, the large bushy Busbys, Club-wigs, Story wigs with their five rows of curls, and Brown Georges favoured by the King. According to Walter Thornbury,

> A city gentleman or actor, about 1775, had three wigs; two being for ordinary wear, and of these one nicely powdered was brought by the barber every morning, when he came to shave the master of the family; and the third being a Sunday wig, which was taken away on the Friday and brought back on the Saturday. At spare times the barber would sit at his shop door, surrounded by his friends, while he wove flaxen curls on a dummy ... The scorching of wigs was ceaseless; the clash of tongs was continuous ...[13]

A day-to-day wig cost a guinea, but some wigs were so expensive they were worth stealing; ne'er-do-wells snatched them, even in daylight, from their wearers' heads.

But then fashions changed. William Turner no doubt heard from his West Country relatives that, deep in the shires, gentlemen were beginning to show their own hair, though parsons, lawyers, doctors, and even actors might still be bucking the trend. Fortunately, as wigs departed, the shaving business continued to flourish. Few gentlemen then shaved themselves. Men with beards were either Jews or Turks, or possibly eccentrics like Lord Rokeby; and it was only soldiers, returning from overseas, who wore a moustache.

William Turner seems to have had a fair business. Customers came to the shop or were visited at their nearby homes and in the local hostelries in Southampton Street and the Strand. His name does not appear in the registers of the Barbers and Surgeons Guild, in which young hairdressers were apprenticed; but perhaps he served his time and acquired his skills in less formal Devon circumstances. William Turner's thrifty nature gave rise to a story that he once pursued a customer down Maiden Lane to recover a halfpenny that he had omitted to charge for soap. One skill a successful hairdresser needed was that of keeping his customers amused, with a copy of the *Daily Advertiser* for those waiting and conversation that genially rattled on about the topics of the day.

When he was three and a half, young William acquired a sister. She was baptized at the parish church of St Paul's on 6 September 1778: 'Mary Ann, Daughter of William Turner by Mary his wife'.[14] By late-eighteenth and early-nineteenth-century standards, William and Mary Turner were unprolific. Many families at this time had a dozen children, not all of whom would have lived. The Turners may have had other children who were stillborn or died in infancy, but no record of them has been found. We know that Mary Ann did not quite reach her fifth birthday; once again St Paul's harboured the ceremony, which this time was tearful, with grieving parents and a perhaps bewildered eight-year-old boy. The burial is recorded on 8 August 1783: 'Mary Ann, daughter of William Turner'.[15]

Mary Turner was now forty-four. The effect of her little daughter's death must have been a great blow, even in a time when child mortality was high. Her temperament was anyway, it seems, never stable. Henry Syer Trimmer, eldest son of the Reverend Henry Scott Trimmer, Turner's good friend, later saw an unfinished portrait Turner had done of his mother, a picture – according to young Trimmer's reporter, Thornbury – which was

> one of his first attempts ... There was a strong likeness to Turner about the nose and eyes; her eyes being represented as blue, of a lighter hue than her son's; her nose aquiline, and the nether lip having a slight fall. Her hair was well frizzed – for which she might have been indebted to her husband's professional skill – and it was surmounted by a cap with large flappers. Her posture ... was erect, and her aspect masculine, not to say fierce; and this impression of her character was confirmed by report, which proclaimed her to have been a person of ungovernable temper, and to have led her husband a sad life.[16]

The boy, now the sole surviving child, took refuge in his own amusements: drawing was one such, early noticed. It was recalled that 'he first showed his talent by drawing with his finger in milk spilt on a teatray'.[17] Another story concerned a professional call the barber made on Mr Humphrey Tomkison, a jeweller and silversmith who lived a few houses away along Maiden Lane. The jeweller's son Thomas used to claim that his father was the first to discover the boy Turner's abilities. Thomas Tomkison told a friend in 1850: 'On one occasion Turner [senior] brought his child with him; and while the father was dressing my father, the little boy was occupied in copying something he saw on the table.' On being shown the drawing, Mr Tomkison refused at first to believe the boy had done it by himself. It was a precise rendering of a coat of arms engraved on a silver tray.[18] From early on, young Turner seems to have had a stump of pencil or piece of chalk always in hand, and would lie on the floor or sit at a table copying pictures, engravings and advertisements in newspapers and handbills.

When he was old enough to leave the house on his own, it was to enter a world that extended further and further away from the barber shop. Down Thatch'd House Alley or Bailey's Alley, long dark slits between the houses, to the Strand. Up Bedford Street and into the railed churchyard that led to the door of St Paul's. Within the church, the huge white ceiling and a golden sun over the altar. Up Southampton Street or along Henrietta Street to the Piazza and the market, where, just after breakfast, the last costermongers were dragging away their laden barrows, or encouraging the donkeys that drew their carts, as they set off to the streets of customers awaiting the day's fruit and vegetables. Empty sieves and sacks and hampers and baskets were being piled up, and streetsweepers were clearing the litter of purply-green cabbage leaves, bits of white-yellow turnip or pale-orange carrot, fragments of red apples and crushed brown chestnuts, shreds of lettuce and sprout tops and onion skins, and discarded paper jackets that had been wrapped around lemons. Maybe even an orange to be rescued from a gutter. He might drift by the caged linnets and larks being sold for a penny on either side of the east end of the church, and then wander through the flowers and flowerpots under the colonnade, where tired porters were perched on their baskets, drinking coffee from a stall. The shoeless flowergirls sat on the steps of the Covent Garden Theatre, tying up their bunches, while others clustered around the pump, chattering and elbowing one another as they watered their wilting violets.

He was small for his age, and, it would seem, something of a loner. Nevertheless he was a Covent Garden native who felt secure exploring his own part of the city. Not far away, in King Street off the north-west corner of the Piazza, was the 'Spectacle Mecanique'. Payment of a small coin allowed you to look at the wonderful Swiss contrivances: a life-size mannikin of a boy, which appeared to write to dictation; a figure which drew landscapes; a mechanical girl who played a harpsichord; and a metal canary in a cage that hopped up and down and whistled a tune. In the market during the day mountebanks performed and, despite the by-laws, wild beasts were now and then exhibited.

One day Turner's territory expanded: he crossed the Strand for the first time, a broad thoroughfare filled with clattering hackney coaches and private carriages. He made his way down through the tight streets and alleys to the river. In front of the tall fancy houses of the new Adelphi a stone quay had been built for barges and lighters to land and embark cargoes. But in many places the old foreshore was unimproved, with stretches of beach, rotting wharves and the remains of pilings. At low tide you could clamber down on to the shingle and strongly smelling mud and find treasures among the detritus: white clay pipes, a ship's block, lumps of coal. Boatmen with skiffs and wherries plied for hire from the steps called 'stairs'- Salisbury Stairs and York Buildings Stairs were the nearest. The boatmen waved and shouted to anyone who looked as if they wanted to be rowed on the river. Not far away, at Hungerford, there were wharves where you could watch coal, timber, stone and marble being landed. With the tide, lighters and barges – sails down and steered by long sweeps – shot beneath the three bridges (Westminster, Blackfriars and London). The Thames surged by, thick rippling water, with the occasional herring barrel or tree stump swirling past. Down east, he learned, was the Pool, Wapping, Greenwich, Gravesend and the sea. Up west, inland, was Lambeth, Vauxhall, Chelsea, England.

At the age of ten he went that way, west to Brentford on the Thames, to stay with his butcher uncle Joseph Marshall. The reason for the journey is obscure; it may have been 'a fit of illness' arising from 'a want of air'[19] – a hearsay explanation suggesting bronchitis or asthma brought on by life in a city where 900,000 people used coal fires to try to keep warm in winter. It may have been that his parents feared that their only child would follow Mary Ann into the grave unless they got him out of the gritty urban atmosphere. Or the departure for Brentford may have come about because of the domestic difficulties, springing from his mother's 'ungovernable temper', that appear gradually to have shattered the Turner household. Whatever the reason, young William was taken in by the Marshalls and sent to school.

Until this moment, education doesn't seem to have been to the fore. How much reading and writing he learnt at home is uncertain. But in Brentford in 1785 Turner went to John White's school. This establishment had some sixty pupils – fifty boys and ten girls – and stood in Brentford High Street opposite an inn called The Three Pigeons; it was a few minutes' walk from the market place, where the butcher and his wife lived next door to another inn, The White Horse. Also living in Brentford were Mr and Mrs James Trimmer and their expanding family. Mrs Trimmer had been Sarah Kirby, from Suffolk, daughter of a friend of the artist Thomas Gainsborough, and as well as bringing twelve children into the world she wrote books, did good works and in particular promoted Sunday schools: the Brentford Sunday school was founded in 1786 at her urging. Many of those who supported her Brentford Sunday school were dissenters, but her own son Henry Scott Trimmer was eventually ordained in the Church of England.

It may have been at the Brentford Sunday school or at John White's academy that young William Turner first met Henry Scott Trimmer, who was a few years younger but was to become a close friend.[20] It may have been in the Trimmer household, where Gainsborough was a cherished name, that Turner first realized that artists could be greatly honoured. Henry Scott Trimmer's eldest son passed on his father's story that Turner, on the daily plod between home and school, amused himself 'by sportively drawing with a piece of chalk figures of cocks and hens on the walls as he went to and from that seat of learning'. The graffiti artist got more orthodox practice within White's establishment, drawing 'birds and flowers and trees from the schoolroom windows'.[21] He was known by now as a boy who enjoyed being kept busy with pencil and paint. While at Brentford, a friend of his uncle, a distillery foreman named John

Lees, asked him to colour the engravings in a copy of *The Antiquities of England and Wales*, by Henry Boswell. According to Lees family tradition, the foreman paid Turner twopence for each of the seventy or so plates he thus livened up.

The huge, heavy tome whose tall pages he turned was a leather-bound compendium of separately printed parts; it incorporated 'a general history of antient castles' and was illustrated with simple engravings of weapons, the habits of religious orders and the elements of early Norman architecture. It pictured churches, chapels, abbeys, priories and cathedrals, ruined castles and old palaces. Among the 'antiquities' presented with no great sophistication were Friar Bacon's Study at Oxford, Dover Castle, Rochester Castle, Bolton Castle in Yorkshire, Carisbrooke Castle on the Isle of Wight, Stonehenge, St Michael's Mount, Holy Island and Caernarvon Castle. Nearer to home were St Paul's Cathedral, Lambeth Palace and Syon House, the Duke of Northumberland's mansion, just up the Thames from Brentford. Young William Turner washed in the skies with blue, the lawns and grassy slopes with green. He painted the walls of castles and churches a sandy yellow and the flags flying from towers bright red and blue. The figures of people strolling on the swards or rowing in boats were picked out: ladies' dresses in pink or red, men's coats in blue (or, for a change, vice versa). He carefully filled out in flat colours the leaves and branches of trees.

It was rainy-day work but it made a dent. Here, attentively studied and dramatized with colour, were all the elements and indeed the subjects, in very straightforward form, of what he was going to do in a few years' time. Here is a crude but memorable engraving of the bizarre rock formations inside Fingal's Cave, on the Scottish island of Staffa, and the exclamatory text: 'Compared to this, what are the cathedrals or palaces built by man!'[22]

The grind at John White's school can be imagined with some help from Captain Marryat's young hero, Jacob Faithful, who attended a charity school in Brentford. Jacob was an unlettered orphan of Thames waterfolk, planted abruptly at the school. Despite the bullying that new boys attract and the beatings that those who seem stupid or recalcitrant are subject to, he succeeded in acquiring from the usher, the headteacher's assistant, the rudiments of written language and then, from the dominie, a good deal of basic learning: the Greek gods, the ancient heroes; stories from the Bible and

Shakespeare; the kings and queens of England. It was the right age for impressions to be made on a boy, and many of these tales and legends were, like Boswell's castles and cathedrals, fixed in Turner's mind. Here he would have heard of Ulysses and the Cyclops, Dido and Aeneas. Here, like Jacob Faithful, he 'was doomed to receive an education ... in reading, writing, and ciphering'.[23]

However, in William Turner's case, perhaps because of his late start, perhaps because he lagged in some areas and was hyperactive in others, the effects of this instruction were not altogether successful. In syntax, in spelling, 'must try harder'. Sometimes memories of his city life may have crowded out present moments when he should have been memorizing a times-table or declensions of a Latin verb. There were overwhelming feelings which could not be framed in words, written or spoken, but which prompted drawings. Many of his sketches 'were taken by stealth ... His school-fellows, sympathising with his taste, often did his sums for him while he pursued the bent of his compelling genius.'[24] Some of his Brentford schoolmates, less sympathetic, may have laughed at the city boy for 'talking funny'. In some verse jotted in a guidebook which he also used as a sketchbook in 1811, Turner – then aged thirty-six – seemed to be remembering this time with a gawkiness he could not throw off:

> Close to the millrace stands the school,
> To urchin dreadful, on the dunce's stool
> Behold him placed behind the chair
> In doleful guise twisting his yellow hair
> While the grey matron tells him not to look
> At passers by thro' doorway, but his book.[25]

Brentford had features that may have made up for the trials of education. The village was on the river opposite Kew, with several islands called eyots which – muddy-sided and freighted with willows – like huge moored barges briefly divided the waters of the Thames. It was a historic spot, as Uncle Joseph or Mr White must have pointed out: at the ford here, of Brent*ford*, where the twisting River Brent joined the Thames, British tribesmen under Cassivellaunus had opposed Julius Caesar's legionaries as they marched north. Hereafter, the river was to figure powerfully in Turner's imagination, and was to well up constantly in the poetry he attempted to write in his thirties and early forties.

By eleven he had had a city childhood and, courtesy of Brentford, a country one. Going back to Maiden Lane he may have had a sense of London, 'the extended town' as he later called it, with its 'high raised smoke', reaching out to envelop the surrounding farms, fields and commons.[26] London at this point stretched from Tyburn Lane in the west, at the edge of Hyde Park, to Wapping by the river on the east. The streets and squares were spreading northwards above Oxford Street and Holborn to Marylebone, Bloomsbury and Sadler's Wells. Islington, where many of the Marshalls lived, was still a distinct village but would not be so for long. Westminster was expanding to the south-west through Tothill Fields. South of the river, the Borough was growing towards Newington and along the Kent Road to Hatcham and Deptford. Yet Turner came back and felt at home again among the great buildings and the life that pulsed under the canopy of smoke.

It might have been good to stay at home for a while but he was soon sent off again – and once more the reasons are obscure. This time he went east, downriver. Margate was his destination, where his mother had another relative, this one a fishmonger.[27] That it was his mother's rather than his father's family that seemed most concerned to look after him perhaps suggests that her mental health was a large factor in these evacuations from Maiden Lane.

Margate was known for its bracing air, and people were beginning to go there for sea-bathing. You could reach the resort by land or sea, but the latter was the popular way. From the Tower of London you took a hoy, a bluff-bowed sloop-rigged vessel that – weather permitting – made the trip in twelve hours. It was an exciting voyage for the first-time passenger, down the winding river past the oyster boats unloading at Billingsgate, past the ship-building yards at Deptford and the palatial seamen's hospital at Greenwich, past the skeletons of criminals or pirates hanging in chains at Blackwall Point, past the old fort at Tilbury and then along the edge of the Blythe Sands, as the river opened up to the sea. Then along the north Kent shore – Sheerness, Sheppey – bouncing in the chop, spray flying back over the tilted deck, seasick passengers crammed in the cabin. But Turner apparently took to it, with sea-legs from the start. Margate came into view, a collection of houses set back along the beach and around the little harbour, formed by an L-shaped stone jetty or pier. Here the hoy landed amid great bustle: hotel waiters and porters touted for custom; small urchins offered to carry the bags.

In Margate, Turner – eleven going on twelve – went to Mr Coleman's school. Thomas Coleman, a native of this Thanet part of Kent, had lived for a time in London and been converted to Methodism by John Wesley's preaching. In Margate, Coleman established a chapel and small school and preached in the streets; he was regarded as a man 'of great boldness and great fluency of speech', and antagonized many of Margate's residents. Nevertheless, he made many converts to the Wesleyan brand of evangelical Christianity; his chapel was well attended, as was the schoolroom in Love Lane.[28] The effect of Mr Coleman's 'fluency' and religious ardour on young Turner is indeterminable, but the boy's knowledge of the Bible was certainly improved. Whatever Turner's later beliefs, there is no doubt that in many respects he was a non-conformist of a taciturn kind, and the teaching of the bold dissenter may well have helped fix his burgeoning sympathies for the unorthodox.

The journey to, and the stay in, Margate also made him like the sea. Standing on the harbour jetty or playing on the north-facing beach, building sand-castles, breathing salt air, he watched the tide run in and out; he saw the sunlight striking through loose cloud the sails of ships that were making along the Thanet coast or fetching out for Ostend and Calais. He watched the waves break on the sand and the fishermen launching and hauling out their boats. And he drew. One of his first original works that survives is a drawing of a street in Margate, a downhill prospect over roofs to the masts of ships and the sea beyond. The complicated perspective of the descending street, with house fronts, rooftops and an empty cart beside a fence, is handled with remarkable skill; only the sash windows of the right-hand houses seem a bit awry, but maybe they were so in the actual houses. By the time he returned to Covent Garden again, Turner was a child not only of the city and the rural Thames but of the seaside.

The boy brought back a healthier complexion for his reimmersion in the full tide of human existence that Dr Johnson believed to be concentrated at Charing Cross. He also brought his folder of drawings to show his parents. His father had intended him to follow in the barbering trade, and William Turner senior must be congratulated for *not* saying, as he looked through the folder, 'What a waste of time, young fellow! You'll be better off helping me.' On the contrary, William Turner gazed at his son's work with pride and hung the drawings in the shop window and doorway, 'ticketed at prices varying from one shilling to three'.[29] Long afterwards, a few such drawings – signed 'W. Turner' – were cherished by customers whose perspicacity had been keen at the time, even if blended with goodwill. The hairdresser now had an answer for the common question, 'What's William going to be?' He told such clients as Humphrey Tomkison and the Academician Thomas Stothard, 'William is going to be a painter.'[30]

2: Up and Coming

I n fact, William Turner, aged twelve, seemed more inclined
to become an architect, as he turned out sketch after sketch
of churches, abbeys, country houses and city streets. The two
earliest drawings that he signed, though copied from prints, are *The
North-West View of Friar Bacon's Study and Folly-Bridge, Oxford*, after
an engraving in the *Oxford Almanack* of 1780, and a *View of Nuneham
Courtenay from the Thames*; both are inscribed 'W. Turner, 1782'.[1]
Much later, Clara Wheeler, the daughter of his good friend William
Frederick Wells, said that Turner had often declared that 'if he could
begin life again, he would rather be an architect than a painter'.[2]

The dormer windows and tiled roofs that he could see from
his small bedroom in Maiden Lane, and the sky above, gave him
subjects and new ways of making pocket money. In addition
to his barber-shop sales, he began to earn small sums by adding
backgrounds to the designs of architects, washing in 'rolls of white
clouds and blue wastes of summer sky'.[3] He was hand-colouring
prints for the engraver John Raphael Smith in nearby King Street,
putting to work the simple techniques he had learnt while doing
Mr Lees' job in Brentford. Many of Smith's mezzotints were of
portraits of belles painted by Reynolds, Gainsborough and Romney
– a different challenge for the colourist. In any event, if most of the
suggestions we have are true, for the next few years young Turner
was rarely without a pencil, pen or brush in his hand. Most of his
part-time jobs made use of his sympathy for buildings and his skill
in drawing them.

In the roll of architects who figure in the by no means substantially
documented history of Turner's apprenticeship are found the names
of Bonomi, Porden, Dobson, Repton and Hardwick. His possible
association with Joseph Bonomi comes a little later – Bonomi, an
Italian who had been working in England since 1767, is alluded

to as a fashionable architect in Jane Austen's *Sense and Sensibility*. One account has Turner actually articled to an architect for a fee of £200 put up by William Turner senior; but the architect after a short trial decided that the youth's talents lay elsewhere and returned the boy and the money. In a similar story, a barber-shop customer left a bequest of £100 to the hairdresser, and Humphrey Tomkison made the enterprising suggestion that the sum be used to article the lad to the topographical illustrator Thomas Malton. The result (according to Thornbury) was that Malton 'in sheer desperation' took 'his unpromising pupil' back to Maiden Lane and told the barber, 'It is no use. The boy will never do anything … Better make him a tinker, sir, or a cobbler, than a perspective artist!'[4] One gets the feeling that there are elements of truth in these stories, though the names attached to them could be shifted around without harm.

William Porden may provide firmer ground. The son of a Hull labourer, he studied with James Wyatt and went on to acquire a reputation as a neo-Gothic architect, though he failed to be elected as an associate of the Royal Academy in 1806. He designed several buildings for the Prince of Wales in Brighton: the stables at the Pavilion, the Prince's pleasure palace, and a house on the Steyne for Mrs Fitzherbert, the Prince's mistress. Porden is said to have nobly offered to take young Turner as an apprentice without any premium being paid. Thornbury, apparently unaware of Porden's fondness for the Gothic, says that for him Turner 'swept in gravel walks winding up to … Grecian porches, floated blue skies over his composite pediments, and pencilled in grass-tufts and patches of dock as the foregrounds to his Corinthian mansions'.[5] Alaric Watts writes that, on leaving this employer, Turner 'furnished Mr Porden with a liberal stock of skies for future use'.[6]

The notion that Turner found the lowest rung of the architectural ladder uncomfortable is given substance by the tale that, when colouring the perspective drawing of a mansion for a 'Mr. Dobson', the boy did the windowpanes in a way that showed the reflected light from the sky contrasting with the dark of the room within. Mr D objected to this novelty: the panes should be a plain dark grey, the glazing bars white; this was the recognized practice. 'It will spoil my drawing,' said the young artist. 'Rather that than my work,' answered the architect. Turner obediently finished the colouring in the way he was commanded but then 'left his employer altogether'.[7]

STANDING IN THE SUN

Turner's association with Thomas Hardwick has a definite base and appears to have been helpful to both parties. Hardwick's father – also a Thomas – was a builder and architect in Brentford; once again, Uncle Joseph and family may have provided the connection. Thomas Hardwick junior had been a pupil of Sir William Chambers, whose new Somerset House was going up at the east end of the Strand, and had studied at the Royal Academy Schools. He worked for several years with the young John Soane in Rome, and according to James Wyatt was 'a regular bred classical architect'.[8] Hardwick's classicism was cool and direct. Despite the building downturn that now began with the French Revolution and continued through the ensuing wars, Hardwick seems to have had steady surveying work and to have been kept busy designing public buildings, especially churches and jails. From 1787 to 1790, he was in charge of rebuilding St Mary the Virgin Church in Wanstead, north-east of London, and Turner did watercolours of the edifice before and after the changes. Hardwick also superintended the remodelling of St Paul's, Covent Garden, after the disastrous fire that engulfed it in 1795; he recased it in Portland stone, while adhering closely to Inigo Jones's original design. He drew up improvements for the Duke of Northumberland's Syon House, and Turner may have helped with the plans. Turner evidently left Hardwick's office on good terms, for Hardwick later bought some of his work, and his son Philip, also an architect and businessman, remained closely connected with Turner to the end of the artist's life.

The bleak outlook for aspiring architects at this time may have been one factor that dissuaded young Turner from carrying on in the profession. Perhaps, too, he eventually found the job uncongenial in terms of the inspiration he got from it. In his meticulous early drawings and watercolours, architecture was the nub of things.[9] His eye was taken not only by grand buildings but by humble, whether farm cottages or inns like the Swan, at Lambeth, which intruded its more homespun form in front of the Archbishop's Palace, the purported subject of his first watercolour to be shown at the RA in 1790. And architecture remained an absorbing interest with him. It was a specific category to which he devoted many of the works for his great engraving project that began in 1807, the *Liber Studiorum*. In later years he designed several buildings: a neo-classical gatehouse for a friend; a country villa and a townhouse-cum-gallery for himself.

He owned and read a number of books to do with the profession, Sir Henry Wotton's 1624 *Elements of Architecture* being one. And the knowledge of perspective acquired in drawing buildings was to be put to further instructional use. Certainly the love of buildings never left him. C. R. Cockerell, architect and archaeologist, encountered Turner in 1825, when the artist was fifty, and remained 'more than two hours with him talking of Vanbrugh, Hawksmoor & others, he as usual standing with his hat on'.[10]

As well as working for architects, Turner was associated with at least one architectural illustrator. Before he was fifteen, he had gone to evening classes at the studio of Thomas Malton, a scene-painter at Covent Garden Theatre and draughtsman of elegant topographical views. Malton had a wooden leg, following a childhood accident; he too had been a student at the Royal Academy Schools and may have told his pupil enticing tales of life on the Somerset House lower deck. Thornbury's account of Malton saying that the boy was 'no use'[11] is evidently false. Malton's influence is to be seen in early Turner works, such as the watercolour of the south front of Radley Hall, elaborated from rough drawings he made on a trip to Oxford in 1789. Malton's own work of that year is nicely illustrated in a drawing of St Dunstan's in the West, Fleet Street. In a lecture some twenty years later the pupil gave credit to Malton for his help: 'His mode of instruction was divested as much as possible of prolixity … Whatever he saw in nature [was] incontravertible.'[12] And further homage was heard 'in after life' when Turner described Thomas Malton as 'my real master'.[13]

Whether he jumped or was pushed out of the architectural profession, Turner had mentors who had definite ideas about where the fourteen-year-old should be spending some hours of his day. Thomas Hardwick may have proposed that he attend the Royal Academy Schools. Thomas Malton may have fired the same ambition. And a barber-shop customer then facilitated the process. One client of Turner senior was a clergyman from Foots Cray in Kent, the Reverend Robert Nixon, who had seen the drawings hanging in the shop while his whiskers were being lathered or his wig dressed. Nixon introduced the youth to John Francis Rigaud, a forty-seven-year-old portraitist and member of the Royal Academy. Rigaud made the necessary moves to recommend Turner as a probationary student at the Academy Schools.

The Turners at this point, 1789, were at 26 Maiden Lane and remained there for the next ten years, until the end of the decade. Although 'William Turner', presumably senior, does not appear by name in the rate books until Lady Day 1795, he stays in the books thereafter until 1800–1, second in the list for the north side of the Lane, a property – valued at £30 – next to Hand Court; this was a T-shaped alley running back from the street. The doorway to the hairdressing shop and house was set back on the left under an arch which gave entrance to the Court. That the Turner family was there before the barber actually became responsible for the Poor Rates is indicated by the 'place of abode' given for young Turner in a 1790 Royal Academy catalogue – 'Maiden-lane' – and the even more specific 'No. 26 Maiden-lane' in a catalogue for 1791.'[14] Thornbury claimed to have visited Hand Court before these Maiden Lane buildings were demolished around 1860 and he described it as 'a sort of horizontal tunnel, with a low archway and a prison-like iron gate'.[15] Turner's room, where he painted and slept, was at the top of the house, looking out over the Lane at the houses opposite, in one of which he had been born.

It was a five-minute walk down Southampton Street and along the busy Strand to the large greystone pile of Somerset House, where the Royal Academy had its quarters. The Academy itself was just over twenty years old – an institution, approved by the King, that had finally met the claims of British painters and sculptors for status and royal patronage. From its beginning in December 1768, the Academy had declared the free training of artists to be one of its duties, meaning to replace the various 'academies' for drawing and painting from life that came and went in London; one of the most recent of these was William Hogarth's, in Peter Court off St Martin's Lane. From 1771 the Royal Academy Schools had been housed in a portion of old Somerset House, the palace designed by Inigo Jones, along with the Academy's Council Room and Library, though exhibitions had to be held elsewhere. But after the opening of the Chambers-designed buildings in 1780, all the workings of the Academy took place in the new Strand block of Somerset House.

To be admitted to the Schools, young Turner had to make a drawing of an antique plaster-cast and submit it to the Keeper, Agostino

Carlini. Carlini, approving it, passed it on to the Academy Council, which could give or withhold admission. The decisive Council meeting was chaired by the Academy President, the distinguished portrait painter Sir Joshua Reynolds. The Academy's admission register for 11 December 1789 listed six successful candidates in alphabetical order: Dixon, Willm, age fifteen; Gyfford, Edw., age seventeen; Rosetti, Jno Baptista, age twenty-five; Sherridan, Jno, age twenty-five; Turner, Willm, age fifteen; and Wingrave, Fran. Chas., age fourteen. Turner was the Royal Academy's 544th student. In pencil, after the 'Willm.', someone in the office had added to the register 'Jos. Mallord'. If his 23 April 1775 birth-date was correct, he was in fact still fourteen.

Sir Joshua had declared that the Academy Schools must have 'an atmosphere of floating knowledge' and 'an implicit obedience to the Rules of Art'. Furthermore, the President said, 'every opportunity should be taken to discountenance that false and vulgar opinion, that rules are the fetters of genius. They are fetters only to men of no genius.'[16] Among the rules that young William Turner had to subscribe to were those 'for preserving order and decorum' in the Schools. If he defaced a 'Plaister [plaster] Cast, Model, or Book', he would be expelled. He was to go on drawing 'after the Plaister' until judged fit to draw 'after the living models'. The Plaister Academy was open all day, except on Sundays and holidays and during vacations. The School of Living Models – also called the Life School, Life Class or Life Academy – functioned in the evenings, in summer after 4 p.m., in winter after 6 p.m. There were two terms, in summer from 26 May to 31 August, in winter from 29 September (which was Michaelmas) until 9 April. About twenty-five students were admitted each year and were permitted six years of study. The admission policy was egalitarian: talent rather than family background counted for most. (John Soane's father was a bricklayer.)

Although the regulations decreed that new students spend at least a term drawing from the plaster-casts before moving on to live models, Turner spent nearly two and a half years doing chalk and stump studies of the Apollo and the Antinous of the Belvedere, the Venus de Medici, the Diskobolus and the Dying Gaul, before being admitted to the Life Class in June 1792. Did he need to work harder at the antique, or was he thought to be too young to look at live flesh? The casts themselves were somewhat battered. When the Prince Regent twenty years later decided to give twenty-six better casts from the Vatican marbles to the Academy rather than to the British Museum, the editor of the *Annals of Fine Arts* lamented that 'such fine casts ... should be destined to the smoky, dingy rooms of the Royal Academy, liable to the carelessness of housekeepers, porters, and idle boys'.[17]

In the Life Academy, which Turner attended from June 1792 to October 1799, at first regularly, later on and off, two models at a time were 'set' by the Visitor in poses adopted from Old Master paintings, and continued for two hours, measured by an hour-glass, with several rest periods. Naked female models were introduced in the early 1770s, but were – as the painter and Academician James Northcote remarked – 'much disapproved of by some good folks'.[18] No students under the age of twenty, unless they were married, were permitted to draw female models. What seems to be Turner's first drawing of a nude woman appears in a sketchbook of 1796–7: she is seated with legs crossed and hair in a turban; the drawing is nicely coloured, the anatomy well-rendered.[19] One highly regarded male model was a serving soldier, Sam Strowger, who was afterwards taken on as an Academy porter. Students drew lots for their places, to give all an opportunity of the best drawing positions, though in winter a spot near the coal stove was most coveted by those trying to draw with chilblained fingers. While the models posed, the students were admonished to 'remain quiet in their places'.

All these rules may have struck the new boy – no idler – as forbidding, but in reality the fetters were less confining. The sculptor Joseph Wilton, who succeeded Carlini as Keeper in 1790 and remained in the post until 1803, was elderly and lacked a firm grip. Conditions in the Schools were crowded and standards low. Joseph Farington, the governessy Academician who kept a diary through these years, noted on several occasions what he considered to be the deplorable activities of the students, drinking, loitering and behaving badly: for instance, throwing at one another the pieces of bread they were supposed to use for rubbing out mistakes.'[20] Farington seems to have forgotten that boys will be boys.

Apart from those who signed on with him, Turner's Schoolmates in the early 1790s included Martin Archer Shee, George Chinnery, Joshua Cristall and Robert Ker Porter, who was admitted at the tender age of thirteen. Bob Porter had a reputation for cheekiness; on one occasion he embellished his drawing of the antique Gladiator with a sword and helmet the cast didn't have, knowing that 'Squire' Wilton would be aggravated by this. Porter went on to paint a vast 2800-square-foot *Battle of Agincourt*, shown at the Lyceum in 1805, and thereafter sailed to Russia where he married a princess. Another contemporary was Henry Aston Barker, son and assistant of Robert Barker who in 1789 created the panoramic display in the Haymarket of the Grand Fleet anchored in Spithead, that Turner may have gone to see. Queen Charlotte, visiting the spectacle, said it was so real it made her feel seasick. One anonymous Academy student of the time later recalled:

> With the smoke from the candles and the lamps, and the dust from the chalk, the dresses of our respected instructors used seldom to exhibit any marks of splendour after their attendance in the schools. Mr Wilton, for example, was a man of very great personal neatness, frills and ruffles forming a prominent feature of his costume. Soon, however, the ardour of the artist would overcome the exactness of the beau, and if by chance a student made an error in his drawing by too powerful an outline or too marked a development of muscular action, Mr Wilton would gently come up to the draughtsman's side, and collecting his delicately white ruffles between the tips of his fingers and the palm of his hand, begin to rub over the offending parts, smudging the white with the black chalk, saying, 'I do not see those lines in the figure before you.'[21]

James Barry, the Irishman who was Professor of Painting and who lived in a dilapidated old house in Castle Street, near Oxford Street market, had none of Wilton's sartorial standards. He was thought uncouth and sardonic, but was popular with the students, to whom he was invariably helpful; yet he got on badly with his fellow Academicians, who took away his membership of the Academy in 1799. (He had publicly criticized Reynolds, and in his lectures violated the rule that no allusion be made to works of contemporaries.) Turner probably attended Barry's lectures, in one of which Barry made a 'long parallel between Poetry and Painting'.[22]

Turner is said also to have been on hand on 10 December 1790, the twenty-second anniversary of the Academy's foundation, when the President gave the last of his series of Discourses. The audience in the Exhibition Room – including Edmund Burke and James Boswell – was several hundred strong and, according to Dr Charles Burney who was there with his daughter Fanny, 'very turbulent', particularly the 'young students ... who seemed unable to hear and diverted themselves'. Turner, presumably attentive, would have heard Sir Joshua in his marked Devon accent recommend to students 'a rational method of study', with not too much indulgence for 'peculiarity', and citing Michelangelo as an example of the 'mechanick excellence' needed before painting could become boldly poetic. Reynolds praised 'indefatigable diligence' as the basis for inspiration.[23] But while the President spoke, ignoring the less than diligent students, there was a 'violent and unaccountable crack', which suggested to Dr Burney that one of the main beams supporting the floor of the Exhibition Room was about to give way. Sir Joshua ignored this, and a second crack which shortly followed. After his address ended, safely, Fanny Burney met James Barry on the stairs and was told by him that the 'danger had been very real, and our escape fortunate'. And she added, 'We are universally abused by our friends for our foolhardy complaisance to Sir Joshua in not making the best of our way out at the first warning.'[24] Sir Joshua, asked what he had thought when he heard the cracks, replied grandly, 'I was thinking that, if we had all perished, the art in England would have been thrown back five hundred years.'[25]

What effect did his Academy training have on the adolescent Turner? It is hard to imagine him openly mocking his teachers or doing anything other than what was asked of him. There are hints, rather, of a head-down dutifulness, within which his own as yet barely suspected fires were banked. He sketched the antique figures; he drew the posed models; and he attended some of the lectures, and fitted in his many part-time jobs. Along the way, he made notes of useful technical tips. On the back of one black and white chalk drawing done in the Schools he wrote:

Well Hot
{
1. Get an Etching Ground, 26
2. Heat the Back of the P [plate?]
3. Rub it over with the Ball
4. Dab it over with the Dabber of[f]
5. Smoke it over with the Wax Tapur
6. Put some ... at back of the Palte [plate?]
7. Re. of Wax
}

Turpentine Varnish and Lamp Black[26]

The Academy provided a different discipline from his work copying topographical illustrations or washing-in architectural backgrounds. John Ruskin, who became Turner's most passionate advocate half a century after this, thought the effect of the Schools had been dire:

> Turner, having suffered under the instruction of the Royal Academy, had to pass nearly thirty years of his life in recovering from the consequences ... The one thing which the Academy *ought* to have taught him (namely, the simple and safe use of oil colour), it never taught him; but it carefully repressed his perceptions of truth, his capacities of invention, and his tendencies of choice. For him it was impossible to do right but in a spirit of defiance; and the first condition of his progress in learning was the power to forget.[27]

But other experts have stressed the Academy's positive effects. It 'taught him all it knew', said Cosmo Monkhouse.[28] Philip Hamerton thought that, even for one who was a budding landscape artist, the advantage of academic figure study was that 'it thoroughly educates the eye to the perception of line, projection, and colour. It does not educate the special faculty of the landscape painter, which is a peculiar kind of memory, but it prepares him for his future work by a steady training in the elementary business of art.' For that matter, 'a figure, placed in a certain light, is as much an object under an effect as a near mountain in clear weather; it is, therefore, an initiation in the laws of effect as well as in those of form and colour'.[29] The Academy gave him other things, too. Frequent association with young painters – camaraderie – was good for a youth with somewhat solitary inclinations. Competition with them spurred him on. And from the start the Academy gave him recognition: his Lambeth Palace watercolour, an exercise in Malton's manner but immensely skilful for a fifteen-year-old, was hung on the walls of Somerset House for the Academy exhibition of 1790.

One other indoor element of Turner's education as an artist came from visits to other painters. He is said to have sat in occasionally at Sir Joshua's 'octagonal, snuff-strewn' studio in Leicester Fields, watching the master create his highly polished portraits.[30] C. R. Leslie, who was to become an Academician and a friend of Turner's, wrote that Sir Joshua 'kindly allowed young artists to call on him early in the morning before he had himself commenced painting. He criticised their works ... and he most readily lent them his finest works to copy. Turner ... told me that he copied many of his pictures when he was a student.'[31] Turner may also have studied briefly with a far less successful portraitist named Mauritius Lowe, the natural son of an Irish peer, who recognized Turner's talent. In 1781 Fanny Burney called Lowe 'a certain poor wretch of a villainous painter, who is in some measure under Dr Johnson's protection'. Lowe's studio was off-putting, at least to potential clients. A Mr Crutchley, bullied by Johnson into going there for a sitting, was 'so horrified by the dirt and squalor that he thrust the price of the portrait into the artist's hands and ran away'.[32] Lowe's widow and daughters later applied to the Royal Academy for charitable help, and Ruskin later still organized an annuity for the daughters, partly on the strength of Lowe's connection with Turner.

Young Turner's 'steady training' by now involved him in trips into the countryside. It was a time when almost every artist was – not just in his journeyman years – a taker of journeys. It seemed as if every meadow, hillside, abbey lawn and castle courtyard in Britain sooner or later had an itinerant artist seated in it, busily sketching in pursuit of picturesque beauty. Turner did not mean to be left out. Those two copy-drawings he made in 1787 of Friar Bacon's Study and Nuneham Courtenay House foretell his way westward. Two years later, aged fourteen, he visited his uncle Joseph Marshall at the house he had retired to at Sunningwell, near Oxford, and sketched several views in the locality: Sunningwell Church; Radley Hall, near Abingdon; and Nuneham Harcourt. His sketchbook labelled 'Oxford'[33] was a home-made affair of twenty-six pages stitched within a marbled paper cover. He filled it for the most part with light pencil sketches that showed an eye not only for perspective and architecture but for natural detail. He drew the tall chimneys of a big house and rendered with clever squiggles the leaves of a tree. He sketched a herd of cows, a dog pointing, a stable lad holding the reins of a stiff, merry-go-round sort of horse, and a boat under sail on the river. At least one Oxford sketch furnished material for a watercolour when he returned home.[34]

In 1791 he got further west, to Bristol and Bath. While still in his teens he went several times to Wales, the West Midlands and the Isle of Wight, as well as to nearer-at-hand Kent and Surrey. The habit of a summer or early-autumn sketching tour was set, and stayed with him. By stagecoach, on hired or borrowed horses, but often on foot, he travelled considerable distances. The writer Lovell Reeve, his contemporary, later wrote, 'He would walk through portions of England, twenty to twenty-five miles a day, with his little modicum of baggage at the end of a stick, sketching rapidly on his way all striking pieces of composition, and marking effects with a power that daguerrotyped them in his mind. There were few moving phenomena in clouds and shadows that he did not fix indelibly in his memory, though he might not call them into requisition for years afterwards.'[35] His baggage usually contained a book or two – early on, perhaps a volume by that apostle of the picturesque, the Reverend William Gilpin. In 1792–3 he seems to have carried a copy of *Don Quixote*, for in two drawings the Spanish knight and his faithful Sancho Panza appear in their 'enchanted boat' in the unlikely setting of a Welsh millstream. Thornbury tells us that on one early tour on foot to Oxford, Turner had 'the company of a poor artist named Cook, who afterwards turned stonemason. Cook's feet got sore, and I believe he was soon left behind by the indefatigable Turner. [When Thornbury says 'I believe', the reader may suspect some invention.] As for sleeping, the thrifty lad, careful never to affect prematurely the style of the fine gentleman, rested in any humble village public-house whereat he could obtain shelter.'[36]

Sometimes the shelter was free. In 1791 he stayed for several weeks with friends of his father's, the Narraways, in Broadmead, Bristol. John Narraway was a well-to-do dealer in animal hides and a maker of glue from animal bones. While there, Turner clambered up the steep banks of the Avon gorge. He drew the distant Welsh coast and the ruins of a chapel on an island in the Severn. One high, bird's-eye-view drawing, with a few preliminary washes of yellow and blue, shows the topsails of an otherwise unseen boat running downriver, sails lifting above the craggy Avon banks; the power of selection, of deciding what is not shown, is already impressive. Because of his mountain-goat-like pursuits, the Narraways nicknamed their young guest 'the prince of rocks'. John Narraway also noted, on the frame of a watercolour of a Bristol church that Turner gave him, 'NB he has crooked legs.'[37] Turner sketched some members of the family and at their request grudgingly portrayed himself, from the waist up. A miniature which Ruskin later owned is said to be the self-portrait done by the sixteen-year-old artist, though the pop-eyed, long-haired stripling in a jacket much too small for him looks not just unwilling but younger than sixteen. Turner defensively told the Narraways, 'It's no use taking such a little figure as mine. It will do my drawings an injury. People will say such a little fellow as this can never draw.'[38]

Turner's self-consciousness about his fairly small size was obviously matched by his fear of damage to his reputation as an up-and-coming artist. Ruskin's informant was Ann Dart, a niece of John Narraway. When she wrote to Ruskin in 1860 – nearly seventy years later – her memory may not have been certain about dates, but she retained (and had perhaps rehearsed on and off through the intervening years) a definite impression of a youth for whom his art was everything. Indeed, her account of conversations about the self-portrait may have been based on Narraway family gossip, since she herself seems to have first met Turner on a later visit he made to Bristol, *en route* to Wales, in 1798. But one way or other Miss Dart concluded that Turner was

> not like young people in general, he was singular and very silent, seemed exclusively devoted to his drawing, would not go into society, did not like 'plays', and though my uncle and cousins were very fond of music, he would not take part ... He had no faculty for friendship and though so often entertained by my uncle he would never write him a letter, at which my uncle was very vexed.

Is it possible that old Miss Dart had never got over being ignored as a girl by the grumpy young prodigy? Yet she noted, on the plus side, that 'he would do anything my uncle or cousins would ask him in the way of taking sketches in the neighbourhood [and] he gave us many of these drawings'. And despite being 'very difficult to understand, he would talk so little ... people ... could not help but like him because he was so good-humoured'. On the debit side once again, 'he was very careless and slovenly in his dress ... He would talk of nothing but his drawings, and of the places to which he should go for sketching. He seemed an uneducated youth, desirous of nothing but improvement in his art ... Sometimes [he] would go out sketching before breakfast, and sometimes before and after dinner ... He was not particular about the time of returning to his meals.'[39]

This unfriendly yet good-humoured, hard-to-understand but singular, slovenly and at the same time ambitious youth most often came back to Maiden Lane with crammed sketchbooks to work on during the winter. Some sketches were studies for work he had been commissioned to do for Walker's *Copper-plate Magazine* and Harrison's *Pocket Magazine*, which published engravings (based on drawings) that helped satisfy a popular demand for picturesque topographical views. The cathedrals, castles, old bridges and abbeys provided paying material; but Turner also sketched showmen's vans, a donkey and watercart, a ploughman, a sleeping dog. In his late teens, some of the sketchbooks became more substantial: leather-bound, with brass clasps. In his notes within, his handwriting didn't seem uneducated but rather a serviceable copperplate, with slightly ostentatious curlicues to the capital letters. In some places he made notes to help his recall: 'The distance last with the sky a lovely tint of Blue Lake and Indian – more as it approaches.'[40] In others he noted architectural details: 'Wollaton Hall, Lord Middleton. Tuscan, Doric and Ionic with E.B.P. to each. The wings have niches.'[41]

On the backs of some pages he recorded the names of clients. In his 'South Wales' sketchbook of 1795, for instance, he proudly reminded himself of 'Order'd Drawings' for Dr Mathews of Hereford; Viscount Malden of Hampton Court, Herefordshire; Mr Landseer; and Sir Richard Hoare.[42] He also made little lists of art materials needed: 'wood slab, brushes, I. rubber, Bells Ink, Slab book, pencil'.[43] A friend inscribed for him in the South Wales sketchbook a list of places against some of which he put an X, explaining, for future reference, 'X places mark'd thus have good Inns.' It seems his early frugality was now not always adhered to. But next to St David's he pencilled the warning 'no Inn'.[44] Where did he spend the night?

In most places he was attracted to water: to mill races, to streams where men were fishing, to beaches and foreshores where boats were setting out or being hauled up. Sometimes his destinations met the contemporary picturesque requirements, as with the multicoloured cliffs at Alum Bay, on the Isle of Wight, while fulfilling his own need simply to get close to the sea. Occasionally among the useful topographic sketches something utterly personal impends, like the head of a sleeping woman, wearing a mob-cap.[45] The woman has, it seems, features in common with Turner. Is this his mother, for once peaceful in sleep?[46]

*

Much of his education in these teenage years still came from making copies. But now his masters were not the makers of handbills and silver serving trays but Thomas Gainsborough, Philippe-Jacques de Loutherbourg, Michael Angelo Rooker and Paul Sandby, among others. Later, looking over some prints with his friend Henry Trimmer, he picked up a mezzotint of a van de Velde showing a large seventeenth-century warship running before the wind in stormy seas. Turner said to Trimmer: 'Ah! that made me a painter.'[47] But it could have been said that the close study or copying of works by a score of other artists 'made' him, or to be exact helped make an artist of a youth who had every instinct for and every intention of becoming a painter. The topographical artist and engraver Edward Dayes wrote in 1804, not long before his death by suicide, that Turner – whom he knew quite well by that stage – was

> indebted principally to his own exertions for the abilities which he possesses as a painter, and ... he may be considered as a striking instance of how much may be gained by industry, if accompanied by temperance, even without the assistance of a master. The way he acquired his professional powers was by borrowing, where he could, a drawing or a picture to copy from; or by making a sketch of any one in the [RA] Exhibition early in the morning, and finishing it at home.[48]

Dayes was frequently to be found at the London house of Dr Thomas Monro, a medical man who specialized in nervous and mental problems. (He was principal physician to Bethlehem Hospital for the insane and briefly had King George III as a private patient.) From 1794 to 1820 the doctor lived in the Adam Brothers' new Adelphi development, facing the river, south of the Strand and not far from Maiden Lane. There, at 6 Adelphi Terrace, he patronized the arts. Other residents included Robert and James Adam, who had managed to rescue their costly building scheme from financial collapse by a lottery; James Graham, notable quack doctor and impresario of Emma Lyon, later Lady Hamilton; and David Garrick and his wife. Dr Monro had inherited wealth; he collected pictures and their makers, whether senior artists of the time or young men of promise like Tom Girtin. Turner's name first appears in the doctor's diary in 1793, though it seems Monro had already come across the youth's work on show in the Maiden Lane barber shop and had bought several drawings at an extravagant two guineas apiece. The doctor also bought a watercolour of St Anselm's Chapel in Canterbury Cathedral, which Turner exhibited at the Royal Academy in 1794.

Joseph Farington may have taken an interest in Turner from the start because he, Farington, had attended the life classes of the artists' society that met at 20 and 21 Maiden Lane, just before number 21 became William and Mary Turner's first home. At the end of 1794 Farington was told by his friend Dr Steers that 'Dr Monro's house is like an Academy in an evening. He has young men employed in tracing outlines made by his friends, etc. – Henderson, Hearne, etc., lend him their outlines for this purpose.'[49] The evenings were generally on Fridays in winter. Later Farington heard further gossipy details of the Monro 'school' or 'manufactory':

> Turner and Girtin told us they had been employed by Dr Monro 3 years to draw at his house in the evening. They went at 6 and staid till Ten. Girtin drew in outlines and Turner washed in the effects. They were chiefly employed in copying the outlines or unfinished drawings of [J. R.] Cozens etc., etc., of which copies they made finished drawings. Dr Monro allowed Turner 3s. 6d. each night. Girtin did not say what he had. Turner afterwards told me that Dr Monro had been a material friend to him, as well as to Girtin …[50]

The rewards of these Friday evenings included oysters for supper.

Where the two rising stars, Turner and Girtin, first met is unclear. It may have been at John Raphael Smith's shop in King Street, where both worked at colouring prints by hand. Tom Girtin, born 18 February 1775, the son of a Southwark ropemaker, had studied under Edward Dayes. Like Turner, he toured the English countryside and the Welsh mountains, and showed genius even earlier than Turner. At the good Dr Monro's, Girtin sometimes copied works by Malton, Turner's 'master', and Turner copied works by Dayes. Increasing the chances of their evening work being confused, they were both influenced by John Robert Cozens, who had travelled to Italy with the wealthy art patron and novelist William Beckford and there painted seemingly tranquil watercolours that had a powerful impact. In 1776 Cozens showed at the RA a painting called *Hannibal, in his march over the Alps, showing to his Army the Fertile Plains of Italy*, a subject that stuck in Turner's mind. Poor Cozens was one of several artists of these times who cracked up under the strains of life – Dayes and Haydon are others. Cozens lost his reason and for his last three years of life was confined under the care of Dr Monro, who also helped him out financially.

Turner and Girtin struck people as dissimilar characters, Turner 'reticent of his knowledge, and close as to his methods of work; Girtin ... of an open, careless, and sociable disposition'.[51] However, Girtin complained to Cornelius Varley of Monro's habit of making him do outlines, while Turner got to do the tinting, which did not give Girtin the same chance of learning to paint. But Girtin did paint his own watercolours as well as collaborate with Turner on joint productions. William Henry Pyne, a watercolourist, engraver and critic, later noted:

> The water colour drawings of Turner and Girtin, which Dr Munro [sic] possessed, were very remarkable for a strong resemblance to each other; and it is only after a severe search and scrutiny of both, that it becomes perceptible how to mark the difference. Turner's are distinguished by an elaborate and careful detail of every object, whether of buildings, figures, trees, or distant scenery; yet combining altogether exquisite taste, breadth, harmony, and richness. Some of Girtin's are almost as careful, but he seems to have soon launched out into that free and bold style which carries with it an imposing effect, by its being executed with apparent ease. Turner never seems to have aimed at this seductive style of execution; all his drawings display the utmost feeling for finish and detail, but at the same time preserving the breadth and harmony of nature.[52]

Another, slightly younger artist, William Havell, considered the Girtin–Turner phenomenon and decided that both were

> great experimentalists in rendering paper and water-colours subservient to the expression of light, which they found to be chiefly dependent on gradation ... In such matters, there was no trick they were not up to. Turner used to cut out figures in paper and paste them on his drawing. If his experiments spoiled one part of a drawing, he would paste the good part upon another piece of paper, rub down the edges of it, and work on the new surface till he brought the whole into harmony. He and Girtin would also seek to create gradation by pumping water upon their drawings.[53]

Girtin is thought to have discovered how to 'wipe out lights' in a watercolour when he accidentally spilled water on a drawing and then sopped it up with a handkerchief. The places where the water had lain were left white, the colours removed. According to Pyne, Turner worked out how to do the same thing by using pieces of bread as mops.

Various people then and since have wondered what so talented a young artist as Turner got out of his three years or so of Friday evenings at Dr Monro's art-factory. One scholarly biographer believed it 'taught him little, for it only exercised the skill he already possessed', though he also admitted that 'the regular performance of these academical exercises was probably beneficial at first', and noted a 'marked access of confidence noticeable in his work in the latter half of 1795', when he was twenty, that may have been due to his 'pictorial gymnastics' at Monro's.[54] At the time William Turner senior thought his son could have been doing more profitable work; he 'often grumbled' about '*Him* making drawings for Dr Monro for half a crown'.[55] A drawing, perhaps done by the doctor–patron, shows the young Turner earning his half-crown, seated at a desk, long hair tied in a sort of queue or pony-tail, cravat wrapped around his rather truncated neck, his gaze concentrated down his long nose, and pen or watercolour brush poised over the paper. Two candles set on a shelf above the desk provided light as Turner worked, copying perhaps a drawing by one of the many 'professional Picturesque tourists' of the time.[56] Dr Monro eventually owned several hundred 'Turners', most based on the works of other artists, some done in collaboration with Girtin. Many were of places in Switzerland, France and Italy, where neither he nor Girtin had yet gone.

Yet Turner was not forced to go to Dr Monro's, and he must have felt he needed the apparently humdrum experience. There was something to be said for the fact that he was absorbing – by copying – works of art, rather than working from nature, in company with fellow students, and doing so for pay. The painter Walter Sickert thought that

> The habit thus early forced upon him, of regarding himself as an actual producer, i.e. as a maker of articles with a definite market value, must have been beneficial to him. The existence of a class of real patrons, whose tastes had to be consulted, and whose pockets contained actually interchangeable coin of the realm, must have placed some insistence upon the social aspect of art, and have helped the boy from making the mistake which so many subsequent artists

have made, of considering their work merely as a means of super-individual or universal communication.[57]

In later life, when colleagues expressed amazement that he had spent all that time at Dr Monro's for mere pocket money, Turner said, 'Well, and what could be better practice?'[58]

But it was not just indoor copying work at the Adelphi. 'Dr Monro also encouraged the young artists to sketch from nature, and to bring their sketches and to work them into pictures at these evening meetings.'[59] Turner and Girtin sketched at the nearby ruins of the old Savoy Palace and on the Thames, from boats. The river banks were still mostly ragged, with here and there the bones showing through of old hulks and ancient wharves. Watermen, bargemen and lightermen steered their craft under sail or sweep, up and downstream, past the anchored artists. The doctor was keen on landscape – hence the many picturesque pictures he bought, executed by his friends Hearne, Dayes and de Loutherbourg. John Linnell, a younger artist later taken up by Dr Monro, said that the doctor himself led Turner and Girtin on drawing trips in the country, probably while they were staying at his cottage at Hadley, in Surrey.

At some point in the mid- to late-1790s Turner found the parental home uncongenial enough to cause him to move out. But he did not go very far. At first it was only to separate studio space and living quarters, which he could now afford, along Hand Court.[60] His mother's mental disorder may have been a crucial factor. Moreover, the once welcome habit of barber-shop customers extending their largess to the young artist must have become irksome. Well-intentioned people would keep barging in, like the Reverend J. Douglas, a chaplain to the Prince of Wales, who lived in Rochester but stayed with a bookseller in the Strand when he came up to town on court occasions. Douglas would have his hair dressed at William Turner's, and once found young Turner drawing in the back sitting room behind the shop. He looked at Turner's work and invited him down to Rochester to paint – which Turner did. (A resulting watercolour of Rochester Castle, with fishermen drawing boats ashore in a gale, is now untraced.)

On another occasion, in the spring of 1798, also in Kent, he stayed with another clergyman and barber-shop customer. This was the Reverend Robert Nixon, who had introduced him to J. F. Rigaud and hence to the Royal Academy. His fellow Schools pupil Stephen

Rigaud was already at the Nixons' in Foots Cray when Turner arrived unexpectedly and was heartily welcomed at the little parsonage – though he declined to go to church. Two days later they set off on a sketching party. Rigaud later recalled:

> It was a lovely day, and the scenery most delightful. After having taken many a sketch, and walked many a mile, we were glad at length to seek for a little rest and refreshment at an inn. Some chops and steaks were soon set before us, which we ate with the keen relish of appetite, and our worthy friend the Clergyman, who presided at our table, proposed we should call for some wine, to which I made no objection, but Turner, though he could take his glass very cheerfully at his friend's house, now hung his head, saying – 'No, I can't stand *that*.' Mr Nixon was too polite to press the matter further, as it was a pic-nic concern; so, giving me a very significant look, we did without the wine. I mention this anecdote to show how early and to what extent the love of money as a ruling passion, already displayed itself in him, and tarnished the character of this incipient genius; for I have no hesitation in saying that at that time he was the richest man of the three ...[61]

Turner's refusal to share a bottle with his pious companions may not have been plain churlishness. He may have been impelled by the thrift he had got used to on his own longer sketching tours; he may also have not wanted to drink while working – a constraint which, as the years went by, did not seem to matter so much. His already entrenched custom of concentrating on his art, even at the expense of friendliness, was once again demonstrated. And although his ability, whether inherited or nurtured, to put by money seems strongly attested here, one should remark, as is often the case with Turner, an opposing tendency: in a sketchbook of around 1795 is to be found a note, 'Lent Mr Nixon 2.12.6.'[62]

Apart from all his hackwork for architects, magazine publishers, country-estate owners and Dr Monro, Turner was now earning by giving instruction. Although a student, he was a teacher. In fact, one of his pupils in landscape painting was Reverend Nixon, whom young Rigaud taught figure-drawing. In 1798 Nixon sent Turner an ink-and-wash sketch of some buildings, seen through an arch, and Turner wrote back apologizing for not having been able to walk out to Lewisham to see him – eight miles – because he had fallen and hurt his knee. He advised Nixon to be sparing with his colours till Turner was able to see him again. Below the sketch he added helpful instructions for his amateur pupil: 'Get all the Shadows in Ink – except the Sky, Blue and Ink. The Arch was'ht with Bistre after the Shadow of Ink.'[63] Although Nixon lived in Foots Cray, he perhaps met Turner in Lewisham, half-way between them, as Turner had another Lewisham pupil. In the mid-1790s, from about the age of nineteen to twenty-three, Turner had numerous pupils who paid him between five and ten shillings a lesson,[64] quite a large sum at a time when printing compositors, for instance, earned fourpence an hour. The names of some of his pupils were jotted in his sketchbooks, such as the 'Marford Mill' sketchbook of 1794, where on the back of one drawing one finds 'Major Frazer. April 6. 1 hour & Half. 8 lessons.'[65] In the 'Smaller South Wales' sketchbook of 1795 he has written 'Teaching' alongside a squad of names: Mr Murwith; Mr Jones of Lewisham; Mr Davis ditto; Miss Palin; Miss Hawkins; and Mr Goold.[66] Another name is that of William Blake, though this is not the great poet and illustrator but a gifted amateur who lived in Portland Place, London, and commissioned a watercolour of Norham Castle, in Northumberland, from Turner in 1797.

Thornbury in 1860 wrote of 'old people still living who remember Turner in 1795 or 1796 ... when he taught drawing ... One of them describes him as "eccentric, but kind and amusing".'[67] This informant was possibly Lady Julia Gordon née Bennet, the widow of Sir John Willoughby Gordon, former Army Quartermaster General. As a young woman – a few months younger than her teacher – Julia Bennet took watercolour lessons from Turner. Two watercolours showed their joint handiwork. One, of Cowes Castle, is inscribed 'First with Mr Turner, 1797'. Another, larger, is of Llangollen Bridge, and has written on the back 'Julia Bennet – with Mr Turner. May 1797'. The background looks like Turner's work, the foreground is very amateurish. Like Catherine in *Northanger Abbey*, Julia Bennet may have 'confessed and lamented her want of knowledge' as she learnt of foregrounds, distances, perspectives, lights, and shades, and 'soon began to see beauty in everything admired' by her teacher.

Yet he did not want to let such work dominate his life. He apparently wasn't very talkative as a teacher; he told Farington on one occasion that his practice 'was to make a drawing in the presence of his pupil and leave it for him [or her] to imitate'.[68] Although he continued to teach throughout the next year, in November 1798 Farington reported that Turner was 'determined not to give any more lessons in drawing'. 'Mr Turner' evidently didn't need the status of teacher or the extra income. Perhaps, too, he was making such artistic advances of his own that dealing in fairly basic terms with beginners and hobbyists exasperated him. However, in the years to come he went on helping RA students as a Visitor in the Schools, and he often gave tips to colleagues on sketching trips or when preparing canvases for exhibition. Even so, he always seems to have found it easier to show rather than tell someone what to do: articulating the problem and the solution was more difficult.

One pencil drawing he did in 1798 shows the interior of Covent Garden Theatre. The view, with figures, is from the gallery, presumably while Turner attended a performance there. But his interest in theatre was not only that of a spectator and had been evident for some years. At the age of sixteen he had been recruited as an assistant to the Academician William Hodges, who was the designer and scene painter at the Pantheon, the domed assembly rooms-cum-theatre-cum-opera house in Oxford Street. Turner is missing from the RA Schools attendance registers from 22 April to 18 June 1791, and the name of William Dixon, one of his classmates, is listed as a Pantheon assistant. The signature 'Wm. Turner', similar to that in the RA registers, appears on Pantheon receipts of that time. At the Pantheon Turner would have helped paint the backcloths with clouds, city walls, village houses and stormy seas. He must have been particularly dismayed on the freezing cold morning of 14 January 1792 to hear that the Pantheon, overnight, had been gutted by fire. His reportorial instinct was strong – and quickly aroused by catastrophe – and he dashed up to Oxford Street to sketch the scene. The upsetting rumour was that the fire had started in the scene room, where he had worked: musical scores, instruments, costumes and scenery had been destroyed.

Despite the bitter cold, Turner drew the façade of the wrecked building and the adjacent shops, whose names he noted. Back home he squared the sketch[69] to make it easier to transfer to a larger size as a watercolour, *The Pantheon, the morning after the fire*, which he showed at the RA exhibition in the late spring.[70] The scene is done in his best Malton-derived manner, though with icicles from the frozen fire-extinguishing water hanging from the cornices, and the devastated interior visible through the windows with their broken sashes. Several firemen with their hand-pump are still emptying buckets in the foreground, while small bunches of spectators gawk and gossip. Their conversation is indicated by a few rather stilted gestures. But the morning light slants in cleverly from the upper-right back (of the stage, as it were), which allows the artist to render the front-facing undamaged windows of several neighbouring buildings in solid black, without highlights or reflections, in a manner some of his architect employers would approve.

Turner's experience in the theatre made a lasting impression on him. It was to be demonstrated in paintings in the following decades in which he indulged his fondness for bright lights and flaring colours. Even his first exhibited oil (RA 1796), *Fishermen at Sea*, has a moonlit mood of melodrama about it, although the motion of the fishing boats rolling in a heavy swell off the Needles, at the western end of the Isle of Wight, is brilliantly observed. The influence of the seventeenth-century Dutch painters is to be detected in the sea, and that of the Strasbourg-born, London-resident, eighteenth-century scene painter and RA Philippe-Jacques de Loutherbourg (whom Turner may have met at Dr Monro's) in the rather stagy moonlit clouds. One wonders if as a boy Turner went to not only the nearby Spectacle Mecanique but to de Loutherbourg's Eidophusikon in Spring Gardens. The name means more or less 'same-as-nature image', and the Eidophusikon gave the viewer the impression that he was watching a sort of moving picture, displayed within a stage about six feet wide and eight deep, and depicting calm and storm, on land or sea, with accompanying sound and light effects produced with tambourines and sheets of copper, Argand lamps and stained glass. Thornbury repeats a tale that 'Mrs Loutherbourg grew very jealous of Turner's frequent visits to her husband [in Hammersmith], and ... at last, suspecting the young painter was obtaining all her husband's secrets from him, she shut the door in his face and roughly refused him admittance.'[71] Moonlight and water also figure prominently in the oil Turner showed at the RA in 1797, as the title indicates: *Moonlight – a study at Millbank*.

Although his early oils suggest that Turner knew he had to prove his worth as a painter in that medium to be accepted as a potential member of the Royal Academy, through most of this period of apprenticeship his reputation was that of a rising and innovative watercolour artist. The rather flatly washed pencil outlines he did to begin with gave way to much bolder work. The boundaries of the craft were technically and even physically pushed back. He started to use coloured paper or paper stained with dark washes and to employ gouache or bodycolour, an opaque watercolour paint thickened with gum or clay. He worked out ways of preserving areas of white paper as white through his technique of blotting and 'stopping out', and he built up complicated structures with layers of wash, opposing warm and cool colours, defining lights and shadows with dampenings, abrasions and scrapings. He learnt idiosyncratic short-cuts for fluently conveying the bits which some artists make obviously tedious work, like leaves of trees and waves at sea. The 'tinted drawings'[72] which were – though precocious – a bit finicky in the totality of the record they made (e.g. *The Cathedral Church at Lincoln*, RA 1795) were supplanted by work that was altogether more free and truly assured. The 'mappy'[73] topographical illustrations are replaced by an energetic autobiographical art.

The boy was now a man. At the age of twenty-one, in the summer of 1796, he went to Brighton, perhaps to recuperate from sickness, from overwork or from family turmoil in Maiden Lane. He also went to Margate again. In both places he sketched and painted, but only thirty in the hundred pages or so of his small leather-bound Brighton sketchbook[74] were used, and some of those are tentative sketches that to Finberg 'look like the work of an invalid'.[75] Others, however, in simple pencil and colour, have a thrilling sense of discovery about them: the ribs and planking of a beach-boat, seen from inside; a litter of pigs; suckling their mother; and a labouring couple, seen from behind, walking rather wearily with various burdens, a small girl in a striped dress grasping her parents' hands. As with the pigs, there is a fond or maybe rueful observation of family solidarity. Moreover, a slightly later sketchbook,[76] which he used from the autumn of 1796 into 1797, and which is known as the 'Wilson' sketchbook after the copies of some Richard Wilson pictures in it, is full of marvellously confident coloured drawings that make bold use of the book's small red-brown pages; despite its tiny format, it reveals – as do some of the Brighton sketches – a more emotional, less constrained artist than we have seen before.

While there was talk in the country of a French invasion, which caused the militias to be doubled in strength, Turner seems to have been having his own strenuous ups and downs. In Margate, presumably visiting his Marshall relatives, if not his old teacher Mr Coleman, he was apparently distracted one moment and fired up the next. Even Finberg, no enthusiast for the personal, believes that 'Something unusual must have happened [to him] in 1796.[77] Thornbury concluded that 1796 was the year that Turner caught 'the old ailment', love.[78] The girl was the sister of a former school-comrade, 'vows of fidelity were exchanged', but the affair was blighted by a separation: Turner left on a tour; she received no letters from her lover, possibly because they were kept from her by her parents, and she then yielded to the importunities of another more proximate suitor. Turner turned up again too late, and the disappointment – he had been jilted – soured him for life.

Although this romance as recounted by Thornbury is improbably stretched out, Turner may have failed to write promised letters to his love object and paid the price. An independent source, Robert C. Leslie, son of Turner's friend and fellow artist C. R. Leslie, wrote later that when he was living at Deal around 1869, 'my next-door neighbour was an old lady of the name of Cato; her maiden name was White; and she told me that she knew Turner well as a young man, also the young lady he was in love with. She spoke of him as being very delicate, and said that he often came to Margate for his health. She seemed to know little of Turner as the artist.'[79] That may be the way the young artist wanted it.

3: Rising Star

People saw Turner in different ways. And Turner saw himself in a way no others did. Fellow artists who tried to draw him found it difficult to catch a likeness – for one thing, he didn't want to be portrayed by others; it was almost as if he feared the effect of an evil eye. In public, he seemed to create an aura around himself that repelled the sizing-up gaze of would-be portraitists. It made him a hard subject to get hold of. About some of his chief characteristics there might be, in conversation if not in portraiture, ample agreement. He was fairly short – about five feet four inches in height. (This has been determined from a tailor's pattern for some of his trousers. His waist measurement was thirty-five inches.) He had a great beak of a nose, like that of a parrot or, putting it more admiringly, an eagle. His head seemed large, though with a low forehead that sloped back under a shock of brown hair, roughly parted in the middle. His eyes, in various lights, were blue, or bluish-grey, or grey, and, though they rarely met the eyes of other people, his gaze was described as penetrating. The lips were full, the complexion – at any rate in later life – ruddy. He was somewhat bandy-legged and had big feet. (Delacroix, whose Paris studio he visited on one occasion in either 1829 or 1832, remarked on his big shoes.)

'An odd little mortal,' was how one woman described him.[1] Dayes wrote in 1805: 'The man must be loved for his works; for his person is not striking, nor his conversation brilliant.'[2] Others called him 'homely'.[3]

When trying to describe his appearance in maturity, people often used down-to-earth analogies: 'he had the look of an English farmer', said Delacroix.[4] The Redgraves believed he looked like 'a long-stage coachman'.[5] Many at most stages of his life were made to think of a seafarer: 'A short, sturdy, sailor-like youth', said Lovell Reeve;[6]

'the captain of a river steamboat', wrote C. R. Leslie;[7] 'a North Sea pilot', was the view of Leslie's son Robert.[8] The profile appealed to those who wanted to make a quick study, for seen from the side the Punch-like nose was an unforgettable feature: one example was the drawing done on 31 March 1800 by George Dance. But the future engraver Charles Turner a few years earlier caught his fellow RA student full-face and – perhaps in consequence of what was going on – in an unforgiving mood. Charles Turner wrote at the bottom of his study the ironic title, 'A Sweet Temper'. Under beetling eyebrows the very widespread eyes seem to be enfilading the presumptuous draughtsman with musket fire.

Turner's vision of himself at the age of twenty-three or twenty-four was less hostile. He is not known to have painted any other portraits, or indeed any other self-portraits, so the oil painting he did of himself between 1798 and 1800 must have sprung from a strong feeling at a particular time. It was as if he wanted to put on record a J. M. W. Turner who was his own man. He, too, chose the front view, which diminished the impact of his nose. He wore the same accoutrements that Dance and Charles Turner sketched him in, a high-collared dark jacket, a waistcoat and a white cravat wound several times around his neck and then knotted in front: the effect is almost that of a heavy bandage or a sort of adult swaddling to prevent coughs and colds. For someone who in the painting of human figures sometimes showed a haphazard sense of anatomy, this head-and-shoulders is a remarkably skilful piece. Clearly the subject interested him. There is no hint of his less than average height or jockey's legs. He catches the self-absorption and also the self-assurance, the ambition and the intransigence. For a moment, too, he seems to have had a young man's normal interest in clothes: in a sketchbook of 1799, he listed the apparel he needed on a tour, including three coats, ten waistcoats (five coloured, four white, one black), four under-waistcoats, six shirts, eight cravats, six cotton stockings and three silk stockings.[9]

Turner's career as a professional artist continued to be bound up with the Royal Academy – with its politicking, its exhibitions, its friendships and animosities. And in 1798 and 1799 he went on making use of the Life Academy, for although portrait painting was never going to be his *métier* he wanted to practise his sketching of figures, in chalk and watercolour.[10] For a young man whose own family life provided little stability or ease, the Academy offered a sure point, a professional home from home. It was also an arena in which, without too much damage to his reputation as a difficult introvert, he could perform and shine. He could do this more easily because by and large it was not a high moment in English art. Great honours and great prices were awarded to Benjamin West, the American-born President of the Academy, whose gloomy, staged and stilted paintings met a contemporary mood. (West's unenterprising inaugural presidential address in 1792 dwelt on two subjects, 'the excellence of British art, and the gracious benevolence of His Majesty', George III, the Royal Academy's – and West's – great patron.) Henry Fuseli, another incomer (from Switzerland), achieved celebrity for his highly mannered and theatrical pictures (and among Academy students for his flamboyant behaviour as Keeper of the Plaister Academy and then Professor of Painting). Thomas Lawrence's portraits were fashionable and de Loutherbourg's landscapes popular. But the only threat to Turner would have been Thomas Girtin, had he painted in oil.

Within the Academy, Turner's name was being bandied about. Joseph Farington's diary, full of Academy and Whitehall gossip, first alludes to him in 1795, but towards the end of the century his name appears often. During the 1798 exhibition Opie and West were both talking of him. According to Northcote, Farington 'was no painter; he cared nothing at all about pictures, his great passion was the love of power',[11] and on 24 October 1798 the diarist was apparently pleased with the coming man's recognition of him as a mentor and guide to his Academic future:

> Turner has called. He talked to me about his present situation. He said that by continuing to reside at his Fathers he benefitted him and his Mother: but he thought he might derive advantages from placing himself in a more respectable situation. He said, he had more commissions at present than he could execute and got more money than he expended. The advice I gave him was to continue in his present situation till he had laid aside a few hundred pounds, and he then might with confidence, and without uneasy apprehensions, place himself in a situation more suitable to the rank he bears in the Art.

Farington soon afterwards went to call on Turner in Maiden Lane:

> The apartments, to be sure, small and ill-calculated for a painter.

He shewed me two books filled with studies from nature – several of them tinted on the spot, which he found, he said, the most valuable to him ... He requested me to fix upon any subject which I preferred in his books, and begged to make a drawing or picture of it for me. I told him I had not the least claim to such a present from him, but on his pressing it I said I would take another opportunity of looking over his books and avail myself of his offer.[12]

Turner, quietly and pragmatically currying favour with the Academy hierarchy, had also put aside his inclinations for working undisturbed to invite John Hoppner to call. Hoppner, portrait painter to the Prince of Wales, chose a study Turner had done in Durham, but was not inhibited by the gift from giving the younger man some advice. Turner told Farington that Hoppner had suggested Turner's paintings were a bit too *brown*. Turner was therefore 'attending to nature' to try to correct this tendency. The humility is startling, and perhaps rather suspect.

Via the Academy, Turner was also coming to public notice. In 1797 the art critic of the *Morning Post*, Anthony Pasquin, wrote about Turner's *Fishermen coming ashore at Sunset previous to a Gale*, which was displayed at the RA exhibition:

We have no knowledge of Mr Turner but through the medium of his works, which assuredly reflect great credit upon his endeavours. The present picture is an undeniable proof of the possession of genius and judgment and, what is uncommon in this age, it partakes but very little of the manner of any other master. He seems to view nature and her operations with a peculiar vision, and that singularity of perception is so adroit that it enables him to give a transparency and undulation to the sea more perfect than is usually seen on canvas. [13]

An Ipswich amateur of the arts, Thomas Green, wrote in his diary:

June 2, 1797. Visited the Royal [Academy] Exhibition. Particularly struck with a sea view by Turner – fishing vessels coming in, with a heavy swell, in apprehension of [a] tempest gathering in the distance, and casting, as it advances, a night of shade; while a parting glow is spread with fine effect upon the shore. The whole composition, bold in design, and masterly in execution. I am entirely unacquainted with the artist; but if he proceeds as he has begun, he cannot fail to become the first in his department.[14]

A wider acquaintance is suggested by a Gillray print of this same year. A woman named Mary Ann Provis claimed to have rediscovered Titian's secret colouring methods, which she sold to several gullible Academicians. Gillray's satire showed Sir Joshua Reynolds rising from the grave (Sir Joshua had devoted much time in trying to find out the Venetian methods), while a monkey, representing Fashion, urinated on a stack of works by artists who had not succumbed to Mrs Provis's lures: the artists included Beechey, Loutherbourg and Turner.

Among the enterprising patrons of the day, the word was 'Keep an eye on this man Turner.' In 1797 Edward Lascelles, heir to Lord Harewood, wanted drawings from him of the family mansion in Yorkshire.[15] The banker and amateur artist Sir Richard Colt Hoare, also of Adelphi Terrace, invited him to his country estate at Stourhead, Wiltshire. In 1798 Lord Yarborough got him to make some drawings of the new mausoleum that the architect James Wyatt had designed for his estate in Lincolnshire. William Beckford asked him to the great Gothic abbey he was building at Fonthill in Wiltshire, to make a watercolour record – and Turner went. More distant subjects were proffered by Lord Elgin, who in early 1799 paraded the idea that Turner – recommended by Benjamin West – should accompany him to the Ottoman Empire to draw sculptures and buildings in Athens, with the understanding that Elgin would keep all his work and Turner would give Lady Elgin free drawing lessons. But they could not agree on a price. The mean Elgin had offered Girtin £30 a year for the job; Turner – with big ideas of his own value – apparently wanted £400 a year, though later Elgin claimed he had asked £700 to £800 a year, plus expenses. A more satisfactory patron shortly appeared in the shape of John Julius Angerstein, timber trader, insurance broker and art collector. Turner told Farington in May 1799 that Mr Angerstein was to give him forty guineas for a drawing of Caernarvon Castle in north Wales – a price greater than he would have asked – which he had rendered as if it were a seaport by Claude, with the river and Menai Strait beyond illumined by sunset. Angerstein had asked him to come and see his pictures, which included Claude's *Seaport with the Embarkation of the Queen of Sheba* (1648). The magnate came into the room while Turner was looking at this picture, so Turner's colleague George Jones later recalled. 'Turner was awkward, agitated, and burst into tears. Mr Angerstein enquired the cause and pressed for an answer, when Turner said passionately, "Because I shall never be able to paint anything like that picture." '[16]

Not every patron of the arts thought Turner could do no wrong. In 1799, Dr Whitaker, a local historian and vicar in the north of England, took up Turner to illustrate his history of the parish of Whalley, but had problems with the young artist, whom he condescendingly called 'the draftsman'. Turner refused to copy a 'very bad painting' which a friend of Whitaker's wanted used in the history instead of a Turner sketch, and Whitaker had trouble soothing his 'draftsman', who had 'all the irritability of youthful genius'.[17]

Turner put his name down for associate membership of the Royal Academy in 1798. There were twenty-four candidates, including his teacher Thomas Malton; two would be chosen. Farington had promised his vote. Turner came third in the ballot, after Shee and Charles Rossi. It was a good result for the first attempt, and particularly since he was standing in defiance of an Academy rule, adopted two years before, that artists were not eligible for election until they were twenty-four; he was twenty-three. (Thomas Lawrence had been the youngest Associate to date, being elected in 1791 when he was only twenty-two.) But the following year Turner had no age barrier. He continued to call on Farington, asking his advice again about whether he should take separate lodgings and telling him about his recent sketching tours in Yorkshire, Wales and elsewhere. At the end of October 1799 Farington noted in his diary that Turner 'has been in Kent painting from Beech trees. Very anxious about the election.' Farington told him he had no reason to worry, and he was right. At the election in November Turner came first in both of two ballots and was elected Associate. He went next day to thank Farington. At the Council meeting on the last day of the year, the Secretary of the Academy read out Turner's obligation, which Turner signed. Benjamin West, the President, who had not in fact voted for him, handed him his diploma.

Turner and those who backed him both deserved congratulation: Turner for his success in concealing what might have been seen as selfish characteristics; his supporters in recognizing the overwhelming strength of his art (which outweighed any doubts about his personal charm and acceptability as a member of their club). Turner at this stage could readily manifest different attributes on different occasions, an ability that was not necessarily consciously directed but was simply a part of his natural shrewdness and drive. To Angerstein he no doubt appeared a man wonderfully moved by great painting. To Farington he seemed not prickly and surly but 'modest and sensible'.[18] Turner's protective colouring was also to be seen in his work, which – despite Hoppner's strictures against its brownness – continued sombre in tone, as if reflecting the dark and desperate times: naval mutinies; war with France; rebellion in Ireland; more and more talk of a French invasion. His pictures also reflected the aesthetic prognostications of Edmund Burke, the author, orator and member of Parliament, and of Sawrey Gilpin, the animal painter who had supported Turner in his first attempt to become an Associate in 1798 and had written an influential essay on landscape colouring.

The northward thrust of Turner's sketching tours at this time fitted this tendency. His works from the fells of the Lake District, from the River Tweed in Northumberland, and from the mountains of north Wales met contemporary demands for art that prompted mysterious evocations and profound thrills, and for which the term 'Sublime' made a convenient label. Observing 'fearful sights' and striking a note of 'gloomy grandeur',[19] Turner even while fitting the fashion (if not slavishly following the theory) began to capture landscapes that embodied deeper human aspirations.[20] In writing, Wordsworth and Coleridge were treading the same mountainous paths in search of the powers immanent in high places. The rather tight, ceremonious eighteenth-century world of witty cliques and classical learning was giving way to a more expansive, 'romantic' time. Meanwhile across the Channel the divine right of kings was being supplanted, to the accompaniment of bloodshed and terror, by the natural rights of the people.

During the 1790s, the members of the London Corresponding Society held their meetings at the Bell Tavern, in Exeter Street, a hundred yards or so from Hand Court. Over a supper of bread, cheese and porter they discussed the hardness of the times, the dearness of all the necessities of life, and the business before them: Parliamentary Reform. The Society helped organize provincial groups that shared its goal, worked to spread the revolutionary ideas of Tom Paine, and corresponded with members of the French National Assembly and Jacobin Clubs. They terrified the British government, which in the course of the decade became so fearful of revolution that it suspended Habeas Corpus and prohibited 'seditious' meetings. In 1799 it banned the Society and other radical groups. By the Combination Act of that year, the formation of trades unions was prohibited and summary trials were allowed. The journalist William Cobbett, returning from eight years in the young United States to what he thought was Merry England, was soon enlightened. In 1800 he set up the offices of his newspaper the *Porcupine* in Southampton Street and began to cast his fierce eye on government corruption, on place-mongering and other features of what he called the deadweight system.

Turner's politics cannot be inferred from the proximity of this radical activity. It is not known if he read the short-lived *Porcupine* or its long-lived successor, *Cobbett's Political Register*. But there are grounds for suspecting that the barber's son – Mr Coleman's pupil – hid a quirky dissidence under the deference and sensibleness that Farington was shown. Farington at this time thought that a number of Royal Academicians and Associates had radical sympathies. William Beckford was one of the earliest of a line of Turner's patrons who had forward-looking political inclinations. Now, at the end of the century, Turner was interested in the story of the extermination of the Welsh bards by King Edward I: the artist-performers who were the guardians of the language and hence the spirit of a small nation, wiped out by an absolute monarch. Thomas Gray had given this theme an airing in his poem 'The Bard', and other painters had also taken it up as a subject. Turner didn't finish either of the watercolours he started on this theme, but his *Caernarvon Castle* watercolour of 1799–1800, shown at the RA in the latter year, has in the foreground a bard prominently chanting under a Claudean tree. The lines of verse the painter attached to this picture referred to Edward I as 'the tyrant'. (The verse is doggerel enough to be by Turner, as we shall see; and if it is his, it is among the first of his poetic effusions to be put before the public.)

In the same year, he exhibited the darkly brooding *Dolbadern Castle*, also a north Wales subject, and the verse – from the cloudy syntax and random punctuation presumably also by him – struck the note of the tremulous sublime once again, while making a less oblique reference to political freedom:

How awful is the silence of the waste,
Where nature lifts her mountains to the sky,
Majestic solitude, behold the tower
Where hopeless OWEN, long imprison'd, pin'd
And wrung his hands for liberty, in vain.

The Welsh prince Owain ap Gruffydd was held captive in Dolbadern Castle from 1255 to 1277, but the man who kept him there was his brother Llywelyn – to the Welsh 'the Last Prince', but to Owain no doubt a tyrant, too. And while it alludes sadly, even romantically, to the difficulty individuals have in effecting political change, the painting's most powerful and most fatalistic suggestion concerns the power of nature. This puny, ruined castle doesn't match up to the surrounding mountains.

Turner made his own leap to freedom at this time. The hints Farington had been receiving from the younger artist about looking for his own establishment in the expanding area north of Oxford Street were not just idle talk. In late 1799 Turner moved to lodgings in Harley Street. The house, number 64, stood on the south-west corner of Harley Street and Queen Anne Street. His landlord was the Reverend W. Hardcastle, who had recently taken over the lease from Robert Harper, a schoolmaster. Harper's school in a garden building had been attended by Turner's friend William F. Wells, the watercolour painter and drawing master, when a boy. Wells, a friend for the last seven years or so, may have alerted him to the possibility at 64 Harley Street, but the rooms were not problem-free. Turner dropped in to see Farington on 16 November. He talked with unusual forthcomingness about painting – 'Turner has no settled process but drives the colours about till he has expressed the ideas in his mind' – and also about his new quarters, where much painting was going on. Farington noted, 'J. Serres is to have the use of a parlour and a room on the 2nd floor in the house in which Turner lodges in Harley St., which he much objects to as it may subject him to interruption. Serres to use these rooms from Ten in the forenoon till 3 or 4 in the afternoon, when the Rev. Mr Hardcastle is to have the use of them … Serres' wife etc. are in other lodgings where his family concerns are carried on.'[21] John Thomas Serres was the son of Dominic Serres, a Frenchman who had been marine painter to George III. John Thomas followed him in this job and also became marine draughtsman to the Admiralty, using a specially provided boat to sketch the French coast. But Turner's worries probably centred less on the marine painter, whose interest in the sea he shared, than on Serres's wife, Olivia. Turner wanted a house where he could work without distraction. Even though Mrs Serres was in 'other lodgings', these were not very far away at 81 Wimpole Street, and she might well invade his life at Harley Street. Olivia Serres was a tall, well-built and most often heavily rouged woman who claimed to be the daughter of the Duke of Cumberland, brother of the King; she believed that she therefore deserved the title of princess. As a young girl she had been Serres's student and had fallen for him. Turner, having moved out of Maiden Lane, did not need another disturbed woman in his life.

W. F. Wells's daughter Clara was about twelve years old at this point and an altogether less disconcerting member of the fair sex. She later recalled Turner's 'constant and almost daily' visits during this period. Her father was regarded by Turner 'as an able counsellor in difficulties' and the Wells house as 'his second home, a haven of rest from many domestic trials too sacred to touch upon'.[22] The Wellses had a London residence in Mount Street, off Grosvenor Square, a fifteen-minute walk from Harley Street.[23] They also had a tile-hung country cottage at the village of Knockholt, on the North Downs in Kent, where Turner studied the beeches and the northward views back to London; on a clear day you could see the dome of St Paul's Cathedral and the hills of Hampstead. In town, Turner 'usually spent three or four evenings in every week at our fireside', Clara said, more than half a century later. 'I can still vividly recall to mind my dear father and Turner sketching or drawing by the light of an Argand lamp, whilst my mother was plying her needle and I, then a young girl, used to read aloud some useful and entertaining work.' Clara added that 'Turner loved my father with a son's affection; and to me he was as an elder brother.' When at Knockholt, 'many are the times I have gone out sketching with him. I remember his scrambling up a tree to obtain a better view, and there he made a coloured sketch, I handing up his colours as he wanted them.'[24]

His move out to his own separate lodgings and his eagerness to spend time with the happy Wells family may have been prompted by the implosion of the Turner household in Maiden Lane. His once pre-eminent need – expressed to Farington – to be of help to his parents seems to have been set aside for the sake of self-preservation and undisturbed work a little while before the final calamity. This occurred on 27 December 1800, when his mother was admitted to Bethlehem Hospital for the insane. It must have been a terrible Christmas. Mary Turner was said to have led her husband William 'a sad life',[25] and this was the saddest moment in it. At the crunch, neither husband nor son appears to have wanted to take full responsibility, for the petition to the hospital governors to admit Mary Turner was made not by William senior or junior but by one of the hairdresser's brothers, Joshua. (Joshua had also made the jump from Devon to London, where he worked in the Storekeeper's Department of the Excise Office.)

The petition may not have been entirely truthful; it stated that Mary Turner 'has been disordered in her Senses – about 9 months, was not so before, is in a healthy condition, has not attempted Mischief'. But if, as some believe,[26] her problem was schizophrenia, she may well have been violent. A security bond for Mrs Turner was given by Robert Brown, an upholsterer from Bedford Street just around the corner from Hand Court, and Richard Tremlouw, a wig-maker from Air Street off Piccadilly.[27] These bondholders pledged that they would remove the patient if the hospital governors asked them to. However, after a year in Bethlehem, or Bedlam as it was familiarly called, Mary Turner was moved to the ward for females considered incurable. Mary Turner remained in the incurable ward for over two years. She did not leave Bedlam alive.

Bethlehem Hospital – originally the Hospital of St Mary of Bethlehem – was an elegant building in Finsbury Circus, backing on to the north side of London Wall and facing out on Moorfields. On the piers of its gates were carved two figures – one representing 'Raving', the other 'Melancholy' – sculpted by Gabriel Cibber, the Danish artist who settled in England and fathered Colley Cibber, the playwright. But the site and the architecture were the only magnificent features of this ghastly institution. Patient-care was primitive. Although by this time the hospital had ceased to allow visitors on Sundays and holidays to gaze at the inmates, a popular mid-eighteenth-century leisure activity at a charge of a penny, the therapeutic regime at Bedlam still involved cages, chains, beatings, blood-lettings and straitjackets. Fuseli blithely told Farington not long after this that he had learnt from a medical man that 'the greatest number of those confined there were *women in love*, and the next greatest class was *Hackney and Stage Coachmen*, because of the effect on the pineal gland of constant shaking they are subject to'.[28] Roughly 120 patients in various states of dementia, peaceful and violent, were managed by four keepers. A Parliamentary report on the hospital not long after this revealed that a 'resident' apothecary visited at the most for half an hour a day. The steward and the matron were both seventy years of age and let the servants run everything. The sole physician came infrequently and recommended such remedies as 'bleeding, purging, and vomit', though not in winter, 'when the house is excessively cold'[29] – so cold, indeed, that some inmates lost fingers and toes from frostbite.

The admission of Turner's mother to this snakepit was facilitated by a special relationship. The hospital physician was Dr Thomas Monro. The job, which he held from 1791 to 1816, was a cushy sinecure that had been handed down from his grandfather to his father and then to him. Thomas Monro, a specialist in mental disorders, was, as noted, called in early during George III's reign to look at the King, and consulted again in 1811–12 when he is said to have prescribed a hop-pillow for the uneasy royal head to rest on. After a Parliamentary enquiry in 1815–16 into the running of Bethlehem Hospital had determined that there were gross inadequacies, Dr Monro was compelled to retire. Among the faults, at least as far as the doctor was concerned in the case of Mary Turner, seems to have been a free-and-easy way with the hospital admission regulations.

She was of course the mother of his star protégé. That may have been the main criterion governing her admission to Bedlam, for she appears to have met none of the other qualifications. 'She was *not* violent, dangerous, or suicidal,' writes Cecilia Powell, though this is taking the possibly biased word of her sponsors. 'She was *not* in the position of having nobody to care for her, since she had a husband six years her junior who was so strong and healthy that he outlived her by over a quarter of a century; and she had an equally healthy son aged 26. She was *not* a pauper.'[30] William Turner senior was working as a hairdresser until 1801. William Turner junior was doing extremely well as an artist and already had money invested in Government Funds. Father and son could have afforded to put Mary Turner in a private asylum, at a cost of roughly a pound a week, and there she might have had more considerate care than in

Bedlam. It would seem that, thanks to Dr Monro, she was confined at no cost to her husband and son. We have no sure way of entering their minds and hearts on this matter. Maybe they were at the end of their tether and grasped – without much thinking – Dr Monro's offer to have Mary looked after. Maybe they acted like poor people and Bedlam was the destination they would have expected for one of their kind if mentally ill. But it is doubtful whether the Marshalls, worthy tradespeople, would have been happy with this. *They* might well have considered that the Turners were being cheap, mean-spirited and unloving.

Maybe, too, Mary's son was scared that he would also become mad – feeling, as many did then, that madness was infectious or ran in the family. Did he think of J. R. Cozens, also a Monro patient, and other demented artists, waiting for him to join their benighted group? Perhaps he felt he had 'assisted' on the domestic scene long enough. Or it could be that the rising star was simply ashamed of his mad mother. Hereafter Turner seems never to have mentioned her. Indeed, he reacted badly if others mentioned her. Some years later a Dr Shaw, who believed he was related to Turner on his mother's side, paid him a visit; he said, 'May I take the liberty of asking you whether your mother's name was Marshall?' Turner immediately looked furious. 'His manner was full of majesty, accompanied with a diabolical look.' He replied that the liberty Dr Shaw had taken was unwarrantable and his presence was an obtrusion.[31] Yet Dr Shaw managed to quieten the fiery artist with an apology, and the doctor was invited to make another visit.

Some anguish persisted. Long after, he told John Ruskin that the young writer's first duty in life was to his mother. When with the Wells family, he seems to have warmed in the convivial atmosphere and to have realized that much of it was due to his friend Wells's wife, Clara's mother. He noted in a sketchbook in 1806, for no benefit but his own memory: 'There is not a quality or endowment, faculty or ability, which is not in a superior degree possesst by women. Vide Mrs. Wells. Knockholt. Oct.'[32] Turner's mother died in Bedlam on 15 April 1804. From the start his relations with women were characterized by loss: his sister; the Margate girl; and now his mother. In many respects, he seems never to have got over her.

As one woman was moving away from him, another was moving closer. We don't know how and when he met Sarah Danby. It took

Farington, the diligent busybody, until 11 February 1809 to find out about her. On that date he recorded that the artist A. W. Callcott had commented to him in regard to Turner, 'A Mrs. Danby, widow of a musician, now lives with him. She has some children.' As far as his Academy colleagues were concerned, Turner had been successfully covering his tracks for the previous nine or ten years.

He may have met Sarah by way of her husband John Danby. Danby was a Catholic, a composer of songs and masses, who held the post of organist at the Chapel of the Spanish Embassy in London and perhaps also at the Sardinian Chapel. He married Sarah Goose in Lambeth in April 1788; she was about twenty-two, with Lincolnshire connections. The Spanish Chapel, in Manchester Square, was designed by Joseph Bonomi around 1793. Possibly as a result of doing work on the backgrounds of Bonomi's drawings, Turner was introduced to Danby. The Danbys were Covent Garden residents, for some years after their marriage living at 26 Henrietta Street, a block away from Maiden Lane. Another link may have been through the Callcotts. The brother of Turner's friend and follower Augustus Wall Callcott was a musician, John Wall Callcott, who like Danby composed glees – short, serious and not always gleeful choral pieces for unaccompanied male singers. Danby's glees won prizes; he received a medal for one of his best known, 'Awake, Aeolian Lyre'. In 1789 his second collection of glees was published and in the list of subscribers is a 'Mr Turner'.

Another point of contact may have been the Pantheon, where Danby performed at a concert in February 1791, not long before Turner's scene-painting stint there. Although Miss Ann Dart told Ruskin that young Turner, when staying with the Narraways, 'had for music no talent',[33] this may have been because he was too shy to display any; certainly he was interested in music. Some of his sketchbooks have pages that have been ruled for music, a few with notation, and one setting out a 'gamut for flute'.[34] In several sketchbooks of these years, he jotted down ballads he heard and some he may have invented: 'swains', 'longing arms' and other unoriginal elements are put into play. One lengthy song whose words he laboriously inscribed had to do with a sailor and his Nancy; it must have touched him – perhaps he wanted to share it with a Nancy or Sarah of his own when he returned from his sketching tour.

Sarah was about nine years older than Turner. She was a practising Catholic and if he was attracted to her on first meeting he no doubt had to wait for John Danby's death before expressing his desire. Danby died on 16 May 1798 at 46 Upper John Street, near Fitzroy Square, on the evening of a concert for his benefit, possibly from the effects of severe rheumatoid arthritis. Since her marriage, Sarah had been busy bearing children: three out of six or seven survived at the time of her husband's death, and she was a month or so pregnant with another. After the loss of her husband, Sarah went on living for the next couple of years at Upper John Street, not far from Whitfield's Methodist Chapel, with her daughters: Louisa Mary, born 1792; Marcella, born 1796; Caroline Melissa, born July 1798; and Teresa, born January 1799. She was probably hard-strapped and quickly turned to the Royal Society of Musicians for help. From the Society she received a pension of £2 12s 6d a month, together with a payment of between fifteen shillings and one guinea a month for each of the girls until they were fourteen, when the Society paid for them to be apprenticed as schoolteachers. The laws of the Society provided that a widow's allowance should cease if she 'be found in illicit intercourse'. It was evidently to her advantage not to have it known that she was cohabiting, and this fell in nicely with Turner's keen sense of privacy.

His affair with Sarah Danby remained a love-in-a-corner thing, and despite Farington's record of Callcott's comment and several other clues it has been denied by some writers ever since. Thornbury does not mention Sarah Danby. Finberg, referring to 'Mrs Danby' without a 'Sarah', apparently confuses her with her niece Hannah, who came to work for Turner as a servant in 1809 at the age of twenty-three, and claims this 'Mrs Danby' was only a housekeeper, whose 'children came to be regarded by the gossips as Turner's offspring'.[35] Jean Golt suggests that Hannah, rather than Sarah, was Turner's mistress and the mother of the two daughters he sired.[36] Although this takes us somewhat ahead, in order to establish once and for all the Sarah Danby–J. M. W. Turner connection it is worth stating a few relevant facts.

In Turner's second will and various codicils to it he referred to Sarah Danby and to 'Evelina and Georgiana T', who were 'her daughters' or 'her natural daughters'. Evelina, born about two and a half years after her Danby half-sister Teresa, was baptized in the church of Guestling, near Hastings, East Sussex, on 19 September 1801, where the baptismal register records her as 'Evelina, daughter of William and Sarah Turner'.[37] In a Sussex sketchbook used a few years after this event, Turner wrote on the label, 'Lewes, Hurstmonceux, Pevensey, G., & Winchelsea'- all the place-names in full except the 'G.' Guestling, near Winchelsea, is the only name beginning with a G that is possible. Turner seems to be suppressing some of the evidence, as if he didn't dare spell out the full name for fear of giving something away, even to himself. But other clues to the link later emerged. When Evelina got married, in October 1817, it was under the name of Evelina Turner; one of the two witnesses was Sarah Danby. In a letter of 15 December 1853, Evelina's husband refers to his wife as Turner's daughter, and in a letter of 24 November 1865 to a lawyer acting for Turner's relatives in claims against his estate, Evelina mentions 'my father's will'.[38] Despite suggestions by several writers other than Jean Golt that Turner was the lover of Hannah Danby, there is absolutely no evidence to that effect. Sarah's position, whether as his mistress or as the mother of his children, cannot be challenged. Yet it is not known what he did in the way of keeping her and the girls; probably he did as little as possible.

For a while after Turner started his affair with her, Sarah Danby went on living with the four Danby girls at 46 Upper John Street. But the Danby name disappeared from the rate books at that address in 1800. It seems likely that they moved in that year to 75 Norton Street, not far from John Street, off Portland Road. This is the address Turner gave for publication in the 1801 Royal Academy catalogue; he had vacated his rooms in Harley Street for the time being, whether to avoid the Serreses or to be with Sarah. He took the Norton Street house together with a merchant named Roch Jaubert, a friend of the Danbys, who had been a witness at the wedding of John and Sarah in 1788. Jaubert, a cheesemonger at one stage, published a book of John Danby's glees after the composer's death. In May and June 1802 William Turner senior wrote from this address to his brothers Price and John in Devon about their mother's will. Whatever his attachment to Sarah, Turner was soon back at 64 Harley Street, where he bought a lease of the entire house and planned to build a gallery for showing his pictures.[39] It would seem from Callcott's remark to Farington in 1809 that Sarah and the girls (now five in number, one being his) went with him, at least for a few years, or were brought thereafter to see him from time to time. The Reverend Trimmer visiting Turner's later residence around the corner in Queen Anne Street occasionally saw a girl whom, 'from her resemblance to Turner, he took to be a relation'.[40]

Turner of course looked at women not only as a man but as an artist. A woman was a form of flesh and muscle and bone. In one sketchbook of 1798,[41] he drew a female nude with coloured chalk and watercolour: high-lit conical breasts, puppety head lowered, hair falling behind, with one leg and knee raised awkwardly across the other; and on the next page, as if getting closer, he concentrated on a smaller area of the woman, from one shoulder to one knee. A couple of years later a sketchbook[42] contains two pen-and-ink and white chalk female figure-drawings on coarse blue paper: one seated, quite chubby, mostly clothed, though her loose dress reveals a breast; the other kneeling, holding a prone man in her arms, his head in her lap. Rightly or not, one thinks of Sarah Danby.

Their relationship was evidently not smooth. In another sketchbook he used in 1799 and 1800, containing drawings of Salisbury and of barges and sunsets, Turner jotted some memoranda about money at one end and at the other several stanzas of a poem:

> Love is like the raging Ocean
> Winds that sway its troubled motion
> Women's temper will supply
>
> Man the easy bark which sailing
> On the unblest treachrous sea
> Where Cares like waves in fell succession
> Frown destruction oer his days
> Oerwhelming crews in traitrous way
>
> Thus thro life we circling tread
> Recreant poor or vainly wise
> Unheeding grasp the bubble Pleasure
> Which bursts his grasp or flies.[43]

On the stormy seas of life, the poor artist-sailor goes around in circles, vainly seeking pleasure, and, time after time, runs into deep trouble as he does so. With Sarah, he seems to have asked himself now and then, What have I taken on? Turner's interest in *The Aeneid* grew in the ensuing years and a particular theme from it that he developed in his works was the passion of Dido and Aeneas – fatal for Dido, whom Aeneas, pushed hither and yon by the gods, abandoned. His painting *Dido and Aeneas*, probably begun in 1805, was exhibited at his gallery in 1806, and as if to mark an occasion was shown again at the Royal Academy in 1814. Were there several sunderings of his attachment to Sarah?

If Turner's qualities as a partner were not to be relied on and if – as we shall see – his attributes as a parent were extremely poor, he was a good son to his father. The old man had encouraged him; he would, after his mother's departure, look after his father. William Turner senior used to tell anyone who would listen that when the Tory government of William Pitt the younger imposed a tax on hair powder in 1795, it drove out wigs and ruined his trade. Fashions were changing, too, and queues and powdered hair were on the way out. As a result of his declining business and possibly of his son's success, the older Turner gave up his shop and house at 26 Maiden Lane and went to live with William junior – at Harley Street, at Norton Street and then at Harley Street again. He became the odd-job man or factotum, preparing canvases for painting and varnishing them afterwards, running errands, and in his West Country accent chatting with visitors as his son rarely did. However, his free and easy ways did not extend to overlooking the behaviour of his brother Jonathan in regard to their mother's estate. She died in April 1802 and Jonathan, a baker, who had been caring for her at his house in Walcot, near Bath, claimed most of her money. The four other brothers and their sister Mary didn't like this at all, and William wrote from Norton Street to insist strenuously that Jonathan be brought to heel and all share alike as their mother had intended. The estate was worth less than £300. After some squabbling, Jonathan was paid his expenses for looking after difficult old Mrs Turner and the remaining assets were split equally among the six heirs. The episode has been seen as indicating the hard-headed, grasping nature of the Turners, but it may well be that they were not unlike most people where family money was concerned.

On 12 February 1802, Turner was elected a full Academician. There had been vacancies as a result of the deaths of several members of the Academy. Farington lobbied for Turner, and he was elected to fill the first vacancy by a clear majority over the opposing candidate, Joseph Bonomi. (Curious that on becoming an Associate Turner had triumphed over his former teacher Malton, and on this occasion prevailed over a presumed part-time employer and possible early contact with the Danbys; but it was a small, competitive world.) Turner sent his 1800 painting of Dolbadern Castle as his Deposit or Diploma picture and on 14 April 1802 received his Diploma as an Academician, signed by the King. Until that time, only one man, Thomas Lawrence, had been elected a full Academician at a younger age. As with Turner's election to associate status, this success seemed based almost wholly on the other members' perception of his artistic ability; 'his manners were not ingratiating'.[44] When Stothard suggested to Turner that he call on his supporters to thank them for their votes, Turner bluffly replied that he 'would do nothing of the kind. If they had not been satisfied with his pictures, they would not have elected him … Why thank a man for performing a simple duty?'[45] But Turner himself felt the moment worth celebrating and signalling. 'W. Turner' was now replaced in the Academy catalogue by his full name, 'Joseph Mallord William Turner, R.A.' On election to full membership, the new Academician was expected to make a present to the Academy. Turner gave the Academy twelve silver dessert spoons. In fact, he went on being more generous to the Academy than to any of the women in his life.

Numerous paintings and many drawings and sketches of this time demonstrate what the members who voted for him evidently felt: he was now a master. He was attacking the art world on several fronts, as a maker of history paintings, of landscapes and of marine paintings. He was taking on rivals past (for the most part) and present (where he had few competitors). His first very large painting in oil was called *The Fifth Plague of Egypt*. It shows a thunderstorm breaking over the pyramids while a pair of Old Testament characters in the heavily shadowed foreground strike attitudes of classic doom and lamentation. In the RA catalogue (for 1800) Turner attached a quotation from Exodus: 'And Moses stretched forth his hands towards Heaven, and the Lord sent thunder and hail, and the fire ran along the ground,' which suggests that his knowledge of the Bible wasn't perfect; he was mixing up the fifth with the seventh plague. Two years later Turner painted *The Tenth Plague of Egypt* and cavalierly set the catastrophe in what looks like an Italian hill-town. In the *Fifth Plague*, the mood is one of sublime terror owing much to Poussin; the storm is derived from one Turner had experienced in the north Wales mountains the year before. The *Morning Chronicle*, reviewing the RA show, said the painting gave Turner 'a new character in his profession'.[46] The *Monthly Magazine* described Turner as a master whose name could be coupled with Claude's and Gainsborough's. A patron agreed with the critics: William Beckford bought the picture for 150 guineas and also bought for 35 guineas each five large watercolours Turner had done of Fonthill Abbey, the Gothic extravaganza which Beckford himself was building.

In the following year, however, there were amid the plaudits intimations of criticism to come. In Turner's *The Army of the Medes destroyed in the Desart by a Whirlwind* (a painting now lost), viewers had trouble finding the Medes. One writer said that Turner 'seems to have buried his whole army in the sand of the desert with a single flourish of his brush'. And the *Porcupine*, Cobbett's paper, declared, 'Mr Turner has doubtless heard that obscurity is one source of the sublime, and he has certainly given to the picture a full measure of this kind of sublimity. Perhaps his work may be best described by what a lady said of it – that it is all flags and smoke.'[47]

No one complained about several seascapes of these years, in which the flags were ensigns and wimpels and the smoke was spume and spray. In 1800 the immensely wealthy coal and canal magnate Francis Egerton, the Duke of Bridgewater, commissioned a seapiece from the painter of the moment to hang in his collection with a painting by the seventeenth-century Dutch artist Willem van de Velde the younger. Shown at the Royal Academy in 1801, the picture was called *Dutch Boats in a Gale: fishermen endeavouring to put their fish on board*; its dark, louring clouds, breaking seas and nearly colliding boats made a great impression. The picture was the hit of the show, 'a peculiar favourite of the spectators'.[48] Some who would later be less enthusiastic about Turner talked it up strongly. According to Farington, the amateur painter and connoisseur Sir George Beaumont thought very highly of it, though he was aware of Ludolf Backhuysen as an influence and thought 'the water rather inclined to brown'.[49] Beaumont's protégé John Constable thought highly of it, too, though it seemed to him much in debt to van de Velde. Fuseli told Farington after the Academy dinner on 25 April that Turner's picture was the best in the exhibition and was reminded of another Dutch painter; the picture, he thought, was 'quite Rembrandtish'.[50]

A boat in imminent danger was also the subject of one of his two marine works in the 1802 exhibition. During his sketching tour the previous summer he had gone up the north-east coast making studies of waves, boats and beaches, but earlier experiences as a boy watching the fishermen at Margate, and going out with them in their boats, may have also been invested in *Fishermen upon a Lee-Shore, in Squally Weather*. The boat being pushed out through breaking surf into 'waves in fell succession' is barely under control – will the sea win this little battle? Although this brilliant rendering of the dangers of a leeshore got most of the viewing attention, its companion seapiece now seems the more impressive picture. This was *Ships bearing up for anchorage*, a more spacious and less melodramatic work than the Bridgewater Seapiece, that its purchaser Lord Egremont took to his great country house at Petworth in Sussex. The impact of the Egremont Seapiece is so all-encompassing that a viewer may neglect to consider the preparatory work that went into its making. A sketchbook of 1800–2 called 'Studies for Pictures'[51] has some of the rehearsing. Four or five drawings in pencil, pen, white chalk and wash on light-blue-grey paper are of ships, some possibly done at sea, some perhaps from a beach. Turner occasionally added a note, for example: '2nd ship at a greater distance ... wet sand ... figures'.[52] He catches with a few lines and shadows the scend of the sea, the sense of a ship rolling under bare poles, another heeling in a gust of wind. The essence of ships, sky and water, and a few figures on the shore, delivered with – as Fuseli would have noticed, had he seen the drawing – Rembrandtian economy.

4: Fair Winds and Foul

The war with France had been going on and on, sapping Britain's energies and spirits; but in March 1802, the Treaty of Amiens was ratified between the two ancient rivals. In the ensuing period of peace it became possible for the first time in nine years for English travellers freely to visit their neighbour across the Channel. Hundreds jumped at the chance. Among them were many with artistic inclinations: the actor John Philip Kemble, the banker-poet Samuel Rogers and a number of Academicians, including the President Benjamin West, Martin Archer Shee, Joseph Farington, Henry Fuseli, Robert Smirke and the new full member, Joseph Mallord William Turner, twenty-seven years old that April and bursting to see France. Leaving his mother in Bedlam, and his father, his mistress Sarah Danby and baby daughter Evelina in Norton Street, Turner went abroad. It was his first foreign journey. That he had been looking forward to it for some time is evident from his small 'Dolbadarn' sketchbook of 1799, in which – amid lists of castles, clothes and meteorological terms and of course pages of sketches – are found jottings of basic French grammar: pronouns personal, possessive, demonstrative and relative; the verb *donner*, with the imperfect spelt wrongly *je donnerios*. 'What have *you* given me?' Sarah might have said as the artist, clutching his portmanteau, sketchbooks, new passport and letters of credit, made his *au revoirs* and went out of the door.

Farington and Fuseli set out a month after Turner, but the three met while in Paris and compared notes on their journeys. Farington recorded in his diary how he haggled with the packet master at Dover over the fare to Calais, in the end bringing the price down to half a guinea. A supper of chickens and pigeons at Montreuil cost fifteen pence per person. Burgundy was expensive – four shillings and sixpence a bottle – but the beds at their inn were 'very well'.

They set off next morning at 5.15. 'At the barrier going out of town, a Savoyard girl played on a Mandoline, which catching the ear of the Drivers, they stopped their Horses a little. The musick, the appearance of the warm rays of the rising sun, and the freshness of the air caused very agreeable sensations.'[1]

Turner, starting in mid-July, had for companion on this trip no poor workman but rather a well-to-do country gentleman, amateur artist and antiquarian from Durham named Newbey Lowson, two years older than himself. The professional and the hobbyist had probably been introduced by the Earl of Darlington, for whom Turner later did drawings of his place, Raby Castle, and who with Lord Yarborough now took a helpful interest in the new Academician. The noblemen seem to have subscribed funds for Turner to make the journey to the Continent, and Lowson may have assisted. Yarborough also provided a reference for Turner when he applied for his British passport. As Farington was to hear, Turner and Lowson travelled in some style, buying their own two-wheeled carriage – a 'cabriole' – in Paris for thirty-two guineas and selling it there on the way back; they stayed in good inns and took their own Swiss servant, also acquired in Paris, who was paid five livres a day.

But such a journey at this time was never altogether comfortable, and the initial stages were particularly onerous. It generally took a full day to reach Dover by a more than averagely expensive coach from London. At the harbour, the porters who carried luggage to be cleared at the customs house were notoriously avaricious. The town charged passengers several shillings to cross the gangplank to the packet. Tobias Smollett some years before called the route from London to Dover the worst road in England: 'The chambers are in general cold and comfortless, the beds paltry, the cooking execrable, the wine poison, the attendance bad, the publicans insolent, and the bills extortion.' Dover was a den of thieves; the inhabitants lived by piracy in time of war and 'by smuggling and fleecing strangers in time of peace'.[2] The Dover-Calais crossing was the shortest (other packets started from London and landed at Dunkirk or Boulogne), but even then could take as long as fourteen hours. Passengers wishing to be out of the elements were crowded into a single cabin. Turner's friend the journalist Cyrus Redding in 1815 found 'beds in tiers, male and female in confusion together … there was no moving without trampling upon the prostrate, even the floor occupied'. Redding spent most of the voyage on a coil of rope, near the cabin door, wrapped up in a cloak, drinking hot water and brandy, and munching biscuits. If low tide or contrary wind or sea conditions made difficult the packet-boat's entry into Calais harbour, passengers were often transferred into smaller boats, rowed by apparently fearless desperadoes.[3]

This happened to Turner. A good sailor who did not suffer from *mal de mer*, he travelled as ever with all his senses vibrantly alert and recording mechanisms immediately at hand. Deluges of spray may have kept his sketchbook closed in the small boat that ferried them in, but it was open the moment he set foot on shore. Next to a bold black and white chalk sketch of breakers and boats, he noted, 'Our landing at Calais – nearly swampt.'[4] He then went out along the pier in order to watch and draw his packet – or another like it – as it came charging in through the tormented seas of the congested entrance. Waves broke over the pier. The usual pier-head crowd of gawkers and fisherfolk were this day crouching as much out of the wind and spume as possible. The arriving English packet, forced over to the west side of the entrance by a bluff French fishing boat reaching out with scandalized mainsail, looked as if it was going to run down a smaller boat being rowed desperately across the channel. Imminent shipwreck – man against the raging ocean – was still his matter (and never ceased to be), and in this case the viewers at the Royal Academy next summer would see the result: *Calais Pier, with French Poissards preparing for Sea, an English Packet arriving.* Here were his favoured comings and goings, with near collisions and imminent disaster, rendered in a way that was both a personal tribute and a toss of the gauntlet to the old Dutch sea-painters. 'Poissards' was a typical Turner off-the-cuff piece of Franglais, derived it would seem from the actual French word *poissarde*, which meant fish-wife.

Turner's touring experiences this year we know about largely through the somewhat formalizing filter of Farington's diary. Possibly because he was travelling in unaccustomed upgraded style with Mr Lowson, Turner failed to make in and around his sketches his usual jottings about the weather, distances and expenses. His sketchbooks on this trip were comparatively hefty – the 'St Gothard and Mont Blanc' sketchbook[5] was nineteen by twelve inches and leather-bound – and the carriage and servant were therefore useful. Yet Turner apparently felt his usual secretive urges. One of the rules of the companionship said to have been laid down by him was that Lawson was not to draw any view that Turner was sketching. It has also been claimed that Turner failed to show his generous fellow traveller a single sketch he had made. Given the enforced proximity of their coach-sharing, this seems unlikely.

Turner got back to Paris from Switzerland towards the end of September and Farington encountered him on the 30th sketching in the Louvre. On this day and the next, Turner unburdened himself of various terse travel tips and complaints. He told Farington that on the outbound journey they had taken four days to go from Paris to Lyon and the countryside was 'very bad', though from his sketchbooks it certainly didn't look that way around Mâcon. He was three days in Lyon. He thought little of what he saw of the River Rhône there but the views of the Saône were fine. Scotland – where Turner had toured the previous year and Farington had also been – came to mind: though the buildings of Lyon were better than those of Edinburgh, there was nothing so good as Edinburgh Castle. But generally in Lyon he felt unsettled; the place was 'very dear', and the nightly price of a bed was eight livres. In the vicinity of Grenoble, 'about a day's journey beyond Lyons … there are very fine Scenes'.

As for 'Swisserland', as Farington (and Jane Austen) spelt it, Turner found that country in 'a very troubled state, but the people well inclined to the English'. In particular, Grindelwald was fine. Lawson didn't seem to figure in Turner's account, at least as Farington reported it, of his journey through the defile of the Grand Chartreuse, nine miles long, which abounded 'with romantic matter'. Then Chambéry–Geneva–Chamonix–Bonneville. Still the Prince of Rocks, Turner climbed the Montanvert at Chamonix and made a tour around Mont Blanc over the Col du Bonhomme and Col de la Seigne to Courmayeur and then Aosta via a road over which French and Austrian forces had battled in 1796. He regretted not going to Turin, only a day distant from Aosta. He (and presumably Lawson) crossed by the Great St Bernard Pass to Martigny – 'Road and accomodations … very bad' – but thereafter things improved on the way to Chillon and Vevey. He saw the Reichenbach Falls and the great fall at Schaffhausen – eighty feet deep, and 'the width of the fall about four times and a half greater than its depth', the observant tourist told Farington. 'The rocks of the fall are inferior to those above the fall of the Clyde but the fall itself is much finer.'

The information that passed between the senior and junior Academicians was for the most part professional artist-talk. Turner thought Switzerland offered 'rather broken' lines in the way of landscape features, though 'there are very fine parts … [with] fragments and precipices very romantic and strikingly grand'. However, Swiss trees were 'bad for the painter', except for the walnuts, and the houses had 'bad forms – tiles abominable red colour'. It seems that despite his well-to-do companion, carriage and servant, Turner kept his thrifty habits to the fore. 'He underwent much fatigue from walking, and often experienced bad living and lodging.' He told Farington that his living expenses amounted to seven shillings a day and it was 'necessary to make bargains for everything, everywhere, or imposition will be the consequence'. Swiss wines were also bad for this painter: 'too acid for his constitution being billious'. Yet 'the weather was very fine' – that is, as far as Turner was concerned, for 'he saw very fine thunderstorms among the mountains'. Turner worked hard, as always; in his three months away he made about 400 drawings, over four a day, of which a score were in colour. He was trying to put it all down, perhaps a little unselectively, bowled over by Alpine scenery.

These sketches are his real memories of the tour, and Farington would have got a better sense of Turner's journey by looking at them rather than listening to him. But he hadn't just sketched mountains, passes, meadows, rivers and waterfalls. In one vellum-bound sketchbook with a few drawings of Swiss local people is a fairly detailed drawing, brightly coloured, of a young woman in a rumpled bed, with another person lying behind her.[6] The almost spotlit young woman is bare-breasted, and her festival dress lies on the floor. Although two women's hats are among the litter of clothes, the person in shadow close behind the Swiss girl looks to this viewer like a man – with tousled hair, eyes closed, his left arm under her head and his hand on her naked shoulder. Indeed, if one puts aside scholarly notions of a brothel frolic or lesbian entanglement, it is possible to see in the cartoon-like features of this 'companion' the rudiments of a self-portrait by the artist–tourist himself. He sleeps, after his romp with the chambermaid, while the young woman, bemused, looks at the dawn light flooding in through the window. How soon afterwards, one wonders, did he make this drawing – turning *amor* into art? This sketchbook, by the by, has scribbled inside its back cover Turner's rendering of the ribald old song 'I am a Friar of Orders Grey'.

Many English travellers felt awestruck when arriving in post-revolutionary Paris and seeing everywhere relics of bloody times. Haydon, travelling with Wilkie at the end of the war, noted places that brought to mind 'murders in the name of liberty' but also felt some insular bemusement: 'The first impression of Paris ... on an Englishman used to the regularity of London streets was that of hopeless confusion; cabs, carts, horses, women, boys, girls, soldiers, carriages, all in endless struggle; streets narrow, houses high, no flat pavement ... ' On the other hand, the people had vitality, and 'though most men enter Paris with disgust, no man ever left it with disappointment'.[7]

Turner knew where he wanted to concentrate his attention. During his several weeks in Paris he often went to the former Royal Palace of the Louvre. There, in what Farington called 'the Picture Gallery', works were to be seen which the Corsican upstart's armies had recently 'liberated' from Italy – for example, Titian's *Death of St Peter Martyr* from the Church of SS Giovanni and Paolo in Venice. Turner made rough sketches of the masterpieces and noted the way colours were used and effects were achieved. He sometimes – as with Titian's *Christ crowned with Thorns* – recorded details of the thickness of paint and the process by which the picture had been painted, but he also felt with the subject, Christ, remarking how 'the position of the legs indicates excessive pain and exertion to sustain it'.[8] He copied Titian's *The Entombment*, and of the *St Peter Martyr* he wrote in his sketchbook (which he labelled 'Studies in the Louvre'), 'The characters are finely contrived, the composition is beyond all system, the landscape tho natural is heroic, the figure wonderfully expressive of surprize and its concomitate fear. The sanguinary assassin striding over the prostrate martyr who with uplifted arm exults in being acknowledged by heaven. The affrighted Saint has a dignity even in his fear ...'[9] There is something touching about this earnest analysis, this identification with the characters, in words put down only for himself.

These Titian studies were to bear fruit in his own attempt at a biblical Old Master, *The Holy Family*, exhibited at the RA the following year, 1803. But other masters made their impression in the Louvre. He looked hard at Raphael's *Infant Jesus caressing St John* and

Correggio's *St Jerome*. He studied the works of Giorgione, Guercino and Domenichino. He was unhappy about Rembrandt's *Susannah*, 'finely coloured but ... miserably drawn and poor in execution', and the Rubens *Landscape with a Rainbow* was characteristically 'defective as to light and the profusion of nature'. He could see ways of making better even the works of artists he particularly admired, like Ruysdael's *A Storm off the dikes of Holland*; in his sketch of this picture, Turner improved things by leaving out a house that he thought spoilt the 'dignity' of the right side of the painting. One artist – one of his heroes – unaccountably missing from his Louvre sketchbook was Claude Lorrain, despite being the obvious influence on another large canvas he was thinking about at this time, and showed in 1803, *The Festival upon the Opening of the Vintage at Mâcon*. (On seeing this picture, the influential patron and amateur artist Sir George Beaumont said it was 'borrowed from Claude but all the colouring forgotten'.[10] What Sir George did not notice was that Turner for his Claudescape had with cross-Channel panache taken more from an earlier sketch he had done of the Thames at Richmond than from his recent studies of the Saône at Mâcon.)

However, another French seventeenth-century painter was fully though not uncritically regarded. Turner approached Nicolas Poussin, a master, on remarkably equal terms. He admired his *The Israelites gather manna* ('the grandest system of light and shadow in the collection') but declared of Poussin's *Deluge*, 'The colour of this picture impresses the subject more than the incidents, which are by no means fortunate either as to place, position or colour, as they are separate spots untoned by the under colour that pervades the whole. The lines are defective as to the conception of a swamp'd world and the fountains of the deep being broken up. The boat on the waterfall is ill-judged and misapplied, for the figures are placed at the wrong end to give the idea of falling ...'[11] He wrote as someone who had recently been gazing at waterfalls, who knew boats and had looked – not long before, off Calais Pier – into the fountains of the deep.

With Farington he also went to an exhibition of contemporary French painting and 'held it very low – all made up of *Art*'. But his taste was eclectic; he made a sketch of P.-N. Guérin's *Return of Marcus Sextus*, a painting of 1799 that Haydon would have liked, and he approved as 'very ingenious' the small domestic paintings of Madame Marguerite Gérard, the wife of the historical painter Baron François

Gérard: she had studied with Fragonard, her brother-in-law, and liked painting young mothers with children. Turner, Farington and Fuseli called on the sculptor Jean-Guillaume Moitte at the Louvre but found the Frenchman 'cold and dry, apparently little disposed to conversation', at least with the three Royal Academicians. And they visited Mademoiselle Jaullie, said by Farington to be an Irish pupil of David, and apparently a more genial person, for Fuseli began to talk about how he had got started as an artist, stealing bits of candle at the age of eight so that he could sit up all night drawing.

At the end of 1802 the King, George III, took against those supposedly royal Academicians who had been seduced into travelling to France that year, believing them to have 'democratical' tendencies.[12] Turner might have felt the not uncommon impatience for reform, but no one questioned his patriotism. All the same, like many others he was fascinated by the Frenchman – 'the Giant Usurper' as the British press called the First Consul – who dominated the times. Napoleon and his wars figured obliquely in such works of Turner's as *The Army of the Medes destroyed in the Desart by a Whirlwind* (RA 1801) and *Hannibal crossing the Alps* (RA 1812). Less oblique and more contemporary were a number of canvases: *The Battle of Fort Rock, Val d'Aouste, Piedmont, 1796* (RA 1815), several with the Battle of Trafalgar and its sailor casualties as a subject, and one showing the bloody aftermath of Waterloo. Much later, in 1842, he exhibited *War. The Exile and the Rock Limpet*, a quirky comment on the banal end of Napoleon's career. Although he was generally unaffected by the trappings of class or title, he did not reject occasional contact with great names. He later got to know Louis-Philippe, son of the Duke of Orléans, while he was living in English exile in 1815 near his own house in Twickenham.

The Peace of Amiens came unstuck. Rightly suspicious of Bonaparte's empire-building intentions in the Near East, Britain hung on to Malta, despite the treaty provisions. In May 1803 the two countries were at war again. By then, another closer-to-home calamity had affected Turner. His fellow apprentice Tom Girtin had also gone to France during the truce to draw and etch Parisian scenes. Critics and colleagues had sometimes boosted Girtin or Turner at the expense of one another. Hoppner reported to Farington on 9 February 1799 that 'Mr Lascelles as well as Lady Sutherland are disposed to set up Girtin against Turner – who they say effects his purpose by industry – the former more genius. Turner finishes too much.'[13] Four years on, Farington listened to Northcote discuss the merits of various artists, including Lawrence, Hoppner and Beechey: 'Turner has a great deal of painter's feeling, but his works too much made up of pictures, not enough of original observation of nature: Girtin had more of it.'[14]

Yet Turner himself was in no doubt of his old friend's talent. Whether or not he made the oft-quoted remark, 'Had Tom Girtin lived, I should have starved,'[15] or declared to a collector named Chambers Hall that he would have given one of his little fingers to have made a drawing like Girtin's *White House*, Turner greatly admired the mature work of his companion-worker at Dr Monro's and John Raphael Smith's. He was naturally aware of Girtin as a competitor in the landscape business. Hearing him say that he was planning to go sketching at St Albans, Turner didn't dally. He had gone and come back with a book of sketches before Girtin got around to making the excursion. Yet much later he told the Reverend Trimmer, 'We were friends to the last, although they did what they could to separate us.'[16]

In 1802, however, poor Tom Girtin was in the grip of severe pulmonary disease, and on 9 November, despite the ministrations of the ubiquitous Dr Monro, he died. The funeral took place at what by now seemed to be Turner's church, St Paul's, Covent Garden, and Turner was among Girtin's friends who were there, inevitably thinking about fate and fortune. Poor Tom, despite his immense talent, was gone at twenty-seven.

Turner was not only alive but pushing for promotion in the workings of the Academy. Farington that December noted: 'Turner was very urgent to be a Visitor'[17] – that is, a Visitor in the Academy Schools; but Farington tried to cool his ambitions. Turner was in the thoroughly committed stage of the new volunteer, pitching in for every assignment. Unfortunately the way ahead was not straight, acceptance not easy. The institution to which he wanted to give his all was riven by dispute; pleasing one faction of the forty oil-painters, sculptors and architects who were members meant annoying another faction. The Academy was both a club and a trade union. Its members met constantly and exchanged useful tips, gossiping about patrons and prices. Its functions included an annual dinner. At that of 1803, the first toast as usual was to 'our founder and patron', the King, and was followed by the singing of the national anthem. Other toasts were accompanied by airs and glees, among them 'The Wooden Walls' and 'To love I wake'. After the final toast, to 'the Patrons of the Arts', came the air 'Inspire us Genius of the Day'. At the 1804 dinner, with the Prince of Wales as the guest of honour, the actor John Philip Kemble competed with the Duke of Norfolk in a battle of Greek and Latin quotations and then entertained the company with recitations from Shakespeare.

The Academy gave financial relief to elderly artists and their families, and bolstered the status and sales of its active members. Academicians often did good turns for each other, as Thomas Lawrence did in 1809 when he suggested to a collector named Penrice who was thinking of buying some Old Masters that he instead patronize living artists, in particular 'Mr Turner'.[18] And they also indulged in the back-biting and bitchiness that members of most clubs are susceptible to. Probably, all in all, it was better to be a member, on the inside, not necessarily taking it all too seriously (though that was not Turner's way), than to be on the outside, not a member, taking it extremely seriously, as did Benjamin Haydon-a man whose genius unfortunately (for someone who was sure he was a great painter) flourished most richly in words. Too often for the sake of his career these were words of invective against the Royal Academy.

The royal patronage of the Academy was one cause of internal dispute at this time. How much influence should the King (who provided its home at Somerset House) have in Academic business? Secondly, what were the rights of Academicians, and should their General Assembly – made up of all forty members – have the power to approve and disapprove the decisions of the eight-strong Academy Council? Malcontent members used these questions about hitherto undefined matters to make trouble and forward their own interests. A court party formed which wanted to get rid of the Academy President, Benjamin West. West's supporters, keener on the independence of the Academy from the Crown, were led by Farington. In 1803 the court party had a slim majority on the Council. There was a great deal of politiciking over items that now seem very dusty indeed. West – a former royal favourite but now one of those the King believed to be admirers of Napoleon – lost a large commission for paintings at Windsor Castle and had his royal pension stopped, and there was a further attempt to do him down by leaking to the press an accusation that one of his paintings for the 1803 RA exhibition had already been exhibited in 1794 (second showings were not allowed); West claimed that he had repainted and altered the picture.

This was the year that Turner was on the exhibition hanging committee for the first time, along with Soane, Rossi, Bourgeois, Richards and Wilton. It was also the year he joined the Academy Council for a statutory two-year term. To begin with he faithfully attended Council meetings, and usually voted with the Democrats against the Royalists, but soon he was absenting himself – it was as if he couldn't stand this almost domestic acrimony. Through much of 1804 he failed to show up at Council meetings. The disagreements often became hotly personal. Farington reported an argument – overheard by William Daniell – between Turner and his fellow Council member the painter Sir Francis Bourgeois. The dispute took place after the Academy General Meeting on Christmas Eve 1803, and was notionally about whether to give a gold medal for architectural drawings at the annual prize giving, with Turner among the majority who voted not to give one on this occasion. Farington wrote:

> Bourgeois had said that when premiums for Architecture & for Models [Sculpture] were to be adjudged, he attended to the opinions of those who were more conversant in these studies. Turner hinted that [it] might be well that he [Bourgeois] should [do the same] in what related to the figure, signifying his incompetency. This caused Bourgeois to call him a *little Reptile*, which the other [Turner] replied to by calling him a *great Reptile* with *ill manners*.[19]

Turner's self-importance – or was it simply independence? – was asserted on 7 February 1804, when he refused to tell Farington how he planned to vote in the upcoming election for the post of Keeper of the Academy. Farington himself had a fight with the small-statured artist at a Council meeting on 11 May. Turner arrived late, after some of the other members – Farington, Bourgeois and Smirke – had briefly adjourned for a private chat. When they came back into the room, it was to find (wrote Farington) that Turner 'had taken *my chair* and began instantly with a very angry countenance to call us to account for having left the Council. On which, moved by his presumption, I replied to him sharply and told him of the impropriety of his addressing us in such a manner, to which he answered in such a way that I added his conduct as to behaviour had been cause of complaint to the whole Academy.'[20] This from his old mentor! That Turner's brilliance as a painter might be accompanied by what some of his colleagues saw as big-headedness seemed now to affect their judgement of his pictures. Hoppner, after seeing Turner's works at the 1803 Exhibition, 'reprobated the presumptive manner in which he [Turner] paints, and his carelessness. He said that so much was left to be *imagined* that it was like looking into a coal fire, or upon an old wall, where from many and undefined forms the fancy was to be employed in conceiving things ... His *manners* so presumptive and arrogant were spoken of with great disgust.'[21] On the way home from a dinner at Hoppner's on 13 May 1803, Farington talked with other guests on the subject of artists 'being like their works ... Turner confident, presumptuous, – with talent'.

There was a sudden burgeoning of disapproval for the works of this ill-mannered genius. Fuseli – generally an enthusiastic supporter – joined Sir George Beaumont in using the term 'blot' about parts of some of Turner's pictures,[22] and these critics meant something accidental and messy, and not products of chance disposed to produce 'one comprehensive form' in the way that Alexander Cozens had used blots.[23] Even the press was no longer full of praise. The *Sun*, commenting on *Calais Pier*, said that 'The sea looks like soap and chalk ... All the figures are flat and are by no means enlivened by *dabs* of gaudy colour.' On 16 May the *True Briton* wrote, 'A certain artist has so much debauched the taste of the young artists in this country by the empirical novelty of his style of painting that a humorous critic gave him the title of *over-Turner*.' This indicates that he already had followers, even disciples – which must have annoyed some of the senior Academicians all the more.

John Constable, the landscape artist who in 1802 exhibited his first picture at the RA but who, despite being only a year younger than Turner, had seventeen years still to go before he became an associate member of the Academy, talked to some of the younger artists and was startled to hear that they thought Turner's work was 'of a very superior order' and not 'in any extreme'.[24] The novelty of

Turner's colouring and the drama of his compositions threatened the static world of his older colleagues; there was something confusing in much of his work ('incongruity and confusion' – the *Sun* on *Calais Pier*).[25] He presented wreck and catastrophe, sometimes averted, sometimes witnessed and participated in. It was enough to make one want firm, ordered, understandable works to hold on to. And perhaps it was also confusing that he would then provide just that, producing pictures of such splendid serenity as the Mâcon harvest festival.

There were rumours at this time of members seceding from the Academy. If Lawrence, Opie, Fuseli and Shee pulled out, wouldn't Turner go as well? Word got around that he was building his own gallery, and would fail to exhibit at the Exhibition in 1804. But Turner, despite all these ups and downs, went on loving the Academy and wanting 'to be useful' to it, as he afterwards declared in a lecture.[26] Some of the ways in which he served the Academy will be looked at in greater detail later on, but at this point it is sufficient to note that although he continued to express disgust at the Academy's self-inflicted troubles – as he did to Farington in January, 1807 – he went on thrusting himself into prominence within its hierarchy: in the same year, 1807, he volunteered for the Academy's vacant Professorship of Perspective. And his affection for it lasted too. He felt for it, like a son for a mother.

As for his own mother, she died, still in Bedlam, on 15 April 1804. Where she was buried, or whether her son attended her funeral, we do not know.

5: Aladdin's Cave

April 1804 was important in another respect: it was the month in which Turner opened a gallery for exhibiting his own work. The reasons for this venture were numerous. The idea for it may have come from his friend William F. Wells, whose house in London and cottage in Kent had provided frequent refuge. Wells founded the Watercolour Society this year, and he may have prodded Turner into entrepreneurial activity; he was to do so even more notably two years later. Another factor in the establishment of the gallery was Turner's unhappiness with the way things were going at the Royal Academy, which had led to the rumours – heard by Farington – that he was not going to exhibit there this year 'but was painting pictures to furnish a gallery ... where he means to make an exhibition and receive money'.[1] He in fact took refuge in one of the Keeper's Rooms at the Academy this same spring to work on a painting, *Boats Carrying Out Anchors and Cables to Dutch Men of War, in 1665*, because of the turmoil at Harley Street.

In having his own display room Turner was not unique. Other painters – such as Fuseli, Northcote and West a few streets away – had their own galleries, and some, like Haydon, were forced to rent rooms for the purpose when they had completed a work that they wanted to receive special attention. Turner was not very fond of dealers, apart from one man later in life. Like many artists, he didn't always seem to want to *sell* his pictures, even though that was what his professional life and sustenance depended on, and what a gallery would seem to be designed to expedite. But the gallery may also have been a manifestation of the pleasure he increasingly took in keeping his pictures together; in a codicil he made to his will in 1832, the gallery became a fall-back position for effecting this if certain other measures were not adopted.

The gallery was the first of two he was to have near this corner of Harley Street and Queen Anne Street.[2] It extended from the rear of the house into the back garden; Turner, inviting Farington to see it, told him it was seventy feet long and twenty feet wide. The building works may have been one reason (Sarah Danby possibly another) that had kept him at 75 Norton Street, but in 1804 he resumed giving 64 Harley Street as his address in the Royal Academy catalogues. The proud painter sent out printed invitations to colleagues and collectors and the gallery was apparently opened by 18 April, three days after his mother's death. Evidently he was not in mourning, at least in terms of the public; it seems he wanted no one to know that his mother had died, or where.

Farington could not go to Harley Street at once but recorded Sir George Beaumont's carping verdict that Turner was displaying too many pictures – pictures, moreover, with overly 'strong skies and parts not corresponding with them'.[3] Another critic took a contrary tack, accusing Turner of sending inferior works to the Academy and keeping the best for his gallery. The gallery struck some members of the Royal Academy as part of a threatening tendency, seen in the formation of such rival bodies as the Watercolour Society and – in 1805 – the British Institution for Promoting the Fine Arts. A few artists made comments in which envy had an obvious role. Hoppner, in 1805, was to remark that the gallery 'appeared like a Greens stall, so rank, crude, and disordered were his pictures'[4] – and the implication may have been that Turner hadn't come that far from his origins in Covent Garden, near the vegetable market. But Turner, however proud of his profession, also could not help but treat it as a trade. In a letter to his friend James Holworthy in April 1827 he refers to his gallery as 'the shop'.[5] Callcott later told Farington that 'when Turner first opened his gallery, he hesitated whether he should ask one or two hundred guineas for about a Half Length size picture, and determined on the larger sum, as in that case if he sold only half the number he might otherwise do, his annual gain would be as much and his trouble less'.[6]

At least to begin with the gallery seems to have been a success. Influential buyers were forthcoming. Lord Auckland wrote to thank Turner for his invitation and to say that he and his family planned a visit. (Never one to waste a piece of paper, Turner did a quick pen-and-ink sketch of a shipwreck on the back of Auckland's note.) John Soane, the architect, came and Mrs Soane bought a drawing.

In May 1805 Sir John Leicester toured the gallery and decided he wanted Turner's new marine stormpiece, *The Shipwreck*, though it was the following January when he paid Turner the £315 price for it. In 1805 Turner thriftily used the Academy porters to hand-deliver to Academicians his invitations to his 'Exhibition *at home*', in what was also a way of showing he was on good terms with them as individuals, despite being miffed enough with the Council not to exhibit at the Academy that year.

In 1808 most of the paintings and drawings he sold were from the gallery, nearly two thousand pounds' worth. The gallery's 1809 opening was pompously announced in a newspaper on 23 April: 'Tomorrow Mr Turner the Academician will gratuitously open to the classes of Dilettanti, Connoisseurs and Artists, his gallery in Queen Ann Street West ...' The catalogue for that year's show listed the titles of eighteen oils and watercolours, several of which had poetic quotations attached, one being 'Thomson's Aeolian Harp'. The gallery seems to have stayed open for about two months, during the RA exhibition season, until the end of June. A note of pride as well as of anxiety was to be detected in a letter of 2 May 1810 to James Wyatt, an Oxford printseller, asking for the swift dispatch of a frame, 'because my Gallery opens on Monday next'.[7] But in 1811 he seems to have had no show; apparently the builders were in and he wrote to Wyatt again, saying he was so surrounded 'with rubbish and paint that I have not at present a room free'.[8]

The gallery was shut down in 1816 because Turner had a new scheme in mind. In 1820 he set to work in Queen Anne Street on a site behind the Harley Street buildings. This new place, an expansion and conversion of a mews cottage into a house and gallery, encroached a little on the land of his Harley Street properties – the gardens of the house he was living in and of the two houses adjacent to it, whose leases he also acquired. (The freehold was owned by the Duke of Portland; in 1823 Turner was granted new leases of sixty years from April 1822.) Turner was his own architect for the Queen Anne Street establishment, though Soane seems to have been an influence. He was also his own contractor and had to spend a good deal of time dealing with workmen.

On 13 November 1820, at which time he owned a house in Twickenham as well, he wrote from a disrupted Queen Anne Street to his friend Wells, who was then living in Mitcham, Surrey, and who, as a boy, had been a pupil in the school run by a Mr Harper in part of Turner's Harley Street property. The letter is characteristically full of half-jokes, crowded associations, confused allusions and literary references, for example to *King Lear* at the end of the first paragraph:

Dear Wells
Many thanks to you for your kind offer of refuge to the Houseless, which in the present instance is humane as to cutting you are the cutter. Aladdins palace soon fell to pieces, and a lad like me can't get in again unsheltered and like a lamb. I am turning up my eye to the sky through the chinks of the Old Room and mine; shall I keep you a bit of the old wood for your remembrance of the young twigs which in such twinging strains taught you the art of wiping your eye of a tear purer far than the one which in revenge has just dropt into mine, for it rains and the Roof is not finish'd. Day after day have I threatened you not with a letter, but your Mutton, but some demon eclypt Mason, Bricklayer, Carpenter &c. &c. &c. ... has kept me in constant osillation from Twickenham to London, from London to Twit, that I have found the art of going about doing nothing – 'so out of nothing, nothing can come.'
However, joking apart, if I can find a day or two I'll have a peep at the North Side of Mitcham Common, but when, it is impossible to say. Whenever I have been absent either something has been done wrong or my wayward feelings have made me think so, or that had I been present it would not have occurred, that I am fidgetty whenever away. When this feeling has worn *itself* away, at least I shall become a better guest. But in whatever situation I may be ... believe me to be
With sincere regard
Yours most truly
J. M. W. Turner[9]

He was allowed to rebuild the front part of the house to a depth of about twenty feet, so a letter from the Duke of Portland's office informed him, 'the front wall of which is to be built with new picked Stocks neatly pointed'.[10] The drawing room was upstairs, facing north on to Queen Anne Street, and Turner used it not for 'withdrawing', in the conventional after-dinner sense, but for his studio, for drawing and painting. Behind this room a new nineteen-foot-wide gallery extended fifty-five feet to the rear. A fireplace was centrally located in one of the long side walls; the walls themselves were painted dark red. A central skylight, with canopy-like blinds, provided diffused lighting.[11] In a sketchbook he had first used at Tabley House in 1808, he drew a diagram of heating pipes in a picture gallery and wrote, 'Flues from the back parlour or kitchen to warm the Gallery. Ventilation of Gallery – and the blinds to bow and set behind a moulding to exclude the Sun's rays.'[12] Turner's new house struck most visitors as dark – they suspected that he had designed it with minimal fenestration in order to avoid paying taxes, introduced in 1792, on houses with more than six windows. However, one visitor in the 1840s thought he was first led through darkened downstairs rooms in the house so as to be more responsive to the dazzling pictures in the gallery. [13]

The new gallery was opened in 1822 and as time passed Turner encouraged his artist-colleagues to visit it not just in the exhibition season. In a letter to Clarkson Stanfield, he writes, 'Pray make it any day most convenient to you and your friends to see the Gallery.'[14] Whether invited formally or by an impromptu hail in the street, visitors often felt a strange mixture of privilege and bewilderment. Some artist friends, like Charles Leslie, having visited on their own, later took their children to the gallery, as a treat, as to an Aladdin's cave. Several enthusiasts who were up from the country or newly arrived from abroad made it a prime point of call. Admirers like John Ruskin gained entrée to the gallery for their friends. Cyrus Redding, the journalist who accompanied Turner on parts of a West Country tour in 1811 or 1813,[15] encountered Turner some time later in Harley Street. 'He told me, in his rough way, that if I would come to his gallery in Queen Anne Street, I should see something with which I was acquainted, meaning a scene that I knew. I did not fail to call … I found that the work to which he alluded was his picture so much noticed, since called "Crossing the Brook". This picture, except the immediate foreground, was taken from a height on the Cornish side of the Tamar, above the Weir Head, and the inclined bridge, yet higher, connecting Cornwall and Devon.'[16] For Redding, as for a few others who had been with Turner in the field, the gallery provided a personal view of large-scale work that transfigured outdoor sketches. For many visitors it was an intimate manifestation of the results of what was mostly hidden, the daily industry with oil and watercolour, canvas and paint. They did not see his studio, where he stood at the easel lifting a brush to and from the palette over and over again, gazing, squinting, rarely standing back, following the dictates of eye and hand. And therefore for most who came to the gallery this was the next best thing, a dazzling experience.

But the gallery's glory days were soon gone. As the years passed the palace of pictures failed to give visitors a sense of brightness or splendour. 'Dingy',[17] 'dusty', 'dimly-lit'[18] and 'dilapidated'[19] were common descriptions. The neo-classical lines of the exhibition room were gradually obscured by clutter and even wreckage, as the artist seemed to lose interest in how his paintings were presented. Turner was aware that the gallery which had once been new and clean, with a skylight that did not leak, had become 'a dark abode',[20] but one wonders if he knew the full extent of its reputation. By the second part of his life, when we have most accounts of visits to his gallery, many art-lovers had the impression that it – and the house it was part of – was an ogre's castle, where a witch assisted with spells, and semi-wild cats, her familiars, stalked among rotting canvases.

This 'witch' was Hannah Danby, Sarah's niece, his house-keeper and general servant, whom time also treated badly. Elizabeth Rigby, an intellectual young amateur artist and writer on art topics who became the wife of the painter and Academy President Charles Eastlake, called her 'a hag of a woman, for whom one hardly knew what to feel most, terror or pity …'[21] The artist George Lance called by invitation in the 1840s but found entry difficult:

> After knocking and waiting for rather a long time, [the door] was slowly unchained and partially opened, so partially as to reveal only a portion of his servant – an old woman, one eye bandaged and the other seeming to require the same kind of protection. After some parleying, on my assuring her that I came by Mr Turner's own appointment, she let me in. Directly my name was announced, the great painter came into the hall, gave me a most hearty welcome, and conducted me at once into his gallery … It was one of those deluging days which we experience now and then … Guess my astonishment and concern to find the floor strewed with old saucers, basins, and dishes, placed there to catch the rain, which poured in from broken panes, cracks and crevices.

But Lance concealed his anxiety: 'indeed, so much was I impressed by the pictures which covered the walls that I soon forgot the danger they were subjected to'.[22] One picture in particular danger was Turner's watercolour *The Battle of Fort Rock, Val d'Aouste, Piedmont*, which the Reverend William Kingsley – a Yorkshire clergyman and friend of Ruskin – saw blocking up a window in an outhouse, 'no doubt to save window tax'.[23]

The thought of meeting the fearsome ogre bothered the Scots painter William Leighton Leitch. In 1842 Leitch had a conversation with one of the daughters of Turner's good friend and patron Walter Fawkes. Miss Fawkes asked Leitch if he had been to Turner's gallery, and Leitch said no – in fact, he had heard that Mr Turner objected to artists seeing his pictures. Miss Fawkes replied that this notion arose from Turner once catching an artist rubbing or scraping one of the pictures in his gallery (presumably to see how thick the paint was); his reaction can be imagined. But for Leitch there would be no difficulty, since Turner would know who he was. She would write to Turner that afternoon.

Leitch said, 'I would like the answer to keep as an autograph.'

Miss Fawkes said, 'There is little chance of that. Mr Turner is a very singular person and very chary of writing now. It appears that he once heard of an autograph of his having been sold for fifteen pence. Rather than let you have such a chance, he'll come all the way down from Queen Anne Street and leave his answer verbally at your door.'

Leitch said later that Miss Fawkes turned out to have been right:

> Turner himself came to Wilton Place and left word that he was going out of town, but that his housekeeper would let me see the pictures. Miss Fawkes told me that I was highly favoured, as Turner hardly ever allowed visitors to see his gallery except when he was on the spot himself. She told me that he had a 'peep-hole' from his painting-room to the gallery, so as to be able to see what people were doing, and hear what they were saying.
>
> So I went. I had heard of dirty rooms and of the mysterious house-keeper, and my curiosity was excited. The house had a desolate look. The door was shabby and nearly destitute of paint and the windows were obscured by dirt.

Hannah clearly was out of touch with Victorian values, possibly at this point because of the disfiguring disease she had, possibly from a bloody-mindedness she shared with her employer. Or was it that having been ordered not to rearrange things in his studio, where he feared the effect of interference under the guise of tidying and cleaning, she had gradually adopted a hands-off policy to the gallery and the rest of the house above stairs?

> When I rang the bell the door was opened a very little bit, and a very singular figure appeared behind it. It was a woman covered

from head to foot with dingy whitish flannel, her face being nearly hidden. She did not speak, so I told her my name, and that Mr Turner had given me permission to see the pictures. I gave her my card and a piece of silver with it, on which she pointed to the stair and to a door at the head of it, but she never spoke a word, and shutting the door she disappeared.

It was a raw, wet autumn day and it still felt like that indoors. Leitch wished he had brought a companion to this weird place. Turner's hall was not like any that he had seen in other London houses. It was square, empty of furniture, the walls a dingy brown with some casts of the Elgin marbles mounted on them. In the gallery, the rain was coming in through the broken and missing panes of the skylight. He put his umbrella up and kept it up. Although the whole place looked wretched, he was particularly shocked by the state of some of the pictures. In *The Rise of Carthage*, the sky was cracking, 'not in the ordinary way, but in long lines, like ice when it begins to break up. Other parts of the picture were peeling off – one piece just like a stiff ribbon turning over.'

The lone visitor walked back and forth, cold and uncomfortable. Finally he sat down on a dirty chair in the middle of the gallery, his umbrella over his head, and abstractedly contemplated a picture.

> From this state I was brought back to myself by feeling something warm and soft moving across the back of my neck; then it came on my shoulder, and on turning my head I was startled to find a most peculiarly ugly broad-faced cat of a dirty whitish colour, with the fur sticking out unlike that of any other cat. The eyes were of a pinky hue, and they glared and glimmered at me in a most unearthly manner. The brute moved across my chest, rubbing its head and shoulders against my chair. I put up my hand to shove the creature away, and in doing so let my umbrella fall, and this startled four or five more cats of the same kind, which I observed moving about my legs in a most alarming way.

Leitch took fright, made for the door and dashed downstairs. 'On looking back I saw the cats at the top glaring at me, and I noticed that every one of them was without a tail. As I could see nothing of the housekeeper, I opened the door for myself and shut it after me with a bang, so that she might hear I had gone.'[24]

The cats were on hand one day when Mrs Thomas Rose called to see the gallery. She was the wife of an art lover, Thomas Rose of

Cowley Hall, Uxbridge, and had brought along a woman friend. They 'were shown into a large sitting-room without a fire', Mr Rose later told Thornbury, and

> lying about in various places were several cats without tails. In a short time our talented friend [so Rose or Thornbury condescendingly refers to the artist] made his appearance, asking the ladies if they felt cold. The youngest replied in the negative; her companion, more curious, wished she had stated otherwise, as she hoped they might have been shown into his sanctum or studio. After a little conversation he offered them wine and biscuits ... One of the ladies bestowing some notice upon the cats, he was induced to remark that he had seven, and that they came from the Isle of Man.[25]

Turner's lovely *Fishing upon the Blythe-Sand, Tide setting in*, exhibited in his first gallery in 1809, was one of the stars of the second (Thornbury claimed Turner had refused to sell it to the generally antagonistic Sir George Beaumont); but it didn't for that reason always get looked after. According to Thornbury, it for a while 'served as the blind to a window that was the private *entrée* of the painter's favourite cat, who one day, indignant at finding such an obstinate obstacle in her way, left the autograph of her "Ten Commandments" on the picture ... All Turner said to Hannah Danby was "Oh, never mind."'[26] In December 1851, it was still among the twenty-five pictures in the gallery, one of two pictures, it seems, hanging to the left of the fireplace.

The stock of pictures in the gallery changed but slowly: some sold, yet some did not; a number of the very best remained, the results of abortive sales or simply too prized by their creator to be let go. The twenty or so paintings were hung close together, in some cases with their frames nearly touching. From the period 1800–10 were *The Tenth Plague of Egypt, The Death of Nelson* (later known as *The Battle of Trafalgar, as seen from the Mizen Starboard Shrouds of the Victory*), *The Garreteer's Petition, London from Greenwich, Kingston Bank* and *A Cottage destroyed by an Avalanche* – as well as the *Blythe-Sand*. Lady Pauline Trevelyan made several visits to the gallery in the later years and spoke of seeing, amid the darkness and dust, 'those brilliant pictures all glowing with sunshine and colour – glittering lagunes of Venice, foaming English seas, and fairy sunsets, all shining out of the dirt and neglect, and standing in rows one behind another as if they were endless'.[27]

Some visitors to the gallery never saw the proprietor; he was possibly away, on tour or at one of his homes-from-home, or else was busy in his adjacent studio, the holy of holies into which almost no one was allowed to intrude. A first cousin of his from Devon, Mary Ann Widgery, was shown around the gallery by her uncle, William Turner senior, perhaps in the 1820s, and thought it noteworthy that she did not set eyes on the artist. She later declared that, while in the gallery, her uncle told her that his son was 'an eccentric person'. (He also told her that his wife, the painter's mother, had been out of her mind.)[28] But once in a while the master made a sudden appearance. In 1822 he pounced, like one of his cats, on a young student. David Scott had been making a little 'memorandum' of a Turner picture,

> when a servant entered and said, 'Master don't allow sketching.' I was somewhat surprised, as no one had been in the room, and the door shut. However, I hardly considered what I was doing to be sketching, so I put in the line of the distance, which took two moments. Immediately in bounced a short stoutish individual, the *genius loci* himself. He said he was sorry I had not desisted, and I replied that what I had done was a mere trifle. He muttered something about memoranda and first principles, whereon I showed it to him and tore it up. He must have a peep-hole. And yet he is really a great painter.[29]

Others were luckier: John Sell Cotman managed to sketch a 'furtive copy' of Turner's painting *Harvest Dinner, Kingston Bank* at the first gallery in 1809; maybe there was no peep-hole there.

Frith told of one well-known 'picture merchant [who] though ... aware of Turner's dislike of the fraternity', determined one day to see the famous gallery in Queen Anne Street. 'Forgetting – or perhaps not knowing – that his card must be given to the servant before admission could be obtained, or believing, possibly, that the maid merely took it as a matter of form, he was proceeding leisurely upstairs into the gallery, when he found himself pulled backwards by his coat-tails, and on looking round saw the irate face of the great artist who, without a word, pointed to the front door, through which the dealer made an ignominious retreat.'[30]

Others saw a more affable Turner in his exhibition room. Young Robert Leslie made many visits to Queen Anne Street with his father, a member of the Academy. The senior Leslie, so his son thought, had leave to go to the gallery whenever he pleased. Robert

Leslie recalled several occasions when Turner, hearing friends at hand, would pop out of his studio

in a mysterious way … and then leave us again for a while …I particularly remember one visit, in company with my father and a Yankee sea captain, to whom Turner was very polite, evidently looking up to the sailor capacity, and making many little apologies for the want of ropes and other details about certain vessels in a picture. No one knew or felt, I think, better than Turner the want of these mechanical details, and while the sea captain [whose name was Morgan] was there he paid no attention to any one else, but followed him about the gallery, bent upon hearing all he said. As it turned out, this captain and he became good friends, for the Yankee skipper's eyes were sharp enough to see through all the fog and mystery of Turner, how much of real sea feeling there was in him and his work. Captain Morgan, who was a great friend of Dickens, my father, and many other artists, used to send Turner a box of cigars almost every voyage after that visit to Queen Anne Street.[31]

We learn occasionally that life went on elsewhere in the house. Robert Leslie also retold a story he had heard

of how Turner was one day [before 1830] showing some great man or other round his gallery, and Turner's father looked in through a half-open door and said, in a low voice, 'That 'ere's done,' and that Turner, taking no *apparent* notice, but continuing to attend his visitor, the old man's head appeared again, after an interval of five or six minutes, and said, in a louder tone, 'That 'ere will be spiled.' I think Landseer used to tell this story as having happened when he and one of his many noble friends were going the round of Turner's gallery about the time that Turner's chop or steak was being cooked.[32]

Turner was self-absorbed, self-preservatory, and even fierce when cornered, like a cat – sometimes cool, sometimes responsive. But he didn't lie around; he worked hard. As noted, the studio that adjoined the gallery – the hard-work room where the exhibited marvels were created – was off-limits to all but a favoured few. Clara Wells called it 'emphatically his sanctuary, his harbour of refuge'.[33] G. D. Leslie, brother to Robert, wrote later of going into the studio from the gallery to look at a painting on an easel that Turner wanted to show his father, and seeing, too, 'on a shelf a row of fat glass bottles, closed by bungs, with brilliant colours in powder inside them. These most likely contained orange and yellow chrome, orpiment, emerald green, red lead, or other pernicious pigments which the great genius delighted in and recklessly employed.'[34] The room – the 'drawing room' of the house – had the correct-for-a-painter north-facing outlook, giving daylight with less shadow.

According to Thornbury, the room 'was remarkable for a dusty and dirty buffet ... In this he kept the immemorial sherry bottle with the broken cork that served him for a decanter ... A friend who called upon him was treated to a glass of sherry from the old bottle and the old buffet – one glass. About the same time next year the artist came again, had another glass, and praised the wine. "It ought to be good," said Turner; "it's the *same bottle* you tasted before."'[35] (However, this is not a story that seems to fit with Thornbury's other stories about Turner's heavy drinking. And other visitors recalled the sherry bottle as being kept in a cupboard on the stairs.) Thornbury further claimed that 'the chief furniture' of the drawing room 'was a common oak-grained table, once, it is believed, the property of Lawrence; a huge paint-box, sheaves of uncleaned short brushes in a tin case, and a palette that also once belonged to Sir Thomas'.[36] Several more reliable witnesses saw a few models of full-rigged ships, which he kept close at hand to provide details of rigging arrangements and perhaps also simply as touchstones.

Yet, for most who came to 47 Queen Anne Street, the studio remained – as it did for a long time for the Reverend Trimmer's son, Henry Syer Trimmer – 'enshrined in mystery, and the object of profound speculation'. It was not until after the painter's death that the younger Trimmer gained entry to 'the august retreat'.

> I entered. His gloves and handkerchief lay on a circular table, which had in the middle a raised box (with a circle in the centre) with side compartments; a good contrivance for an artist, though I had never seen one of the kind before. In the centre were his colours, the great object of my attraction. I remember, on my father's observing to Turner that nothing was to be done without ultramarine, his saying that cobalt was good enough for him; and cobalt to be sure there was, but also several bottles of ultramarine of various depths; and smalts of various intensities, of which I think he made great use. There was also some verditer. The next object of interest was the white; there was a large bottle of blanc d'argent, and another of flake white. Before making this inspection I had observed that Turner used silver white. His yellow pigments consisted of a large bottle of chrome. There was also a bottle of tincture of rhubarb and

some iodine, but whether for artistical or medicinal use I cannot say. Subsequently I was told by his housekeeper that ultramarine was employed by him very sparingly, and that smalt and cobalt were his usual blues.

Hannah also informed Henry Syer Trimmer that she often set Turner's palette. The palette he saw

was a homely piece of square wood, with a hole for the thumb. Grinding colours on a slab was not his practice, and his dry colours were rubbed on the palette with cold-drawn oil. The colours were mixed daily, and he was very particular as to the operation. If they were not to his mind, he would say to Mrs. Danby [that is Hannah], 'Can't you set a palette better than this?' Like Wilson, Turner used gamboge; simply pounded and mixed with linseed cold-drawn oil.

His brushes were of the humblest description, mostly round hog's tools, and some flat. He was said to use very short handles, which might have been the case with his water colours; but I observed one very long-handled brush, with which I have no doubt he put in the effective touches in his late pictures. According to his housekeeper, he used the long brush exclusively for the rigging of ships, etc. However, there were a great many long-haired sables, which could not have been all employed for rigging. She also said that he used camel's hair for his oil pictures; and formerly he showed my father some Chinese brushes he was in the habit of using. When he had nearly finished a picture, she said, he took it to the end of his long gallery, and there put in the last touches.

In Turner's travelling box, together with some books, Henry Syer Trimmer found many deeply worn cakes of watercolour and a few sable brushes and lead pencils. His belief that Turner had used wax in his early pictures, 'from their having turned yellow', was confirmed – to his mind – by finding in the studio 'a jar of wax melted with rose madder and also with blue, which must have been used very recently, though it might have been for water-colours. There was also a bureau of old colours and oils ... a bottle of spirit varnish and a preparation of tar, tubes of magilp, old bladders of raw umber and other dark earths.' The remaining contents of the studio were numerous unframed pictures and a large assortment of well-thumbed 'views of foreign scenery ... the drudgery of art, of which master minds avail themselves'.[37]

6: Golden Apples, Silver Thames

Although Queen Anne Street – and its Marylebone surroundings – might be a satisfactory though sedate place for a successful artist to live, it had one great disadvantage for Turner: it wasn't close enough to the water. He was a child of the Thames, and, by way of the river, a child of the sea and the seashore. He needed to be able to get to one or the other. He needed flowing water, fresh or salt. He needed the sound of a rushing weir or of a grating shingle-beach. His presence in London was now bolstered by his gallery, at least in the exhibition season; even when closed, it was there, standing in for him and awaiting fresh pictures. In July 1805, he felt free to leave town and take deep breaths of fresh air. He was getting away from the squabbling of his acrimonious fellow Academicians – who called forth *his* acrimony – and putting himself at a distance from constant talk of the French and the likelihood of invasion. The armies of Napoleon – now Emperor – were still drawn up on the north coast of France, poised to strike England once the French fleets had been gathered there to control the Channel. The art treasures of London would then be added to the other loot in the Louvre.

Putting such concerns to the back of his mind, Turner rented a house on the banks of the Thames in the village of Isleworth. This was a mile upstream from Brentford, where since his boyhood stay the Grand Junction canal had been built to join London to Birmingham, part of the spreading waterway network that served a rapidly industrializing nation. Between Brentford and Isleworth elegant parkland surrounded Syon House, the crenellated home of the Duke of Northumberland. Across the river from Isleworth, spanned by Syon Ferry, was the equally sylvan deer park of Richmond. Downstream on the south bank, in Surrey, was Kew, where King George III was having a new palace built (the King, it was hoped, was recovering from the mental disorder which had overwhelmed him in 1804). Not far away on Richmond Hill was Sir Joshua Reynold's former out-of-town residence, Wick House, while across from Richmond at Twickenham, a little way upriver in Middlesex, stood Horace Walpole's fantasy Gothic edifice called Strawberry Hill, Alexander Pope's riverside villa, and the Palladian Marble Hill House, which George II had built for his friend Mrs Howard and which had more recently been the abode of Mrs Fitzherbert, putative wife, by secret marriage, of the Prince of Wales.

Turner thus followed the aristocracy and leaders of culture when choosing an out-of-town house. And as he did so he seemed to have a high, even noble, purpose in mind for his art, meaning to emulate Reynolds's attempt to place portraiture in the tradition of European history painting, in his own case by bringing landscape painting into the same fold. On the concave bend of the Thames at his new abode, Syon Ferry House, he could see not just the river and the working life on it but – a few hundred yards downstream, as if in a time-warp – a classical temple. This was the Pavilion, a small, cylindrical structure the Duke of Northumberland had had built for riverside parties.

At Isleworth, the smattering of classics Turner had been treated to as a boy was vastly enlarged. Now, at the age of thirty, he did a boot-strap further-education job on himself. The 'Greek Craze' was at its height, affecting all the arts. Flaxman's illustrations for Homer and Aeschylus were much admired. Fuseli was to be heard exclaiming 'The Greeks vere Gods! The Greeks vere Gods' – indeed, both Farington and Haydon heard him do so, the former to the students of the Academy's Antique School, the latter when seeing the marbles that Lord Elgin had brought back from the Parthenon in 1804 to his house in Park Lane.[1] (They were not unpacked until 1806 or exhibited publicly until the summer of 1807.) Benjamin West was among the artists who went to see them. Turner had a privileged private view of the marbles in August 1806; he wrote fulsomely if clumsily to thank Lord Elgin:

> your Lordships collection is perhaps the last that will be made of the most brilliant period of human nature –
>
> Graiis ingenium. Graiis dedit ore rotundo
> Musa loqui

showing that he had read Horace's *Ars Poetica* ('It was the Greeks to whom the Muse gave genius and polished speech'). Turner went on: 'I shall be run away with, so must with the rest of mankind who venerate the arts, pay my homage to your Lordships exertions for this rescue from barbarism.'[2] As we have seen, Turner was sufficiently run away with to purchase casts of the marbles, which he displayed, dustily, in his front hall at Queen Anne Street.

Turner's pictorial interest in man's 'most brilliant period' had begun before Isleworth. Several works of the previous few years have classical subjects, Greek and Roman, among them *Tivoli – Temple of the Sibyl and the Roman Campagna* and *Diana and Callisto*, free copies of paintings by Richard Wilson. All his own work were *Aeneas and the Sibyl, Lake Avernus* of 1798 and *Jason* (1802); the latter seems to have sprung from his reading of the English translation of part of Apollonius Rhodius's *Argonautics* in the 1795 fourteen-volume set he owned, edited by Robert Anderson, entitled *Works of the British Poets*. He had been dipping into Ovid by way of Addison's translation of the *Metamorphoses*, and his *Narcissus and Echo* (1804) arose from this source. Anderson's large anthology made up part of the library Turner brought to Isleworth; it also contained Pope's translations of the *Iliad* and *Odyssey*, and Dryden's *Aeneid, Eclogues* and *Georgics*.

Ideas for paintings were generated by his reading, and as he sketched the scenery near Syon Ferry House he jotted down in his sketchbooks the titles of possible subjects that seemed to fit a chosen landscape. Looking at a spot on the riverbank, overhung by a few trees, the scenery might prompt 'Jason: arrival at Colchis' or 'Ulysses: arrival at Crusa'. It seemed to be the composition and the place that came first and the 'subject' could be one of several vehicles he had in mind. It was the same with 'The Meeting of Pompey and Cornealia' – or, it might be, 'The Parting of Brutus and Portia' or 'Cleopatra sailing down to Cydnus'. He was clearly obsessed with farewells – Portia, Cleopatra and Cornelia, three heroines in Plutarch's *Lives*, were widows, whose loves 'sailed away to fulfil a fateful destiny'.[3] Was he currently estranged from Sarah Danby or preparing himself for such a state? Aeneas and Dido provide a parallel of tragic love and separation, and Aeneas was the hero he most identified with. One rough drawing in his 'Studies for Pictures, Isleworth' sketchbook[4] is inscribed 'Eneas and Evander'. In Virgil's *Aeneid*, book VIII, Aeneas sails up the Tiber and encounters the river god, who informs him that this is going to be his home. Then King Evander greets him and allies himself with Aeneas. Turner perhaps hoped for a similar encounter with Old Father Thames.

In another sketchbook he used at the time,[5] he penned a note concerning 'The Fall of Rome'. Isleworth hovered between now and then, with drawings of Windsor Castle or Kew Palace on one page, classic temples or Carthaginian harbour fronts on another. Among the sketches is one of a Thames-side glade with figures to which he attached the word 'Hesperides', and which would be the seedcorn for a large Poussinesque painting, *The Goddess of Discord choosing the Apple of Contention in the Garden of the Hesperides*. He exhibited this in 1806 at the British Institution, and though the subject came from classical legend, it may have struck him as a likely one just then because of Royal Academy bickering. Some sketches in another book[6] are of murder and mayhem: 'Death of Achelous', 'Death of Nessus' and 'Death of Liseus'. Turner was evidently still reading Ovid's *Metamorphoses*, which provided enticing and possibly useful – for pictures – stories of bodice-ripping and costly passion among the gods and their companions: the nymph Syrinx, pursued by Pan; lovely Salamancis, joined eternally to the lustful Hermaphroditus; and Phaeton, who went joy-riding in the chariot of his father, the Sun, and fell dead into the River Evidanus, which Turner couldn't help but picture as resembling the Thames.

Despite what seems an almost total immersion in the classics, he did not neglect other books. He read the Bible, at least Genesis, where the story of devious Jacob and honest Esau appealed to him. He read the poetry of John Milton, James Thomson, Edward Young and Mark Akenside; he had begun to attach to his paintings catalogue citations or epigraphs from such poets. And following his memo in a sketchbook about Esau, he noted – as if for future use in this way – some lines from Alexander Pope's pastoral *Summer*: 'A Shepherd's Boy, he seeks no better name / Leading his Flock beside the Silver Thames'.[7]

Verse filled the interstices of his teeming mind, by notable poets and by himself – although (as will be seen) it was not to J. M. W. Turner that the Muse gave poetic genius and polished speech. For some of his friends, it seemed part of his oddness that he was so fond of talking about poetry. Sometimes while on sketching expeditions from Isleworth the weir of his imagination overflowed and he scribbled alongside his drawings short fragments and longer snatches (now often hard to decipher). That a painter could also be a poet was impressed on him in 1805 by his portrait-painting colleague Martin Archer Shee, who published a successful satirical collection called *Rhymes on Art*. Would-be poets generally feel the poetic impulse in their late teens, but Turner's urge came later, following his interest in songs. One of his early brief bursts of poetic inspiration went first into a sketchbook:

> Discord dire sister – of Ethereal Jove
> coeval hostile even to heavenly love[8]

and then, somewhat refined, into a notebook he started to keep about this time specifically for his verse. Here, where the theme was once again the Goddess in the garden of the Hesperides, the choice of the 'apple of contention' led on implacably to the Trojan War:

> With vengeful pleasure pleas'd the Goddess heard
> of future woes and then her choice preferred
> The shiny mischief to herself she took
> Love felt the wound and Troy's foundations shook[9]

From the sketchbooks emerges a picture of his life at Syon Ferry House. In the Hesperidean garden of Isleworth he had All Saints Church as a near neighbour, with a wharf in front of it at which small river barges and lighters collected market produce and delivered grain, coal and timber. The riverfront pub the London Apprentice furnished legends of smugglers and liquid solace for visiting watermen, locals and recently arrived artists. Turner wrote his new address in his new top-of-the-line calf-bound sketchbook,[10] which he labelled 'Studies for Pictures, Isleworth', and set forth to fill its pages – grey-washed so that they gave off less glare when he worked out-of-doors in bright sun. He sketched the riverbanks, the King's never-to-be-completed palace at Kew, the castle at Windsor, the trees and meadows and swans and fishermen. At some point near Windsor he picked a leaf from a bush and pressed it between the pages. And he drew the craft which moved up and down the river by sail, quant pole and oar, or were plucked along by the current or the tide (below Teddington) or were towed by men called halers or by horses – or by any combination of these. Among the workboats and fishermen's skiffs, his gaze fell on such special craft as royal barges, propelled by oars and used for state occasions; and his eye imagined other vessels that would indeed have been rare on the Thames, like Greek triremes.[11]

Wherever Turner was he drew boats, whether in the West Country, in Wales, in Scotland, in France or in Italy – on the Avon and the Seine, the Severn or the Tweed, on the beach at Brighton or at Margate, under castle walls or on city foreshores. There was always a sail, a mast or a hull whose shape and sheer required the attentions of his pencil. Even an 1804 sketchbook apparently devoted to academic figure drawings[12] has boats in it, almost as if a chore had been relieved by delight. Here at Isleworth boat-ownership became a possibility; he wanted a boat of his own. Among the sketches of craft of all kinds now appear strictly two-dimensional drawings of small boats, showing them side-on, bows-on, in elevation and plan, and with various rigs for which he drew sail-plans with measurements attached. These pipedreams sometimes combined characteristics of Thames craft, Dutch fishing boats and Mediterranean vessels; they had low freeboard, leeboards and lateen rigs – that is, with a large wing-like sail hung from a single yard that inclined upward from just above the bow. Reef points were a feature that Turner added to such a sail, with northern caution making provision for reducing sail-area in bad weather. On one boat the mainsail, forward, is lateen-rigged while the smaller mizzen sail, aft, has the more conventional – for the Thames – sprit-rig.[13] Several rough sketches show his cogitations on how a lateen sail would perform when hard on the wind and actually head to wind, shaking vigorously. In one more considered drawing, the helmsman sits on the weather gunwale, slightly crouched as if trying to reduce his own windage or protect himself from spray. On a sketchbook page he worked out the costs of various items for a boat:

Sails £10. Mast 3. Bows[prit?] 1.　Booms (?) 2.
Rigging 5. Iron[work?] 1.　Pump 1. -: [total]23.[14]

What Turner's 'easy bark'[15] looked like is not certain but one sketch[16] may give an idea: this was more or less a Thames wherry, clinker- or lapstrake-built, with low topsides, a raking stem and broad stem. The fact that a lateen rig would be unhandy when obliged to tack frequently in confined waters may have convinced him to have lugsails or spritsails for main and mizzen, and perhaps a jib for extra windward drive and help in bringing the boat about from one tack to the other. An orange-sailed sprit-rigged craft in his 1808 *Sheerness as seen from the Nore* is painted almost with pride of ownership.

Word of Turner's boat-ownership soon spread. Lord Egremont, the great Sussex estate-owner who had bought his first Turner, *Ships bearing up for Anchorage*, in 1802 or shortly thereafter, and *Narcissus and Echo* in 1804, was heard to assert that Turner had 'a yacht'.[17] Turner's friend the Reverend Trimmer, who lived at this point at Kew, told his son (who told Thornbury) of a boat Turner kept on the Thames, though he mentions Richmond as its mooring place. Thornbury himself claimed that 'a good deal of [Turner's] knowledge of seamanship was picked up during his trips to the North, to which he always went by a collier',[18] but it is more likely that he began to acquire his boat-handling skills as an eighteen-year-old, out sketching on the tidal river at Battersea with Edward Bell, the engraver, when they at least once got stuck on the mud. (Thornbury elsewhere claims that Turner 'beat about year after year in all sorts of smugglers' boats'.)[19]

What was his Isleworth boat called? *The Owner's Delight* was the name he inscribed on the stern of a small boat, on the river near Battersea Bridge, in a watercolour by him once owned by his friend Walter Fawkes at Farnley – *November: Flounder-Fishing*. But a sketchbook of around 1809 contains a draft of a long poem, or series of verses, about the building of a British *Argo* on the Thames. The man behind this project is an 'artificer' 'Whose pregnant mind long in confusion lay'. Ingenuously but touchingly Turner conveys the excitement of this *Argo*'s launching:

> All ready, ready let her go
> Long as the Thames shall flow
> May thou be blest my dear Argo
> All ready, ready every'one replies
> O Goddess hear my ardent sighs
> Swift as an arrow from a bow
> She goes she goes then let her go
> Long as the Thames shall flow
> O Goddess bless the ship *Argo*[20]

This summer, as he rowed and sailed his *Argo* or *Delight* upriver and down, the weather was unsettled. There were standard English sunny periods and showers and several severe thunder-storms. And there were rainbows. It was good weather for watercolours, particularly of the sort Turner painted, with wet paint often deployed on wet paper. Sailing his boat from Isleworth to Kew, Richmond, Kingston and Hampton Court, he often pulled into the bank in order to sketch and sometimes paint the ordinary with extraordinary touches; many sketches were hasty, even rudimentary, but captured something he wanted to remember; others – also rapidly done – were much more detailed watercolours. His subjects were moving clouds, passing light, shadowed or sunlit trees and grass, people in boats or standing on the riverbanks. He painted his own house, to which he came back in the evening, where his father – all being well – would have supper ready. He went further up the Thames to Eton and Windsor, and then up its tributary, the Wey, to Guildford. In some places he moored for the night along the riverbank, cooked supper on an open fire and slept on the bottom boards of his boat; in others he stayed at inns, like the White Lion at Guildford or the Swan at Walton.

On one such cruise he took along some mahogany boards on which he made oil sketches, working in the boat or on the bank, and the paintings that resulted seem spontaneous, moment-catching; he carried a travelling paint-box, outfitted for the purpose, with linseed oil and a dozen or so bladders of oil colour. He spent more time apparently on some larger ten-by-fifteen-inch drawings[21] and oil sketches that he made on four-foot-by-three-foot canvases – taken into his boat rolled up and then pinned to a board when he painted on them in the more settled autumn weather. He was in the vanguard of a movement towards painting in the open air – a movement that included several Thames Valley painters he knew, such as William Delamotte and William Havell, and the East Anglian John Constable. Turner on these occasions deployed his oils almost as if they were watercolours, sometimes not using a ground on the wooden panels, letting the wet paints blend together. In mood, he seems a long way from *The Shipwreck*, which he had displayed in his gallery only a few months before (and for which he may have summoned memories of the wreck of the East Indiaman *Mars* on Margate Sands in 1787). Claude and Poussin are well off-stage. The effect is original and unshadowed by predecessors; it is one of exhilaration and gratitude for being where he was, doing what he liked doing – sailing, rowing, fishing, having a good time in the open air, with painting and drawing almost by-products of his voyage rather than its purpose.

Many of the oil sketches on canvas show evening scenes, painted after he had tied up for the night. If he had to stop to wait for a lock gate to open, or felt like fishing or calling at an inn, he often fitted in a painted sketch. He camped out on one occasion close to some bargemen who had tied up in Cliveden Reach and had their dinner fire going as the sun went down, and the artist caught the scene.[22] As a river excursionist, one man in a boat, he was as much a pioneer as in his art, though unlike the later writer Jerome K. Jerome he did not memorialize his misadventures – except perhaps in the *Argo* poem. He happily persevered past Marlow, Henley, Reading, Caversham, Pangbourne, Goring, Wallingford, Shillingford and Dorchester. It was ninety-seven winding miles from Isleworth to Oxford, where he painted (for reproduction in the *Oxford Almanack*) Christ Church from the river, a mistier, more distant version of his 1798–9 study of the college.

He also sailed downriver, away from rural agricultural confines. By now he was convinced of the seaworthiness of his craft and his own boat-handling abilities. There is no evidence that he had a crew, but perhaps his father accompanied him on some voyages. Between Isleworth and the City he made no sketches or paintings until he reached London Bridge and Billingsgate market, where the fishing smacks unloaded their catches. For a watercolour here,[23] his point of view along the foreshore suggests that he beached his boat – whether to draw or spend the night. He navigated the ship-crowded Pool of London and followed the bends of the river down past Deptford and Greenwich, down Bugsbys Reach and Gallions Reach, marshes and creeks on either side, to Tilbury and Gravesend where the river widens into the estuary. There, slopping about in the waters between Sheerness on the Kent side and Southend and Shoeburyness on the Essex shore, he sketched small craft and larger ships. Here, at the confluence of the Thames and the River Medway, was the historic naval anchorage of the Nore, and the sea was choppy. His sketchbook[24] has water-stains on most pages. He drew warships and guardships, passenger-carrying hays and barges bearing hay from country to city. He was stocking up with material for marine paintings. He drew boats with all sails set, sails reefed, sails brailed up, sails furled. He noted dimensions, proportions. He sketched boats passing dramatically close to one another and recorded the interaction of wakes and waves, wind-driven seas and tidal currents. He noted passing clouds and changing light. Putting these things on paper helped fix them in his visual memory. Meanwhile the breeze tried to turn the pages of his sketchbook, damp spray flew, and his own boat pitched and lurched in the seaway.

He now observed these happenings as a sailor as well as an artist. When it came to making a record in paint of something he had actually seen on the water, he got things right. For instance, in the painting he called *Fishing upon the Blythe-Sand, Tide setting in* (RA 1809), the title in its finicky way establishes the time and whereabouts of painting in almost logbook fashion: the tide was flooding over the Blythe Sand, a six-mile-long, one-mile-broad shoal area in the southern half of a section of the Thames known as Sea Reach – Canvey Island to the north, Cliffe Marshes and Yantlet Spit to the south. The title asserts the fact that he, the artist and boatman, had been there. A broad patch of sunlight falls on the shallow waters where the fishing boats flock – it is a favourable time for sprats or whitebait. In the nearest boat, beating out towards the sunlight from the shadowed foreground close to the beach, the helmsman sits to leeward under the orange-tan mainsail, looking attentively forward to the luff of the jib. The observation is more than matter-of-fact; the identification of artist with subject is moving. He understood how boats sit in the water, how they move in a calm or angry sea, and how the men on board them sat or stood at particular tasks, perched on a thwart, standing with one hand gripping a mast-shroud; and he instilled this knowledge into his work, in no braggadocio way but infusing it, so that seamanship became part of the painting's essence.

Among other examples of this nautical and artistic 'rightness' are *Sheerness and the Isle of Sheppey* of 1807, in which the foredeck hand is backing the jib to help his boat come about, and the Bridgewater Seapiece of 1801, *Dutch Boats in a Gale: Fishermen endeavouring to put fish on board*, which was one of his more overtly dramatic 'are they going to crash into each other?' pictures – in this, the viewer's eye is drawn to the helmsman of the smaller, nearer boat, who is at that moment putting his helm down, turning his craft to pass under the leeside of the larger vessel, which is otherwise going to run it down.

Although summer ended, Turner stayed with the river and maritime matters. Tired of waiting for his navy, Napoleon moved his troops eastward to defeat the Austrians at Ulm; but the news of this calamity was more than balanced in England by reports of the British victory over the combined French and Spanish fleets at Trafalgar on 21 October. The country was enraptured by accounts of the tragic but splendid battle in which the nation's great sea commander had laid down his life. Haydon reflected the mood, writing in his journal how Nelson's death 'affected me for days. But all fears of invasion were now over, and we looked forward to our pursuits with a degree of confidence which only those can estimate who passed their early days among the excitement of perpetual war.'[25]

Turner was no exception to this interest and the feelings that mixed mourning with celebration. In his case, there was almost a regret that he had not been on hand. As with the Pantheon fire, the occasion brought out the reporter in him. When, in late December, the *Victory* reached Sheerness with Nelson's body preserved in a cask of spirits, Turner took two sketchbooks, one almost used up, one new,[26] and went down to Sheppey and the Nore again. He sketched the battered first-rate ship-of-the line from various angles. He did several large drawings in pencil, watercolour and ink: one[27] of the *Victory*'s quarterdeck had notes attached – 'Guns 121 lb. used in the Ports marked i.x.', 'Splinter hitting marks in pencil / 9 inches thick', and 'Rail shot away during the action' – while another[28] showed the battered masts and rigging. In the sketchbooks, he recorded dimensions and drew details of naval uniforms. Talking to the officers, he took notes about the battle: 'After the ST [presumably the *Santissima Trinidad*] … passed some other ship with a White Lion Head raked the Victory.' He jotted down the characteristics of the ship's master, Mr Atkinson: 'square, large, light hair, grey eye, 5-11'. After noting that Nelson's stalwart aide Captain Thomas Hardy 'wore B. gaiters', he wrote: '4 sailors carried some officer down about the time L. N. fell, on his left arm. Some one forwarded to help him. A marine to every gun stands aft. 8 others. C. Hardy rather tall, looks dreadful … fair, about 36 years.'[29]

Turner knew that he had to put these things – relevant or not – on paper as they flowed in conversation, faster perhaps than he could cope with, otherwise back in Isleworth or Harley Street he would realize that he needed a detail whose lack would impede the picture or, as would prove to be the case, pictures. One assumes that he was among the crowds in London for Nelson's funeral on 9 January 1806, when the Admiral's coffin under a great black canopy was borne – in a funeral car built like a small *Victory* – from the Admiralty past Somerset House to St Paul's, amid what one onlooker called 'awful silence', broken only by the rustle made as people respectfully removed their hats.[30] Haydon noted: 'At the conclusion of the funeral service in the Cathedral, the old flag of the *Victory* was torn into a thousand shreds, each of which was carefully preserved by its fortunate owner as a relic of the hero.'[31]

The Battle of Trafalgar was a subject Turner wrestled with these first months of 1806 and thereafter could not shake off; it haunted him for another eighteen years. To begin with he painted a view of the battle 'as seen from the Mizen [sic] Starboard Shrouds of the *Victory*'[32] – a title that seems to suggest the artist actually climbed into the rigging to size up the view. He has Nelson in white breeches lying on the deck at the base of the main mast, like Christ removed from the Cross. Gunsmoke billows up on all sides. Most of the picture is a great jumble of the masts, yards and sails of the embattled ships. Compressing the occasion, Turner shows a sailor bringing forward a French flag to the dying Nelson, as evidence that victory has been won. (Turner made a key for the picture for visitors to use when viewing it in his gallery, with a description of the action at the moment Nelson was shot and a list of the names of various officers and crew who are portrayed.) Farington, coming to the gallery to see the picture on 3 June 1806, wrote, 'It appeared to me a very crude, unfinished performance, the figures miserably bad.' Perhaps it *was* unfinished. The critic of the *Examiner* was also caustic, suggesting that it looked as if all the men on Turner's *Victory* had been 'murdered'.[33] Turner's attempt to get across the confusion of battle, and indeed not only the course but result of the battle, was a brave one, but neither Farington's nor the *Examiner*'s judgement seems wildly unfair.

A more oblique reflection on the great event was a smaller oil he apparently painted and exhibited at this same time: *The Victory returning from Trafalgar*. This picture – and a similar watercolour he made[34] – shows three views of a ship, allegedly the *Victory*, off the south-west shore of the Isle of Wight, though she does not seem to have a jury-rig, as the *Victory* did following a temporary refit at Gibraltar after the battle, or an ensign at half-mast, as would be expected with the Admiral's body on board. Turner once again put some fishermen in a small boat directly in the path of the warship, which is running eastwards up the Channel under topsails and main topgallant; it was his customary device for bringing the spectator into a small drama, but here also seems to suggest that, even at this tragic moment, ordinary life goes unthinkingly on.

Although he sometimes put the facts aside when they offended his compositional needs, Turner's grasp of naval detail was often admired in the press. For example, on 8 May 1808, the *Examiner* wrote – this time with enthusiasm – of his painting the *Confluence of the Thames and Medway* (which Lord Egremont bought): 'The ships in ordinary, or which are taking on board their heavy stores and rigging, display considerable technical knowledge of marine affairs, and are painted with great care, as are also the machinery for swinging in the masts and guns, and the small vessel, laden (we suppose) with hay.' This knowledge was something the usually secretive artist could be generous with, beyond what he imparted in his paintings, to the right person. As we will see, Robert C. Leslie, as a boy of eight, found this out while staying with his father at Lord Egremont's mansion at Petworth, when Turner made a model boat for him. Turner himself never forgot having been a lonely child who had liked playing with a toy vessel. In a sketchbook of 1809, he penned some verses about a poor cotter's child:

> The daring boy …
> Launches his paper boat across the road
> Where the deep gullies which his father's cart
> Made in their progress to the mart
> Full to the brim deluged by the rain
> They prove to him a channel to the main
> Guiding his vessel down the stream
> The pangs of hunger vanish like a dream.[35]

In these years, Turner's sketchbooks contained – apart from sketches and poems and letters and lists of materials and numbers of banknotes – jottings to do with the techniques of commercial fishing; in one he notes, 'Fleet of Fishermen. Smelting', and records how they set about this: 'One throws out the net – then rows round and while is pulling up another net runs out, so one net is always down.'[36] In another he remarks that 'Large Eeel Hooks' – note the three 'e's – are 'Patent Yellow'.[37] He was also interested in the appearance of water and the effect of light on and in it, reflected and refracted; his awareness that reflections do not necessarily appear uniform is demonstrated in one of several paintings he did of Walton Bridges, possibly exhibited in his gallery in 1807, where the curves of the reflected bridge arches are a good deal more squashed than the actual arches above.

In a sketchbook he used between 1806 and 1808,[38] he tortuously attempts to define in words such matters: 'Reflection in water [:] tho' the real shadow is nearly the same from the plane of the Horizon in near Objects, yet when the whole of the light lays behind it frequently streaks a shade 3 times its hight.' On the River Dee, while visiting his patron Sir John Leicester's country house at Tabley in 1808, he sees a white body floating (whether human or not he doesn't say; perhaps 'body' meant object) and observes, 'yet the reflection of the white body had not any light or white reflection but on the contrary had its reflection dark'.[39] And he goes into a long and convoluted disquisition on reflections that can be condensed to the propositions that, on water which is rippled, reflected objects are elongated; that the theory of a looking-glass is not relevant when dealing with reflections in flat water; and that, if they are treated in terms of such a theory, they are 'most fallacious to the great book of nature'. This is a point, he concludes, poignantly, 'When panting art toils after truth in vain'.[40]

After his short lease came to an end at Isleworth, Turner did not give up the river. Farington wrote in his diary for 10 May 1806: 'Turner is going to reside abt. 10 or 12 miles from London, & proposes only to retain in London His Exhibition Gallery. This he does from an economical motive.' Although Turner – uneconomically – went on paying the Isleworth rent until March 1807, he had by then taken on the lease of another house on Upper Mall in Hammersmith, a little closer to town than Isleworth and once again with a Thames view. Young Trimmer recalled 'a garden [which] ran down to the river, at the end of which was a summer house. Here, out in the open air, were painted some of Turner's best pictures.' When the Reverend Trimmer expressed 'his surprise that Turner could paint under such circumstances, he [Turner] remarked that lights and a room were absurdities, and that a picture could be painted anywhere. His eyes were remarkably strong. He would throw down his watercolour drawings on the floor of the summer-house, requesting my father not to touch them, as he could see them there, and they would be drying at the same time.'[41] According to the Pre-Raphaelite artist and critic F. G. Stephens, who later lived in the vicinity, the house was painted white and 'was of a moderate but comfortable size'.[42] The front garden that extended to the river was traversed by a tree-lined public pathway to the church. Market gardens lay behind the house. Looking downriver Turner could see the sun rise and looking upriver see it set.

The immediate neighbourhood had stronger artistic associations than Isleworth. William Hogarth had lived and died nearby. James Thomson the poet, whose work Turner had been devotedly reading, wrote his *Seasons* in his lodgings at the Dove, a riverfront inn along Hammersmith Terrace, where Charles II and Nell Gwynne used to meet. In the Terrace, too, lived P. J. de Loutherbourg, whose career as a successful painter was now being matched by his popularity as a prophet and 'healer'. So many would-be patients thronged to the Terrace that de Loutherbourg's neighbours were annoyed; some threatened to wreck his house, and indeed a few windows were broken. After this, de Loutherbourg scaled down his practice, and agreed to see new clients only on Thursdays and his established patients on Monday and Friday evenings. Whether Mrs de Loutherbourg continued to hold a grudge against Turner for – as she had alleged – filching her husband's artistic secrets is not known. Certainly Turner in later life retained an affection for the Swiss painter's work, which had several times spurred him to competition, Alpine or marine; he bought some small drawings of Welsh and Shropshire subjects by him at the sale of Dr Monro's collection in 1833.

Although Turner kept a much lower profile than de Loutherbourg, he and his father were well known on the Hammersmith waterfront, particularly to Mr Sawyer, a local boatmaster. Presumably Turner brought his boat down from Isleworth and had it moored where he could get at it for excursions and sketching trips. And he saw a good deal of the Trimmers. Henry Syer Trimmer remembered walking as a boy with his father and Turner 'under the blaze of the great comet' one night in 1811,[43] the last year he had the Hammersmith house.

One of his riverside winters was fierce with cold. A sketchbook[44] has pencil drawings of barges and small boats imprisoned in the frozen Thames. The coalman's deliveries would have been more frequent, as the fireplaces at West End, Upper Mall, added their quota of smoke to the Hammersmith air and the painter tried to keep his hands warm enough to wield a brush. When boating weather returned, Turner was out on 'the happy river'[45] again, jotting down verse that constantly paid homage to Pope and Thomson, refought the Trojan War and dribbled on about swains and meads and azure skies. All the while he drew the river craft and riverside vegetation and naked boys fishing. On a sketch of sky he noted, 'Light stationary clouds with blue at the bottom.' In a cottage along the river he hastily drew the interior with figures and wrote, as if to help him remember what it was all about: 'Girl breaking off sticks and putting them on the grate.' 'Girl filling the tin kettle out of a large brown jug.' On a narrow canal barge, he sketched a woman holding an infant while a man did the cooking. In another sketchbook of river scenes and boats[46] a subject occurs to him: 'Ulysses and Poly' – the Cyclops Polyphemus was to be encountered several decades later on a larger scale.

In the years to come Turner continued to look at water both as artist and as boatman: the height and heft of waves was doubly meaningful to him. On one occasion he was spotted near Westminster Bridge by someone who passed by again half an hour later, and there was Turner still squatting on his heels, staring at the ripples at the edge of the river current. Effie Ruskin, fascinated by her first husband's god, said of Turner: 'The way in which he studied clouds was by taking a boat which he anchored in some stream, and then lay on his back in it, gazing at the heavens for hours and even days, till he had grasped some effect of light which he desired to transpose to canvas.'[47] And he hung on to his boating skills. Mary Lloyd, later to write a book named *Sunny Memories*, was staying at Thames Ditton with the Carrick Moore family – friends of Turner's – one summer when Turner, by then well into old age, was also a guest. She recalled that 'when the ladies proposed to go over the river to Hampton Court Gardens, Turner said "and I will row you". This was an offer difficult to refuse, so we got into the boat and started … There was some difficulty in landing by the sedgy bank, but we said it would do very well; however, Turner insisted on taking us further on to a more convenient spot, because, he said with his shrug, "None but the brave deserve the fair."[48] 'His shrug' seems to have been well known.

He may well have looked back to his period at Isleworth and Hammersmith as a sort of golden age – with his Hesperidean front gardens facing out on a sunlit river, with Thames aits or eyots for classical islands, and with time framed by tide. For some six hours the river's current flowed towards the sea and for some six hours it was stopped and thrust back by the incoming flood. One of the Hesperides – the sweet-singing nymphs who guarded the golden apples in their garden on the river Oceanus – was Aegle or Brightness, a granddaughter of the Sun, called by Ruskin 'the healing power of living light'.[49] For Turner, the river offered reflected light and moving water, a double blessing.

7: Boxing Harry

For most of Turner's nine million countrymen, this was a depressed time. Trade was flat. In new building, in commerce, the war created no boom. If he had followed his first inclination and become an architect, he might well have starved. As it was, a number of his painting contemporaries found it hard to make ends meet. George Morland, landscape and animal painter – and heavy drinker – was frequently in and out of debtor's prison, as Haydon was later. James Barry, like Haydon a troublesome person, an ex-professor of Painting at the RA, died in reclusive poverty at the age of sixty-five in February 1806.

Yet for Turner money rolled in. He asked high prices for his pictures and, if buyers cavilled, he asked higher prices. (This was generally a shrewd bargaining ploy, giving his clients the impression that, if they resisted his first price, his pictures would cost more, not less.) In May 1804 Sir John Leicester offered him 250 guineas for *The Festival upon the Opening of the Vintage of Mâcon*, a painting for which Turner wanted £300. By the time Sir John agreed to pay the £300, Turner had upped the ante to £400. The Earl of Yarborough paid this price. 'Opie said to Thomson he did not see why Turner should not ask such prices as no other person could paint such pictures,' wrote Farington;[1] but a few months later he noted with a trace of malicious pleasure that Turner 'was to have painted 2 pictures for Mr [Thomas] Barnard [a founder of the British Institution] at a certain price, but on hearing Daniell had that price, *demanded double*, and the pictures were not painted'.[2] Farington also thought that Turner's pictures ought to have had a lot more work done on them to suit the prices he was asking. Whether enviously or sincerely, other Academicians shared this judgement about Turner's finishing skills. In July 1809 Farington enquired of Thomas Hearne and Henry Edridge '"what might be reckoned a fair price for one of those pictures [of Turner's] for which Lord Essex gave 200 guineas?" Hearne said "For a person a full admirer of his pictures 50 guineas, but for myself I would not give fifteen.'"

Despite Hearne, full admirers were on hand, and not only Sir John Leicester and the Earl of Yarborough; other 'exalted personages'[3] lined up in 1805 to subscribe to the engraving Charles Turner did of the painting Sir John had purchased, *The Shipwreck*, among them the Duke of Argyll, the Earl of Essex and the Earl of Carlisle. Other less exalted subscribers were the artists John Varley, Thomas Stothard and William Havell, and, among the art-lovers, 'Miss Wells' – probably Clara[4] – and Daniel Lambert, a celebrated fat man of the age, who in April 1806 came from Leicester to London in a specially constructed large coach and had a portrait painted from which Charles Turner made a mezzotint print.

Turner's gallery was a money-spinner, producing sales far greater than those he achieved in such venues as the Academy and the British Institution: in 1808, for instance, he sold through his gallery four paintings to Lord Egremont and three to other buyers for a total of £1417 10s, an average of £200 a picture; Further sales in this year brought his earnings up to roughly £2000. (One can multiply this figure by about forty to get an equivalent for today – say, £80,000 or $130,000.) He was a good salesman for his work; for much of his career, until the art dealer Thomas Griffith came on the scene in the 1840s, he handled his own business. In a letter of 21 November 1809 written from his house in Hammersmith to James Wyatt, carver, gilder and printdealer in Oxford, he set forth his prices for certain standard sizes of oil paintings he could make for a Wyatt print. 'My pictures are all 3 feet by 4 feet, 200 gs., half which size will be 100, but shall not mind an inch or two. A drawing I will do you for 80 gs.'[5] (Turner's syntax was weak, as usual; he meant not that all his pictures were 3 by 4, but that for all 3 by 4s he charged – at this point – 200 guineas.) And there were occasions when for diplomatic reasons he was less straightforward. In 1811 Earl Grey wanted to buy his *Mercury and Herse* (just over six feet by five feet) for 500 guineas, but, as Farington noted, there was a report that the Prince Regent had purchased it, 'which not being the case, Turner was embarrassed about it, and under these circumstances, with his usual caution, will not name a price when asked by his acquaintance[s]'.[6]

Turner's caution or prudence about money was demonstrated in many a sketchbook, where he listed at the front or back the serial numbers of banknotes taken along or spent on his tours. He continued to jot down from time to time his daily expenses, as on a trip to Leeds in 1816: 'Porterage, 2s. 8d. Fare to Leeds, £2. 2s., Coachman, 1s., Dinner at Eaton 5s. 6d., Coachman – Scrooby, 1s. 6d., Ditto 1s., Breakfast Doncaster, 2s. 3d., Brandy & Water, Grantham, 1s. 6d., Coachman & Guard, 4s. 6d. Total £3. 2s. 11d.'[7] (In fact, he added it up wrongly: the total was a shilling less.) In a scruffy little notebook[8] used between 1809 and 1814 he made a comprehensive account of his financial worth and also placed in a pocket inside the cover a statement of various stock-holdings. On 17 August 1810, his investments in government bonds, usually called 'the Funds', were:

	£	s.	d.
Reduced 3% Annuities	2,283	9	3
Consolidated 3% do.	823	5	7
Navy 5%	4,110	1	4
	7,216	16	2

This time he got his sums right.

Tucked in with this statement was another from his stockbroker, William Marsh, showing various transactions made for Turner in government stock for the period 3 January to 26 July 1810. Turner added to Marsh's penned figures a pencilled record of the name of the work or patron whose purchase had enabled him to buy a certain block of stock. Neither now nor later did he have a bank account, but got Marsh to buy Funds when he had money to hand and sell some when he needed cash. 'Dad never praised me for anything but saving a ha'penny,'[9] he said once, and Dad must have been constantly delighted as the man who had looked after half-pennies as a boy now squirrelled away pound upon pound. Turner's interest in money led him to read about counterfeiting, possibly with a view to ensuring that he did not accept any dud notes; in his library in later years was to be found a work by Thomas Carson Hansard et al., *Report on the Mode of Preventing the Forgery of Bank Notes*, 1819. However, the only note in his handwriting in the book, scribbled upside down inside the front cover, is about the genuineness of a different article:

> To ascertain whether what is called mushrooms is real or not – Take
> a little salt and sprinkle it on the spunge or spongy side. If it turns
> yellow it is poison; if it turns black it is the real mushroom.[10]

Of course his interest in the production of banknotes, real or forged, may have come about also from his study of engraving methods.

The same notebook records two purchases of land in 1809, at Richmond for £400 and at Lee Common in Buckinghamshire for £102. The land at Richmond – in fact across Richmond Bridge, in Twickenham – fitted in with his liking for the Thames, but the reason for his purchase of the Lee land – on the edge of the Chiltern Hundreds, west of Berkhamstead – isn't known. (This property still belonged to him at his death: 'A cottage or tenement situate at Lee Common in the parish of Great Missenden in the County of Bucks and an Orchard or Meadow Plot thereto belonging'.)[11] Clearly he had no intention of keeping his savings under his mattress. A note in his hand on another page in this notebook says, 'Brick earth of 6 feet deep is worth £200 per acre – 5 yard of gravel 2 feet deep. 1 load.' Another investment of this time was the purchase of ten £5 shares in the Atlas Fire Office. Outstanding amounts owed him for pictures were £1000 by the Yorkshire landowner Walter Fawkes, £200 by John Fuller MP, and £400 by Sir John Leicester. Turner also made an inventory of a number of unsold paintings, valuing them at between £50 and £100 apiece; it was as if he didn't feel very hopeful of getting rid of them.

Whatever the reason for Turner's survey of his financial standing at this point, at the age of thirty-five, it must have cheered him: he was worth between £12,000 and £13,000. He was able to put behind him the gloomy doubts of the year before, expressed in the 'Cockermouth' sketchbook:

> Adverse frown[s] my wayward fate
> Fast telling on my poor estate
> O Heaven avert the impending care
> O make my future prospects fair.[12]

He felt buoyant enough to extend his Harley Street empire along Queen Anne Street into the mews property for his new house and gallery, and rich enough to start building a new house on his Twickenham land.

*

It can be said that Turner always acted like someone who had been poor when young. But it is probably truer to see him as someone who had seen both hard and good times, bread-and-dripping at home, and a thick slice off the Sunday joint at the Marshalls' in Brentford, and this may have accounted for his own fitful nature where money was concerned: now generous, now niggardly. Sometimes he felt rich; sometimes, despite being rich, it seemed to him that he might have a desperate need for all the money he could lay his hands on in the near future – and he was, in consequence, very tight. A few of his colleagues were spendthrift. Thomas Lawrence, for instance, who also got high prices for his work, was generous to women and to needy fellow artists (like James Audubon) and was frequently in deep debt. Turner undoubtedly had his Scrooge-like moments. He hated waste. He reused lines of poetry; he painted on scraps of salvaged board; much of the paper he used for watercolours was 'not of the highest quality'. Some of his blue paper was grocer's sugar-loaf wrapping paper. However, as time went on Turner often splurged on relatively costly pigments, such as Indian yellow and madder. In the 1830s and 1840s, he used natural ultramarine, which cost eight guineas an ounce, when a much cheaper synthetic substitute existed.[13]

Even so, his fellow artists for the most part traded examples of his economical disposition. Edridge in 1804 talked of Turner's 'narrowness of mind' – meaning his parsimony. Turner had received 250 guineas from the Duke of Bridgewater for his *Dutch Boats in a Gale*, the Bridgewater Seapiece, but was understood to have badgered its next owner, one of the Duke's heirs, for the cost of the frame, a further twenty guineas; Edridge thought this counter-productive. But it was Turner's custom to charge for his frames at cost-price, and he expected the client to return the frame if he did not wish to pay for it. Others used to talk about how he often demanded his travel expenses – as on the occasion when he delivered his painting *Rosehill Park, Sussex* (c.1810) to John Fuller MP, and asked for his cab fare. His friend George Jones, exasperated by yet another example cited by Thornbury of this sort of behaviour, commented, 'It is very doubtful if JMWT ever asked for his coach fare but often talked of it when joking with his friends.'[14] But was he simply trying to put on a smiling face when forced to acknowledge a well-known habit? To Turner's credit, a northern manufacturer named Henry M'Connell denied another Thornbury story that Turner had claimed an extra eighty guineas for going to Venice expressly to paint a picture for him. The picture was *Venice* (RA 1834), for which M'Connell paid Turner £350. He also bought *Lightermen heaving in Coals* (RA 1835), for £300, which M'Connell said was more than Turner had asked for it. M'Connell added, 'No one could have behaved with less parsimony – I may almost say with greater generosity – than did Turner in his transactions with me.'[15]

It is doubtful whether Lord de Tabley, formerly Sir John Leicester, would have said the same. The artist William Jerdan was at Tabley Hall once when Turner – 'our prince of landscape painters', Jerdan called him – was staying as a guest. Jerdan wrote:

> In the drawing room stood a landscape on an easel on which his Lordship was at work as the fancy struck him. Of course, when assembled for the tedious half hour before dinner, we all gave our opinions on its progress, its beauties and its defects. I stuck a blue wafer on to show where I thought a bit of bright colour or light would be advantageous; and Turner took the brush and gave a touch, here and there, to mark some improvements. He returned to town, and – can it be credited! – the next morning at breakfast a letter from him was delivered to his Lordship containing a regular bill of charges for 'Instruction in Painting'. His Lordship tossed it across the table indignantly to me and asked if I could have imagined such a thing; and as indignantly, and against my remonstrances, immediately sent a cheque for the sum demanded by 'the drawing master'.[16]

Did Turner have his tongue in his cheek? If it was a joke, of the kind Jones credited him with, Lord de Tabley didn't get it; and yet what compelled Turner to make it was obviously a mercenary streak. It is a pity we don't know whether he cashed Lord de Tabley's cheque.

Turner hated to pay for anything that was not specifically delivered as contracted for. (His relations with his engravers, which will be looked at separately, were riven by disagreements on this score.) On one occasion he refused to pay the fare on an omnibus when it didn't go to the Bank as promised. The Reverend T. J. Judkin saw him near St Paul's, admonishing the conductor, who allowed the irate passenger to walk off without paying. His 'repugnance to part with money', as Alaric Watts characterized it, was demonstrated when, allegedly, 'after volunteering to erect a monument over the remains of his early companion, Girtin … he retracted on finding that it would cost rather more than ten pounds'.[17] A tablet that did finally get erected in St Paul's, Covent Garden, was that to his parents; this, as we shall see later, also showed up his parsimony. The architect T. L. Donaldson, who climbed Vesuvius with Turner on the artist's first Italian tour in 1819, told an acquaintance who reported on it afterwards that in Rome they 'were all invited to dine with the British Ambassador ... White waistcoats were the fashion at that time; but Turner, not being provided with one, rambled about and found one at a second hand clothes dealer's shop. The price asked was 5 shillings. Turner thought it too much: not being able to converse in Italian, he asked Donaldson to accompany him to the shop and try to obtain the waistcoat for a less sum. Donaldson and Turner went to the dealer's and succeeded in buying the article for 3 shillings and 6 pence.'[18]

A writer named Edward Dubois clearly hoped to raise a laugh when he suggested sardonically in the *Observer* on 22 December 1832 that Turner was *not* known for his 'overweening love of filthy lucre'. But Alaric Watts noted that although Turner – 'the astute bargain-maker' – often sent in a bill for his expenses when working on a commission, these were generally very moderate, 'confined to absolute necessaries'. One item in such an expense account puzzled the recipient: 'Boxing Harry, 2s. 6d.' Boxing Harry, he discovered, 'was the slang phrase on "the road" for making one meal answer the purpose of two, that one being tea with meat "fixings"'.[19]

Some, then and later, thought Turner's mercenariness ran in the family. There was the time, for example, when Turner's uncles squabbled about their mother's small estate. But in fact that matter was amicably resolved, and it doesn't seem very different from the disputes that many families go through. Turner's carefulness about money did not prevent him from seeing wider implications. George Jones wrote: 'Turner was a holder of Bank Stock at the time of the reduction of interest from 5% to 4%. I inquired of [him] what he thought of the reduction ... He replied, "I like 5% for my money and the quartern loaf at a shilling [12 pence]. Ask the poor man what he likes: he would say, 'I like the quartern loaf at eight pence and interest at 4%.'"'[20] His business sense was considered valuable by several institutions. The Royal Academy put it to use; he often prompted the Academy to economies, as in October 1811 when he proposed that the Academy buy rather than hire twenty-four chairs it needed, to save money in the long run. He worked for many years as a trustee, Treasurer and Chairman of the Artists' General Benevolent Institution. Once Turner went to solicit a subscription to the artists' charity from the sculptor Joseph Nollekens, whose reputation for tightfistedness exceeded his own. (Nollekens was known for sending his tenants frequent reminders of rent due, for scrimping on coal and candles, and for getting his servants to pick up scraps in the street for his dog Cerberus.) But like Turner he could also surprise. On this occasion Nollekens asked Turner how much he wanted. 'Only a guinea,' said Turner; upon which the sculptor immediately opened a table-drawer and gave Mr Turner *thirty* guineas, saying, 'There, take that.'[21]

George Jones was aware that Turner had a problem about money, in terms of normal civilized behaviour, but he felt there were grounds for it. Jones wrote:

> His education had been defective … He had no one to impress upon him that disdain of mercenary feeling which ought to accompany genius. He never in early life felt the tendered hand of generous friendship: the hands extended to him sought to profit by his talents at the smallest expense possible … He became suspicious and so sensitive that he at length dreaded the motives of all by whom he was approached on business. He desired to be wealthy and took every honourable means to be so, and was indefatigable to become independent of the world.

Jones also made a further point:

> However great Turner's desire to accumulate money, he never betrayed the slightest envy of the wealth or success of others; he never disparaged the works of his contemporaries, nor ever sought to supersede them in obtaining employment.
>
> Mr [Samuel] Rogers gave him a commission to illustrate his *Pleasures of Memory* and his *Italy*. Turner was so satisfied with the elegant way the works were published that he would only receive five guineas a piece for the loan of the drawings. [Thomas] Campbell, the poet, desired Turner to make a set of drawings for an edition of his works, for which [drawings] Campbell's circumstances did not allow him to pay, and he had the honesty to confess that it would be inconvenient for him to discharge the debt; on which, Turner with kind sympathy told the poet to return the drawings [after they had been engraved] and he should be satisfied. These drawings Turner afterwards gave a friend.[22]

Others heard other sides to this. Campbell claimed that he had paid Turner 500 guineas for the drawings, which Turner bought back for 200. According to Cyrus Redding, Campbell found he couldn't get rid of the drawings for a decent price and, running into Turner, told him jokingly that he was going to put them up for auction. Campbell told Redding: 'Turner said, feeling annoyed, I suppose, at my remark, "Don't do that; let me have them." I sent them to him accordingly ... and he has just paid me for them.' Campbell seemed to think that he had put one over on Turner. But Redding decided later that Turner might well have done this out of a desire to be friendly to Campbell. 'He was just the character to do such an act silently and bluntly.'[23]

Jones believed that 'Turner's heart was replete with charitable feelings, though his manner was not inviting to the prosperous or the poor.' He didn't like appearing kind. 'He was rough in his manner to suppliants, yet I have known him give his half-crown where another would have offered a penny.' Moreover, although he, Jones, had never needed assistance from Turner, 'I am certain no one would have given it to me more willingly.'[24] George Lance, a still-life and history painter who had been a pupil of Haydon's, called Turner 'a strange compound – so much natural good-heartedness, so much bad breeding. I do believe what Boswell said of Johnson may quite as truly be applied to him, that if he was a bear, it was only in the skin.'[25] Despite the retrospective strictures of Ann Dart, Turner in later life helped John Narraway's son and daughter with a loan.[26] Jones declared that 'in one instance he returned a bond for £500, which was never again asked for or paid'. Furthermore, 'At the Royal Academy it was so difficult to get him to attend and take the sums due to him for duties performed in that Institution, that, while I was the Keeper, the Treasurer consented to pay Turner's earnings to me, and receive my receipt for the same, that the accounts might be made up; and I kept the money until I found an opportunity of making Turner take it.'[27]

Yet Turner's colleagues, puzzled by his bearishness, frequently debated the depth of his generosity. How real was it? Like Stephen Rigaud earlier, Charles Cope, an Academy student in the 1820s, had the impression Turner was a 'pincher',[28] and it was generally accepted that sherry and biscuits were the only hospitality anyone ever received in his house. But on one occasion when he was part of a large group dining out at Blackwall, below Greenwich, the sculptor Chantrey at the head of the table was presented with the hefty bill and, to raise a laugh, threw it to Turner. Turner paid it and allowed no one else to contribute. Cyrus Redding said that during their jaunts in Devon in 1813 Turner paid his quota 'cheerfully' at the inns where they stopped for refreshment. Turner was also the host at a picnic party at Mount Edgcumbe, near Plymouth, at which 'cold meats, shellfish, and good wines abounded', according to Redding, who was a guest.

> In that delightful spot we spent the best part of a beautiful summer's day. Never was there more social pleasure partaken by any party in that English Eden. Turner was exceedingly agreeable for one whose language was more epigrammatic and terse than complimentary upon most occasions. He had come two or three miles with the man who bore his store of good things, and had been at work before our arrival. He showed the ladies some of his sketches in oil, which he had brought with him … The wine circulated freely … My opinion is, that this great artist always understood the occasion and was prepared to meet it as any other individual would do.[29]

The impression builds of a man whose shyness got in the way of his liberality and sometimes camouflaged it. George Jones again: 'When we dined out, I always insisted on paying half the coach hire, but when we went to parties in the country, he always ordered the fly and would never say what it cost, so I used to put half a sovereign into his waistcoat pocket, which was very rarely half the expense.'[30] Thomas Rose recalled the first time Turner stayed with him and his family at Cowley Hall, near Uxbridge, Middlesex: 'On the morning after he left, one of the servants came to Mrs R. with several shillings in her hand, stating she had found the silver under the pillow where Mr Turner had slept, and asking her mistress what she should do with it. She was told it was doubtless intended for herself, but on his next visit she would soon learn if it had been left by mistake. Such, however, did not appear to be the case, for under the pillow was always a little mine of the *argentum vivum*, or silver that will slip through the fingers.'[31]

Jones thought that Turner's reputation for 'love of money' – as Rigaud put it, 'a ruling passion which tarnished the character'[32] – had come about because for much of his career he was saving with a specific object: the charity he intended to establish for the relief of impoverished artists. Clara Wells exclaimed,

> Surely the man is to be honoured who, denying himself almost the comforts of life, could steadily devote the accumulated wealth of long years of toil to so noble a purpose. And let it not be thought that Turner's heart was closed to the many appeals to his benevolence which came before him. I know he gave ungrudgingly, but he was no boaster of his good deeds.[33]

Turner's 'liberality', as Clara called it, could be seen in his attitude towards other artists. Ruskin wrote that he had never heard Turner 'say one depreciating word of living man, or man's work; I never knew him let pass, without some sorrowful remonstrance, or endeavour at mitigation, a blameful word spoken by another'.[34] Frith was once with several artists discussing the shortcomings of a picture, when Turner joined them. 'After hearing much unpleasant remark from which he dissented, he was forced to confess that a very bad passage in the picture, to which the malcontents drew his attention, "was *a poor bit*".' Frith applauded Turner's generosity toward younger artists, 'his kindness in expressing his opinion of all contemporary work', and he noted that such remarks were 'in exact opposition to the general notion of his disposition'.[35] The Reverend Trimmer, on a fishing excursion with Turner, was shown an illustration in Thomas Campbell's *The Pleasures of Hope*, which Turner had brought along to read while angling. Turner thought the illustration pretty. Trimmer queried this: 'Nothing first-rate, is it?' Turner reiterated his judgement: 'It is *pretty*, and he is a poor man with a large family.'[36]

George Lance attended a dinner where he met the then elderly Turner. 'On the wall was a picture of mine, so elaborated that it approached to decided hardness: Lord Mornington [one of the guests] remarked the fault, appealing to Turner for a corroboration of his judgment; but the only remark he could extract from the kind old man's lips was, "Oh, my lord, you should see it by daylight."' On a later visit to Turner's gallery, Lance thanked Turner for a statement in which Turner had mentioned Lance along with Etty and Mulready as 'the three greatest colourists' in British contemporary art. Turner replied, a bit stiltedly but with feeling, 'I have many times endeavoured to serve my brother artists, but you are the first that has ever expressed gratitude for it.' Of course, as Lance realized, his friendly supporter was the 'greatest colourist' of all.[37]

Turner wasn't celebrated for giving away his own work, though he left a sketchbook with the Narraways. He is also said to have presented a seapiece to a Margate boatman to settle an account for taking him out, and to have given 'a drawing of great value' to the man who kept the local ale-house near his friend Walter Fawkes's Farnley Hall 'in liquidation of a trifling score of some four or five pounds'.[38]

He was known for giving practical help to his colleagues in the Academy, but other instances were talked about. W. J. Broderip, an acquaintance of the engraver and watercolourist J. W. Archer, called at Chantrey's studio one Sunday morning to see a maquette for a statue Chantrey was working on of George Canning, who had been Prime Minister. Turner was there, with other artists. Archer wrote:

> While they were discussing the merits of this fine statue, Turner was to be observed casting his eye round the studio, till, discovering the object of his quest, he seized upon and poised a long pole which stood in a corner, and advanced with it pointed at the clay model, as if threatening the destruction of its plastic fabric. Mr Broderip, uncertain whether to suppose the great painter influenced by sudden frenzy, stepped forward to arrest the apparently rash deed; but Chantrey laid a hand upon his arm, saying, 'Let him alone, he knows what he is doing.' And Turner, having dug the end of the stick among the folds of drapery in front of the statue, drew a long vertical groove down to the base of the figure. Chantrey then approached the model smiling, lovingly thumbed the gashed clay, and said 'Thank you, Turner! That straight line among the folds will make my figure stand firmly on his feet.'[39]

At the Trimmer house one day when Turner was on hand, Henry Howard RA painted a portrait of one of the boys holding a cat. The older Trimmer son told Thornbury that the cat gave the artist some problems. 'The head and fore-legs were capital; but the hind-legs and tail caused the difficulty. What to do with them? "Wrap them up in your red pocket-handkerchief," said Turner, who was looking on; and not only was the cat difficulty disposed of, but the picture was improved and it is one of Howard's best works.'[40]

Turner could be brusque one moment and considerate the next. John Sell Cotman, the brilliant watercolourist and etcher, was offended when Turner, with apparent rudeness, declined to join him in undertaking a commission for the pair of them to do some drawings. Cotman said, 'I am truly sorry to find such a man with such a mind.' But Turner later recommended the hard-up Cotman for the post of drawing-master at King's College School, paying £100 a year. The school authorities asked Turner – it seems not for the first time – whom he would propose for the job, and Turner said, 'Why of course Cotman. I have already said Cotman. I am tired of saying what I say again: "Cotman! Cotman! Cotman!"'[41] And despite his dislike of Haydon's antagonistic attitude towards the Royal Academy, Turner out of artistic interest or compassion for the wilful and desperate artist called in at the special exhibition Haydon put on in 1814 for his *Judgement of Solomon*. Haydon exempted Turner from the bitter wrath he felt for Academicians in general: 'Turner behaved well and did me justice,' he wrote.[42]

Clara Wells saw both sides of Turner, miser and giver. She was sure that 'there was more hidden good and worth in his character than the world could imagine'. She thought 'he had a tender, affectionate heart, such as few possess'.[43] Some who had business dealings with him, like the writer Walter Scott, might conclude that 'Turner's palm is as itchy as his fingers are ingenious.'[44] But Clara had seen a different man. Under 'that rather rough and cold exterior', she detected strong affections and – perhaps more surprising – one of the most 'light-hearted merry creatures'. When staying with the Wellses at Knockholt around 1807–9, Turner didn't stand on his pride or parade his suspiciousness. Being with them seemed to take him out of himself. Clara – who was about twenty at this time – wrote later: 'I remember one day coming in after a walk, and when the servant opened the door the uproar was so great that I asked the servant what was the matter. "Oh, only the young ladies [my young sisters], ma'am, playing with the young gentleman [Turner]." When I went into the sitting-room, where Turner was seated on the ground, with the children winding his ridiculously large cravat round his neck, he exclaimed, "See here, Clara, what these children are about!"'[45] A pencil-and-oil sketch he did of an armchair while *chez* Wells seems to express the sense of solid comfort he felt when with them.[46]

'Turner was fond of children,' said the younger Trimmer, and children realized this and were fond of him in return.[47] But to his own children he appears to have been a barely, or at the best fitfully, interested father. Someone else whose opinion one would like to have had on whether Turner was generous or mean was his children's mother, Sarah Danby – but she left no recorded comment on the subject. Inside the cover of a sketchbook he used in 1809–11 for some scenes around Hastings,[48] he noted various sums of money received and paid out: £210 came in from 'Phillips'; payments were to 'Platt 17–10'; 'Mrs W 6–6'; and 'Mrs D 4–4'. Sarah, assuming she is 'Mrs D', gets the least of the payments. That she was getting a pension from the Royal Society of Musicians while living with Turner may have given him an excuse for handing out less to her; she obviously kept it quiet that they had a 'relationship' for fear of losing her Society benefits. As we have seen, Turner apparently helped Sarah fiddle the books; it suited his secretiveness and fears of too definite an entanglement. During the years in Hammersmith when she was – according to Callcott – living with him, her daughter Marcella Danby began her apprenticeship as a teacher at the nearby Mrs Wyatt's Catholic school for girls. Sarah Danby often sent deputies up to town to the Royal Society of Musicians offices in Lisle Street, Soho, to collect and sign for her monthly benefit of £4 14s 6d: one of her Danby daughters, generally Marcella, or her niece Hannah, or even Turner's father went on these errands.

Sarah was about forty-three in 1810. In 1811, rather late to be bearing another child, she gave birth to her second Turner daughter, Georgiana; the birth apparently took place south of the River Thames 'in Surrey', according to a census return Georgiana made later, though perhaps untruthfully.[49] (When Georgiana married in 1840, she gave her father's name as 'George Danby, deceased'; and John Danby had, as far as is known, no relatives named George.) It is worth noting that Turner in 1811 was in Hastings and its vicinity, as he had been in 1801 when Evelina was baptized in Guestling, Sussex. It is a 'Hastings' sketchbook which records his payments to Platt, Mrs W and Mrs D. Was Platt a doctor, Mrs W a midwife? On a later page of this sketchbook he scribbled 'Guestling. Calld 3 Oaks. Cook.' In another sketchbook used in 1811[50] is a small drawing of a wooden cradle. Perhaps it sheltered the infant Georgiana, who twenty-nine years later would refuse to name her real father.

That Sarah about this time ran into trouble with the Musicians Society may not be coincidental. Her monthly allowance was abruptly reduced. In January 1812 it was cut to one guinea, with an extra fifteen shillings every quarter for 'school' for one of the girls. The guinea-a-month was most likely a specific maintenance payment for the last Danby daughter, Teresa, who was still below the apprenticeship age of fourteen. In August 1813 Sarah wrote to the Society asking that her full allowance be paid once again. Why had it been interrupted? Had the Society heard of Georgiana's birth and found out that Sarah was living with JMWT? Her address in 1813 was given as 10 Warwick Row, possibly in Southwark, which was Surrey in those days. In any event, the Society's acting Secretary Mr Cordell 'informed the Board that Mrs Danby had been sworn by Mr Wm. Parsons who is satisfied with her statements. Ordered that Mrs Danby's allowance be paid her including last month.'[51]

It seems that Georgiana's arrival in the world was something Turner couldn't handle. It apparently precipitated the final break-up with Sarah Danby. Perhaps, too, Sarah made him think of his mother – he didn't want to be possessed by a woman. In any event, her successful appeal for her pension may well have depended on establishing that she was not in a state of 'illicit intercourse', and therefore she decided the time had come to move out. Neither Hannah nor Turner's father helped her collect her widow's allowance after 1813; she went on receiving it from the Society for another forty-eight years, until her death, aged about ninety-four, in 1861. (John Danby had certainly got his money's worth for his modest payments into the Society's pension fund before his death.) If Turner gave further financial help to the mother of his two daughters, there is no record of it. He would eventually consider assisting Evelina and Georgiana. For the moment his verdict was a few words scribbled lightly in a sketchbook: 'Woman is Doubtful Love.'[52]

8: The Bite of the Print

Turner was staying with the Wells family in 1806 when the idea of doing a series of engravings, to be called the *Liber Studiorum*, came to the fore. The prints Charles Turner had done from his painting *The Shipwreck* were evidently going to be a success. He had, as we have seen, quite a few unsold paintings on hand and the publication of further engravings might well be worth his time and trouble; it was a medium in which, shooting for the moon as always, he could try new things. It must also have occurred to him that while oil colours faded and cracked, and canvases decayed, engravings were a way to gain posterity's attention.[1] According to Clara Wells, her father for a long time had been urging Turner to make a selection of his works for reproduction in print form, 'telling him that it would surely be done after his death, and perhaps in a way that might not do him that justice which he could ensure for himself'.[2] Wells, at that point teacher of draughtsmanship at the East India Company's College at Addiscombe, Kent, kept on at Turner about this, until one autumn day at the Knockholt cottage the artist gave in. He said, 'Well, Gaffer, I see there will be no peace till I comply; so give me a piece of paper. There now! Rule the size for me, and tell me what I am to do.'[3]

Turner no doubt had some preconceptions of what he was going to do, above and beyond reproducing 'a selection' of works he had painted; but Clara had the impression that it was her father – the 'gaffer' or foreman – who set up the structure of the project, in particular the way in which the prints were going to be placed in rather eighteenth-century-sounding subject categories, such as pastoral, architectural and mountainous. Turner then and there did some drawings for what would be the first set of prints to be published.

The title for the project – *Liber Studiorum*, the 'Book of Studies' – was an obvious obeisance to Claude Lorrain, one of his heroes.

Claude (1600–82) had made 195 drawings as a record of his own works, so that posterity would be better able to identify fakes of his pictures. Thus the title of Claude's collection of drawings, *Liber Veritatis*. The original of this was now in England, owned by the Duke of Devonshire, and had been reproduced by the engraver Richard Earlom for publication in London in the 1770s. Turner's reverence for Claude was frequently visible in his landscape paintings – in his classical Thames-side idylls, for example – and was noticed by colleagues who saw him spellbound or even moved to tears in front of Claude paintings. An audience at a convoluted lecture Turner gave at the Royal Academy in 1811 heard one passage of surprising clarity as he declared:

> Pure as Italian air, calm, beautiful and serene, spring forward the works and name of Claude Lorrain. The golden orient or the amber-coloured ether, the midday ethereal vault, the fleecy skies, resplendent valleys, campagnas rich with all the cheerful blues of fertility, trees possessing every hue and tone of summer heat; rich, harmonious, true and clear, replete with all the aerial qualities of distance (aerial lights, aerial colour) – where, through all these comprehensive qualities and powers, can we find a clue to his mode of practice?

Turner's answer was: in a 'continual study of the parts of nature'.[4] Through his own *Liber*, Turner meant to show the effects of such a study, to do so by following Claude's method of drawing and washing in with pen and brush using sepia ink, and – in the wake of Earlom's print versions of Claude that had been successfully published by Boydell – to have his drawings translated into engravings, the most common reproductions of the time, which would make his *Liber* publicly accessible.

His Brentford hours spent colouring the prints of Boswell's *Antiquities* for John Lees had made their mark. The *Liber* would also be in great part Turner's Antiquities: it would feature castles, temples, abbeys, mills and old bridges, located by rivers and streams, and attended by herds of animals and small groups of people – both structures and persons often given an antique cast by being in classical guise or garb. As noted, he had been an illustrator from the start of his career, turning out drawings which had been engraved for magazine and periodical publication. The *Copper-plate Magazine* and the *Oxford Almanack* had both used his services. Covent Garden while he grew up had seemed as full of printmakers and printdealers as it was of fruit and vegetable merchants; two engravers, Vere and Woodfield, had worked in Maiden Lane. Ackermann's well-known printshop was not far away in the Strand. Turner had done his stint colouring prints for John Raphael Smith. He may have picked up tips from the engraver Edward Bell, with whom he toured Kent in 1793. His interest in the processes of printmaking was evident in sketchbook memoranda of materials needed for the craft. Now he meant to do a good deal of the actual print-creating work himself.

The 'plate' used for printing was at this time still copper. (Steel, which was more durable and hence better for making many impressions, only came into use in the 1820s.) The copper was heated and coated with a waxy varnish; on to this was traced the bare bones of the drawing being reproduced; and then the design was cut into the wax with an etching needle, a fine point which exposed the copper beneath. The plate was next dipped in acid, which bit into the exposed, wax-free lines; these lines would hold ink and thus produce black marks when the plate was used for printing. Further refinements to the plate, after the wax was removed, could be achieved by engraving – incising or gouging more lines directly on the plate with a burin or graver, and burnishing the copper to produce whiter, lighter areas – and by mezzotinting; this was a way of achieving strongly contrasting tonal effects by roughening the plate to produce little burrs that held the ink to make shade and by scraping or burnishing away the burrs to give the effect of light. Engraving was hard physical work and took time; it was generally left to professional engravers who were proud of their craft in translating artists' drawings into prints by way of lines, hollows and dots. After being inked, the plate was wiped with muslin so that the ink remained only in the declivities. A dampened sheet of paper was laid on the plate, and then plate and paper put in a press and squeezed together. Early impressions of the print were called proofs; the artist could note or 'touch' corrections on these that he wanted the engraver to make. Engravers had the right to keep some of these early versions for themselves as a supplement to their fee.

Turner put out a prospectus for the *Liber Studiorum*. He displayed a copy of this inducement in his gallery together with examples of the drawings that would be engraved in the first set he intended to publish. He promised subscribers a hundred landscapes, designed and etched by him, and engraved in mezzotint. The publication – so the *Review of Publications in Art* for June 1808 declared – would describe 'various styles of landscape, viz., the historic, mountainous, pastoral, marine, and architectural'. A capital letter on the print would denote the classification. Turner shortly came up with a sixth category, with the initials EP, apparently signifying 'Elevated Pastoral' – and, by the way, indicating his own ambition to elevate landscape art above 'map-making'.[5] He intended to bring out the work in sets or parts, each of which would have five engravings stitched into blue folders. On the front was a printed title, a written-in part number and his signature.

He did not get around to a frontispiece until well into the project, in 1812, but now, with his mind full of the *Liber*, he saw ideas for it everywhere he travelled. In 1807, in the late autumn, he went to Portsmouth to watch some captured Danish ships sail into the harbour, and sketched and wrote poetry on the way down and back; his painting *Spithead*, exhibited at his gallery the following spring, came from this trip and so did some sketches that were transformed into four finished drawings for the *Liber*. One was of Hindhead Hill, crossed by the Portsmouth road, with its gibbet on a mound in the middle distance and sheep in the foreground; this – *Liber* plate number 25 – combined a pastoral calm with intimations of highway villainy and cruel retribution. His Isleworth time provided other subjects. In one sketchbook[6] he noted the names of subscribers and the expected costs and profits of the venture.

In the end, Turner produced fourteen parts of his *Liber*, one of which had a sixth print in the shape of the frontispiece: making a total of seventy-one of the intended hundred. Only nineteen of the prints were based on works – oil paintings or watercolours – he had done in the past. In the first few years he brought out two parts annually. Sometimes there were longer intervals in publication. To begin with he charged fifteen shillings for a set of prints, and one pound fifteen shillings for a set of the earlier proofs, but after a couple of years these prices were increased. John Pye, an engraver who greatly admired Turner and remained friendly with him perhaps because, not using mezzotint, he didn't work on the *Liber* and had none of the grudges of engravers who did, wrote later: 'Turner's own selling price of lettered proofs was two guineas each number of five, or upwards of eight shillings each proof for ready money only.' And he gave no discounts, even to good friends.[7] He wanted the prints of each part of the *Liber* to be seen as a set, and he called buyers of separate prints 'a pack of geese'. Irritated, he demanded, 'Don't they know what *Liber Studiorum* means?'[8] On another occasion, when he was told that some prints from the *Liber* were being picked out as of special value, he said to Ruskin, 'What is the use of them but together?'[9] Production of the *Liber* was effectively over and done with in the early 1820s, though afterwards he worked on some smaller mezzotints to which the title 'Little *Liber*' has been given.

Whether from his suspicion of printdealers or his desire to encompass as much of the printmaking business as he could, Turner's *Liber* was very much a do-it-yourself thing, albeit with frequent help from professionals. And, like many such projects, it had problems. After making his working drawing or cartoon with pen and brush, sometimes boldly mixing the sepia ink with watercolours, he usually had an engraver make a tracing of the main structure of the drawing in red chalk. This tracing Turner used in reverse (turned over, that is, so that the plate would produce prints with left and right as in the original drawing), as a pattern for cutting the line work into the wax. The plate was then sent back to the engraver for biting in with the acid, and proofs were taken at this stage so that Turner could direct the engraver in changes needed for the next. The engravers occasionally complained that Turner, when etching the line work, hadn't followed his own designs but had changed an emphasis here and there.

In the course of the project, Turner – already a proficient etcher – mastered engraving techniques; he engraved eleven of the seventy-one plates himself.[10] This hard work also required immense precision of touch with the engravers' tools. When engravers were working for him, he kept them busy altering the plates, whether or not they had counted on so many requests for changes. While James Lahee was doing the final printing from a plate, Turner often went down to Lahee's workshop to watch the prints come off the press, to check on the effect of alterations he had made, and with burin or scraper to make further changes on the copper. Much of his correspondence of this time is with engravers, full of fussy comments about outlines, proofs or parcels of plates going to or from Hammersmith or Queen Anne Street. Engravers received willy-nilly an education from Turner, and he from them.

For many of the first parts of the *Liber*, Charles Turner, his former fellow student, made engravings and also acted as publisher, accepting subscriptions at his home at 50 Warren Street. But from 1811 the artist took over the sales side as well; he had a good base for this at his gallery. Nevertheless, despite having a hundred subscribers in 1810, as a sketchbook note recorded,[11] the project was unprofitable at the time. It is unclear how many proofs Turner actually had made from each plate, but after eight or so proofs a copper plate could produce only some thirty prints before being in need of considerable repair work. Not only did Turner have too many prints and/or proofs printed, but, as we will see, he seems on occasion to have passed off prints as proofs, taking extra cash for what unsuspecting customers believed were pressings from the more prized early states. As doubts were raised about these 'proofs', buyer confidence was shaken.

Moreover, Turner's distribution system was faulty. Printdealers increasingly declined to handle the *Liber* for Turner because he allowed them too small a discount. Colnaghi's allowance was cut back from 20 per cent to 10 to 5 to zero. The parts were published erratically. His advertising was either too little or too late. He wrote an irritated author-to-publisher note to Charles Turner on a proof of the *Lake of Thun, Liber* plate number 15, brought out in 1808: 'Respecting advertizing you know full well that everything ought to have been done long ago!! I have not seen a word in the papers … if you can get advertized anywhere DO SO … the plates not done – not advertized, in short everything has conspired against the work.'[12] When it came to doing it himself, there were similar problems. In June 1811 he advertised the sixth and seventh parts of the *Liber* in the *Sun* and felt bound to tell subscribers who had not received part five to contact him.

Although the *Liber* may not have been the lucrative venture he had hoped for, it had an impact on his fellow artists. A few, jealous of Turner's versatility, might have scoffed at it, as John Constable did when he mockingly referred to it in a letter as the 'Liber stupidorum'.[13] But others – particularly those in the landscape business – were impressed. John Varley was one such and David Cox another; Cox was an early subscriber to the *Liber*. Turner seems to have meant the work to have instructional value and also to boost the status of landscape painting, which – despite Wilson and Gainsborough – in many academic minds still played second- or third-string to the schools of history and portrait painting. (Reynolds and West still mattered; there were those who shared the alleged opinion of the French painter François Boucher who died five years before JMWT was born, that nature was 'too green and badly lit'.)[14] Turner took up Reynold's challenge to put things in a proper order by 'establishing the rules and principles of our art on a more firm and lasting foundation'.[15] Landscape, he wanted to show, could express profound and diverse ideas, associations and emotions.

His ability to think in light and shade, that Ruskin later admired,[16] was one that made him, as a painter, the maker of work perfectly suited for translation into print form. It was said that, seeing a proof lying with the top of the paper towards him on a table some distance away, he could diagnose its tonal faults and prescribe remedial changes without turning it around. John Pye – who went on to engrave thirteen non-*Liber* plates after Turner's work, the first being *Pope's Villa* in 1809–10 – wrote with a fan's enthusiasm:

> He would turn his proofs, after touching them, from side to side and upside down that the key of colour might be maintained and carried into effect. He was wont to say that engravers have only white paper to express what the painter does with vermilion. He was never tired of going to Hampstead and would spend hours lying on the Heath studying the effects of the atmosphere and the changes of light and shade, and the gradations required to express them. The great principle he was always endeavouring to advance was that of the art of translation of landscape, whether in colour or black and white, [and] was to enable the spectator to see through the picture into space.[17]

His admirers saw other things in the *Liber*. Pye thought Turner's success with it lay in his 'government of chiaroscuro'. Pye also regarded it as 'the depository of true principles belonging to a school of landscape which was in danger of passing away'.[18] Indeed, it seems now a final eighteenth-century work of Turner's; the 'Little *Liber*', by contrast, is less precise, more expressively 'romantic'. Ruskin detected 'decay and humiliation' in the *Liber*, giving 'solemnity to all its simplest subjects'. And he thought 'the meaning of the entire book was symbolized in the frontispiece … Tyre at Sunset, with the Rape of Europa' – suggesting the decay of European civilization, 'its beauty passing away into terror and judgement'.[19] One may also perceive a 'landscape of conflict'[20] – possibly between the classical idyll and the real life of hedgers, ditchers, watercress gatherers, bargees and fishermen; but Turner in the *Liber* doesn't seem *that* interested in the people who provide scale and focal points; they are simply components of the scene. John Lewis Roget, the editor of Pye's papers, took a more down-to-earth view than Ruskin:

> We may look at the plates in the *Liber Studiorum* for indications of Turner's views of life, and of human pride, his hopelessness and sadness, and his sense of humiliation and decay. We may trace in them his keen perception of the phenomena of nature, and his firm grasp of their various characteristics; the growth of wood, the hardness of stone; the swell of waves, and evanescent forms of vapour. But the practical artist will do well to remember that they are, at the same time, a set of very careful 'arrangements in brown', and to observe how much of their effect upon the mind is due to the so-called 'tricks' of contrast and gradation, of balance and harmony of parts and masses, which preserve a unity in their variety, and enabled the painter to place each subject plainly and impressively before the spectator.[21]

Some of the 'sadness' of the *Liber* may in fact spring from the fact that those 'arrangements in brown' are brown – there is a quality in prints, over and above their worlds-that-are-lost subject matter, that lies in their very brownness or monochrome condition and evokes a subdued response. Whether this was felt by the artist is not known. Turner may on the contrary have felt, on top of the usual mixture of dissatisfaction and satisfaction that creation brings, an exhilaration in demonstrating his range and power. His project was a lot less like Claude's than the word *Liber* suggested. The engravings he had done from his own paintings and watercolours were very different from those models. And, above all, he must have felt with pride that he had shown what he could do without the aid of colour.

Yet, putting away his etching needle or the chalk with which he touched a proof, the short-tempered artist was not necessarily in a good mood. The cantankerous element in Turner, never far below the surface, frequently bubbled over in his dealings with engravers; the hard bargainer seemed to become ever more implacable. With F. C. Lewis, the first engraver he got to work on the *Liber*, a price of five guineas was agreed for Lewis's work in putting areas of Turner's etched outline into aquatint. (This was a form of etching that created flat tones to produce something of the effect of a watercolour wash.)

Trouble soon followed the agreement. Turner wanted twelve proofs from the plate before Lewis started his aquatinting work. He also sent a drawing for a second plate and wanted Lewis 'to get on with it' before he, Turner, had done the original etching of the plate. When Lewis showed reluctance to do this, Turner proposed that the engraver do the initial etching and then he would add any further etching he felt was needed. Lewis quite rightly thought the agreed fee, just acceptable for the first plate, was insufficient for the second. He told Turner that the charge would now be eight guineas. At the time, Lewis was making engravings from works in the Royal Collection by Claude and Raphael and getting between fifteen and forty guineas a plate, depending on their size. The proper charge for the Turner work should have been fifteen guineas, Lewis thought. But Turner dug his heels in. He wrote to Lewis:

> Sir
>   I received the Proof and Drawing – the Proof I like very well but I do not think the grain is so fine as those you shewed me for Mr Chamberlain [John Chamberlaine, the publisher of the Royal Collection engravings] – the effect of the Drawing is well preserved, but as you wish to raise the Price to eight guineas I must decline having the other drawing engraved therefore send it when you send the plate, when they have arrived safe, the five guineas shall be left in Salsbury St where you'll be so good as to leave a recept for same.
>   Yours,
>   J. M. W. Turner
>
> 14 Dec. 1807,
> Hammersmith.[22]

Turner moved his custom to Charles Turner, who had done such a successful job with *The Shipwreck*, and – poor Lewis! – agreed to pay eight guineas a plate. The terms between the two Turners were tightly drawn: JMWT personally to begin the plates by drawing the subject in outline through the etching ground on to the copper; CT to etch these outlines and perform the subsequent mezzotinting. Charles Turner also acted as publisher over the next two years, bringing out parts 1 to 4 of the *Liber*, twenty plates in all. Each plate took him about two weeks to engrave. In 1809, however, Charles Turner ran into extra trouble with a plate and told JMWT that he ought to be paid more – twelve guineas, according to a Pye memo on the subject, ten guineas according to CT's account.

Whatever the additional sum, the artist wouldn't pay it. He was already in a bad humour with the engraver. Charles Turner was also a grumpy character, short in height like his namesake, and with a limp because of a congenitally damaged foot. The artist called on the engraver between the publication of parts 3 and 4 of the *Liber* and, according to Pye, said, 'This is a pretty business. Why, I find that some of the *Liber* prints have been stolen.'

CT: 'Well, do you suppose I stole them?'

JMWT: 'I don't say who stole them!'

CT: 'How do you know that some of them have been stolen?'

JMWT: 'Why, because many proofs are about that have never been published. I have seen some of them for sale without needle holes in their margins – which could not be if they had not been stolen.'[23]

The upshot was that after the engraver's demand for a higher fee the two Turners did not speak to one another for a number of years – nineteen, Charles Turner used to say, though in fact he engraved plate 57 of the *Liber*, *Norham Castle on the Tweed*, in 1816, so the quarrel seems to have been patched up after nine years. In 1810, the artist – believing that he had reserved to himself the sole right to colour prints – wrote the engraver a peremptory note about another alleged offence: 'Mr Turner requests Mr C. Turner to explain through what cause the Print of the Shipwreck now in a shop in Fleet St., late Macklin, happens to be *coloured* when Mr C. Turner expressly agreed that none should be coloured but by J. M. W. Turner *only*.'[24] During these moments, Charles Turner may well have recalled the drawing of a scowling JMWT he had executed around 1795, entitled 'A Sweet Temper'.

And yet the scowl was not permanent; as we have seen, the artist's grudges didn't last forever. When Charles Turner was elected an Associate Engraver at the Royal Academy in 1828, JMWT wrote to him from Rome, where he was painting:

> Dear Charles
>   I have just received a letter from Mr Jones and I sit down to congratulate you or rather myself, for without Sir Tho[mas's] casting vote your losing the election by my absence would have

made me miserable – I do not mean by saying so to take any credit to myself but on the contrary do beg that you regard with truly worthy and not an obsequious respect the Members who so nobly supported you and particularly to the President who may have had some cause of yore of displeasure, for the flattering manner which he bestow'd it, your never to be *forgotten* esteem and regard, and now do think what a shame the clamour of the love of money caused, dismiss it now unworthy of yourself, your family need it not and will readily account [?] for your honor and your *name*.

Belive me most truly yours

J. M. W. Turner

P.S. You see I am acting the Papa with you but it is the last time of asking.[25]

(JMWT was in fact a year younger than the engraver.)

The identity of the culprit in the 'stolen proofs' drama later came to light. Pye wrote:

The great painter having threatened with an action the dealer in whose shop-window the proofs had been exposed for sale, he [the dealer] brought forward a woman of whom he had bought them. She proved to be the person the great painter employed to stitch together the prints of the *Liber* in numbers. This person declared that the prints she had sold were her own, for that Mr Turner had given them to her instead of money, when she pressed him for the amount due to her for the labour she had performed, and that she sold them to enable herself to get bread.[26]

In other words, the villain of the piece was 'the great painter' himself.

However, it was eventually revealed that Charles Turner did keep a large stock of Turner proofs. He explained to John Pye how he had come by them: 'While I was engraving the plates of the *Liber*, the great man often called upon me. When my first plate was finished, and I showed my great namesake a proof of it, he said, "I like this, Charley, you must get me a dozen proofs of it." Several times he said, "Charley, I should like to have a dozen proofs of that plate." Of course I got the proofs, and paid for them, and also the like number of all the other plates which I engraved for the work. But, some years afterwards, when I quarreled with him, I asked for the money that I had paid for the printing of the proofs. He said, "I shan't pay you, for I never ordered 'em." So they remained in my hands.'[27] And Charles Turner eventually was well repaid for the money he had laid out. In 1852 he sold some *Liber* and *Shipwreck* proofs to the dealer Colnaghi for more than £800. At this point he was cross with himself, since in time past he had (so he claimed, not altogether plausibly) let his servants light fires with such proofs, when they didn't seem to have any resale value. He exclaimed to Pye, 'How unconscious was I that I was robbing my children of a fortune!'[28]

Other engravers found relations with their taskmaster equally tricky. For Thomas Lupton, who had just served an apprenticeship with George Clint, the engraver of *Liber* plates 41 and 45, work on a plate took nearly two months and the materials cost over a pound – Lupton's fee of five guineas did not go far. Clint himself, who received six guineas a plate, gave up the commission because the fee was not enough. And though one might have thought that, once Turner had got the *Liber* and all his responsibilities for it out of his system, he would mellow, his relations with the engraver and publisher W. B. Cooke proved the contrary.

Cooke was the publisher of *The Southern Coast* and various other riverine and coastal subjects done by Turner; engravings continued to meet the curiosity of armchair travellers, and Turner remained the artist of choice for publishers of topographical series. Cooke bought or rented the use of Turner drawings. In the case of *The Southern Coast* the rental fee was to be £7 10s each for fifty or so drawings; in addition Turner wanted twenty-five sets of proofs. By the end of 1826 some heat had been engendered in communications between artist and engraver. On 1 January 1827 Cooke wrote to regret that Turner was persisting in his demand for the twenty-five sets of proofs. He pointed out to the artist that *The Southern Coast* was his – Cooke's – original idea and that he had invested much in it, including a commission of more than £400 to Turner. He had persuaded him to take a share in it, which brought Turner profits on top of his fee. And although he had recently offered to pay for further drawings in the series at twelve and a half guineas each, Turner had shown his gratitude by demanding two and a half guineas more for the drawings already done. The artist had come into Cooke's office and in front of several members of the staff had declared, 'I will have my terms! Or I will oppose the work by doing another "Coast"!' Cooke quoted this declaration back to Turner, 'These were the words you used; and everyone must allow them to be a *threat*.'

Cooke recalled an earlier injury. Turner had *given* him, so he thought, a drawing called *Neptune's Trident*,[29] used on the wrapper of *Marine Views*, of 1825 – a drawing which the engraver had presented to Mrs Cooke. 'You may recollect afterwards charging me two guineas for the loan of it, and requesting me, at the same time, to return it to you; which has been done.'

Cooke, thoroughly wound up by now, concluded:

> The ungracious remarks I experienced this morning at your house, when I pointed out to you the meaning of my former note ... were such as to convince me that you maintain a mistaken and most unaccountable idea of profit and advantage in the new work of the 'Coast'; and that no estimate or calculation will convince you to the contrary. Ask yourself if Hakewill's 'Italy', 'Scottish Scenery' or 'Yorkshire' have either of them succeeded in the return of the capital laid out on them ... There is considerable doubt remaining whether they will ever return their expenses, and whether the shareholders and proprietors will ever be reinstated in the money laid out on them. So much for the profit of works.
>
> I assure you I must turn over an entirely new leaf to make them ever return their expenses.
>
> To conclude, I regret exceedingly the time I have bestowed in endeavouring to convince you in a calm and patient manner of a number of calculations made for *your* satisfaction; and I have met in return such hostile treatment that I am positively disgusted at the mere thought of the trouble I have given myself on such a useless occasion.[30]

About this same time, the engraver Edward Goodall was involved in a quarrel Turner had with W. B. Cooke's brother George, who had engraved many plates after Turner's work in the previous years. Turner encountered George Cooke at a meeting of the Artists' Conversazione, a discussion society that met at the Freemasons' Tavern; Turner said he wanted the return of some touched proofs that Goodall – who had been working for the Cookes – was hanging on to. Cooke declined to press Goodall to do this. According to Thornbury, 'Turner grew white with rage, and Cooke red as fire; and presently Cooke came up to Mr Goodall and said, "If you give them up, I shall call you a mean fellow." Next day Mr Goodall went to Turner's house about a plate, when the storm commenced. Turner lamented that the Conversazione should have no more pleasure for him since these quarrels, and demanded the proofs. Goodall [who for some reason had the proofs with him] refused to give them up, and even half thrust them into the fire, when the blaze caught them.

In terror of fire, Turner, whose chimney was never swept, ran with shovel and tongs to save the house, exclaiming, "Good God! You'll set the house on fire!"[31]

But relations with Goodall were also patched up. In 1842 he had the immense job of making a plate from Turner's painting *Caligula's Bridge* (RA 1831). For this Goodall was paid the goodly fee of 700 guineas by the artist (for what, however, might be several years' work of line engraving). In the course of Goodall's labours, Turner asked for a number of alterations – to the size of the engraving and to the buildings and people in the design. At one point Turner made some quick chalk marks and said, 'Mr Goodall, I must have two more boys in here, and some goats. You can put them in for me.' Goodall replied that he could not engrave from such slight indications, and Turner therefore painted in what he wanted in watercolour over the oils of the painting.

Turner dug his heels in when an arrangement suited him, and he was quick to push an advantage, even retroactively, as in the price of the *Southern Coast* drawings, when an opportunity appeared. What he did not seem to take into account was the riskiness of the print business – although his own experience with the *Liber* should have showed him how slow a profit might be in coming. It may well have been craftiness that sometimes led him to wrap himself in his fame and temperament as an artist and thereby stand aloof from the commercial reality that affected others. But of course he knew that print publishers went broke. (He was personally affected, in money terms, when the Finden brothers became insolvent in 1842, while working on several large plates after his paintings; he wrote to Clara Wells, now Mrs Wheeler, '*Woe is me.*')[32] Although Charles Heath was thrilled to bring Turner into a series called *Picturesque Views in England and Wales* in the 1820s and 1830s – for which the artist was to be paid thirty guineas each for 120 drawings – the series was not a financial success. Heath's partners, Hurst and Robinson, who put up all the capital, went bankrupt.

As an example of what the publishers were up against with Turner, George Cooke used to talk about another occasion when Hurst and Robinson's profit margins had been threatened. After some haggling, Turner agreed to 'make them a series of drawings for a topographical work at the rate of twenty-five *pounds* a piece, and he went away expressing his entire satisfaction with the arrangement.

He came back, however, a few minutes afterwards, and thrusting his head in at the door of the room he had just left, ejaculated "Guineas." "Guineas let it be," responded the publishers, and he once more retired. He soon returned, however, and added, "My expenses." "Certainly," was the answer. This facility of disposition he seemed determined to test to the utmost, for he came back a third time to remind them that he must have in addition twenty-five proofs.'[33]

Avarice and respect for an old friend seemed to go hand in hand on an occasion in the 1820s. For a new Cooke series, *The Rivers of England*, Turner's work was to be joined by designs by Thomas Girtin and William Collins. Turner was asked to work on some of the prints made after Girtin's watercolours. According to Thomas Miller, Turner said to W. B. Cooke,

> 'I'll touch them for Poor Tom. Poor Tom!' and he continued repeating the words 'Poor Tom' as if to himself. Cooke took the proofs to him, and [Turner] worked upon them for a long time, bestowing great care and 'making them', as Cooke said, 'quite his own'; and, at last, after holding them individually at arm's length, throwing them on the floor, turning them upside down, and flinging them in every direction, he said, 'There, Poor Tom! That will do. Poor Tom!' and Cooke was about to take the impressions away, when Turner, clapping his arm upon them, exclaimed – 'Stop! You must pay me two guineas apiece first.'[34]

Part of the money problem with the *England and Wales* series was that Turner resisted Heath's plea that it be printed from steel plates, which would have allowed a longer run, that is more copies. To begin with, he was not keen on steel engraving. Thornbury suggested that this was because Turner didn't want to supply prints 'by the million'. Talking with Sir Thomas Lawrence one day about engraving, Turner was said to have declared that he hated steel.

'Why?' asked Lawrence.

'I don't like it. Besides, I don't choose to be a basket engraver.'

'A basket engraver? What's that?'

Turner mischievously explained that, when he had got off the coach in Hastings not long before, a woman had come up to him with a basketful of prints of Lawrence's portrait of Mrs Peel, and wanted to sell him one for sixpence.[35]

Something about engravers – or the print business – seemed to bring out Turner's most prickly reactions. When Heath discontinued the *England and Wales* series in 1838, after its twenty-fourth part, the stock of unsold prints and the copper-plates were put up for sale for £3000. The printdealer H. G. Bohn offered £2800, but this wasn't enough, so the prints and plates were sent to auction. Many looked forward to buying various items, but when the day came Turner bought the whole lot at the reserve price of £3000. As Thornbury recounts the story, Turner said to Bohn, 'So, Sir, you were going to buy my "England and Wales" to sell cheap ... But I have taken care of that. No more of my plates shall be worn to shadows.'

Bohn replied that he was not interested in the plates, only in the stock of prints. Turner perked up at this and said *he* only wanted the plates. He invited Bohn to breakfast the next day to talk about it. Bohn came to Queen Anne Street and found the offer of breakfast no longer stood. Nevertheless, he offered Turner £2500 for all the prints, on the understanding that the plates and the copyright – which had been valued at £500 – were to remain with the artist. But Turner, obdurate, wanted £3000 for the prints *and* to keep the plates. 'Thus', says Thornbury, 'the interview closed.'[36]

Frith told of a 'superior' printseller in Rathbone Place who greatly appreciated the *Liber Studiorum*. He acquired prints of it whenever he could. On one occasion he purchased a print that had been damaged by stains and rough use, and, feeling that it could not be much further injured, displayed it in his shop window. Turner came by, saw the damaged print and bounced into the shop. He said crossly, pointing to the window, 'It's a confounded shame to treat an engraving like that! What can you be thinking about to go and destroy a good thing – for it *is* a good thing, mind you!'

'*I* destroy it!' said the shopman in a rage. 'What do you mean by saying I destroyed it? And who the devil are you, I should like to know? I didn't ask you to buy it, did I? You don't look as if you could understand a good print when you see one. *I* destroy it! Bless my soul, I bought it just as it is – and I would rather keep it till Doomsday than sell it to you. Why you should put yourself out about it, I can't think.'

'Why, I did it,' said Turner.

'Did what! Did you spoil it? If you did, you deserve—'

'No, no, man! My name's Turner, and I did the drawing, and engraved the plate from it.'

'Bless my soul!' exclaimed the printseller. 'Is it possible you are the great Turner? Well, sir, I have long desired to see you. And now that I have seen you, I hope I shall never see you again. A more disagreeable person I have seldom met.'[37]

A printdealer named Halstead had a story with a happier ending:

> Turner and I had many a quarrel. He used to be so angry with me because I broke up many of his 'Libers', and sold the plates [prints] separately. He could not stand that. One day in my shop in Bond Street we had a worse quarrel than ever, and he went out furious, having used very strong language. I had a corner by my window which commanded the street, and from whence I could see all that passed. Being much overcome by what had happened, I crept into that with a paper, and tried to read. He saw me from the outside, and presently came running back into the shop and said, 'Well, God bless you! God bless you!' 'Your words come very pleasantly, sir,' said I, 'after a most unpleasant morning!' 'God bless you!' said he once more, and ran off.[38]

*

Turner's pride in his own work was, with prints as with paintings, most often immense. Now and then, he ceased to be painstaking; but he had a better right than anyone else to decide whether care or neglect was the order of the day. Generally his perfectionism prevailed. Indeed, it has been suggested that money may have sometimes been merely the excuse for terminating arrangements with engravers about whose skills he had doubts. He occasionally tried to balance with compliments any requests for improvements he wanted made. In 1824, when he was in Yorkshire, he received from the then publishers of the *Southern Coast*, J. and A. Arch, an early proof of the plate George Cooke was making from his picture *Hythe*. Turner did some pencil corrections, made a note in the margin for Cooke and added a postscript:

> P.S. You ask me for my opinion. First I shall say in general *very good*, secondly the Figures and Barracks excellent; but I think you have cut up the Bank called Shorne Cliff too much with the graver by lines [another diagram] which are equal in strength and width and length, that give a coarseness to the quality, and do not look like my touches or give work-like look to the good part over which they are put – The Marsh is all a swamp. I want flickering lights upon it up to the sea, and altho' I have darkened the sea in part yet you must

> not consider it to want strength ... Get it into one tone, flats, by
> dots or some means, and let the sea and water only appear different
> by their present lines.[39]

Two more proofs passed back and forth between Cooke and Turner, being touched and commented upon, before the plate was put through the press for prints.

In another piece of correspondence from this time, Turner wrote to one of the Arches about the Scottish engraver William Miller, who was also engraving a plate for the *Southern Coast*: 'There is so much good work about Miller and it would [be] but justice to tell him so from me if you like.' Miller saw another result of Turner's acute perception one day at W. B. Cooke's house, when, among others, Turner and Thomas Lupton were on hand. Turner was talking to an artist named Hugh Williams about an engraved scene, when, 'differing in opinion as to the forms of some lines in the subject, a piece of paper was produced, upon which each artist made a slight sketch in pencil to elucidate his views. At the conclusion Lupton was somewhat slyly appropriating the sketch, a proceeding which Turner's keen eye disappointed by transferring it to his own pocket, notwithstanding Lupton's claim of property as having furnished the paper.'[40]

The painter William Leighton Leitch claimed that Turner 'got his things so beautifully engraved by terrifying the men out of their wits ... [J. C.] Allen and Lupton have both told me what a fright they used to be in when Turner appeared.'[41] But some engravers, enthusiastic about Turner's work from the start, stuck with him through thick and thin. Heath declared that in spite of Turner's 'exactions and the difficulty of bringing him to any reasonable terms, he had greater satisfaction in dealing with him than any other artist ... Once he had pledged his word as to time and quality, he might be implicitly relied on.'[42] According to Thornbury, Turner returned a thousand pounds Heath had advanced to him for work on an issue of *The Keepsake*, one of the then popular annuals that were issued around Christmas, suggesting that Heath pay him when his business picked up. Hugh Munro of Novar, amateur artist and friend of Turner, told of an occasion when, far from harassing an engraver, an engraver harassed Turner. Munro had visited Turner on a Sunday afternoon, 'when the painter was often at leisure', and one of the Cookes had burst in on them. The engraver, 'with all the air of a bullying tailor come to look after a poor sweating journeyman, wanted to know if those drawings of his were never to be finished. When the door closed behind him, the big salt tears came into Turner's eyes, and he murmured something about "no holiday ever for me".[43]

If he was not in a defensive or tetchy mood, Turner could be amicable and even show heartfelt sympathy with his engravers. Charles Turner got used to him arriving with his large umbrella, saying he couldn't stop more than a couple of minutes, but then keep the engraver talking at his sitting-room door for an hour or so. George Jones recalled that when Charles Turner's son was dangerously ill the artist 'went constantly to enquire after the health of the youth and of the family; he never left his name, and this solicitude was not known to the parents until, after the son's death, the servant then reported that a little short gentleman of odd manners had called every evening to know the state of the sufferer'.[44] And after the death of Charles Turner's wife in 1836, Turner wrote to the engraver, his always tortuous syntax further distorted by emotion:

> My Dear Charley
> I must break through the rules of propriety to ask you, 'to throw myself upon your kindness' – only – think what I suffered at Sir Thomas Lawrence's [death] and for so long an illness – that I beg of you to yield to my fears against my will – which believe me Charley is with you in your present misery and do not think a particle of respectful regret is wanting to your amiable [?] loss or in any want of attention to your request by a note yet now arrived from Mr Chittendon [the undertaker] 43 Greek St. Soho – that I do again beg of you to let me feel at home all that true concern!! Without any alloy of apprehension.[45]

Puzzling this out must have momentarily taken Charles Turner's mind off his loss.

Edward Goodall also had experience of Turner's good side. His son told Richard Redgrave that his father on one occasion 'unwittingly signed an agreement, in that careless manner too common with artists, to engrave a series of book illustrations from designs by Turner, and ... when he came to study this agreement he found it contained clauses which laid upon him very serious terms, such in fact as he had never contemplated. He became much alarmed, and on seeing Turner he told him of his fears, and said,

"You alone can help me out of my difficulties."'

'How is that?' asked Turner.

'Why,' replied Goodall, 'by refusing to complete or to make the illustrations I have engaged to engrave.'

'That is a bad alternative,' said Turner; 'it would cost me £500 worth of work.'

'True,' said Goodall, 'but I have been engraving your works for the last twenty-five years with increasing pleasure, and would you bind me to work on these to my great loss, and in misery as I work? You will fill up your time in an equally profitable manner, and you will relieve me from engagements which, on signing the agreement with the publisher, I certainly never understood.'

Turner agreed to do as he asked, but he added, 'I have done that which I never did before, and would not do for another.'[46]

If Turner pushed his engravers hard, it was not only because he was acquisitive of cash but because he was anxious for fame. In his 1822 negotiations with Hurst and Robinson, he invoked an illustrious predecessor, Richard Wilson, four of whose pictures had been engraved by William Woolett for Boydell. Hurst and Robinson, successors to Boydell's business, were proposing to print 500 impressions from a plate after a Turner painting. Turner, envisaging himself in a titanic struggle with past masters, wrote: 'Whether we can in the present day contend with such powerful antagonists as Wilson and Woollett would be at least tried by size, security against risk, and some remuneration for the time of painting.'[47] Although no agreement apparently was reached on that scheme, Hurst and Robinson commissioned John Pye to engrave Turner's *Temple of Jupiter Restored* (RA 1816). In 1825 they also made an attempt to buy Turner's *Dido building Carthage* (RA 1815). Alaric Watts went along with Robinson to Turner's house to negotiate the purchase, Turner having named 750 guineas as his price a few days before. But when Robinson got to Queen Anne Street he found the ante had been raised to 1000 guineas. 'Mr Robinson objected that he could not consent to so large an increase of price, without obtaining the sanction of his partners; but before they had time to make up their minds, Mr Turner sent them a verbal message, declining to dispose of it at all; he considered it, he said, his *chef d'oeuvre*.'[48] As such, it seems he did not want it to be sullied by any form of translation into print. Later, again according to Watts, Turner refused an offer of 5000 guineas from a group of benefactors who wanted to present the *Dido* to the National Gallery. He had by then an even greater interest in the afterlife of his work than he did in a sale and had decided to leave the painting to the nation on his death.

Despite the difficulties of working with Turner, those in print-selling and publishing recognized how much of a draw his name could be. Robert Cadell, the Edinburgh publisher, met Turner on a visit to London in June 1831 and found him 'a little dissenting clergyman-like person – no more appearances of art about him than a ganger'. But this look of a workers' foreman did not prevent Cadell from talking Sir Walter Scott into the idea of having Turner illustrate an edition of Scott's *Poetical Works*. Cadell believed that the engravings of Turner drawings would help sales: 'With his pencil I shall insure the subscription of 8,000 – without, not 3,000.'[49]

As time passed, and the clamour of the love of money faded for him, too, his Queen Anne Street house filled up with engravings; at the end there were dusty heaps and boxes-full, numbering over 5000 prints and proofs. He was right to be nervous of a chimney fire. He went on making new prints from old *Liber* plates – and unlike his engravers, who used solid black capital letters (such as M, EP, H, for his categories of landscape) to denote prints, and outline capital letters to denote proofs, Turner ignored such niceties. The actual categories may never have had much point, other than to frame the tumble of notions fermenting in his imagination; the engraver and writer John Landseer was one who doubted their value. Part of his plan had been to put one print from five of the six categories in each set, to give subscribers a range of subjects, and he tried to keep to this. On the blue wrappers of the sets, he had filled in the part numbers and added his initials, using black ink for prints and red for proofs; and sometimes he actually put the word 'Proof' in the upper-left corner. But subscribers who paid for a set of proofs rarely got a full set; they were lucky to get one proof per set; the rest were in fact prints.

To some, Turner's reuse of the old *Liber* plates seemed to involve a similar lack of honesty. He repaired worn spots and reissued prints that, as mentioned, he called proofs, charging the higher – by a few shillings – prices that proofs fetched. 'Sham proofs', Thornbury called them, while noting that this sharp practice required Turner to make alterations 'with consummate art'. He hid 'the wear and tear of the copper, the faintness, the blur, or the pallor of the plate's old age', and 'devised new beauties'.[50] In *Liber* plate number 50, *Mer de Glace*, he turned a smooth glacier into sharp waves of ice; in *Aesacus and Hesperie*, number 66, he changed the way the sun came through the trees in the glade where Hesperie sits, and altered her head.

Perhaps Turner really thought that in these alterations, repairs and reissues he was making things anew, and that this deserved a proper recompense. As usual, his logic was rather twisted. His genius for sleight of hand sometimes got the better of his adhesion to the conventional rules of the trade. But if one looks at the experimental engravings which didn't get into the *Liber* or which were produced after he terminated its publication and which he didn't bother to sell, one can see how far-reaching a genius it was. Some of these engravings – like *Stonehenge at Daybreak*, *Moonlight at Sea*, *Sandbank with Gypsies*, and the twelve of the so-called 'Little *Liber*' series in the 1820s – were more than translations of drawings into print. They showed not only 'signs of struggle and dissatisfaction',[51] but an intensity and accomplishment which resulted from the power of creation at full stretch.

After the 'Little *Liber*', whose twelve mezzotints he engraved himself, he lost some of this interest in personally putting his own work in engraved form; but he went on being an illustrator for the projects of others – for poetry by Milton, Byron, Scott, Campbell and Rogers; for topographical works and annuals. For these Turner did his original drawings in watercolour – colour replacing the monochrome of the *Liber* drawings – and the engravers had their work cut out to convey the deep complexities of his colour; they also had to cope with Turner's continued requests for changes to the plate. Ruskin thought some of the plates done for *The Harbours of England* (earlier issued as *The Ports of England*) were 'among the very finest that had been executed from his marine subjects'[52] – though he added of the plate called *Portsmouth* that the artist had spoiled the original power of the work by retouching the proofs, forcing the engraver – Thomas Lupton once more – to tame what had been 'a gaunt, dark, angry wave'.[53] In the 'Little *Liber*', with numerous stormclouds and thickened skies, the dark angry waves were untameable.

9: Deep Puzzles

At 8 p.m. on Monday, 7 January 1811, a short, beaky-nosed thirty-six-year-old man wearing a frock coat and a bulky white cravat – which made him look neckless – appeared on the rostrum of the lofty-ceilinged Great Room of Somerset House. Alongside him were a stack of drawings and a bas-relief for use as examples in the address he was about to give, while high on the walls hung huge copies of Raphael's tapestry cartoons – permanent visual aids. The chairman for the evening was the elderly Academy President, Benjamin West, his Pennsylvanian origin still detectable in his voice despite nearly half a century in London. West had just introduced the speaker to the assembled Academicians, Associates, students and curious members of the public who had managed to get tickets for this long-awaited occasion: the first lecture by the Professor of Perspective. The spirits of the audience, precariously balanced between anticipation and dread, took an immediate dip as the speaker began with a hesitating, garbled apology: 'Alacrity should have appeared earlier in my behalf, but when the continual occurrences and ardours of the profession crowd around, it too often happens that they prevent the completion of greater concerns, and therefore I must waive, saying I am ready that I have pleased myself, or can please.'[1] The eyes of various listeners met, or tried to avoid meeting. 'Alacrity' should have had him standing there at least three years before.

Next day, the *Sun* newspaper's John Taylor gave the Professor's inaugural discourse a kindly thumbs-up: it 'was written throughout in a nervous and elegant style, and was delivered with unaffected modesty'.[2] Taylor, an unofficial press spokesman for the Academy, was right about 'nervous'. Turner read much too fast from his script. He mumbled. His voice was deep – a higher tone would have been more distinct. His accent was still closer to a costermonger's than a courtier's; in the best Cockney manner, he dropped 'h's where they were needed and added them where they were not. Those members of the audience who were hard of hearing, like the engraver John Landseer and the Academy librarian Thomas Stothard, could understand little or nothing of what he was saying, but neither could many of those who were not at all deaf.

Things did not improve in his second lecture the following week. Charles Rossi, on hand with some other RA Council members, told Farington that Turner 'got through with much hesitation and difficulty'. Farington himself was in the chair for lecture number four and seemed relieved that it 'lasted [only] 35 minutes'.[3] Later professorial performances showed no success in mastering such basic public-speaking skills as voice projection. Richard Redgrave, who was in the audience on several occasions, wrote: 'Half of each lecture was addressed to the attendant behind him, who was constantly busied, under his muttered directions, in selecting from a huge portfolio drawings and diagrams to illustrate his teaching.' Moreover, Turner's 'naturally enigmatical and ambiguous style of delivery [rendered the lectures] almost unintelligible'.[4]

The job had become his in November 1807, when twenty-seven members of the RA Assembly voted for him and one – in perceptive, solitary minority – voted against. A 'Teacher of Perspective', Edward Edwards, had instructed in the Academy Schools from 1788 until his death in 1806, but the Council then decided to elevate the post. Even so, Turner was the only candidate. Presumably the post would give him an opportunity to sort out all his ruminating about art, and it might help focus his reading. It would give him status as one of the nabobs of the Academy. In late 1809 he was clearly upset that he had not been accorded his title in a recently published edition of John Opie's *Lectures on Painting*, to which he had subscribed, and asked that, if there were another printing, 'all the *Proffessors* may be alike in the Subscribers list'.[5] He had proudly begun signing pictures with 'P.P.R.A.' after his name and listed the title, Professor of Perspective, along with his current address, in the Academy exhibition catalogues. But, as he also said in that first lecture in 1811, he had another motive: he wanted 'to be useful to an institution to which I owe everything'.[6] For a while he may have hoped to emulate Sir Joshua, whose *Discourses* – at least as learned texts – had acquired immediate renown.

'Alacrity' in getting to the rostrum was not habitual with Academy professors. George Dance, Professor of Architecture until 1806, had *never* lectured. When John Soane was elected to the post that year, Turner congratulated him in a letter and quoted from Charles Churchill's poem *The Ghost*:

> Professors (justice so decreed)
> Unpaid must constant lectures read;
> On earth it often doth befall
> They're paid and never read at all.[7]

Soane waited three years to give his first lecture, and then, for the occasion, got Turner to help arrange and exhibit the illustrations. Both men were asked by the anxious Council in December 1808 when they were going to start lecturing. They were also, in Turner's words, 'tickled up' by a letter-writer to the *Examiner*, who in January 1809 told the editor of that paper to thrash all the Academy professors – 'these sons of indolence' – for failing to deliver a single lecture the last season.[8] Later that year, as if to indicate that he was brooding about the arena for his as yet unspoken thoughts on perspective, Turner made suggestions for better lighting in the Great Room; Soane proposed improvements to the seating. When Soane did get started, he was soon in trouble: his colleagues did not approve of his critical remarks in a lecture of 1810 on his fellow Academician and architect Robert Smirke. (Soane didn't like Smirke's designs for Covent Garden Theatre.) Soane's lectures were suspended, and in 1813 his post was declared vacant, though the Council later backed down and let him resume. Soane, according to one listener in 1813, was the worst reader he had ever heard, but this comment may have been from someone who hadn't attended the lectures of the Professor of Perspective.

Justice decreed that a few professors were worth hearing. John Flaxman, elected Professor of Sculpture in 1810, was good at getting his message across, though his lectures, often reprinted, were considered 'heavy reading'.[9] The biggest draw at this period was Anthony Carlisle, surgeon at Westminster Hospital and a medical adviser to the Prince Regent, elected Professor of Anatomy in 1808, and knighted in 1821. At one lecture Carlisle's illustrative matter lay on two dinner plates, which were passed around an enthralled and somewhat unnerved audience, one plate bearing a human heart, the other a man's brains. Hazlitt, who was there, almost fainted. Carlisle often brought on people to pose, sometimes nude. Prize-fighters, Chinese jugglers and Life Guards were among his models. He generally appeared at the rostrum in full court dress, including a cocked hat, and he packed the audiences in. At one of his Life Guards lectures, when the soldiery wielded their swords to demonstrate the flexing of certain muscles, a squad of Bow Street constabulary had to be summoned as would-be members of the audience stormed Somerset House, some attempting to get in through the Great Room skylights.

Turner went to Carlisle's lectures and alluded to them in his own; he believed that perspective and anatomy complemented one another and shared a foundation in geometry. Like the other Academy professors, Turner was paid £10 for each performance; sixty pounds a year if he fulfilled his duties. Being Turner, he must have found the money an enticement. Being Turner, he sometimes didn't bother to collect his fees.

There were no Life Guards in Turner's tardily started lectures, but much to do and not to do with his nominal subject. There were chunks of poetry. Claude – as we have seen – and Sir Joshua were much in evidence. He gave the impression of having done a lot of research in the three years since his election, and a great number of authors were brought to bear, including Pliny the Younger, Franciscus Junius, Guidobaldo del Monte, Bernard Lamy and Gérard de Lairesse. He owned a copy of *Leçons de perspective positive*, by the sixteenth-century French architect Jacques du Cerceau and had been reading the works of the English portrait painter and art theorist Jonathan Richardson. As a former architectural draughtsman, Turner had a sound working knowledge of perspective. Thomas Malton senior, the father of one of his own teachers, had written an influential treatise on the subject, whose definitions Turner borrowed; some of Euclid's axioms he acquired from the same source. He quoted – and argued with – Charles du Fresnoy's *The Art of Painting* and paraded many of the ideas of John Joshua Kirby, the maternal grandfather of his friend the Reverend Henry Trimmer and popularizer of the perspective theories of the mathematician Dr Brook Taylor. The standard notion of perspective was that of a view as it would be if traced on the glass of a window, by someone looking from one spot with one eye closed. But Turner shared with Kirby a distrust of 'standard perspective'. On the one hand, as an artist he appreciated the value of structure: 'The knowledge of rules begins to create a confidence unattainable by any other method, which ... enables the mind not only to act for itself but to duly appreciate with truth and force what nature's laws declare.'[10] On the other hand, it was the truth of nature that one was really after.

Standard perspective was dominated by straight lines; Turner – the landscapist – believed art had to take into account the curvature of things, and he tried to incorporate this: 'The meandering river and the rushing cataract appear sometimes not wholly unapplicable [to perspective], but they evade such weak control – turning aside like graceful elegance, defying all rules.'[11] In his own work, he often bent the rules, sometimes having two viewpoints or 'points of sight' in a picture. However, George Leslie said that 'His pictures always *looked right*, even if the perspective in them was theoretically faulty.'[12]

In his lectures, Turner also examined various architectural elements – spires and towers, columns and colonnades. He discussed his own experiences with reflections and refraction. (He found such matters moving: sketching Bolton Abbey in Wharfedale, he writes on his drawing of the river water, 'Beautiful Refln.')[13] Many aspects of the science of optics and human perception interested him, for example the author Richard Payne Knight's account of a boy, born blind, who gained sight with the removal of cataracts but needed 'the gradual employment of impressions received through the other senses ... to learn to distinguish near from far'.[14] One knew what one saw as a result of all sorts of associations. His own chief aim, the painting of landscape, was acknowledged. He stressed its value once again; even in history paintings by the old masters the landscape backgrounds were 'part of the subject and equal in power'.[15]

In spite of the fascinating material in them, the lectures – six in all that winter season of 1811 – were generally agreed to be a let-down. Part of the problem lay in the scripts Turner read from, and lost his way in. Long insertions were crowded in the margins. Capital letters and numbers provided keys, indicating where he should use an insert or show an illustration, but he frequently got confused about where he was and what came next. He amended his original drafts, had fair copies made, and then further revised them. One neat version of his fourth lecture was written out by a copyist named W. Rolls, but soon it was added to and corrected.

The cultured script of Henry Howard, the Secretary of the RA from 1811, has been detected in a draft of another lecture, possibly giving the anxious Professor a helping hand, while the script of others seems feminine: did he get Sarah Danby to be his unpaid clerk? As Turner's additions mounted and his sentences rambled on, he put in marks with red watercolour to show where he should pause for breath and let his listeners catch up.

If they could. In fact, the associations of facts and ideas that Turner made were not easily grasped by his audience. His leaps of mind were *his* and were put in his own way. Sometimes the trouble was that he had not understood the text he was quoting from. His scholarship was often suspect: he would give credit to primary sources, which he hadn't read, rather than to the secondary sources in which he had found his material. He paraphrased Sir Joshua Reynolds, who in turn had adapted the ideas of Roger de Piles – when it might have been simpler to quote de Piles or Sir Joshua. In his reading, Turner now and then fixed his attention on the footnotes rather than on the main text, and, when planted in his lectures, the resulting information seemed not only pedantic but astray. He borrowed pompous terms and wrapped them in involved, even inscrutable sentences. Yet his curiosity could not be faulted. John Constable – an RA exhibitor since 1802 but still waiting to be an Associate – sat next to Turner at an Academy dinner in 1813 and reported: 'I was a good deal entertained with Turner … He has a wonderful range of mind.'[16] The trouble was that, when not encountered on a one-to-one basis, that mind manifested a magpie-like voracity. The material Turner gathered made for a cluttered compost heap. He had no training in how to sift and distribute it. It might eventually help to generate pictures, but it did little for rational discussion of artistic strategies and principles.

He had some supporters in his audiences. His father proudly came to several lectures. John Linnell, an RA student from 1806 to 1810, was in the Great Room on 27 January 1812 and drew the senior Turner, lips compressed, his mind no doubt wandering on to things other than perspective. Thomas Stothard, too deaf to hear Turner's words, faithfully attended his lectures. When a fellow Academician enquired why, Stothard explained, 'Sir, there is much to see at Turner's lectures – much that I delight in seeing, though I cannot hear him.'[17] The illustrations, sometimes displayed at the relevant moment, were often 'a rare treat' and 'truly beautiful', thought Richard Redgrave, 'speaking intelligibly enough to the eye, if his language did not to the ear. As illustrations of aerial perspective and the perspective of colour, many of his rarest drawings were … placed before the students in all the glory of their first unfaded freshness.'[18] Turner eventually compiled a collection of some 200 pictures: drawings to demonstrate types of shadow; coloured drawings of water-filled glass balls, some of which showed reflections from one another; watercolours of steeples and spires, of façades and screens and pediments; and even more elaborate watercolours of prison and mausoleum interiors. Most of the lecture illustrations were his own work, but he also showed pictures by Dürer and Raphael.

Diagrams and sketches for the purpose of his lectures crowd his sketchbooks of this period. The 'Perspective' sketchbook of 1809[19] has not only perspective diagrams – and the ever-present sketches of boats and barges – but a line from Virgil's *Eclogues*, which he may have jotted down for quoting at a lecture, or else simply to bear in mind as a crutch: *Non omnia possumus omnes* ('Not everyone can do everything'). But with some of his listeners the titbits of poetry he proffered were popular – even via the fog-creating medium of Turner's voice. He quoted Milton. He recited lines from *The Pleasures of the Imagination* by Mark Akenside. And he worked bits of Akenside into lines purportedly his own:

> Reclaims their fleeting footsteps from the waste
> Of Dark Oblivion, thus collecting all
> The various forms of being to present
> Before the curious aim of mimic Art.[20]

*

Over the twenty-seven years that he held the post, Turner's six lectures were repeated in varying forms. He went on rewriting them, as though striving for purity. He tried to fit them together more effectively with his illustrations. But 'mutability' – an Akenside term – was strong, and his heart wasn't always in it. At one lecture in early 1812, according to Soane, who was there, 'No drawings … very thin audience … the word Perspective scarcely mentioned.'[21] He gave the lectures in 1811, 1812, 1814, 1816, 1818, 1819, 1821, 1824, 1825, 1827 and 1828. In 1827 there were four rather than the customary six lectures, and he was paid only £40. Why didn't he give the lectures every year? Did he feel they needed greater improvement but had no time for it? Was he overwhelmed by sour moods of feeling unwanted or of not wanting to face the public? The midwinter lecture season may sometimes have given him the genuine alibi of poor health. On 28 December 1812 the minutes of the RA Council recorded that a letter had been read 'from the Professor of Perspective asking to be allowed to postpone his course of lectures until the season of January, 1814, on account of indisposition'. The postponement, of a full year, was allowed; nothing was said about the nature of the indisposition.[22] And when the year passed, Turner again had difficulties. Although his first lecture of 1814 was set to be delivered on 3 January, it did not take place. An advertisement, placed by the errant Professor, appeared in the *Morning Chronicle* two days later:

> LEFT in a Hackney Coach which stopped at Somerset House on Monday night (January 3rd) a PORTFOLIO containing demonstrations, etc., etc., etc., of the Science of Perspective. Whoever will bring the same to Mr Turner's, Queen Anne Street, W., corner of Harley Street, shall receive TWO POUNDS reward, if brought before Thursday, afterwards only ONE POUND will be given for them at the end of the week. No greater reward will be offered nor will this be advertised again.

The absent-minded Professor apparently meant to deal as firmly with greedy finders of his property as he did with hungry engravers.

But another advertisement – placed by someone who hadn't read Turner's – appeared in the *Morning Chronicle* on 6 January:

> PORTFOLIO FOUND. A gentleman having engaged a Hackney Coach on Monday evening last, from the Strand, opposite Somerset House, found therein a large portfolio (much damaged) containing some drawings of the Science of Perspective. They will be restored to the owner on his giving a proper description of the contents, and defraying the expense of this advertisement. Should no application be made within fourteen days they will be disposed of as waste paper, being considered of little value. Apply at Messrs Boore and Bannister's Don Cossack Warehouse, New Street, Covent Garden.

No doubt fuming, 'Waste paper! Of little value!', Turner recovered his precious portfolio with its fifteen or so diagrams and drawings. The course of lectures was rearranged to begin on 10 January but apparently did not. A correspondent in the March issue of the *New Monthly Magazine* reported 'something laughable' at Somerset House: although the Perspective lectures had been meant to start at 8 p.m. on the 10th, the audience had to wait until 9 p.m. before the Professor appeared. Then – 'oh, sad disaster!' – it was to hear him announce that he had lost his lecture. 'In this dilemma Mr Turner held a conference with the Keeper, Mr Fuseli [who was in the chair that evening], and the latter informed the company that his friend had left the lecture in the hackney coach which conveyed him.'

Fuseli, apologizing for his own lack of preparation, stepped into the gap and gave a talk on painting in his usual spirited manner, and thus spared the audience the usual 'grunts and groans' of dismay and disbelief he himself was known for uttering during Turner's lectures. Lightning shouldn't strike the same spot thrice, but in 1818 (when Turner delivered two of his lectures within a week) those attending his fourth lecture were told by the Professor as he mounted the rostrum that he had again left his lecture in the hackney coach bringing him here. This time no other speaker stood in for him. The audience – including John Sell Cotman – sportingly applauded the Professor and went home. Some must have speculated on what lay behind his neglectful behaviour: was he losing his mind?

In 1817 a new form of lighting came to Somerset House. The Great Room's immense bronze chandelier, a gift of the Prince Regent, was fitted with gas jets. But it did not illuminate Turner on the rostrum. Late in 1816 he dickered with the Council, asking that he be allowed to postpone the 1817 series for a year; he seemed to expect immediate permission. The Council indeed replied with speed, but wanted to know why. The Council members felt there should be good reason for suspending 'any part of the regular routine of education in the Royal Academy'. Turner answered that he had pressing engagements. The Council reluctantly went along with this but reproved their Professor, telling him his reasons had not been 'satisfactorily stated', and reminding him 'that it is incumbent on the Professors of the Academy not to enter into any engagements which may preclude them from fulfilling permanent duties'.[23]

In 1827, his fifth lecture was called off. Advertisements in the *Morning Post* and *Morning Chronicle* explained the cause of cancellation as a 'domestic affliction'. *The Times* on 13 February ascribed it to 'the death of a near relation' – though who this may have been is unclear. His nearest and dearest at this time was his father, and though he may have been ill he did not die in 1827.

John Taylor's flattering remarks on Turner's inaugural lecture in 1811 were welcomed in a note from the artist. Taylor's review of the second lecture (which discussed theories that reflected light 'makes a regular parabolic kind of curve' and Malton's dissent from this) said that it 'manifested deep investigation'. But Taylor added, 'From the nature of the subject, it was not probable that the lecture would afford much gratification to those who were unacquainted with the subject.'[24] To this, Turner replied with some fifty lines of doggerel which made flattering play with a satire Taylor had written on Walter Scott; clearly he had read Taylor's *The Caledonian Comet*. Taylor was more than kind in his comments on the next four lectures, calling the Professor 'a rare example of scientific knowledge and practical excellence'.[25] Other commentators, in ensuing years, were less generous. A writer in the *New Monthly Magazine* in 1816 made fun of Turner's speaking and his accuracy:

> Excellent as are Mr Turner's lectures, in other respects there is an embarrassment in his manner approaching almost to unintelligibility, and a vulgarity of pronunciation astonishing in an artist of his rank and respectability. Mathematics he perpetually calls 'mithematics', spheroids 'spearides', and 'haiving', 'towaards', and such like examples of vitiated cacophony ... He told the students that a building not a century old was erected by Inigo Jones; talked of 'elliptical circles'; called the semi-elliptical windows of the lecture room semi-circular, and so forth.[26]

His last Perspective lectures were delivered in 1828. He had lost interest; he had other things to do; everyone had heard what he had to say on the subject. Yet he remained Professor of Perspective for the next ten years. A Parliamentary Committee in 1836 looked at art instruction and, turning to the Royal Academy – evidently aware of a lack of lectures – asked if the 'school of perspective' was being properly conducted. The Academy President, then Sir Martin Archer Shee, replied that Turner had not been pressed to deliver his lectures, in part because some Academicians thought that lecturing was ill calculated to convey the science of perspective. But they had also forborne to do so 'from a delicacy which cannot perhaps be perfectly justified, but which arises from the respect they feel for one of the greatest artists of the age in which we live'.[27] At the end of 1837, when he was sixty-two, Turner told the Council that he proposed to resign the professorship, doubtless to the relief of most members, though his decision was received 'with great regret'.[28] This sentiment was shared by the General Assembly on 10 February 1838, when his resignation was formally announced. The Academy went back to having a 'Teacher of Perspective'.

In later years Turner took no great pride in what he had achieved as professor. According to David Roberts, his health was proposed at one occasion by an Irishman who had attended the lectures, and Turner replied in a jocular way that 'he was glad this honourable gentleman had profited so much by his lectures as thoroughly to understand perspective, for it was more than he did'.[29] But his diffidence had always been a crucial part of his public speaking. At the end of one lecture he had admitted, 'After all I have been saying to you, gentlemen – the theories I have explained and the rules I have laid down – you will find no better teachers than your own eyes, if used aright to see things as they are.'[30]

For all of his omissions and failures as a professor, Turner went on being a thoroughly useful teacher in the Academy Schools. Former students talked of the practical help he gave them. He was repeatedly appointed a Visitor in the Life School because of his instructional ability, although his advice might be conveyed with gesture and example rather than in carefully phrased language; to some, his assistance seemed to be given almost telepathically. Richard Redgrave observed:

> A few indistinct words, a wave of the hand, a poke in the side, pointing at the same time to some part of the student's drawing, but saying nothing more than a 'Humph!' or 'What's that for?' Yet the fault hinted at, the thing to be altered was there, if you could but find it out; and if, after a deep puzzle, you did succeed in comprehending his meaning, he would congratulate you when he came round again, and would give you some further hint; if not, he would leave you with another disdainful growl, or perhaps seizing your porte-crayon, or with his broad thumb, make you at once sensible of your fault …The schools were usually better attended during his visitorships than during those of most other members.[31]

*

Turner's inarticulate nature was complicated by his infatuation with words. His art was an insufficient means of release for what boiled inside him. As if it were beyond his control, he poured forth floods of verse. The art world first became fully aware of his serious intentions concerning this other art form in 1812. The Academy had revived in 1798 an earlier dispensation allowing painters to quote lines of poetry after the listings of their picture titles in the exhibition catalogue – and Turner had taken immediate advantage of this to append snatches of Milton and Thomson. In the ensuing years some of his pictures were so honoured with verse, sometimes credited, sometimes not. The thirty-two lines that accompanied his picture *Thomson's Aeolian Harp*, a Thames-at-Richmond classical landscape exhibited at his gallery in 1809, were unattributed but were written by him – the result of several sketchbook drafts.

Three years later at the Academy exhibition he showed along with three other landscapes a large (nearly five feet by eight feet) oil entitled *Snow Storm: Hannibal and his Army crossing the Alps*. In this a dark swirl of cloud sweeps over the cowering figures of Hannibal's force; puny men humbled by nature, as Napoleon's Grande Armée had been by the Russian winter just past. And in the 1812 Academy catalogue readers were treated to a passage from an 'M.S.P.' – in other words, a manuscript poem, all his own work – called 'Fallacies of Hope':

> Craft, treachery, and fraud – Salassian force,
> Hung on the fainting rear! then Plunder seiz'd
> The victor and the captive, – Saguntum's spoil,
> Alike became their prey; still the chief advanc'd,
> Look'd on the sun with hope; – low, broad, and wan;
> While the fierce archer of the downward year
> Stains Italy's blanch'd barrier with storms.
> In vain each pass, ensanguin'd deep with dead,
> Or rocky fragments, wide destruction roll'd.
> Still on Campania's fertile plains – he thought,
> But the loud breeze sob'd, 'Capua's joys beware!'[32]

It is a good example of Turner's poetic talent or mimetic skills: echoes and borrowing from other poets, in this case Thomson, and words lacking necessary antecedents or without evident meaning, used as they are – in this instance, 'alike' in line 4, 'in vain' in line 8, 'Or' in line 9, and 'he thought' in line 10. It is verse that tries too hard and falls embarrassingly, tumbling from an intended sublime to a ridiculous end – bathos the effect. But this didn't bother him.

Many young people are 'poets' in their late teens and early twenties and wisely give up thereafter. Turner, having dabbled in verses before, took to poetry in a big way in his thirties. Verses gushed from him indoors and out; he scribbled it mostly by pencil in his nearly illegible handwriting, in sketchbooks and guidebooks, sometimes using pen and ink for a passage that he particularly fancied, and copying out a favoured draft in a special notebook – strange in having no sketches in it – that he reserved for his verse. Staying at inns on his own, riding in coaches with other passengers, sitting on hillsides: nowhere was he immune to the fever. Even on a riverbank, with a fishing rod in one hand, he wrote poems with the other – if only, along with the fish, he had thrown some of the words back in! His determination was admirable, even when the results were dire (one thinks of Yeats's definition of rhetoric, 'Will doing the work of the imagination'.) He slapped the words down like blobs of paint, but they refused to meld, to contrast, to work together. He knew something else was needed and numbered the syllables in his 'Ode to Discord' as he apparently tried to improve the metre. He did several drafts of this, and of other favourites of the moment, such as 'On Thomson's Tomb' and the 'Dear Molly' love poem of 1809:

> By thy bosom so throbbing with truth
> Its short heavings to me, speaks reproof
> By the half blushing mark on each hill
> O Molly dear Molly be still.[33]

The 400 lines of mostly rhymed travel notes written in 1811 on blank pages interleaved amid the gazetteer information of his copy of *The British Itinerary* (a tiny pocket companion for travellers) represent the most determined adhesion to banality and cliché, indeed to doggerel:

> Then the famed Icknield Street appears a line
> Roman the work and Roman the design.

Needy labourers, peaceful streams, sportive sea nymphs, dreadful monsters and parching heat also make an appearance in this work.

The patriotic artist–poet, heading westward on his own itinerary, considers in passing the merits of lobster fishermen, captive British prisoners, bold British seamen and the gallant Nelson.

The word 'fallacious' cropped up first in his 'Tabley Hall' sketchbook in 1808, as he prepared for his lectures; it never goes away. 'Hope' is also ever-present: 'What hope appeared ever to deny' in *The British Itinerary*; 'in hope of less inclement skies' in a sketchbook[34] – but the skies usually let loose a downpour and hope is not only denied but blasted and blighted. Much of this was convention, but it was one that Turner adopted willingly. He didn't have that much to complain about as far as fame and fortune were concerned; but clearly his emotional life – his life as a son or lover – had let him down. Hope was not to be trusted; neither were women. If you look on the sun with hope, look out! The fierce archer will smite you.

Turner's 'M.S. Fallacies of Hope' was never a consecutive, finished work, though he may have wanted to give that impression. Rather it was a scrapbag of bits and pieces he added to over the years, and made use of in the Academy catalogues at exhibition time. 'Hope's delusive smile'. 'Hope's harbinger, ephemeral …'[35] His colleagues staunchly tried to throttle their expressions of amusement. Now and then they couldn't take it any longer and tried to stifle the poem. In 1834 the Council seems to have allowed his verses – meant to have been appended to his picture *The Golden Bough* – to vanish from the catalogue, leaving only the reference to the 'M.S. Fallacies of Hope'. When he refused to sell his picture of *Carthage* and declared he would be buried in it, a friend told him, 'But they will dig you up, and get your picture for nothing. If you really want to rest in one of your works, be buried in the *Fallacies of Hope*. No one will dig you up then.'[36]

Thackeray, in 1845 in *Fraser's Magazine*, made gentle fun of what he called 'that sybilline book of mystic rhymes', and said of its author, 'I don't like to contemplate him too much, lest I should actually begin to believe in his poetry as well as his paintings, and fancy the "Fallacies of Hope" to be one of the finest poems in the world.'[37] In 1840, *Punch* took note of the lines from 'Fallacies' that Turner had attached to his RA exhibit *Slavers throwing overboard the Dead and Dying – Typhon coming on*:

Aloft all hands, strike the top-masts and belay;
Yon angry setting sun and fierce-edged clouds
Declare the typhon's coming.
Before it sweep your decks, throw overboard
The dead and dying – ne'er heed their chains.
Hope, Hope, fallacious Hope!
Where is thy market now?

Punch retaliated with:

A Typhoon bursting in a Simoon over the Whirlpool of Maelstrom,
Norway: with a ship on fire, an eclipse, and the effect of a lunar
    rainbow.
O Art, how vast thy mighty wonders are
To those who roam upon the extraordinary deep!
Maelstrom, thy hand is here.

From an unpublished Poem[38]

A lesser man would have taken heed of the public mood and kept his poetic output to himself. But Turner was not to be silenced by criticism or parody. His last four exhibits at the Academy in 1850 were accompanied by four poetic fragments, one of which – to go with *Aeneas relating his Story to Dido* – was:

Fallacious Hope beneath the moon's pale crescent shone
Dido listened to Troy being lost and won.

*

It was part of the stock in trade of the eighteenth-century artist to consider painting and poetry hand in hand; they were sister arts; they were twins. 'Painting is poetry,' wrote Jonathan Richardson, Britain's first art theorist; elsewhere he opined, 'Methinks it would not be amiss if a painter, before he made the least drawing of his intended picture, would take the pains to write the story' – though he does not mention writing it in verse.[39] Sir Joshua, in his third Discourse, said that an art of animating figures with 'intellectual grandeur ... can only be acquired by him that enlarges the sphere of his understanding by a variety of knowledge, and warms his imagination with the best productions of ancient and modem poetry'.[40] In his 'Perspective' sketchbook of 1809, in several dense and foggy pages of prose writing, Turner tried to grapple with the differences between what painters and poets do. Near the end of one draft of his first lecture, he got it a bit clearer; he wrote (reworking Akenside): 'Thus Painting and Poetry, flowing from the same fount mutually by vision, constantly comparing Poetic allusions by natural forms in one and applying forms found in nature to the other, meandering into streams by application, which reciprocally improved, reflect, and heighten each others beauties like ... mirrors.'[41]

Some of his fellow artists were demonstrating that reading and quoting poetry were not enough; one should write it too. Fuseli wrote verse, in German. William Blake was a double threat, though Turner may not have known his poetry. He certainly knew the written work of Martin Archer Shee, portrait painter and Academician, whose *Rhymes on Art* appeared in two parts in 1805 and 1809 (the second under the title *Elements of Art*), satirizing philistinism, attacking critics of modern art and promoting the idea of a great public collection of painting. Shee's *Rhymes* attracted much attention.

Of course, there was more to Turner's poetic impulse than a desire simply to compete with Shee or even a desire for public attention, of which he was already getting a fair quota. His ambition – his intention to be a self-made poet as well as a painter – can be seen in the fact that he copied out in the 'Frittlewell' sketchbook (1809) a passage from Lord Holland's 1806 *Life* of the Spanish poet and playwright Lope Félix de Vega Carpio (1562–1635): 'The chief object of Poetry is to delineate strongly the characters and passions of Mankind, to paint the appearances of Nature and to describe their effects to our imagination. To accomplish these ends the versification must be smooth, the language pure and impressive, the images just, natural and appropriate.' If Turner thought that, by writing this down, he would accomplish such an end, it was a vain hope. But he ploughed on regardless. Writing poetry was a way of working off some of his misanthropy and pessimism, of burning up his moody displeasure with the world:

> Misanthrope stalks the soul in silent shade
> On the bold promontory thrown at length he lies
> And sea mews shrieking are her obsequies.[42]

Although bad poetry was the first and obvious product, the act of writing helped his painting. He came to sketchbook, watercolour paper and canvas with a less burdened spirit.

In one respect, Turner's verse seems to indicate his desire to seem better educated than he was. But it also has another quality characteristic of the man: it respected the past. His literary heroes were of the eighteenth century. He admired the Augustan, pastoral style of Thomson and Akenside; he liked their classical allusions, allegorical personifications and vague, abstract concepts. He didn't seem to notice the new writers, his young contemporaries, such as Wordsworth, Coleridge, Shelley and Keats, though he took to Byron later on.

In his thousands of words of tin-eared verse, Turner rarely put together any that had the intensity and rhythm and surprise of a real poem. His 'Hastings' sketchbook[43] of 1809–11 contains a well-organized chunk of blank verse:

> World I have known thee long & now the hour
> When I must part from thee is near at hand
> I bore thee much goodwill & many a time
> In thy fair promises repos'd more trust
> Than wiser heads & colder hearts w'd risk
> Some tokens of a life, not wholely passed
> In Selfish strivings or ignoble sloth
> Haply there shall be found when I am gone
> What may dispose thy candour to discover
> Some merit in my zeal & let my words
> Out live the Maker who bequeaths them to thee
> For well I know where our possessions End
> Thy praise begins & few there be who weave
> Wreaths for the Poet brow, till he is laid
> Low in his narrow dwelling with the worm.

This hangs together too successfully to be Turner; whom is he echoing? (Herbert? Cowper?) The essential Turner, heard when not trying hard to be Thomson or Akenside, gives voice in 'Dear Molly', with its orgasmic climax:

> By the touch of lip or rove of my hand
> By the critical moment no Maid can withstand
> Then a bird in a bush is worth two in the hand
> O Molly dear Molly   I will

The muddle of much of Turner's poetry prompts questions about how his brain worked. How 'normal' was his thinking? His contrariness may have had physiological as well as psychological roots. He painted with his right hand, but was he naturally a left-hander who had been forced to use his right? It has been remarked that two of his Perspective illustrations that demonstrate a triangle fitted inside a circle have headings that reverse the situation: 'Circle (or circles) within a triangle'.[44] His friend George Jones said, 'Turner's thoughts were deeper than ordinary men can penetrate and much deeper than he could at any time describe', though he put a generous gloss on this by noting that 'the indistinctness of his thoughts, like the indistinctness of his pictures, always indicated either greatness or beauty'.[45] On numerous occasions in his company, people did not know what Turner was talking about. David Roberts said, 'The same mystery that pervades his works, seemed to pervade his conversation.'[46]

In many of the notes that he wrote in the margins of books – conversations as it were with himself or with the authors – the same mystery is present, though presumably *he* was privy to it. Sometimes his reading was thorough. As noted, he had subscribed to the *Lectures on Painting* of John Opie, which Opie as Professor of Painting had given at the Royal Academy. Turner wrote to the Plymouth artist Ambrose Johns that he was 'troubled with a fit of scribbling' as he read them, and the margins of the first third of the book are crammed with what he called his 'marks of gall'.[47] The marks were in fact unusually cogent. When Opie wrote that for artists, 'nothing is denied to persevering and well-directed industry', Turner says, 'It is right to hold out such a hope to light the weary artist on the way,' but suggests that perseverance and industry are not enough. And when Opie later hedges his first claims in this matter, Turner notes the qualification: 'the acknowledgement of an innate power that enforces, that inspires, and without which labour would be fruitless and a vain drudgery'. When Opie declares that students should not just study nature but attentively study 'the peculiar manner of each master', Turner responds with a *cri de coeur*, a bit rambling now, but clearly something he had to say, even for his own benefit:

> He that has that ruling enthusiasm which accompanies abilities cannot look superficially. Every glance is a glance for study: contemplating and defining qualities and causes, effects and incidents, and develops by practice the possibility of attaining what appears mysterious upon principle. Every look at nature is a refinement upon art. Each tree and blade of grass or flower is not to

him the individual tree grass or flower, but what [it] is in relation to the whole, its tone, its contrast and its use, and how far practicable: admiring Nature by the power and practicability of his Art, and judging of his Art by the perceptions drawn from Nature.[48]

His disparate character was drawn to hopes of synthesis and fusion. Just as, in the 1809 'Cockermouth' sketchbook,[49] he had quoted Tom Paine to the effect that the sublime and the ridiculous were 'so nearly related that it is difficult to class them separately', so he now feels that nature and art can be brought close, at least by the able artist who has 'that ruling enthusiasm'.

He was also thinking about the interrelations of painting and poetry, and when Opie mentions the 'contrariety of means' of the two arts, Turner adds, 'though drawn from the same source and both feeling the beauties of nature'. But not all his annotations to Opie are either as sensible or as sensitive as that passage where he declares that 'Every glance is a glance for study.' When Opie calls beauty 'a word to the full as indefinite, if not as complex, as the word nature', Turner pens in the margin, 'Beauty is compleatly a term of intimacy for no two agree when what is beautiful even in as to letch [lechery?] if possible even exceed the above end function in nature for what is pleasing to one optic is disgusting to others ...' And he proceeds into further obscurity and illegibility. But let us agree with him that beauty is in the optic of the beholder.

His swings between cogency and nonsense were as dramatic as those between generosity and niggardliness, furtiveness and ostentation. If he had been truly dyslexic,[50] he would have been so continuously – and his letters demonstrate similar bouts of indistinctness and precision. Frequent Jekyll and Hyde tussles went on in Turner's brain. Much of his art paid homage to the past; much of it increasingly did so in a revolutionary way. He loved his pictures, and let many moulder with damp and dust. His visions were one moment foggy, the next radiantly clear. He lacked 'higher' education but had a strong desire for learning. His mother's mental collapse may have caused reverberations in the son, and who knows what genetic predisposition he had to similar psychic storms? He was driven into himself at an early age and spent the rest of his life making fitful attempts to unroll, to say 'Here I am, this is me.' His inchoate strivings to express complicated thoughts were in contrast to his father's simple shrewd loquacity. Turner wanted to be up to date with contemporary thought on aesthetics – with the sublime, the picturesque and the interleavings of painting and poetry – and often waded in way out of his depth.

And yet he should be given credit for trying. His reading, not always incisive, was wide. As well as the classical and eighteenth-century poets, he dipped into works of ancient history and made notes about Roman emperors and Assyrian kings. In the 'Tabley no.3' sketchbook he jots down details about the first Christian church supposedly built in Glastonbury in AD 44. Giraldus Cambrensis, the Welsh ecclesiastical chronicler, interests him on the subject of the building of Pembroke Castle. In the 'Finance' sketchbook[51] he transcribes part of a Hindu account of the Creation of the World from Alexander Dow's *History of Hindoostan* (1768), along with notes on essays he had been reading by Sir William Jones about Hindu chronology and Indian, Greek and Roman gods. (Some of this was fed into several *Liber* engravings.) He read the *Travels* (1805) of James Bruce, who reached the source of the Blue Nile in the early 1770s. He bought Thomas Hope's *On the Costume of the Ancients* (1809) and in his notes on Shee took issue with Hope's call for national patronage for historical painting, with art being seen as a vehicle for enhancing British commerce. Turner thought art should have higher goals. He read Hugh Blair's *Lectures on Rhetoric and Belles-Lettres* (1783), in which the 'Nature of Poetry' and 'Sublimity' were considered, and he copied out in his 'Derbyshire' sketchbook of 1807–9[52] a passage from Blair on writing style:

> Perspecuity in writing is not to be considered as merely a sort of negative virtue, or freedom from defect. It has higher merit. It is a degree of positive beauty. We are pleased with an author, we considered him as deserving praise, who frees us from all fatigue of searching for his meaning; who carries us through this subject without any disarrangement or confusion, where we see to the very bottom.

Poor Turner! He took this to heart, enough so to write it down, and it didn't do him much good. But he would have been a different person, and artist, if it had.

Turner was aware of his lack of perspecuity in writing. He often brooded about what he wanted to say in a letter or speech and drafted passages in a sketchbook. Before an Academy dinner in 1809, he evidently wanted to get his witticisms right, in referring to the *Examiner's* suggestion that Academy professors were 'sons of indolence', and worked up a reply. But his pride was nevertheless sometimes touched. In 1813 he wrote some caption material for the *Southern Coast* series, which W. B. Cooke sent to the journalist William Coombe for copy-editing. Coombe wrote to Cooke that it was 'the most extraordinary composition I have ever read. It is impossible for me to correct it, for in some parts I do not understand it.'[53] Turner, miffed, withdrew his contribution and Coombe wrote his own.

In his correspondence Turner frequently repeats words unnecessarily, misuses words, omits words. Drafting a letter to Sir John Leicester on the back of a drawing of donkeys on a hillside, he leaves many blanks in the text;[54] it is as if there were gaps in his thought processes. Often his punctuation is idiosyncratic, his spelling haphazard. But suddenly the clouds part, the wind drops, the sun shines and he spells difficult words correctly. In 1811 John Britton sent him a copy of the letter-press he was planning to use with the Pye and Heath engraving of Turner's *Pope's Villa* he was publishing, and Turner's reply to Britton – despite a few mis-spellings and distensions of sense – is in the main well thought out and well expressed:

> Sir
> I rather lament that the remark which you read to me when I called in Tavistock Place is suppressed for it espoused the part of Elevated Landscape against the aspersions of Map making criticism, but no doubt you are better acquainted with the nature of publication, and mine is a mistaken zeal. As to remarks you will find an alteration or two in pencil. *Two* groups of sheep, *Two* fishermen, occour too close – baskets to entrap eels is not technical – being called Eel pots – and making the willow tree the identical Pope's willow is rather strained – cannot you do it by allusion? And with deference: – 'Mellifluous lyre' seems to deny energy of thought – and let me ask one question, Why say the Poet and Prophet are not often united? – for if they are not they ought to be ...[55]

A letter of March 1812 to James Wyatt in Oxford about the plate Pye was making of his *View of Oxford from the Abingdon Road* makes similar cogent points about details in a proof. Wyatt had apparently been suggesting the introduction of a 'venerable Oak or Elm' and

Turner writes, 'Fancy to yourself how a large Tree would destroy the character! That *burst* of flat country with uninterrupted horizontal lines throughout the Picture as seen from the spot we took it from! The Hedgerow Oaks are all pollards, but can be enlarged if you wish ...[56]

One area where Turner's love of words consistently did not cause him to fall on his face was that of the titles he gave his pictures. Some of these – particularly the marines – have the poetry of exact observation and briny detail: *Entrance of the Meuse: Orange-Merchant on the Bar going to Pieces; Brill Church bearing S.E. by S., Marensluys E. by S.* (1819); *Life-boat and Manby Apparatus going off to a Stranded Vessel making Signal (Blue Lights) of Distress* (1831); *Van Tromp, going about to please his masters, ships a sea, getting a good wetting* (1844).

Hazlitt, referring to the slips of the pen and slovenliness of style in Northcote's *Fables*, said that he did not hold Northcote at all accountable, 'since an artist wrote with his left hand and painted with his right'.[57] Fortunately Turner's art depended on a creative power of altogether different strength and focus than that which brought forth his words. In his pictures, his 'optics' and brush-holding right hand played their part, and his reasoning or intellectual faculty had less to do. Making his paintings, as a famous admirer was to point out, Turner worked with 'inspired unconsciousness'.[58]

10: Crossing the Brook

Whatever his ambitions as a professor, Turner never looked like one. Nor was there, for this knockabout poet, any ivory-tower pallor. As we have seen, he had the appearance of someone with an out-of-doors job – a seaman or a coachman. He indeed made many of his British coach journeys as an outside passenger. Except in winter, when in his studio, he spent a good deal of the year in the open air. His complexion was a ruddy red from exposure to sun, wind and rain. Young G. D. Leslie, meeting him in later life, said, 'His large grey eyes were those of a man long accustomed to looking straight at the face of nature through fair and foul weather alike.'[1] To the journalist Cyrus Redding, who got to know Turner in 1811 or soon after, the artist (then aged thirty-six) was 'rather stout and bluff-looking' and 'somewhat resembled the master of a merchantman'.[2] His short stature and bandy legs enhanced the impression of one whose centre of gravity was – for a mariner – usefully low to the deck. The side-whiskers he allowed to grow at this time added to the effect.

In the summer of 1811, Turner set off on his first considerable tour for some years. Since his Scottish expedition of 1801, his only extended travels had been to France and Switzerland in 1802. In the following nine years he had been preoccupied with the Thames, and his country jaunts had for the most part taken the form of visits to friends like the Wellses, at Knockholt, or to places where he had been invited to paint a great house and the surrounding landscape. In 1807 such a trip was to one of the houses of the Earl of Essex, Cassiobury Park, near Watford, in Hertfordshire; in 1808 he visited Tabley Hall, Sir John Leicester's place in Cheshire; and in 1809 he travelled to Petworth House, in Sussex, and Cockermouth Castle, in Cumberland, both belonging to Lord Egremont. In 1811, he kept his gallery closed while he contemplated changes to it. He had a good show at the Academy, where the Prince of Wales – made Regent this year – had been among those who praised his *Mercury and Herse*. Now the Cooke brothers wanted many drawings from him for their proposed *Southern Coast*; it would require a 'professional tour' of nearly three months to the Dorset coast, to Devon and Cornwall, giving him a chance to see new ground and also to pause on his ancestral territory near Barnstaple. He did some preliminary reading. Then, taking sketchbooks, paint-box, clothes, books and fishing rod, and leaving his father and Hannah in charge at Hammersmith and Harley Street, he shook off the worries of Somerset House and the dust of the Strand.

On the way he did a lot of hill-climbing and beach-walking, for better views of castles such as Corfe and St Michael's Mount and the cliffs at Lulworth Cove. He sketched and scribbled – in his own fluent shorthand for one and his less legible longhand for the other. He imagined gallant tars and sportive sea nymphs. In Plymouth he drew the ships at anchor in the harbour off the Hoe and the hulks moored up the River Tamar; he was as interested in the whale-shapes of the moribund vessels as he was in those full-rigged, in fighting trim. These were the wooden walls that kept England safe from Boney.

He was to make follow-up trips in 1813 and 1814, but it was apparently on this first south-west expedition that he met Redding, then editor of a local paper. Redding, Cornish by birth, had grown up in the West Country; he was a knowledgeable companion and got on well with the crusty artist. He had reformist political views and shared with Turner an interest in shipwrecks. Turner was also befriended by a wealthy Quaker merchant named John Collier, afterwards the member of Parliament for Plymouth, who on Fridays and Saturdays held open house for a cosmopolitan crowd of ships' captains, import and export dealers and local worthies. With Collier and Redding, Turner went sailing on the St German's river and talked of his Devonshire origins. Redding had a privileged glimpse of the artist at work and remarked how little, 'to the unpractised eye', his first sketches showed of the after picture. Perhaps, thought Redding, he bore much away in memory which helped him decipher his sketches back in his studio.[3]

In 1813 Redding accompanied Turner on a coastal voyage to Burgh Island, in Bigbury Bay, about twelve miles east of Plymouth.

Other members of the party were Collier, an Anglo-Italian scene painter and panorama artist named James De Maria, and an army officer. The boat was of Dutch build, undecked, crewed by one sailor and its owner-master, Captain Nichols, 'a fine old weather-beaten seaman'. They had all been invited to a lobster feast at their destination. However, it was a nasty-looking morning, with a heavy swell and rising wind. 'The sea', wrote Redding, 'had that dirty puddled appearance which often precedes a hard gale.' Off Stoke Point, where the sea rolled in grand furrows from the Atlantic, the conditions became stormy, but the boat ran before the wind, mounting the ridges bravely. Turner seemed to be enjoying himself.

> He sat in the stern sheets intently watching the sea, and not at all affected by the motion. When we were on the crest of a wave he now and then said … 'That's fine! Fine!' Two of our number were ill. The soldier, in a delicate coat of scarlet, white, and gold, looked dismal enough, drenched with the spray, and so ill that at last he wanted to jump overboard. We were obliged to lay him on the rusty iron ballast in the bottom of the boat, and keep him down with a spar laid across him. De Maria was silent in his suffering. In this way we made Burgh Island. The difficulty was how to get through the surf, which looked unbroken. At last, we got round under the lee of the island and contrived to get on shore.'[4]

They were pretty wet when they landed. Nevertheless, while the lobsters were being boiled, Turner clambered up despite the wind towards the summit of the island. It seemed to Redding that he perched there writing rather than sketching. Then he joined the others for the picnic and 'did ample justice' to the lobsters. The journalist noted that the artist drank porter with his food but afterwards liberally took his share of the wine. Meanwhile the gale increased. Captain Nichols declared that he was going to sail back – his boat would defy any sea – but the landsmen in the party had had enough. They proposed to walk at low tide across the sands to the mainland and spend the night at Kingsbridge, three miles away. This they did, and Turner accompanied them. Redding wrote: 'We rose at seven the next morning in Kingsbridge and went before breakfast to Dodbrook, to see the house that had belonged to Dr Walcot [Dr John Wolcot, the writer 'Peter Pindar'], and where he was born. The artist made a sketch of it and of another house … We had now more than twenty miles to travel home. A vehicle was provided, but we walked much of the way, for Turner was a good pedestrian, capable of roughing it in any mode the occasion might demand.'

Trudging on, they met a local peer named Lord Boringdon who invited Redding, Turner and De Maria to spend the night at his house, Saltram. Its parkland provided views over a broad passage of the River Plym. At Saltram another guest was the singer Madame Catalani, who evidently found the weary travellers an appreciative audience, treating them to some of her favourite airs. The rooms of the great house were full of pictures, but Turner when being shown round was in one of his taciturn moods. The old masters – according to Redding – 'seemed to attract little of his attention, though they might have drawn more than I imagined, for it was not easy to judge from his manner what was passing in his mind'. As to the flimsy, picturesque landscapes of the Florence-born Francesco Zuccarelli (1702–88), a founder member of the RA, Turner refused to express an opinion; he would have felt it disloyal to criticize a fellow Academician. However, in the billiard room, in front of Stubbs's *Phaeton and the horses of the sun*, he let slip the one word 'Fine.' And later he warmed up a little. Redding wrote: 'Turner on retiring to rest had to pass my bedroom door, and I remarked to him that its walls were covered with paintings by Angelica Kauffmann – nymphs and men like nymphs, as effeminate as possible. I directed his attention to them, and he wished me "Good night in your seraglio."' In the morning, Turner and Redding walked in the park and Turner found a high spot again from which he sketched.[5]

On another day near Plymouth, Turner, De Maria and Redding were standing just after sunset beside the Tamar river. Turner had earlier remarked that, when the sun went down, the gunports of a seventy-four-gun ship lying in the shadows of a hill below Saltash would be indiscernible. De Maria now said, 'You were right, Mr Turner, the ports cannot be seen. The ship is one dark mass.'

'I told you so,' said Turner. 'Now as you can see it – all is one mass of shade.'

'Yes, I see that is the truth, and yet the ports are there.'

'We can take only what we see, no matter what is there. There are people in the ship – we don't see them through the planks.'

'True,' replied De Maria.[6]

But if De Maria had been more knowing, he would have pointed out to Turner that he sometimes set aside this empiricism for a different sort of artistic realism – as his 1823 *Trafalgar* was to demonstrate, with the people of the *Victory* being disposed to show various moments of the battle.

On another boating excursion, this time a long way up the Tamar river, with four in the party and Redding once more as guide, they were surprised by nightfall. Redding recalled:

> To go down the river in the night was impracticable, on account of the chance of getting on shore upon the mud banks. There was an inn hard by at which beds could not be obtained; and some course must be resolved upon. We might walk to Tavistock, three or four miles off but a vehicle which had come from Plymouth that day with two of our party could do no more than carry two to the town. Turner said he would rather stay until the morning on the spot where we were debating the subject. He did not mind sitting up – would anyone volunteer with him? The horse would come over fresh in the morning with those who might then leave: I volunteered. Our friends drove off, and the painter and myself soon adjourned to the miserable little inn. I proposed to 'plank it', in the sailors' phrase – that is, to go to sleep on the floor; but some part of it was damp, and the whole well sanded, so that it was not a practicable couch, however hard.

At this point, Turner said that, before anything else, he had to have some bread, cheese and porter.

> Very good bread and cheese were produced, and the home-brewed suited Turner, who expatiated upon his success with a degree of excitement which, with his usual dry short mode of expressing his feelings, could hardly be supposed. I pleased him further by inquiring whether bacon and eggs could be obtained; and getting an affirmative reply, we supped in clover, and sat until midnight in conversation. I found the artist could, when he pleased, make sound, pithy, though sometimes caustic remarks upon men and things with a fluency rarely heard from him. We talked much of the Academy, and he admitted that it was not all which it might be made in regard to art. The 'clock that ticked against the wall' sounded twelve; I proposed to go to sleep. Turner leaned his elbow upon the table, and putting his feet upon a second chair, took a position sufficiently easy, and fell asleep.

Redding laid himself at full length across some chairs, and followed Turner's example.

Before six in the morning we rose, and went down towards the bridge. The air was balmy; the strong light between the hills, the dark umbrage, and the flashing water presented a beautiful early scene. Turner sketched the bridge, but appeared, from changing his position several times, as if he had tried more than one sketch, or could not please himself as to the best point.[7]

Redding, as already noted, found Turner unniggardly, cheerfully paying his way at inns when often more than bread, cheese and porter were involved. The journalist was also a guest at the picnic party Turner gave at Mount Edgcumbe near Plymouth, as a return for all the hospitality he had received. He went with Turner on various inland excursions. 'It was during these rambles that I imbibed higher ideas, not only of the artist, but of the man, than I had previously held.' He was also pleased to have had a chance to appreciate Turner's mind: 'Concealed beneath his homely exterior, there was a first-rate intellect.'[8]

Others gave help to Turner during his Devon visits. The young Plymouth-born painter Charles Eastlake, who studied with Haydon but did not adopt any of that artist's anti-Academy feelings, took Turner to his aunt's cottage at Calstock, up the Tamar. The local artist Ambrose Johns was a member of the party and fitted out a portable painting-box for Turner, containing among other materials paper already prepared for oil sketches. Eastlake later recalled that Turner made his first sketches in pencil and in a stealthy fashion, and his companions didn't intrude. But he then relaxed. Perhaps feeling a Devonshire man among other Devonshire men, he let down his guard:

> When Turner halted at a scene and seemed inclined to sketch it, Johns produced the inviting box, and the great artist, finding everything ready to his hand, immediately began to work. As he sometimes wanted assistance in the use of the box, the presence of Johns was indispensable, and after a few days he made his oil sketches freely in our presence. Johns accompanied him always ... Turner seemed pleased when the rapidity with which those sketches were done was talked of; for, departing from his habitual reserve in the instance of his pencil sketches, he made no difficulty of showing them. On one occasion, when, on his return after a sketching ramble to a country residence belonging to my father near Plympton, the day's work was shown, he himself remarked that one of the sketches (and perhaps the best) was done in less than half an hour.[9]

According to a member of the Turner family, Turner called on his relations in Barnstaple during his West Country travels. He also visited his uncle Price Turner, who lived in Exeter. Uncle Price thought his son Thomas had artistic talent and was told by his brother, William Turner senior, to get the boy to make some drawings to show JMWT. Turner called at the Price Turners but apparently offered no encouragement to young Thomas, whose talents lay elsewhere. In fact, Turner back in London reverted to his customary reclusiveness where his Devon relatives were concerned. When Thomas Price Turner came to London in 1834 to sing in the chorus at a Handel commemoration concert, he called twice on his famous cousin before getting to see him. On the third occasion, the painter gave him a cool reception and didn't even ask him to sit down.

Turner's souvenirs of the West Country included the lovely ink-and-wash drawing of Berry Pomeroy, which he did for the *Liber* series – the castle misty in the distance to the right; a frail wooden bridge over a stream; a Turner-out-of-Claude tree almost centre stage, with more boskiness behind and to the sides. Although some of the oil sketches done with the aid of Johns's box were seen by the ladies at the Mount Edgcumbe picnic, they seem to have disappeared afterwards into his Queen Anne Street stockpile. It was of course the *Southern Coast* commission which had set him off, and the watercolours he did over a number of years for this – with London, not Devon, water – were important products of these tours. In these, by his now experienced alchemy, the shorthand of his sketches was transformed with brilliant colour and energetic line into full-fledged visions. They were done on white paper, about ten inches by seven and a half – slightly smaller than his usual practice. The play of light, the movement of clouds and trees, the placing of people at work in fields or on beaches, were for the most part called up in his studio from the store of images and data in his well-stocked imagination. He brought the Devon weather on to his paper. His brush evoked dewy grass, damp air, hazy sun.

His watercolour methods involved both a production line and a kind of baptism by immersion. At one point the painter W. L. Leitch observed Turner working on several watercolours at once. First, he pencilled in light outlines. Then 'he stretched the paper on boards and, after plunging them into water, he dropped the colours onto the paper while it was wet, making marblings and gradations throughout the work. His completing process was marvellously rapid, for he indicated his masses and incidents, took out half-lights, scraped out highlights and dragged, hatched, and stippled until the design was finished. This swiftness ... enabled Turner to preserve the purity and luminosity of his work, and to paint at a prodigiously rapid rate.'[10] The boards to which the paper was attached had handles at the back to facilitate plunging them into water-filled pails. Turner washed in the principal hues on one and while it dried began similar washes of groundwork on the next, so the first would be ready for finishing by the time the fourth drawing had been 'laid-in'. In some watercolours that came from his West Country tours, he painted for himself alone, not for engravers: *Hulks on the Tamar: Twilight*,[11] for example, where detail and 'finish' have been forgotten and hues and shapes are everything.

Turner liked conceiving things in groups as well as doing things in bunches and series. The boy who had become an only child seemed to want to surround himself with families of pictures, almost protective phalanxes. One view of something was rarely enough; he needed different aspects of it, at different times of day, in different moods or atmospheres – such as calm and storm. One river or bridge was insufficient; he had to have many bridges, many rivers. And then he didn't like them separated, as pictures most often are when sold to individual buyers. Once again: 'What is the use of them except together?' Engravings were therefore valuable to him since they made a sequential record; and Turner's willingness to tackle large groups of related subjects made him the perfect illustrator for print publishers like the Cookes and Charles Heath, who kept on dreaming up new series of 'Views' for what they hoped – somewhat recklessly – was an ever-expanding market. After the *Southern Coast*, for instance, the Cookes decided to do a series called *The Rivers of Devon*. Turner did them four watercolours, from which engravings were made, but the project did not reach publication stage.

The greatest single memento of his Devon days was *Crossing the Brook* – a title he purloined from Henry Thomson RA, whose 1803 picture of that name had been bought by Sir John Leicester. In his studio, sketchbooks lay on a table near at hand, ready to consult. On his easel, a tall stretched canvas, roughly six feet high and five and a half feet wide, faced him in the mornings as he stood there at work: brush to paint to canvas, brush to paint to canvas, over and over again. Much of the scene – the low valley receding gently out of the foreground hills; the winding river spanned by a high, multi-arched bridge; the soft Tamar countryside with its thick mantle of woods; the horizon at mid-height with a hint of distant sea – is assembled from his recent tours. In the immediate foreground is the brook, which here widens to a shallow pool. A young woman leans against a large block of stone, which may be part of an old bridge. Her feet are ankle-deep in the water and she looks back at an unkempt dog which is loyally following her across the brook, bearing her hat in its mouth. Five or six yards away on the right a girl sits at the water's edge, pensively watching – behind her, a little lane leads into a dark tunnel formed by overhanging trees. On the left, out of deep shadows rises one of Turner's trees – hard to imagine he had never been to Italy – which was now almost his trademark, though still an act of homage to Claude. It is tall, slim and sinuously trunked, lacking boughs until it branches out in a broad-brimmed mass at the top. A less emphatic sister tree stands behind it. The two trees reach into the luminous sky above the two young women.

When they got to see the picture, Turner's Devon companions claimed knowledge of many of the elements. Redding wrote: 'Meeting him in London one morning, he told me that if I would look in at his gallery I should recognize a scene I well knew, the features of which he had brought back from the west.' Part of the foreground, thought Redding, was taken from a spot near New Bridge on the Tamar.[12] He felt proud to have been part of its making. Eastlake looking at the same scene said with his own sense of attachment, 'The bridge is Calstock Bridge.'[13] Others believed they saw a resemblance to Turner's daughter Evelina in the girl sitting on the edge of the brook. Evelina was thirteen in the winter of 1814–15, when the picture was probably painted. (Georgiana was then only three years old.) The young woman paddling on the left is too old to have been modelled by Evelina. As for the dog, was it Eastlake's aunt's?

Although *Crossing the Brook* received high praise from most viewers when shown at the Academy in 1815, Sir George Beaumont, as we shall see, did not like it. And though it was more spacious than any Claude, *Crossing the Brook* did not sell. In 1818 Turner quoted prices for it and *Frosty Morning* to the Norfolk banker and antiquarian Dawson Turner: 550 guineas for *Crossing the Brook*, 350 guineas for *Frosty Morning*. But the other Turner didn't take the bait. (He did, however, buy a set of the *Liber*.) Much later, in 1845, the artist thanked Dawson Turner for a generous comment on *Crossing the Brook* and added, 'Thank Heaven which in its kindness has enabled me to wade through the Brook' – of life, one supposes. He concluded, referring to the painting, 'it I hope may continue to be mine – it is one of my children'.[14] Kept in his gallery, it was despite his possessiveness in fact looked after by him like one of his children – with lofty indifference.

Soon there were other commissions, other parts of Britain, and much water that wasn't always nicely confined in brooks and rivers. He was in the north of England in the torrentially wet summer of 1816, sketching subjects for a *History of Richmondshire*, staying with his friends the Fawkeses, and travelling hundreds of miles in mud and rain; but this will be looked at in detail in Chapter 12. In the following summer of 1817 he had already been across the Channel, to Waterloo and up the Rhine, when he journeyed north again, staying with the Fawkeses near Leeds and calling at Raby Castle, the Earl of Darlington's seat, to do some sketches for a commissioned oil painting. He went to Durham for another local history for which he had been asked to make illustrations. There was more travelling 'deep strewed paths and roads of mud to splash in and be splashed'.[15] His touring equipment generally included an umbrella. Samuel Rogers, the poet-banker, recalled an occasion when Turner left his umbrella behind at a dinner in town. 'He was very anxious about it as it was the one he used when out sketching. Mr [Charles] Babbage returned it, who had taken it in mistake for his own. It was a very shabby one, and in the handle (like a bayonet) there was a dagger quite two feet long.'[16]

Scotland saw him in late October 1818. He went on assignment: to make sketches for thirteen drawings for the *Provincial Antiquities of Scotland*, for which the author Walter Scott was providing the text. Turner stayed in Edinburgh and its vicinity for several weeks, hard at work, and didn't go out of his way to sweet-talk the local arts folk. Jane Schetky, whose brothers were both painters, reported in a letter, 'Turner breakfasted with us, and was very gracious; he saw Alick's pictures and mine, and condescended to praise my copies of Havell. We are all, however, provoked at the coldness of his manner.

We intended to have a joyous evening on his arrival, but finding him such a *stick*, we did not think the pleasure of showing him to our friends would be adequate to the trouble and expense.'[17] Turner evidently didn't want to be lionized by the Scots. According to Miss Schetky, he further displeased the Edinburgh portrait painter William Nicolson, who prepared a feast for Turner and invited 'ten fine fellows to make merry with him'. Turner didn't show up.[18]

In August 1822 he was again in Edinburgh. On this occasion he had a busy social life. He met the architect Charles Cockerell, dined with Henry Raeburn the portrait painter, and went to banquets and church services. One has the impression that this time he *did* want to be noticed, and in particular by George iv, king since 1820. A royal ceremonial progress was being made in Scotland, and Turner planned twenty pictures for engraving. William Collins RA was on the quay at Leith when the royal yacht, the *Royal George*, sailed in and Collins was surprised to find Turner there too. Like the King, Turner had made the trip by sea, since another commission he was gathering material for was the Cooke venture dealing with English rivers and ports, and he took the opportunity to reconnoitre the east coast of England by way of the boat from London to Leith.

Although nothing directly came from the ceremonial-visit drawings, Turner's time was not wasted. Some sketches provided the groundwork for title-page vignettes he did for Scott's *Provincial Antiquities*. Two oil paintings, never finished, depicted the King at the Lord Provost's dinner and a service in St Giles's Cathedral. Instead of helping create a published record of the King's Scottish progress, he took up a royal commission in 1823 that Sir Thomas Lawrence helped him acquire: to supply St James's Palace with one of several paintings celebrating the success in battle of the House of Hanover. Turner was to do another *Trafalgar* for the King's Levée Room. As usual, he got stuck into the research. He borrowed drawings of ships which had fought in the battle from John Christian Schetky, now the King's Marine Painter in Ordinary and handily placed at the Naval Academy in Portsmouth. (Schetky had accompanied the King on his Scottish progress and presumably met Turner then.) Schetky now offered him sketches of the *Temeraire* but Turner needed a specific view of the *Victory*, 'three-quarter bow on starboard side'.[19] He looked up his sketches for the painting he had done of the battle in 1806. He revisited the Medway and sketched details of warship hulls, spars and rigging.[20]

He had been down to Portsmouth in June 1814 when the then Prince Regent had attended a naval review in Spithead, that splendid protected anchorage for Britain's wooden walls. The Emperor of Russia and the King of Prussia, Britain's allies in the last stage of the Napoleonic struggle, were guests to view the fleet and attend a 'collation' in the great cabin of the *Impregnable*. Turner, afloat in a small boat, was on hand, enjoying himself as a reporter, listing the names of the ships and their captains, and making light, rapid sketches of the vessels.[21] The results seem meagre. But then many of his sketches were the merest jottings: the bare bones of a possible picture; a few quick lines to prompt in the studio his recall of a scene, which he could generally conjure up in as much colourful complication as he wanted. Yet sometimes fairly simple sketches were more than rudimentary in effect, for example a landscape in one of his 'Devon Rivers' sketchbooks[22] where a few pencil lines of varying weight and emphasis suffice to suggest wonderful recession. And sometimes he felt the need to use his time on the spot to make detailed, even elaborate, pencil or pen drawings, like that of Christchurch Abbey in Hampshire,[23] or precise studies of plants, weeds and flowers,[24] done for his satisfaction at the moment.

Some of his southern country excursions in the decade from 1810 in Kent and Sussex were for oil-painting commissions, and in several sketchbooks he made panoramic views of Rosehill Park, the home of the member of Parliament and Jamaica landowner John 'Mad Jack' Fuller; the oils followed the drawings closely, conveying the soft folds of the Sussex downland. Where the landscape offered him the slightest opening, he showed glimpses of the sea. Except in Yorkshire, he gives the impression of following every brook and river to the coast, the *seaside*, to sketch the new Martello towers and old castles, to draw the fishing boats that were moored in harbours or pulled up on beaches. He was constantly attracted to Hastings, Deal, Ramsgate and Margate – particularly the last. It was as if he knew it had not only been part of his childhood but had a further role to play in his life. He was going to continue to visit it and sketch there until he found out what that role was.

In the lists he made in his sketchbooks of what to take on his tours, one item often figures among the painting kit and clothes:

'Fishing Rod'. Wherever Turner first baited a hook and dropped it into the water – on the Thames foreshore below the Strand, upriver at Brentford while living with his uncle and aunt Marshall, or off the beach at Margate – the pastime caught him; he was an angler for life. One reason he wanted to live beside the Thames was so that he could go fishing. One of the attractions of country-house commissions was that natural lakes or architect-designed ponds were an essential part of the scenery, nicely enhancing the landscape but also usefully stocked with tench, pike and carp. When he visited Tabley Hall in the summer of 1808, another visitor, Henry Thomson RA, told Callcott (who told Farington) that Turner's 'time was occupied in *fishing* rather than painting'.[25] Most likely, Turner, up at dawn, had done his sketching and drawing and then gone fishing by the time Thomson got up and noticed.

His friends generally admired his perseverance at the sport. He fished in all weathers. George Jones went fishing with him at Petworth and on a visit to Sir J. Wyattville at Windsor Castle on the Thames. Jones said, 'His success as an angler was great, although with the worst tackle in the world. Every fish he caught he showed to me, and appealed to me to decide whether the size justified him to keep it for the table, or to return it to the river. His hesitation was often almost touching, and he always gave the prisoner at the bar the benefit of the doubt.'[26] The Trimmers went fishing with him – the eldest son recalled as a boy accompanying him one day when he went fly-fishing from the banks of the Thames: 'He insisted on my taking the fish, which he strung on some grass through the gills, and seemed to take more pleasure in giving me the fish than in taking them ... He threw the fly in first-rate style.'[27]

His tackle was not always poor; a favourite rod in his later years could be assembled out of ten sections, with a brass reel and hefty line. Clearly Turner's ambition was to catch fish, not to break records by using lightweight line. However, according to Thomas Rose of Cowley Hall, Uxbridge, Turner on one visit brought along an umbrella that didn't contain a bayonet but became 'by some contrivance' a fishing rod. Rose saw him with this 'sitting patiently for hours by the side of a piece of water belonging to the property ... perhaps without even a single nibble'. But when he got a bite, he 'appeared as much pleased as a boy from school'.[28]

As a boy in the early 1830s, Robert Leslie was at Petworth with his father when, walking in the park, they saw a solitary man pacing to and fro, watching over his lines strung out beyond the water-lilies that grew near the bank.

> 'There', said my father, 'is Mr. Turner, the great sea painter.' He was smoking a cigar, and on the grass, near him, lay a fine pike. As we came up, another fish had just taken one of the baits, but, by some mischance, this line got foul of a stump or tree root in the water, and Turner was excited and very fussy in his efforts to clear it, knotting together bits of twine, with a large stone at the end, which he threw over the line several times with no effect. 'He did not care,' he said, 'so much about losing the fish as his tackle.' My father hacked off a long slender branch of a tree and tried to poke the line clear. This also failed, and Turner told him that nothing but a boat would enable him to get his line.

Charles Leslie, the day before, had seen Chantrey trolling for jack, rowed about by a man in a boat. Thinking it hard that Turner should lose his fish and a valuable line, Leslie and Robert went across the park to a keeper's cottage, where the key of the boathouse was kept.

> When we returned, and while waiting for the boat, Turner became quite chatty, rigging me a little ship, cut out of a chip, sticking masts into it, and making her sails from a leaf or two torn from a small sketch-book, in which I recollect seeing a memorandum in colour that he had made of the sky and sunset. The ship was hardly ready for sea before the man and boat came lumbering up to the bank, and Turner was busy directing and helping him to recover the line, and, if possible, the fish. This, however, escaped in the confusion. When the line was got in, my father gave the man a couple of shillings for bringing the boat; while Turner, remarking that it was no use fishing any more after the water had been so much disturbed, reeled up his other lines, and slipping a finger through the pike's gills, walked off with us toward Petworth House.

Young Robert walked behind, admiring the great fish, and noticing as Turner carried it

> how the tail dragged on the grass, while his own coat-tails were but little further from the ground; also that a roll of sketches, which I picked up, fell from a pocket in one of these coat-tails, and Turner, after letting my father have a peep at them, tied the bundle up tightly with a bit of the sacred line. I think he had taken some twine off this bundle of sketches when making his stone rocket

apparatus, and that this led to the roll working out of his pocket. My father knew little about fishing or fishing-tackle, and asked Turner, as a matter of curiosity, what the line he had nearly lost was worth. Turner answered that it was an expensive one, worth quite half a crown.

Turner's fish was served for dinner that evening; and, though I was not there to hear it, my father told me how old Lord Egremont joked Chantrey much about his having trolled the whole of the day without even a single run, while Turner had only come down by coach that afternoon, gone out for an hour, and brought in this big fish ... I have often thought that Turner went out to catch that pike because he knew that Chantrey had been unsuccessful that day before.[29]

While he fished alone, his mind free-wheeled over many subjects, but it was not so relaxed that useful ideas didn't swim through it. Lines of verse came to him and were sometimes written down. It was while looking at the River Dee, for instance, when at Tabley Hall, that he had noted the effect of ripples on reflections. He acquired a good deal of angling lore: he knew that while fishing you should sit facing the sun, so that your body didn't cast a shadow out over the water and alert the fish. He owned a copy of *The Compleat Angler* and sometimes took it with him on his travels. Isaak Walton's book, first published in 1653, conveyed the obsessive quality of angling and the dreaminess that an angler is subject to. It gave all sorts of handy tips – about, among other things, the making of fishponds, which he seems to have taken note of when digging one at his new house at Twickenham, on which he started work in 1812. The book told the reader how to make and then colour – for camouflage purposes – a fishing line, using a pint of strong ale, half a pound of soot, some walnut-leaf juice and a little alum, the sort of recipe that Turner was fond of. It also described times and places for catching particular fish, surveyed types of hooks and bait, and suggested ways of cooking one's catch. It is a book of homespun wisdom and reflection, interspersed with poetry, and Turner no doubt approved of it on that score too.

Like John Donne, whose love poem 'The Baite' makes good use of fishy metaphor, Turner enjoyed figures of speech derived from angling. He evidently had rod as well as pencil and sketchbook in hand in 1809 when making drawings for his Perspective lectures and jotted down the words:

Below the Summer Hours they pass
The water gliding clear as glass
The finny race escapes my line
No float or slender thread entwine.[30]

Other doleful lines from this time include a lament from a 'hapless' fisherman driven by rain under a tree 'in doubtful shelter', while 'the anxious angle trembles in his hands'. This is in a long screed that ends with a true *cri de coeur*: 'Written at Purley on the Thame rainy morning no fishing.'[31]

Particularly when corresponding with his good friend (and fellow fisherman) James Holworthy, after Holworthy moved to Hathersage in Derbyshire in 1822, Turner's language was coloured by their common interest. In the freezing January of 1826, and in the wake of a financial collapse in the City of London which had helped precipitate the failure of his printsellers Hurst and Robinson, Turner wrote to Holworthy; he compared Holworthy's position in the country with his in town, where the Thames

> is impeded below bridge; St James' and Serpentine both frozen in spight of every attempt to keep them open by folly and rashness; so the advantage is by the side of the trout stream in more ways than one. Look at the crash in the commercial world of mercantile speculation, and the check which must folow, but the trouts will be found in the pool and the gudgeon in the shallow, but every-one seems to have had a nibble, and experience so bought will last longer than a day or its day ...[32]

And at the end of the same year, in a letter to Holworthy, Turner alluded to wild talk that he, Turner, had been blown up in the explosion of a powder magazine that autumn near Ostend, where he had planned to stop, and notes that the rumour does not seem to have reached Holworthy in his quiet valley at Hathersage: therefore 'the lake babbled not or the wind murmured not, nor the little fishes leaped for joy that their tormentor was not ...'[33]

Even though addicted to angling, Turner was not the sort of fisherman who when doing it excluded all else. As noted, sketching and verse-writing went well with fishing. He could put down his rod, as at Petworth, to make the model boat for young Robert Leslie. He could even talk: again at Petworth, he was sitting by the pond one day fishing with J. E. Carew, the sculptor who did restoration for Lord Egremont, when Carew broke the companionable silence to say, interrogatively, 'Turner – they tell me you're very rich.'

With a chuckle, Turner replied, 'Am I?'

'Yes – everybody says so.'

'Ah. Well, I'd give it all up to be twenty-five years of age again.'

'What? Do you like it so well as all that?' Carew asked ironically.

'Yes, I do.'[34]

Fish and fishing got into his work. There were the fishermen off the Needles, by moonlight; flounder-fishing at Battersea; fishing off the Blythe Sand; Dutch fisherfolk cleaning and displaying their catch; fishing boats off Hastings; eel hooks and smelt catching and crab pots ... He was interested in those who made their living out of fish. Personal, amateur fishing too: a rod that looks to be waiting for its owner to show up lies in the foreground of his painting *The Fountain of Indolence* (RA 1834). One of the *Liber* subjects was *The Young Anglers*; the boys in this are shown fishing in the pond of Marylebone Fields, a short walk from Queen Anne Street – Turner no doubt was reminded of himself at that age, happily hoping to hook a chub with improvised tackle. He sketched anglers whenever he saw them, with fellow-feeling, a nice example being those who reappear in *Trout Fishing in the Dee*, a mountainous–pastoral painting that resulted from his Tabley Hall stay and was exhibited in 1809. The look of fish – the iridescence and translucence; the shine and wetness of scales; the aggrieved appearance of eye and mouth – was captured in a study of four fish, a sort of still-life, he did in pencil and watercolour, maybe at Farnley in the early 1820s.[35]

Turner's 'piscatory propensities'[36] were a source of humour for his friends and patrons. Elhanan Bicknell, whose art collecting was funded by his whale-oil business, bought a painting, the *Ehrenbreitstein*, from Turner in the early 1840s but had trouble taking delivery because John Pye was engraving a plate from it. Bicknell wrote to Pye in June 1845:

> My getting the painting *appears* as distant now as it was in March 1844. I thought I had only to send to Queen Ann St. to have it – but the grim master of the Castle Giant Grimbo shakes his head and says he & you must first agree that all is done to the plate that is

necessary, & the picture will be wanted to refer to. Now as I know he goes out a good deal fishing at this season – & then leaves town for some months tour in the Autumn, I hope you will do what is required while he is in town. He is at home today and tomorrow, for he is to dine with me tomorrow – he said he should then get off after fish.

Pray fasten your strongest hook into him before he fairly takes water again or he may get so far and so deep that even a harpoon will not reach him ...[37]

Turner, writing to Bicknell in January 1845, fell into the same cosy mode, on one occasion telling him to call at Queen Anne Street at his earliest convenience, 'for I have a whale or two on canvas'.[38]

Turner painted fish, wrote fish, thought fish and dreamt fish. Some of his dream fish were the sort he would have loved to catch; some, as he grew old, were monsters, spawned by nightmares. A misshapen fish, seen head on, appears to have popped up out of the sea, at the water's edge, as the artist stood looking out from Margate or Deal beach. One painting he entitled *Sunrise with Sea Monsters* (c. 1845). The fish that devour the human food in *Slavers throwing overboard the Dead and Dying* (RA 1840), beneath a lurid tropical sky, are not so much sharks as chub and goldfish grown to fiendish size, avenging representatives of all the fish he had sought and caught. He would have read in Izaak Walton 'of the monsters, or fish, call them what you will', to be found in various rivers and seas, and of the strange marine creatures collected by John Tradescant and Elias Ashmole in the seventeenth century and to be seen in London in their private museum of natural curiosities. Like Walton, Turner seems to have felt 'that the waters are Nature's store-house, in which she locks up her wonders'.[39]

A waterbound place in southern England to which he returned in the 1820s was the Isle of Wight. He had been a little-known young artist when he sketched there in 1795, visiting the western end of the island, and storing impressions for what would be his first oil exhibited at the RA, *Fishermen at Sea*, the following year. In 1827 he went back as a famous painter at the invitation of the most celebrated architect of the time, John Nash. The island was a place for admiring the picturesque rather than the sublime, but Turner by his second visit was less in thrall to such concepts. However,

Nash, aged seventy-five, had built his own picturesque creation, East Cowes Castle, in which his castle-loving guest must have had a happy time. It was a hilltop mansion-cum-folly, with towers and battlements, overlooking the waters of Cowes Roads and the Solent. Nash was brilliant and unorthodox – the sort of man who took to Turner, possibly because Turner responded to him. Nash since just before the turn of the century had been a member of the Prince of Wales's set. By 1827, with royal backing, he had changed the face of central London: laid out Regent's Park (named after his good friend and patron) and its surrounding terraces of grand houses; converted Buckingham House into a palace; developed St James's Park; and was now preparing to reshape the top of Whitehall and the old Royal Mews into Trafalgar Square.

Turner went on to the Nash castle after a short visit to Petworth, and was treated as a valued guest. Nash set aside a room for him to paint in. Boats and the water were on hand. Cowes Regatta, started by the Royal Yacht Squadron the year before, took place while he was there, and he went afloat to sketch the big white-sailed cutters and ketches fretting like racehorses around the starting line. (On several days he listed the names of yachts and their owners, perhaps prodded by his reportorial instinct, perhaps foreseeing a possibility that the wealthy yachtsmen might buy ensuing pictures.) He had a productive time. He filled three sketchbooks, did a large number of ink-and-chalk drawings on blue paper and painted several oils. In the pencil sketches a few lines suffice to suggest the slant and tilt of masts and sails, as the boats heel to the wind and hobby-horse over the Solent chop. For his sugar-paper drawings he stalked the grounds by day and night, sketching the battlements and bastions in the August sunlight and the statuary set in and around ornamental basins under a new moon.

That he was enjoying himself was shown by the fact that he made a gift of a pencil drawing of the Medina river, showing ships at anchor and a lady sitting in the stern of a skiff; he gave this to Miss Harriet Petrie, then a guest at the castle, and embellished the present with his initials: JMWT. He got on so well that he stayed from late July to early September, longer than he had meant to. On three occasions he wrote to his father, who was looking after things in Queen Anne Street, asking him to send more clothes – 'Light Trouzers' and 'White Waistcoats' – and painting materials – a 'canvass', six feet by four, to be sent rolled up, without a stretching frame; 'some scarlet lake and dark lake and burnt Umber', from James Newman's shop in Soho Square; and, as an afterthought, '1 ounce of Mastic', all to be sent by the Southampton or Portsmouth coach.[40]

Two of the paintings he did for Nash of Cowes Regatta were on view at the RA in 1828; one of the chalk drawings was worked up into another subject with nautical overtones (and a long title), *Dido directing the equipment of the Fleet, or The Morning of the Carthaginian Empire*. It was intended for a collector called John Broadhurst, but it remained unsold, in the artist's gallery. Turner's Carthaginian fantasies overlapped with those of being at the helm of a racing yacht. While at Nash's castle, he painted on two lengths of the canvas his father had sent down nine vibrant oil sketches of yachts competing out in the Solent. Figures from a sketch at the castle also came in handy for a painting he called *Boccaccio relating the Tale of the Birdcage*, a Watteauesque scene that puzzled Boccaccio readers, the *Decameron* having no birdcage tale in it. His real power was shown in a slightly later painting, never exhibited in his lifetime, called *The Music Party*. This apparently shows a small evening party in the castle's Octagon Room, with long red drapes hanging in a window embrasure, and a piano being played by a lady in an off-the-shoulder black dress; Mrs Nash was a skilful pianist.

He also made time on the Isle of Wight to catch up with an old friend and former pupil, Julia Bennet. Now married to Sir James Willoughby Gordon, who owned a house at Niton, near the southern tip of the island, she and her sister had inherited a manor house called Northcourt, near the island village of Shorwell. The previous year he had shown at the Academy a painting titled *View from the Terrace of a Villa at Niton, Isle of Wight, from Sketches by a Lady*; so it may be that Julia Gordon, by getting him to work up her sketches, had reinterested him in the island. The fact that he did for her something that he would not have done for most hostesses suggests that an affection persisted for his pupil. Moreover, in one of the sketchbooks he used on the island is found a draft of a note: 'Give my love to Miss Wickham. Hopes that windows are now fully squared, and seen through in. Perspective JMWT.'[41] Was Miss Wickham a friend of Julia Gordon's who had also studied with him, in particular how to draw houses? However, it seems dismal that he felt the need to write a trial version of such a message. At the Gordons on the island he painted *Near Northcourt in the Isle of Wight*, a limpid landscape showing two women washing clothes at a stream beside a sunken lane, with a black dog in attendance. Perhaps down at St Catherine's Point, below Niton, he sat on the beach and absorbed the empty Channel for the oil *Study of Sea and Sky, Isle of Wight*, painted on a section of his roll of canvas, which was never exhibited in his lifetime but was the precursor of many similar shipless marine paintings that expressed the immensity of the elements, the smallness of man – all part of crossing life's brook. Then he went back to the bustle of the house-party at the Nashes overlooking the crowded Solent.

In the course of his home tours, Turner displayed not only a predilection for the Elevated Pastoral but an interest in subject matter that might be called Humble Parochial. Great storms at sea, great classical setpieces and great Claudean exercises were for a moment set aside. On his travels he captured an essence of England. Although much of the work that came from those journeys rose well above the level of illustration, it provides a first-rate record of rural and provincial Britain at the time. The watercolours he did for the various series of engravings are landscapes often populated by working people: soldiers and smugglers, sailors and their women, shepherds and shepherdesses, colliers and keelmen, milkmaids and washerwomen; they are usually at their specific tasks, such as the fisherman seeking flounder and the miller mending the sails of his windmill. Others, not so hard at work, were tramps, bathers, market-shoppers and children playing. He looked only briefly at the industry that was changing the face of the North and the Midlands, and the lives of many people: in one watercolour, smoke drifting diagonally up from the chimneys of the mills and factories of Leeds provides a backdrop for a scene that suggests an attractive busyness – cloth being dried in a field; masons at work on a wall; various people on errands coming up a rutted roadway – but hardly anything oppressive or satanic. In another, a little less oblique in its approach to the Industrial Revolution, nightfall at Dudley with a new moon discloses flames as well as smoke from a chimney, but the artist still finds charm in a rather dingy waterway and barges moored bow to stern along the right bank, where a white tow-horse is being tended after its day's labour.

The writers of the time did a better job than the artists of portraying the massive changes happening in Britain. Turner was no Elizabeth Gaskell or Charlotte Brontë, or Disraeli even. His references to the new age are generally either tangential or almost commemoratively rueful, as we will see when he paints the *Temeraire* and the Great Western Railway. Although he registered signs of change, he was not the illustrator equivalent of an impartial social historian. He was clearly happier in the persisting British countryside. He was interested in its livestock, both managed and wild: horses pulling timber wagons and coaches or carrying packs; cattle, sheep, pigs; rabbits, hares, deer; pheasants, geese, ducks, swans, woodcock, gulls; many dogs but – surprisingly given Queen Anne Street – no cats (perhaps he thought of them as suitable only for interiors). Similarly, the structures in his landscapes are for the most part of long standing: old inns, venerable castles, great country houses, ancient churches and monuments. Stonehenge was an artefact he responded to in a way that was not at all antiquarian; rather he caught its archaic immanence.

Compared with his then far less celebrated contemporary John Constable, Turner sometimes seems a victim of his immense range and ambition. He is not satisfied with the reality of nature but has to transfigure it by brilliant colour and energetic line into an ideal. Occasionally the brilliance and energy seem to lack heart. But more often he presented observations that have the intensity of visions, caught in the moment when a cloud passes across the sun or when a shower has just dampened the grass. Watercolour was the perfect medium for such spontaneity – even if the spontaneity was hard worked for, brought about as ever in his winter studio from the shorthand of his sketches and the deep reserves of memory.

But he could achieve similar effects in oil. *Frosty Morning* is a case in point: wintry sunlight, leafless trees, hard ground, rime in the furrows, a chill in the air. On a journey to Yorkshire his coach had paused; Turner had got out for a stretch and taken all that in. At his easel, all that was expressed, and more. The melancholy of a rural morning in winter is heightened by two of the figures: the young girl – Evelina perhaps – has a rabbit-stole for warmth over her shoulders, giving the viewer the strange feeling that the animal has just been shot by the man with a shotgun – her father? There is something curious and uncertain about the relationship between her and him. She stands more or less behind him but close to him, almost sheltering, though there is no contact with him. He, leaning on his gun, seems more interested in the two horses (for which the model – according to the eldest Trimmer son – was the old crop-eared bay he kept at Twickenham). Man and girl are not talking to one another but brooding separately.

Constable's friend and patron Archdeacon John Fisher saw *Frosty Morning* at the Royal Academy in 1813 and felt it was 'a picture of pictures'. It was the only painting at the exhibition he liked better than Constable's. Fisher wrote to his friend, 'But then you need not repine at this decision of mine; you are a great man like Buonaparte, and are only beaten by a frost.'[42] The Reverend Trimmer prized the picture, and said that Turner had once talked of giving it to him. But Turner did not part with it – it remained in the gallery, one of the painter's favoured children.

11: Sir George Thinks Otherwise

Turner as a natural force, as formidable as the Russian winter – that was one way of looking at him; and Archdeacon Fisher was not alone in seeing him that way. In 1815 Turner was forty. He was of all British artists the hardest to ignore. Most of the attention he received continued to be in the shape of praise. The newspaper and periodical writers generally raved about his exhibition entries. At the Academy this year four of his watercolours were joined by three oils: the 1809 *Fishing upon the Blythe-Sand* (so far only shown in his gallery); *Crossing the Brook*; and *Dido building Carthage*. The latter two paintings were hailed in the *Champion*, on 7 May 1815, as 'achievements that raise the achievers to that small but noble group, formed of the masters whose day is not so much of today as of "all time"'. Thomas Uwins, an artist who later became an RA, went to see the exhibition at Somerset House and wrote to a friend 'in praise of Lawrence's portraits, of Wilkie's "Distress for Rent", and of that greatest of all living geniuses, Turner, whose works this year are said to surpass all his former outdoings'.[1]

The following year, William Hazlitt, trained as an artist but the most perceptive literary critic of the time, mixed praise with criticism that seemed to have been helped by a crystal ball. He called Turner 'the ablest landscape-painter now living'. But he went on – in the *Examiner* – as if he was aware of how Turner was going to paint in the near future. Hazlitt thought that Turner's

> pictures are however too much abstractions of aerial perspective, and representations not properly of the objects of nature as of the medium through which they were seen. They are the triumph of the knowledge of the artist, and of the power of the pencil, over the barrenness of the subject. They are pictures of the elements of air, earth, and water. The artist delights to go back to the first chaos of the world, or to that state of things when the waters were separated

from the dry land, and light from darkness, but as yet no living thing nor tree bearing fruit was seen upon the face of the earth. All is 'without form and void'. Some one said of his landscapes that they were *pictures of nothing, and very like*.[2]

Others felt differently. Sir George Beaumont was a perfect gentleman, landowner, amateur artist, collector, member of Parliament from 1790 to 1796, and a patron usually most generous to artistic talent, but his sensibilities were rubbed the wrong way by the professional painter from Covent Garden. It was remarkable that the hero of both men was Claude Lorrain. The baronet owned – along with pictures by Poussin, Bourdon, Rubens, Rembrandt and Richard Wilson – three Claudes, one of which, *Hagar and the Angel*, he took everywhere with him. And yet in 1815, faced with two large, well-formed Turners – *Dido building Carthage* and *Crossing the Brook* – that showed Claude's beneficent influence, Sir George bristled. He poured out his feelings to Farington. Of the *Dido*, he complained:

> The picture is painted in a false taste, not true to nature; the colouring discordant, out of harmony, resembling those French Painters who attempted imitations of Claude Lorrain, but substituting for his purity and just harmony, violent mannered oppositions of Brown and hot colours to cold tints, blues and greys: that several parts of Turner's picture were pleasingly treated but as a *whole* it was of the above character.
>
> Of his picture *Crossing the Brook*, he said it appeared to him weak like the work of an Old Man, one who no longer saw or felt colour properly; it was all of *pea-green* insipidity. These are my sentiments said he, and I have as good a right and it is as proper that I should express them as I have to give my opinion of a poetical or any other production.[3]

Sir George had early on been intrigued by what he heard of the new Covent Garden talent. He had sent John Britton to Maiden Lane on a reconnaissance, to look at the young artist's sketches and report back to him, and he had no doubt heard from Britton that Turner had declared: 'Tell Sir George Beaumont that I don't show my unfinished works to anyone.'[4] Sir George's pride had perhaps been hurt by this rebuff. Yet, in 1799, he had admired *Dutch Boats in a Gale*. Farington reported that the baronet thought 'very highly' of this painting, though 'the sky [was] too heavy and the water rather inclined to brown'.[5] Sir George seemed to be straining here to find a point to criticize, since he was normally fond of – even passionate about – brown. He was celebrated for saying, 'A good picture, like a good fiddle, should be brown,' for then it would have the look of a much varnished Old Master.[6] He was also reputed to have said, 'There ought to be one brown tree in every landscape.' (And Turner's paintings should have made him happy on that score.) By 1803 Sir George had cooled further. He told Farington that Turner 'finishes his distances and middle distances upon a scale that requires *universal precission* throughout his pictures, but his foregrounds are comparatively *blots*, and faces of figures without a feature being expressed'.[7] The water in *Calais Pier* looked to him like veins in a slab of marble. The following year he agreed with Edridge that Turner 'never painted a good sky'.[8]

Sir George may have been on surer ground in 1806 when he declared that Turner 'is perpetually aiming to be extraordinary', though he went on, 'but rather produces works that are capricious and singular than great'. Moreover, opined Sir George, his colouring was now 'jaundiced'.[9] At a dinner in June that year, over cold roast beef and pigeon pie, Sir George, Farington and Edridge had 'a strong conversation on the merits of Wilson as a Landscape Painter and the vicious practise of Turner and his followers'.[10] In 1811 Augustus Wall Callcott – one of the followers – talked to Farington about Sir George's 'continued cry against Turner's pictures, but said Turner was too strong to be materially hurt by it. Sir George, Callcott said, acknowledged that Turner had merit, but it was of a wrong sort, and therefore on account of the seducing skill displayed should be objected to, to prevent its bad effects inducing others to imitate it'.[11] And in 1812 more of the same: Sir George thought that Turner was doing 'more harm in misleading the Taste [the art world] than any other artist … he had fallen into a manner that was neither true nor consistent. His distances were sometimes properly finished, but when he came to the foreground it bore no proportion in finishing to the distance beyond it.'[12]

Yet Sir George could now and then set aside this somewhat antiquarian didacticism; he had the discernment to want to buy *Fishing upon the Blythe-Sand*, one of the most seductively direct seascapes Turner did at this period. According to Thornbury, Turner refused to sell it to 'his old enemy'.[13] Turner in 1810 proffered it, along with three other marine pictures, to Sir John Leicester, in a note with tiny sketches to illustrate the paintings, but it remained in his gallery.

Some contemporaries thought Sir George's damaging effect on Turner's clientele was considerable. But Sir John Leicester remained a faithful purchaser – indeed, in 1818 he bought one of the four pictures Turner had advertised in his note, the 1807 *Sun rising through Vapour*, which Turner, in a little title above the sketch, had called 'Dutch Boats'. At this point the Yorkshire squire Walter Fawkes was well into his long career as a Turner collector, and had in the last few years bought *London*, the view from Greenwich that Turner exhibited in 1809. Lord Egremont bought thirteen oils from Turner between 1806 and 1812. However, some of the dukes and earls who had given his career such a flying start had fallen away, and the new wealthy manufacturers had yet to make up the gap. Sir George's criticism of *Crossing the Brook* was given as a reason why it didn't sell. Callcott, who had not sold a picture at the Academy exhibition for three years, told Farington that Sir George Beaumont's 'persevering abuse of his pictures had done him harm',[14] and that Turner had suffered from the same cause. Turner had thought of not exhibiting at the RA this year, but had since changed his mind; he was 'determined not to give way before Sir George's remarks'. Two years later, Thomas Phillips RA talked to Farington 'of the great injury done to Turner by the reports of Sir George Beaumont and others of his Circle. He said Holwell Carr [the Reverend W. Holwell Carr, a director of the British Institution and collector who had subscribed to the engraving of *The Shipwreck*], 'speaking … of Turner's picture of *Dido building Carthage*, observed that "Turner did not comprehend his art." By such speeches Philips [sic] thought Turner was greatly injured and the sale of his works checked.' Farington himself thought that what he considered to be Turner's high prices were more to blame.[15]

In fact, of more than seventy oils painted between 1803 and 1815, twenty-six failed to sell during the lifetime of the painter; half a dozen or so sold some years after being painted. But roughly half of his output of that twelve-year period did find a purchaser before, on, or soon after first exhibition. The main negative impact seems to have come in the years 1813–15, when none of his five big pictures sold. These were *Frosty Morning*, *Apullia*, *Dido and Aeneas*, *Crossing the Brook* and *Dido building Carthage*. From 1812, *Snowstorm: Hannibal crossing the Alps* also remained on his hands.[16]

Seen from Turner's and Callcott's point of view, Sir George seemed an ogre. For many artists, on the contrary, he was pure benevolence. He helped many young painters with gifts and commissions. He was a patron to John Jackson, son of a Yorkshire tailor, providing him with £50 a year till he gained a footing in London. He went on helping B. R. Haydon, ordering pictures from that difficult man, even though Haydon in his megalomania insisted on painting canvases that were too big for the Beaumonts to cope with. He was one of those who generously supported J. R. Cozens in his lunacy, when Cozens – whose father Alexander had been Sir George's drawing master at Eton – was in the care of Dr Monro for three years in the mid-1790s. He bought work by the young George Lance. He had the perception to collect more than thirty Girtin watercolours, and to show them to the young John Constable – who was, brightly, sent by his mother to see the helpful baronet. Beaumont also showed the aspiring East Anglian painter his Claude *Hagar* and the pictures he himself had painted, which, friends of Farington told the diarist, 'looked like pictures painted more in imitation of pictures than of nature'.[17] (But a drawing of a lady, probably his wife Margaret, shows ability, and perhaps love.) Sir George went on over many years to encourage Constable's career, even though the artist told him that he would never put brown trees in *his* landscapes. (Constable thought that the passion that collectors like Beaumont had for the darkened canvases of old paintings was a threat to 'God Almighty's daylight'.)[18] Beaumont befriended Coleridge and Wordsworth. The latter helped Sir George lay out the new gardens at his Leicestershire country seat, Coleorton. Sir George left Wordsworth a yearly pension of £100, which made up a fifth of the poet's income.

Haydon – in his calmer moments not unmindful of Beaumont's generosity – called him 'a tall, well bred handsome man with a highly intellectual air'.[19] C. R. Leslie thought him 'a very delightful person', although he later wrote that this 'sincere friend to the Arts' was in many respects 'a mistaken one'.[20] Sir George's range of taste in art was fairly narrow. He had a high opinion of his own connoisseurship, an opinion which struck some as conceit. Northcote, not taken up by Sir George, said the baronet was 'all for fashion and novelty, took people up and then dropped them'.[21] Dorothy Wordsworth, the poet's long-suffering sister, found the Beaumonts 'so good and kind-hearted'.[22] And they certainly dropped neither Coleridge nor Wordsworth during the long estrangement between those former friends. Sir George in a lasting act of generosity left many of the masterpieces in his collection – including his beloved *Hagar* – to the nation, as part of the basis for a National Gallery. Haydon was moved at hearing of Sir George's death in 1827 and praised his love of art, while not ignoring his weaknesses, especially as they seemed to apply to B. R. Haydon: 'His great defect was a want of moral courage; what his taste dictated to be right he would shrink from asserting if it shocked the prejudices of others or put himself to a moment's inconvenience. With great benevolence he appeared, therefore, often mean; with exquisite taste he seemed often to judge wrong; and with a great wish to do good he often did a great deal of harm.'[23] Sir Walter Scott at the same time called Sir George 'by far the most sensible and pleasing man I ever knew – kind, too, in his nature, and generous – gentle in society, and of those mild manners which tend to soften the causticity of the general London tone of persiflage and personal satire'.[24]

Did Sir George have a genuine case against Turner – a case based on something other than a personality conflict? The fact that he had not been with the vanguard of those who encouraged the young Turner, and had not been able to make a protégé of him, may have had a bearing on his attitude. Despite his high Tory politics, Sir George appeared sympathetic to the new emphasis on personal feelings and inner vision that swayed Wordsworth and Coleridge, and was labelled Romantic; why didn't he care for it in Turner too? Wordsworth wrote, in *Resolution and Independence* (published 1807):

> All things that love the sun are out of doors;
> The sky rejoices in the morning's birth;
> The grass is bright with rain-drops; – on the moors
> The hare is running races in her mirth;
> And with her feet she from the plashy earth
> Raises a mist, that, glittering in the sun,
> Runs with her all the way, wherever she doth run.

Turner's work of this time, particularly his watercolours, strikes a similar note of gladness at creation, though with hints of the possibility of what Wordsworth in a following stanza saw as the final despondency and madness poets (and presumably all artists) were subject to. Defending Wordsworth against the strictures of the critics of the *Edinburgh Review*, Sir George showed that he had accepted Coleridge's notion that a new and original writer had to form the taste by which he was to be appreciated. Sir George said to Farington: 'All men who write in a new superior stile must *create a people capable* of fully relishing their beauties.'[25]

That he could not see Turner in the same light, as an artist needing to create an audience to understand him, may have been because his own knowledge of traditional painting got in the way. He, George Beaumont, was an artist. He knew how it should be done. He could see that Turner was no longer dedicated to eighteenth-century clarity and precision; he was – as the prescient Hazlitt had noted – beginning to pursue the unclear, the indefinite, the imprecise (all of which were of course harder to get at and render, but Sir George did not give credit for that). Turner had stopped trying to be an old master and was, on his own terms, seeking to be a new one. To Sir George's mind, it seemed that Turner was doing harm 'by endeavouring to make painting in oil to appear like watercolours, by which attempting to give lightness and clearness the force of oil painting has been lost'.[26] In the *Dido building Carthage*, Turner's liberal use of yellows bothered some critics at the time, and Sir George was not alone in finding the colouring 'discordant'. Lawrence and other colleagues at the Academy told Turner that something was wrong, and Turner seems to have agreed. During one of the varnishing days that had been established in 1809 for artists to put final touches on their pictures hanging in Somerset House, he altered the picture, painting an entirely new sky, according to Trimmer, and making the sun white rather than yellow.

Although the *Dido building Carthage* was ranked by Robert Hunt, in the *Examiner*, beside the best works of Poussin, Rubens and Claude, its 1817 sequel led Hunt to complain of 'the false splendour' of its colouring.[27] Turner's second study in imperial ambition would have won him the prize for longest title, had there been such a trophy: *The Decline of the Carthaginian Empire – Rome being determined on the Overthrow of her Hated Rival, demanded from her such Terms as might either force her into War, or ruin her by Compliance; the Enervated Carthaginians, in their Anxiety for Peace, consented to give up even their Arms and their Children.* For those hungry for more, he appended in the catalogue seven lines of his verse – 'At Hope's delusive smile

...' and so on. Both *Carthage*s, rising and falling, were in his grand manner, and their frames functioned as prosceniums: Carthage looks like a stage set. The lighting is theatrical, even operatic; the curtain has just gone up and the orchestra is going full blast.

And yet Turner loved them, particularly the first of the pair. They were his classical dream writ large: the gladness of creation, the despondency of failure, hymned with all the stops out. As we have seen, he rebuffed offers for *Dido building Carthage*. He wanted the nation to have it (and possibly the *Decline*) if he wasn't going to be rolled up in it for burial. For an artist whose figure-painting was not consistently wonderful, the figures on the waterfront of this rising Carthage are admirably done, and the dream becomes real or at least common property by way of the boys sitting at the edge of the stone quay. They watch their toy boat – properly rigged for the Mediterranean with a lateen sail – sail across the harbour basin, while Dido turns aside from supervising the construction works to glance their way, as if seeing in them the hopeful future of her new city. The morning sun glints in long beams down the crowded harbour towards us. But when this painting is hung alongside a similar subject by Claude, as Turner also wanted, we see the inherent restlessness that was in Turner and not in Claude; and which Sir George was perhaps reacting to when he talked of Turner 'perpetually aiming to be extraordinary'. Turner's truly great performances came when he did not try so hard to outdo and update his idol.

Turner's response to criticism was, as we might expect, rarely uniform. Ruskin was later given the impression that his enthusiastic commentaries weren't read by their subject. Earlier, Turner had thanked writers such as John Taylor for their remarks. At this time, when he was forty or so, he was used to praise and blame; sometimes he greeted both with a grunt or a shrug; but on other occasions, according to his friend the Vicar of Heston, Henry Trimmer, critical comments brought tears to Turner's eyes. Were these lachrymose reactions brought on by suggestions that he was tending to imbecility, as West had suggested? In 1806 James Boaden of the *Oracle* looked at Turner's *Schaffhausen* at the Academy exhibition and declared, 'That is madness. He is a mad-man,' and Turner's old supporter John Taylor, editor of the *Sun*, agreed. As time went on, the word 'maniac' cropped up. 'Bedlam' was mentioned.[28] Sir George's remark that Turner's works were those of an old man who had lost his power of execution carried the implication of pre-senile dementia. In 1809 Thomas Hearne, Henry Edridge and Farington were looking at one of the Earl of Essex's three Turners at Cassiobury Park when Hearne said, 'The sky was painted by a mad man.'[29] Perhaps the fate of Turner's mother had become known, and the condition was assumed to be hereditary. Turner's tears may have been of anger at such comments or of unhappiness that he could not forfend such madness if it was – like some nightmarish demon of Fuseli's – waiting to embrace him.

Turner was concerned about his reputation. Talking with Farington on 17 August 1810 he complained about the use of his name in a print-publisher's advertisement. He did not mind his name being associated with Farington's or Hearne's, 'but would not have it united with the names of artists taken up accidentally and not of established respectability'. (The pomposity may well be Farington's rather than Turner's.) When it came to Sir George Beaumont's attacks, he didn't quail; they brought out the competitor in him. In 1806 Sir George had taken up the young Scottish painter David Wilkie, who did homely Dutch-type scenes – popular examples being *Village Politicians* and *The Blind Fiddler*, the latter commissioned by Sir George. The rural genre paintings of the recently deceased George Morland were also in vogue. Turner determined to show that he could produce pictures in the same category. One result was – another lengthy title – *A Country Blacksmith disputing upon the Price of Iron, and the Price charged to the Butcher for shoeing his Poney*, shown at the RA in 1807. Turner had evidently read in the papers that wartime inflation had hit the cost of iron, and had used those stalwart British characters the blacksmith and butcher to show the grassroots effect of rising prices. However, the picture could perhaps have been subtitled 'The Painter sticking his Tongue in his Cheek, and challenging the attention given to newly fashionable Scottish Artists by Regency Patrons'.

There was gossip at this time of Sir George being made President of the once again riven Royal Academy, no doubt furthering his shocking ambitions to get Wilkie elected an Academician without first being elected an Associate. One can read Sir George's name into a note Turner scribbled in the margin of a page of Shee's *Elements of Art*: 'It is natural that there should be more dictators than encouragers, more critics than students, more amateurs than artists.'

And next to a passage by Shee referring to the Academy's rival, the British Institution, Turner noted: 'to have no choice "but that of the Patron" is the very fetter upon Genius, that every coxcomb wishes to rivet but Choice should even a Beggar stand alone. This stand is mine and shall remain my own.'[30]

In 1814 Sir George held sway as one of the directors of the British Institution, which had offered a prize of one hundred guineas for a landscape to be a proper companion to the Old Masters. Ten days later than the date specified in the rules, and thus cleverly disqualifying himself, Turner sent in a picture which largely *was* an Old Master: at first sight it appeared to be a replica of Lord Egremont's Claude, *Jacob with Laban and his Daughters*. (Lord Egremont was also a director of the BI and on its prize-giving jury, but didn't turn up on the day the jury voted.) Turner called his version *Apullia in Search of Appullus vide Ovid*. The reference was to Ovid's poem 'The Transformation of Appullus', which he had found in his edition of Anderson's *Complete Poets* – in the translation therein Appullus was a 'bold buffoon' who mimics the motions of the wood nymphs 'with gest obscene' and is turned into a wild olive tree, a shrub which retains 'the coarseness of the clown'.[31] For that matter, one of the nymphs in Turner's picture seems to be looking out at the viewer – and the prize judges – in a saucy or scornful way.

Turner's beautifully painted near-Claude thus seems to have been a bright piece of mockery at Sir George and his cronies for their doctrinal attitudes towards contemporary art. If they wanted unoriginal Claudes, he could paint them – and tease his antagonists. But he could also – *vide* his Didos, his Carthages – paint scenes that showed he had read his Virgil, his Goldsmith's *Roman History*, and had thought about the influence of individuals and human relationships on what had happened in the past. The British Institution gave its hundred guineas to T. C. Hofland, a not very lively landscape painter who specialized in close imitations of Claude and Poussin, Wilson and Gainsborough. Yet Hazlitt did not detect any leg-pull; he was happy with the *Apullia*, in which 'all the taste and all the imagination being borrowed, his [Turner's] powers of eye, hand, and memory are equal to anything'. And he added, 'We could almost wish that this gentleman would always work in the trammels of Claude or N. Poussin.'[32]

The strained relations between the RA and BI factions were

much in evidence in 1815 (a year in which the end of the great war brought about enormous financial uncertainty, with Government Funds falling in value, and prices of day-to-day goods starting to shoot up). Two years before, Turner, Robert Smirke and Callcott had declared their disapproval of the BI's plan to display the works of Reynolds at the same time as the annual RA exhibition. Now the Academicians were worried that a BI exhibition of 'foreign old masters' would harm their own exhibition sales. They counter-attacked. An anonymous seventy-four-page polemic entitled *A Catalogue Raisonné of the Pictures now Exhibiting at the British Institution* lambasted though didn't name the 'pretended patrons' – Sir George, the Reverend Holwell Carr and Richard Payne Knight – and defended Turner. Callcott was suspected of being one of the *Catalogue's* authors and Walter Fawkes one of its backers. Smirke told Farington that he approved the remark in the *Catalogue* 'that there had been a *virulence of criticism* on the pictures painted by Turner, such as should be reserved for Crime ...'[33]

Despite these distractions, and despite the faltering sales of some of his big canvases that may have impelled him towards the engravers and watercolours, Turner's standing in 1815–16 was immense. He had put landscape painting in the front rank. His genius and hard work had brought him fame and the money to build his gallery and, more recently, a new house near the Thames in Twickenham, and also to publish the *Liber Studiorum*, a fanfare for landscape, a salute for his own talents. At this moment of national victory over Napoleon, he was – as Sir George ruefully acknowledged – influential, too, among other artists. He had founded what was almost a school – 'the White Painters' – whose members had given up the old black and brown tones of landscape painting. 'The Taste' brought into being by, in particular, the Reverend William Gilpin, author of *Observations relative chiefly to Picturesque Beauty*, disapproved of white. Gilpin thought the chalkiness of its coast made the Isle of Wight objectionable; similarly the glaciers of Savoy. Turner, using white grounds for large parts or even all of his oil paintings, as if they were watercolours on white paper, was achieving effects that offended connoisseurs brought up to consider a prospect of countryside improved if seen through a Claude Glass, which gave things a dusky-gold Old Masterish hue.

As Sir George put it, Turner was 'misleading the Taste' with the

STANDING IN THE SUN

help of such 'followers' as William Havell, William Daniell and Callcott. (Sir George had criticized the 'white look' of Callcott's two coast scenes shown at the Academy in 1806; seeing these, James Northcote had commented that Callcott 'had founded himself on Turner's manner, which several others had adopted, and "had leapt out of the frying-pan into the fire" – to avoid the appearance of oil in their pictures, they now seemed as if executed with mortar'.)[34] Sir George's BI crony Richard Payne Knight had bought several of Callcott's works, but that may have been a deliberate ploy to advance Callcott at Turner's expense. Callcott himself later recalled that he had been a 'devout admirer' of Turner's work from the moment he saw it, though this did not prevent him from lamenting about his old hero 'that a species of perversity induces him to court public outrage ...'[35]

Turner and Callcott became friends – good enough friends for Callcott to know that Sarah Danby was living with Turner in 1809. They worked together on Academy Councils and committees, and were both elected to serve among the Visitors at the Academy's new School of Painting in 1815. They sat together at the Academy dinner that year with their ally the artist James Ward, who shared with Turner a passion for Yorkshire and an interest in the sublime. Also at their table were the collectors Walter Fawkes, Sir John Swinburne and Thomas Lister Parker, another Yorkshire landowner who was a patron of Turner's and had bought one of Callcott's 1806 coast scenes. Turner's influence over young painters continued into the next generation. David Roberts, who came from Scotland to London in 1822, to begin as a theatre-scene painter, thought of Turner as 'the mighty painter of the day that all spoke of, and whose works were the all-in-all to every young artist'.[36] Roberts' friend and Drury Lane and Covent Garden rival Clarkson Stanfield shared these feelings. Turner's *Carthage*s were lessons in colour and composition to the scene painters. Art writers in the 1820s and 1830s saw Turner's influence in the works of Roberts and Stanfield, one in the *Art-Union* claiming that the brilliance of their scenery was due to colour-lessons learnt from Turner.

One of the first of Turner's oils to be painted on a white ground was *Petworth from the Lake, Dewy Morning*, done for Lord Egremont in 1809; Turner had found a way of making country-house portraiture new and luminous. But white was not everything for the dean of the White Painters. Turner once told the Reverend Henry Trimmer that yellow was his favourite colour; he had more varieties of it in his studio than he had of reds, browns, blues or greens. Sir George in 1806 had observed that Turner's colouring was now 'jaundiced' and we have seen how annoyed viewers were by the yellows in *Dido building Carthage*. In his 'Chemistry & Apuleia' sketchbook[37] used around 1813, Turner recorded the formulations of various yellows, along with a method for waterproofing linen (possibly to keep him dry while sketching and fishing) and a description of the symptoms of and a remedy for the Maltese Plague – should he ever encounter that dread disease. Hazlitt in 1816 noted critically that Turner was putting blue and yellow paint side by side on his canvases 'to produce the effect of green at a distance' – a procedure Hazlitt thought 'quackery',[38] though the Impressionists were to follow suit. The artist William Westall once spotted a yellow palm tree in a Turner picture and felt bound to approach the painter, albeit timidly.

'I have travelled a great deal in the East, Mr Turner,' Westall ventured, 'and therefore know of what I am speaking, and I can assure you that a palm-tree is never of that colour: it is always green.'

'Umph!' grunted Turner, almost transfixing Westall with his glance. 'Umph! I can't afford it – can't afford it.' And with those words he walked away.[39]

Turner wasn't only respected by people who were influenced by his kind of painting; artists who worked in quite different ways admired him too. Haydon, unsympathetic to most Academicians, was impressed by the fact that Turner dropped in to see his *Solomon*, when Haydon exhibited it to the public in 1814 – the ardent paranoiac wrote, calmly for once, 'Turner behaved well and did me justice.'[40] The following year Haydon took the celebrated Italian sculptor Antonio Canova round town to 'show him the lions'. They went to Turner's gallery and Canova as he looked at the pictures kept exclaiming 'Grand genie!'[41] Another artist who took to Turner's work was Thomas Lawrence, the handsome and fashionable portrait painter, who was knighted by the Prince Regent in 1815 and elected President of the Academy in 1820 in succession to West. It was after his visit to Turner's gallery in 1809 that Lawrence had tried to interest a Yarmouth collector named Penrice, who wanted to acquire some Old Masters, in buying the work of a living artist instead: Turner, he told Penrice, being 'indisputably the first landscape painter in

Europe'. The picture Lawrence had in mind – which Penrice didn't buy – was *Near the Thames Lock, Windsor*, which Lawrence described as 'full of sentiment, and certainly of genius ... It is in his own peculiar manner, but *that* at its best.'[42] Turner, as we shall see, had his loyal way of returning such gestures.

The engraver and writer John Landseer had visited Turner's gallery in 1808 and had been bowled over by the new lightness of key. He wrote, in his quarterly *Review of Publications of Art*, 'The brightness of his lights is less effected [sic] by the contrast of darkness than that of any other painter whatever, and even in his darkest and broadest breadths of shade, there is – either produced by some few darker touches, or by some occult magic of his peculiar art – a sufficiency of natural clearness.'[43] And four decades later, John Burnet declared, 'The light key upon which most of our present landscape painters work owes its origin to Turner; the presence of his pictures on the walls of the Academy engendered this change from the darker imitations of Wilson and Gainsborough, or the contemplation of the landscapes of the Dutch school'[44] – though he went on to wonder whether the English school wasn't 'extending this principle to excess'.[45] The light key had a brilliant adherent in John Constable, who was finally making an impression in 1815. Constable, who in conversation now and then made envious remarks about Turner, once exclaimed to C. R. Leslie, a friend he had in common with Turner, 'Did you ever see a picture by Turner and not wish to possess it?'[46] In the battle against the White Painters, Sir George couldn't win.

It was curious that the influential baronet did not attack more effectively what really might have been Turner's artistic Achilles' heel: his depictions of human beings. As we have seen, a critic in the *Examiner*, after viewing Turner's *Battle of Trafalgar* in 1808, thought that all the crew members of the *Victory* had been 'murdered',[47] and Farington had described the figures in the same painting as 'miserably bad'.[48] And yet in *Dido building Carthage* the figures are successfully done: naturally arranged, anatomically drawn, doing their bit in the picture. His trouble seemed to be not that he couldn't draw and paint the human figure, as some critics complained, but that he wasn't consistent in this respect. Sometimes he seemed to want to get his figures right, sometimes he gave the impression he didn't care.

Turner – it is clear – never gave up practising his figure-drawing.

'Academy studies' from nude models appeared from time to time in his sketchbooks, among the sketches of boats and trees and country houses. The 'Lowther' sketchbook of 1809–10[49] contains several accomplished drawings of female nudes: one woman, wearing only a head scarf, is lying on her back with one knee raised, one hand to her turned-aside face, and there is a suggestion of something more intimate than a life-class study – is this Sarah posing for William? (The fact that the following four pages of the sketchbook were torn out prompts thoughts that he went on to draw even more intimate sketches, which someone later removed.) In the 'Hastings to Margate' sketchbook of the years 1815–16,[50] there are several simply drawn nudes that are first-rate – one, done from the back, in which the woman has her left hand touching the top of her head, hair piled high; another, from the front, in which the drawing is equally direct and convincing, though the thick rendering of pubic hair might not have been regarded as academically proper. His colleagues presumably felt he was competent in figure-drawing, because they continued to appoint him as a Visitor to the Life School, giving him the opportunity to draw from the model while monitoring the students. He was still a Visitor there at the age of sixty-nine. But though much of his life-drawing was skilful in the disposition and moulding of the body, it could seem careless or uninspired, with a too-regular line for the curves of arms and thighs.

Now and then he sketched clothed figures in a way that showed he could respond to the human frame with empathy: barefooted Scottish girls in big shawls, seen in Edinburgh; the family group in an early Brighton sketchbook[51] with a weariness in the way they walk. At Cowes in 1827 he drew the women in big hats and long dresses; he painted Mrs Nash at the piano, no face, vague in detail, but – in terms of the painting – right. The figures in many of his paintings work as part of the scene to which they have been assigned: fishermen in boats, shepherds on hillsides, Carthaginians on a quay, children on a beach. In such paintings as *The Country Blacksmith* and *Pope's Villa*, the figures are perfectly serviceable and don't draw attention by looking wrong. The Redgraves believed 'his effort is rather to give the right treatment to his figures – the true effect of light and sun and air, their true keeping in the picture, and the indefinite mystery of sunshine upon them – than to define their forms or to complete their outline'.[52]

Yet close attention was not sought. Expressiveness was often wanting in faces; people seemed denied an individuality by being drawn without a look of their own. He drew human beings much of the time the way he drew animals – cows or pigs, say, and certainly granting them less uniqueness than he gave to crop-eared horses. People if not anonymously wooden might be grotesque, with bodies as cartoonish lumps or sticks, eyes like currants. The reviewer for the *Monthly Magazine* in 1803 declared that the Joseph (who was shown bald) in Turner's *Holy Family* looked like a Chinese mandarin. Striking a similar note, the *St James's Chronicle* of 12–15 May 1804 said that the sailors in *Boats carrying out anchors and cables to Dutch men of war in 1665* were 'all bald or like Chinese'.[53] His increasingly conservative contemporary Wordsworth, seeing Turner's *Jessica* at the Academy in 1830, thought the artist had painted it after he 'had indulged in raw liver when he was very unwell'.[54] Viewers of other Turner pictures with figures in them were reminded of stuffed fish; dummy heads like those in the window of the Maiden Lane barbershop; bags of potatoes; Punch and Judy characters …

The same painter who did the figures in *Dido building Carthage* produced such a freakshow as *What you Will!*, another Watteau-influenced picture, this time a study of characters from Shakespeare's *Twelfth Night* that he exhibited in 1822; here the figures look like ill-made puppets. The statuary in the garden where Turner has placed them seems a lot more life-like than the purported people. His great exemplar Claude was no help in this respect: Claude's weirdly elongated figures often look as if they have their heads on backwards. At the beginning of Turner's career, many of the figures in his paintings had an affinity with the low-life characters of Teniers and Rowlandson, but as time goes on other less down-to-earth models come into play, and his figures often have a gnome-like or goblin-like appearance reminiscent of Bosch, or seem unearthly like Blake's. Many are short. Dido and Aeneas are exceptions. Something there was in Turner, surfacing at least some of the time in his work, that didn't love people – their personality, their feel, their human nature – and didn't want to look at them too closely.

There is indeed a curiously detached quality to the few 'erotic' drawings that survived excision by the executors and destruction approved by John Ruskin, and which we will consider again. A voyeurism – a sense of looking on rather than involvement – is evident, as in that drawing of the Swiss girl in bed with a companion, her costume on the floor. Of course, the artist is perforce a watcher and recorder, but Turner does not convey any affection or pleasure of the sort Rembrandt did in his etching showing a couple making love, *Het Ledekant*. Ruskin justified 'the *want* of drawing' in his hero's representation of people as being a proper 'indecision', faithful to the way the eye at a distance takes in partial impressions of forms and figures in a landscape.[55]

Certainly, 'indecision' was in the air. It was possibly an aspect of the times that offended Sir George Beaumont, though it didn't seem to bother him in the sister art of poetry. Turner was both captive and master of it, aiming to be extraordinary, and catching reverberations of 'the first chaos of the world'. Despite the Congress of Vienna's attempts to restore many features of the pre-revolutionary status quo in Europe, some crowns would never be put back on heads; some crowned heads were off altogether. Nineteenth-century steam was filling cylinders, pushing pistons, moving machinery, turning wheels and paddle-wheels. The reform of franchises and the redistribution of legislative power were being demanded. The deep distress of many city and country folk after the end of the long war helped produce an unstoppable force. The old order was crumbling, and Sir George – a member of Parliament for a rotten borough which had but one elector – was part of that structure. He must have sensed in Turner, despite his early sublime and picturesque trappings, a support for the forces of change.

12: Dear Fawkes

I f Devon was one focal point in Turner's world, Yorkshire was another, even more important – the magnetic North to which, when he wanted to get out of town, he felt himself pulled. Almost every year between 1808 and 1824 he went north to Yorkshire, to Farnley Hall, to be with the Fawkes family and to stay in the rooms they kept ready for him. From there he made sketching expeditions in the vicinity and further afield. Going to Farnley in summer or autumn was often both a working trip and a holiday. He went to breathe deeply the air of the river-furrowed Dales, in the North Riding of Yorkshire; how much he enjoyed himself was to be seen in the work he did there.

By 1816 he had known Walter Fawkes for some fourteen years. Fawkes, enthusiastic about the Alps, had commissioned three watercolours that arose from Turner's 1802 Swiss tour.[1] Turner went to Farnley for the first time in 1808 after staying at Tabley Hall in Cheshire, and Fawkes made this visit particularly memorable by ordering twenty watercolours: ten of the Alps, ten of Yorkshire. Between 1804 and 1810 Fawkes also bought six oils from Turner, setting aside his resolution only to buy watercolours from contemporary artists. These oils included the painting showing three views of the *Victory* coming up the Channel and the misty prospect of London from Greenwich. Slowly the relationship changed from being simply one between generous patron and favoured artist to one between good friends.

On 4 November 1812, at the Academy Council, Turner told Farington that he had 'a nervous disorder, with much weakness of the stomach. Everything … disagreed with him – turned *acid*. He particularly mentioned an aching pain at the back of his neck. He said he was going to Mr Fawkes's in Yorkshire for a month.' Farington in his avuncular way told Turner that 'air, moderate exercise and changing his situation would do most for him'.[2] Turner had not made a summer tour in 1812. He was involved in building his new house in Twickenham, close to the Thames. Builders; his work; the split with Sarah; another impending course of perspective lectures – all may have brought on dyspepsia or an incipient ulcer, or have excited his hypochondria, which was probably aggravated by the fact that he was without a wife or lover to complain to. A month at Farnley would set him up for the rest of the smoggy London winter.

If you judge a man by his closest companions, Turner does well. The friend of Wells, Trimmer, Holworthy and Fawkes appears in a different light from when seen in the lonely gloom of Queen Anne Street. At Farnley Hall he was almost extrovert: 'merry' and 'playful' were words used to describe him there.[3] What brought him out of his shell was in great part the personality of his host, Walter Ramsden Hawksworth Fawkes. Fawkes, of an old Yorkshire landowning family, had inherited Farnley from his father in 1792, at the age of twenty-three. Six years older than Turner, he had an income of some seven to eight thousand pounds a year. After being a happy-go-lucky undergraduate at Cambridge, he settled down to running the Farnley estates, marrying, becoming a father (with eventually four sons and seven daughters) and collecting art. He also held left-of-centre political views; as an 'advanced' Whig, he represented Yorkshire in Parliament from 1802 to 1807; at one election in 1806 he defeated the Tory candidate and Turner's previous patron Edward Lascelles. Fawkes successfully bred short-horn cattle and helped run the local agricultural society. He not only painted and drew, as many country gentlemen did, but wrote on various historical and political topics. His *Chronology of the History of Modern Europe*, published in 1810, was a meticulous compilation of crowned heads and rulers, including the Carolingians, Ostrogoths, Mercians, and Moors in Spain, 'from the Extinction of the Western Empire AD 475 to the Death of Louis the Sixteenth'. John Varley did a pencil portrait of Fawkes a few years later that showed his double chin, compressed lips and heavy eyebrows. Fawkes looked like a bulldog.

Farnley Hall was the right sort of house for such a man, multi-faceted, time-encrusted, sweetly placed. Onto a rambling late-sixteenth-century manor an elegant neo-classical mansion had been recently attached by Fawkes's father; the architect of the new 1786–90 addition was John Carr of York. Both sections were built in the local millstone grit, the old part a rough grey, the new more smoothly dressed and gold in colour, with quartz adding to its sheen. Farnley, not far from the little market town of Otley, was set in well-treed parkland with open prospects of the River Wharfe to the south, green pastures and, from the upstairs rooms, the moors around Ilkley.

Fawkes was turning the old part of the house into a private museum for his collection of things from the seventeenth-century English Civil War. He had a number of items that had belonged to Thomas Fairfax, who had lived at nearby Menston Hall and served as a general in Cromwell's army. Fairfax's sword, boots, candlestick and wheelchair were kept in an oak-panelled room with a mullioned bay window. Parliamentary banners and pikes were hung among antlers and stags' heads on the old staircase. In Carr's balustraded Palladian building the rooms were larger, with high ceilings, elaborate plasterwork and fancy fireplaces, but still gave a feeling of domestic intimacy and, despite the large staff, privacy. Two sets of finely made double doors were hung in each doorway in the three-foot thick interior walls. The skylit grand staircase had columned landings and fine friezes. A small upstairs drawing room was octagon-shaped – a Carr feature. Turner's big bed-sitting-room and adjoining smaller room, a suite which Fawkes insisted the artist use at any time, whether or not he and Mrs Fawkes were in residence, were at the south-east corner of the new house – the smaller room, for painting in, looked east towards the stables.

Turner felt at home at Farnley. The Fawkes girls recalled seeing the door to one of his rooms open one day, 'with cords spread across the room as in that of a washerwoman, and papers tinted with pink, and blue, and yellow, hanging on them to dry'.[4] He felt free to shoo the girls off if they pestered him when sketching in the grounds, saying to them 'Go away, you little baggages!' Did they – girls were bothersome – remind him of his own daughters? However, he helped illustrate a five-volume ornithological scrapbook for the Fawkes children, making watercolour studies of birds for them to stick in opposite the pages on which feathers from similar birds were fastened. His bird portraits tended to be most effective, even most 'life-like', when the birds were dead; his watercolours of a live robin and goldfinch have a slightly hesitant touch. But he went to some lengths for the bird collection. When seven-year-old Richard Fawkes – later a military man – asked especially for a cuckoo, Turner got one for the purpose; he remembered in 1851, 'A Cuckoo was my first achievement in killing on Farnley Moor in ernest request of Major Fawkes to be painted for the Book.'[5]

For Fawkes senior he did watercolours of the house and grounds, his training as an architectural draughtsman never put to better use, though Hardwick and Malton might not have approved his informal touches: a sash-window open at the bottom to reveal a woman looking out into the side garden; a carriage halting in the drive, to allow Fawkes and one of his dogs to get out; and two girls sitting in the drawing room, sewing or reading, while a third is playing the piano, and three Turner oils are shown hanging on the end wall around the fireplace. In the Oak Room, General Fairfax's wheelchair seems to be awaiting an occupant. At the foot of John Carr's staircase a footman bears a tray into the dining room. In the Conservatory, Chinese lanterns hang over an assortment of plants. He also drew the flower garden, the carriage drive, the old dairy, the Avenue, the Wood Walk, and the summer house seen from the Wharfe riverbank. (He went fishing along the Wharfe, which provided excellent angling up to Bolton Abbey.) He got involved in his host's enthusiasms – particularly Fawkes's antiquarian obsession. One coloured drawing was of the oak cabinet in which many of these relics were housed, and in this drawing Turner, like a small boy making a model, cut cupboard doors which could be opened so that they revealed the interior of the cabinet – this, and the items in it, were painted on another piece of paper stuck on the back of the first. He and Fawkes evidently had fun.

At Farnley Turner got more than moderate exercise; his appetite picked up. Years later he recalled the 'culinary exploits' of Hannah Holmes, a cook there.[6] There were frequent picnics. He went grouse-shooting with his host on Hawksworth Moor and made his usual sketchbook record of the guns and dogs and dead game. After one such occasion, Turner was allowed to take the reins of a tandem carriage for a rough passage over some fields on the way back to Farnley, and the carriage capsized – no one hurt, much laughter, and the driver celebrated as 'the Over-Turner'.[7] (Walter Fawkes may have known that Turner, as we have seen, had already been given this nickname by the *True Briton* in May 1803.)

For his host, Turner also put to work his talent as an architect; he designed a pair of neo-classical lodges for the east gate of the Hall, and made a watercolour to commemorate the finished product. Turner was to be bumped into in the house or grounds at any time of day, sometimes down by the river with his rod, but most often with a sketchbook and pencil in hand, sketching, say, one of the peacocks. (He identified with peacocks perhaps even more than with mallards, putting one in the frontispiece of the *Liber* and another on a chunk of classical masonry in *The Thames at Weybridge*, painted c. 1807–10; there was something about their searching eyes and hooked beaks that may have reminded him of what he saw in the mirror when shaving.) Young Hawksworth, the eldest son, came across him on one of his sketching prowls and drew a funny caricature of the honoured guest.

Turner's secretiveness about his working habits was undermined at Farnley. Perhaps emboldened by seeing his 'laundry-line', one of the Fawkes girls sought hints on painting watercolours and was told to first soak the paper in a jug of water. Hawksworth always remembered one stormy day when, he said, 'Turner called to me loudly from the doorway, "Hawkey! Hawkey! Come here! Come here! Look at this thunderstorm. Isn't it grand? Isn't it wonderful? Isn't it sublime?" All this time he was making notes of its form and colour on the back of a letter. I proposed some better drawing-block, but he said it did very well. He was absorbed – he was entranced. There was the storm rolling and sweeping and shafting out its lightning over the Yorkshire hills. Presently the storm passed, and he finished. "There, Hawkey," he said. "In two years time you will see this again, and call it *Hannibal crossing the Alps*."'[8] Out of his experience of a Wharfedale thunderstorm and his knowledge of Alpine scenery, Turner contrived the elements that began to shake up his classical compositions: swirl and vortex. Claudean serenity and certainty hit the fan of change and doubt. The 'first chaos of the world' was revisited.

On hand at the first day of creation of *Hannibal*, Hawkey also had the good fortune to be there at the making of a watercolour masterpiece – seeing it all, from start to finish. As Edith Mary Fawkes – Walter Fawkes's great-niece – related, at breakfast one morning Fawkes said to Turner,

'I want you to make me a drawing of the ordinary dimensions that will give some idea of the size of a man of war.' The idea hit Turner's fancy, for with a chuckle he said to Walter Fawkes's eldest son, then a boy of about fifteen, 'Come along, Hawkey, and we will see what we can do for Papa,' and the boy sat by his side the whole morning and witnessed the evolution of *The First Rate taking in Stores*. His description of the way Turner went to work was very extraordinary; he began by pouring wet paint till it was saturated, he tore, he scratched, he scrubbed at it in a kind of frenzy and the whole thing was chaos – but gradually and as if by magic the lovely ship, with all its exquisite minutia, came into being and by luncheon time the drawing was taken down in triumph.[9]

At Farnley Hall, about sixty miles from the sea, Turner drew a sea picture, retrieving from his memory the towering sides of the ship and its immense tumblehome, and prompting a sense of its spars and rigging mostly out of sight above.

Hawksworth saw Turner on another morning, watching a housemaid at work pipeclaying some outside steps. He talked her into giving him some, which he carried off to his rooms, and afterwards said it made a 'capital white' in a drawing.[10]

In July 1816 Turner took one of the coaches he by now knew well that went to Leeds, with names such as *Lord Nelson*, *Highflyer* and *True Briton*. The fare for an outside seat behind the coachroof was two guineas, with a few extras for tips and porters' fees; he saved about a guinea by not travelling inside. At 10 m.p.h. the coach thundered up the now hard-surfaced Great North Road to Grantham, where passengers spent the night. On the journey, hunched down in the wind and rain, Turner may have thought of earlier trips north. His first tour to Yorkshire had been in the summer of 1797, following hard in Tom Girtin's tracks; then, among other things, he had gone to paint watercolours of Harewood House, the home of the Lascelles family, five miles east of Farnley. That year young Edward Lascelles had bought his *St Erasmus and Bishop Islip's Chapels* for three guineas – a sum he didn't scorn at the time. He had gone on from Harewood to other parts of the north: north-eastwards to the Tees, the Tweed and Berwick; over to the Lake District; across the sands of Morecambe Bay to Lancaster at low tide; across to York, Harewood again, and Beverley. Six results of that tour had been displayed at the RA in 1798, including views of *Kirkstall Abbey* and

Norham Castle on the Tweed (the second of these Edward Lascelles also bought).[11] Turner thereafter associated the north with his rapid success; in 1831 he would come again to Norham Castle and be seen taking off his hat and bowing low to it. A companion asked him what all this was about. Turner said: 'I made a drawing of Norham Castle several years since. It took. And from that day to this I have had as much to do as my hands could execute.'[12]

He had also gone north in 1799, when he went to Whalley on the border between Yorkshire and Lancashire to make drawings for Dr Thomas Dunham Whitaker's *History* of that place. He seems to have been introduced to Whitaker by a bookseller and artist in Halifax, Thomas Edwards, who also knew Walter Fawkes, and may have introduced Turner – 'the draftsman' – to him as well.

Sixteen years later, memories of being irritated by Whitaker were no doubt far from Turner's mind as he was borne north. He now had an immense commission for another Whitaker project: a *History of Yorkshire,* the first part of which was to be a *History of Richmondshire*, and all to be illustrated with engravings after his watercolours. Farington, ever agog for such news, noted that Turner was to be paid 3000 guineas for 120 drawings, though he shortly scaled down the fee to 2000 guineas – still a tidy amount. Farington added, 'After making his agreement with Messrs Longman & Co he returned to them and told them he had omitted to mention his expences in travelling. They replied that they considered that expences to be included in the agreement, but he would not allow it. It ended in their proposing to give him twenty pounds which he assented to, but added that *it must be made guineas.*'[13]

On the second day of his 1816 journey north he travelled from Grantham to Doncaster to Leeds and finally reached Otley before nightfall. There was a hearty welcome at Farnley, and then three days to get over his coach ride before the Fawkeses took him along on a family holiday, westward, up into the Pennines. Mrs Fawkes wrote in her always sparsely worded diary an entry for 17 July: 'Left Farnley with Walter, Maria, Amelia, Ayscough, Richard and Mr. Turner.' The four children rode with her in a carriage; Turner and Fawkes rode on horseback.[14] They stayed the night in Skipton and then journeyed on to Browsholme, near Clitheroe on the Lancashire border. Browsholme was the home of Thomas Lister Parker, an old friend of Fawkes and another patron of Turner; it was a large old house, three storeys high, with a lovingly preserved interior. Mrs Fawkes's diary records days of rain, for example: '*Fri. 19th*. Rained all day. Sat in the house. Late in the evening walked a short way with John Parker and Mr. Turner ... *Tues. 23rd*. Heavy rain. Drove with Walter. Obliged to take shelter in a farmhouse. Walter bought a print of the Prodigal Son ... *Thurs. 25th*. Went to see Gordale Waterfall. Returned home. Heavy rain. Turner went on a sketching tour.'[15]

1816 went into the records as 'the year without a summer'. Mount Tambora, a volcano in the South Pacific, had erupted the year before, its ash clouds affecting the world's climate. But Turner had his Longmans commission to fulfil, and he put up with the rain. After his final jaunt with the Fawkes family to see the great gorge and waterfall at Gordale, he set off for more than two weeks on his own, covering some 500 miles on horseback, exploring market towns like Richmond and Kendal, staying in small inns, clambering up fells and trekking round peatbogs, looking into caves and potholes, visiting more waterfalls or 'forces' as they were called up there, sketching castles and abbeys, the Lake District mountains, Yorkshire moorlands and dales – all picturesque enough, all hard, wet work; three sketchbooks-full.

One day at Mill Gill falls, near Askrigg in Wensleydale, he dropped a sketchbook he was using and got it muddy; he turned the page and kept sketching. A day's ride with halts for drawing was often followed by a quick excursion from his inn for an evening sketch or two. At High Force on the upper Tees he stayed out so long that it grew dark and for a while he was astray, but eventually found his inn. He crossed the sands of upper Morecambe Bay at low tide, presumably in the company of one of the carriages that made the journey (and sometimes got bogged down), their passengers keeping an apprehensive eye on the fast-flooding tide. From Richmond, on 31 July, he dropped a line to his friend the watercolour artist James Holworthy, to tell him that he found it impossible to meet him at a mutual acquaintance's as they had arranged, and added the postscript: 'Weather miserably wet; I shall be web-footed like a drake, except the curled feather; but I must proceed northwards. Adieu!' The weather did not improve; as he wrote to Holworthy a little later, it was still 'Rain, Rain, Rain, day after day ... a most confounded fagg, tho on horseback ... the passage out of Teesdale leaves everything far behind for difficulty – bogged most compleatly Horse and its Rider, and nine hours making 11 miles ...'[16]

He was back at Farnley on Sunday, 11 August. He had made 450 sketches and was glad for a bath, a drying fire and the convivial company of the Fawkes family. Perhaps he recited to Walter Fawkes a song he had heard during his tour and written down in a sketchbook:[17]

> Here's a health to Honest John Bull
> When he is gone, where will ye find such another
> So with Hearts as with Bumpers quite full
> Here's a health to Old England his mother.

He was back in time for the Glorious Twelfth, when the grouse-shooting season began, and Fawkes held a shooting party. 'All the gentlemen', Mrs Fawkes wrote in her diary, 'went to the moors.'[18] Turner recorded the scenes in several sketchbooks, one larger than usual:[19] the bare moors; loose clouds drifting over a valley; the beaters with dogs; the sportsmen on their horses or standing with their guns; the well-organized after-shoot refreshments. He also made several watercolours of the event. One was called *Grouse-Shooting, Beamsley Beacon* – Beamsley Beacon was out on the moors about six miles north-west of Farnley, towards Bolton Abbey. In another watercolour, *Shooting Party on the Moors*, three marquees have been erected, a barrel of ale is waiting to be broached, and dead birds are lying ready to be grilled over a fire. Walter Fawkes stands holding a bird he has shot. The painter has inscribed on the nearby canvas of a tent: W. FAWKES   FARN.

But the holiday mood was shattered next day. Richard Hawksworth Fawkes, Walter's youngest brother, was injured by a shotgun blast. He seemed 'pretty well' the following day, according to Mrs Fawkes, but on the evening of the 15th was said by a doctor to be failing. On the 16th Mrs Fawkes wrote: 'Poor Richard died 5 o'clock in the morning.'[20] The shooting-party guests left the stricken house over the next day or so, though Turner, John Parker and a Miss Coates stayed on a little longer. Then Turner went off for another sketching excursion. He wrote to W. B. Cooke from Farnley on 28 August, acknowledging the receipt of a letter from Cooke and explaining that he had been away again. Richard Fawkes's death had 'made it better for me to leave for a few days'.[21] Though close to the

Fawkeses, he felt the need to let them be on their own to mourn, without having to worry about him as a house-guest.

He made a cover for a sketchbook used at this time out of a tract, on which were printed some Old Testament lines from Exodus; the Lord tells Moses to make coats for Aaron's sons. Perhaps he picked it up on his travels and remembered his schooldays with Mr Coleman. The sketchbook contained a sketch that formed the basis of a drawing for an unpublished *Liber* plate, *The Stork and Aqueduct*. Inside one cover he wrote a poem, first in pencil, then in ink:

> Sweet Independence, rough is thy nature, hardy, sincere,
> Thou gives the humble roof content, devoid of fear
> Even of tomorrow's fate, and adds a blissful joy
> To its perhaps lone inmate, even without alloy.[22]

The Fawkeses, drawing together at this sad moment, made him feel his essential solitariness.

Yet he remained based at Farnley through the first two weeks of September, writing several times to Holworthy to try to arrange a meeting on his way back to London, and sympathizing with his friend, who had been suffering from rheumatism, which Turner called 'the Rumaticks'.[23] Despite the grief at Farnley, despite the weather, it had been a successful summer tour: at least three crammed sketchbooks and a number of preparatory watercolours – some of those 'beginnings' made up of broad washes of colour that he used for setting down the tonal structure of pictures to come, and which the Fawkes girls may have seen hanging from his laundry-lines. Twenty finished watercolours became his contribution to the *History of Yorkshire*, a project which remained incomplete; Dr Whitaker died in 1821. In them, with an occasional nod to the sublime and frequent genuflections to the picturesque, he evoked a landscape which moved him: limestone scars, meandering rivers, tumbling waterfalls, distant valleys.

At some point during this Yorkshire visit he seems to have found time to call on a Leeds bookseller and printdealer, a Mr Robinson, to whom Longmans had given him a sealed letter of introduction. This apparently 'recommended' the artist in unflattering terms, Longmans having experienced the artist's hard bargaining. The letter concluded, 'Above all things remember that Turner is a GREAT JEW.' According to Thornbury, Mr Robinson (no anti-Semite) took this injunction literally and, since it was a Sunday when Turner called, suggested that he amuse himself with some books while he, Robinson, went to church. Later the printdealer apologized when ham was served for dinner.[24]

Turner was at Farnley Hall again the following year, several months after returning to England from a trip up the Rhine and after his intervening expedition to Durham and Raby Castle. He was apparently somewhere in the north on 31 October 1817, when his daughter Evelina married Joseph Dupuis in the fashionable church of St James's, Piccadilly. She was seventeen; he was twenty-eight – an 'older man' and consular official, perhaps met through her mother's musical friends. Sarah Danby was at the wedding and was entered in the marriage register as one of the witnesses. Even if her father was absent, Evelina didn't hide her paternity; she was married in the name of Evelina Turner. But she may have liked the idea of a husband who would also be a father to her; she accompanied him to his next post in West Africa, where they survived the climate of the White Man's Grave but became parents of a child who died in infancy. (They went on to have four other children who lived. Joseph Dupuis was apparently a touchy man, who never became more than a vice-consul in distant posts, though his book, *Journal of a Residence in Ashantee*, published in 1824, was seriously reviewed.) Clearly Evelina didn't need to go to the Gold Coast, far from Turner's sight, to be out of Turner's mind.

It was mid-November when he reached Farnley and found Mr and Mrs Fawkes away. When they got home, Turner was installed in his rooms. He had been working on a series of fifty watercolours of the Rhine, which Fawkes saw and immediately agreed to buy. A colourful account of this transaction has Turner arriving out of the blue one night 'when dinner was ready; he was greeted with delight. "Where have you been?" "Up the Rhine." "Have you done any work?" "Oh yes, a lot." "Where are they?" "In my greatcoat." "May I get them?" said Mr Fawkes, but Turner said "No," went out to the coat – which was described … as one of the sort old hackney coachmen used to wear, [with] any number of capes, one over the other, and a lot of pockets – brought a roll out of one pocket and re-entered the drawing room and began to flatten out the drawings.' Fawkes, 'wild with delight', bought the lot for £500.[25]

Turner seems to have felt he had travelled enough this year and been away too long from his own studio. He wrote to Holworthy from Farnley on 21 November, apologizing for not having been in touch, bemoaning the muddy weather once again and declaring, 'I do wish to be in town ... the day of the season is far spent, the night of winter near at hand; and ... Barry's words are always ringing in my ears: "*Get home and light your lamp.*"' He was remembering a passage from a lecture James Barry had given in 1793, eulogizing Joshua Reynolds, in which Barry had said to the Royal Academy students and his colleagues, 'Go home from the Academy, light your lamps, and exercise yourselves in the creative power of your Art, with Homer, with Livy, and all the great characters, ancient and modern, for your companions and counsellors.'[26]

The Fawkeses also had a splendid house in town – at 45 Grosvenor Place, Belgravia, looking out across the grounds of Buckingham House (as yet unmodernized by Nash). Turner often visited the family there. He did a watercolour of the extensive view eastwards from the upstairs windows, showing Buckingham House, the twin greystone towers of Westminster Abbey and, in the misty distance of the city, the dome of St Paul's. He got involved in many Fawkes family occasions. In June 1818 he went with them to see two of their sons at school. Mrs Fawkes wrote in her diary: 'Thursday, 4th June. Went to Eton to see the boat-race. Dined and slept at Salt Hill. Little Turner came with us.' Her 'Little Turner' suggests not just Turner's lack of height but the affection in which he was held. Turner took the opportunity to make a sepia drawing of another royal residence, *Windsor Castle from Salt Hill* – a drawing which was engraved for the *Liber* but never published.[27] In June 1820 he again went with the Fawkeses and two of their daughters (and a family friend, the amateur artist Edward Swinburne) to the Eton boat-race. The following month he was with a Fawkes party that went downriver to Greenwich and then came back to tea at Grosvenor Place. As time passed, he was invited to Fawkes weddings. When their youngest, Anne, married Godfrey Wentworth, of Wooley Park, Yorkshire, on 20 June 1822, he was one of twenty-three guests who were invited to the dinner after the ceremony. Mrs Fawkes's diary: 'Anne and Godfrey married. A very long day. Had a large party to dinner. All tipsey.' In the first part of 1825 he often had Sunday dinner with the Fawkeses at their new London house in Upper Harley Street, a short walk from Queen Anne Street; he was there on 2 March

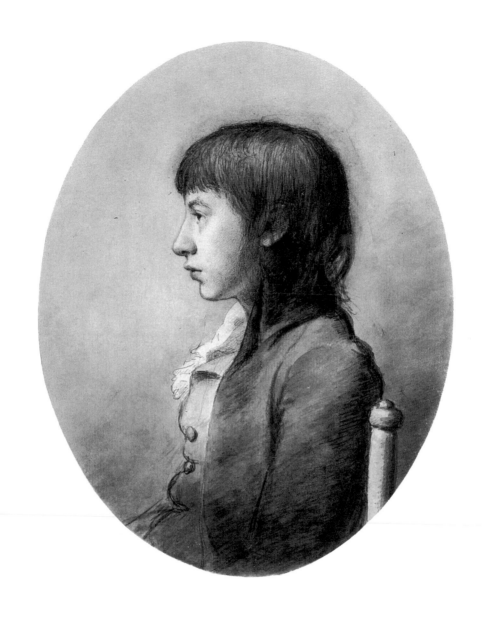

Turner, aged 17, in a portrait by George Dance, 4 August 1792

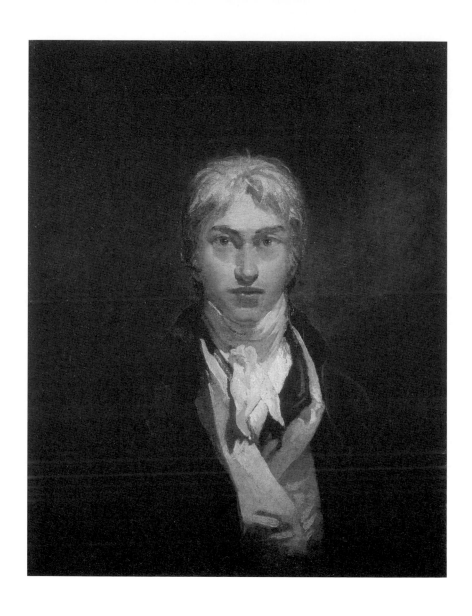

A self-portrait by Turner, aged about 24, c. 1799

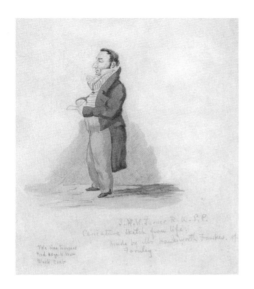

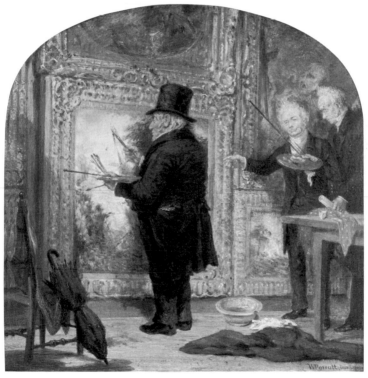

Caricature of Turner, by F. H. Fawkes, c. 1818

Turner on varnishing day, by S. W. Parrott, c. 1840

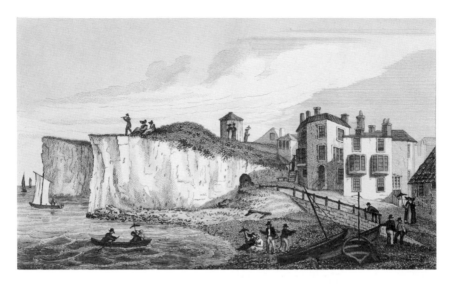

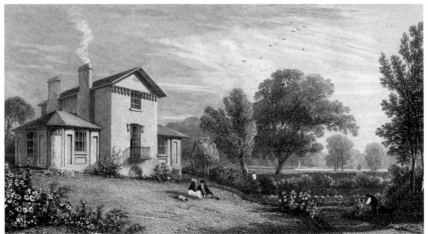

Margate: The seafront at Cold Harbour, Margate,
with Mrs Booth's bay-windowed house on right, 1820

Sandycombe Lodge, Twickenham, by W. B. Cooke
after William Havell c.1814

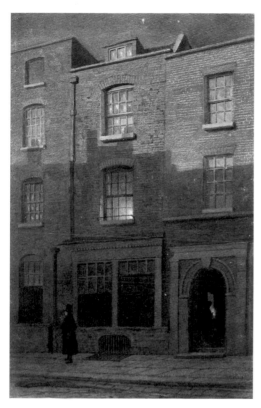

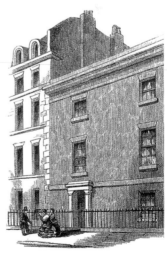

26 Maiden Lane and entrance to Hand Court, by J. W. Archer 1852

47 Queen Anne Street, from the *Art-Journal* c. 1852

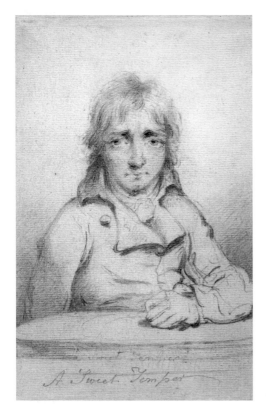

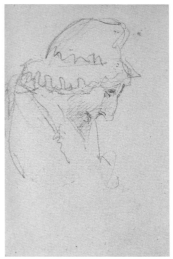

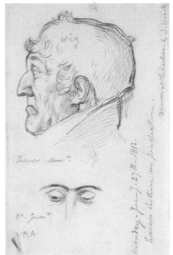

'A Sweet Temper': J. M. W. Turner as seen by his fellow-student
Charles Turner, c. 1795

A sketch by Turner of – probably – his mother, c. 1794

Turner's father, and the eyes of J. M. W. Turner, sketched at the RA
as William Turner listened to his son lecture, by John Linnell, 1812

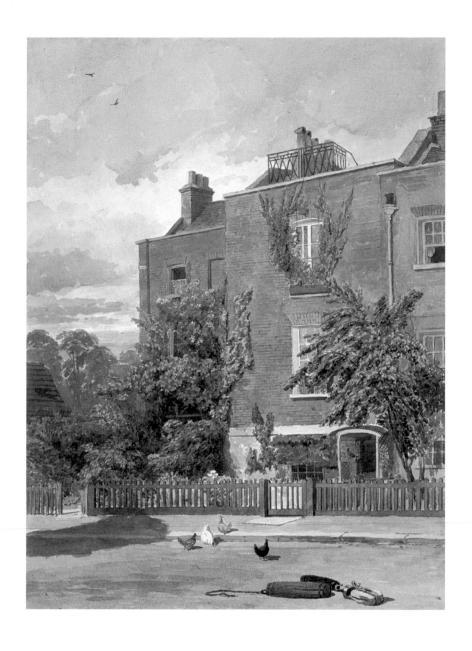

6 Davis Place, Cremorne New Road, Chelsea, by J. W. Archer, 1852

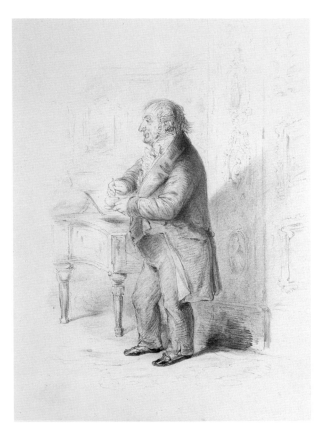

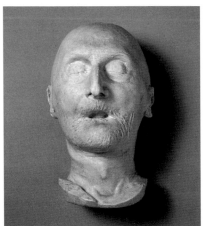

Portrait of Turner, by J. Hogarth after Count Alfred D'Orsay, 1851

Turner's death mask, attributed to Thomas Woolner, 1851

for Walter Fawkes's fifty-sixth birthday, and he was there again on 6 April for the entertainment – which included harp-playing by a four-year-old girl prodigy – after Hawksworth's marriage.[28]

Whether Fawkes and Turner ever got on to Christian-name terms is unlikely. Fawkes, the wealthy landowner, was patron as well as good friend to the professional artist. In one sketchbook of these years, the 'Farnley' of 1816–18, Turner jotted down some dimensions for 'Mr Fawke's Frame'.[29] But Fawkes was certainly a wonderful patron. He bought from Turner works large and small, impromptu studies, studio watercolours and highly worked oils. He subscribed to the print of *The Shipwreck* in 1805. In 1809 he bought the *London from Greenwich* and *Shoeburyness Fishermen*. In 1810 he bought *Lake of Geneva from Montreux*. That year Turner noted in a sketchbook[30] figures indicating that Fawkes owed him £1000, and their friendship didn't stop him recording their business dealings. For example, in late 1821 he wrote in a sketchbook the prices of pictures Fawkes had recently bought: some watercolours of Italian scenes for twenty-five guineas each; the watercolour of the Farnley oak cabinet (with opening doors) for ten guineas; a drawing of swords for five guineas.

Thomas Uwins wrote a little later: 'Fawkes buys from his own feelings. He is a man of sound good sense, with a long purse and a noble soul.'[31] Fawkes bought Turners at the Academy exhibitions and commissioned Turners while walking around Farnley with him – for instance, the watercolour showing him and his dog getting out of his carriage at the east front of the Hall. On another occasion Fawkes and one of his sons, out shooting, overtook Turner with his sketching equipment. One of the Fawkes girls told W. L. Leitch that 'they all walked a little way together, and came to a place where a dead buck was lying. The keepers had shot it, and they and their firelocks made a very striking group. Mr Fawkes said, "Turner, I wish you would make a note of that for me. It is very picturesque." Turner pulled a tiny sketchbook from his waistcoat pocket, and quickly made what Mr Fawkes desired. At night Mr Fawkes said, "Mind, Turner, don't forget to give me the sketch you made for me today."' Leitch said that Fawkes again paid ten guineas – though, as Marcus Huish noted when recording Leitch's memories, this may have been for a more important sketch he worked up from the first slight one.[32]

Fawkes's twenty-first birthday gift to his son Hawksworth in 1818 was Turner's large pellucid Dutch scene of boats and water and immense sky, *Dort, or Dordrecht, the Dort Packet Boat from Rotterdam Becalmed*. Henry Thomson, a fellow Academician, saw it at that year's exhibition and told Farington that it was 'very splendid', with such brilliant colouring 'it almost puts your eyes out'.[33] On 4 May, Farington recorded the fact that Fawkes had bought it for 500 guineas and that William Owen RA had told him Turner could paint such a picture in a month. The painting was hung in the place of honour at Farnley, over the main mantelpiece in the drawing room. Turner had been on the waterway north of Dordrecht in August of the previous year and had sketched the crowded Rotterdam ferry waiting for wind; one word, 'cabbages', was written on the sketch. In the painting, a cabbage drifts on the calm water, and the painter had put his signature on a floating log in the way that seventeenth-century Dutch painters used to do. He was obviously paying tribute to Aelbert Cuyp, whose works included *View of Dordrecht* and *The Rotterdam Ferry* – Turner's packet boat flies the same flag as Cuyp's ferry. The painting was also a reaction to his friend and 'follower' Callcott's 1816 *Pool of London*. The *Dort's* brilliance and 'raised key' seemed unnatural to a few critics but Walter Fawkes's (and Hawksworth's) choice gave great pleasure to the artist.

The private buyer was the mainstay of painters at this time. There were few individual dealers with galleries, and no great museums buying modern art. For his sales, Turner depended on a small number of wealthy landowners and country gentlemen like T. L. Parker, Sir John Leicester, John Fuller and Fawkes. And Fawkes – whom Turner recognized as such by frequent invitations to the annual Royal Academy banquet – was his patron *par excellence*, who bought more than 200 watercolours and half a dozen important oil paintings at a cost of at least £3500. In 1819, a month after Sir John Leicester had put on show eight Turner oils at his London home, Fawkes mounted an exhibition in Grosvenor Place of his own collection of watercolours. This included drawings by John Varley, Peter de Wint, David Cox and Joshua Cristall, but the majority – sixty of those displayed – were by Turner: twenty Wharfedales, forty Alpine and varied British subjects. Perhaps influenced by his wife's concern for their fine furniture and carpets, Fawkes had a warning printed on the entrance tickets, which were good for Tuesdays only: 'No admission if the weather be wet or dirty.' Visitors gave up their tickets in the front hall and were then directed up an ornate staircase, past marble statues standing in niches, to the reception rooms.[34] Eventually, six weeks after the opening, a catalogue was on hand, with a dedication from patron to painter.

For engraving in the catalogue, Turner did a frontispiece with a stone tablet showing the names of the artists and an illustration of the drawing room depicting the furniture, the carpets, the cut-glass chandelier and the pictures displayed. He embellished in watercolour the cover of Fawkes's copy. The novelty of being able to see so many Turner watercolours led to much enthusiasm in the press, and Fawkes included in the catalogue a selection of comments. One reviewer hailed Turner as the best of all living artists – 'For design, for colouring, for strength of conception, for depth of feeling and felicity of execution – for originality, truth, and variety'.[35] The artist was a frequent visitor to the exhibition. W. P. Carey, a writer on the arts, saw him there on several occasions: 'He generally came alone; and while he leaned on the centre table in the great room, or slowly worked his rough way through the mass, he attracted every eye in the brilliant crowd, and seemed to me like a victorious Roman General, the principal figure in his own triumph. Perhaps no British Artist ever retired from an exhibition of his own works, with so much reason for unmixed satisfaction, or more genuine proofs of well deserved admiration from the public.'[36]

Turner and Fawkes got on well with each other not only because of art. They shared political sympathies. Farington claimed that Fawkes held 'republican principles'.[37] Although that was an exaggeration, Fawkes was descended from Guy Fawkes, who in the early seventeenth century was an agent in the Catholic plot to blow up the Houses of Parliament; in May 1812, some years after he ceased to be a Whig member of Parliament, Fawkes spoke at the Crown and Anchor Tavern in London at an anniversary celebration of the election to Parliament of Sir Francis Burdett, an ardent reformer. Fawkes demanded the restoration of the country's constitution, 'so long and loudly extolled in theory, and so strangely perverted in practice'. The Luddite movement was gathering force at this time: the government had enacted legislation that enabled the judiciary to sentence to death those who destroyed machines. There were riots brought about by food shortages. Twelve thousand troops had recently been sent to keep order in Nottinghamshire, where looms had been wrecked. Fawkes in his speech saw revolution approaching, brought on by 'perseverance in this corrupt and inadequate system of government'.[38]

Turner's radicalism was less articulate and less consistent. The youth who had attended Mr Coleman's Methodist school in Margate, and who had grown up in Covent Garden, where various dissident printers lived and worked and members of the London Corresponding Society met, seems as an adult to have developed reformist connections. His friend Callcott's father and half-brother were supporters of the reformer Horne Tooke and the Corresponding Society. By the time he was forty Turner had become interested in the cause of Greek independence: a drawing of the mid-1810s[39] had as one of its two titles *Attalus declaring the Greek States to be free*. He had read the poems of Lord Byron, champion of Greek liberty, and made a watercolour to illustrate Byron's *The Giaour*, showing two enslaved Greek girls with a Turkish guard, which was bought by Fawkes. Another 'Byronic' watercolour which took Fawkes's fancy was that which Turner did of the field of Waterloo, the day after the battle, showing the dead and the dying, friend and foe, 'in one red burial blent'.[40]

One provocative result of Turner's Teesdale slog in August 1816 was the watercolour *Wycliffe, near Rokeby*. This showed Wycliffe Hall, which was believed to have been the birthplace of the fourteenth-century religious reformer and Bible translator John Wycliffe. John Pye, who engraved this picture for the *History of Richmondshire*, had two questions for the artist. One concerned a burst of sunlight Turner had introduced when touching a proof. Turner explained, 'That is the place where Wickliffe was born, and there is the light of the glorious Reformation.' The engraver then asked, 'But what do you mean by those large fluttering geese in the foreground?' Turner replied, 'Oh, those – those are the old superstitions which the genius of the Reformation is driving away.'[41] In another version of this conversation, Pye declared that the geese seemed large. Turner said, 'They are not geese, they are overfed priests.'[42] Turner's friends were often unsure whether he was pulling their legs or had serious allegorical intentions. In this case, it is significant that, perhaps prompted by Fawkes, he introduced into several proof stages of the print the longer title 'The Birthplace of John Wickliffe (*The Morning Star of Liberty*) near Rokeby, Yorkshire', and added a long inscription which informed the viewer of Wycliffe's work translating the Bible into English and of the religious and political persecutions which had ensued to the present day in 1822. However, for publication the title was shortened, the inscription dropped.

Another hint of sympathy with religious dissent is to be found in the watercolour of Launceston, Cornwall, which he painted in the mid-1820s for the *Picturesque Views of England and Wales* series. Launceston Castle had been used as a prison during the Cromwellian Protectorate and George Fox, shoemaker, preacher and founder of the Quakers, had been imprisoned there. The Quakers refused to take oaths, respect judges or remove their hats in court. Turner had several Quaker acquaintances, including the Edinburgh engraver William Miller. The tiny figure of a man in this picture, riding towards Launceston Castle, wears a broad-brimmed black hat of the sort Quakers wore. He is seen from the rear, boots sticking out, his light-grey horse plodding down a stony track and the long ascent to Launceston still ahead of him: nothing assertive; a diminutive pilgrim's progress; maybe even – along with the allusion to Fox – something of a miniature self-portrait. If Turner was a radical, he was a cautious one.

There were later indications that Turner felt strongly about Hungarian independence. His friend George Jones, whom he called Georgey, had a sort of namesake in Görgei, one of the leaders of the movement for a free Hungary. When Görgei betrayed his cause, Turner said to Jones, 'I shall not call you Georgey any more!'[43] This may be a better example of Turner's humour than of his political sympathies. However, more public demonstrations of where he stood came during the struggle for the passage of the great Parliamentary Reform Bill of 1832. A watercolour of *Northampton* the previous year showed the entry into that town of Lord Althorp, Lord Grey's Chancellor of the Exchequer, who was a devoted reformer and was seeking re-election. And in 1832 Turner produced a painting showing William of Nassau, the Prince of Orange, arriving in Torbay in 1688 'after a stormy passage' from the Netherlands – an action which led to the bloodless Glorious Revolution or Dutch takeover of that year.[44]

For Fawkes, passionately interested in the struggles between Parliament and Crown in the seventeenth century and in the restoration of constitutional guarantees that followed, Turner was a more than willing illustrator. During several visits to Farnley

Hall in the early 1820s he made drawings for his host's Fairfax collection. Among some 'Historical Vignettes' were several entitled 'REVOLUTION 1688'. One showed a crown, swords, a Book of Statutes and parchment scrolls inscribed 'King William's declaration for restoring the liberties of England', 'Magna Carta' and 'Bill of Rights' – the latter with a text that declared 'Parliaments ought to be Full, FREE and FREQUENT.' A great amount of close work was involved for the artist, whose heart must have been in it. And talking with Fawkes about such matters, Turner would have kept his end up; his interest in Magna Carta had been evident in his *British Itinerary* poem of 1811, in which he wrote:

> Thus native bravery, Liberty decreed,
> Received the stimulus act from Runnymead.[45]

At Farnley for Christmas 1821, Turner made sketches of other Fawkes relics: Oliver Cromwell's watch; General John Lambert's sword; and the seal of the Commonwealth. He copied various emblems and wrote down political catchphrases of that period: Bad Advisers; Arbitrary Measures; Forced Loans; the King's Will; the Law; Resistance to Oppression; Petition of Rights; and Commons Remonstrance.[46] Fawkes and Turner seemed to have thought that Britain at the present moment had similar problems, and needed a similar radical shake-up.

Fawkes also supported campaigns for the abolition of slavery and for Catholic emancipation. However, he was in no way a Jacobin: reform, not revolution, was his belief. He never ceased to be a member of the county establishment and in 1823 was appointed High Sheriff of Yorkshire – a largely ceremonial post involving the entertainment of circuit judges.

With his Scottish preoccupations, among others, Turner had not managed to get to Farnley in 1822; but in 1823 he was there when Byron's friend the writer and reformist member of Parliament John Cam Hobhouse visited. Hobhouse was amazed to find 'the most celebrated landscape painter of our time' working humbly on designs for Fawkes's Fairfaxiana collection.[47] In 1824 he arrived there on 19 November and stayed until 14 December. While at Farnley he worked on an engraver's proof for George Cooke and made a number of sketches for two watercolours. These were to be his last work for Walter Fawkes; it was to be his last visit to Farnley Hall. Fawkes had been ill a few years before; Turner in a note to Clara Wells Wheeler on 4 May 1820 explained that Fawkes was 'very unwell' and entry to the exhibition this year at Grosvenor Place was therefore restricted: he sent a private invitation for the Wellses and Wheelers. In June 1825 Fawkes was confined to bed in Upper Harley Street by his doctors, and he told his wife he knew he 'never more should get out of it'.[48] However, Turner dined with the Fawkeses twice in August before heading off on a Low Countries tour. In mid-September Fawkes's condition deteriorated, and he died on 25 October. Turner was devastated. In the midst of a long letter to Holworthy a few months later he burst out: 'Alas! my good Auld lang sine is gone … and I must follow; indeed, I feel as you say, nearer a million times the brink of eternity.'[49]

How deeply he felt the loss of Fawkes was shown in the fact that he never went to Farnley again, despite remaining in close touch with Hawksworth Fawkes. Around 1817 he had painted a swirling colour study[50] in preparation for a watercolour showing the loss of a man-of-war, maybe to be a companion of the *First Rate taking in Stores*; and at some point after Fawkes's death he inscribed the study, 'Begun for Dear Fawkes of Farnley'.[51] A decade after Fawkes died Turner was sketching in the Alps with Hugh Munro when, one day in the Aosta valley, Munro found one of his companion's partly used sketchbooks in his own luggage. Munro gave it to Turner. Turner looked it over and then, without a word, handed it back to Munro; he clearly wanted Munro to keep it. The sketchbook had a number of blank leaves, presumably why Hannah had packed it for him to bring on the tour, but those pages that had been drawn on contained sketches from his last Farnley visit. Usually he was as possessive as can be about such work. This time he didn't want reminding about all that Fawkes and Farnley had been to him.

13: The Squire of Sandycombe

A letter of 29 June 1815 to James Holworthy is tersely eloquent:

> Dear Sir
>> I am very sorry I cannot avail myself of your kindness today as I must go to Twickenham, it being my father's birthday.
>>> Yours most truly
>>> J M W Turner

Thursday morning[1]

It was in fact William Turner's seventieth birthday.

Whatever our uncertainty about the depths of Turner's affection for his mother, there is no doubt about the love he had for his father. 'The old man' had encouraged him in his ambitions. Since William Turner had retired from hairdressing he had been his son's Man Friday in picture-making, stretching his canvases, varnishing the finished products, running errands and minding the 'shop'. The house Turner built at Twickenham as his own retreat was also a retirement home for his father, where Turner senior could garden and enjoy his old age.

Turner had bought the land in May 1807, when he was living at Harley Street and Hammersmith. It was a large, triangular plot in an area called Sand Pit Close, not far from the river and Richmond Bridge. He seems to have paid £100 for the ground and hoped to put up a house for £400. Soon he was spending a good deal of time pipe-dreaming and planning. Several sketchbooks used in the years 1810–12 contain figurings about the construction and workings out of the cost of labour and materials. He drew numerous ground plans and elevations. In one sketchbook[2] he made a list: '4 Chimney pieces. 7 Best Doors – 2 got. 8 Common Doors. 12 Windows. 5 Attic

Windows – 2 got. 2 Pr. of F [French?] Window Doors – outward doors.' His favoured house design had an Italian Alpine chalet look about the roof, with broad, overhanging eaves that would create strong shadows on the walls beneath. One version had a prominently roofed porch at the rear of the house, where the ground sloped down past a pond toward the south-east – towards the rising sun. From upstairs, as a climb up a ladder or into a tree may have told him, there would be glimpses of the river.

When staying at Farnley, or travelling on tour, he continued to think about the new house. He outlined the plot; he indicated where he would plant the building; he sketched an enlarged pond. He worked out the dimensions of rooms and sketched designs for such features as an Adam-influenced mantel- and chimney-piece. Altogether he drew more than twenty small plans for his villa and nearly fifty elevations. The delights of ownership were enhanced by the thrill of being his own architect, and seeing the results. However, in architecture as in art he began with models furnished by others: pattern books; designs for ornamented cottages shown at the Royal Academy; the work of architect contemporaries. He wanted a small house that sat nicely on the sloping ground. He liked symmetry and neo-classical formality. His old mentor Dr Monro had a cottage at Fetcham with overhanging eaves and a Palladian treatment of the windows. His friend and fellow professor Soane was probably bothered for advice, though Soane would have been pleased to help: he thought highly of Turner's skills in this field; talking of Turner's architectural drawings that had been used to illustrate the Perspective lectures, he had called them 'dangerous models of excellence'.[3]

Turner seems also to have been his own contractor, hiring and organizing the tradesmen and artisans, and like most owner-builders he was apparently worn down by this. The nervous disorder and stomach weakness he had complained about to Farington on 4 November 1812 may well have been the result of having to deal with his workmen. In the sketchbooks he noted the costs of landscaping: '100 Planting. 20 Garden. 40 Pond.'[4] He reckoned up the labour costs, 'Tayler Wages. 11 weeks 17.10', which was 3s 1d a day, slightly over the three-shillings rate recommended in builders' pattern books of the time. Characteristically he estimated the interest he was forgoing on the sum spent on the property – £30 – and this, with the annual rates of £20, meant the place would lose him about

£50 a year. He eventually also concerned himself with the materials used for house-painting, jotting down what seems to be a recipe for distemper:

> 4 Pounds of Roman Vitriol
> A Kettle of Boiling Water
> 2 Pounds of Peat Ash
> ¼ of Yellow Arsenic makes a good green, for walls equal to oil[5]

The house – in brick, stucco and slate – went up in the course of 1812. In July 1813 it first appeared in the rate books. It had a small central two-storey block and on each side a small one-storey wing with rounded outer corners and sunken panels to give variety to the walls. It was smaller than many of the designs had suggested; it lacked the large roofed porch he had considered for the back, but an iron balcony outside the central French windows gave access to the garden. A 'triglyph-band' of brickwork, a sort of cornice, ran across the main gable-end from eave to eave. Inside, the rooms were small, though the domed entrance hall was nicely proportioned and detailed, with arches, fluted mouldings, and expensive glasswork for the front door. An elegant staircase curved up beneath an oval skylight, like the stairs in Soane's townhouse facing Lincoln's Inn Fields. The main sitting room, overlooking the garden, seems to have been the studio, where he painted in the morning light. The large bedroom above it (one of two rooms upstairs) also seems to have been his. The smaller bedroom at the front was his father's. In the basement were storage rooms, a little informal dining room and the kitchen. A lane ran down the long north-eastern side of the garden towards Richmond Bridge. The garden itself had many shrubs and trees – willows, chestnuts, hawthorn, an oak – in and out of which blackbirds flew.

'Solus Lodge' he first called it; it was for life without Sarah Danby – his Dido left behind. He gave this and Queen Anne Street as his addresses in the 1814 RA catalogue. His surly, reclusive urge was being indulged – even advertised. But his mood lightened; the house was finished, furnished; friends came to call. His father enjoyed life there: memories of an upbringing in a Devon village had never faded despite his years in the hubbub of Covent Garden, and in Twickenham he was closer to the soil. Turner senior may have been brought in on the debate for an alternative to 'Solus Lodge' and as chief gardener promoted the sandy hillocks round about as the basis for a new and more picturesque name. The house had become 'Sandycombe Lodge' when Turner wrote to Ambrose Johns in Plymouth in October 1814. About this time Turner's colleague William Havell sat in the garden and did a watercolour of the house for an engraving in W. B. Cooke's *Thames Scenery* that was entitled *Sandycombe Lodge, Twickenham, the Seat of JMW Turner RA.*

'The Seat'! Turner must have relished that. All sorts of impulses and influences were gathered here. Some thought Sandycombe represented his idea of a nobleman's fishing lodge. Some detected an act of homage in miniature to Alexander Pope's riverside mansion in Twickenham, demolished in 1807; he had felt strongly about its decay and disappearance, with a draft of verses about Pope's 'lost fane' appearing on the back of one of his sketch plans for Sandycombe,[6] and a lovely sad painting, *Pope's Villa During Its Delapidation*. But Sandycombe was also a statement of success: his own Thames villa, just across the river from where Sir Joshua Reynolds had had his suburban residence in Richmond. It was not far from Isleworth or indeed from Brentford, where as a small boy with great dreams he had first enjoyed these reaches of the Thames. He enjoyed as well the artistic reverberations that had already affected so many of his river works. He would not have needed telling by the *Copper-plate Magazine* that the view from Richmond Bridge was 'one of the richest landscapes that nature and art ever produced, strongly reminding the connoisseur ... of some of the best performances of Claude Lorrain'.[7]

Life at Sandycombe for father and son was largely without frills. There might be Grecian statue-niches on the staircase, and a piece by Chantrey – *Paul at Iconium* – placed above the black marble fireplace in the formal dining room, but other prominent and less fancy *objets* were models of ships in glass cases, with their sky backgrounds and sea platforms painted by their owner, who sometimes consulted the shape and rigging of the vessels when working up a marine canvas. The eldest Trimmer boy, Henry Syer Trimmer, recalled visits to Twickenham:

> I have dined with him at Sandycombe Lodge, when my father happened to drop in, too, in the middle of the day. Everything was of the most modest pretensions; two-pronged forks, and

knives with large round ends for taking up the food; not that I ever saw him so use them, though it is said to have been Dean Swift's mode of feeding himself. The table-cloth barely covered the table, and the earthenware was in strict keeping. I remember his saying one day, 'Old Dad,' as he called his father, 'have you not any wine?' Whereupon Turner senior produced a bottle of currant, [concerning] which Turner, smelling, said, 'Why, what have you been about?' The senior, it seemed, had rather overdone it with hollands [that is, spiked it with gin], and it was set aside. At this time Turner was a very abstemious person.[8]

Turner's colleague, the sculptor Francis Chantrey, was often at Sandycombe. Chantrey, who had married his cousin, a wealthy Twickenham girl, had also had a humble start, working as a grocer's boy in Sheffield; he had been bald because of an illness since he was twenty-one. Chantrey and Turner often went fishing during these visits; it seems likely that Turner continued to keep his boat at Isleworth. Other artists and friends came to call. John Pye, who engraved *Pope's Villa*, was 'feasted' with the simple fare of cheese and porter.[9] The Wellses came, bringing others. A close friend of the Wells family and collector of drawings, H. Elliott, who worked as a private secretary in the War Office, seems to have been devoted to Clara Wells. In July 1813 Elliott wrote to another of Clara's admirers, Robert Finch (who owned two Turners, a watercolour and drawing), about a water-trip up the Thames:

> one of the most delightful days I have ever spent – everything went off well, & there was no drawback to our enjoyment. Our four-oared boat just held our party of 17, consisting of the Wells's, Herbsts, Miss Perks, Turner, Wilson, Thos, Chas & Jas Wheeler, Edward & I. The six last only rowed, Wilson all the way there & back, Edw & I provided one oar between us, & the Wheelers for the other two. We dined in a beautiful part of Ham Meadows upon half-made hay, under the shade of a group of elms near the river, & had coffee and tea at Turner's new house. Miss Perks took a guitar and Edward a flute & we had a great deal of music & singing ... we had good veal & fruit pies, beef, salad, &c – but our table cloth being spread on the short grass in a lately mown field we reposed after the Roman fashion on triclinia composed of the aforesaid hay ...[10]

Elliott, a year later, described Clara as lively and unreserved and accustomed to treat her men friends like brothers. He wrote to Finch that some common people might have thought when they saw her together with a man that 'there was a flirtation between them. But so might they say of you the next half hour, of me the next, of Turner the next, of Wilson the next …' Turner undoubtedly felt close to Clara, and she to him, though of her many suitors it was Thomas Wheeler, a surgeon, whom she married. She and Turner kept in touch, but he saw her less often as time passed. Clara alluded to her feelings for Turner in a letter to Elliott in 1853: 'I am sure no two persons (man and wife excepted) ever knew each other to the heart's core better than we did – but enough, it is dangerous to open memory's flood gates.'[11] But, if it was dangerous for her, there seems a good possibility that Clara – about twenty-eight years old to Turner's forty in 1815 – was attracted to Turner, perhaps even more than he was to her.

A letter from Turner in Queen Anne Street to the Reverend Trimmer (on holiday in Southwold) of 1 August 1815, just before the artist set off for Farnley, may refer to Clara. Turner first complained that he wasn't using his Twickenham place enough; he had been forced to return to town the day he had gone out to his retreat. 'Sandycombe sounds just now in my ears as an act of folly, when I reflect how little I have been able to be there this year, and less chance (perhaps) for the next in looking forward to a Continental excursion, & poor Daddy seems as much plagued with weeds as I am with disappointments, that if Miss — would but wave bashfulness, or – in other words – make an offer instead of expecting one – the same might change occupiers …'[12] But, more likely, the unnamed woman was interested in taking over Sandycombe from its proprietor, then suffering the not uncommon worries of a second-home owner who is too often prevented from getting to his little place in the country.

Yet Sandycombe came into its own on at least one occasion for entertaining some of his fellow Academicians. Turner was a stalwart member of the Academy Club, whose subscription cost two guineas a year and had gatherings at which red wine negus was the principal drink. (Joseph Nollekens used to steal the nutmegs needed for the negus on these get-togethers. One day, when the second bowl of negus was being made, the nutmegs were found to be missing. Rossi asked Nollekens to see if they had fallen under the table, at which 'Nollekens actually went crawling beneath upon his hands and knees pretending to look for them, though at that very time they were in his waistcoat pocket.')[13] The Club frequently took to the water, downriver to Greenwich for a whitebait dinner in May, or upriver for a summer excursion. In July 1819 its members went afloat from Westminster Bridge in the Board of Ordnance's barge or shallop with ten professional oarsmen to do the rowing; the weather, starting bleak, improved. Farington recorded:

> The river was a scene of much gaiety from the display of City Barges and Pleasure Boats. We stopped at Barnes, and in the boat had a loaf and cheese while the Boatmen had fare in the Inn. We then proceeded to the Eel Pie House at Twickenham, where we landed, a little after 3 o'clock and about 4 we sat down to excellent fare brought from the Freemasons Tavern under the management of a Clever Waiter.
>
> We dined in the open air at one table and removed to another to drink wine and eat fruit. Everything went off most agreeably.
>
> Before 7 o'clock we again embarked and rowed down the river, the tide in our favour, and a full moon. Turner and Westmacott were very loquacious on their way back ...[14]

When the Club failed to organize a jaunt in 1821, Turner stepped into the gap. He sent out invitations. That to Abraham Cooper RA, postmarked 7 August 1821, read:

> Dear Sir
> The *second* meeting of the Pic-nic-Academical Club will take place at Sandycombe Lodge, Twickenham, on Sunday next, at about three o'clock. Pray let me know in a day or two that the Sec[retar]y may get something to eat.
> Yours truly,
> Jos. Mallord Wm. Turner
> For map, turn over to the other side.

(His sketch map showed Sandycombe in relation to the roads leading to it from Twickenham, Isleworth and Richmond Bridge.[15])

He saw a lot of the Trimmers, who were then four miles away at Heston; Henry Scott Trimmer was the vicar there from 1804 until he died in 1859. His son Henry Syer Trimmer was encouraged in his drawing efforts by Turner – the vicar, as an amateur painter, would have been happy about this, though the boy preferred drawing pictures of armed men, 'all swords and plumes, men slashing and horses kicking'. Turner suggested there wasn't much call for military painting, and later dissuaded him from becoming an artist.[16] As already noted, the elder Trimmer was a grandson of Joshua Kirby, friend of Gainsborough and writer on perspective. After visiting Osterley House to look at the painting collection with the Trimmers, Turner in the evening drew from memory a sketch of a Gainsborough they had seen, and also, a sketch of a woman gathering watercress whom they had seen on the way, on which he wrote '*Checked blue apron*'. 'These', said Mrs Trimmer, seeing the finished drawings, 'are for me.' 'If you take them,' Turner said, 'I must do two more.' But according to Henry Syer, and despite Thornbury's remark that Turner was 'by no means a member of "the give-away family"',[17] Turner actually did give the drawings to Mrs Trimmer, and made copies for his essential store.[18] Moreover, on another occasion Turner did a watercolour of two small cousins of the Trimmer children playing on the floor, which he gave to the parents of the children he had drawn.

Young Trimmer thought Turner liked coming to Heston to fish and talk with his father and also to be close to his old haunts at Brentford. He was remembered for standing in the vicarage garden under his umbrella for two days in pouring rain, fishing with a long rod in a small pond, 'without even a nibble'.[19] While staying at Heston, Turner also respected his friend's occupation and went to church. (This was a change from his behaviour in 1798, when he refused to go to church when staying with the Reverend Robert Nixon, since he was involved in painting.) Henry Syer thought a church interior in the *Liber* was based on the Heston church, where Turner pondered light, shade and architectural detail while listening to the sermon. For a short time he gave the Reverend Trimmer drawing lessons in return for instruction in Latin and Greek; the vicar said Turner 'sadly floundered in the verbs, and never made any progress – in fact, he could not spare the time'.[20]

From Heston, there were sketching expeditions. Henry Syer remembered going out with his father and Turner in Turner's gig, pulled by the temperamental Crop-ear. 'His sketching apparatus was under the seat ... We went at a very steady pace, for Turner painted much faster than he drove. [Perhaps this was particularly true after the Farnley overturning.] He said, if when out sketching you felt at a loss, you had only to turn round or walk a few paces farther, and you had what you wanted before you.'[21] On one excursion Henry Syer went with his father, Turner and Henry Howard to Penn, 'all of them in search of the picturesque ... We came to a halt in a grove or copse where luxuriated wild flowers in profusion. It was a charming day; and, though so many "years bygone", I can now see vividly before me my father and Howard, both standing legs a-straddle, and Turner at a little distance in a ditch, all hard at work at the aesthetical. After a while Turner emerged from his retreat with a capital water-colour, with which Howard and my father were in raptures. He said he got into the ditch to avoid the sun, but Howard whispered to my father that it was to avoid showing his *modus operandi*.'[22] Certainly it was unlike Turner to avoid the sun.

As for Crop-ear, the old bay was variously described as a horse, a pony and a cross between the two. Turner used to say proudly 'it would climb a hill like a cat and never get tired'. However, friends noted that, although he was attached to his model for the horses in *Frosty Morning*, 'the restive creature was always at issue with him. Once, when the pony was ill, Turner prescribed for him himself, having a great objection to farriers' bills. In struggling one night to free himself from his toils, for he had to be fastened up with chains, he got strangled. Turner grieved over him sincerely, and gave him decent burial in his garden.'[23]

The Sandycombe garden was large enough to handle the interment of Crop-ear and cope with much besides. Blackbirds nested in the bushes and small boys crept in to steal their eggs. Turner chased the boys away; they took their revenge by calling him 'Blackbirdy'.[24] The young intruders may also have introduced a young pike or 'jack' into the garden to eat the trout that Turner carried back in a can from the Old Brent for stocking purposes. The pond had figured in his dreams of Sandycombe, recurring on the site plans among the house designs. As extended, the pond was roughly square in shape, the home of many water-lilies as well as fish. In a sketchbook memo he set down the cost of planting trees and digging out the pond at £100 – a lot more than the £40 he had originally estimated for pond works. Another memo[25] suggests that he may also have broken down and *bought* for £2 some trout to put in it.

Turner's father loved the garden. There, according to the Trimmers, he was to be found at work on many days 'like another Laertes'.[26] Not on Tuesdays, though, for that was market day in Brentford, 'when he was often to be seen trudging home with his weekly provisions in a blue handkerchief, where I have often met him, and asking him after Turner, had answer, "Painting a picture of the Battle of Trafalgar".'[27] The old man looked very much like his son, 'particularly as to the nose', and being short, thin and common-looking; but was chattier and more cheerful than JMWT.[28] He was less fond of his son's willows, which, he complained, made the property look like an osier bed. The retired hairdresser kept the grass trimmed, grew vegetables for home consumption and tried to hold the plaguey weeds at bay. By one account, he also did some empire-building: he 'made great exertions to add to his son's estate at Sandycombe by running out little earthworks in the road and then fencing them round. At one time there was a regular row of these fortifications, which used to be called "Turner's Cribs". One day, however, they were ruthlessly swept away by some local authority.'[29] On Sundays Turner senior was a regular attender at Twickenham parish church.

On top of his provisioning and gardening duties, the old man still had responsibilities in town in spring and early summer, when he went up daily to look after the Queen Anne Street gallery. Sometimes, in fine weather, he made his way on foot, as Farington discovered on 24 May 1813, when he and Constable called to look at Turner's exhibition for that season. 'Turner's father was there, who told me that he had walked from Twickenham this morning, eleven miles; his age 68. In two days the last week he said he had walked 50 miles.'[30] Like his son, William Turner was, in Cyrus Redding's term, 'a good pedestrian'. Occasionally he took the Twickenham–London coach, but the cost of this pained him. One day a friend who knew how disconsolate he was made by the expense encountered him in Queen Anne Street looking particularly happy. Asked about his good mood, William Turner explained that he had found an inn near Sandycombe where the market-gardeners baited their horses. He had made friends with one. 'Now, for a glass of gin a day, he brings me up in his cart on top of the vegetables.' The Covent Garden connection may have helped.

In 1812 the old man had written in his clumsy hand to a nephew in Devon:

> Dear Nephew I did not have your letter till the 25 was in Queen Ann street 10 Days   Return here the Day you wrote your letter   I came to town yesterday but Could not Return as it is so far   your

> Uncle J and Wife was very well yesterday   I have not heard some
> time since that Brother Price wife was dead   Jonathan sent to
> Joshua saying nothing would give him more pleasure for to se[e]
> all his Brothers. But at one time as he thought you would be their
> as to Mathews the[y] are Brush makers not Merchants   I went
> to Cartwright & Co in Hatten gardens 22 the[y] said that the[y]
> might be 30 next week   I am glad you are all well as we are Ditto I
> remain yours W. Turner.

Foggy writing ran in the family.

In 1821, he wrote from Sandycombe to the same nephew. His penmanship had improved in the intervening nine years of being factotum to his son.

> Dear Nephew I cannot come to London haveing so short notice   I
> have seen the Coach this morning and I find the[y] Change Horses
> at the Kings Arms Hounslow   the coachman Comes Every Day
> but Sundays   on Friday I will be at the Kings Arms Ready to see
> please God I am till then yours W. Turner.
>   If you dont on Friday send me word I only Read yours Last
> Night[31]

In September 1826 the old man was evidently worried about his son, who was travelling on the Continent; he knew young William planned to come through Ostend, where the powder magazine had exploded, killing several, and, not having had a letter from him since the explosion, feared for his safety. He evidently talked about his worries, contriving – as the artist wrote to Holworthy afterwards – 'to stir up others in the alarm'. But it seems that a provincial newspaper, the Hull *Advertiser*, reporting the explosion in sensational fashion, had first spread the concern, perhaps to the Fawkes family, who enquired of Turner senior – though the news didn't get as far as the Holworthys in Derbyshire.

Father and son shared a number of interests. There is no evidence that Turner senior did any of the simple surgical jobs, like bloodletting, that barbers were accustomed to, but he was – like JMWT – attached to herbal remedies. Turner wrote to his friend Wells in September 1823:

> My Daddy cannot find the recipe, but I have puzzled his recollection
> out of two things … Poppies and Camomole … ½ a cup of poppy
> seeds to a good handfull of Camomile flowers simmer'd from a

Quart of Water to a pint in a glazed vessel ... and used by new
flannel as hot as can be ... alternately one piece soaking, while the
other is applied ... to keep up equal warmth.[32]

What Wells needed the compress for – a sprain, a bad back? – we
aren't told.

When he was twenty-three, Turner had been given directions by
Miss Narraway for making an ointment for cuts that he noted in
a sketchbook.[33] In the 'Chemistry' sketchbook of 1813,[34] he wrote
down a way of tackling the Maltese plague. In verses jotted in the
'Woodcock Shooting' sketchbook of 1810–12,[35] the word 'oculist'
occurs several times, suggesting that he may have been consulting
a specialist for sight problems. Turner seems to have had another
sort of problem in 1820, which led to him calling off his summer
tour; he may have snapped an Achilles tendon. 'I only come to town
once a week,' he wrote from Twickenham to W. B. Cooke, 'owing
to my accident and rebuildings'.[36] (The rebuilding was of his gallery
in Queen Anne Street.) But by this time concern for his father's
health was generally larger than for his own. Sandycombe had the
reputation of being damp, and 'Poor Daddy', as Turner called him
in a letter to Trimmer,[37] was often catching cold. The old man was
now his only family; as a time approached when his father might not
be around, the son may have begun to realize how valuable was his
father's pride in him. At Sandycombe they lived like two bachelors
or two widowers.

Did such a life suit the younger man? His friend Trimmer believed
that Turner's domestic arrangements were 'founded on the models
of the old masters'.[38] The Old Masters were not well known for
their marriages; it was almost an academic convention that such ties
and the painting life did not sit easily together; housekeepers and
mistresses (who were perhaps models) were to be preferred. A happy
marriage could swamp your creative powers. Worrying about how to
support a wife and children could be distracting or destructive. Wives
went mad – think of Mary Turner. As time would show, getting
married didn't help poor Haydon. Sir Joshua – the great role-model
– had never bothered with marriage (a long-suffering sister and then
a niece looked after him for a number of years). There were also
dangers in marrying too well: Nathaniel Dance gave up painting
altogether on wedding a rich widow. The engraver J. T. Willmore
once heard Turner declare: 'I hate married men. They never make

any sacrifices to the Arts, but are always thinking of their duty to their wives and families, or some rubbish of that sort.'[39] At a certain point, too, one gets used to the life one has been leading and fears to change it.

In a letter to Holworthy of 4 December 1826 Turner referred to arrangements that made a visit, and angling, difficult: 'I am fixt by Exhibition's log; in the summer I have to oil my wings for a flight, but generally flit too late for the trout, and so my round of time. I am a kind of slave who puts on his own fetters from habit, or more like what my Derbyshire friends would say an Old Batchelor who puts his coat on always one way.'[40]

Another letter to the well-married Holworthy followed in April the next year, when Turner was no longer in Twickenham. He wrote: 'What may become of me I know not what, particularly if a lady keeps my bed warm, and last winter was quite enough to make singles think of doubles.'[41] Sandycombe may have been absorbing enough for a while, but he seems to have been tiring of the entirely single life. As we shall see, after a stay in Margate, he was thinking of 'doubles', maybe not for twenty-four hours a day, seven days a week, but at least for keeping his bed warm.

At first, while he was the master of Sandycombe, his painting output stayed high, but in the second half of his proprietorship, from 1819 to 1826, the production of oils slackened. Chantrey told Farington in April 1821 that 'Turner has no picture for the Exhibition this year, and ... has not a single commission for a picture at present.' He added, alluding to [Turner] being in good circumstances, "He can do very well without any commission."'[42] Travel to new fields was taking up much time, and there was his work for the printmakers, but he may have felt the need for new patronage. In 1819 he had exhibited a grand painting that exploited his local scene and seemed to be making a push for royal favour. This was *England: Richmond Hill, on the Prince Regent's Birthday*. It showed the winding Thames; Twickenham (and Sandycombe) hidden in the trees on the further bank; a distant field with a game of cricket going on; and, in the foreground, on the summer-shadowed slope under well-spaced tall trees, a genteel crowd of partying people, seemingly borrowed *en masse* from Watteau. Turner presumably knew that the Prince Regent had come from Kew and ridden up Richmond Hill on 10 August 1818, two days before his birthday; and it so happened that the Prince's 'official' birthday and name-day was St George's Day, 23 April, which was of course Turner's birthday. A rapport, therefore, and why not a connection?

The picture was king-size – roughly six feet by eleven. Turner attached some lines from the 'Summer' section of Thomson's *Seasons* that precede some possibly more appropriate lines about 'the matchless vale of Thames; / Fair-winding up to where the muses haunt / In Twit'nam's bowers ...'[43] A few viewers found Turner's pastoral hymn to England a bit unEnglish. The writer for *Bell's Weekly Messenger* (16 May 1819) admired the painting but qualified his praise: 'The distance, the foreground, the trees and the figures are all Italian. On Richmond Hill, and on such a day, John Bull with his dame, with the rustic lads and lasses of the village, sporting under the sturdy oak, would have been more characteristic of England.'[44] But this was to request a different nostalgia. Turner had not yet been to Italy and was – if not simply reverting to his ideal Claudean scenery – perhaps looking forward to that country in paint.

Another large picture (over five feet by eight) exhibited that year had different princely associations: *Entrance of the Meuse: Orange-Merchant on the Bar, going to Pieces; Brill Church bearing S.E. by S., Masensluys E. by S.* In this the painter looked at events from water-level; the viewer feels as if he is about to be soaked by the wind-against-tide chop. Some scavengers in a pulling boat in the foreground are fishing up oranges – part of the cargo of the wrecked Dutch sailing-vessel Turner has placed so precisely (with compass bearings) on a shoal and burdened (in lieu of its spilt cargo) with one of his puns, the ruling house of the Netherlands being that of Orange-Nassau, which at this time was having financial problems. And there may be other more personal associations here. A duck, if not a mallard, is flying out of the picture to the right. The elderly man who is improbably standing up in the boat, leaning slightly forward and to the left, without holding on to anything despite the pitching and lurching of the craft in the short seas, has that high-foreheaded, gnomish, Punch-like look that we have seen before, and which has a 'familiar' feeling – something of the Linnell sketch of William Turner from 1812. The old man must have made a handy model on occasion. The act of standing up in the boat may be a reference to Turner senior's 'habit of nervously jumping up on his toes every two or three minutes ... which rather astonished strangers'.[45] But the picture, one of Turner's most marvellous seascapes, is also a tribute to the old Dutch painters, with a vast sky – more than three-quarters of the canvas – like that in a Philips de Koninck, though with clouds, which Turner had been collecting in various sketchbooks, that are all his own.

One seascape that was less successful was the result of the former Prince Regent, now King George IV, finally bestowing a commission on Turner – which kept him busy in late 1823. This was the *Battle of Trafalgar* which the Reverend Trimmer heard about from Turner's father when meeting him on the way home from Brentford market, and which those in the art world knew was to be part of a scheme for displaying great British victories in St James's Palace, along with a de Loutherbourg of the Glorious First of June 1794 naval battle. Lawrence, royal portrait painter, as already noted, had helped get him the job. Turner did his usual thorough research and borrowed sketches of ships from John Christian Schetky. At eight and a half feet by twelve, it was the largest picture he ever painted, and he laboured hard over it. It succeeded in showing what a confusing bloody mess a naval battle could be – sailors drowning, waves tinged with blood, smoke billowing, spars and sails and rigging falling. As with his earlier picture of the *Death of Nelson* he wanted to compress the events of the battle into a single moment; he showed Nelson's pre-battle signal 'England expects ...' still flying, while fragments of Nelson's motto *Palman Qui Meruit Ferat* loom mysteriously in the sea. While the battle is still going on, some sailors have their hats raised in signals of victory.

Bits of the picture are indeed successful: in the dark lower-left-hand corner, beyond a buoyant stump of a mast, in a ship's launch collecting the wounded a man stands, in black silhouette; disembodied hands reach from the surrounding water as if to hang on to an immense horizontal Union flag. But the main impression is that the *Victory* is a vast piece of scenery that has been trundled into the middle of a stage. The tumbled-together masts and sails look like so many tangled sheets and collapsed laundry-poles.

Very few people liked it. Haydon heard from a member of Parliament that 'the Government was not satisfied' with Turner's performance, and he thought that the chances of getting further state sponsorship for historical painting had been damaged.[46] George Jones, painting two military scenes, worked alongside Turner for nearly a fortnight at the Palace, giving their pictures finishing touches, and said that Turner 'was criticized and instructed daily by the naval men about the Court, and during eleven days he altered the rigging to suit the fancy of each seaman, and did it with the greatest good-humour'.[47] Some naval persons didn't like Turner's scheme of showing different moments of the battle all rolled together. Thomas Hardy, Nelson's captain, declared the picture looked 'more like a street scene than a battle'.[48] An old Greenwich pensioner said, 'It's more like a brickfield. We ought to have had Huggins' – Huggins being a more or less competent painter of ships.[49] Turner told H. A. J. Munro that the Admiralty made him spoil the picture and the only sensible observations were from the Duke of Clarence, a navy man, later King William IV. The Duke, however, is said by another informant to have made 'as a sailor' some disagreeable observations, to which Turner replied rather roughly. 'The Duke finished the conversation by saying, "I have been at sea the greater part of my life, Sir, you don't know who you are talking to, and I'll be damned if you know what you are talking about."'[50] According to Munro, 'Turner once invited Holworthy and myself to dine with him at Greenwich [where in 1829 both Turner's and de Loutherbourg's pictures were relegated from St James to the retired seamen's hospital]. We, after dinner, visited the Hall and were looking at this painting, a Pensioner came up and told us it was like a carpet. "That is the one to look at," pointing to the Loutherbourg. I turned to look at Turner who was gone.'[51]

Although Turner on and off considered Sandycombe an act of folly, and worried about keeping it, such anxieties did not stop him from expanding his Twickenham empire. In the summer of 1818 as a Twickenham property owner he was awarded a small piece – about an eighth of an acre – of an area of common ground that was being enclosed. In August he acquired more of the land: three adjoining plots of 'Freehold Land situate and being on and late part of the waste called Twickenham Little Common'.[52] These plots totalled nearly an acre and were bounded by the Hanworth–Twickenham road on the north and the Hampton road on the south. At this time he was Chairman and Treasurer of the Artists' General Benevolent Institution – he got his friend Walter Fawkes to become a member in 1816, paying annual dues of five guineas – and he was thinking more and more of how to help artists in distress. He had talked to Farington on this subject at an Academy Club dinner in March 1818. Soon he began to think of building a college or almshouse for 'decayed English artists' on this land. 'To his intimate friends he constantly talked of the best mode of leaving property for the use of the unsuccessful,' said his friend George Jones, adding, after noting Turner's occasional closeness in small matters, that he loved to save and accumulate for that one great object.[53] He also owned a small meadow just north-west of Sandycombe, which he had bought at the same time as the Sandycombe site and from the same person: 'a piece or parcel of Copyhold or Customary Land ... at the North West End of ... Holloway Shot'.[54]

This may have been the land he sold to the South Western Railway Company some years later when they were extending their network from Richmond to Windsor. The railway company wanted only a tiny portion of Turner's land, but the artist got the Duke of Northumberland's land steward John Williams to handle the matter for him, and the company was talked into buying half an acre. Williams, wrote Alaric Watts, 'exerted himself so effectively that he obtained, to the astonishment of Mr Turner, who had not the remotest idea of the Railway value of land, £550 for it. "But," said Mr Turner, after recovering from his surprise, "the expenses will, I suppose, swallow up a considerable part of it." "Not a shilling," said Mr Williams, "beyond a small fee to the surveyor; the company will pay the rest."' Turner 'expressed himself highly satisfied, muttered a few thanks, and parted without any further recognition of the service'.[55]

He was fifty in 1825, the year his friend Fawkes and his professorial colleague Henry Fuseli died, and he had begun to think in even greater detail about what should be done with his wealth and possessions on his own death. The year before, feeling the need for order, he had got out all his sketchbooks and labelled, numbered and sometimes named them. (The most up to date was that used in the summer of 1824[56] for sketches of the piling works for the new London Bridge.) His ties with the past needed confirming even as individuals who had been of early help slipped away. His old adviser Joseph Farington had died on the next-to-last day of 1821, falling downstairs from the gallery of a church in Didsbury, near Manchester. He had also been affected by the death of his uncle Joseph Marshall – his Brentford guardian – at Sunningwell near Abingdon in June 1820. From him Turner inherited part of the property once owned by his mother's grandfather, Joseph Mallord. This was a share in four small houses in Wapping that would have been his mother's, had she been alive and competent. These were in New Gravel Lane, near Eastern Dock, one of the new docks into which ships could lock from the tidal Thames and which were changing the nature of cargo-handling.

Turner seems to have got the job of looking after this little estate, making sure the rents were collected for the benefit of himself and his co-heirs. In an 1821 sketchbook he kept a copy of a receipt for the annual rent he had received for 7 and 8 New Gravel Lane from one Isaac Hodgson. Turner sent on shares of the proceeds to his co-beneficiaries – once in 1822 using W. B. Cooke to deliver £20 to Joseph Marshall's widow. At some point the ownership of the houses seems to have been divided, 9 and 10 New Gravel Lane becoming the property of his cousins Henry and Eleanor Harpur. (Henry Harpur served as one of Turner's solicitors; George Cobb was another.) Turner took on 7 and 8 New Gravel Lane and a few years later consented to them being converted into an inn, the Ship and Bladebone; in 1843, its tenant, Thomas Farrell, sent Turner a receipt for £10 which Turner had paid for repairs to its roof.

Owning the freehold of a Wapping pub gave Turner an excuse for jaunts downriver to the docks, to look at shipping, talk to the mariners and stevedores and have a drink. In later years, it also – according to Thornbury, who heard about it from John Ruskin – allowed him sometimes to 'wallow' at weekends. Being Turner, he took his sketchbook with him. Ruskin eventually came across drawings Turner had supposedly done at Wapping, of 'sailors' women ... in every posture of abandonment'.[57]

Certainly the Ship and Bladebone would have given Turner a good base for Wapping research; but just how depraved a hostelry it was is open to question. The twenty-one-year lease (at a rent of £50 a year) which Thomas Farrell had signed, under bond, bound him 'to conduct the place in orderly fashion so as not to imperil the licence'.[58] More innocent drawings possibly of Wapping origin are sketches of mudlarks he did in 1823–4.[59] Even if he did spend a good deal of time there, he wasn't shy of letting the connection be known. He took an open interest in the wording of leases. George Cobb, who acted for him in connection with leases in 1827 and 1831, also visited Wapping on Turner's behalf. In 1827, Turner tried to ensure that work was done on the Wapping properties to make them good to the end of the leases and had his friend Thomas Allason, a surveyor and architect, look them over to see what needed doing. The Ship and Bladebone was still in his possession at his death, though by then it was, like his gallery, in a run-down condition. Indeed, at that stage it was 'unsafe and unoccupied'.[60]

Turner continued to amass property. He eventually had his leasehold houses in Harley Street and Queen Anne Street, the Wapping houses, the Twickenham Common land, the Lee Common cottage and orchard he had bought in 1810, and four acres of marshland in Barking, Essex, which was let to a Mr Choat for £10 a year. But despite an evident desire to keep a portion of his wealth safe in bricks, mortar and land, not all his property investments were a success. J. W. Archer wrote:

> He would occasionally look in at the auction mart by the Bank; and on one of those occasions it occurred to him that two houses were about to be knocked down at a very low figure; he bid, and got them; but on going to view his purchase, he found them situated in Little Clarendon Street, Somers Town – a low back street, whose tenants frequently flit before quarter day [when rents were due]; and he learned, moreover, that the cheapness of the houses was much more than balanced by the heavy ground rent of £12 each. Turner now called upon an associate engraver of the Royal Academy, and took him into counsel as to how he should manage to transfer his purchase to somebody else. His friend undertook to try what could be done, and went to one W——, who held a large amount of similar property in the neighbourhood; but on stating his object, the man of tenements, instead of making an offer, said:
>
> 'I have no objection to take the houses off the gentleman's hands; but what is he willing to offer me for doing so?'
>
> What he paid to be let off his bargain, the writer knows not; but he has little doubt that it was a good round sum.[61]

At any rate, Turner didn't add the worry of being a Somers Town landlord to that of owning a low dive in Wapping. He had trouble enough with some of his tenants. In 1821, there were problems with Benjamin Young, a dentist, who was renting part of his Harley Street domain. Turner asked Holworthy to go with him to 'Hick's Hall', the Clerkenwell sessions house, to give evidence that a second notice had been properly served on Young. In 1827 he was having continued difficulty with one Smith, whom he had 'long ago desired' his father and William Marsh, his stockbroker, to remove from one of his properties.[62] In 1840 there were problems concerning an agreement about a 'frontage' and boundaries with a Mr Wally Strong, and Cobb, the solicitor, was told by Turner to 'watch him … I will not be charged for his ifs and ands'. Strong, it appeared to the angry artist, wanted 'to swell the cost of the lease for him some how or other'.[63] Like many property owners, Turner vacillated between the joys of possession and the pains of administration and maintenance. But his Micawberish habits could be suddenly thrown aside in favour of an extensive magnanimity; at his death, it was found that he hadn't bothered to pursue a tenant for several years of unpaid rent.

Eventually in 1826 he sold Sandycombe Lodge. Rather than the 'Discarded London' he had apostrophized in verses at the beginning of his Sandycombe experience, he decided to discard Twickenham.[64] In a letter to Holworthy in May 1826 he refers to 'us poor Londoners',[65] and first and last he *was* a Londoner. As he rationalized it, the Sandycombe garden had become too much for his father, who was eighty-one that year. The sale didn't please the old man, but Turner went ahead anyway; he may not have wanted to leave him there so much by himself or have him walking the long distance up to town, if his cheap rides failed. This filial concern did not prevent him from continuing to keep his father busy – 'latterly', the young Trimmer noted, 'his son's willing slave',[66] as the various commands from East Cowes showed. Writing to Holworthy in January 1826 to thank him for a turkey, which father and son had evidently eaten together, Turner said, 'Daddy being now released from farming thinks of feeding, and said its richness proved good land and good attention to domestic concerns.'[67]

Sandycombe was sold for £500 'of lawful money' to a retired haberdasher, Joseph Todd of Clapham; this sum was less than he had put into it. Turner looked at the fishpond for the last time. But before leaving Twickenham, he made some trips on the river, revisiting the sites of old sketches and pictures, and making a few more – valedictions, as it were.[68] Yet there was still going to be life on the river to come for him, closer to town.

14: Southern Light

Like Aeneas, Turner finally found Italy. As we have seen, he had been painting Italy before he got there: classical ruins; homages to Claude; and tributes to Richard Wilson, such as *Diana and Callisto* of 1796 and *Tivoli and the Roman Campagna, after Wilson* of 1798. He had wanted to go to Italy in 1816 and expressed his disappointment when he told Holworthy that, as well as Yorkshire being soaked with rain, Italy was 'deluged, Switzerland a wash-pot ... [and] all chance of getting over the Simplon or any of the other passes now vanished like the morning mist'.[1] Italy stayed in his mind as he read Byron's poetry and copied bits of the Reverend J. J. Eustace's *Tour through Italy* of 1813 and made commissioned watercolours to be engraved for James Hakewill's *Picturesque Tour of Italy*. One might have thought, from a watercolour he did in 1817, that he already had been there. The watercolour, which Fawkes bought, showed Vesuvius erupting, full of fire and colour, though it was based on someone else's drawing. His colleagues kept urging him to go. Lawrence, who was in Rome in the summer of 1819, doing portraits of princes of the Church and hanging around the Duchess of Devonshire, wrote to Farington on 2 July, with the advice that he press Turner to get cracking: 'His genius would here be supplied with new Materials, and entirely congenial with it He has an Elegance, and often a Greatness of Invention, that wants a scene like this for its free expression ...'[2]

In fact, Turner – now forty-four – had already decided to go. He set off on the last day of July 1819, and marked the occasion by starting a diary:

> Left Dover at 10 arr. Calais at 3 in a Boat from the Packet Boat.
> beset as usual. began to rain next morn on the setting out of the
> Dil[igence] Conversation in the diligence the Russe 2 Frenchman

and 2 English Cab. 3 Engl. Russe great par Example the Emperor Alexander too ... the French tres bon zens but the English everything at last was bad, Pitt the cause of all, the Kings death and fall and Robespierre their tool. Raind the whole way to Paris. Beaumont sur Oise good[3]

And that was far as the 'diary' got. The grind of travelling took over. He was two days in getting to Paris. From there he went via the valley of the Yonne to Sens, Auxerre and Lyon, and thence to Chambéry and Lanslebourg and over the Mont Cenis pass. Early starts, long days in the coaches; bad inns, poor food, awful beds. But the Alps, wonderful as ever, as always allowed one to encounter what Byron called 'throned Eternity in icy halls / Of cold Sublimity'.[4] Then down to Lake Como, Milan, Verona and Venice – drawing, drawing, drawing during his short stay there. On to Bologna, Rimini, Ancona and over the Apennines – the further south, the more brilliant the light – sketching the streets, squares and gateways of the towns, his fellow-travellers waiting for a diligence or *vettura*, the hillsides with villages and towers. South of Ancona he noted among his sketches colours that reminded him of his heroes:

> color of the Hill Wilson Claude the olives the light of these when the Sun shone grey [turn?]ing the Ground redish green Gray now ... to Purple the Sea quite Blue, under the Sun a Warm Vapour from the Sun Blue relieving the Shadows of the Olive Tree dark while the foliage Light or the whole when in shadow a quiet Grey. Beautiful dark Green yet warm. the middle Trees get Bluish in parts for distance. the aquaduct redish the foreground Light grey in shadow[5]

Now that the long wars were over, Rome was once again luring many foreign artists as visitors and residents, particularly the English and Germans. But Turner was his usual somewhat secretive self, staying in the Palazzo Poli and quietly getting on with the job. From the moment he arrived he was out sketching the ruins and prospects of the city from the various vantage points; he drew the works of art, statues as well as paintings. From the Palazzo Poli, he sketched the extravagantly Baroque Fontana di Trevi with its gods and sea monsters.[6] He determinedly filled sketchbook after sketchbook; he made several hundred larger drawings. His friend Chantrey was also in town, as fond of society as ever, and rather worried because Turner was being stand-offish – Chantrey didn't know where Turner was lodging. However, he was seen at the Venetian Academy of Painting in Rome on 15 November, at an occasion to which Chantrey, Lawrence, Jackson and Thomas Moore, the poet, also went, with the fashionable sculptor Canova, and later in the day at the Academy of St Luke, where Canova had put him up for honorary membership, albeit in his letter of recommendation spelling his name *Touner*. Lawrence had written to Canova to introduce Turner – England's 'finest landscape painter' – and asked Canova to be patient, as Turner was 'unacquainted with the Italian language'. Lawrence, Turner and Canova shared an interest in the Venetian masters: Titian, Tintoretto and Veronese – though ultimately Turner preferred Tintoretto.[7]

Turner was spotted on the tower of the Capitol one stormy day when the Princess of Denmark and a friend of Moore's named Colonel Camac were also sightseeing there. The Colonel noticed that the wind was bothering the Princess and plucked Turner's umbrella from under his arm to shelter the Princess. The umbrella was blown inside out, breaking some of its ribs. The Princess smiled her thanks to the Colonel; Turner scowled. He had presumably been disturbed when sketching *and* had his umbrella wrecked. There were further sightings of him in Naples, to which he had dashed in hopes of observing Vesuvius erupting – the real as opposed to the imagined thing. One of Sir John Soane's sons, then in Italy, wrote home to his father:

> Turner is in the neighbourhood of Naples making rough pencil sketches to the astonishment of the Fashionables, who wonder what use these rough draughts can be – simple souls! At Rome a sucking blade of the brush made the request of going out with pig Turner to colour – he grunted for answer that it would take up too much time to colour in the open air – he could make 15 or 16 pencil sketches to one coloured, and then grunted his way home.[8]

Any who thought that the taciturn Turner would enliven the social scene in Rome soon changed their minds. Hazlitt called Rome 'of all places the worst to study in',[9] and Turner did not want the city's distractions. While Lawrence wrote to Farington on 16 October to talk of Turner's arrival and say how worthy he was of 'this fine City, of all the Elegancy and Grandeur that it exhibits',[10] those who were less in the swim saw Rome's seediness. At least, back in Queen Anne Street, waiting for a letter, Turner senior heard no worrying rumours about his son of the sort that circulated about Chantrey: that the rubicund sculptor had been captured and was being held for ransom by bandits. Brigands were as much a part of the Italian scene as classical ruins, and featured, for example, in the popular paintings of his colleague Eastlake, in Rome since 1816.

Turner, possibly thinking of brigands, had taken the shortest and most frequented road when he went to Naples. On the way, through Fra Diavolo country, he sketched from the moving carriage or when it stopped in the safety of towns. He visited Lake Avernus. There Virgil had placed the meeting of Aeneas with the Sibyl, an old theme of Turner's and the subject of a picture he had done in 1815 for the classically inclined Sir Richard Colt Hoare. His sketchbook was sprinkled with hot ash when he climbed Vesuvius, but there were no fireworks from the mountain. However, there were compensations: the view out over the Bay of Naples and the old Roman resort of Baiae; the excavations at Pompeii; and Paestum's temples. He knew Paestum from the drawings of J. R. Cozens and Piranesi, but the real thing was tremendous; he drew the temples from without and within, from close and afar. On the way back to Naples by boat, he sketched the rugged coastline.

Lord Byron was in Rome – a friend of the poet Thomas Moore and acquainted with Samuel Rogers, the London banker and versifier, whom Turner knew – but there is no record of a meeting between the fashionable, unconventional poet and the moody, unconventional painter. The fourth Italy-centred canto of Byron's world-weary epic *Childe Harold* had been published in 1818, and Turner read it. He owed to Byron the lines adapted from *Childe Harold* III he had attached to his *Field of Waterloo*, shown at the RA in 1818. Byron's work became part of the filter through which his mind sieved his Italian experiences. Shelley's work seems to have performed a similar function. 'Ode to the West Wind' was written at this time and that poet's almost tactile reaction to the time-wrecked beauty of the Italian coast was much like his own.

Well stocked with dreams, Turner went slowly home in mid-winter. Christmas in Florence, then Turin. The ordinary coach service to Savoy was not running because of heavy snow, but Turner joined another voyager in hiring a coach to take them. Later he wrote to Holworthy about this venture, which went well until they reached the top of the pass over Mont Cenis, where the coach capsized:

> Very lucky it was so; and the carriage door so completely frozen that we were obliged to get out at the window – the guide and the Cantonier began to fight, and the driver was by a process verbal put into prison, so doing while we had to march or rather flounder up to our knees nothing less in snow, all the way down to Lancesbyburgh [Lanslebourg] by the King of Roadmakers' Road, not the Colossus of Roads, Mr MacAdam, but Bonaparte, filled up by snow and only known by the precipitous zig-zag.[11]

He got back to London in time for the Academy Club dinner on 2 February 1820 where he gave Farington, sitting next to him, the highlights of his six months' trip, with particular praise for Tivoli, Nemi, Albano and Terni. During his absence John Constable had finally – sixteen years after first exhibiting at the RA – been elected an Associate Academician.

On his return, Turner saw a good deal of the Fawkeses in town, attended numerous RA Council meetings, and was kept 'in constant ossillation'[12] between Twickenham and London while his former mews property in Queen Anne Street was being reconstructed and his new gallery built. His mind was obviously on many things. In fact, the Academy exhibition this year suggested that the first impact of Italy had not been altogether salutary. He had been disoriented by the experience. In the 1820 RA catalogue he gave his titles as Professor of Perspective and – a new source of pride – member of the Roman Academy of St Luke, but for an expert in perspective his one picture on show was a bizarre performance.

Rome was the nominal subject. The full title of the roughly six foot by eleven painting was *Rome, from the Vatican: Raffaelle, accompanied by La Fornarina, preparing his pictures for the decoration of the Loggia*. The background view of Rome was as Turner had recently seen it. The view of the Vatican loggia was a compositional mish-mash, with arches and balustrades disappearing weirdly, the floor slanting upwards as if under pressure, and the viewer's eye led uncomfortably in several directions at once. The figures, to put it kindly, were not his best: Raphael's mistress doll-sized, playing with her jewels, and the divine painter himself comparatively immense and rather posily looking up at his ceiling fresco work. As for the colours: the sky was a vivid blue, the stonework gloriously golden, the foreground a warm red. The overall effect was brilliant and gaudy and the general reaction to the picture that it was an unhappy experiment. Even Ruskin, some years later, thought that Rome had done Turner no good: 'Michael Angelo's sprawling prophets, and Bernini's labyrinthine arcades wholly bewildered him, and dragged him into their false and fantastic world.'[13]

It took him a while to assimilate the Italian experience and the southern light. Having long since lived with the prospect of Italy, he now had to learn to handle the actuality. And it took his viewers time to come to terms with the results. His pictures no longer seemed to fall into simple categories of history painting, landscape or seascape. The categories merged, the complexities multiplied and the subjects became obscure. Turner had always crammed a lot into his paintings: references to work by other artists; innumerable associations picked up from reading; his own experiences, like the Wharfedale storm in *Hannibal crossing the Alps*. But now that great heap of compost seemed to be spread more freely, generally enriching his pictures. He was no longer painting views but visions. 'Golden visions, glorious and beautiful,' said Constable in 1826.[14]

Perhaps the first successful big picture to accommodate his Italian gatherings and what he had accomplished in the previous decade in such pictures as Hawksworth's birthday gift, the *Dort*, was the *Bay of Baiae, with Apollo and the Sibyl* of 1823. (Turner's original spelling was 'Sybil'. The Cumaean sibyl was 700 years old, but Turner represented her as young and buxom.) Baiae was the coastal town near Naples where well-to-do Romans had their winter villas. Wilson and Claude had been here too, but Turner, painting its ruined beauty, got more in. His colour of the moment was an autumn gold. However, according to a well-travelled friend of George Jones, Turner invented 'half the scene'. Jones told Turner that he 'had planted some hills with vineyards [where] there was nothing in reality but a few dry sticks'. Turner replied, 'All poets are liars.' Jones then wrote on the frame, 'SPLENDIDE MENDAX', and Turner laughed and left it there.[15] Unfortunately the inventor in this case was not only imaginative but faulty in his workmanship: the painting's success was soon imperilled by his use of asphaltum, which caused parts of it to darken and crack.

His big Italian picture of 1826 was also golden: *Forum Romanum*, *for Mr. Soane's Museum.* In this, he showed the Arch of Titus and the ancient Via Sacra, a fresco of a Madonna and child and an angel on a ruined wall incorporated in a church, and a procession of monks and a woman kneeling before a monk. The picture subsumed various past and present items to do with religion and reverence beneath a great overhanging arch which was a further bit of mendacity: he had made it up – or maybe borrowed it from Piranesi – but it worked, acting as the arch of history under which we live, and paint, and pray. He had been commissioned to paint the picture by his friend John Soane, but embarrassment soon set in. The painting – five feet by eight – was 'over-size' for the planned spot in Soane's house (every cubbyhole full of antiquities) in Lincoln's Inn Fields. Soane decently sent Turner a cheque for the agreed 500 guineas on 9 July 1826, but Turner, appreciating Soane's predicament, kept the picture and returned the cheque. If Soane had been sensible, he would have cleared out some of the clutter in his house in order to hang a glowing masterpiece. But some contemporary critics also hesitated. After viewing *Forum Romanum* at the RA exhibition, the writer for the *Literary Gazette* declared (13 May 1826): 'The artist ... has combated a very difficult quality of art, in giving solidity without strong and violent opposition of light and shade. [However,] Mr Turner ... seems to have sworn fidelity to the *Yellow Dwarf*, if he has not identified himself with that important necromancer.'[16]

The Yellow Dwarf! Was there a dig here at Turner's height as well as at his extreme fondness for a particular colour? (*Le Nain Jaune* – *The Yellow Dwarf* – was a fairy story by Mme d'Aulnoye, later a pantomime. *The Black Dwarf* was a tale by Walter Scott, published in 1816, and also the name of a radical weekly paper, founded in 1817.) Yellow was by now well known to be his favourite.[17] It had been asserting itself since *The Rise of Carthage*, but in the 1820s there was no avoiding it. Critics rushed to condemn Turner's use of yellow and the ensuing gaudiness and 'meretricious style of colouring'.[18] The winter of 1825–6 was productive for him, and one of his other pictures at the Academy in 1826, *Cologne, the Arrival of a Packet Boat*, albeit unItalian, was also complained about on this score. The *Morning Post* on 9 May said, 'Mr Turner had made very free use of the chrome yellow – will it stand the test of time?'[19] The picture was so bright that a story was told to the effect that Turner generously washed it over with lamp-black, so as to avoid overwhelming two

Lawrence portraits hung near by at the exhibition, and had advised an anxious Lawrence not to worry – it would all wash off after the exhibition. But this seems to have been a fable, generous to Turner. Indeed, Turner's concern for the golden brilliance of the picture, partly achieved perhaps by watercolours as well as oils, was evident in one of the letters he wrote to his father from John Nash's castle at Cowes in 1827, when the picture was about to be sold; he wrote, 'You must not by any means wet it, for all the Colour will come off.'[20]

In 1827 his second Mortlake Thames-side picture, *Mortlake Terrace, the Seat of William Moffat, Esq. Summer's Evening*, was condemned for its yellowness. This time the *Morning Post* on 15 June wrote that Turner was getting worse from 'what we may call a yellow fever'. Moreover, switching diseases, it thought that when, as in this case, every part of a picture 'should be afflicted with the jaundice, it is too much to be endured'. The painting represented a sad and needless 'falling-off'.[21] He had hitherto been called mad but now – aged fifty-two – he had to put up with the suggestion that his powers were failing.

Writing to Holworthy in May 1826 he joked about his notoriety. His colleague Thomas Phillips had just come back from Italy. Turner wrote: 'Professor Phillips returned quite a carnation to what he went [–] jumbling about did him good, at least in complection. Tho the executive, alias hanging committee at the Royal Academy this year has brought him back to his original tone of colour – but I must not say yellow, for I have taken it *all* to my keeping this year, so they say, and so I meant it should be …'[22] In another letter to Holworthy in December that year he referred to his friend Callcott's forthcoming marriage in Italy to the widowed Maria Graham, 'a very agreeable Blue Stocking; so I must wear the yellow stockings'.[23] This was an allusion to a speech of Malvolio's, in *Twelfth Night* – Turner knew his Shakespeare – but of course it also came aptly from one in the thrall of the Yellow Dwarf.

He continued in following years to harp good-humouredly on the subject. In a letter to George Jones of 22 February 1830, after some melancholy reflection on some recent deaths, he brightened up:

I wish I had you by the button-hole, notwithstanding all your grumbling about Italy and yellow. I could then tell freely what has occurred since your departure of combinations and concatenations [at the RA] somewhat of the old kind, only more highly coloured, and to my jaundiced eye not a whit more pure ... Chantrey is as gay and as good as ever, ready to serve; he requests, for my benefit, that you bottle up all the yellows which may be straying out of the right way ...[24]

On an occasion at the sculptor Richard Westmacott's, a fellow member of the Academy Club, Turner was asked by someone who was leaving for Italy if he could do anything for him there. 'No,' said Turner, 'unless you bring me back some Naples yellow.'[25] The joke by now was part of his fame. A caricature by Dicky Doyle in the *Almanack of the Month*, in 1846, showed a small top-hatted Turner wielding a mop between a canvas and a bucket labelled YELLOW.

Italy and the ensuing liberation had an impact on his technique. It seemed to Samuel Redgrave that Turner now 'adopted a principle of light with a small proportion of dark, used a light ground, and by scumbling obtained infinitely delicate gradations'.[26] Yet there was a downside to this free and easy brightness as he placed watercolour on top of oil and oil on watercolour, added resin to paint, and used pigments that were bound to fade or grow dark; and he didn't care. He wanted to capture the moment and put practical considerations aside. He was impatient to get effects, to try all sorts of things, sound and unsound. His paints sometimes dried unevenly and soon cracked. The ground was not always well prepared: that of one of his Cowes Regatta pictures was a sort of tempera, which caused the oils on top to flake constantly. Now and then he had to call in a cleaner or restorer to bring back to life a picture he had painted not many years before. One of his main paint suppliers, Mr Winsor, was unhappy at the fugitive colours Turner was buying and 'plucked up courage one day to remonstrate with him for so doing. Turner's answer, in spite of the friendship between the two men, was somewhat uncompromising ... "Your business, Winsor, is to make colours for Artists. Mine is to use them."'[27] John Constable, having been to see the Turners John Sheepshanks had at his Blackheath house in 1836, wrote to C. R. Leslie, 'Turner is very grand ... but some of [his] best work is swept up off the carpet every morning by the maid and put into the dust hole.'[28] The *Bay of Baiae* was soon a wreck – 'a beautiful wreck it is true, of a picture that is past', wrote Richard Redgrave in 1866.[29]

The pictures of his that generally stood up best were watercolours, if preserved from exposure to constant sunlight. The light inherent in them was less obstreperous than in many of the oil paintings. For Robert Hunt, reviewing in the *Examiner* of 3 February 1822 an exhibition of watercolours at W. B.Cooke's in Soho Square, it was 'a diffusive, lustrous, and mild light that … shines into the mind, blending … power with gentleness … The wonder-working Artist has produced this sweet effect by colour, almost independently of chiaroscuro, and by keeping the edges of the forms all tender. They hold a bland but luminous communion of light with each other, and with our minds …'[30] While in Italy in late 1819 he made some lovely watercolours and preliminary colour-studies at Como, Venice, Rome and Naples – his brushwork increasingly bold and direct, the results fresh and immediate. Among the eight watercolours of Italy he painted for Fawkes when back in England in 1820 and 1821, one showed a coach crossing Mont Cenis in a snowstorm, two were of Venice, one was a morning view of Vesuvius across the Bay of Naples, and four were of Rome. Among the latter, *The Colosseum* and *The Interior of St Peter's* were done from without and within, and were studies in scale. They were brilliant exaggerations, in which Turner juggled with the architectural facts and made the viewer feel puny. In his first Venice watercolours, water was the important element, reflection and shimmer the keynotes, the buildings seen as in a mirage. But many of the watercolours done at this time remained in their large sketchbooks.

The public saw the results of others he did between 1826 and 1828: small vignettes for engravings in an edition of poems about Italy by his patron–friend Samuel Rogers, which the illustrations helped to make a commercial success, and three watercolours for a Charles Heath print series which didn't come to pass – the three were instead engraved for publication in a Heath annual, the *Keepsake*. One, *Lake Albano*, contained three Turneresque figures, a woman and two men, one of whom was a pedlar, the other obviously a bandit. If young Eastlake could do well with bandit pictures, why shouldn't he? However, in this picture Turner's non-conformist view of one of the world's great religions has taken a hand. His bandit has laid aside his gun and appears to be discussing with his lady friend which religious print to buy from the pedlar. A temple of Catholic piety, the Pope's summer place, Castel Gandolfo, can be seen in the background.

Not long after this, he was heading back to the Mediterranean. He had moved out of Sandycombe, Walter Fawkes was dead, and it was eight years since he had been in Italy. He would be away for Christmas; his ageing father and Hannah would have to look after things, and each other, in Queen Anne Street. Setting off in August 1828, he took a different route from 1819, this time down through France to Marseilles and then along the coast. On 13 October, he wrote an amiable letter to George Jones from Rome:

> Two months nearly in getting to this Terra Pictura, *and at work*; but the length of time is my own fault. I must see the South of France, which almost knocked me up, the heat was so intense, particularly at Nismes and Avignon; and until I got a plunge into the sea at Marseilles, I felt so weak that nothing but the change of scene kept me onwards to my distant point.
>
> Genoa, and all the sea-coast from Nice to Spezzia is remarkably rugged and fine; so is Massa. Tell that fat fellow Chantrey that I did think of him, *then* (but not for the first or the last time) of the thousands he had made out of those marble crags which only afforded me a sour bottle of wine and a sketch; but he deserves everything which is good, though he did give me a fit of the spleen at Carrara ...
>
> Hope that you have been better than usual, and that the pictures go on well. If you should be passing Queen Anne Street, just say I am well and in Rome, for I fear young Hakewell has written to his father [James Hakewill] of my being unwell; and may I trouble you to drop a line into the twopenny post to Mr C. Heath, 6 Seymour Place, New Pancras Church, or send my people to tell him that, if he has anything to send me, to put it up in a letter ... directed for me, No. 12 Piazza Mignanelli, Rome, and to which place I hope you will send me a line? Excuse my troubling you with my requests of business. Remember me to all friends. So God bless you. Adieu.
> J. M. W. Turner[31]

He seems to have been saving postage, and time, writing to Jones rather than Queen Anne Street. However, Clara Wells Wheeler was also keeping an eye on things. She wrote to Robert Finch in Rome on 4 November: 'Will you have the kindness to give my kindest regards to Turner, and tell him I sent to his father's house to enquire after his father's health, that I might send him the latest intelligence, and that the old gentleman was very well, but was out of town.'[32] As for Turner's restorative plunge into the azure Mediterranean, it prompts the idea that this amateur

Thames waterman – and child of Margate beach – could swim.

He had written from Paris to Eastlake, who was still at 12 Piazza Mignanelli, where Captain Thomas and Maria Graham had also lived in 1819. (Widowed while on a voyage to Chile, Maria had married Turner's friend Callcott in 1827, and, after a year-long honeymoon tour of Europe including Rome, had just got back to the Callcott house in Kensington.) Addressing him as 'Signor Carlo', Turner asked Eastlake to order basic painting materials for him, including two canvases with 'the best of all possible grounds'. He wanted to get cracking on a painting for Lord Egremont, hoping that the 'first brush in Rome on my part should be to begin for him con amore a companion picture to his beautiful Claude'.[33]

His convivial mood continued. Once at Eastlake's apartment near the Spanish Steps, where he was lodged in a spare study, he led a more social life than he had during his first stay in Rome, despite 'working literally night and day', as Eastlake told a friend.[34] Eastlake, by now well established, got him welcomed by the artistic community. Turner visited a number of the brotherhood of British sculptors and painters and said friendly things to them; he seemed to be enjoying himself. But there were petty difficulties *chez* Eastlake. His host wrote to Maria Callcott in London that Turner was having trouble with other residents of the house: 'He does not quite agree with Ugo, and Albina plays the piano wretchedly close to his bed-room, so that he is not very comfortable. We tried dining at home for a while, but they did not use us well, and we now go out – he is used to rough it.'[35]

In December, after he had moved to more spacious and apparently quieter rooms near the Quattro Fontane, he held an exhibition to stop people 'gabbling', so he wrote to Chantrey.[36] He showed three of the canvases on which he had been working so hard. These were *The Vision of Medea*, a *View of Orvieto* and *Regulus*. Eastlake, who may have talked him into this show, wrote to a friend in Liverpool:

> More than a thousand persons went to see his works when exhibited, so you may imagine how astonished, enraged or delighted the different schools of artists were, at seeing things with methods so new, so daring, and excellences so unequivocal. The angry critics have, I believe, talked most, and it is possible you may hear of *general* severity of judgment, but many did justice, and many more were fain to admire what they confessed they dared not imitate.[37]

For one thing, artists and art-lovers had never seen pictures displayed, as Turner's were, unframed but instead with ropes nailed around the stretchers, painted with yellow ochre tempera. One viewer was Byron's friend J. C. Hobhouse, later Lord Broughton, who had met Turner at Farnley Hall, and who now said, 'An ignorant man like myself would find it difficult to believe them to be the production of the very first of living painters. The chief of these strange compositions, called the Vision of Medea, was a glaring extravagant daub, which might be mistaken for a joke – and a bad joke too.'[38] Thomas Uwins, painting in Naples, heard the rumours and wrote to Joseph Severn, who had helped look after the dying Keats in Rome in late 1820. Uwins asked if Turner was 'trifling with his great powers'. Severn answered: 'Turner's works here were like the doings of a poet who had taken to the brush.'[39]

The gossip persisted. Eastlake – unexciting as a painter but an extremely perceptive colleague – wrote to Maria Callcott in March 1829, after Turner had left:

> The Romans have not yet done talking about the Paesista Inglese – *how* they talk would be worth relating if they knew anything of the matter. When you see his 'Vision of Medea', you may imagine with what astonishment the modern Italian school would look at it … The one called 'Regulus' is a beautiful specimen of his peculiar power, yet the wretches here dwelt more on the defects of the figures, and its resemblance to Claude's compositions than on its exquisite gradation and the taste of the architecture. The latter was perfect for beauty of design, more Italian that Italy itself.[40]

The 'picture for Lord Egremont' was *Palestrina – Composition*, which the noble Earl in the end didn't buy and Turner held on to possessively for another sixteen years. This was indeed a specimen of Turner's peculiar power, though perhaps imperfect in design and 'composition'. Turner's eight-foot-wide canvas contained many echoes of Egremont's Claude, *Landscape with Jacob, Laban and His Daughters*: a bridge, a town, a mountain, some pastoral figures. But *Palestrina* seems the product of a split vision, two pictures, as it were, each lovely in its way, joined down the middle. A hill, castle, town, bridge and river to one side; figures and cattle and a receding avenue lined with tall trees on the other. The conjunction is unsettling. The viewer's attention is taken in two directions at once. Turner seemed to be working on several different levels in terms of perspective, paint-handling and mood. A more satisfactory Italian venture for Lord Egremont was the purchase of a piece of antique sculpture – a Dionysus – which Turner examined for him and – with Eastlake's help – had shipped to England, eventually to join the Petworth collection. (The Dionysus took its time to reach England, as did Turner's own paintings that he shipped back; at one point he lamented that they must be 'among the fishes' and wondered about making an insurance claim.)[41]

A simpler and nobler picture than *Palestrina* was a large red-brown-and-yellow landscape he did of the hill country south of Orvieto. One can just make out a ruined village, Civita di Bagnoregio, on its lonely crag. A road undulates across the treeless foreground – also bereft of peasants and *banditti*. It is a warm and hazy day. The picture feels, like some of his Thames oil sketches, as if it was done on the spot, though they were conjured up in Queen Anne Street, and this was probably begun in Rome.[42] He seems to have put it aside before working out quite how to finish it. It lacks picturesque flourishes or 'poetical' content. It is the work of a painter with a brush.

He set off for home at the New Year. Before he left he began a poem 'Farewell a second time the land of all bliss'. He went on to refer, among many obscurities, to two of his touchstones: 'the lost greatness of Imperial Rome' and 'that great being of long versed renown ariel Claude'.[43] A young fellow Englishman in the coach between Rome and Bologna wrote *en route* to Thomas Uwins in Naples:

> I have fortunately met with a good-tempered, funny, little, elderly gentleman, who will probably be my travelling companion throughout the journey. He is continually popping his head out of the window to sketch whatever strikes his fancy, and became quite angry because the conductor would not wait for him whilst he took a sunrise view of Macerata. 'Damn the fellow!' says he. 'He has no feeling.' He speaks but a few words of Italian, about as much of French, which two languages he jumbles together most amusingly. His good temper, however, carries him through all his troubles. I am sure you would love him for his indefatigability in his favourite pursuit. From his conversation he is evidently *near kin to*, if not *absolutely*, an artist. Probably you may know something of him. The name on his trunk is, J. W. or J. M. W. Turner![44]

There were troubles enough in the course of the journey for the fifty-four-year-old 'near kin to' an artist. Winter had set in. Turner a few weeks later wrote to Eastlake, describing the trip:

> Snow began to fall at Foligno, tho' more of ice than snow, that the coach from its weight slide about in all directions, that walking was much preferable, but my innumerable tails would not do that service so I soon got wet through and through, till at Sarre-valli the diligence zizd into a ditch and required 6 oxen, sent three miles back for, to drag it out; this cost 4 Hours, that we were 10 Hours beyond our time at Macerata, consequently half starved and frozen we at last got to Bologna ...

There, his troubles did not diminish:

> the Milan diligence was unable to pass Placentia. We therefore hired a voitura, the horses were knocked up the first post, sigr turned us over to another lighter carriage which put my coat in full requisition night and day, for we never could keep warm or make our day's distance good, the places we put up at proved all bad till Firenzola being even the worst[,] for the down diligence people had devoured everything eatable (Beds none) ... crossed Mont Cenis on a sledge – bivouaced in the snow with fires lighted for 3 hours on Mont Tarate while the diligence was righted and dug out, for a Bank of Snow saved it from upsetting – and in the same night we were again turned out to walk up to our knees in new fallen drift to get assistance to dig a channel thro' it for the coach, so that from Foligno to within 20 miles of Paris I never saw the road but snow![45]

Crossing Mt Cenis by sledge was fairly common practice in winter; carriages, unable to negotiate the conditions, were often dismantled and their parts carried over by mules. The alternative Simplon route offered the dangers of avalanches. Turner's good humour and indefatigability, sorely tested by the journey, were on record that year at the RA when he showed a watercolour of the diligence in a snow drift.

At home again in Queen Anne Street in the dark mists of a London winter, he stayed for a few months in spirit in the south. (The country was in political turmoil, with the movement for Catholic emancipation finally about to achieve its objective.) Turner worked hard finishing paintings for the Academy exhibition. He was too busy even to dine with Clara Wheeler and her family on a Saturday in mid-March; he decorated his note of regret with a sketch of a knocked-over jar of varnish, pouring out its contents, and a palette which he turned into a dismayed-looking head. He added a rush of words: 'Time Time Time so more haste the worse speed.'[46] One of the pictures he was most preoccupied with was one that had been in the back of his mind for more than twenty years. *Ulysses deriding Polyphemus* was the resolution of a dream.

Turner had long been enthralled by the *Odyssey* and in particular by the story of the hero's encounter with the giant one-eyed son of Poseidon, the Cyclops, Polyphemus. Did Turner identify, one wonders, with Ulysses, whom Polyphemus at one point refers to as 'small, pitiful, and twiggy'?[47] The painting was a trumpet blare of triumph, celebrating the escape of Ulysses and his surviving men. Ulysses' burnished, lateen-rigged ship is being rowed strenuously away from a rocky shore; its strange bows, like the mouth of a huge fish, gape open most usefully to house an anchor. Ulysses stands on a raised platform just aft of amidships, taunting the giant, while an ensign aloft flourishes his name in Greek. Polyphemus himself, in blinded agony, rises out of purple smoke and cloud above a volcanic peak. Meanwhile the horses of the sun-god Apollo prance above the sea. The early-morning sun irradiates the water towards which Ulysses' ship bustles, and phosphorescent Nereids frolic like porpoises in its bow-wave. The colouring is wild but wonderful. '*Colouring run mad*,' said the *Morning Herald* on 5 May 1829. But as the *Times* noted on 11 May, 'No other artist living … can exercise anything like the magical power which Mr. Turner wields with so much ease.'[48]

Part of the magic lay in the mixture of fact and fancy, his reading and his imagining. The sky could be that seen after a volcanic eruption – one he had never witnessed. The coast could be the Bay of Naples – with perhaps a few rocks from the English south coast, like the Needles or the Thurlestone, thrown in. Some of the detail is as described by Homer: the Cyclops, for example, who 'seemed no man at all … he seemed rather a shaggy mountain reared in solitude'.[49] Turner properly places the other ships in the Greek squadron at an offshore island waiting for their leader's return. Moreover, he may have come across in some journal or other discussion of recent investigations into phosphorescence – hence the nearly transparent Nereids. But other things are not as in the text of the *Odyssey*. The Cyclops's cave Turner puts at sea-level rather than up in the mountains. The crew members seen in profusion up on the lateen spars as they unfurl the sails look more like stage-hands than sailors.

Indeed, the ship coming towards the middle of the picture from the left, while the sun beams out of the right-hand side, was a theatrical formula he was to use again, maybe with even greater success, ten years later. A *gesture*, echoing Ulysses' dramatic brandishing of the olive branch with which he had blinded Polyphemus, is implicit in the high stem of one of the waiting craft at the right, looking like a raised fist, and mocking the Cyclops's anger.

Turner went on having a good time with this painting after he had finished it. When the amateur artist and collector Reverend T. J. Judkin met him at a dinner party soon after the 1829 exhibition and started going on about the *Odyssey*, Turner mischievously denied that Homer, or Homer via Pope, was his source. He took his theme rather from that later interpreter of the Ulysses and Polyphemus story, the comic theatre and song writer, Tom Dibdin:

> He ate his mutton, drank his wine,
> *And then he poked his eye out!*[50]

Turner's theatregoing was noted by his friends. He talked about Shakespeare and the acting of William Macready. But if he knew his Dibdin from visiting the music halls, *Ulysses deriding Polyphemus* seems to show that he knew his Shelley too:

> Half the sky
> Was roofed with clouds of rich emblazonry
> Dark purple at the zenith, which still grew
> Down the steep west into a wondrous hue
> Brighter than burning gold.[51]

The painting did not find a buyer. It remained his own dream. But, like Ulysses, Turner must have rejoiced to have got this far in his voyage. The painting like a banner flaunted that success.

He had kept his rooms in Rome, hoping to return this year. But the thought of the summer heat there worried him, and his father was ailing, so in the end he didn't go – in fact, he never went back to central or southern Italy. He wrote to Eastlake to ask him to sort out any problem in getting new tenants for his rooms and to make arrangements for the continued rent of a closet in which he had left some things. Mutual aid among the British artists in Rome, and those coming or going there, was a happy commonplace, but

Turner's helpfulness might have had a high price. Clara Wheeler, thinking Turner was still planning to go again to Rome, wrote in August 1829 to Robert Finch, who was out there: 'The second chance you mention, viz. Turner, by whom to send the books, is a broken reed;he coming overland, will not increase his luggage, and if he would, I should be quite sorry to trust him, for he would be quite sure to lose your books, as he invariably does, more than half his own baggage in every tour he makes, being the most careless personnage of my acquaintance.'[52] (During his 1817 tour to the Low Countries and Germany, he noted in a sketchbook: 'Lost in the Walett. – A Book with leaves. ditto Campbell's Belgium. 3 shirts. 1 night ditto. A Razor. A Ferrell for Umbrella. A pair of Stockings. A Waistcoat. ½ Doz. of Pencils. 6 Cravats. 1 Large ditto. 1 Box of Colours.')[53] Instead of Italy, Turner made a quick trip to France and then stayed at Petworth for a few days in early September.

His father died on 21 September. Two years before, Turner had told Holworthy that he had begun to think of being truly alone in the world, and now the moment had come. The funeral took place on the 29th at St Paul's, Covent Garden, which made for a sort of homecoming: William Turner had married Mary Marshall there on 29 August 1773. He had seen his son started as an artist and on his way. So much of what Turner first did was with the knowledge that it gave his father pleasure and pride. And that knowledge, though overtaken by much else, remained part of the deep momentum, a sustenance. Now he would have to do without the old man's pride in him.

Fearfully low, he went to stay with the Trimmers at Heston. With the years, the father–son relationship is reversed; the son acquires an almost parental concern for the father; and now, as he told the Trimmers, he felt as if *he* had lost an only child. It was a moment when *The Aeneid* might have provided a refuge. Turner, like Aeneas, had carried his father, not out of burning Troy but from Maiden Lane. In mid-voyage, like Anchises, his father forsook him by dying.

Another dream, or nightmare, of this time shows a spectral horse, seemingly high in the air, its lower parts enveloped by cloud, with wild orange sky above. The horse bears a human skeleton, arched across its back, arms outstretched, head upside down – the head wears a rudimentary crown. Death, terrible and fearsome, filled his mind. He may have been reading the Bible too, and this *Death on a Pale Horse* may have been provoked by the Book of Revelation. He laid on the oil paint and then frenetically scratched away at it, as he had done at the watercolour *A First Rate taking in Stores*.

The day after the funeral he signed a will; it was his first. Obviously his father's departure had made him decide to set his estate in order, in case the pale horse came for him as well. In this will, he left small amounts to several uncles and nephews and small annuities to his ex-mistress and children and housekeeper. (These annuities were to be interest from capital, at 5 per cent amounting roughly to £25 per year to Sarah Danby; £25 to Evelina and £50 to Georgiana, 'natural daughters of Sarah Danby'; and £50 to Hannah Danby – whose father's name he couldn't remember when he tried to identify her.)[54] Evelina was about twenty-eight and married at this point; Georgiana was unmarried and about eighteen. Turner himself seems to have drawn up this will, although William Marsh, his stockbroker, was one of the witnesses. In the will Turner also left £500 to the Artists' General Benevolent Institution and funds to the Royal Academy to provide for a Professor of Landscape Painting and a Turner Gold Medal. The rest of his estate was to go towards setting up a charity for distressed landscape painters and single men. (He presumably meant landscape painters who were single men, a category close to his heart, but legal exactitude was unfortunately not his forte.) This charity was to take the form of a 'college' and gallery built on his land at Twickenham. His two Carthage paintings were to go to the new National Gallery, which had opened five years before in Pall Mall, as long as they were hung next to Claude's *Mill* and *Seaport*. His own fame remained a prime concern. However, his wealth was not much increased by his father's death. In the probate letters of administration of December 1829 for his father's tiny estate, Turner was referred to as 'the only child of the said deceased' and the effects were described as 'under £50'.[55]

Other deaths cast a gloom on this time. Turner was a pallbearer at the funeral of the painter and engraver George Dawe in October 1829 – Dawe had been six years younger than him. Harriet Wells, one of the three daughters of his good friend W. F. Wells, went next. Turner wrote to her sister Clara on 3 January 1830:

> Your foreboding letter has been too soon realized. Poor Harriet, dear Harriet, gentle patient amiability. Earthly assurances of heaven's bliss possesst, must pour their comforts and mingle in your

distress a balm peculiarly its own – not known, not felt, not merited by all.

I should like to hear how they are at Mitcham, if it is not putting you to a painful task too much for your own misery to think of, before I go on Friday morning. Alas I have some woes of my own which this sad occasion will not improve, but believe me most anxious in wishing ye may be all more successful in the severe struggle than I have been with mine.[56]

Then Thomas Lawrence died, aged sixty, and after lying in state overnight in Somerset House was buried in St Paul's Cathedral on 21 January. Turner wrote to George Jones, who was in Rome, to tell him

of the last sad ceremonies paid yesterday to departed talent gone to that bourne from whence no traveller returns. Alas! only two short months Sir Thomas followed the coffin of Dawe to the same place. We then were his pall-bearers. Who will do the like for me, or when, God only knows how soon. My poor father's death proved a heavy blow upon me, and has been followed by others of the same dark kind. However, it is something to feel that gifted talent can be acknowledged by the many who yesterday waded up to their knees in snow and muck to see the funeral pomp swelled up by carriages of the great, without the persons themselves.[57]

Turner's respect was immense for 'gifted talent' among his colleagues. During the service in St Paul's, his pew neighbour Wilkie at one point whispered about some element of the spectacle, 'Turner, that's a fine effect,' and Turner looked away in disgust. Constable noticed this, and talked approvingly of Turner's reaction.[58] Turner not long after paid his own tribute to the Academy's late President in a watercolour showing the crowds and carriages standing in the cold outside St Paul's: *Funeral of Sir Thomas Lawrence, a sketch from memory*. Along with *Palestrina* and the *View of Orvieto*, it was among the half-dozen pictures he showed that year at the RA. (But he didn't hold Wilkie's remark against him to the bitter end. Wilkie would eventually have his tribute too.)

Although, as it turned out, he had said farewell to Rome for ever, Italy kept surfacing in his work. He went on reading Byron (who had died at Missolonghi in 1824), studying Piranesi and consulting the classic authors. The golden light shone in paintings on Italian themes, both ancient and modern. He made watercolours for engraved illustrations to Byron's collected works. He was the right man for the job, since he and Byron had similar artistic temperaments

– they were fast workers; they responded to immediate stimuli; they both saw beauty and decay bound up in Italy.

One such painting, *Childe Harold's Pilgrimage – Italy*, made the connection brilliantly clear. The Childe – or noble youth – was the romantic, melancholy narrator of Byron's poem of that name, a poem taking the form of a reflective tour of Europe past and present. The painting, exhibited in 1832, contained one of Turner's favourite river-bend scenes, a single tall pine tree and sundry crumbling ruins. It was a homage to Italy and a bravura performance, as the *Morning Chronicle* told its readers on 7 May: Turner 'performs wonders on a single string – is as astonishing with his chrome, as Paganini [who had been giving concerts in London] is with his chromatics'.[59] Turner, slightly editing, attached Byron's lines from *Childe Harold*:

> and now, fair Italy!
> Thou art the garden of the world, the home
> Of all Art yields, and Nature can decree;
> Even in thy desert, what is like to thee?
> Thy very weeds are beautiful, thy waste
> More rich than other climes' fertility;
> Thy wreck a glory, and thy ruin graced
> With an immaculate charm which cannot be defaced.[60]

Unfortunately the charms of Turner's picture were in one sense not immaculate: his pigments were unsafe, the ground soon absorbed the colours put upon it, tints dried and turned to powder and fell off; the picture went to pieces and restorers were needed. Critics asked why he wouldn't take 'simple, easy, and well-known precautions'[61] to secure the permanence of such magic.

The Golden Bough of 1834 had similar ingredients and a similar golden glow, though no Byron – there was a reference to the 'M.S. "Fallacies of Hope"', but no actual lines from the work; gossip had it that the RA Council suppressed the dreaded verse. Lake Avernus, Claudean stone-pines, a temple, a brilliant landscape and Deiphobe, the Cumaean sibyl, holding the bough which enabled Aeneas to visit the underworld without harm. In this painting, signs of decay also soon appeared. A few years on, Vernon Heath, the nephew of the purchaser, the wealthy horse-dealer Robert Vernon, noticed that one of the figures was coming away from the canvas. The artist was called in and the figure was discovered to be made of paper, like the dog in *Mortlake Terrace – Evening*. According to Vernon Heath, Turner exclaimed,

> I now remember all about it. I determined, the picture being all but finished, to paint a nude figure in the foreground, and with this intention went one night to the Life School of the Royal Academy, and made a sketch in my notebook. Finding, next day, that it was the exact size I required my figure to be, I carefully, by its outline, cut it out of the book and fixed it on to the picture, intending, when I had time, to paint the figure in properly. But I forgot this entirely, and do not think I should have remembered but for you.[62]

The picture went back to Queen Anne Street and the artist properly painted the figure in. Turner in his usual contrary way could take infinite pains; he could also – as Clara Wheeler noted – be extremely careless.

And now Venice. Turner went there for the second time in 1833. The *Gazzetta Privilegiata di Venezia* of 9 September 1833 announced the arrival in the city from Vienna of 'Turner, gent. inglese.' He stayed just a week.[63] The watercolour sketches he had done in 1819 during his five days or so in the city were evocative and simple – a few dashes of colour, some sweeping wash-filled brushstrokes, and there for example was *Looking east from the Giudecca, sunrise*. His almost calligraphic way with paint was powerfully evident in *Venice: A Storm on the Lagoon* – though this was painted during his last visit to Venice in 1840. Certainly Venice went on bringing out the absolute best in him. There the temptation to be florid and fanciful, over-allusive and genuflecting to influences this way and that was avoided, at least in the watercolours which the watery city demanded when he was on the spot. (Finished oils of the place, back in London, got more finicky; some of his large, late oil studies were as free as the watercolours.) Perhaps Venice was already unreal and fantastic enough not to need further mystification or complication. 'There,' wrote a fervent admirer, 'he found freedom of space, brilliancy of light, variety of colour, massy simplicity of general form.'[64]

In 1840 he apparently stayed at the Hotel Europa, at the entrance of the Grand Canal, as he had in 1833. It was a great step-up from north of England village inns or Alpine hostelries. But there was no wallowing in luxury; he took his usual exercise, after supper climbing out on to the hotel roof to draw and paint the prospects: the Campanile of St Mark's, for instance, during a thunderstorm, lit up by lightning, or the night sky spangled by fireworks and rockets. He haunted the canals by gondola, going back to places he had sketched in 1819 – churches, palaces, bridges, the lagoon. He went to the theatre and – judging by watercolours he did – saw *Romeo and Juliet* and *Othello.* He thought about Tintoretto, for whom his admiration had been noted by Thomas Moore and Lawrence. He brooded about Venetian history – the death of the Republic at the hands of Napoleon's army in 1797 and the city's existence now under repressive Austrian rule. There was the sense of vain striving that he got with the thought of Carthage and yet also the thrill, the delight, from what all his senses were reacting to: sketch after sketch, turning the pages, pencil or brush in a fast flurry of strokes, the days and nights not long enough to get it all down. In 1840 the watercolour artist William Callow was a fellow guest at the Hotel Europa. They sat together at meals and talked. Callow later recalled Turner as 'a short, dark man, inclined to stoutness, with a merry twinkle in his eye ... One evening whilst I was enjoying a cigar in a gondola I saw in another one Turner sketching San Giorgio, brilliantly lit by the setting sun. I felt quite ashamed of myself idling away the time whilst he was hard at work so late.'[65]

In Venice Turner did without his old props, or prompters, Claude and Wilson. He knew his Canaletto but wasn't oppressed by the slightly claustrophobic painstakingness of the Venetian painter. His own Venetian pictures were wide open. Here for the first time he matched in his watercolours the vigorous economy of Rembrandt drawings. And back in London he went on pursuing the Venetian theme along with his usual sea scenes and classical subjects. Venice made for sales, as – in Byron's wake – Bonington, Etty, Prout and Stanfield had discovered. From 1833 to 1837, and from 1840 to 1846, the Royal Academy exhibition had at least one Turner painting of Venice every year. Many of these pictures sold to merchants and manufacturers like Robert Vernon, John Sheepshanks, Elhanan Bicknell, Benjamin Windus and Henry McConnel, and to his Scottish landowning friend Hugh Munro, with whom he went to the Italian Alps in 1836.

One such oil painting, bought by Munro, was among his three Academy exhibits in 1836: *Juliet and her Nurse.* Why Juliet and her nurse should be standing on a balcony overlooking St Mark's Place in Venice, and not a piazza in Verona, was one of many questions that came to the mind of a writer for *Blackwood's Magazine*, the Reverend John Eagles, an amateur artist. For him the picture was 'a strange jumble ... thrown higgledy-piggledy together, streaked blue and pink and thrown into a flour-tub. Poor Juliet has been steeped in treacle to make her look sweet, and we feel apprehensive lest the mealy architecture should stick to her petticoat and flour it.'[66] But other viewers saw it as 'a perfect scene of enchantment'. The aesthetic seventeen-year-old son of a London wine importer was so angry that he wrote an impassioned reply to Eagles's piece. John Ruskin had gone to Venice the year before. He thought Turner's imagination was "Shakesperian in its mightiness ... The spires of the glorious city rise indistinctly bright into those living mists like the pyramids of pale fire from some vast altar ... This picture ... ought only to be viewed as embodied enchantment, delineated magic ...'[67] Ruskin's father recommended that young John first send this case for the defence to Turner himself. Turner replied on 6 October 1836: 'I beg to thank you for your zeal, kindness, and the trouble you have taken in my behalf in regard to the criticism of Blackwoods Mag for Oc respecting my works, but I never move in these matters. They are of no import save mischief and the meal tub which Maga fears for by my having invaded the flour tub.'[68]

Ruskin's letter did not go to 'Maga', a nickname for *Blackwood's*, but his enthusiasm was not thwarted, and many hundreds of thousands of words, on and around Turner, were to follow. Turner sent the letter to Munro. When an engraving of the painting was made in 1842, Turner changed the title to *St Mark's Place, Venice (Moonlight)*; perhaps he realized that seeing a performance of *Romeo and Juliet* in Venice was not quite a sufficient justification in the eyes of people who had altogether different associations for the play. Four lines of verse were attached to the second state of the print, adapted from *Childe Harold's Pilgrimage*, as if to reiterate his deep affection for the city:

> but Beauty doth not die -
> Nor yet forget how Venice once was dear -
> The pleasant place of all festivity
> The revels of the earth, the Masque of Italy[69]

15: Figures on the Shore

L ike most of us, Turner felt urges that were by turns outward
and inward; he was impelled by the need to seek new places
and to return to those he had been close to. But, despite the
attractions of Devon and Yorkshire, Italy and Switzerland, Margate
remained an essential element in his life. Throughout the late 1820s
and the 1830s – through his own middle age, when he was no longer
beholden to Sandycombe – he went to Margate for weekends and
longer stays.

Mr Coleman's school had been sold in 1805. The bluff-bowed
sailing hoys were replaced by paddle-wheel steamers, speedier and
less impeded by contrary winds. Gas-lighting was introduced in
1824. The old windmill – Hooper's mill – which had dominated
the town skyline was damaged in a gale about this time and pulled
down, ceasing to figure in Turner's sketches. By 1829 the little seaside
town had 9000 inhabitants. Its fresh air and sea-cures still beckoned
invalids and genteel holiday-makers – Keats went there in May 1817
and stayed at the Bell. Margate's Benjamin Beale had invented the
bathing machine – a sort of shed on wheels – in which the bather's
modesty was preserved while he or she was hauled in and out of the
sea by horses. Margate's bathing rooms, where bathers booked their
machines, were regarded as good places for meeting the other sex.
Margate also had its Assembly Rooms, with a band which played
from noon to one, three circulating libraries, from which the works of
Miss Burney, Miss Austen and Lord Byron could be borrowed, and
a Theatre Royal, with performances from very light to semi-serious.
But it was Brighton on the south coast and other small resorts like
Sidmouth and Aldeburgh that gradually acquired the fashionable
visitor, while Margate got more and more of *hoi polloi*. Mrs Sarah
Trimmer had taken her children to Margate; her son the Reverend
Henry Trimmer took his to Southwold. But Turner stayed loyal.

In 1829 he could still catch the so-called Safety Coach that left Charing Cross at 8 a.m. and, via Canterbury, reached Margate at 6 p.m., horses, coach and road permitting. Thornbury's ubiquitous informant the Reverend Judkin 'met him once on a Margate coach. They had, he found, been travelling together for some time. Mr Judkin reproached him with his shyness, and Turner said, in fun, "Why, how could I venture to speak to a great divine?"'[1] But by the late 1820s Turner was more likely to be found on one of the new paddle-steamers that left from the Tower at 9 a.m. and got to Margate pier by 4 or 5 p.m.: flush-decked, with two raking masts and a slender, equally raked funnel (which had to be stayed like a mast to keep it up) belching coal smoke. Alaric Watts recalled: 'Mr Turner was very fond of Margate, and in the summer often went there on Saturday morning by the *Magnet* or *King William* steamer. Most of the time he hung over the stern, watching the effects of the sun and the boiling of the foam. After two o'clock he would open his wallet of cold meat in the cabin, and, nearing himself to one with whom he was in the habit of chatting, would beg a clean plate and a hot potato and did not refuse one glass of wine, but would never accept two. It need hardly be added that he was no favourite with the waiters.'[2] On a later occasion, he was seen on one of the steamers, eating shrimps like any holidaymaker out of an immense red silk handkerchief laid across his knees. Once, on the *City of Canterbury*, he had his portrait done in silhouette, complete with top hat. One suspects the insistence of a companion in this case, possibly female, for – as noted before – Turner was not keen on having others portray him. Meanwhile the other passengers paced the decks, ate their sandwiches, read novels, looked down the hatchway at the valves and connecting rods of the steam engine, or talked about where they were going to stay.

At Margate, new arrivals still had to push their way through the porters, sightseers and urchins on the pier. If Turner was heavily burdened with baggage, he may have splashed out the porter's fee of 3d per item. His choice of inns included the York, the Ship and the Queen's Arms, but he seems to have preferred the greater seclusion and domestic comforts of boarding houses. Just when he first came to the lodgings run by Mrs Sophia Caroline Booth is not known.[3] Mrs Booth is listed in the local rate books for a house over-looking the promenade from 1827 to 1836. She was also there for the 1841 census. This property was just east of the little harbour, part of a terrace of buildings known as Cold Harbour that included the Customs House and the Foy Boat Inn, and had an oblique view of the sea. Nearby steps led up to the fort on the cliff top. At first he would seem to have been an intermittent lodger *chez* Booth, but the old bachelor gradually became a regular and cosseted guest.

In the 1841 census Sophia Caroline Booth was recorded as being 'of independent means'.[4] Also in the Cold Harbour house was a female servant, Judith Hollam, age twenty-two. Mrs Booth gave her age as forty. Like some women at that watershed, she seems to have deducted a year or two, for other indications are that she was born just before rather than just after the turn of the century; at her death in 1878 her age was given as eighty. Her birthday was 9 January. (Ruskin later wrote to her on that day to wish her many happy returns. The year was probably 1799, since 'Sophia Caroline Nolt' was baptized at Dover on 3 February of that year.)[5] Mrs Booth was therefore about thirty when she first met the short, preoccupied and rather odd London artist; he was roughly twenty-five years older than she. But 'older men' presented no problem for Sophia Caroline, already twice a widow in 1830. And Turner, as we know from his liaison with Sarah Danby, had no problem about widows.

First time round, Sophia married in 1818 Henry Pound, a Margate mariner; by him she had a son, Daniel John. About four years after Pound's death by drowning in 1821, she was snapped up by John Booth, a fairly well-to-do Kent man then in his early sixties. They too had a son, who was christened John Pound Booth in the church of St John-in-Thanet, Margate, on 13 November 1825. However, this boy died in Margate when only six and a half, and less than a year later, on 13 April 1833, John Booth senior was buried, aged seventy-one. Her second husband left Sophia Caroline the household effects, £1200 in cash, and the income on the rest of his property, with £200 to be paid to his stepson Daniel Pound when he reached the age of twenty-five. So Mrs Booth was, unlike Sarah Danby, not hard up when Turner became more than a paying guest. From various later descriptions, she seems to have been a comfortably buxom woman, not well educated, and with an earthy country accent. Evidently she soon made Turner think of doubles instead of singles; Mrs B might keep his bed warm.

In one respect he was even more successful with Mrs Booth than with Mrs Danby: no one in the London art world knew about his Kent widow while he and she were cohabiting in Margate in the 1830s and 1840s. Few suspected even when he had moved her up to Chelsea after that. It was one of his cleverest pieces of subterfuge. Indeed, his arrangement with Mrs Booth seems to have driven him to ever deeper concealments. In the summers of 1837 and 1838 he now appears to have been in Margate a lot but also perhaps went touring in Europe; he covered his tracks neatly. Charles Turner, the engraver, seemingly a bit miffed that he had not found out about Mrs Booth during JMWT's lifetime, later complained, 'What a Pity so great a Man in talent should not have made a more Lady like choice – he could not have introduced *Her* to *his Friends*.'[6] But Turner, being who he was, didn't want to. Margate was at a useful distance from most of his Academy colleagues.

At what point Turner made the passage from lodger to lover is not known. While staying in Margate with her, Turner when occasionally taken ill was attended by Dr David Price, who had been John Booth's physician and executor, and Price's prescriptions for the artist were made out in the name of Booth – Turner seems to have been passing in Margate as a new 'Mr Booth'. David Roberts, the artist, had the impression shortly after Turner's death that Turner and Mrs Booth had been together for about eighteen years, during which 'they lived & passed together as husband & wife, under the name of Mr & Mrs Booth'.[7] Roberts talked to Mrs Booth in the summer of 1852 and thought her 'a tall, lusty woman'. She told him that she knew 'from the first' who Turner was. But it is doubtful whether she knew what she was letting herself in for. She told Roberts – something he regarded as 'extraordinary' – that 'with the exception of the first year [Turner] never contributed one shilling towards their mutual support!!!' However, he did give her numerous scraps of his poetry – 'Verses in honour of herself and her personal charms'.

Roberts, though sensible of Turner's talent and even of his 'profound greatness', couldn't help but conclude that, as a man, Turner 'was selfish to an extream … [and] cunning, penurious & sensual'. Roberts believed that he saw more of Turner 'in latter years' than did Turner's other professional brethren and was more of a friend to him than many, but still Turner went on making a

'Mistery' of his life, resisting all attempts to find out how and where he was living, and delighting 'in mistifying others'.[8] This need to keep secrets went back to his childhood; he was the sort of boy who wouldn't tell his mother everything she wanted to know about his doings. He seemed to want to divide his life into watertight compartments, so that, if one was pierced, the others would keep him afloat. The pleasure he took in going incognito wasn't simple: sometimes it seemed the reverse of a desire for fame; sometimes it seemed as if it heightened for him the fact that he was famous. He and Mrs Carrick Moore, a London surgeon's wife, had fun with the name 'Jenkinson', which he now and then used with her, as in a letter in 1844: 'Mr Avalanche Jenkinson presents his thanks to Mrs Moore …'[9] Mrs Moore called him this in return, to humour what George Jones referred to as Turner's 'jocose love of mystery.'[10]

For Turner, the pleasure of knowing things that he kept to himself was greater than any pleasure he might have got from revealing them. He stayed several times with Mr and Mrs Thomas Rose at Cowley Hall, near Uxbridge, generally walking the fifteen miles from London. Rose recalled that Turner came in,

> heated and tired, carrying a small carpet-bag, which was kept like a sealed book, never allowing the key out of his possession. The ladies tried various means to induce him to give up its possession, ostensibly to arrange his articles of clothing which they presumed it contained, though it must be confessed that female curiosity was the predominating cause; but he clung as tenaciously to his key as a miser to his gold.

On one occasion at the Roses, Turner came in wet and tired from fishing in the rain.

> The servant was sent to the bedroom for his slippers; only one was to be found. Here was an opportunity not to be missed. The ladies ordered the servant to bring down the carpet-bag, hoping doubtless to obtain a glimpse of its contents; but a sly glance from our friend, with a peculiar shrug of his shoulders, and the two monosyllables 'No, no,' effectually put to flight their hopes. As a *dernier ressort*, one then offered to take his key and bring down the slipper. To that he replied, 'I never give it up'; and they never learnt its contents.[11]

Some of Turner's secretiveness about Sophia Booth and Sarah Danby may have sprung from a fear that, by carrying on with them, he would prejudice his standing as a Royal Academician. The Academy's founding instruments required its members to be 'men of fair moral character' as well as artists of distinction.[12] But Turner's need for mystery was in his bones. He also knew its value in terms of his art. The Redgraves observed that Turner 'ever studied to preserve a sense of *mystery* [in his pictures] ... The suggestiveness of a work of art is one of its richest qualities; and the veriest blot of Turner is suited to suggest more than the most finished picture of imitative details.'[13] As for his taciturnity, Ruskin found it 'very strange and sorrowful' that Turner would only 'hint ... at these undermeanings of his; leaving us to find them out, helplessly ...'[14] But perhaps Turner was helpless, too; he could not help being the way he was, not wanting to spell things out. In any case, the 'meaning', if it were forced out of him, might not always be as profound as some thought. The simplest answer might be the most correct. George Lance attended a dinner at which Turner was one of the distinguished guests.

> When we adjourned to the drawing room, our interest was fixed upon that lovely picture of Venice, which Turner painted expressly for Chantrey [*Ducal Palace, Dogano, with part of San Giorgio, Venice*, RA 1841], in the centre of which is a gondola, or rather gilded barge, in which are grouped a crowd of ladies and gentlemen, children and boatmen. Floating near this vessel is an object which I conceived must be, from its size and colour, a gorgeous turban. Just as I had suggested that belief, Turner came up, and Professor Owen said diplomatically: 'We are enchanted with that glorious work of yours, sir, but are divided in opinion as to what that object is floating so buoyantly on the water.'

Was it a buoy, a barrel, a seaman's cap, or some other highly coloured piece of flotsam?

Turner took his time in answering. Then, 'after two or three twitches of his lips, and as many little half *hmms*, he replied, "Orange – orange."'[15]

Although it would have had more shock potential in the prudish age into which he was now moving than it might have done earlier or later, Turner's choice of an 'unladylike' friend had a lot to recommend it.

Sophia Booth was a Margate woman when he met her, and Margate was his favourite resort. With its bow-fronted terraces, plentiful taverns and eel-and-pie shops, 1830s Margate was not stuffy – it was like the cheaper seats in a theatre, where the customers took their coats off and laughed out loud. All day the streets were noisy with the cries of vendors of cockles, bloaters, muffins, souvenirs and sermons. Organ-grinders and itinerant bands played at street corners. The air smelled of brine, fish and beer. The arrival of the Saturday evening 'Husbands' Boat', bringing down from London the spouses who had been working there all week to their holidaying wives and children, was the source of much badinage.

Seaside landladies – often widows, known for their frugality – were also the butt of coarse jokes. But we have no evidence that Sophia Booth, after taking in Turner, went on harbouring paying guests in Cold Harbour. This sailor ashore was no spendthrift, but she may have decided that the late Mr Booth's estate provided enough for her to live on. Like Turner, she was presumably glad of an occasional partner to keep her bed warm. That he wanted his identity to remain secret – that he sometimes had the furtive ways of a bankrupt – was in the end no great matter. It seems fitting that in the place where, by the account Mrs Cato gave to Robert Leslie, the first love of Turner's life had been blighted, he now found a good companion.

From Mrs Booth's point of view, it may have been an advantage that he was not around all the time. The sailor went to sea. He returned to Queen Anne Street, still his homeport, albeit little cared for, with Hannah (and the cats) in residence. Except once, Margate doesn't figure in his correspondence; he tried to leave his business affairs in town. But Margate was a practical jumping-off point for Europe. Sketchbooks might begin with Margate and go on with French or German subjects. And from Margate he roamed the Kentish coastline from the Medway round to Folkestone; he sketched at Whitstable and Ramsgate, Deal and Dover. He walked the beaches and headlands in fair weather and foul. He hired boats to take him a little way offshore, so that he could sketch the harbours, cliffs and towns. He observed and drew waves breaking, or running up and then noisily retreating over the shingle. A sailing ship stranded ashore was still a promising subject; so was a steamer bucking into the chop and scud off the North Foreland, black smoke blown skyward. For watercolours, there was nothing like Thanet

STANDING IN THE SUN

skies – 'the loveliest', as he once told Ruskin.[16] From the fields west of Margate he made a watercolour of the town rising behind the bay and harbour, with a verdant foreground where sun-hatted children and attendant girls with parasols picked nosegays. He had done a painting of the old pier nearly thirty years before (*The Old Pier, Margate*, c. 1804). Now he sat with a sketchbook at the upstairs front windows of Sophia Booth's house and looked out over the esplanade and rebuilt pier to the waters where North Sea and Thames Estuary converged. The sea's energy, its relaxed moments, its beauty and the sense it gave of being dangerous, ready to pounce, offered him a profusion of subjects for sea paintings.

He dipped into Dutch history at this time. He read about the Anglo–Dutch conflicts of the seventeenth century and the way in which British constitutional monarchy had been secured by the accession of a Dutch prince to the British throne. And in his usual manner – part homage, part competition – he set about a sequence of seapieces that would have been 'history paintings' if they had not been so fresh and vivid – it was as if the sun-drenched spray was still wet on them. He seemed to be on the Dutch side (it was a period in which, as we shall see, while visiting Petworth and fulfilling commissions for the Earl of Egremont, he was also taking a great interest in Rembrandt). The Academy exhibition of 1831 saw his *Admiral van Tromp's Barge at the Entrance of the Texel, 1645*. (Turner's interest in things Dutch did not extend to getting Tromp's name right – there was no 'van'.) The following year he exhibited three Dutch paintings: *The Prince of Orange, William III, embarked from Holland, and landed at Torbay, November 4th, 1688*; *Van Tromp's Shallop, at the Entrance of the Scheldt*; and *Helvoetsluys; – the City of Utrecht, 64, going to Sea*. In 1833 there were *Van Goyen, looking out for a Subject* and *Van Tromp returning after the Battle of the Dogger Bank* (followed eleven years later by *Van Tromp, going about to please his masters*).

The seas in many of these seascapes could have been painted from studies of those off Margate, though the colouring of the *Van Goyen* was more Venetian than northern. However, *The Rotterdam Ferry Boat*, exhibited in 1833, was thrashing through waters remembered from his last trip to the Low Countries in 1825. Where historical fact or contemporary reality did not provide a Dutch 'subject', his imagination stepped in, as in two paintings of 1827 and 1844 with

Port Ruysdael in their titles; this was a harbour he invented to convey his admiration for the Dutch master, though neither were very like Ruysdael, and the earlier of the two pictures, at any rate, showed that he could paint the North Sea better than Ruysdael or the Willem van de Velde who he had once claimed had made him a painter.

But pictures with Dutch themes were only a part of his immense marine production of these years. From the age of fifty to sixty-five, between 1825 and 1840, he gave the impression of viewing the sea daily, from ashore or afloat, whether he was actually in Margate and Deal, or in Queen Anne Street listening to the rut of the waves in his head. The 'space' he found at Venice was in many of these seascapes, and so was the salt breeze and slapping spray of British coastal waters. No one till now had got so fully within the movement of air and water. His hours of watching and sketching had brought him into the heart of the elements, and if he had never painted a single landscape or Carthaginian picture, these seapieces would have merited for him the title of Master. He continued to be engaged by the sea's destructive force and a good many of his marines were of storms and squalls, wrecks and ships aground. One such oil painting was his lengthily titled *Life-boat and Manby Apparatus going off to a Stranded Vessel making Signal (Blue Lights) of Distress*, exhibited in 1831. This may have represented a scene on the Norfolk coast near Yarmouth, where George Manby had invented his life-saving device, a mortar that fired a rope from lifeboat to craft in distress. The picture showed that he could paint in his old darker manner when he chose. From the same part of the East Anglian coast came a later watercolour, showing a sailing ship approaching Yarmouth harbour entrance through heavy seas while several groups of drenched fishermen haul small boats up the beach.[17]

A number of these pictures did not have conventional subjects; human beings were often not visible in them. If they were 'about' anything, it was the elements and man's place in the elemental mess, hanging on to the rigging, the bare bones of order. He went a trifle reluctantly to Scotland in 1831, to see Sir Walter Scott at his home at Abbotsford and then on tour to collect materials for the illustrations he was to make for a complete edition of Scott's poetical works. Robert Cadell, the Edinburgh publisher, as we have seen, had told Scott that Turner would 'insure the subscription of 8,000 [copies] – without, not 3,000'.[18] Cadell paid the expenses and Turner put aside his talk of not feeling well, of having already enough appropriate Scottish drawings to work from, and of being short of time, since he wanted to make if possible a summer trip across the Channel.

Turner declined Scott's offer of a pony on account of what he called his 'bad horsemanship', [19] which seems to indicate that he had lost some of the abilities or confidence that had taken him over hill and dale in the north of England out of Farnley; but he seized the opportunity of a new steamboat service to get out to the Western Isles. From Tobermory he embarked on the *Maid of Morven*, bound for Staffa and Iona. However, as he wrote in a letter a number of years after the event,

> a strong wind and head sea prevented us making Staffa until too late to go on to Iona. After scrambling over the rocks on the lee side of the island, some got into Fingal's Cave, others would not. It is not very pleasant or safe when the wave rolls right in. One hour was given to meet on the rock we landed on. When on board, the Captain declared it doubtful about Iona. Such a rainy and bad-looking night coming on, a vote was proposed to the passengers: 'Iona at all hazards, or back to Tobermoray.' Majority against proceeding. To allay the displeased, the Captain promised to steam thrice round the island in the last trip. The sun getting towards the horizon, burst through the rain-cloud, angry, and for wind; and so it proved, for we were driven for shelter into Loch Ulver, and did not get back to Tober Moray before midnight.[20]

On Staffa, Turner, a rock-climber since youth, showed none of his horse-riding hesitation. He was one of the party that scrambled into Fingal's Cave, where he sketched the interior. The cave, a place of Romantic pilgrimage, had been discovered in 1772 by the great naturalist Sir Joseph Banks, and featured in the fashionable works of Ossian – the purported ancient Gaelic epic that turned out to have been forged by the Highland-born poet and publicist James Macpherson. Turner, back home, did a vignette of the cave from within for the Scott *Poetical Works*. And he recorded on canvas with stormy brushstrokes the offshore scene that had prevented the *Maid of Morven* reaching Iona: the oncoming foul weather, the sun low on the murky horizon, the steamer plugging away from the steep-cliffed island, smoke streaming sideways in the wind. Despite the title – *Staffa, Fingal's Cave* – it was the rough sea and threatening sky he was interested in.

Although the critics generally admired this masterpiece at the 1832 RA exhibition, the picture remained in his dusty gallery until 1845, when his friend C. R. Leslie, acting as agent for Colonel James Lenox of New York, bought it for £500. But a complaint followed – and controversy thereafter. Turner asked Leslie how Colonel Lenox liked *Staffa* and Leslie felt bound to say that Lenox thought it indistinct. According to Thornbury, Turner replied to Leslie, 'You should tell him indistinctness is my *forte*.'[21] A later reading of Leslie's letter to Lenox suggests that Leslie in fact quoted Turner as saying the 'indistinctness is my fault' – he perhaps felt he should take the blame because the picture's varnish had bloomed on the sea voyage to New York. But in a sense Thornbury's mistake was a lucky hit: indistinctness had become Turner's *forte*.

Whatever his feelings about the times in which he lived, now going with them, now harking back away from them, Turner liked steamboats. A lovely watercolour from around 1830 shows one – a paddle-steamer – bustling along perhaps towards Margate with a thunderstorm looming towards it, a slash of lightning scribed across a wall of falling rain.[22] A paddle-wheel tug goes about its undertaking in the *Fighting Temeraire* of 1839, which will be discussed in a later chapter. Another paddle-steamer appears, more or less, in another bad-weather oil painting that demonstrated his genius for the indistinct. This was the 1842 *Snow Storm – Steam-Boat off a Harbour's Mouth*, a title that went on, and on, in his inimitable fashion, *making signals in shallow water, and going by the lead. The author was in this storm on the night the Ariel left Harwich*. Just how much of a fiction 'the author' perpetrated in this tumultuous seascape is moot. Since *Staffa* the weather had worsened. Indeed, in the 1842 picture an Alpine storm had apparently hit the North Sea; the steamer was in an avalanche of waves, going downhill, possibly going under.

The Reverend William Kingsley told Ruskin the story of how he took his mother (who, he claimed, knew nothing about art) to Turner's gallery:

> As we were passing the 'Snowstorm', she stopped before it, and I could hardly get her to look at any other picture; she told me a great deal more about it than I had any notion of, though I have seen many sea storms. She had been in such a scene on the coast of Holland during the war. When, some time afterwards, I thanked Turner for his permission for her to see his pictures, I told him

STANDING IN THE SUN

that he would not guess what had caught my mother's fancy, and then named the picture; and he then said, 'I did not paint it to be understood, but I wished to show what such a scene was like; I got the sailors to lash me to the mast to observe it; I was lashed for four hours, and I did not expect to escape, but I felt bound to record it if I did. But no one had any business to like the picture.' 'But,' said I, 'my mother once went through just such a scene, and it brought it all back to her.' 'Is your mother a painter?' 'No.' 'Then she ought to have been thinking of something else.'[23]

Prior to that final bit of churlishness, was he concocting some exciting background for Kingsley? One remembers, as he may have done, Ulysses bound to the mast to prevent him heeding the sirens' voices. There was apparently no *Ariel* sailing out of Harwich at this time. But a packet of that name operated from Dover, and in 1840 had brought Prince Albert from the Continent to England. A government survey vessel, the *Fairy*, which had set out from Harwich, was one of a number of ships lost in a great storm that devastated the south-eastern coasts of England on Friday, 13 November 1840 (a storm which figured in *David Copperfield*). Turner's wonderfully associative mind could easily have exchanged the *Fairy* for the *Ariel*, also a sprite, and from *The Tempest* at that! We note that he didn't specifically state in his title that he was on board the *Ariel*, but says, rather differently, he 'was in this storm'. He might have been on the beach at Margate, braced against the wind, watching the breakers roar, and perhaps watching a paddle-steamer trying to gain ground against the seas. If he had been aboard such a ship, he would have realized how impossible it would have been for any seaman to cast a lead to take soundings in the nearly terminal weather he painted.[24] And yet he definitely *felt* that he had been in this storm. He told Ruskin, his mind again drifting quickly from one idea to another, 'I hope I may never be out in another. Anything but snow: like the King of Sweden – anything but a bear – he wouldn't have minded a lion; but he didn't like a bear.'[25]

The critics had their easy way with *Snow Storm*. The writer for the *Athenaeum* (14 May 1842) said derisively: 'This gentleman has, on former occasions, chosen to paint with cream, or chocolate, yolk of egg, or currant jelly, – here he uses his whole array of kitchen stuff.' The *Art Union* (1 June 1842) wanted to wait for the storm to clear a little before giving a full account of the picture. One commentator claimed the picture was nothing but a mass of 'soapsuds and whitewash'.[26] Turner had by then become acquainted with the Ruskin family, and young John Ruskin got the artist's reaction to this. 'Turner was passing the evening at my father's house on the day this criticism came out: and after dinner, sitting in his armchair by the fire, I heard him muttering to himself at intervals, "soapsuds and whitewash! I wonder what they think the sea's like? I wish they'd been in it."'[27] What it was like was, as he had shown, a vortex of hurtling water and screaming air – sea and sky conjoined. He was sixty-seven when he exhibited this picture. He must have felt he was heading into the vortex.

Yet, as was always the case with him, two poles presented themselves: calm alternated with storm. It was sometimes 'the morning after' as he walked the beach and saw a ship aground, small boats in attendance, anchors placed ready to try to haul her off at the next tide. He saw and sketched a peaceful and exceptional game of cricket being played at low tide on the sometimes murderous Goodwin Sands. He watched children on the beaches and sketched them flying kites, building sand castles or looking for shells and crabs. 'Marine Dabblers' had been a subject in the *Liber* and cropped up again as a faint label in a sketch in 1829–30 of small figures on a beach, along with others of Margate and its harbour.[28] A painting of 1840 was called *The New Moon: or 'I've Lost My Boat, You shan't have Your Hoop'*. In this the children are on Margate beach – cliff and pier in the background, the smoke from a steamer's funnel trailing into the sunset beneath the new moon, a white dog looking at a boy with a stick and a black dog scampering towards the water.

He found another sunset scene on a beach on the other side of the Channel – women bent crab-like over the wet sands – and from it painted *Calais Sands, Low Water, Poissards collecting Bait*, exhibited in 1830. (After twenty-eight years, he still had Calais linked with poissards.) Any sort of fishing activity continued to catch his eye, at any time of day, whether of a catch being sold on the beach or the boats themselves at work. One immediate oil sketch, two foot by three, showed a cream-sailed cutter ghosting through the mist past a shore on which vague figures sort white shapes, presumably the morning haul. The sky above has a vivid Mediterranean-blue intensity but the small high-bowed, steep-sheered vessel is of authentic English shape.[29] Many of the great number of pictures he did at this time of inshore seas and calm beaches were unpopulated and painted for his own pleasure, with no thought of exhibition. A gentle sea laps the beach in *The Evening Star*, painted around 1830.

The edge of the sea formed a parallel for 'the brink of eternity', the closeness of which he had already felt. Hard to look at the sea without thinking of immensity, mortality, futility. And yet the beauty of it! In the 1830s, as he took the steamers to and from Margate for long weekends or summer weeks, he sometimes thought about his parents, who had first sent him there. In the summer of 1832 he finally got around to having a memorial to them erected in St Paul's, Covent Garden:

IN THE VAULT
BENEATH AND NEAR THIS PLACE
ARE DEPOSITED THE REMAINS OF
WILLIAM TURNER
MANY YEARS AN INHABITANT
OF THIS PARISH, WHO DIED
SEPTEMBER 21st 1830.
TO HIS MEMORY AND OF HIS WIFE
MARY ANN
THEIR SON I. M. W. TURNER R.A.
HAS PLACED THIS TABLET
AUGUST 1832

He evidently composed this rather confused epitaph himself. He got the year of his father's death wrong. He seems to have decided at the last minute to include his mother in the tribute to his father. There was an element of self-advertisement though also some truth in his pointing out the achievement of his parents in having such a son, an Academician. And the making of the monument resulted in one of his fits of pettiness. A mason was owed 7s 6d for his work on it, and a churchwarden at St Paul's, Mr Cribb, paid the bill, 'feeling certain that Turner would repay him when he came to look at the tablet. Turner called, and seemed satisfied with everything; until Mr Cribb mentioned the 7s 6d, when Turner told him to come some day and bring a receipt for the money, and said "he shouldn't pay it without he did". The money was not worth the trouble, so Turner got the mason's work without paying for it.'[30]

His old foe Sir George Beaumont had died in 1827. In the 1830s, the 'catalogue of death'[31] included his former mentor and his mother's physician, Dr Thomas Monro, who died in 1833. In 1836 his friend of so many years William Wells died, aged seventy-five. A rather terse note on black-edged paper from Turner to Wells's daughter Clara, by then Mrs Wheeler, says:

> I am much bothered and much agrieved by your injury and Mr Wheeler calling yesterday Evening hope you have written to Mitcham with my best regards
> Believe me most truly
> tho in great haste
> J M W Turner[32]

But in person he allowed his feelings to show. Clara recalled that Turner came round to her house 'in an agony of grief. Sobbing like a child, he said, "Oh, Clara, Clara! these are iron tears. I have lost the best friend I ever had in my life."' Clara thought Turner would have been 'a different man ... if all the good and kindly feelings of his great mind had been called into action'.[33] That point – the partial rather than total deployment of those feelings – had been demonstrated in the new will he made in 1831; or, possibly, what was shown in this instance was how grand his generosity could be on a large, institutional scale, how meagre in terms of real people.

This, his second such testament, was drafted by his solicitor George Cobb, and William Marsh, his stockbroker, who had witnessed his will in 1829, gave no help this time. Cobb evidently had pondered some of the legal problems involved in Turner's desire to set up a charity for 'Poor and Decayed Male Artists born in England and of English Parents Only and lawful issue'. The Mortmain Act of George II's time prohibited bequests of land for charitable purposes. So this second will directed Turner's executors to sell his land and invest the proceeds in a fund from which, after bequests were paid, the balance could be used to set up and maintain his charity for decayed artists, the charity to be called 'Turner's Gift'. The executors were to be Wells, the Reverend Henry Trimmer, Samuel Rogers, George Jones and Charles Turner. However, in this will, and in a subsequent codicil of 20 August 1832, his niggardly legacies to his ex-mistress and their daughters made a strange contrast to that munificent 'Gift'. Although like most people Turner realized that you can't take it with you, he was not about to give pleasure to individuals he actually knew and had blood ties with by leaving them generous amounts; there clearly wouldn't have been any pleasure for him in contemplating such action. So Hannah Danby, 'niece of John Danby, musician', and 'Eveline and Georgiana T the daughters of Sarah Danby' were by this 1831 will to get £50 a year for life, and Sarah herself a miserable £10 a year – sums increased in the 1832 codicil for Hannah and the girls to £100 a year. (Hannah was also to get an extra £50 a year for looking after 47 Queen Anne Street and keeping the 'Gallery in a viewable state ... concurring with the object of keeping my works together'.)

After various such bequests and the setting up of Turner's Gift, the residue of his estate was left by him to the Royal Academy as long as they had a dinner on his birthday, paid for a professor in landscape painting, and gave a biennial 'Turner's Medal' for landscape painting. If the Academy did not accept this arrangement, so the 1832 codicil declared, 'I give the same to Georgia Danby or her Heirs after causing a Monument to be placed near my remains as can be placed'.[34] Georgiana's name he or Cobb got wrong, although this mistake might not have worried her if she had indeed received the residue. Evelina had had her Christian name misspelled in the 1831 will and in this codicil her married name was given as Dupree rather than Dupuis. Though mentioned last, the monument (and its proximity to his remains) seems to have been high on his agenda now. So was the disposition of his paintings in the new National Gallery in a room to be called 'Turner's Gallery', with the paintings he referred to as *Dido building Carthage* and *The Sun rising through Vapour* to be always hung between Claude's *Seaport* and *Mill*. Turner had an Anglo-Saxon appetite for fame after death – after the battles of life. What his relatives, his ex-mistress and his daughters thought of him was less important.

Death, the final shipwreck, might be in his thoughts: now and then, as at the times of making these testaments, in the forefront of his mind, but mostly at the back of it. Meanwhile he embraced life, in the ample form of Sophia Booth or in snacks of shrimps eaten out of his handkerchief. He went on with untempered energy painting oils and watercolours, touring and sketching. Most professional artists continue to do what they do best, refining their craft, but not really changing form and subject. Turner was different – although his land and sea subject matter might seem the same, overall his way of presenting it changed. Despite occasional forays in past methods and styles, he was not satisfied with the mixture as before, however celebrated it had made him. What he had achieved was possible; he wanted to take the next step, to achieve the impossible. The *sine qua non* of great art is *dis*satisfaction, and Turner had an abundance of it.

At some point his restlessness affected his enjoyment of Margate. The railways began to bring more and more trippers. Perhaps he was spotted by a colleague, for he wasn't the only artist who liked the Thanet coast, and then had to put up with joshing questions. Although Margate was Mrs Booth's home, they may have moved on, seeking privacy; they seem to have spent a month or so in Deal in 1850. Alaric Watts heard that they sojourned in that town for a time after the move to Chelsea. A sketchbook of the 1840s contains sketches of Margate, Sandwich and Deal,[35] and also has jottings by Turner that have to do with building or fixing up a house. There is a rough ground plan showing several rooms. A list of work and materials mentions roofs, stairs and window-sills: thirty-eight window-sills, in fact, a number which seems implausible. Perhaps he planned a longer seaside stay in a new abode. But the Eastlakes were also in Deal in August 1850, and this might have given Turner a fright.

The 'wizened' and 'odd little mortal'[36] with his sun-reddened face remained in Mrs Booth's favour, whatever his eccentricities and stinginess. To his credit, he took an interest in the upbringing of Daniel John Pound, her son by her first marriage and a well-set-up youth, who 'took after' Turner to the extent of training as an engraver.[37] Eventually, at least when Turner was in her company, the artist's appearance was less untidy and unbrushed; she seems to have taken him in hand. There are hints to be gathered of their days together: he rarely let a subject for a drawing slip by undrawn, and he did three mackerel waiting on the Margate kitchen table.[38]

And there are hints of their nights together too. Those who later were suddenly made aware of Mrs Booth and claimed that all she had been was his housekeeper not only have to face David Roberts's remark that they passed as husband and wife, but have to ignore a number of drawings and oil sketches from these years. One little sketchbook[39] of the 1830s contains a number of blurry 'Colour Studies' – coloured mists or curtains, almost, that are waiting to be lifted or pulled; and when they are, at least partially, there are to be seen in a number of them forms, sometimes hard to make out: bodies, alone or together; legs up, limbs tangled; a woman lying on her side, buttocks exposed, vulva highlighted with a single dash of red paint; and what could be a tall dark toadstool seen from above but is – in the context of the limbs and nudes on surrounding pages – most likely an erect phallus. At fifty-nine or so he still had a powerful sex-drive, though he didn't seem altogether free about revealing it, even for his own viewing.

Most of these 'studies' are not well drawn; only a part of him seemed involved. Some have a voyeuristic feeling: one shows two extra-terrestrial-looking figures watching a naked sleeping woman. The sensuality and cunning that David Roberts remarked are more evident than any ability to draw the human form. But now and then things become more straightforwardly clear – and more ably done. There are several pictures of the same period that seem to be of one woman – flat-faced, though with rounded cheeks and soft somewhat undershot chin, her hair in a bun at the back. One watercolour of a woman's head, eyes closed; one red-chalk sketch of the same woman sleeping, her full bare breasts visible above rumpled sheets; and a rough oil sketch, perhaps done by oil light or candlelight, of the woman's head as she sleeps.[40] Some of these pictures were left with Mrs Booth and they could only be of her. It seems obvious that their intimacy was such that Turner could get out of bed, after love-making, and draw or paint Sophia while she slept.

16: Varnishing Days

A lmost as if he deliberately wanted to overturn the central assumption about his character – that he was a 'mistifying' recluse – Turner for a short period once a year came forth and performed as an artist before his colleagues. The hedgehog turned briefly into a peacock. This occurred at the Royal Academy, on the days before the annual exhibition that were allotted for members to put the finishing touches to their works. The privilege to do this had been slowly built up, particularly by Turner since 1798, when he was twenty-three, and had been given some formality in 1803, when Turner was on the Council; in that year a day was actually set aside for members to varnish their exhibits. In 1809, the RA General Assembly accepted Martin Archer Shee's proposal that three or more days be granted – 'previous to the day appointed for the Annual Dinner in the Exhibition Room'[1] – for members to retouch or varnish their pictures. It remained an Academy tradition for more than forty years, complained about in the press as a form of favouritism and resented by non-Academician exhibitors who did not have the same opportunity; it was thought unfair that they were not even allowed to dust their pictures. The number of varnishing days expanded at one point to five. Although, towards mid-century, there was a move to get rid of them, they were retained until 1852, largely because Turner so manifestly made use of them.[2]

Despite some ups and downs in the relationship, the Academy remained at the heart of his professional life. He went on taking his turn on the Council; he served a twenty-three-year term as Auditor, putting his canniness about money to the Academy's service, and he continued to be a Visitor in the Schools. He took part in debates in the Assembly, though sometimes he did not speak publicly but – according to his friend George Jones – tried to get acrimonious proceedings peacefully resolved. (Perhaps he had had early practice in this, mediating between his parents.) Occasionally Turner's confused attempts to speak had a similar effect; heated debates sputtered to an end and matters later received calmer consideration. Farington on 21 January 1819 recorded Callcott's complaints that 'little business was done at the Academy Council owing to the improper behaviour of Soane, jeering at what was said by members and treating business with ridicule; added to which the incessant talking of Turner made it impossible to proceed with any dispatch'.

However, Jones also recalled Turner's 'exemplary' conduct and 'zealous' attendance; he 'never made his excursions abroad until the business of the Academy was suspended by vacation ... At the great dinner before the opening of the Exhibition and at the Exhibitors' dinner at its close he invariably attended, deeming the latter a most important opportunity of getting acquainted with the artists likely to become members of the institution.'[3] In a typically foggy speech at one such end-of-exhibition dinner, he finally got to his point, which was loyalty to the Academy. Addressing the younger exhibitors, he said, 'When you become members of this institution you must fight in a phalanx – no splits – no quarrelling – one mind – one object – the good of the Arts and the Royal Academy.'[4] And his working year – touring in the summer and autumn, painting hard all winter – generally built to the late spring when the exhibition filled the immediate future. The pictures he intended for it crowded his mind, although they did not necessarily get close to completion; the opening day was his one real deadline.

The Academy remained, increasingly cramped, at Somerset House until 1836. Turner was on the committee set up in 1832 to consult with government officials about the new National Gallery to be built overlooking the new Trafalgar Square, with rooms and galleries for the Academy in the east wing of the structure. But he may not have been happy about the move; he was absent from the farewell dinner in the Great Room of Somerset House on 20 July 1836, with the exhibition pictures still hanging, when Chantrey made a toast: 'The old walls of the Academy!'[5] Did he stay away because he would have been too upset? Was he down in Margate? (He set off with his friend and patron Hugh Munro for France and Switzerland shortly after the exhibition closed, but he was still in London on 26 July.) The Academy exhibition of 1837 was the first to be held in its new quarters. Until the opening of the National

Gallery in 1824 in Angerstein's house in Pall Mall, the Academy show was the chief venue at which the British public could look at art. Yet, whatever Turner's sense of loss aroused by the move from Somerset House, he was among those members who presented pictures to the Academy for its new quarters: he gave a portrait group by Rigaud of three Academicians, to be hung in the new Council room. He was also on the hanging committee for the first exhibition in 1837 at Trafalgar Square.

Farington in 1803 had remarked on Turner's behaviour on 'the day appointed at the Academy for varnishing the pictures'. Wyatt had told Farington how Turner had been seen to '*spit* all over his picture, and, then taking out a box of *brown powder*, rubbed it over the picture'. Farington knew that picture restorers used tobacco juice to tone a recently cleaned picture and assumed that Turner was using snuff for this purpose.[6] As time passed, Turner got more and more out of the concession. By 1819 there were three varnishing days, and in that year he exhibited the *Entrance of the Meuse: Orange-Merchant on the Bar* and *England: Richmond Hill*. Farington happily noted the backbiting brought about by the effect of 'the flaming colour of Turner's pictures' on neighbouring paintings. The diarist went on to mention 'the pernicious effects arising from Painters working upon their pictures in the Exhibition by which they often render them unfit for a private room'.[7] Before the curtain went up on the RA show, Turner got his value out of the varnishing days; and, despite what Farington called 'pernicious effects', many of Turner's colleagues got much benefit and amusement too.

By the 1830s, his performance was a virtuoso act, mingling instruction, entertainment and brazen rivalry as he applied scumbles, glazes and impasto to his unfinished sketches. He worked alone, although artists were allowed to bring an assistant to run errands and clean their brushes, and some like C. R. Leslie took their sons. Robert and George Leslie were impressed by what they saw. Robert remembered that around 1832

> I first went with my father to the Royal Academy upon varnishing days, and, wandering about watching the artists at work, there was no one, next to Stanfield and his boats, that I liked to get near so much as Turner, as he stood working upon those, to my eyes, nearly blank white canvases in their old academy frames. There were always a number of mysterious little gallipots and cups of colour

ranged upon drawing stools in front of his pictures; and, among other bright colours, I recollect one that must have been simply red-lead. He used short brushes, some of them like the writers used by house decorators, working with thin colour over the white ground, and using the brush end on, dapping and writing with it those wonderfully fretted cloud forms and the ripplings and filmy surface curves upon his near water. I have seen Turner at work upon many varnishing days, but never remember his using a maul-stick. He came, they said, with the carpenters at six in the morning, and worked standing all day. He always had on an old, tall beaver hat, worn rather off his forehead, which added much to his look of a North Sea pilot ... His way of work was quite unlike that of the other artists ... His colours were mostly in powder, and he mixed them with turpentine, sometimes with size, and water, and perhaps even with stale beer, as the grainers do their umber when using it upon an oil ground ... Besides red-lead, he had a blue which looked very like ordinary smalt; this, I think, tempered with crimson or scarlet lake, he worked over his near waters in the darker lines.[8]

Turner used a bench or a tea chest to stand on for dealing with the upper parts of a picture – working, so George Leslie said, 'almost with his nose close to the picture'.[9] It was a podium for conducting his own score. On these occasions his demonic energy was fully displayed. The writer and painter E. V. Rippingille – generally hostile to Turner – saw him working before the opening of a British Institution exhibition in 1836 on a painting of the burning of the Houses of Parliament, a picture which

when sent in was a mere dab of several colours, and 'without form and void', like chaos before the creation ... Such a magician, performing his incantations in public, was an object of interest and attraction. Etty was working by his side ... sometimes speaking to some one near him, after the approved manner of painters: but not so Turner; for the three hours I was there – and I understood it had been the same since he began in the morning – he never ceased to work, or even once looked or turned from the wall on which his picture hung ... In one part of the mysterious proceedings Turner, who worked almost entirely with his palette knife, was observed to be rolling and spreading a lump of half-transparent stuff over his picture, the size of a finger in length and thickness. As Callcott was looking on I ventured to say to him, 'What is that he is plastering his picture with?' to which inquiry it was replied, 'I should be sorry to be the man to ask him.' ... Presently the work was finished: Turner gathered his tools together, put them into and shut up the box, and then, with his face still turned to the wall, and at the same distance from it, went sidling off, without speaking a word to anybody, and when he came to the staircase, in the centre of the room, hurried down as fast as he could. All looked with a half-wondering smile, and Maclise, who stood near, remarked, 'There, that's masterly, he does not stop to look at his work; he *knows* it is done, and he is off.'[10]

C. R. Leslie used to say that Turner looked upon varnishing days as one of the greatest privileges of the Academy; the days gave him a lot of opportunity for his mysterious little jokes and fun with his brother artists. The man who wasn't above cadging a clean plate and a hot potato on the steamer to Margate, here 'borrowed' materials. Richard Redgrave saw him at it:

Such was his love of colour that any rich tint on a brother painter's palette so tempted him that he would jokingly remove a large portion of it to his own, and immediately apply it to his picture, irrespective of the medium with which it was made up. From our own palette he has whisked off, on more occasions than one, a luscious knob of orange vermilion, or ultramarine, tempered with copal, and at once used it on a picture he was at work upon with a mastic magylph. Such a practice, productive of no mischief at the moment, would break up a picture when the harder drier began to act on that which was of a less contractile nature.[11]

Redgrave knew Turner from the early 1830s and thought that at this stage of his life, from his mid-fifties, he did not look like a genius.

His short figure had become corpulent – his face, perhaps from continual exposure to the air, was unusually red, and a little inclined to blotches. His dark eye was bright and restless – his nose, aquiline. He generally wore what is called a black dress-coat, which would have been the better for brushing – the sleeves were mostly too long, coming down over his fat and not over-clean hands. He wore his hat while painting on the varnishing days – or otherwise a large wrapper over his head, while on the warmest days he generally had another wrapper or comforter round his throat – though occasionally he would unloose it and allow the two ends to dangle down in front and pick up a little of the colour from his ample palette. This, together with his ruddy face, his rollicking eye, and his continuous, although, except to himself, unintelligible jokes, gave him the appearance of that now wholly extinct race – a long-stage coachman.[12]

Richard Redgrave also had first-hand experience of the help

Turner gave on these occasions to younger colleagues, even though 'it was conveyed in dark hints and ambiguous phrases'. He recalled that during the first varnishing days in 1841 to which he was admitted on being elected an associate, he was 'trying to *spoil* his picture, *The Castle Builder*, when Henry Howard came up to him and said, 'in his most frigid manner', that the bosom of his figure was indelicately naked, and that some of the members thought he should paint the dress higher.

> Here was a dilemma for a new associate. Of course, with due meekness, I was about to comply with his advice, although greatly against the grain, and with a sort of wonder at myself that I could possibly have been ignorantly guilty of sending an immodest contribution to the Exhibition. Meanwhile, Turner looked over my shoulder, and, in his usual sententious manner, mumbled out, 'What-r-doing?' I told him the rebuke I had just received from the secretary. 'Pooh, pooh,' said he, 'paint it lower.'

Redgrave thought Turner was trying to lead him into trouble. Turner added, turning on his heel, 'You want white.'

> What could he mean? I pondered over his words, and after a while the truth struck me. The coloured dress came harshly on the flesh, and no linen intervened. I painted at once, over a portion of the bosom of the *dress*, a peep of the chemise. Howard came round soon after, and said, with a little more warmth, 'Ah! you have covered it up – it is far better now – it will do.' It was no higher however; there was just as much of the flesh seen, but the sense of nakedness and display was gone. Turner also came round again, and gave his gratified grunt at my docility and appreciativeness, which he often rewarded afterwards by like hints.
>
> Now this was not a mere incidental change, but it was a truth, always available in the future, the value of linen near the flesh – a hint I never forgot, and continually found useful. Many such have I heard and seen him give to his brother landscape painters – either by word of mouth or with a dash of his brush.[13]

In fact, Turner did not confine his help to landscapists. Wandering around the exhibition rooms on a varnishing day in 1847, he stopped at a picture by the history painter Solomon Hart, showing Galileo in a Florence prison being visited by John Milton. Galileo's head in the picture was against a light, bare background. Turner with a piece of chalk sketched in Galileo's solar system behind his head. 'Turner was upon the point of effacing his addition,' Hart wrote later, 'but Stanfield, who was much interested, hastened to me, to persuade me to preserve the lines. He mixed up some paint and stood over me whilst I secured them with colour. All thought that Turner's suggestion had much improved my picture.'[14] As a 'fixer', Turner was busy that year. He was working on his own picture of the making of a statue of the Duke of Wellington, *The Hero of a Hundred Fights*, and one of its neighbours in the hanging arrangement was Daniel Maclise's *Sacrifice of Noah after the Deluge*. The following conversation was recorded by George Jones:

Turner: 'I wish Maclise that you would alter that lamb in the foreground, but you won't.'

Maclise: 'Well, what shall I do?'

Turner: 'Make it darker behind to bring the lamb out, but you won't.'

Maclise: 'Yes I will.'

Turner: 'No you won't.'

Maclise: 'But I will.'

Turner: 'No you won't.'

Maclise did as Turner proposed and asked his neighbour if that would do.

Turner (stepping back to look at it): 'It is better, but not right.'

He then went up to the picture, took Maclise's brush, accomplished his wish and improved the effect. He also introduced a portion of a rainbow, or reflected rainbow, much to the satisfaction of Maclise, and his work remains untouched.[15]

On a varnishing day during an earlier year the landscape painter W. F. Witherington was having trouble with a picture of a road passing through a wood, with some prominent white wild flowers in the foreground. It wasn't quite right, and Witherington asked some Academicians how to improve it. William Hilton said, 'I will fetch a man to tell you.' Turner came over. According to T. Sidney Cooper, who was on hand, Turner 'dipped his brush into some blue that he had on his palette [and] glazed over the white flowers. They all immediately exclaimed, "That's it!" And certainly the effect was magical. It at once put the whole picture in tone.'[16]

The same ability to see how a small change could significantly make or break a picture came to the aid of Cooper himself. Stanfield on this occasion, possibly in 1846, had suggested to Cooper that he lower the tone of the background on which some sheep were painted, as it was all too much the same colour. Cooper was just about to do this when Turner came by, looked at the picture, added some colour from his palette and walked on. Stanfield said, 'Don't touch it – he has done all that it wanted.' When Cooper left the RA rooms, he ran into Joseph Gillott, the wealthy pen manufacturer, and told him what had happened. Gillott, after being reassured that Turner had really 'touched' the picture, immediately agreed to buy it unseen for £300.[17] Assisted in a similar way was the landscapist Thomas Creswick, who in 1848 exhibited at the RA a picture called *Squally Day*. The American artist and journalist William J. Stillman wrote:

> Near the centre of the landscape was a white horse, forming rather a conspicuous object. On the varnishing day, one of the academicians advised him to paint out the horse, and a difference arose with regard to it, when it was agreed to refer the point to Mr Turner, who was in another room, and had only once walked hastily through the room in which the picture was, making it impossible for him to have given it more than a passing glance. He replied, without going [again] into the room, 'Keep it in.' 'But,' said they, 'something is wrong.' 'Well,' said Turner, 'you have got him turned the wrong way' – and on seeing the picture they discovered that the horse had turned his head towards the storm instead of his tail, as he should have done.[18]

Other young painters received encouragement from Turner – one of them, Frith, thought modestly that Turner had overpraised him on one occasion. When young Robert Leslie became an exhibitor at the Academy in 1850, with a rather sentimental picture called *A Sailor's Yarn*, Turner came over and after a minute of looking at it said, 'I like your colour.' One imagines that Turner felt the need to be kind and this was the most honest compliment he could pay; at any rate, it remained in Robert Leslie's memory, a source of pleasure.[19] If there were small boys around, like Robert and George Leslie when younger, Turner didn't mind them watching him, and even now and then explained things to them. George Leslie, aged nine, observed him in 1844 when he was working on *Rain, Steam, and Speed*:

> He used rather short brushes, a very messy palette, and, standing very close up to the canvas, appeared to paint with his eyes and nose

as well as his hand. Of course he repeatedly walked back to study the effect ... He talked to me every now and then, and pointed out the little hare running for its life in front of the locomotive on the viaduct.[20]

Young Leslie then had lunch in the Council Room, sitting between his father and Turner. Turner helped him to slices of tongue and made him feel at home. The boy didn't 'understand all the jokes and fun that went on', but got the impression 'that Turner held his own in it all remarkably well'.[21] (According to George's father, Turner – despite his singularly secretive habits – had a social nature, and on these occasions 'was the life of the table'.)[22] Frith was at one of these varnishing-day lunches when R. R. Reinagle came in late and somewhat drunk and sat down next to Turner. Turner asked where he had been – 'You were not in the rooms this morning.'

'*Been*, sir?' said Reinagle. 'I have been in the City. I have invented a railway to go up and down Cheapside. Omnibuses will be done away with. I shall make millions, and' – looking round the table – 'I will give you all commissions.' Then looking aside at Turner, 'And I will give you a commission if you will tell me which way to hang the picture up when I get it.'

'You may hang it just as you please,' said Turner, 'if you only pay for it.'[23]

At another lunch, when an engraver stood up to carve some beef, another member appropriated the engraver's chair, with the result that when the engraver sat down he did so, with a shock, on the floor. At this – J. W. Archer wrote – 'Turner growled out: "Come, come – this is too bad, I cannot have one of my best engravers spoilt in this way"; and going round to his prostrate ally, assisted him to rise, with an earnest expression of condolence, and recommended a mixture of oil and turpentine, which he said he had in his colour-box, as an efficient lineament.'[24]

There was also of course an element of rivalry at the Academy on these days; Turner zestfully entered into the spirit of competition. George Leslie noted that other artists used to dread having their pictures hung next to his, on which he piled, 'mostly with the knife, all the brightest pigments he could lay his hands on, chromes, emerald green, vermilion, etc.' His neighbours said that 'it was as bad as having their pictures hung next to an open window'.[25] Chantrey as a sculptor could afford to be better humoured about this Turner effect;

one cold day, he stopped before one of Turner's paintings 'in which orange chrome was unusually conspicuous, and affecting to warm his hands before it, said, "Turner, this is the only comfortable place in the room. Is it true, as I have heard, that you have a commission to paint a picture for the Sun Fire [Insurance] Office?"'[26]

Not only did Turner make his own pictures 'blaze with light and colour'; there were reports, said George Leslie, that he occasionally worked on pictures hung next to his to make them less so. 'It is said that he was once discovered, by a fellow-member, rubbing tone over a small picture that was above one of his own, and on being asked if that were his picture he was working on, he replied, "No, but it is spoiling mine." Most probably the toning was put on with watercolour only, for he would hardly have been so unjust as to use oil. Yet Turner was, as Voltaire said of the prophet Habakkuk, *capable de tout*.'[27]

His younger colleagues Stanfield and Roberts followed him in treating varnishing days as occasions for working on their pictures and having a good time. In 1826 Callcott exhibited a picture entitled *Dutch Fishing-Boats running foul, in the endeavour to board, and missing the painter-rope* – the last phrase of which was taken to be a jocular reference to Stanfield's failure to finish a picture called *Throwing the Painter* in time for the exhibition. The following year, Turner – with whom jokes could ferment for a long time – took up the challenge with his *'Now for the Painter', (Rope). Passengers going on Board*. (The rather flat-footed '(Rope)' seems to have been for the benefit of landlubberly viewers, though it may have been Turner simply milking the pun to the last drop.)

Frith was on hand when David Roberts needed all his sense of humour to handle Turner as a varnishing-day neighbour. Roberts's *A View of Edinburgh* – 'a long, narrow, delicately-coloured picture' – was hung next to Turner's *Masaniello and the Fisherman's Ring*. Frith wrote that when first placed on the wall, Masaniello's 'queer figure' was relieved by a pale grey sky, the whole effect being almost as grey and quiet as Roberts's picture. Turner's face was muffled 'to protect it from the draughts' for which the rooms were celebrated.

> Both he and Roberts stood upon boxes, and worked silently at their respective pictures. I found myself close to them, painting some figures into a landscape by Creswick. I watched my neighbours from

time to time, and if I could discover no great change in the aspect of 'Edinburgh', there was no doubt whatever that 'Masaniello' was rapidly undergoing a treatment which was very damaging to its neighbour without a compensating improvement to itself. The gray sky had become an intense blue that even Italy could scarcely be credited with it. Roberts moved uneasily on his box-stool. Then, with a sidelong look at Turner's picture, he said in the broadest Scotch:

'You are making that varra blue.'

Turner said nothing; but added more and more ultramarine. This was too much.

'I'll just tell ye what it is, Turner, you're just playing the deevil with my picture, with that sky – ye never saw such a sky as that!'

Turner moved his muffler to one side, looked down at Roberts, and said:

'You attend to your business, and leave me to attend to mine.'

And to this hour 'Masaniello' remains – now in the cellars of the National Gallery – with the bluest sky ever seen in a picture, and never seen out of one.[28]

Yet he let Jones win a similar contest in 1833, when Turner added more blue to a picture one day to outblue the sky in Jones's picture, and Jones the next day made his own sky *whiter*, which made Turner's sky look much too blue. Turner slapped Jones on the back and told him to enjoy his victory. When Jones before the 1832 exhibition told Turner that he was going to paint Shadrach, Meshach and Abednego being delivered from the fiery furnace, Turner said, 'A good subject. I will paint it also.' He asked what size Jones intended to paint it, and said he would paint it the same, got Jones to order two panels for them both, and said he would make sure not to look at Jones's while he was painting it. 'Both pictures were painted and exhibited,' wrote Jones. 'Our brother Academicians thought that Turner had secretly taken an advantage of me and were surprised at our mutual contentment, little suspecting our previous friendly arrangement.'[29]

Others, faced with Turner's competitiveness, were less contented. C. R. Leslie was on hand when Turner's *Helvoetsluys*, to start with 'a grey picture, beautiful and true, but with no positive colour in any part of it', was hung next to Constable's *Opening of Waterloo Bridge*. Leslie wrote that Constable's painting looked as if painted with liquid gold and silver, and Turner came several times into the room while Constable was heightening with vermilion and lake the decorations and flags of the city barges. Turner stood behind Constable, looking from the 'Waterloo' to his own picture, and at last went and got his palette from the Great Room where he had been touching another picture. He then put a round daub of red lead,

> somewhat bigger than a shilling, on his grey sea, [and] went away without saying a word. The intensity of the red lead, made more vivid by the coolness of his picture, caused even the vermilion and lake of Constable to look weak. I came into the room just as Turner left it. 'He has been here,' said Constable, 'and fired a gun.' ... The great man did not come again into the room for a day and a half; and then, in the last moments that were allowed for painting, he glazed the scarlet seal he had put on his picture, and shaped it into a buoy.[30]

There has been some discussion as to whether the jaunty black dog that was put on the parapet in Turner's *Mortlake Terrace ... Summer's Evening* was added as an afterthought by Turner himself on a varnishing day or by a fellow artist doing him a good turn. One viewer, the writer and editor of *Punch* Tom Taylor, called the dog 'a proof of Turner's reckless readiness of resource when an effect in art was wanted. It suddenly struck the artist that a dark object here would throw back the distance and increase the aerial effect.'[31] But Frederick Goodall RA, the son of one of Turner's engravers, said it was the work of the twenty-five-year-old Edwin Landseer: 'He cut out a little dog in paper, painted it black, and on Varnishing Day, stuck it upon the terrace. All wondered what Turner would say and do when he came up from the luncheon table at noon. He went up to the picture quite unconcernedly, never said a word, adjusted the little dog perfectly, and then varnished the paper and began painting it. And there it is to the present day.' However, it seems more likely that it was Turner himself who originally placed the paper dog on the canvas, and perhaps it fell off and Landseer stuck it back again.[32] Turner, we recall, also employed a paper figure in *The Golden Bough*.

Landseer admired Turner's helpfulness and teaching skills on varnishing days. He said later:

> I should think no man could be more accurate in his observation, or more thoroughly grounded in the education of the artist than Turner. I have seen him detect errors during the days when we met at the Academy, after the pictures were placed; and whatever he suggested was done without question, and it was always an improvement, whether in proportion or chiaroscuro, or anything

else. He was thoroughly grounded in everything, and, without exception, I should say, the best teacher I ever met with.[33]

Doubts also are cast on two stories about his 1826 exhibit, *Cologne, the Arrival of a Packet Boat, Evening*. One had it that Chantrey heard that during varnishing days Turner had been toning the picture with watercolour. Chantrey was said to have rubbed a wet finger across one of the packet boat's sails and realized he had removed some glazing. Another was that the vividness of this picture – one of his 'yellow dwarf' products – overwhelmed two portraits by Lawrence that hung on each side of it, and Turner therefore generously gave the *Cologne* a wash of lamp-black; this horrified Lawrence, though Turner was said to have assured him it would wash off after the exhibition. Despite George Jones and Ruskin standing by this story, it has been pointed out that Turner, for all his acts of helpfulness to his colleagues, would never have diminished to such a degree the impact of one of his main exhibits. He had, moreover, specifically told his father to take care of the surface of this painting – not to touch it with water or varnish and to wipe it only with a silk handkerchief. A more typical incident occurred the following year, when his *Rembrandt's Daughter* was hung close to a Martin Archer Shee portrait of an academic in a bright-red university gown. Turner piled on the red lead and vermilion to 'checkmate' Shee.[34]

The operation of hanging the pictures involved a good deal of politicking, diplomacy and – it could not be helped – ill-feeling. Pictures were hung close together all over the walls, which in the case of the Great Room were extremely high. They could be hung 'on the line', at roughly a viewer's eye height; 'below the line', as many small pictures were, packed in like 'little bricks', as the hangers called them; or 'skied' up to the ceiling, tilted forward to make them more visible.[35] Turner served from time to time on the hanging committee, whose membership changed every year. In 1811 when he and Callcott were on the committee, they were criticized for exceeding the limits of eight works allowed members (Turner showed nine, Callcott ten), 'all placed in the very best positions', it was noted.[36] (In 1818, Callcott moved his *Mouth of the Tyne* to make room for Turner's *Dort*.) In 1812 there had been ructions at Somerset House. Big historical pieces by West and Fuseli (who was on the hanging committee) were given the best positions. Farington was also on the hanging committee that year and wrote in his diary (10 April):

Turner's large picture of 'Hannibal crossing the Alps' was placed over the door of the new room (but in the great room) & it was thought was seen to great advantage. Mr West came & concurred in this opinion with Smirke, Dance & myself. Calcott came and remarked that Turner had sd. that if this picture were not placed under the line He wd. rather have it back; Calcott also thought it wd. be better seen if under the line. He went away & we took the picture down & placed it opposite to the door of the entrance, the situation which Calcott mentioned.

There, so Farington thought, it appeared to the greatest disadvantage. It injured the whole effect of that part of the arrangement, and the committee therefore decided to replace it. On the following day,

While we were at dinner Turner came and took a little only having dined early. He asked me 'What had we done with His pictures?' I told Him we had had much difficulty abt. His large picture 'Hannibal crossing the Alps'. He went upstairs & staid a while and afterwards returned to us with an apparently assumed cheerfulness but soon went away and took Howard out of the room, who soon came back & informed us that Turner objected to His picture being placed above the line. Howard assured Him it was seen there to better advantage, but He persisted in saying that if it were not to be placed below the line He would take it away; that as He saw us cheerfully seated He would not now mention his intention to us, but would come on Monday morning to have the matter finally determined.

On the Monday Turner duly repeated his threat to take the *Hannibal* away. Farington then got it hung 'at the head of the new room' below the line. Here, after some more indecision from Turner, which presumably served to irritate the hanging committee, the artist approved its situation, 'provided other members shd. have pictures near it'. His friend Leslie in fact thought that at this location it was hard to see the *Hannibal* 'at the proper distance, owing to the crowd of people' in front of it. The crowd, at any rate, seemed to indicate that Turner got for his picture what he wanted, the maximum of attention.[37]

Turner was also unhappy about the way his other exhibits of that same year, his two Oxford pictures, were hung, because of their neighbours, but despite complaints about this to James Wyatt, for whom he had painted them, he left them at the exhibition. His interest in the surroundings of his pictures extended beyond the neighbouring paintings. Alaric Watts thought this concern 'that everything should aid the effect of his pictures' lay behind his offer one year to pay for cloth to recover the seats of the room in which one of his paintings was hung.[38]

As always with Turner, his inner barometer soon swung from stormy to fair. Jones noted his generous behaviour as arranger one year when he 'took down one of his own pictures to give a better place to a picture by the late Mr [Edward] Bird, before that artist was a member of the Academy'.[39] And Jones recalled that on the occasion of their competition with fiery-furnace pictures, when the hanging committee gave Turner's picture a superior position, Turner 'used his utmost endeavours to get my work changed to the place his occupied and his placed where mine hung, as they were exactly the same size'.[40] David Roberts contrasted Turner's modesty about his own abilities with Constable's disposition to talk about himself and his works. Roberts met the two one night in 1831 at 'dear old General' Phipps's house in Mount Street, where the walls were covered with fine paintings:

> Constable a concealed egotistic person, whatever Leslie may have written to the contrary, was loud in describing to all the severe duties he had undergone in the hanging the Exibition. [He was on the hanging committee that year.] According to his own account nothing could exceed his disinteredness or his anxiety to discharge that Sacred Duty. Most unfortunately for him a Picture of Turner's [*Caligula's Palace*] had been displaced after the arraingment of the room in which it was ... Turner opened upon him like a ferret; it was evident to all present Turner detested him; all present were puzzled what to do or say to stop this. Constable wriggled, twisted & made it appear or wished to make it appear that in his removal of the Picture he was only studying the best light or the best arraingment for Turner. The latter coming back invariably to the charge, yes, but why put your own there? [This was *Salisbury Cathedral from the Meadows*.] I must say that Constable looked to me and I believe to every one else, like a detected criminal, and I must add that Turner slew him without remorse.[41]

Despite Roberts's allegation that Turner 'detested' Constable, there is evidence that in this, as so often, a contrary case can be made: Turner went to call on Constable in February 1829, after he was finally elected a full member of the Academy, and talked with him till one in the morning, although it is uncertain whether

Turner actually voted for Constable or for his good friend Eastlake. According to Cosmo Monkhouse, Turner gave Constable some varnishing-day help 'on one occasion by striking in a ripple in the foreground of his picture – the "something" just needed to make the composition satisfactory'.[42]

It was a matter of dispute among his fellow artists just how much of his pictures Turner painted when they were hanging on the walls of the Academy, though most agreed that his virtuoso performances on varnishing days greatly reduced the longevity of his paintings. Frith said it was 'an erroneous notion that Turner occasionally had painted the *whole* of some of his pictures during varnishing days', though he acknowledged 'seeing great effects in the way of change and completion produced by Turner in a very short time'.[43] But as the Redgraves noted, his habit of pinching knobs of colour from other painters like Stanfield and applying it, 'irrespective of the medium with which it was made up', caused a number of his later paintings to fail.[44] His *Rembrandt's Daughter*, with much last-minute brilliance, soon cracked up. Concern for the longevity of the surface of his pictures was less in his mind than concern for immediate impact and sometimes any medium would do. Stanfield told the restorer F. P. Seguier: 'I saw Turner apply watercolours with his fingers as a finishing glaze to certain of his oils.'[45]

George Leslie, with his own and his father's knowledge of the subject, wrote of Turner's later work:

> Turner used to send these pictures into the Academy with only a delicate effect, almost in monochrome, laid on the canvas, and very beautiful they looked, often like milky ghosts. They had probably been painted for some time, as they were quite dry and hard; all the bright colour was loaded on afterwards, the pictures gradually growing stronger in effect and colour during the ... varnishing days.

Leslie believed that Turner for a long time had been preparing works for future exhibition, by laying in, with simple colours, the effect and composition, painting them solidly and very quickly with considerable impasto, and allowing the whole to dry and harden together.

> He would use no fugitive pigments in these preparations, contenting himself with the ochres, siennas, and earth browns,

with real ultramarine, black, and a very liberal allowance of white. He must, I think, have had many works thus commenced laid by in his studio, from which he would take one, from time to time, to send to the Academy for exhibition. I have formed this opinion from having seen the remarkable series of Turner's works that were recently discovered and since hung in the National Collection. The preservation of these pictures is remarkable, and I have a very strong conviction that they were probably painted very quickly. Perhaps any one of them represents little more than a day's work. That the safest and simplest pigments alone were used, accounts for their good preservation, their mellow tone being merely the effect of time. If I am right ... we ought to be thankful that they were never exhibited, for, if this had been the case, they would, most likely, have by this time been ruined through the deleterious pigments with which he would have overlaid them on the varnishing days.[46]

As for those that were exhibited in Turner's later years, Ruskin limited their excellence to the time at which they made their exhibition appearance:

No picture of Turner's is seen in perfection a month after it is painted. The *Valhalla* cracked before it had been eight days in the Academy rooms; the vermilions frequently lose lustre long before the Exhibition is over; and when all the colours begin to get hard a year or two after the picture is painted, a painful deadness and opacity come over them, the whites especially becoming lifeless, and many of the warmer passages settling into a hard valueless brown, even if the paint remains perfectly firm, which is far from being always the case ... The fact of his using means so imperfect, together with that of his utter neglect of the pictures in his own gallery, are a phenomenon in human mind which appears to me utterly inexplicable ...[47]

But perhaps there was an explanation. As Turner aged, he was less and less interested in the accomplishment, the results, of painting. He knew that what the *Morning Chronicle* in 1831 called his 'freaks and follies' were often regarded – as Richard Westmacott regarded them – as 'unintelligible to the multitude'.[48] Anyway, he was going to die. Nothing lasts forever. But he *was* interested in the act of painting; he enjoyed it; and he didn't mind people watching him wound up and bound up in the performance. *He* was the exhibition.

Just as he had with one of the burning of the Houses of Parliament paintings, he brought his *Regulus* to the British Institution to finish on its walls. He had painted and first shown this picture in Rome in

1828; it showed one of his Claudean harbours again, with a blinding dazzle of sunlight on the water. The Roman general Regulus, a captive in Carthage, had been sent home to negotiate an exchange of prisoners, and when his leaders refused this, he nobly returned to Carthage where the Carthaginians cut his eyelids off and left him in the sun, blinding him. Quite where Regulus was in the picture none of the viewers could make out, nor what point in the general's comings and goings the scene represented. In 1837 at the British Institution Turner was watched by the twenty-year-old John Gilbert, who had a picture opposite, as he reworked *Regulus*:

> He was absorbed in his work, did not look about him, but kept on scumbling a lot of white into his picture – nearly all over it … The picture was a mass of red and yellow of all varieties. Every object was in this fiery state. He had a large palette, nothing on it but a huge lump of flake-white; he had two or three hog tools to work with, and with these he was driving the white into all the hollows, and every part of the surface. This was the only work he did, and it was the finishing stroke. The sun, as I have said, was in the centre; from it were drawn – ruled – lines to mark the rays; these lines were rather strongly marked, I suppose to guide his eye. The picture gradually became wonderfully effective, just the effect of brilliant sunlight absorbing everything and throwing a misty haze over every object. Standing sideways of the canvas, I saw that the sun was a lump of white standing out like a boss on a shield.[49]

It has sometimes been suggested that the viewer is meant to imagine himself in Regulus' position, being blinded.[50]

At the Academy, there had been intimations of a crack-down on varnishing-day privileges. Martin Shee may have harboured a grudge against Turner for 'checkmating' him in the battle of reds in 1827, because, on succeeding Lawrence as President in 1830, Shee – once an enthusiast for the varnishing days – tried to reduce the number of them. Constable wrote to C. R. Leslie on 27 April 1832:

> I am in the greatest alarm for the Academy. No notice of varnishing has yet come – therefore we shall not be allowed the five days. This is a sad affair to me – but I am rightly served – I should not have sent my scumbling affair. As to Turner (to whom no doubt the blow is levelled) nothing can reach him, he is in the clouds

The lovely Jessica by his side
sat like a blooming Eastern bride

I cannot complain. We set the example by cutting off a day last year – & Shee would cut off all but one if he could. His pictures are always 'hard' before they are sent off his easil & will bear *anything being put upon them*.[51]

In 1852 the varnishing days were suspended, and Charles Eastlake said it was the thought of Turner that had prevented the Academy taking that action until after his death. Leslie wrote that 'had the varnishing days been abolished while Turner lived, it would almost have broken his heart. When such a measure was hinted to him, he said, "Then you will do away with the only social meetings we have, the only occasions on which we all come together in an easy unrestrained manner. When we have no varnishing days we shall not know one another."'[52] David Roberts observed Turner's increasing antipathy to innovations at the Academy, such as the admission of the press to the Academy's private view, and Roberts's daughter Christine Bicknell in 1845, riding home with her father and Turner in a fly, noted Turner's bad temper on the subject of the Academy: he 'grumbled at everybody the whole way particularly at the "Italian" as he called Eastlake & my father who he called "Young England" for attempting Reforms in the Academy'.[53] Turner, according to the Redgraves, was proved right. The varnishing days were reinstated in 1862, their value recognized again as a time when knowledge and experience and advice could be exchanged.

17: Liberty Hall

Anyone looking for a place and a person that embodied what was – albeit quirkily – best about the highest level of English society in the first half of the nineteenth century needed to look no further than Petworth House, Sussex, and its master, George O'Brien Wyndham (1751–1837), the third Earl of Egremont, the nobleman who became one of Turner's greatest patrons. William Cobbett, that scourge of unrepresentative governments, sinecure holders and bad landlords, recorded his arrival in Petworth in 1823, while on one of his Rural Rides to examine the condition of British agriculture; it sounded as if he had reached the Earthly Paradise:

> As you approach Petworth, the ground rises and the soil grows lighter ... Petworth is a nice market town; but solid and clean ... Lord Egremont's house is close to the town, and, with its outbuildings, garden-walls, and other erections, is, perhaps, nearly as big as the town; though the town is not a very small one. The Park is very fine, and consists of a parcel of those hills and dells, which Nature formed here, when she was in one of her most sportive moods ... A most magnificent seat ...[1]

And two years later, on a fine sharp November morning, Cobbett rode through Lord Egremont's park, which Lancelot 'Capability' Brown had laid out in 1752:

> In a very fine pond not far from the house and close by the road, there are some little artificial islands, upon one of which I observed an arbutus loaded with its beautiful fruit (quite ripe) even more thickly than any one I ever saw even in America. There were, on the side of the pond, a most numerous and beautiful collection of water-fowl, foreign as well as domestic ... Everything here is in the neatest and most beautiful state. Endless herds of deer, of all the varieties of colours; and, what adds greatly to your pleasure in such

a case, you see comfortable retreats prepared for them in different parts of the woods.

A gatekeeper tells Cobbett that the whole area of enclosed parkland is '*nine miles round*'. As for the owner, says Cobbett, 'Lord Egremont bears an excellent character. Everything that I have ever heard of him makes me believe that he is worthy of this princely estate.'[2]

The house itself was an immense greystone edifice, twenty-one windows wide, three high. The total effect from the park was monotonous. It sat with its back pressed against the western edge of the town, with a grassy slope in front running down to the lake, or 'upper Pond' as it was called. On the ground floor lay a sequence of splendid rooms; these included the White Library, the Marble Hall (which had a billiard table in it), the Carved Room (with lime-wood panels by Grinling Gibbons), the Square Dining Room, the Red Room and the North Gallery, where many items of the great Egremont art collection not placed elsewhere in the house were displayed. There were two staircases, one called Grand. It was a house so large it made for the unexpected; the inhabitants never knew whom they might encounter in one of the long corridors or going up and down stairs. Visitors were invariably amazed. One such was Thomas Creevey, former member of Parliament (for the rotten borough of Thetford), and Treasurer of Greenwich Hospital for Seamen, who often had no home of his own but went from friendly house to house. In August 1828, he visited Petworth with his friends the Earl and Countess of Sefton, and wrote in his diary:

> Nothing can be more imposing or magnificent than the effect of this house the moment you are within it, not from that appearance of comfort which strikes you so much at Goodwood [where he had just been staying], for it has none … Every door of every room was wide open from one end to the other, and from the front to behind, whichever way you looked; and not a human being visible … but the magnitude of the space being seen all at once – the scale of every room, gallery, passage, &c., the infinity of pictures and statues throughout, made as agreeable an impression upon me as I ever witnessed. How we got into the house, I don't quite recollect, for I think there is no bell, but I know we *were* some time at the door, and when we were let in by a little footman, he disappeared *de suite*, and it was some time before we saw anybody else. At length a young lady appeared, and a very pretty one too, very nicely dressed and with very pretty manners. She proved to be a Miss Wyndham,

but, according to the custom of the family, *not* a legitimate Miss Wyndham, nor yet Lord Egremont's own daughter, but his brother William Wyndham's, who is dead ...[3]

The owner of this establishment showed up after Creevey and the Seftons had been looking at pictures for half an hour:

In comes my Lord Egremont – as extraordinary a person, perhaps, as any in England; certainly the most so of his own caste or order. He is aged 77 and as fresh as may be, with a most incomparable and acute understanding, with much more knowledge upon all subjects than he chuses to pretend to, and which he never discloses but incidentally, and, as it were, by compulsion. Simplicity and sarcasm are his distinguishing characteristics. He has a fortune, I believe, of £100,000 a year, and never man could have used it with such liberality and profusion as he has done. Years and years ago he was understood to be £200,000 or £300,000 out of pocket for the extravagance of his brother Charles Wyndham, just now dead; he has given each of these natural daughters £40,000 upon their marriage; he has dealt in the same liberal scale with private friends, with artists, and, lastly, with by no means the least costly customers – with mistresses, of whom Lady Melbourne must have been the most distinguished leader in that way.[4]

A descendant of the Percys, the Earls of Northumberland, Lord Egremont inherited Petworth – which stood on the site of an old Percy castle – at the age of twelve. In time he became a dashing young man about town and a great catch; but his engagement to Lady Maria Waldegrave was broken off – her uncle, Horace Walpole, called George Egremont 'a most worthless young fellow'.[5] The third Earl lived for some years with Elizabeth Iliffe, whom Farington described as a farmer's daughter who had been 'with his lordship at 15 years of age'.[6] She was known as Mrs Wyndham, and although he finally married her in 1801, the marriage – never made public – did not legitimize the six children she had given him by then. The marriage in fact seemed to upset their relationship; he needed a mistress rather than a wife. By 1803 the Countess was jealous, Farington thought, since she 'apprehends that his Lordship is not faithful to her ... at present they do not cohabit'. After separating from her, Lord Egremont did not marry again. (In London, after selling Egremont House in Piccadilly, he took a house in Grosvenor Place, not far from the Fawkeses, but his heart always seemed to be in Sussex.) As Lady Melbourne's lover, he was thought to have been the father of William Lamb, who became Lord Melbourne and Prime Minister. Lady Blessington, staying at Petworth in 1813, wrote to Earl Granville: 'Nothing will persuade Lady Spenser that Lord Egremont has not forty-three children, who all live in the House with him and their respective Mothers; that the latter are usually kept in the background, but that when any quarrels arise, which few days pass without, each mother takes part with her Progeny, bursts into the drawing room, fights with each other, Lord E., his children, and, I believe, the Company, and makes scenes worthy of Billingsgate or a Madhouse.'[7] Lord Egremont's nose was as much a feature of his face as Turner's, though perhaps a little less hooked; in any event, because of the Earl's amorous propensities, it was said to have become 'a distinct feature of the locality for miles around'.[8]

In these years of agricultural depression, Lord Egremont's liberality sustained the Sussex countryside. He had a strong sense of *noblesse oblige* as well as of *droit de seigneur*. Although he appeared rarely in the House of Lords, he was a stalwart member of the Society for the Betterment of the Conditions of the Poor, set up in 1799. He invested in canals. Like Walter Fawkes, he was a radical land-improver. He planted turnips as a rotation crop instead of leaving the land fallow and grew opium and rhubarb for medicinal purposes. The size of Petworth eggs astonished visitors who had them for breakfast. He bred prize cattle and race-horses – he won the Derby five times and the Oaks the same number, more than any other owner. Cobbett admired the black Petworth pigs, which were kept in an up-to-date piggery built surprisingly close to the house. At one point a sow and her litter got in and galloped through the great rooms. Over 500 deer grazed in the well-managed park.

He was good with his people too. C. R. Leslie noted that at one point Lord Egremont closed the main entrance gate to Petworth, because the gatehouse porter and his wife were both old and ill, and he didn't want them disturbed. He spent about £20,000 a year on charitable work; he helped finance a new County Hospital at Brighton and an Infirmary at Chichester; in Petworth he set up a surgeon–apothecary and paid for the training of a midwife and an inoculation nurse. He also assisted impoverished farm folk to emigrate to Canada, by paying for their passages. (However, he had one blindspot: he opposed Catholic emancipation.) A visiting Frenchman was shocked that local people were allowed into the grounds to play cricket and bowls on the lawn between the house and pond.

The house itself under Lord Egremont's benign rule, according to a family chronicler, 'was like a huge inn with visitors coming and going as they pleased: they were welcome without notice. There was no leave-taking either: you didn't say goodbye, you just left. Guests found themselves confronted with nurses and babies, girls exercising the pianoforte, boys exercising ponies. Nobody was sure whose children they were. There were artists all over the place, some doing original works, others copying Vandycks.'[9] It was a 'strange medley', thought Lady Holland in 1828 – wealthy guests, poor relations; painters and politicians. C. R. Leslie brought his wife and children to Petworth on the first of many visits in the autumn of 1826 and stayed a month. Leslie admired his host for the complete lack of ostentation that went with his munificence. 'Plain spoken, often to a degree of bluntness, he never wasted words, nor would he let others waste words on him. After conferring the greatest favours, he was out of the room before there was time to thank him.'[10] His servants wore plain livery or none at all; some were as venerable and distinguished-looking as Lord Egremont in his old age. The maid of one lady visitor, crossing the hall one evening as the bell rang for the servants' dinner, took the arm of an elderly man and said, 'Come, old gentleman, you and I will go to dinner together, for I can't find my way in this great house.' Lord Egremont gave her his arm and took her to the servants' dining room where he said, 'You dine here. I don't dine till seven o'clock.'[11]

Charles Greville, a political diarist and frequent visitor to Petworth, was staying there at Christmas 1832 and found Turner among the guests, along with 'the Cowpers ... Lady E. Romney, two nieces, Mrs Tredcroft a neighbour, Ridsdale a parson, Wynne ... and a young artist of the name of Lucas'. Lord Egremont, noted Greville,

> liked to have people there who he was certain would not put him out of his way, especially those who, entering into his eccentric habits, were ready for the snatches of talk which his perpetual locomotion alone admitted of, and from whom he could gather information about passing events; but it was necessary to conform to his peculiarities, and these were utterly incompatible with conversation, or any prolonged discussion. He never remained five minutes in

the same place, and was continually oscillating between the library and his bedroom, or wandering about the enormous house in all directions: sometimes he broke off in the middle of a conversation on some subject which appeared to interest him, and disappeared, and an hour after, on a casual meeting, would resume just where he left off. [12]

(Turner had probably been at Petworth for Christmas 1831 as well; Hannah and Queen Anne Street could evidently manage without him.)

The bedrooms at Petworth excited comment from several guests. Creevey in 1828 measured his and found it 'to be 30 feet by 20, and high in proportion. The bed would have held six people in a row without the slightest inconvenience to each other.' Benjamin Haydon had occupied the same room two years before, on his visit in 1826, when he was in raptures at the splendour of his surroundings and at the 'Live and let live' atmosphere engendered by Lord Egremont. He admired the portraits in his room (which included one of 'Bloody' Queen Mary), the velvet and satin bed curtains and the view of the park out of the high windows. Always the outsider, he felt a grateful wonder:

> There is something peculiarly interesting in inhabiting these apartments ... which have contained a long list of deceased and illustrious ancestors. As I lay in my magnificent bed, and saw the old portraits trembling in a sort of twilight, I almost fancied I heard them breathe, and almost expected they would move out and shake my curtains. What a destiny is mine! One year in the Bench, the companion of gamblers and scoundrels – sleeping in wretchedness and dirt, on a flock bed low and filthy, with black worms crawling over my hands – another, reposing in down and velvet, in a splendid apartment, in a splendid house, the guest of rank, and fashion and beauty! As I laid my head on my down pillow the first night I was deeply affected, and could hardly sleep. God in heaven grant my future may now be steady. At any rate a nobleman has taken me by the hand, whose friendship generally increases in proportion to the necessity of its continuance. Such is Lord Egremont. Literally like the sun. The very flies at Petworth seem to know there is room for their existence, that the windows are theirs. Dogs, horses, cows, deer and pigs, peasantry and servants, guests and family, children and parents, all share alike his bounty and opulence and luxuries. At breakfast, after the guests have all breakfasted, in walks Lord Egremont; first comes a grandchild, whom he sends away happy.

Outside the window moan a dozen black spaniels, who are let in, and to whom he distributes cakes and comfits, giving all equal shares. After chatting with one guest, and proposing some scheme of pleasure to others, his leathern gaiters are buttoned on, and away he walks, leaving everybody to take care of themselves, with all that opulence and generosity can place at their disposal entirely within their reach. At dinner he meets everybody, and then are recounted the feats of the day. All principal dishes he helps, never minding the trouble of carving; he eats heartily and helps liberally. There is plenty, but not absurd profusion; good wines, but no extravagant waste. Everything solid, liberal, rich and English. At seventy-four he stil shoots daily, comes home wet through, and is as active and looks as well as many men of fifty ... I never saw such a character, or such a man, nor were there ever many.[13]

Lord Egremont commissioned two paintings from Haydon – *Alexander the Great taming Bucephalus* and *Eucles* – but unfortunately that was Haydon's only visit to Petworth.

Among other artists who enjoyed Lord Egremont's hospitality were Thomas Phillips, the portrait painter and an especial favourite; William Beechey; Sir Thomas Lawrence; David Wilkie; Sir Richard Westmacott; Augustus Callcott; George Jones; and John Constable. (For some reason Lord Egremont didn't buy any of Constable's work.) The sculptors Francis Chantrey and J. E. Carew were often there. Indeed, Carew – with whom Turner had an enigmatic conversation by the pond one day about money and age – once admitted that during the 1830s he 'lived more at Petworth House than with my own family'.[14] Lord Egremont said of Carew, 'When I am gone, he will be a beggar.' And the Earl was right. Carew was ungrateful enough after Egremont's death to sue his former host's executors, lost his case and was declared bankrupt. Leslie – who brought his family to Petworth most autumns in the early 1830s – wrote to Constable on 5 September 1834: 'Today 40 people dine here, most of them magistrates, and the house is as full as it can hold. Among them is the Duke of Richmond. I have just been looking at the table as it is set out in the Carved Room, covered with magnificent gold and silver plate ... Callcott has been here, and went today.'[15] On several occasions the banker-poet Samuel Rogers was also a guest at the same time as the Leslies. 'One evening, all the young ladies in the house formed a circle round him, listening with extreme interest to a series of ghost stories which he told with great effect.'[16]

Turner came to Petworth for a number of stays in the decade after 1827. Lord Egremont and his 'Liberty Hall', as some called it, gave a further liberating boost to Turner's art. With Walter Fawkes and – a few years later – his father both dead, and only Mrs Booth to serve as a sheet anchor through the lonely storms of his fifties and sixties, Petworth provided a place where he could be himself, could enjoy himself and could produce some of his most original and most moving work.

Lord Egremont, with his eye for the best, had taken him up early on. In the first years of the century he bought Turner's 1802 Royal Academy exhibit, the tremendously dramatic *Ships Bearing Up for Anchorage*, which became known as the Egremont Seapiece. Over the next ten years the Earl seems to have been a regular visitor to Turner's gallery; many of the further dozen or so oil paintings he purchased – he never bought any Turner watercolours – were exhibited at Harley Street and only three at the Academy. (Two direct commissions from Lord Egremont in 1809 were for views of his properties, Petworth House and Cockermouth Castle in Cumberland.) The sort of Turner pictures that Egremont fancied were for the most part those that had a classical flavour – elevated pastoral, as it were. Indeed, even in 1827, when Turner had in many ways moved on, Egremont showed his fondness for the poetic landscapes of the earlier period by buying at the de Tabley sale in that year the painting *Tabley House and Lake – Calm Morning* of 1809, which Turner had painted for Sir John Leicester, as he then was.

Turner had passed through Petworth town in 1792, drawing the church, but he apparently first stayed at Petworth in the summer of 1809, when Egremont asked him down to make the portrait of the house. He had a happy time poring over the family collection, including works by van Dyck, Titian, David Teniers the younger, Paul Bril and Cuyp. Claude's *Landscape with Jacob, Laban and his daughters* seized his attention. Paintings by English masters such as Reynolds, Gainsborough and Richard Wilson were also to be seen. Lord Egremont went on buying Old Masters until a few years before his death in 1837, when he told Thomas Phillips that he was resolved to buy only contemporary works thenceforth. At his death the Egremont collection contained 170 paintings and twenty-one pieces of sculpture.

But after that first decade of patronage, something happened between artist and Earl. From 1812, there was a strange gap of thirteen years or so when Lord Egremont seemed to take no interest in Turner's work, and Turner – of course busy with Sandycombe, absorbed by the Fawkeses, discovering Italy and getting on with many engraving commissions – didn't visit Petworth. Was Lord Egremont cross because Turner made such direct use of the Petworth Claude in his *Apullia in search of Appullus* of 1814? This picture, as we have seen, Turner submitted to the British Institution (of which Lord Egremont was a governor), although too late to qualify for the annual prize. Lord Egremont, as it happened, failed to show up for duty on the award jury. Moreover, he was generally known for his equanimity. Yet he could lose his temper when he felt he was being taken advantage of. Leslie wrote that Egremont occasionally ordered people to leave his house who 'encouraged by his good nature and the easy footing on which they found themselves ... had forgotten where they were, and behaved as if that noble mansion were but a great hotel'[17] – a hotel where no bills ever had to be paid.

Turner probably visited Petworth after long absence in 1825. And he and Lord Egremont may have run into one another at Christie's in July 1827, when the late Lord de Tabley's pictures were sold. Turner often showed up when his pictures came back on the market, to see how they did, even to bid for them. At any rate, he was once again at Petworth in late October that year; he wrote a letter from there to George Cobb about his Wapping property. He also seems to have been there on 18 December, when he wrote to Cobb again, this time about a Harley Street tenant. In the next year, before he set off for Rome, he started work on a large new commission from Lord Egremont: four paintings to be hung in long rectangular spaces in the Grinling Gibbons panelling of the Carved Room. For these he made four full-sized oil sketches. Creevey seems to have seen one sketch and one finished painting in the Carved Room in August 1828; he wrote: 'in one of these compartments you have Petworth Park by Turner, in another Lord Egremont taking a walk with nine dogs, that are his constant companions, by the same artist'.[18] Egremont may have taken an active interest in these pictures for – perhaps at his behest – some details in the finished oils have been changed from those in the sketches (which Turner kept): a cricket match was introduced in one in place of what Creevey saw, Egremont in fact returning across the park and being met by a stream of dogs. The oils that stayed at Petworth were largely painted in a golden tone which harked back to Turner's earlier work and which the artist may have thought more agreeable to the Earl, as well as suiting the pictures' rather low positions amid the dark panels.

Turner, as we have noted, was also thinking about Lord Egremont while in Rome, making his first brush *con amore* for him and helping to arrange the shipment of the Dionysus torso to him. But the Earl didn't return any love for Turner's *Palestrina*; it may not have struck him as the companion he had expected for his Claude. Perhaps to make up for his failure to buy this, he bought *Jessica*, which was exhibited at the Academy in 1830. There is nothing Claudean about this picture, the last he was to buy from Turner – a woman at an open window. Rembrandt comes to mind. Despite having sold one family picture, *A Philosopher*, said to be by that master, in 1794 (for £1 9s), Egremont still had several reputed Rembrandts, one – a real one – being the 1633 *Lady with a Fan*, which Turner seems to have been brooding about when he painted *Jessica*.

Indeed, his stays at Petworth seemed to provoke an interest in the great Dutch painter – though there may have been other things in his life that also made him susceptible to this influence just then. One curious picture of 1827 was direct about the interest. *Rembrandt's Daughter* shows Turner not only thinking about Rembrandt but thinking about a father breaking in on the relationship between his daughter and a young man – the father being a painter, though at that point in 1827 it wasn't known that Rembrandt actually had had a girl child. Turner seems to have made an imaginative leap. His heart was also in the painting as regards the figure of the daughter: so much more alive and anatomically well rendered than his figures often were. Did some past incident with Evelina, now ten years married – or some more recent one with Georgiana, still single – fire his fancy? And the Rembrandtian theme and chiaroscuro of this picture were followed by further Rembrandtian reverberations in the 1830s, in pictures with biblical or Jewish subjects, such as *Pilate Washing his Hands*, and a number of works done apparently at Petworth or East Cowes Castle (occasionally his next stop after Petworth), in which red and black were boldly used and the lighting was highly dramatic. *The Music Party, Dinner in a Great Room* and *Figures in a Building* suggest that Rembrandt played a part in Turner's Petworth liberation.

The *Jessica* qualified in this respect in subject matter and composition, but hardly in colour. An Egremont family story has it that, when Turner and some other artists were at Petworth on one occasion, a painter who did figure-subjects told Turner (still famed for his fondness for yellow) that a yellow background was 'all very well in landscapes, but would not be possible in our kind of pictures'. Turner, with a nod to their host, replied, 'Subject pictures are not my style but I will undertake to paint a picture of a woman's head with a yellow background if Lord Egremont will give it a place in his gallery.' Lord Egremont did give Jessica such a place, despite almost unanimous abuse from the commentators who saw it at the Academy. The *Morning Chronicle* declared (3 May 1830): 'It looks like a lady getting out of a large mustard pot.' The *Athenaeum* thought (5 June) that Turner was afflicted with 'jaundice on the retina'. And, as we have noted, Wordsworth grumbled, 'It looks to me as if the painter had indulged in raw liver until he was very unwell.'[19] Sounder criticism might have been levelled at Jessica's physique: the strange foreshortening of her left arm; the wooden nature of the right; the troubling spread of her shoulders. But the head – for a Turner head! – was well done. Something in the gaze reminds us of the way Turner addressed the viewer in his c. 1800 self-portrait.

Turner, with the freedom of the house, was to be seen everywhere at Petworth, prowling through the rooms and along the corridors, poking around in the huge cellars, drawing paper in hand. He made sketching excursions through the meadows around the town and in the parkland of the house, where deer browsed on the swards among the old oaks, beeches and chestnuts. He frequently fished in the little lake – the upper pond. This is where young Robert Leslie saw him at sunset one September evening in the early 1830s, with a fine pike that he had caught lying on the bank, but het up because his line was snagged. And this is where Turner gave Robert 'an early lesson in seamanship by rigging scraps of paper, torn from his sketchbook, upon three little sticks stuck in a board to represent a full-rigged ship, which, to my great delight, he then launched upon the lake.' Robert Leslie later remembered that Constable – who had also been at Petworth some days before – had stuck a sail on the same toy ship: 'I must have mentioned this to Turner, as I have a recollection of his saying, as he rigged it, "Oh, he don't know anything about ships," or "What does he know about ships? this is how it ought to be," sticking up some sails which looked to my eyes really quite ship-shape at that time.'[20] Robert went on to become not only a painter but an amateur boat-builder and a passionate but unpretentious yachtsman, and was always grateful to Turner for this early encouragement.

When he wasn't to be seen indoors or out, it was because he was tucked away in the Old Library, over the chapel. Other artists like Leslie and Beechey used this room from time to time, but once Turner had got into the habit of visiting Petworth after 1827, it was his to work in when he was there, with the door locked from inside, and only Lord Egremont allowed the privilege of interruption. Chantrey had been one of the guests at Petworth when Turner was occupied with his paintings to hang on the Carved Room panels. The sculptor decided to check on what Turner was doing in the Old Library. 'He imitated Lord Egremont's peculiar step,' wrote George Jones, 'and the two distinct raps on the door by which his Lordship was accustomed to announce himself; and the key being immediately turned, he slipped into the room before the artist could shut him out.'[21] The two friends enjoyed the joke.

Turner and Lord Egremont got on well. They were both in their own ways old bachelors, nonconformists, uninhibited by many of the conventions of the day. They had their own types of generosity, one narrowly focused, one nobly expansive. Turner admired Egremont, one imagines, for his style of living and directness, and Egremont admired Turner for his painting ability and determination. They talked and argued on equal terms. On one occasion they had a dispute about the number of front windows in a local house. 'Seven,' said Lord E., 'Six,' maintained Turner, at which point Egremont ordered a carriage and they went to count the windows; Turner was found to be wrong.[22] On another occasion their argument was whether Turner had been right to show some vegetables floating in his painting for the Carved Room, *Brighton from the Sea*. Egremont maintained that carrots wouldn't float, Turner that they would – and this time Turner was proved right.

The liberties Turner took at Petworth included using parts of a cupboard door to paint on when he hadn't got a suitable canvas or panel; one result was *Watteau study by Fresnoy's rules* (1831), a rather weak picture of an artist painting among several spectators. Once in a while he took on the mantle of host. Jones recalled that, when he hurt his leg during a visit to Petworth, Turner's 'anxiety to procure for me every attendance and convenience was like the attention of a parent to a child; his application to the house-keeper, butler, and gardener for my comfort and gratification was unremitted'. Indeed, thought Jones, 'Turner's tenderness towards his friends was almost womanly; to be ill was to secure constant attention and solicitude from him towards the sufferer.'[23] In October 1837 Lord Egremont said to Turner, 'I have written to Jones to join us but he won't come.' Jones reported later: 'Turner felt this remark as important to me and wrote instantly to tell me of the generous Earl's observation. Of course I did not hesitate, but went. Fortunately I did so, for in three weeks the kind and hospitable nobleman ceased to be.'[24] Once when Samuel Rogers and his sister were staying at Petworth, probably in 1827, Rogers at breakfast asked Turner to make him a drawing of a terrace overlooking a lake, bordered by cypress trees. At lunch Turner handed him the drawing, which Rogers later had engraved as a vignette in his book *Italy*. The night before the banker–poet and his sister left, they said farewell to Lord Egremont, as they planned an early departure. Rogers recollected that next morning, 'to my surprise I found Turner at the door, ready to see me off. "How kind of you," I said. "I could not think of letting two such old friends go away without saying Goodbye," he replied.'[25]

Egremont was good at giving his guests the feeling that the house and grounds were, for the time being, their own; in Turner's case, the largess paid off in some of his finest work. It was all the finer for being unencumbered by the need to compete or dazzle. (His competitive instinct was perhaps satisfied by such incidents as beating Chantrey at fishing.) The Petworth effect was felt in full in a series of coloured drawings made, it seems likely, in the late summer of 1827 – more than a hundred, done in gouache or bodycolour, in other words watercolour made opaque with lead or Chinese white, on small rectangular sheets of coarse blue sugar-paper.[26] These were for no client but himself. One word that seems to describe them is 'happy' – not a word that always suits Turner, though it does so when as here he is immersed, with his ambition and its sometimes florid results set aside. Here the economy he had discovered in Venice was again to the fore: a few dabs of colour, a few broad brushstrokes; the solid colours contrasting vividly with the coarse paper; indications rather than outlines; unplanned, done then and there; small epiphanies.

Wandering through the 'pleasure grounds' – to use the term with which one Petworth plan describes the land outside the house – he took pleasure in the views. Walking, breathing, seeing and brushing the colours on paper were, if not quite a single act, a continuous process in which movement, perception and enjoyment became creation. He noted oxen drawing a wagon; some of Egremont's spaniels barking at a pair of donkeys; the Petworth hunt forming up; some deer – almost calligraphically rendered. He captured the evening sky over the park, a *Ulysses deriding Polyphemus* sort of radiance around the sun. He sketched the lake at twilight, with the silhouette of a nearby hillside reflected in it: the reflected hillside darker and shallower than the hillside itself. He produced the strokes that meant a boat on the lake, two men in it. This was a true garden of the Hesperides, English landowning variety.

When he came indoors, he caught with similar boldness the atmosphere of the ground-floor rooms. Some sketches he did with more detail, though never fussily. The much used White Library featured in seven drawings. He showed the bookcases, a piano, busts of philosophers, paintings (including portraits by Thomas Phillips), a cradle, the candelabra. Egremont in his later years used an adjacent room as his bedroom, with a concealed door in a bookcase. For one sketch, Turner stood in the alcove at the southern end of the White Library and looked through it and through all the doorways that linked the seven grand rooms along the western side of the house. The picture-crowded walls of the Somerset Room and Square Dining Room were shown with banners of sunlight streaming across their carpets from the high windows. He noted the massive billiard table that stood in the marble hall and placed at it two dark figures, one wielding a cue. Musicians played in the Little Dining Room, while in the Carved Room next door a banquet was taking place, many people seated at a long table. In the North Gallery he chose to sketch Flaxman's immense marble sculpture *St Michael and Satan*, the scale suggested by two much smaller figures looking up at it.

In some of these blue-paper studies his attention was given to objects, like the large porcelain vases set around a gilt table in the Carved Room. In others, what attracted him were people – talking, playing backgammon or cards, listening to music, waiting for dinner. A young woman plays a spinet. Three women sit at a table while three dogs lie on the floor near by. A man sits with one leg up on a sofa – George Jones convalescing, perhaps. In one, *Spilt milk*, a young woman in a blue dress is wiping her lap. Turner, it seems, knocked over a milk jug at breakfast, and some of the contents landed on Egremont's niece, Mrs Julia Hasler. Two drawings, this and a parkland study, given to her at lunch, were his way of making amends. The humour inherent in the *Spilt milk* drawing and the fact that he actually gave away two sketches shows Turner less socially constrained than he often was.

The figures in many of these gouache drawings are simply sketched, rough silhouettes, cartoons almost; but they give a far better sense of physique and personality than Turner's usual grotesques or even his 'ideal' Claudean forms. Although mostly without obvious features of countenance, these are human beings, with plenty of stance and shape. In their presence, the jumble of life in the great house comes through, with its formality and informality. In some groups one can make out Egremont, white-haired, wearing black evening attire, in the centre of things; his son Colonel Wyndham in his scarlet military uniform, standing near a fireplace; or the tall gawky form of the Petworth rector, the Reverend Thomas Sockett. Sockett began as tutor to Lord Egremont's sons and, since ordination required a degree, was sent to Oxford by the Earl when he decided to make Sockett a clergyman. For many years Sockett enjoyed the opulent Petworth living (at least £1700 per annum); he catalogued the Earl's art collection and ran his assisted-emigration scheme. But finally, after a row about politics, he ceased to be on speaking terms with his patron. There may also have been religious difficulties: Egremont seems to have been less of a practising Christian than the Reverend Sockett might have hoped. Arthur Young, the agricultural reformer, noted while staying at Petworth, 'In the chapel, no worship.' However, Egremont spent over £16,000 on improving Petworth parish church, including the building of a new spire.[27]

Upstairs the mood changes, the intimacy intensifies. Turner painted the bedrooms as warm refuges of privacy: four-poster beds with curtains; fires burning in fireplaces; figures clothed and unclothed; a woman in a black low-cut evening gown at her dressing table, absorbed by what she sees in her mirror; a woman seated at the foot of a bed, doing her hair – she is naked from the waist up.

Who are these women who allowed Turner to sketch them at such moments? Was he granted the freedom of Egremont's alleged harem as well as of the house? It seems unlikely that, given the way Turner kept much of his life in separate compartments, he would have brought a woman to Petworth. But there are hints of eventful goings-on in some of these sketches: a glimpse of a bare body above the sheets; red satin bed-curtains parted as if in amorous invitation; the bed-curtains of what seems to be the same room now green, now yellow, lovingly lingered on. One little pencil sketch in a sketchbook of this time shows a woman who may also be seen in these Petworth bedrooms. Turner has written alongside the pencil sketch the two words, 'Brown Eyes'.[28] Who had brown eyes?

Also upstairs, above the chapel, was the Old Library. A large east-facing semicircular topped window brought in plenty of daylight. Except when Egremont – or Chantrey, on at least that one occasion – wanted to see what he was up to, he had here all the privacy he needed. But, at least in his imagination, this room was populated once by three women who watched as the artist, facing the morning sun, applied his brush to a canvas on an easel.[29] He has turned the window into a great fanlight. In another gouache done in the same room, he concentrated on a vase of lilies, dahlias and other flowers that stands on a table, with a print and some books lying beside it, and in the background a plaster-cast of the *Seated Venus* by Joseph Nollekens. This vase of flowers and the pile of books appear in a third drawing, which showed the portrait painter Sir William Beechey busy with his picture of Egremont's niece, *Mrs Hasler as Flora*. The flowers were a prop in this, and Turner appropriated them as he eventually did the Old Library.

Most years Lord Egremont gave a feast for his tenants and the needy of the area on his birthday, 18 December. Church bells rang to celebrate the occasion. Fireworks concluded it. But in 1834 His Lordship was ill at the time and the feast was put off until the following spring. Charles Greville was there and – a touch condescendingly – recorded in his diary what a fine sight it was:

> fifty-four tables, each fifty feet long, were placed in a vast semi-
> circle on the lawn before the house … Plum puddings and loaves
> were piled like cannon-balls, and innumerable joints of boiled and
> roast beef were spread out, while hot joints were prepared in the

kitchen, and sent forth as soon as the firing of guns announced the hour of the feast. Tickets were given to the inhabitants of a certain district, and the number was about 4000; but, as many more came, the Old Peer could not endure that there should be anybody hungering outside the gates, and he went out himself and ordered the barriers to be taken down and admittance given to all. They think 6000 were fed … Nothing could exceed the pleasure of that fine old fellow; he was in and out of the windows of his room twenty times, enjoying the sight of these poor wretches, all attired in their best, cramming themselves and their brats with as much as they could devour, and snatching a day of relaxation and happiness.[30]

The next great event at Petworth was the last of the third Earl's epoch. Eighty-six years old, he was ailing in early November 1837; in the presence of the sculptor Carew he declared, 'I feel myself likely to go this time – I shall slip through.'[31] Soane had died in January, Constable in March. Lord Egremont died on 11 November. On the 15th, Thomas Phillips wrote to the Reverend Sockett – who, despite the row over politics which had led to him being banned from the house, was in charge of the funeral – to tell him that he and Turner would attend: 'Pray in your arrangements reserve a mourning cloak for me, and another for Mr Turner who is deeply affected.'[32] The *Brighton Patriot* reported at the end of the month that on Tuesday, 21 November, 'the remains of the deeply lamented and sincerely beloved Earl of Egremont were consigned to the silent tomb. The body had not lain in state, but all who desired were permitted to view the remains of one who will be long remembered as a liberal benefactor …' The *Patriot* listed the mourners in their categories, including churchwardens, gamekeepers, clergymen, chaplains, the Earl's physician, artists, servants, head groom and head gardener, valet and steward, bailiffs, surveyors, clerks, chief mourners and their servants, tenants, school children, teachers, friends. The hearse was pulled by sixteen men. Turner walked at the head of the group of artists, and saw the third Earl's body buried in a family vault.

The Earl's death had its effect on Turner. He caught cold, either at the funeral or while attending a life class at the Academy, and, feeling low, turned down an invitation from J. H. Maw, a surgical-instrument manufacturer, amateur artist and purchaser of four of his watercolours, to come and stay in Guildford. He wrote to Maw: 'Sir Anthony Carlisle, who I consult in misfortune says I must not stir out of door until it is dry weather (frost) ... or I may become a prisoner all the Winter.'[33] Another of his patrons, the Norfolk banker Dawson Turner, seems to have thought Turner might benefit from Lord Egremont's will. Turner wrote on 20 December to thank his Yarmouth namesake for the gift of a barrel of herrings, which he had as yet been unable to taste because of his illness, and said: 'Phillips and myself have to thank you for your *good wishes* but he says Lord Egremont has left but few or scarcely any legacies, his Lordship having been his own Almoner during life doing good to all around him.'[34]

Despite a sharp touch of fever following the cold, he kept working while confined to 47 Queen Anne Street. (The herrings he sent on to Eastlake, two days before Christmas.) Indeed, his most profound response to the final slipping away of his noble patron may have been by painting. A rapidly done picture – *Interior at Petworth* as it has been called – shows no specific room in the house but seems rather to be an assemblage of Petworth elements. The oil painting has a bright blood-red ground. Light fills a large arched doorway. What may be the Earl's black-topped catafalque, with the coat of arms on its side, stands amid pieces of sculpture, mirrors, an overturned stool, and a number of dogs, seemingly out of control, who jump, yap and pull at an orange table-cloth. Colour runs riot; order is dissolving into chaos.[35] Turner never exhibited this picture: possibly a final work for Lord Egremont *con amore* and also with grief. As with Farnley after Walter Fawkes's death, he never went to Petworth again.

18: Home and Away

On the second day of August 1839, Turner wrote from Queen Anne Street to the portrait painter Henry Pickersgill RA, a fellow Visitor to the Life Academy, 'My dear Pickersgill[,] Pray forgive me but excuse my [not] being with you on Wednesday next for I am on the Wing for the Continent (Belge) this morning.'[1] Although Petworth and Margate had figured greatly in his life away from Queen Anne Street for the previous ten years, he had also spent a good deal of time abroad, 'on the wing', during many of the summers. His sketchbooks of the period are filled mostly with European subjects. A restlessness seized him after the Academy exhibition closed in July, and could be appeased only by organizing his money (dunning, say, a print-publisher like one of the Findens who owed him), telling Hannah not to expect him back for so many weeks, and packing his 'wallet', a long duffle bag generally carried over the shoulder, with sketchbooks, pencils, box of colours, guidebooks, razor, nightshirt, stockings, cravats, waistcoats, shirts and even a spare ferrule for his umbrella, before setting off for the Channel packet. His planning for what he thought of as 'my summer tour'[2] was not rigorous; his destinations seem often to have been picked at the last minute; and even then, when *he* knew where he was going, his friends and colleagues generally didn't – Pickersgill was fortunate to be given a hint. One consequence of this is that his 'on the wing' movements in the 1820s and 1830s remain a little blurred. Even when places in his sketchbooks have been recognized, the years in which he visited them are occasionally uncertain. How different he was from the altogether domestic John Constable, who never went abroad.[3]

Turner's cross-Channel venturing had begun in 1802; until the Napoleonic wars were over, his restlessness – perhaps partly the result of being shipped hither and yon as a child – had to be appeased by tours within Britain. In 1817, he went to the Rhine by way of Ostend and the battlefield of Waterloo. In 1819–20 he made his six-month trip to Italy and back, but didn't dally on the way through France. He took a mid-September jaunt to northern France in 1821, travelling along the Normandy coast and the Seine between Rouen and Paris. He sketched some Claudes in the Louvre, boats in Dieppe, the cathedral at Rouen and various Channel prospects. In 1824 there was a more extensive journey to the Meuse, Mosel and middle Rhine, with a side trip to Dieppe, which had caught his fancy. In the summer of 1825 he toured Holland and then went on to the Rhine and back via the Meuse. In August and September 1826 he visited Paris and the Loire.

In his sketchbooks he continued to write notes to himself about the distances between places, inns worth staying in and fragments of French or German that might come in handy – in one case, he listed the days of the week in French; in another, in his copy of *Handbuch den Englischen Umgangssprache* used in the 1830s, he noted the German for 'I am very hungry' and 'Will you take a glass of wine?' In the post-war years the means of long-distance travel greatly improved: coaches lost their close kinship to top-heavy farm wagons and became the steady, stately vehicles John Ruskin later remembered, with underseat store-cellars, secret drawers, padded linings, perfectly fitting windows, and four stout, good-humoured horses to pull them. But Turner's travels could still be arduous and even dangerous: he walked for more than twenty miles between one Rhine village and another; a diligence overturned and was, he noted, 'dug out of a ditch between Ghent and Brussels'. 'Dogs and Cats' he wrote beneath a sketched shop-front – a butcher's shop – at Trarbach on the Mosel; the dogs and cats were presumably window-shopping. Most of what he recorded in quick pencil sketches was the usual selection of castles, spires, river scenes, rock formations, aqueducts, boats and harbourfronts, and some of it seems merely compulsive, hardly worth the repetition, until suddenly out of the forest of hurried drawings emerged for the Academy exhibition a luminous oil painting that wouldn't have occurred otherwise: *Harbour of Dieppe (Changement de Domicile)* (RA 1825) was one such, *Cologne, the Arrival of a Packet Boat, Evening* (RA 1826) another, both commissioned by John Broadhurst. Even in a place new to him there were continuities and connections. *Dieppe* has overtones of Carthage – harbour, boats, quaysides, reflected sun. *Cologne* omits the great landmark, the cathedral, and concentrates on the riverfront. Its close relation is the *Dort, or Dordrecht*, by then hanging at Farnley.

In 1828–9 he was back in Italy again, but in the late summer of 1829, when he could not get to Rome, he seems to have been happily, busily, drawing on the Normandy coast, along the Seine, in Paris and on the Channel Island of Guernsey. Unrest on the Continent may have kept him at home in 1830; the July Revolution in France finally replaced the Bourbon dynasty with the more liberal House of Orléans – Louis-Philippe, whom he knew from Twickenham, came to the throne. But Turner was back on the Seine and in Paris in 1832. He was partly occupied with a commission to illustrate Walter Scott's *Life of Napoleon*, and was diligent with his research; he wrote to the publisher Robert Cadell that he had been to Brienne, not far from Troyes, south-east of Paris, where Napoleon had studied at the Military Academy, had then gone looking for Bonaparte's early lodgings in the capital, and had acquired material from which he could make drawings to do with various Napoleonic battles.

He carried a copy of Edward Planta's *A New Picture of Paris, or, the Stranger's Guide to the French Metropolis*; underlinings and notes in the margins marked his interests. Thus he drew attention to the guidebook's declaration that most French inns were 'not very careful in airing their linen', thereby endangering the health of English travellers. Similarly he ticked Planta's statement that 'half a bottle of most of the best wines may be had at any of the restauranteurs', which suggests that despite his earlier biliousness, he was no longer averse to the produce of Bordeaux and Burgundy. Another mark emphasized the guidebook's warning that 'the tradesman of the Palais Royal will unblushingly demand considerably more than the value of his commodities'. At least by now the French had ceased to call Englishmen by such abusive terms as 'Monsieur Pomme de Terre' and 'Monsieur Goddam'.[4] Turner noted in his copy of Planta's *Guide* that a bronze statue of Napoleon was now to be seen that the guidebook said had disappeared. In the back of the book he listed places that for various reasons specially interested him: the Prefecture of Police in the Rue Jérusalem; the Museum of Natural History; the Jesuit church; the Ecole des Beaux-Arts; the Pantheon; and the Tivoli pleasure gardens. In 1829 or 1832 he called on Delacroix at his studio on the Quai Voltaire. As noted, Delacroix recalled that

Turner 'made a mediocre impression on me. He had the look of an English farmer, black clothes, gross enough, big shoes, and hard cold demeanour'.[5]

Meuse, Mosel, Rhine, Elbe, Danube, Seine, Loire and Rhône – his journeys in Europe between 1817 and 1840 depended on rivers. They provided attractively wet and winding ways into a landscape. In England too, for the watercolours he did in the 1820s for engraving in Cooke's *Rivers of England*, he had a chance to revisit old haunts on (and old sketches of) the Tweed, Tyne, Aire, Dart, Arun and Medway. At home or abroad, the juxtaposition of riverside buildings caught his eye. When he felt in the mood for detail, his architectural drawing could still be very precise, as at Coutances, in Normandy, in 1829 or thereabouts, where he drew the two towers of St Pierre Church, with houses between.[6] Norham Castle, on the Tweed, a favourite subject, provided the opportunity to capture atmosphere in watercolour and experiment prismatically by placing primary colours next to one another.[7] He continued to climb heights to look down wooded slopes to sinuous stretches of water and boats in their element. Sails, as on the Avon in his time with the Narraways, still drew his attention, and so did such features as the large rudders and sweeping tillers on the vessels on the Loire.[8] Canal locks attracted him, as they did many artists who drew in the English countryside in the first decades of the nineteenth century, and a windmill might demonstrate an older technology to be contrasted with the new.

Now on coastal and inland waters smoke from tall funnels was an aspect of the scene. Steam packets were introduced on the Dover–Calais run in 1821, when the *Rob Roy* made the crossing in two hours and forty-five minutes. A year later one could avoid the time-consuming land journey to Dover by taking a paddle-wheeler from the Tower to Calais; his c. 1825 watercolour *The Tower of London* shows the paddle-steamers *Lord Melville* and *Talbot*, with their candy-striped funnels, that ran a regular service 'within twelve hours' several times a week.[9] On the Seine by 1829 one could take a *bateau à vapeur* from Le Havre to Rouen. Turner, doing so, took along M. J. Morlent's little guidebook, *Voyage sur la Seine, en bateau à vapeur*, though he used it more as a sketchbook for marginal memoranda of churches and rivercraft; most of the pages remained uncut. Perhaps he found himself on board without a sketchbook.

Steamboats became part of his life – going to and from Margate, for example – and part of his sketching agenda, along with castles and bridges. He liked the thrusting blackness of them, their symmetrical bow waves, the bossy priority they took on waterways. It would be easy to assume that he thought of these steamboats as symbols of the new age. But they may simply have appealed to his eye. He admired their shapes and was grateful for the way their dark smoke made evident the currents in the air. He had noted in a sketchbook around 1808: 'One word is sufficient to establish what is the greatest difficulty of the painter's art: to produce wavy air, as some call the wind ... To give that wind he must give the cause as well as the effect ...'[10] And 'wavy air' became visible by way of coal smoke from the steamers in *Staffa, Fingal's Cave* and in the lovely Seine watercolour of 1832, *Between Quilleboeuf and Villequier*.[11] Of course, he generally fitted in on these river trips one of his other preoccupations. On the Seine in the 1820s he reminded himself about bait for fishing: 'Provide yourself with plenty of gentles [that is, fly-maggots]. If the aforesaid be old so much the better because they will work through the same cleaning themselves the while.'[12]

His travels along French rivers came to fruition in three 'annuals', volumes published for the Christmas and New Year trade that came out in the late autumn but were dated in the following year. *Turner's Annual Tour: Wanderings by the Loire* (1833) was the first; *Wanderings by the Seine* appeared in two parts in the two following years. All three were gathered together in a bumper volume, *Liber Fluviorum or River Scenery of France*, in 1853. Leitch Ritchie, the journalist who wrote the travelogue that accompanied Turner's illustrations, didn't much mention his artist in the text. They may not have travelled together a great deal, 'their tastes in everything but art being exceedingly dissimilar', according to Alaric Watts, whose biographical sketch accompanied the *Liber Fluviorum*.[13] But Ritchie told Watts that when he was in Turner's company he 'was frequently surprised to find what a forcible idea he conveyed of a place with scarcely a single correct detail. His exaggerations, when it suited his purpose to exaggerate, were wonderful, lifting up, for instance, by two or three storeys, the steeple, or rather stunted cone, of a village church.' When Ritchie good-humouredly chided him for this habit, Turner took the offensive, 'his little sharp eyes glistening the while', and gleefully drew attention to Ritchie's insistence that the beard of the notorious wife-killer Gilles de Retz, known as Bluebeard, 'was so intensely black that it seemed to have a shade of blue'.[14] Ritchie must have been affected by Turner's sardonic chant, 'Blue Beard! Blue Beard! Black Beard!', because this observation of Ritchie's, assuming a painter's prerogative to analyse colour, disappeared from the letterpress of the 1853 edition. One such exaggeration of Turner's was to be seen in *Light Towers of the Heve*, a watercolour and gouache he did after his 1829 trip for engraving as a vignette frontispiece for the Seine *Wanderings*. In this the height of the cliff with its two lighthouses at La Hève, near the mouth of the Seine, was shown as far higher than it actually was.

Ritchie was lucky to see anything of Turner; much of the time he travelled on his own, more or less incognito. When he was off on tour, few of his friends or family had an exact idea of where he was. Sometimes, one suspects, Turner himself may not have known where he had got to – on the Loire in 1826 when he jotted down a place name as 'Boulancy', he was in Beaugency, it seems.[15] His solitariness would have been increased by his lack of fluency in other languages. But, apart from that, there was a good deal of the Scarlet Pimpernel about him, spotted here and rumoured there; he didn't want to be pinned down. Despite its characteristic embroidery, a story of Thornbury's rings true; it tells of 'Turner meeting a well-known water-colour painter on the Moselle, and fraternising with him. He [Turner] even went so far as to invite him to rather a handsome dinner, whereat the wine passed freely as the comrades discussed the scenery with enthusiasm. At last it was time to separate, and Turner and his guest exchanged friendly farewells. The next morning the weaker vessel arose late. His first enquiry was if Monsieur Turner had gone out sketching yet. "Left for good at five o'clock this morning, and said you would settle both bills," was the petrifying answer.'[16] In other places the man who enjoyed playing this sort of 'rough practical joke' would simply be missing from the inn come morning because – as this watercolour painter suspected – Turner had got up at dawn and was on the beach or mountainside, filling his sketchbook. The Reverend Judkin once encountered Turner at Boulogne and found that the artist did not relish his cheery 'Why, who would have expected to see you here?' Thornbury reported that 'Mr Judkin saw no more of him till just as he was leaving, when he caught a glimpse of him in a boat bobbing off the shore, drawing in an anxious, absorbed way, and heedless of all else.'[17]

Even when illustrating, Turner was an artist; and, whatever his reportorial instincts, he didn't confront his times. He lived through industrial revolution, agricultural depression and political reform; but his expression of interest in such matters was an artist's, properly oblique, or so combined with historic compost, painterly reference and artistic innovation that the impact of the modern never seemed journalistically sensational. The social and political ramifications of a subject almost always remained incidental to what he was trying to achieve in a picture by way of colour and light.

By 1835, when he was sixty, he had seen a lot of changes in English life. Parts of an empire may have been lost but the bulk was still growing, was further flung than any in human history, and produced vast wealth for the mother country. There, hard roads and fast coaches were followed by iron rails and locomotives. More and more people filled the British Isles and tumbled out overseas; the population of Britain had nearly doubled since the turn of the century and about a tenth of it – nearly two million – was making London burst at the seams. The old market gardens and marshes towards Chelsea and Wapping were being covered with new streets, new houses. A contemporary, Sydney Smith, remarked on all that had happened since he was born in 1771, including smooth streets (which saved him £15 a year on repairs to his carriage springs), gas lighting, effective policing, cheap cabs, medicines like quinine, umbrellas, the penny post and savings banks. And then there were all the effects of Watt's steam engine.

One has the impression that Turner took on most elements of his time quite happily: cotton mills and steam engines produced colourful effects; he enjoyed the contrast between factory fires and rural greenery, such as he had recorded at Dudley around 1832 and was to paint in watercolour and gouache in Liege, Belgium, around 1839. Darwin – still a believer in the biblical account of Creation – went to sea on HMS *Beagle* in 1831 for nearly five years and though neither his 1839 volume on the voyage, which led him to the theory of evolution, nor Sir Charles Lyell's influential *Principles of Geology* appeared on Turner's bookshelves, he had the fifth volume (concerning fishes) of Sir John Richardson's *Zoology of the Voyage of HMS Erebus and Terror*, 1845. It was an age of aggressive enquiry, with religious faith in question and a growing awareness of the immensity of natural processes.

Turner went with his time, taking in its facts through his senses and daily needs. But often in his art other things rose to the surface: his dreams superseded the realities of the day. They could be dreams of Carthage or Venice, of past or present. They could be intimate glimpses, say of Petworth or the Seine, that had an inherent buoyancy, or larger views – some of his oils, for example, of the Kent sea coast – within whose brilliance one detects a dark centre. Man was a puny thing, dwarfed by time and nature. And yet the despair at the heart of this vision did not stop him. If he didn't have hope, he had energy; in late-middle age that energy was stupendous still.

He enjoyed being a journeyman – travelling to fulfil his commissions to illustrate books for armchair tourists. So he went on crossing the Channel, listening to the paddle-wheels thrash and smelling the gritty smoke and salt air; getting up early to catch a coach or train; walking and sketching and arriving tired out late in the day at an unknown inn. But in 1836 he had company – he made his summer tour with Hugh Munro, wealthy landowner and laird of Novar in Easter Ross, Scotland, who had been collecting Turner pictures for at least a decade, and whose vocation as an amateur artist Turner had done much to foster. When John Green's collection in Blackheath was sold by Christie's in April 1830, Munro bought Turner's *Venus and Adonis* (c. 1803–5) and his *Bonneville* (exhibited 1803). According to Alaric Watts, they were 'among the most attractive lots, though neither important in size nor of his best time. In those days their market value might have been about eighty guineas each. They would, however, have been knocked down for considerably less, but for the impetus given to the biddings by one of Mr Turner's agents, whose personal appearance did not warrant the belief that he was in search of pictures of a very high order. He was, in fact, a clean, ruddy-cheeked butcher's boy, in the usual costume.'[18]

Munro had a different story. Turner, he recalled, had alerted him to the Green sale:

> He then knew I had bought anything of his which had come to the hammer. He asked me, if I meant to bid for these pictures, for said he it would be most inconvenient & impossible for me to go there during the varnishing days. I said I should. He asked me how far I should go; as far as I recollect I said £200 for each, probably more for the large one 'Adonis leaving the couch of Venus'. He seemed much pleased – [he said] 'then I shall leave it entirely to

you ...' I was at the sale but did not bid in person. The agent who bid for me said his only opponent was a boy & he could not find out who he was. A long time after, Peacock, a dealer of much taste in Marylebone St. said to me 'Had I been able to be at Blackheath you would have had to pay more for those Turners but I could not go myself & *sent my boy.*' I got the pictures for £75 each. (Turner's prices were then as you know £250 for 3f. by 4f.) On my return to town I called at Somerset House to tell Turner what I had done. He shook his head & said I had got them too cheap – but thanked me for what I had done.[19]

Munro had also gone down the river to Greenwich with Turner and Holworthy in the early 1830s. It was Turner's idea, though he appointed Munro 'commodare' of the jaunt.[20] It seems to have been on this occasion that they visited the Painted Hall of the Naval Hospital after dinner and looked at Turner's *Battle of Trafalgar*, and while they were doing so the forthright pensioner said the picture looked like a carpet and that they should look at the de Loutherbourg *Glorious First of June* instead. Munro was a shy man, not the sort to bid at an auction. Turner had written to Holworthy about him a few years before: 'He has lost a great deal of that hesitation in manner and speech, and [when] spoken to [, does] not ... blush as heretofore.'[21] Turner was to be seen at Munro's house in Park Street, where David Roberts now and then encountered him. At one point Munro was being pressed by Scottish friends to take up politics, but he didn't have the outgoing qualities. In 1836 he was depressed, and Turner out of friendship 'proposed to divert his mind into fresh channels by the expedient of travel'.[22]

They set out after the Academy exhibition closed – it was the last to be held at Somerset House, and Turner, feeling the loss, an old tie broken forever, may have been glad to have Munro along. From Dover they travelled to Calais, and then to St Omer, the old market town on the road south. There, Munro later told Ruskin, Turner sketched 'with great eagerness ... I especially remember an old abbey [St Bertin] which he was sketching in a remarkable way with a bit of plumbago [graphite].'[23] On their way to the Alps Turner wanted to call at places he had not seen before as well as to revisit places like Bonneville. They went through Arras and Rheims, Dijon and Dole, before reaching Lausanne. Munro said of Turner, 'All along, whenever he could get a few minutes, he had his little sketchbook out, many being remarkable, but he seemed to tire at last and got careless and slovenly. I don't remember colouring coming out till we got into Switzerland.'[24] Near Salanches, at the bridge of St Martin's, when Munro was having difficulty with a coloured sketch, Turner asked to borrow a block of paper. 'He reappeared in about two hours and throwing it down, where he had taken it up, said he could make nothing of my papers. I expressed my regret that he had thrown away his time. But it was some days before I had occasion to open the block again (so little did I expect to find what I did, viz. the 4 sketches in it). He *never asked me for them or ever said a word about them*.'[25] Was this an object lesson or a gift – or both, furtively expressed? As Ruskin later remarked, Turner had 'a curious dislike to *appear kind*'.[26]

Munro saw Turner in various moods on this trip. He got to know his aloof way of concentrating, rarely talking, never rhapsodizing about the Alpine scenery; but, once used to that taciturn manner, he found it easy to get on with him. Sometimes Turner was evidently disgruntled: he didn't like the way a coloured sketch had turned out and wished he had used a pencil. He often preferred a higher viewpoint to the one Munro chose. For a sixty-one-year-old, this meant a lot of climbing. In the Aosta valley, many of Turner's sketches were made from spots on the mountains that were reached by arduous ascents. The companions parted in Turin, with Turner intending to return alone by the Rhine route, but before they did so Munro tried to buy from Turner some of his Aosta drawings. Turner would not sell them. Munro felt a little hurt by this. But somehow or other, the sketchbook that Turner had partly used on his last visit to Farnley in 1824 – and was perhaps too saddened by to want to use again – got into Munro's luggage before Turner left. Another mysterious present from one inhibited person to another.

In the course of the 1830s Turner went into Central Europe by way of Copenhagen, Berlin, Dresden and Prague.[27] As mentioned, he went again to Venice. Other than when calling on Delacroix in Paris, he seems to have avoided meeting notable people on these trips and travelled with his usual quiet concentration. An inn-keeper in the Jura had an unfavourable impression of his guest. An English traveller who knew Turner saw his name in the inn's visitors book and asked what sort of man had registered. The patron answered, 'A rough clumsy man, and you may know him by his always having a pencil in his hand.'[28] During his journey home from Venice in

1840, he paused on the Danube near Regensburg, sometimes called Ratisbon, and drew a tower built on a rock, writing next to it 'Tom Girtin'. So far from home, so many years on, his old friend and challenger came to mind.[29]

In 1837, following the deaths of John Soane and Constable, King William IV died, not long after opening the new National Gallery and Royal Academy buildings, and the young Victoria became queen. Turner, like the rest of the country, evidently felt that the throne was safe beneath that plump and tidy form – he took wing for the Continent again. He was away from late July until 5 September, leaving few marks to blaze his trail.[30] In 1839 he made his second long Meuse–Mosel–Rhine expedition – a five-sketchbooks tour into the country Wordsworth had called 'War's favourite playground'.[31] He was invited to Hastings for Christmas by J. H. Maw and he replied on 11 December that he could not come because he had been 'so idle all summer'.[32] In fact he remained busy all winter, finishing his lovely blue-paper gouaches – about eighty in all – that captured the essence of his recent river travels. He also painted hard: seven oils were shown at the Academy exhibition the following May. Idle indeed!

They were busy years, but he had time for Britain too; not only for Petworth and Margate, but for Scotland – two trips in 1831 and 1834 – and Oxford, which he visited on the way to the Midlands in 1830 and again in 1834 to see James Ryman, successor to the print-dealer James Wyatt. Sketches for watercolours which would be the basis of engravings were the reasons for these trips: a typical product the watercolour he did of the Merton Street façade of Merton College, with some workmen cutting timber and dressing stone; a splendid by-product five radiant colour studies or 'colour beginnings' he did of Oxford High Street. The 1831 Scottish trip was the one which took him to Staffa on the *Maid of Morven*, but its main purpose was Cadell's commission to him to illustrate Scott's *Poetical Works*. Turner, as noted, went reluctantly, feeling out of sorts, and believing that he had enough Scottish material already; but Cadell paid his expenses. Scott, although seriously ill, was hospitable at Abbotsford and had Turner shown around various historic and picturesque sites; but Turner seems to have been an awkward guest. Cadell wrote to Sir Walter afterwards: 'I am sorry that Mr Turner should have annoyed you all so much – it was most absurd to be in such a pother.'[33] He had presumably calmed down by the time he visited Hugh Munro at his Novar seat on the east coast of Scotland, overlooking Cromarty Firth. Back home in October 1834 he was involved in outside work much closer to Queen Anne Street.

Turner's interest in the elements – air, earth, fire and water – was life-long, but in several pictures of this time it was fire that preoccupied him. Blazing rockets and fireworks took his fancy on the English coast and over the Venice rooftops. The fires of industry and the flames of hell figured in several watercolours (*Dudley* and *Satan Summoning his Legions*, a preliminary study[34] for a vignette for Milton's *Poetical Works*). His act of genial Rembrandtesque rivalry with George Jones, the *Burning Fiery Furnace*, showing Shadrach, Meshach and Abednego within, was exhibited in 1832. Two pictures of the mid-1830s were an oil, *Fire at Sea*, and a watercolour, *Fire at Fenning's Wharf*. Fenning's was a timber yard next to the Thames that caught fire on the night of 30 August 1836 – and Turner's watercolour makes it look as if he had been an eye-witness. But it isn't clear whether he was in fact back by then from his Swiss trip with Munro (in the course of which a conflagration in Lausanne caught his eye); the seemingly on-the-spot spontaneity of *Fenning's* may have been the result of his veteran artifice. However, he was certainly present at *the* great fire of the decade. On the night of 16 October 1834, he hurried along with many other Londoners to Westminster: the Houses of Parliament in the old Palace of Westminster were burning.

The blaze broke out in the House of Lords shortly after 6 p.m. and spread rapidly in the strong wind. A stock of ancient wooden tallies – notched sticks on which exchequer receipts were once recorded – was being burned in the Lords' furnaces, and the heat became so intense that timbers adjacent to the chimneys ignited. The medieval palace was full of woodwork – beams, rafters, laths, panelling – and much of it went up in flames and smoke, though the great structure of Westminster Hall, which dated from Norman times, was saved. Turner was among a number of members and students of the Royal Academy who were drawn to the fire. One student named John Waller wrote in his diary that some of his fellows were 'on the river in the same boat with Turner and Stanfield ... it must have been a magnificent study for them'.[35] (Poor Waller missed it and regretted it.) Turner's shorthand sketches, done at night by the light of the blaze, were indeed sketchy. He drew the scene not only from a boat but from Westminster Bridge and from the far Surrey riverbank. But back in his studio he put his memories and reactions into a number of watercolour studies, most of them quick, but a more considered one shows the firefighters in Old Palace Yard and a crowd of spectators.[36] He then painted not just one oil but two of the disaster. The first was the painting he was seen working on before the opening of the British Institution exhibition in February 1835. Among the admiring reviewers, the *Spectator*'s writer thought it 'wonderful' – a picture that 'transcends its neighbours [including Chalon's view of the same fire] as the sun eclipses the moon and the stars'.[37] His second fling at the subject was shown at the Academy in May. In this he viewed the inferno from the southern end of Waterloo Bridge, further downstream, which was from a greater distance. There was more water in this picture and hence the great fire was redoubled by its reflection on the surface of the Thames. The fiery colour struck some as almost celebratory, if not inflammatory, and the *Morning Herald* suggested that 'the Academy ought, now and then ... to throw a wet blanket over either this fire king or his works'.[38]

Turner may have felt, as many did, that this calamity was poetic justice: Parliament was being punished for its tardiness in reforming the franchise and for the moderation of its efforts in that respect two years before. He may have been happy to see this headquarters of the old regime of rotten boroughs and the landowner-dominated place-system go up in smoke. (But England was still two nations, and Parliament spoke most directly for just one of those two.) He may have wondered wryly what his Radical friend Walter Fawkes would have said as the buildings his ancestor Guy Fawkes had failed to blow up were now so dramatically incinerated. But the reporter of the Pantheon's morning-after was more likely in the first instance to have been thrilled to witness and record so catastrophic an event – heat and flames consuming the accretion of centuries, and the firemen (still working for private insurance companies) unable to do more than confine it by hosing down, for instance, Westminster Hall, which they saved with the help of a wind shift that blew the fire back towards the riverside buildings. (In his second oil Turner showed the floating fire-pump, labelled 'Sun Fire Office', arriving rather late; because of low water in the Thames, it had run aground on the way; this was the sort of detail that stuck in his mind.) His pictures of the occasion certainly underline his belief that man, faced with great natural forces and human folly, was going to be in deep trouble. But it was the fire itself – its shape, movement and colour – that was his subject, and the associations were condiments to the main course. (Turner also wanted to visit the Tower of London after a serious fire there on 30 October 1841. The Duke of Wellington curtly declined to assist Turner in gaining entry.)

He was still having trouble in the mid-1830s in selling many of his most ambitious pictures. In stock, in his gallery, were *Dido building Carthage*; *Crossing the Brook*; *Bay of Baiae*; *Ulysses deriding Polyphemus*; *Palestrina*; *Staffa, Fingal's Cave* and *Helvoetsluys*, among others. Some friends remained faithful purchasers. Soane bought *Admiral van Tromp's Barge* for 250 guineas in 1831 and Hugh Munro took the *Rotterdam Ferry Boat* in 1833 and *Juliet and her Nurse* in 1836. If, in the public eye, a painter is only as good as the reception of his last picture, his fame was tottery. But the two Houses of Parliament paintings struck a chord and sold quickly: the close-up was bought on the last day of the British Institution show by a Mr Chambers Hall and the more distant view of the fire by a Leeds collector, James Garth Marshall. Marshall's grandson (who inherited the picture) later described a visit his grandfather and father made in 1835 to Queen Anne Street:

> My grandfather asked Turner what his price was and he said he could have anything in his studio for £350. My grandfather then turned to my father and said, 'which do you like best?' and he pointed to the picture now in my possession. But Turner said: 'Well, young man, that is the one you cannot have, as I have decided to give that to the nation,'- but my grandfather, who was a hard-headed Yorkshireman, said: 'No, Mr. Turner, you gave me the offer of anything in your studio at a price and I must hold you to it.' And so the picture came into the family.[39]

Fame, Dr Johnson famously opined, is a shuttlecock, and Turner's celebrity as an eccentric, indeed erratic, genius was heightened by the fact that some critics believed in him and others did not. One writer in *Arnold's Magazine of the Fine Arts* in 1833 recalled Fuseli's verdict – 'Turner is the only landscape painter of genius in Europe' – and went on to judge his most recent work as far superior to his earlier; Turner had 'emerged as a meteor in colouring'.[40] The contrary position was put in *Blackwood's* three years later, when the Reverend John Eagles denounced Turner's Juliet and her Nurse as 'a strange jumble' and an example of the glare and glitter delighted in by modern British artists (as opposed to the shade and depth of the Old Masters).[41] And this brought the seventeen-year-old John Ruskin into the field to defend his hero for the first time – although, as we have seen, Turner dissuaded him from sending on his overwrought reply to *Blackwood's*. But that, as time would show, was not going to shut Ruskin up.

In one respect, Turner was an undoubted success: he made money. The new Victorians respected wealth and those who supported themselves by their own efforts. Although some of his big pictures did not sell, others did, for goodly amounts. George Jones detected Turner's arrival at a level of uniformly 'large prices' when he received 200 guineas from Robert Vernon for *Bridge of Sighs, Canaletti Painting* in 1833, and Turner said to Jones, 'Well, if they will have such scraps instead of important pictures, they must pay for them.'[42] His standard price for three-by-fours was 200 guineas in 1837, but for the larger *Fountain of Fallacy* he charged twice that price in 1839, 'exclusive of frame and copyright of Engraving'.[43] In 1843 he told a would-be client for a commissioned three-by-four painting that the price would be 200 guineas but that the same work 'afterwards', that is bought during the Academy exhibition or at his gallery, would be 250 guineas.[44] Cadell paid him twenty-five guineas each for twenty-four designs for the Scott poems in 1831, a total of £630 (roughly £22,000 today).

In these years he was also engaged in providing illustrations for Samuel Rogers's *Poetical Works* and for the Findens, whose Byron volumes (1832–4) and *Landscape Illustrations of the Bible* (1833–6) he illustrated. (For the latter, he worked from drawings and prints by artists who had travelled to the Holy Land; he did not do so himself.) For the series *Picturesque Views in England and Wales*, for Charles Heath, he got sixty to seventy guineas a drawing. That Turner was 'doing all right' was evident in the fact that he could afford to spend £3000 in buying up the remaining stock of this series in 1840, when Heath had financial troubles, in the process outsmarting the publisher and print-dealer Mr Bohn. And he could also afford to lay out over £2500 in fees to engravers for making five large plates of his own work around this time, on top of which he had to pay for the paper and printing costs of the engravings.

While his work and his name were circulating in the form of prints to a large public, those collectors who were buying his larger works had ceased to be the aristocracy or – Munro excepted – great landowners. One of his new patrons was the Bishopsgate coachmaker Benjamin Windus, who put together a celebrated watercolour collection at his house in Tottenham; there, by 1834, he had some fifty Turners – by 1840, around 200. (He went on to buy Turner oils as well.) The watercolours included drawings from *Southern Coast*, from *England and Wales*, and many of the Byron, Scott and Bible illustrations. Visitors were welcome to see Windus's library and drawing room and view the Turners on display. Other patrons of this time were the Leeds clothing magnate John Sheepshanks, who bought *St. Michael's Mount* (RA 1834), *Line-Fishing off Hastings* (RA 1835) and *Venice, from the Canale della Guidecca* (RA 1840); Henry McConnel, a Manchester textile manufacturer, who commissioned the *Venice* of 1834 and *Keelmen Heaving in Coals by Night* (RA 1835); and Robert Vernon, the horse dealer, who bought among others *Bridge of Sighs* (RA 1833), *The Golden Bough* (RA 1834) and *Neapolitan Fisher Girls* (RA 1840). These men were not buying 'safely' – there was plenty of more conservative painting around to decorate their houses. They were buying with the panache with which they made money; but they weren't throwing their money away.

Considering what a lonely grouch he could sometimes be, Turner was from time to time found in distinguished company. He seems sometimes to have been asked to dinners to provide balance, to be the artist. He may sometimes have gone for the meal, for the talk and for the contacts with people who might provide commissions. In March 1835 he dined with his frequent host Samuel Rogers at his house in St James's Place along with the writer Tom Moore and the editor of the *Times*, Thomas Barnes, who was one of the most influential men in the country. Talking with Moore, Turner said he had often wanted to go to Ireland but had been afraid to. He never went, but he did four vignettes for Moore's book *The Epicurean*, published in 1839.

Yet he was slighted in 1837. The greatest landscape and seascape painter of the age was not on the list of those honoured when Queen Victoria came to the throne and within a month Augustus Callcott, the miniature painter W. J. Newton and Richard Westmacott the sculptor were all given knighthoods. His friend Chantrey had received the accolade in 1835 and David Wilkie in 1836. Why not Turner? His mysterious humour? His lack of social polish? Rumours of unsuitable women? He was perhaps seen simply as too much of 'a character', with his Covent Garden origins still clear. And though he was an intimate part of Lord Egremont's informal court, that apparently didn't carry weight at the west end of the Mall. His sense of neglect may have shown in one of his paintings of 1838, *Ancient History – Ovid Banished from Rome*, and in his 1839 *Cicero at his Villa*. He thought that Cicero had 'died neglected', as he told the listeners to one of his 1811 Perspective lectures – Cicero was in fact forced to flee from his villa and was then murdered. Turner's jocularity may have been clouded for a time but he also may have reflected that British social distinctions broke no bones; they were preferable to cut-throat Roman politics.

He remained staunchly involved with the Royal Academy. He had been on the committee planning the new quarters alongside the National Gallery and in 1837, as already mentioned, he was on the hanging committee for the first exhibition in its new home. He was also on the Council that year along with Chantrey, Leslie and Hilton, though he was not at the meetings that took place through August, September and October – he was away on the Continent, in Margate and at Petworth. After Lord Egremont's funeral he attended the Life Academy as a Visitor. But one aspect of his Academy life now ended. He finally decided to quit his post as Professor of Perspective (his last lectures had been given in 1828). He was formally thanked by Wilkie in early 1838, in a resolution at the General Assembly that Edwin Landseer seconded, expressing – rather pompously – the 'extreme regret they feel upon the loss of the services of a Professor who, by precept and example, has done so much to advance the cause of Perspective in the English School'.[45]

A number of friends never ceased to bear him in mind. Dawson Turner continued to dispatch barrels of herrings to him. John Maw in 1834 sent some Devonshire clotted cream to Queen Anne Street, and Turner twice thanked him for it; once in a formal note that for some reason didn't get promptly delivered, secondly in a note of apology enclosing the first. (In note 1, Turner thanked Maw for the 'Clotted Cream'. In note 2, it was the 'clotid cream'.)[46]

With Turner, as we have seen, charity began largely away from home. It was an age in which private munificence supported many almshouses, hospitals, dispensaries and free schools, though some larger institutions had other support. The Corporation of London looked after Bedlam (which moved to Lambeth in 1815, eleven years after his mother had died in it); Greenwich Naval Hospital was funded by royal, government and personal gift (and by deductions from seamen's wages); and Chelsea Hospital for veteran soldiers was also government-backed. Both Chelsea and Greenwich were grand structures, with Wren buildings facing the Thames, greater than any royal palace in London. Although 'Turner's Gift' was obviously not going to be on that scale, he may have thought of his establishment for decayed artists as emulating, in its smaller, Twickenham way, the great charitable foundations. At some point he bought a book by T. F. Hunt, *Designs for Parsonage Houses, Alms Houses, etc.* (1827), presumably so that he could get ideas for his own charity – which George Jones said 'he did not like to call … alms houses', preferring 'the denomination of "Turner's Gift"'. Jones also said that Turner constantly talked to his intimate friends 'of the best mode of leaving property for the use of the unsuccessful' artists.[47]

Soane – knighted in 1831 – had got a private bill introduced in Parliament in 1833 to ensure that his property went to establish a Soane museum; an ordinary will would not have been sufficient in law to keep his spendthrift son from getting his hands on the estate. But despite Soane's example (successful, as it turned out) in thus getting around the priority usually conceded by English courts to private claims over public claims, Turner failed to take such a precautionary step. Perhaps he thought his relatives would never bother to challenge his intentions. He seems to have been entranced by all the legal language and checks and balances he threw into the codicil drawn up in 1832 for his second will, instructing his executors what to do should there be any objection to setting up 'Turner's Gift' after he died. Although such an institution remained his 'express desire', he declared that 'if it be found impossible to fully carry the same into effect within five years from my death', then he wanted his funds and property used to keep Queen Anne Street going as a gallery, with Hannah as custodian at £150 a year, because a prime object was still 'to keep my pictures together'.[48] A secondary object achieved by this would be to give the faithful Hannah something to do; she had lost some of her *raison d'être* with his father's death in 1829, and his own departure would make her jobless. But whether Turner considered this, or was simply using the most knowledgeable, available and indeed only member of his entourage for such a post, is unknown. Hannah by now was well accustomed to the neglect his pictures received at home.

With Soane, Turner was involved in the Artists General Benevolent Institution. For it they held a joint account in trust. Turner seems to have been one of the founding members of this body in 1814 and for fifteen years was highly active on its behalf, helping negotiate a merger with a rival charity, the Artists Benevolent Fund in 1818. He was chairman of the AGBI board and its treasurer at the time. Both penny- and pound-wise, Turner had financial acumen that was useful. As jottings in his sketchbooks showed, he kept a careful eye on interest rates and the returns to be got from government stock. (The National Debt was funded by individuals like Turner, looking for a safe home for, and steady income from, their money.) The interests of the AGBI were often in his thoughts: he got Walter Fawkes to pay an annual subscription of five guineas in 1816, and he talked up the AGBI to Farington at the Academy Club dinner on 4 March 1818. He paid regular dues and made generous donations on top of them. He was a fairly regular attender of the AGBI's annual dinner. At the dinner in May 1823, at Freemasons' Hall in Great Queen Street (a building whose reconstruction Soane and Philip Hardwick had overseen), Lord Liverpool, the moderate but unthrusting Prime Minister from 1815 to 1827, was chairman for the start of the proceedings. But when he stepped down the AGBI members unanimously called on Turner to take the chair. The *Sun* reported, 'He obeyed the universal desire, and kept up the good humour and conviviality of the meeting.'[49] At the following year's dinner, after the healths of the Secretary and Directors were drunk, Turner – so the *British Press* wrote – 'returned thanks in a neat speech'.[50] This may have been the only 'neat speech' he ever made, and it is a pity no record of it has been found.

David Roberts first met Turner at an AGBI 'stewards meeting' around this time at the Crown and Anchor in the Strand. Turner didn't quite fit the picture that Roberts – then a young scene painter – had built up about him, 'the mighty painter of the day ... whose works were the all-in-all to every young artist'. The AGBI officers were seated around a green-baize-covered table when 'a little square-built man came in, to whom all paid respect. The business having begun, he joined in the conversation, and made some weak attempts at wit – at least I thought so, for no one seemed to laugh at his jokes but himself! So I asked who this very facetious little man was, and my astonishment on being told it was 'The Great Turner' ... turned my head.'[51]

Despite Turner's dedication to the cause, disagreements arose in the 1820s between him and another AGBI stalwart, the Scottish miniature painter Andrew Robertson, about the purpose of the charity. Turner's generous feelings ran, as we have seen, more easily in large institutional channels than they did on a personal scale, and this and his tendency to hoard in case of serious future need came up against the belief of Robertson and others that the AGBI ought to spend more now on widows and orphans. Turner's inflexibility in the face of present individual need had been seen in 1811, when Farington recorded that Mrs Richards, the impoverished widow of John Richards RA, the Academy's former Secretary, had applied to the Academy for help and in the process had, she complained, 'been harshly treated by Turner'.[52] (Was he smarting from the break-up of his own relationship with the widowed Mrs Danby?) According to Thornbury, at the time of Turner's row with Robertson the architect C. R. Cockerell RA went to Queen Anne Street to put the point of view in favour of liberal giving. Turner 'would hardly see him; he growled; he would not relent even when he was warned "that he would one day have to answer to the widows and orphans to whom he had refused bread"'.[53] Turner, we remember, had had some of the benefit from the pension the Musicians Society had given Sarah Danby – there had been less financial pressure on JMWT.

In any event, in 1829 Turner decided to abandon the fight against the majority opinion and secede from the AGBI. He sent a letter to W. L. Roper, the Assistant Secretary, asking leave to resign as Chairman, and despite a quick reply from the Directors, trying to mollify him, his resignation as Chairman and Treasurer was accepted on 24 December 1829, with regret, and with the hope that he might be reinstated in both offices 'at some future time'.[54] Unmollified, in June 1830 he revoked his 1829 bequest of £500 to the AGBI; he seems to have felt that his own charity or Gift was going to require all his spare change. Yet he remained a trustee of the AGBI's funds until 1839, when he failed to respond to a request from the Directors that he continue to act as such and was replaced. But he eventually made up with Andrew Robertson. George Jones at one point told Turner that Robertson regretted their estrangement, and Turner said, "'Let us meet." They did so, and all the past dissatisfaction was forgotten. Turner's heart was replete with charitable feeling, though his manner was not inviting to the prosperous or the poor.'[55]

The American writer Ralph Waldo Emerson, who crossed the Atlantic several times in these years (and in 1848 went to Turner's gallery), thought England was 'the best of actual nations'. It was like a ship anchored in a very effective position 'at the side of Europe, and right in the heart of the modern world'. Emerson saw how the English were tugged two ways, by the past and by the present: 'Everyone of them is a thousand years old, and lives by his memory: and when you say this, they accept it as praise.' And yet the up-to-date was also in evidence if you looked, or listened, hard enough: 'the voice of their modern muse has a slight hint of the steam whistle'.[56]

Turner's love of the English past – and its castles, countryside, sailing ships and heroes – was as great as any Englishman's, but the steam whistle sounded for him too. The man born on St George's Day was 'English-minded', as his young admirer John Ruskin was to observe,[57] in many ways an old-fashioned patriot, and yet he was open to much that the mid-nineteenth century put in his way. This is not to say that all that was happening was reflected in his work. One doesn't see any of the new omnibuses, drawn by two or three horses, that were beginning to trundle along London streets (there were 400 of them in 1837). The gas lamps in town don't show in his pictures. As he walked from the new quarters of the Academy, overlooking what was becoming Trafalgar Square, to the new premises of the Athenaeum Club on the corner of Pall Mall and Waterloo Place – in other words from one great war-memorial site to another – he was passed by cabs, gigs, private carriages and drays jostling each other over the cobbles. He couldn't help but feel the pace of the metropolis of which he was a part, but his artistic interest remained fixed on waves breaking on Kent beaches, palazzos standing alongside the canals of Venice, compositions of trees and people, ships and water, arrangements of colour and light.

Along with steampower at sea, he was interested in lighthouses and life-saving marine innovations, which he drew and painted; but not all the new forms of travel that intrigued him got into his paintings. In late 1836 he heard of a balloon expedition that had been made from London to the Continent by three men, one being Robert Hollond, who was to become member of Parliament for Hastings. Turner wrote to Hollond, with whom he had apparently talked: 'Your Excursion so occupied my mind that I dreamt of it, and I do hope you will hold to your intention of making the drawing, with all the forms and colours of your recollection.'[58]

Turner was taken by the notion of seeing the Channel from high above, the beam of the South Foreland lighthouse on the waters of the Straits, the clouds ahead like battlements, the scattered fires and lights below that gradually formed into a town, and the blackness of night – darker when seen from on high – with the stars 'redoubled in their lustre', shining 'like sparks of the whitest silver', as Monck Mason, one of Hollond's companions, wrote in his account of the trip.[59]

But he was at sea level or rather river level for the one British exhibit he sent to the Academy in 1839 along with four Italian-subject entries, ancient and modern. The title 'Professor of Perspective' after his name was missing from the catalogue this year and would not appear again. He called his riverscape *The Fighting Temeraire tugged to her last berth to be broken up, 1838*. He showed the old warship, a Trafalgar veteran, being towed upriver – a scrimshaw ship with slim ivory masts, bound for the next world and already radiating a magic ghostliness. The *Temeraire* was plucked onward by a thoroughly modern paddle-wheel tugboat, its tall black stack shooting forth a plume of flame and white smoke like a moving pyre, its round-topped black paddle-wheel boxes reminding one of the wheels of a hearse. The tug seems to vibrate with the energy it is using to pull the great corpse of a ship to the breaker's yard. The river is calm. A barge sails gently downstream; a white-canvased square-rigged ship hangs in the distance; a hulk floats near the horizon; and the low sun fires the sky and then, in reflection, the river-surface towards which the *Temeraire* and its tug remorselessly move. They are heading into the flames. It can't be helped.

He saw this in his mind in colourful fragments, in remembered images, that cohered upon the canvas. He stacked his palette with his most ferocious pigments: lemon yellow, chrome yellow, orange, scarlet, vermilion and red lead, hot paints that he laid over an already warm ground of earth colours. A coal fire glowed in the studio grate. Outside, the grey and gritty winter fog swirled along Queen Anne Street. He had glanced at his ship models and some of the hundreds of sketches of warships he had done in the past, including the *Temeraire* when she was laid up in the Medway in the 1820s. Schetky had offered him a drawing of the *Temeraire* when he was working on his second Trafalgar painting in 1823. Turner had been down to Margate in September and he had presumably read in the papers about the old ship being towed from Sheerness to Beatson's yard at Rotherhithe on the 5th and 6th of that month. It was undoubtedly a subject. That the *Temeraire* herself had been denuded for this slow tide-assisted voyage, her masts lifted out, her spars and sails stripped from her, didn't affect his way of telling the story. He had always had a dream of ships in his head; 'floating bulwarks' and 'the saviour of the world' were words of verse he had written in a sketchbook used in 1814 when he watched the Prince Regent and assorted monarchs view the fleet at Spithead.[60] So he left her masts in, her yards aloft, her sails bent on; but no flags or ensigns. There was a fatality to be recorded and the poignant fact that the Admiralty had already sold off this ship for her worth in scrap timber, iron, copper and lead. The *Temeraire* at this point was no longer part of the Royal Navy. He told them to put in with the exhibition catalogue entry two lines, adapted or semi-borrowed in his way from Thomas Campbell's poem 'Ye Mariners of England':

> The flag which braved the battle and the breeze,
>   No longer owns her.

The Fighting Temeraire made a great splash at the 1839 Academy exhibition, only eight months after the ship's last voyage. It tugged at the emotions of many viewers. It evoked the end of the age of fighting sail, the wooden walls and hearts of oak, and the onset of the age of steam and iron. It elicited explication and panegyric. It was, many thought, a splendid poem by the greatest master of the age. 'A magnificent national ode or piece of music,' declared Thackeray, a fluent spokesman for the enthusiasts. In *Fraser's Magazine* he called the *Temeraire* 'a noble river-piece ... as grand a picture as ever figured on the walls of any academy, or came from the easel of any painter'. And he continued with a description of 'the little, spiteful, diabolical steamer' and with a patriotic paean that responded to the ship's service history and battles past:

> We Cockneys feel our hearts leap up when we recall them to memory; and every clerk in Threadneedle Street feels the strength of a Nelson, when he thinks of the mighty actions performed by him.
>
> It is absurd, you will say ... to grow so politically enthusiastic about a four-foot canvass, representing a ship, a steamer, a river, and a sunset. But herin surely lies the power of the great artist. He makes you see and think of a good deal more than the objects before you ...[61]

The Fighting Temeraire indeed made many imaginations work frenetically. The Academicians swapped stories of its origins. One had it that Turner and Stanfield were on an excursion on the Thames, going to Greenwich for a whitebait dinner, when the *Temeraire* came by and Stanfield said, 'There's a fine subject, Turner,' and Turner painted it.[62] But Stanfield himself said this was 'an invention and a lie'.[63] Another theory was that Turner and W. F. Woodington, the sculptor of one of the reliefs at the base of Nelson's Column in Trafalgar Square, were coming back from Margate on a steamer and saw the *Temeraire* in 'a great blazing sunset', at which Turner at once made some 'little sketches on cards'.[64] It was elsewhere claimed that Turner saw the warship go by while he was sitting on Cherry Garden Pier in Bermondsey.

Sooner or later some viewers had problems, and questions, about the *mis-en-scène*: Where on the Thames had Turner placed his ship and tug? Is that Sheerness or Greenwich on the right-hand bank? Is the *Temeraire* being towed southwards in the big U-bend of the river round the Isle of Dogs? Are we looking west or east – in other words, is that a sunset or a *sunrise*? If the latter, was he trying to make us think of the adage 'Red sky in the morning, sailor's [or shepherd's] warning'? Was the picture of the breaker's-bound vessel 'a wry comment that he had been passed over' for honours?[65] Once more, the Fallacy of Hope! Ruskin was in no doubt of the sunset and its portent. Stoked up to full steam he wrote: 'Under the blazing veil of vaulted fire which lights the vessel on her last path, there is a blue, deep, desolate hollow of darkness, out of which you can hear the voice of the night wind, and the dull boom of the disturbed sea; because the cold deadly shadows of the twilight are gathering through every sunbeam ...'[66]

It should be pointed out that *téméraire* means bold; and Turner had got bolder with time. Moreover, he knew that tugs had their masts in front of their funnels but he put his tug's funnel foremost, and to hell with what marine experts would say. Indistinctness was his fault and his forte, and the facts were sometimes what became indistinct as he wrestled to capture an artistic truth. Here, too, he walked a tightrope of sentiment and got to the other end without falling in. The ovations were deserved.

His picture had a price-ticket at first but soon was priceless. A letter from him – of 12 June 1839 – to a potential purchaser of his exhibits at the Academy stated, 'The only picture in east Room unsold is the Marine subject / Price 250 guineas.'[67] In a slightly later letter to Charles Leslie, who had been enquiring what he wanted for the *Temeraire*, Turner wrote that two gentlemen were making up their minds about the picture. Maybe one of the minds to be made up was his own and it was tending toward the idea of not letting the painting go. Rumour had it that the Duke of Northumberland wanted to buy it around 1847 and Turner refused. In 1848, James Lenox, the New Yorker for whom Leslie acted in the purchase of *Staffa, Fingal's Cave*, tried to buy the *Temeraire*. The dealer Thomas Griffith took Lenox to see Turner, and Lenox offered the artist £5000, which Turner turned down, and then a blank cheque, which Turner also rejected. By this stage the painting had become too precious to its maker to be sold or even lent. He had allowed it to be engraved and let the print-publisher J. Hogarth exhibit the painting in 1844. Some time after this he wrote, it seems to Hogarth: 'Dear Sir I have received your note via Margate ... no considerations of money or favour can induce me to lend my Darling again.'[68]

19: The Rigours of Winter

On 22 June 1840 John Ruskin, aged twenty-one, first met his hero J. M. W. Turner, aged sixty-five. The meeting took place at the house of the art dealer Thomas Griffith in Norwood, where Turner talked 'with great rapture of Aosta and Courmayeur'. Ruskin wrote:

> Introduced today to the man who beyond all doubt is the greatest of the age; greatest in every faculty of the imagination, in every branch of scenic knowledge; at once *the* painter and poet of the day, J. M. W. Turner. Everybody had described him to me as coarse, boorish, unintellectual, vulgar. This I knew to be impossible. I found in him a somewhat eccentric, keen-mannered, matter-of-fact, English-minded gentleman: good-natured evidently, bad-tempered evidently, hating humbug of all sorts, shrewd, perhaps a little selfish, highly intellectual, the powers of his mind not brought out with any delight in their manifestation, or intention of display, but flashing out occasionally in a word or a look.[1]

Young Ruskin had first come across Turner's work in an annual *Friendship's Offering* – an engraving of his *Vesuvius Angry* – and had been thrilled. A later gift of Rogers's *Italy* had given him the chance to look carefully at Turner's work. In 1836, as noted, he had tried to reply to the *Blackwood's* attack. By 1840, his father, a prosperous sherry merchant, had begun to collect Turner watercolours, and Ruskin, a highly strung mother's boy with a disdain for the ordinary delights of life, felt that 'whatever germs of better things remained in me, were then all centred in this love of Turner'[2] The prevailing critical hostility to Turner's work was exemplified by the *Literary Gazette*'s comment of May 1842, that his pictures were produced 'as if by throwing handfuls of white, blue, and red at the canvas, and letting what would stick, stick'.[3] Such hostility prompted Ruskin this time into more than a letter, more than a pamphlet. What came into being was *Modern Painters*, at once an impassioned defence of Turner and an intricately wrought – possibly overwrought – five-volume sermon on landscape art. When the first volume, by 'A Graduate of Oxford', was published in May 1843, its author called on Turner. The artist, as if catching Ruskin's desire for anonymity, didn't say anything directly about it but seemed gracious. Ruskin said, 'I think he must have read my book, and been pleased with it, by his tone.'[4]

But Turner waited eighteen months before – at a dinner given by Godfrey Windus – he actually thanked Ruskin for the book, which Ruskin had described to Samuel Prout as 'the hurried writing of a man in a rage'.[5] The Ruskins, father and son, drove Turner home that night. Although it was very late, Turner asked them in for some sherry. 'We were compelled to obey, and so drank healths again, exactly as the clock struck one, by the light of a single tallow candle in the under room – the wine, by the way, first-rate.'[6]

Turner often gave the impression that Ruskin saw more in his work than he himself did. David Roberts once asked Turner 'what he thought of Ruskin's reviews', and Turner assured him that 'he had never read a page of any of his works; this may or may not be'.[7] Mary Lloyd wrote: 'One day Turner took me down to dinner at Mr Rogers, and he said, "Have you read *Ruskin on me?*" I said, "No." He replied, "but you will some day," and then he added with his own peculiar shrug, "He sees *more* in my pictures than I ever painted!" but he seemed very much pleased.'[8] On other occasions Turner laughed off Ruskin's compliments to him and told him that he was too hard on many contemporary artists because he did not know how difficult painting was. (Turner knew that painting was hard work, and both Jane Fawkes and William Kingsley recorded him on the subject: 'The only secret I have got is damned hard work' and 'I know of no genius but the genius of hard work.')[9]

Ruskin was curiously able to extol Turner while disliking Claude and while thinking that Claude had had a 'hurtful influence' on Turner.[10] Ruskin thought Turner's *Liber* print *Severn and Wye*, a lovely Claudean scene, was 'quite useless'.[11] Moreover, Ruskin sometimes seemed oblivious to the *facts* of Turner pictures. W. J. Stillman had to point out to Ruskin that *Juliet and her Nurse* was a moonlight painting. Ruskin hadn't noticed this and indeed disputed it. Stillman therefore called his attention to the fireworks display on the Grand

Canal, and Ruskin then 'admitted that it was not customary to let off fireworks by day, and that it must be a night scene'.[12]

However, Turner was undoubtedly charmed by Ruskin's enthusiasm and buoyed up by the patronage of the Ruskins; soon he was dining frequently at their Herne Hill house. He attended family occasions such as John's birthday. The Ruskins sent fruit, vegetables and eggs from their huge garden to Queen Anne Street. John often visited the gallery, bringing his father or friends. Father and son called on Turner on 28 April 1844, not long after a second edition of the first volume of *Modern Painters* had come out. Ruskin wrote that Turner was 'kinder than I ever remember. He shook hands most cordially with my father, wanted us to have a glass of wine, asked us to go upstairs into the gallery. When there, I went immediately in search of *Sol di Vinezia* [RA 1843], saying it was my favourite. "I thought", said Turner, "it was *Saint Benedetto*." It was flattering that he remembered I had told him this.'[13] It was pleasing for Turner to have a young champion – one of a new generation, who might open the eyes of an as yet untapped public to his merits, and enable him to sell some of his stock of decaying masterpieces.

Like many people in old age, Turner became 'more so'. He did so in his usual contrary fashion. To some he seemed more and more isolated, the gruff recluse of Queen Anne Street. To others, who saw him by the Ruskins' fireside or on Thomas Griffith's lawn, he seemed more sociable than he had ever been, more agreeable and good-natured. And he kept working, working. From 1840 to 1846 paintings continued to pour out of him. Every summer from 1840 to 1845 he went abroad. His energy seemed unabated.

In 1840 he went to Venice again, by way of Rotterdam and the Rhine. He was accompanied part of the way by a married couple, known only by the initials 'E. H.' with which the husband signed a newsy affectionate letter to Turner in Venice. This E. H. wrote from Rome as if to a close friend. It was in Venice that William Callow met Turner, who was staying at the Hotel Europa, and making Callow feel idle by his hard-working habits, out after dinner in a gondola, sketching. Some wonderful watercolours came from this trip, as did nineteen further Venice oils that made their appearances at the Academy over the next six years. One of these was *The Sun of Venice going to Sea*, the *Sol di Venezia* so admired by Ruskin (who got ejected from the Academy for ignoring the regulations and making a sketch of it). The picture was of a sun-dazzled lateen-rigged fishing boat – the *Sun of Venice* – running towards the viewer. Turner had some verse for the Academy catalogue to go with it, lines from his 'Fallacies of Hope', with help from Thomas Gray's 'The Bard':

> Fair Shines the morn, and soft the zephyrs blow,
> Venezia's fisher spreads his painted sail so gay,
> Nor heeds the demon that in grim repose
> Expects his evening prey. [14]

He wanted to let the viewer know that even in the glory that was Venice there was decay. Expectant demons were just around the corner. But what the viewer saw was sparkling beauty.

He was in Switzerland in 1841, 1842, 1843 and 1844. (In 1843 he was also in the Tyrol and northern Italy.) He revisited sketching sites he had first gone to in 1802. He continued climbing. In December 1844 he wrote to Hawksworth Fawkes and alluded to his summer travels:

> I went however to Lucerne and Switzerland, little thinking or supposing such a cauldron of squabbling, political or religious, I was walking over. The rains came on early so I could not cross the Alps, twice I tried, was set back with a wet jacket and worn-out boots and after getting them heel-tapped I marched up some of the small valleys of the Rhine and found them more interesting than I expected. [15]

He was sixty-nine.

On his way back from Venice in September 1840 he called at Coburg, in Bavaria. Out of this visit came a landscape painting, *Schloss Rosenau, Seat of H.R.H. Prince Albert of Coburg* (RA 1841). Queen Victoria had married Albert in 1840 but the monarch didn't take the bait, if such it was, and present her consort with this picture. (The wealthy pen-manufacturer Joseph Gillott bought it several years later – and seven other Turners.) For that matter, the newspaper and periodical critics were not ecstatic. The *Times* said, 'Here is a picture that represents nothing in nature beyond eggs and spinach. The lake is a composition in which salad oil abounds, and the art of cookery is more predominant than the art of painting.' The *Athenaeum* thought it was one of 'the fruits of a diseased eye and a reckless hand'.[16]

Were Turner's eyes in fact diseased? The question had been posed before. Leigh Hunt may have been the writer in the *Tatler* in 1831 who somewhat facetiously attributed Turner's predilection for wild colours – his 'chromatic absurdities' – to an ophthalmic condition.[17] *Blackwood's*, denouncing his RA exhibits in 1837 and in particular *Snow Storm, Avalanche, and Inundation* (a product of his Swiss trip with Hugh Munro), asked: 'Has any accident befallen Mr. Turner's eyes? Have they been put out by the glare of his own colours?'[18] Turner had mentioned several times in some verses in a sketchbook of 1810–12 the word 'oculist', when he was in his mid-thirties,[19] and at some point he acquired spectacles, perhaps for reading. However, he did not wear them in public.[20] To one lady who complained to him about his use of blue, red and yellow, Turner said crossly, 'Well, don't you see that yourself in Nature? Because, if you don't, Heaven help you!'[21] Lady Eastlake, the former Elizabeth Rigby, wrote in 1856: 'Every object he saw, as he himself told us, was outlined to his vision in prismatic colour.'[22]

As he grew older his eagle-like sight may have deteriorated and caused a change in his response to natural colours. It has been suggested that a 'lens sclerosis' and a secondary astigmatism may have caused distortion of vision, a blurring of detail and an overall reddening. A modern eye-surgeon, Patrick Trevor-Roper, discusses the effect of a cataract – 'an opacity of the lens of the eye' – that absorbs 'the shorter spectral wave-lengths, starting with violet and blue', so that 'ultimately it may permit little beyond the red rays to reach the retina'. And he thought that Turner's later pictures became 'more blurred and at the same time increasingly suffused with red and orange light (in Mark Twain's crude description, "like a ginger cat having a fit in a bowl of tomatoes")'.[23] Moreover, 'when such a cataractous painter feels compelled to use blue, he generally exalts it in order to reach through his lowered blue-perception … In this way, perhaps, we can account for the single patch of blue that Turner usually interpolated among the miscellany of reds, right up to the end of his life, but as an almost isolated hue in strong contrast to the seemingly endless variety of reds and oranges which he was using in the same painting.'[24] And yet, even if his eyesight 'failed', and his responses to certain colours changed, the net effect was not necessarily 'bad'. His late watercolours particularly testify, as Monkhouse noted, to a 'perfect perception of the relations and harmonies of different hues … Instead of declining, this faculty of colour seems to have increased in perfection almost to the last.'[25]

For many years his doctor had been Sir Anthony Carlisle, the former Professor of Anatomy at the RA (1808–24). According to Joseph Farington, Carlisle charged a guinea a mile for out-of-town visits and ten guineas a day if detained. He was Joseph Nolleken's doctor and at one period 'visited him at all hours and ... was always with him at the shortest possible notice'.[26] But the diligent doctor abandoned all his patients by dying in 1840 at the age of seventy-two. Turner had had a number of bouts of ill-health in the previous decade, including bad colds and influenza, which sapped his spirits. Now, past sixty-five, there were frequent reports of illness. In April 1842, so 'a lady in Jersey' reported (possibly Thomas Rose's wife), Turner had been 'very ill', and, though 'now better ... it has shook him a good deal. He is living by rule.'[27]

Just what the regimen was, we do not know. Perhaps it was homoeopathic. He might have recalled a remedy he had written in a 'Hastings' sketchbook of 1809–11 using a herb called 'stramonium': 'smoke 2 or 3 pipes every day & swallow the saliva'.[28] His continued interest in such remedies was shown in several sketchbooks in the 1830s, for the bite of a mad dog, for what he called the Colera ('25 Drops of Caje-put oil in a glass of Hot Water, if not relieved in 5 min. take 50 more'), and for some unmentioned ailment that required a prescription of vitriol, rhubarb, soda and some sort of powder.[29] His well-founded nervousness about cholera – which visited London in 1832 – was visible in a letter to Robert Cadell, asking him to send a recent paper on treating the disease, written by Edinburgh medical men.[30] The letter he wrote to Clara Wheeler at her Gracechurch Street home in the City in February 1844 suggests that he was taking some practical measures to keep well:

> I intended to have called in G Church St yesterday but the Enemy beat me. Time always hangs hard upon me, but his auxiliary, Dark weather, has put me quite into the background, altho before Xmas I conceived myself in advance of Mr Time ... Pray accept my concern for the delay of your seeing such kind friends through my engagements at the R.A., which I really do dread. However I have got a Macintosh and with some fur round the shoulders I hope to fare better betwixt the heat and the cold. If not I will give in for everyone feels the variety of the temperature of the Life Academy to be very bad.

In a postscript he added: 'I have been to the R.A. study. It is equal cold and hot like Death.'[31]

By the following December, when he wrote to Hawksworth, the Macintosh with fur didn't seem to be doing the trick: 'for myself, the rigours of winter begin to tell upon me, rough and cold and more acted upon by changes of weather than when we used to trot about at Farnley, but it must be borne with all the thanks due for such a lengthened period'.[32]

Had he had a scare, which made him thus grateful?

He wrote to Ruskin senior in May 1845: 'I have been so unwell that I was obliged to go away from Town to revival by a little change of fresh air.'[33] One wonders about the cumulative effects of working so long with 'pernicious pigments' – particularly chromes and leads – which, as George Leslie observed, Turner 'delighted in and recklessly employed'.[34]

And was he drinking too much? In his Twickenham days, moderation had been the rule, at least at home. The eldest Trimmer son, visiting Sandycombe Lodge, said, 'At this time Turner was a very abstemious person.'[35] Travelling on the Rhine in the late 1830s he noted a day's fare in a sketchbook: 'Bread & Cheese. Bottle of Ale. [That was presumably lunch.] Dinner. 2 small bottles of Stout. Glass of Gin and Water.'[36] Hardly the regimen of a heavy drinker. But 'Mr Time' may have changed him in this respect. 'Bad habits' are mentioned by one of his later physicians, Dr David Price of Margate.[37] Thornbury claimed to have heard from two old boatmen on the Thames, who rowed Turner on sketching excursions, that the artist 'always took a bottle of gin with him for inspiration and never gave them any'.[38] Thomas Rose of Cowley Hall, near Uxbridge, and later of Jersey, told Thornbury of an occasion when, 'after the ladies had retired', Turner and he sat up and talked. On the table stood a large jug of water and a bottle of cognac. Turner had never been very communicative with Rose before, but he now surprised his host by talking about the Pyrenees, various places in Scotland and picturesque scenes on the River Rance in Britanny. 'During the course of the evening his tumbler had never been emptied; first a dash of brandy, then an addition of water, and thus he continued, never entirely exhausting its contents, until it struck two in the morning.' Then they went to bed.[39] (It may have been the Alps rather than Pyrenees, unless Turner was truly drunk.)

As time went on, 'brown sherry' is often mentioned. He did not seem shy about alluding to his fondness for it. In an undated letter to Henry Pickersgill, he wrote, 'Sorry to say I am engaged out of town to-day, so I must be put down on the Black List, instead of the Brown Sherry ...'[40] Wilkie Collins, the novelist and son of the landscape painter William Collins, told Thornbury that he used to attend his father on varnishing days and remembered

> seeing Turner (not the more perfect in his balance for the brown sherry at the Academy lunch), seated on the top of a flight of steps, astride a box. There he sat, a shabby Bacchus, nodding like a mandarin at his picture, which he, with a pendulum motion, now touched with his brush, and now receded from. Yet in spite of the sherry, precarious seat, and old age, he went on shaping in some wonderful dream of colour; every touch meaning something, every pin's head of colour being a note in the chromatic scale.[41]

George Jones was convinced that Thornbury's assertion that Turner in his later years 'gave way to even greater excess'[42] was 'entirely false'.[43] However, although there is no evidence for frequent wallowing in 'some low sailors' house in Wapping or Rotherhithe',[44] there were – Thornbury claimed – other sightings of the great man 'rather the worse for grog' at Offley's in Henrietta Street, Covent Garden. He was said to have resorted frequently in the evening to the Yorkshire Stingo, a well-known tavern in Lisson Grove, in northern Marylebone, with a bowling green, tea gardens and hall where vaudeville acts were performed. But, says Thornbury, he stopped going to the tavern 'on being recognised there by a friend'.[45] One later medical man's diagnosis of Turner's health was that he had 'an alcoholic cirrhosis'. Sir Joshua Reynolds had apparently gone the same way.[46]

Some evenings, after working all day in his studio, he felt like being on his own with his sherry or grog and his thoughts. Some days his mood was low; he did not want company. Colleagues died – old friends like Holworthy, in 1841, and Chantrey, the same year. On the morning of Chantrey's death he went to his house and met George Jones, who recalled, 'He wrung my hand, tears streamed from his eyes, and he rushed from the house without uttering a word.'[47] He declined an invitation from Mrs Carrick Moore and acknowledged that he was 'very low indeed for our loss in *dear* Chantrey'.[48] However, sometimes action followed loss. His old rivalry with Wilkie – who had died on 1 June 1841, during a voyage home from Egypt – was quite set aside in a desire to paint a memorial for his brother painter, although his old competitiveness with a living artist, Jones, remained brisk. Turner had a conversation with Jones.

Turner: 'I suppose nobody will do anything to commemorate Wilkie?'

Jones: 'I shall pay a humble tribute by making a drawing representing his funeral.'

T: 'How will you do it?'

J: 'On the deck of the vessel, as it has been described to me by persons present, and at the time that Wilkie's body was lowered into the sea.'

T: 'Well, I will do it as it must have appeared off the coast.'

And so Turner's *Peace: Burial at Sea* and Jones's 'drawing' appeared at the next Academy exhibition. And there, according to Jones, Stanfield chided Turner on the black sails of the ship, thinking the colour and effect untrue. Turner replied, 'I only wish I had any colour to make them blacker.'

Jones thought Stanfield in the right, but also thought that it was 'very like' Turner 'to have indicated mourning by this means, probably retaining some confused notions of the death of Aegeus and the black sails of the returning Theseus'.[49]

On 26 November 1844, the twenty-nine-year-old artist and teacher James Hammersley visited the Queen Anne Street gallery and was being shown round by an exceedingly taciturn Turner, who was clutching a letter, when the artist exclaimed, '"Mr. Hammersley, you *must* excuse me. I cannot stay another moment; the letter I hold in my hand announces the death of my friend Callcott." He said no more. I saw his fine grey eyes fill as he vanished.'[50]

On the very same day, Turner wrote to Dawson Turner to thank him for a gift of a barrel of bloaters, to tell him Thomas Phillips was recovering from a 'severe attack of something like Bilious Jaundice', to express sorrow at reading in that morning's paper 'that Callcott is no more, *alas*', and to note that 'a great Robbery has been committed upon friend S. Rogers and Co.s Bank, 40,710 in Bank notes'.[51] Callcott's death in context! This is not to suggest that the weepy eyes that Hammersley saw were an act. He was sometimes flooded by sentiment.

Old rivals, old followers and old companions passed on. We

do not always have his reactions. A younger friend, the Reverend Edward Daniell, of the North Audley Street chapel, died aged thirty-nine on a trip to Syria in 1843. (Daniell once told David Roberts that he had known many artists, but none except Turner ever came to hear him preach. 'I never felt more proud than when the great painter passed up the aisle with his old umbrella to take his seat.')[52] And we don't know what he thought in February 1843 when his daughter Georgiana died. She had got married on 18 June 1840 at St Mary Magdalene Church in Bermondsey to one Thomas James Thompson. She was twenty-eight or twenty-nine at the time and said her father was 'George Danby, deceased'. Her husband was only twenty-two and gave his occupation as chemist. (In the 1841 census he was described as a clerk.) They went to live in Park Street, off the City Road, in Southwark, one street from the river, and in the next few years had two sons who died, one at seventeen months, the other at five months, both named Thomas. The first was baptized Thomas William. Evelina's second son was also named William. So the Turner girls' neglectful father – and Grandfather Turner – were in a small way remembered. Georgiana predeceased her second Thomas. He was barely a week old when she died of puerperal fever at the Lying-In Hospital, Lambeth, aged thirty-one.[53]

Georgiana's death caused Turner to change his testamentary arrangements. In the codicil he had made on 20 August 1832 she had been named as a residuary legatee. In the codicil of 29 August 1846 he declared, 'Whereas the residuary legatee mentioned in my Will has died …' and proceeded to replace her, for the time being, with Hannah Danby and Sophia Booth. (This codicil was later revoked, but Hannah and Sophia were given annuities, which remained.) He did not seem to think of Evelina, out of sight and out of mind; she and her husband Joseph Dupuis were in North Africa at this time with their three children. Dupuis – until recently British Vice-Consul in Sfax, Tunisia – had been forcibly detained for a short time, apparently because of a lawsuit, and left the Consular Service in 1842. One has the impression of a cranky man, not ambassadorial material.

Turner continued to go out to convivial dinner-parties. Georgiana's death on 8 February 1843 – assuming he had heard about it – did not stop him from accepting on 12 February an invitation to the Bicknells' for the 25th. He visited the Leslies one evening in the early

1840s and they supped informally on Welsh rarebit. Robert Leslie wrote later:

> At the time my father was engaged upon a portrait of Lord Chancellor Cottenham; and during the evening Turner went into the painting-room, where the robes, wigs, etc., of the Chancellor were arranged upon a lay-figure; and, after a little joking, he was persuaded to put on the Lord Chancellor's wig, in which ... Turner looked splendid, so joyous and happy, too, in the idea that the Chancellor's wig became him better than any one else of the party.[54]

He was also to be seen regularly at the Carrick Moores' house in Brook Street, off Grosvenor Square. James Carrick Moore, a surgeon, had been a good friend of Fuseli, and he and his wife were well acquainted with Samuel Rogers and his sister and such artists as Chantrey, Wilkie, Jones and Eastlake. When Turner could not accept one of Mrs Moore's invitations, he thanked her with one of his jokey letters from Mr Avalanche Jenkinson. He dined with the Bicknells at Herne Hill, with Sam Rogers in St James's Place and with Rogers' sister Sarah in Hanover Terrace. At a dinner at the publisher John Murray's in Albemarle Street in March 1844, he was a guest along with Scott's biographer J. G. Lockhart and Elizabeth Rigby, who wrote for the *Quarterly Review* (and was to become the wife of Charles Eastlake). She wrote in her diary about Turner: 'a queer little thing, very knowing about all the castles he had drawn – a cynical kind of body, who seems to love his art for no other reason than because it is his *own*. Lockhart grew black as thunder when Turner was pertinacious and stupid, and looked as if he could have willingly said, "You blockhead!"'[55] Turner, despite his breadth of mind, was not quick-witted, particularly when among 'intellectuals'.

Sometimes, on social occasions, he was immersed in himself. At a dinner in Greenwich given for Charles Dickens by his friends, before the novelist set off for Italy in the summer of 1844, Turner went with Clarkson Stanfield and sat next to John Forster, Dickens's biographer, who later recalled Turner on that hot day as having his throat wrapped 'in a huge red belcher-handkerchief which nothing would induce him to remove. He was not otherwise demonstrative, but enjoyed himself in a quiet silent way, less perhaps at the speeches than at the changing lights on the river'.[56] At a dinner at the Bicknells' in February 1845, Turner sat next to Clarkson Stanfield's wife, but, according to David Roberts's daughter Christine Bicknell, Turner was 'not in spirits' and Rebecca Stanfield, who could be fairly forbidding, did not enliven him.[57] Yet – as Charles Leslie once observed – 'his nature was social'.[58] There were occasions when he was definitely in spirits. A young artist who met him one evening at David Roberts's house in Fitzroy Square wrote that Turner was 'very agreeable, his quick bright eye sparkled, and his whole countenance expressed a desire to please. He was constantly making, or rather trying to make, jokes; his dress, though rather old-fashioned, was far from being shabby.' Roberts often saw Turner at the Bicknells', at the Reverend Daniell's, at General Phipps's and at meetings of the Academy Club, which were then generally held at the Thatched House club in St James's Street, and he concluded that Turner was 'in reality "a jolly toper"'.[59]

At one dinner *chez* Roberts, Turner was called on to propose his host's health: 'He accordingly rose, hurried on as quickly as possible, speaking in a highly complimentary manner of Roberts's worth and talents, but soon ran out of words or breath, and dropped down on his chair with a hearty laugh, starting up again, and finishing with a hip, hip, hurrah!'[60] At Roberts's on 4 July 1845, so Christine Bicknell wrote in her journal, 'Turner came in after the dinner having dined at Greenwich which was rather visible in his appearance. Upon his health being given he amused them with a very funny speech (& funnier grimaces filling up the pauses) about his whalers, mixing up Mr. Bicknell & fish & ending by proposing his health.'[61] In fact, Christine's father-in-law, the whale-oil magnate, bought Turner's Venice paintings and *Palestrina* (the latter for 1000 guineas in 1844) rather than his whalers. Although he may have commissioned one of the four whaling pictures Turner did, his second *Whalers* of 1845, Bicknell apparently returned it to the artist, angry because some watercolours came off the supposed oil painting when he rubbed it with a handkerchief.

Roberts said that he could 'always get up a pleasant party' for Turner from 'those who loved Art as well as that of men who's profession it was and where the lion of Queen Ann Street was the lion of the party … Turner liked to be amongst men who, like Brackenbury and Ruskin, looked upon him as an inspired being, forgetting the usual accompanyments of the gentlemen, to which Turner did not even pretend; he was uncouth in his manners and curt in reply, until after a good dinner and … wine, he became like other men, always and excepting Keeping up that Mistery, and never, as far as he could help, allowing you to fathom any subject he may have begun if he thought you listened for the purpose of ascertaining his meaning.'[62]

It was Roberts who noted an instance of Turner's secretiveness when he accompanied the old man into the street one night in 1850 after a party. Midnight had struck, Turner was the last to leave, and Roberts went with him to hail a cab. As he helped him up into his seat, Roberts asked Turner where he should tell the cabbie to take him. Turner, not to be caught out so easily in regard to his current domicile (which was no longer in Queen Anne Street), replied with a knowing wink, 'Tell him to drive to Oxford Street, and then I'll direct him where to go.'[63]

Although his connection with the Trimmers seems to have become attenuated, and Hannah Danby appears to have thought the Reverend Trimmer had died some time before 1851, his link with the Wells family, via Clara, remained strong. He frequently visited Thomas and Clara Wheeler's house in the City. He was invited to the wedding of their son James to his cousin Maria Wheeler in February 1844. He wrote:

> Monday night
> My dear Clara,
>   I have been expecting a note for some time and [am] now very awkwardly placed for the 20th. – but I beg to give the Wedding-Cake –
>   Mammy's heart I trust will jump for joy and accept my good wishes for the health felicity and prosperity of the young folks and if I should not be present (but which I mean if possible to be) – give them my love and sip a drop of wine to the better state of Salus Lodge.
>   Believe me most truly
>   Dear Clara
>   your sincely
>   J M W Turner
> Please Don't order the Cake at Birch's   its not a good name for the present occasion.[64]

Eighteen years had passed since he had sold Solus or Sandycombe Lodge, and the reference seems to have been to himself, still *solus* in respect to lawful matrimony (if not to his coastal arrangement with

Mrs Booth) at the age of sixty-nine; and perhaps there is a tinge of regret that he had never proposed to Clara (who was now fifty-six). But it was sweet of him to buy the cake – whatever his drawbacks as a father, he had in him the right, as it were, godfatherly impulses. The jocular reference to the cakemakers named Birch was presumably an allusion to the now almost historic fact – in Turner–Wells circles – that Clara's father W. F. Wells had gone to school at Mr Harper's establishment on the site of Turner's Queen Anne Street house and, also presumably, had been 'birched' while there.[65]

Christine Bicknell continued to see Turner in a happy light. She and her father and her three-year-old son known as 'the Binny' called at Queen Anne Street to collect Turner on 4 January 1845, to take him out to Herne Hill for dinner, and although Turner was at that point out of temper with Academy matters, 'he insisted on our coming in to have a glass of wine! and then toddled off & returned with a piece of *cold plum* pudding for the Binny!' However, after this act of post-Christmas hospitality, he got into the fly and proceeded to grumble about Eastlake and Roberts 'for attempting Reforms in the Academy'.[66]

A number of Turner's letters of these years were written or posted from the Athenaeum, the club of which he had been member since it was founded in a 1824. Turner might not have struck one as a 'club-man', but there were clearly times when he needed cronies and a firm social structure; the Academy, of course, provided some of this. The Athenaeum started as a notion of John Wilson Croker, Secretary to the Admiralty, to provide a meeting place for leading scientists, artists and politicians. It began in a back room at John Murray's, met for a while in the quarters of the Royal Society at Somerset House, and then moved to Waterloo Place. Its neo-classical building, designed by Decimus Burton, rose at the west end of the site of the demolished Carlton House and opened in 1830, providing good food, wine and a magnificent library to read or doze in. Turner seems to have dropped in occasionally at the end of a painting day, as Disraeli's character the lonely lawyer Baptist Hatton did, liking the 'splendour and the light and bustle of a great establishment. They saved him from that melancholy which after a day of action is the doom of energetic celibacy. A luxurious dinner, without trouble, suited him after his exhaustion.'[67] Turner used the free club stationery to write to Clara Wheeler or Thomas Griffith.

He consulted the periodicals in the library, such as the *Edinburgh Review*. Club lore has it that he 'used to dine alone and then insist on the candle being removed from the table while he finished off a bottle of vintage port by himself'.[68] Thornbury, with a similar story, wrote: 'Latterly, Turner was always to be seen between ten and eleven at the Athenaeum, discussing his half-pint of sherry. As his health failed, he became very talkative after his wine, and rather dogmatic.'[69] At least he wasn't wallowing at his Wapping pub.

Frith reported Turner was at the Athenaeum in 1846, reading a newspaper, when Maclise encountered him.[70] Maclise said, 'I have just heard of Haydon's suicide. Is it not awful?'

Turner, without looking up from his paper, said, 'Why did he stab his mother?'

'Great heaven!' exclaimed Maclise. 'You don't mean—?'

'Yes. He stabbed his mother.'[71]

It took Maclise a moment to realize that Turner was speaking metaphorically; he was alluding to Haydon's assaults on the Academy, where Haydon had been a student – assaults which had so overbalanced his career as to help, so Turner thought, bring on his ruin. Turner may also have been speaking from the heart as someone who felt remorse about his failures with and his neglect of his own mother.

Despite Ruskin's championing and despite buyers like Bicknell, Vernon, Windus and Munro, it was evident in the 1840s that the critics and the market generally had gone off Turner's work. It was too hazy, too 'poetic', too imprecise, too romantic, too subjective ... 'Finish' was wanted. Perhaps viewers also sensed in even his loveliest visions a dreadful hopelessness. Thackeray noted that, looking hard at one of his *Whalers*, you could see that the 'beautiful whale' had 'just slipped a half-dozen whale-boats into perdition'.[72] In *Slavers throwing overboard the Dead and Dying – Typhon coming on* (RA 1840), the slave ship seems to be sliding sternwards into a watery chasm, as the tormented sea opens up along the fault line of the setting sun. *All* is about to be lost. His appended verse from the notorious 'Fallacies of Hope' ran:

> Aloft all hands, strike the top-masts and belay;
> Yon angry setting sun and fierce-edged clouds
> Declare the Typhon's coming.

Before it sweep your decks, throw overboard
The dead and dying – ne'er heed their chains.
Hope, Hope, fallacious Hope!
Where is thy market now?[73]

The picture was a passionate presentation of ideas that had been seething in his imagination. Slavery by now was on the way out: in British ships the slave trade had been made illegal by Parliament in 1807 and the institution itself abolished within the British Empire in 1833. Turner may have read the 1839 reprint of Thomas Clarkson's *History of the Abolition of the Slave Trade* (1808), which described the incident twenty-five years earlier when Captain Collingwood of the sailing ship *Zong* ordered sick slaves to be thrown over the side; he could claim insurance on those drowned at sea but not on those who died of disease. But Turner also seems to have had in mind his favourite poet Thomson, whose 'Summer' has a typhoon, a slave ship and sharks waiting for bodies. A biography of the anti-slaving crusader William Wilberforce had been published in 1839 and a Conference of the Anti-Slavery League was opened, by Prince Albert, soon after the RA exhibition in 1840. This was a sort of shipwreck picture for him, though this time the potential wreck seemed particularly encompassing: nature, in the form of the typhoon, had the power as it did in Thomson's poem to destroy the ship, symbol of the tyrannical slave-owners and slave-dealers, as well as the hapless slaves.

Many of the critics thought it a crazy painting. They took note of the bizarre fish and bloody sea, the upraised arms and legs of the slaves with manacles and chains that somehow remained well above the surface although made of iron. The *Art-Union* was put in mind of 'the occasional outbreaks of the madman'. Thackeray could not make up his mind whether the picture was sublime or ridiculous but was certain that it was 'the most tremendous piece of colour that ever was seen; it sets the corner of the room in which it hangs into a flame'. But John Ruskin a few years later was in no doubt that it was the 'noblest sea that Turner has ever painted ... the noblest certainly ever painted by man'. He felt that 'if I were reduced to rest Turner's immortality upon any single work, I should choose this'. Ruskin's father bought it for 250 guineas and gave it to John as a New Year's present in 1844. Ruskin owned it for twenty-eight years, but finally he found it too painful to live with.[74]

In a letter from the Athenaeum of late November 1842, after thanking Dawson Turner for some more Yarmouth herrings, Turner wrote: 'You ask me what "are you doing" "answer endeavouring to please myself in my own way if I can for after all my determination to be quiet some fresh follery comes across me and I begin what most probably never to be finish'd" alas too true.'[75]

Turner's punctuation continued to be idiosyncratic but his pessimism was not totally well founded. Other artists – one thinks of Rembrandt – have pleased themselves in old age, and although fashion may have passed them by, some works have got finished and some have survived to be seen as more than 'follery'. Turner remained on his feet in front of his easel on most days of late autumn, winter and spring, putting paint on canvas. Paintings – particularly of Venice and the sea – came from his studio. There were other productions too, with more rarefied subject matter: follery they might well seem in some eyes. There was his strange Napoleon painting of 1842, for instance – *War. The Exile and the Rock Limpet.* In this the exiled Emperor (looking as if he was on black stilts) stood on a beach pondering the limpet's freedom 'to join his comrades', as the snippet from 'Fallacies' put it. Also thought absurd by many of the art-writers were his 1843 Academy contributions, *Shade and Darkness – The Evening of the Deluge* and *Light and Colour (Goethe's Theory) – The Morning after the Deluge – Moses writing the Book of Genesis.* These maelstroms of colour suggested that he had been reading both the Bible and Goethe; as noted, he had a copy of Charles Eastlake's translation of Goethe's *Farbenlehre*, and seemed to have been brooding on the German polymath's idea of a circle of colours in which reds, yellows and greens had to do with warmth and happiness, and blues, blue-greens and purples prompted 'restless, susceptible, anxious impressions'. The two *Deluge* paintings also made evident that watery catastrophe – the end by inundation – was much in his thoughts, even as the London rain dripped through his gallery sky-light and the cats scampered around the stacks of dusty canvases. Yet the *Athenaeum* magazine (17 June 1843) worked up a reluctant sympathy for these pictures. One could see, it declared, 'a poetical idea dimly described through the prismatic chaos, which arrests the attention and excites the fancy'.

He was indeed pleasing himself. In 1844, aged sixty-nine, he produced seven paintings for the exhibition – a heroic total. There were three Low Countries coastal seascapes (*Ostend*, a second *Port Ruysdael* and a *Van Tromp*), three Venice pictures and, boldest of all, *Rain, Steam, and Speed – the Great Western Railway*. The latter was not flamboyant in size – it was one of his customary three-by-fours – but flaunted the power now abroad in the land: steam harnessed with rail by man, and shown in the natural circumstances of a showery day. The engine, the rail equivalent of the tug in the *Temeraire*, was thundering towards the viewer along a bridge – Maidenhead bridge – over the Thames. A hare could be made out sprinting in front of the locomotive – why doesn't it jump aside and save its life? And below, in Old Masterish calm, some female figures in Claudean costume stand at the river's edge, a man ploughs behind two horses, and a fisherman in a skiff peacefully holds his rod above the limpid water. As noted, George Leslie remembered watching Turner at work on this picture during the varnishing days, nose close to the canvas, wielding his short brushes. Turner pointed out the hare to him:

> This hare, and not the train, I have no doubt he intended to represent the 'Speed' of his title; the word must have been in his mind when he was painting the hare, for close to it, on the plain below the viaduct, he introduced the figure of a man ploughing, 'Speed the plough' (the name of an old country dance) probably passing through his brain.

Thackeray in *Fraser's Magazine* responded with all his empathetic talent blazing. Here, he wrote, is

> a picture with real rain, behind which is real sunshine, and you expect a rainbow every minute. Meanwhile there comes a train down upon you, really moving at the rate of fifty miles an hour, and which the reader had best make haste to see, lest it should dash out of the picture, and be away up Charing Cross through the wall opposite. All these wonders are performed with means not less wonderful than the effects are. The rain … is composed of dabs of dirty putty *slapped* on to the canvas with a trowel; the sunshine scintillates out of very thick, smeary lumps of chrome yellow. The shadows are produced by cool tones of crimson lake, and quiet glazings of vermilion; although the fire in the steam-engine *looks* as if it were red, I am not prepared to say that it is not painted with cobalt and pea-green. And as for the manner in which the '*Speed*' is done, of that the less said the better – only it is a positive fact that

there is a steam-coach going fifty miles an hour. The world has never seen anything like this picture.[76]

Unlike that other great creative spirit of the time, Rossini, who rode a train in Antwerp in 1836 and was so upset he never rode one again, Turner did not turn his back on the locomotive age. There may have been a slight shudder as he watched the Great Western Railway throw a bridge across his beloved river, but the violation was accompanied by a thrill. Moreover, his picture had a participatory feeling to it: it was as though he had been there, as he had claimed to be in *Snow Storm – Steam-Boat off a Harbour's Mouth*, lashed to the mast, or in this case running like the hare. Although there are doubts about the accuracy of its details, the story Lady Simon – a friend of Mrs Ruskin senior – gave to the painter George Richmond and to John Ruskin was of a kind that people could easily believe about Turner. She had got on a train at Exeter, she told Richmond, and in the coach seated opposite her 'was an elderly gentleman, short and stout, with a red face and a curious prominent nose. The weather was very wild, and by-and-by a violent storm swept over the country, blotting out the sunshine and the blue sky, and hanging like a pall over the landscape. The old gentleman seemed strangely excited at this, jumping up to open the window, craning his neck out, and finally calling to her to come and observe a curious effect of light.'[77] Lady Simon went to the next Academy exhibition, saw *Rain, Steam, and Speed*, and realized that the old gentleman, who had had 'the most seeing eyes' she had ever come across, was Turner. And when, standing by the painting, she overheard another viewer exclaim, 'Who ever saw such a ridiculous conglomeration?' she turned and quietly replied, 'I did. I was in the train that night, and it is perfectly and wonderfully true.'[78]

It was a masterpiece. Nobody bought it.

20: Chelsea Harbour

C ramming things in, as if at seventy he knew old time was running out on him, he went twice to France in 1845. In May he was in Margate, presumably with Sophia Booth, and from there he moved on across the Channel to Boulogne, Wimereux and Ambleteuse, drawing busily, trying out broadly brushed watercolour studies. In September he went over again. David Roberts, heading for Brussels, saw him at Dover: 'Who should stumble into the Coffee Room whilst we were at Breakfast but Turner, windbound on his way to Bologne for it blew a huricane and had been for two days previous. He was as mysterious as usual and of course I did not ask him where he was bound for, although he pumped me.'[1]

This time he went on to Dieppe and along the Picardy coast to Tréport and Eu, where the elderly Anglophile King Louis-Philippe often stayed in the Orléans family château. Turner carried only his sketchbooks and a change of linen and was looking, he said later, 'for storms and shipwrecks'.[2] When he reached Eu he needed to have his shoes repaired – he went fast through shoe-leather – and put up for the night at a fisherman's house. According to the Redgraves,

> He had not been long there before an officer of the court inquired for him, and told him that Louis-Philippe, the King of the French, who was then staying at the Château, hearing that Mr. Turner was in the town, had sent to desire his company to dinner (they had been well known to one another in England). Turner strove to apologize – pleaded his want of dress – but this was overruled; his usual costume was the dress-coat of the period, and he was assured that he only required a white neckcloth, and that the King must not be denied. The fisherman's wife easily provided a white neckcloth, by cutting up some of her linen, and Turner declared that he spent one of the pleasantest of evenings in chat with his old Twickenham acquaintance.[3]

He had last seen the King in 1844 when he went down to Portsmouth to watch him land at the start of a visit to the British Queen, and the King had apparently written to him in the meantime. In Eu Turner made some pencil and watercolour studies of the cathedral and the château. (This same month Louis-Philippe received Queen Victoria and Prince Albert there, when they turned up on the royal yacht.) This was Turner's last trip abroad.

Turner managed to avoid the census takers in 1841, when the census was made on 6 June, and in 1851, at the end of March. Although he was still to be found in his Queen Anne Street gallery by appointment, he seems to have been spending more and more time with Mrs Booth. (She, according to the 1841 census, was at home that day in Cold Harbour, Margate.) Indeed, in 1846, they had arrived at a decision that she should come up from Kent to London to look after him.

The question was 'where?' Clearly Queen Anne Street was out – whatever Hannah suspected, she didn't know anything in detail about Sophia. Mrs B, aged about forty-eight in 1846, could not have stood it a minute in that run-down house. In September Turner went to look at his colleague Etty's flat in Buckingham Street, just south of the Strand. It was a top-floor apartment and not far from Maiden Lane where he had begun; maybe a good place to end. Etty, who was going to retire to York in a year or so, said, 'He liked my view, and seemed a little disappointed I was not going sooner. However, he was very good, drank a glass of wine, and, I believe, *sincerely* wished me well, wherever I went; said he should be sorry.'[4] He looked further afield. An important factor was the river – he needed to be close to it. Out across the market gardens beyond Belgravia and Pimlico, down the King's New Road and left to the Thames, he and Sophia Booth went looking. It was a long search. But at last they found a cottage that suited them on the Chelsea riverfront, in the area called World's End. (Mrs Booth – they had this in common – was also a waterfront person.) Chelsea then had a reputation as a resort; Cremorne Pleasure Gardens and Cremorne Pier were a stone's throw to the west, and to the east the wooden structure of Battersea Bridge spanned this stretch of the river. The address of the cottage, which was one of a pair, was 6 Davis Place, Cremorne New Road – a road that was not much more than a country lane along the river bank, forming an extension of Cheyne Walk. For neighbours they had a boatbuilder and two shops selling beer, wine and ginger beer.[5]

They signed up for the cottage in October 1846. There are various accounts of who did the negotiating and paying for the lease. Mrs Booth later told David Roberts that it was she who, for eighteen years, had 'provided solely for their maintenance and living' and that she had 'purchased the cottage at Chelsea from money she had previously saved or inherited ... Turner refusing to give a farthing towards it'. Roberts adds, 'This is a very extraordinary fact if true.'[6] Mrs Booth apparently paid cash for a twenty-one-year lease; the rateable value of the cottage was £11 (a mere sixth of that of 47 Queen Anne Street). John Pye, who like Roberts met Mrs Booth soon after Turner's death, had a slightly different story. In January 1852 Pye visited Chelsea and actually interviewed the owner of the freehold of the cottage. This person told Pye that four or five years before,

> a lady and a gentleman who had seen it, came to the wharf with the intention of renting it, that terms were agreed upon between the parties, but that the negotiation failed in consequence of the proprietor having required to know the names of the applicants, and to have references as to character, which they declined to give. That the gentleman afterwards called at the wharf alone and renewed his negotiations for taking the cottage, by proposing, in lieu of making known his name and giving references as to character, to pay in advance any amount of rent that might be deemed necessary to secure the proprietor against the chances of loss by accepting him as a tenant. To this proposition, influenced by the unproductiveness of the property, the proprietor assented, and hence the unknown gentleman and lady became installed in that quiet retreat of their choice.[7]

The cottage had three floors. There was a low picket fence with a gate to the front garden, an open porch around the front door with trellis sides and a rounded roof, and inside the porch a hanging birdcage for the starling which Turner had caught in the back garden. Virginia creeper grew up the front of the house above the ground-floor window and also around the front second-floor window from a windowbox on the sill. Turner arranged for a railed balcony to be built on the roof at the front, so that he could sit there and look at the river. Mrs Booth told Archer that Turner used to call the prospect westwards his English view, and that downriver or eastwards his Dutch view. Across the road was a small beach that curved round from where the north-west end of Battersea Bridge met the Chelsea shore. In front of Davis Place some steps, covered at high tide, led down to the foreshore, where some skiffs were tied up. On the other side of the river stood the Church of St Mary's, Battersea, where William and Catherine Blake had been married, where the renegade American General Benedict Arnold and his wife the former Philadelphia belle Peggy Shippen were buried, and where – Chelsea tradition has it – some afternoons Turner went to sit in the vestry under the tower and sketch from another angle his English view upriver.

There was a third member of the Davis Place household, at least some of the time: Daniel John Pound, Mrs Booth's son by her first marriage, who was now in his twenties. 'A tall handsome young man', said Roberts, who also found out that Daniel had studied engraving in Germany,[8] perhaps steered towards that profession by his mother's companion. But Daniel must have been sworn to keep that gentleman's name quiet, for few in the art world knew that Turner was in Chelsea. Roberts said, 'In latter years no one, even his most intimate friends, could say how he lived or where he lived.' Moreover, 'it was no use calling at Queen Anne Street as he was seldom there.'[9] Roberts also told Thornbury, 'I and others knew he had another home besides Queen Anne Street, but delicacy forbade us prying further. We all knew that whoever he lived with took great care of him, for he was not only better dressed, but more cleanly and *tidy*, than in former years.'[10] From Sophia Booth, Roberts got the impression that Turner and she were thoroughly involved with one another: 'He, like the great Anthony, seems to have abandoned everything for his Cleopatra, & She, like Cleopatra, seems to have been equaly devoted to him. He would not allow her to see or have communication with any one; they lived & painted together, & to all appearances with the greatest happiness & contentment, the only drawback being that he was jealous of any one approaching her.' Possessiveness now, with his last mistress! Roberts went on: 'On one occasion, when he was ill after taking this house at Chelsea, She had to send for this Dr Price from Marget, who had attended him for many years. On his taking his leave after prescribing for him late at night, She wished to go to show him the way to get a

Cab, or Bus; Turner would not allow it, But got out of bed, dressed & took him himself.'[11]

His secretiveness became more obsessive as he grew older. However, his incognito as at Margate remained the surname of his Sophia. 'In the streets of Chelsea, and all along the shore of the Thames, Turner was known to the street boys as "Puggy Booth", and by the small tradesmen he was designated "Admiral Booth",' Thornbury tells us, 'for the popular notion was that he was an old admiral in reduced circumstances.'[12] The legends of his mysteriousness multiplied. Thornbury again: 'One evening, during a sharp shower, he took shelter in a public-house, where he sat in the farthest corner with his glass before him, when an artist who knew him came in and began with, "I didn't know you used the house; I shall often drop in now that I've found out where you quarter." Turner looked at him, knit his brows, emptied his glass, and, as he rose to go out, said "Will you? I don't think you will."'[13] Someone else recognized Turner on a river steamer going up to town from Cremorne Pier. He was freshly shaved and had well-polished shoes. The man, who was with his son, asked Turner if he had moved to this part of Chelsea. 'Is that your boy?' asked Turner, changing the subject.[14] But, despite Turner's efforts to keep a low profile, Mrs Booth could not help letting slip that 'her husband' was a 'notability'.[15] She confessed to John Pye that she had been unable 'to resist the temptation of whispering here and there that "Booth" was a great man in disguise, and that when he died he would surely be buried in St Paul's'.[16] Even so, in the locality, particularly at the ginger-beer shop, they were known as a very quiet and respectable couple.

Less credence should perhaps be given to the account of Leopold Martin, son of John Martin RA. Leopold in his old age recalled going with his father to Queen Anne Street where they 'found the great painter at work upon his well-known picture, "The Fighting Temeraire"' – exhibited in 1838, as we know – and then, walking to Chelsea where Turner introduced them to 'a small, six-roomed house', with 'a magnificent prospect both up and down river', but otherwise 'miserable in every respect … looking as though it was the abode of a very poor man'.[17] John Martin's visionary paintings showed Turner's effect, but Turner would have been in an especially friendly and forthcoming mood if he let him into the secret of his

Chelsea haven – and even then at a much later date – clearly after 1846 – than Leopold ascribed to the visit.

Turner's sojourn in Chelsea with Mrs B has more romance than any other stage of his life. Pye, visiting the snug little house at 6 Davis Place in the spring of 1852, found Sophia Booth a 'good-looking, dark, and kindly mannered' woman, 'but obviously illiterate'. Turner, she said, had called her 'Old 'un' and she had called him 'Dear'. But Turner's last romance had its practical side. She told Pye 'she used to act as studio boy, cleaning Turner's brushes, setting his palette, and so on'.[18]

Not before time he got in more assistance in this realm. He had been thinking for several years that he ought to find someone to perform some of the functions his father had done. He wrote to Thomas Griffith in February 1844 about various large pictures of his that were 'subject to neglect and dirt', and continued, 'If I could find a young man acquainted with picture cleaning and would help *me* to clean accidental stains away, would be a happiness to drag them from their dark abode.'[19] Occasionally Turner used to go to a Chelsea barbershop for a shave and a haircut – memories of Maiden Lane. The barber, named Sherrell, one day in 1848 or thereabouts mentioned his young brother Francis, who hoped to be an artist. 'Let me see his drawings,' muttered Turner from under the lather. Francis Sherrell then nervously brought along a parcel of drawings. Turner received him kindly and didn't dampen his hopes. He told young Sherrell that he would give him artistic advice in return for studio services. Francis was impressed by Turner, and later used to tell of how the master used his hands for mixing his chromes 'in a bucket' and for laying on his ground work.

Francis was helping out in Queen Anne Street one day when word came upstairs that an artist desired an introduction to Turner.

'Show him in,' growled Turner.

A gentleman entered. 'You're an artist?' demanded Turner. The gentleman bowed assent.

'Show me your hands, then.'

The gentleman obeyed. Turner looked at the outstretched hands and waved his visitor off with the words, 'Get out – you're no painter.'[20]

Turner's contentment in Davis Place comes through obliquely in a note he wrote to Harriet Moore in June 1847, cautiously headed as from 47 Queen Anne Street. He says he is glad to hear that her father had got over an illness, thanks her for news of the George Joneses, and ends: 'How we all grumble in search of happiness or benefits for others yet find Home at Home.'[21] And it is a man who apparently had personal experience of happiness who wrote in November 1848 from the Athenaeum to young Ruskin, at this point upset about the state of the world and possibly uneasy in his relations with his new wife Effie:

> My dear Ruskin
> !!! Do let *us* be happy
> Yours most truly and sincerely
> J. M. W. Turner[22]

Turner's almost paternal anxieties about Ruskin had been evident three years before, when he argued against Ruskin's plan to go to Switzerland in the spring of 1845 *without his parents*, to look at places where Turner had sketched. Ruskin wrote later:

> he feared my getting into some scrape in the then disturbed state of the cantons … Everytime Turner saw me during the winter, he said something to dissuade me from going abroad; when at last I went to say good-bye, he came down with me into the hall in Queen Anne Street, and opening the door just enough for me to pass, laid hold of my arm, gripping it strongly. 'Why *will* you go to Switzerland – there'll be such a fidge about you, when you're gone.' … I made no answer, but grasped his hand closely, and went. I believe he made up his mind that I was heartless and selfish; anyhow he took no more pains with me.[23]

He was still often at the Academy and wrapped up in its affairs. In 1845, for example, he attended Council meetings and served on the hanging committee. He continued to be a Visitor in the Academy Schools, helping students. One aspiring artist, Charles Hutton Lear, encountered Turner for the first time in early May 1847 and wrote in his diary:

> He is not at all 'Turner' as I should have expected to find him, but he is a little man dressed in a long tail coat, thread gloves, big shoes, and a hat of a most miserable description made doubly melancholy by the addition of a piece of broad shabby dingy crape encircling two thirds at least. Thus clad and with his hands behind him appeared in outward form the greatest landscape painter that ever

existed and one of the greatest geniuses, perhaps the world's greatest genius, in Art. There is no evidence of unhealthy biliousness in his face; it is red and full of living blood, and although age has left its mark upon him it does not seem to have taken his energy of mind, for this lives in that observant eye and that compressed mouth, the evidence of an acute, calculating, penetrating intellect.

Lear remembered that T. S. Cooper had told him that when any of the members of the Academy were 'in a mess' with their pictures, a single application to Turner would put everything right.

> An instance of that occurred this morning. I was standing near [J. R.] Herbert's picture watching him introduce an object to the left of his figure of Christ, when a little old man who stood close by me made a gruffly low sort of remark to him. Herbert turned round and with a very reverential air told him that he was going to introduce something to fill up the space to the left, at the same time showing him in his sketchbook the thing he intended. The little old man stood silent for a few seconds and then in a low but very decided tone said, 'You'll spoil your picture, you'll spoil your picture' and in a lazy sauntering movement with his hands behind him walked idly out of the room. Herbert seemed to hesitate and put down his palette, and I turned away. In a few moments I observed the little man return, with a lazy indifferent air walk up to the picture, glance slyly at it, turn round and saunter out again.

When Lear looked at the canvas again, he saw that Herbert had followed Turner's advice. He also noted that there was talk of Turner's pictures being the wreck of a great mind. Rather, he thought, 'They are the glorious setting of a glorious sun.'[24]

At one end-of-exhibition dinner around this time Turner made the speech about sticking together for the good of the Academy that Frith found memorable for 'the stammerings, the long pausing, the bewildering mystery of it'.[25] Because of his age, he was probably not among the Royal Academicians who were sworn in as special constables on 10 April 1848, when the authorities feared that revolution was going to spread from Europe and civil strife was expected in London. Richard Redgrave wrote: 'All day long did we watch anxiously for the coming of the rabble.'[26] In July 1848 he sat on the Academy committee that examined the case of Reinagle, who was accused of exhibiting as his own a painting by another artist; the committee found against Reinagle, who lost his membership of the Academy. But there were indications that the Academy had

had just about all Turner had to give it. David Roberts sensed that 'latterly, he became much more estranged from the Royal Academy', and cited various reasons for this: the death of friends and his belief that the Academy should save money so that it could build its own independent quarters.[27] He had been an Auditor of the Academy since 1824, but he declined to be re-elected in December 1846. He did not like such innovations as allowing the press into the Private View. And his pride must have been hurt when he wasn't asked to become the Academy's President. Martin Archer Shee's health had collapsed in 1845; the younger Academicians wanted Eastlake for President; and Turner – the oldest member at the time – soldiered on for several years as deputy to the President, presiding over Council meetings and presenting diplomas. The job took it out of him. He wrote to Hawksworth on 26 December 1846 thanking him for the customary excellent Christmas pie, and going on: 'in regard to my health sorry to say the tiresome and unpleasant duties of [presiding] during the continued illness of our President for two years – viz my rotation of Council – and being senior of the lot made me Pro Pre – it distroyd my happiness and appetite [so] that what with the business and weak[ness] I was oblidged to give [up] my Summer's usual trip abroad – but thank Heaven I shall be out of office on Thursday the 31 of this month'.[28]

When Shee died in August 1850 a new President had to be elected. Turner was no longer in the running. Charles Leslie wrote later: 'greatly as his genius would have adorned it, on almost every other account he was incapable of occupying it with credit to himself or the institution, for he was a confused speaker, and wayward and peculiar in many of his opinions, and expected a degree of deference on account of his age and high standing as a painter, which the members could not invariably pay him ...'[29]

Leslie called some colleagues to his house to talk over the situation. Turner was there, and Philip Hardwick, architect and Treasurer of the Academy, the son of his old employer Thomas Hardwick. Young George Leslie recalled Turner being

> full of spirits on the evening, and apparently in his usual good health. He quite won the hearts of my two sisters, pretty girls of twenty-two and twenty at the time, flirting with them in his queer way, and drinking with great enjoyment the glass of hot grog which

one of them mixed for him. He always had the indescribable charm of the sailor both in appearance and manners; his large grey eyes were those of a man long accustomed to looking straight at the face of nature through fair and foul weather alike.[30]

The competent, articulate and polished Charles Eastlake was elected President (and knighted). Turner was not in good health and did not attend the meeting that voted Eastlake into the Presidency or the dinners for Academicians Sir Charles and Lady Eastlake gave in early 1851. But the moment had passed when he might have wanted the job. However, his old friend Jones, Keeper of the Academy, who had been acting President after Turner, was miffed at not being asked to stand, and resigned his post.

Organizing one's life as one gets older takes an effort, part of which is the need to think about life after one has gone. In July 1844 he had an indenture drawn up between himself and Samuel Rogers, Hugh Munro, Charles Turner and Martin Archer Shee, to sell them the land in Twickenham for his artists' charity hospital or almshouses, of which they were to be trustees. The institution was to be called 'Joseph Mallord William Turner's Charity for the relief of decayed and indigent Artists', with provisos about the artists being painters in oil, aged fifty-five or older, Academicians, Associates or exhibitors at the Academy for more than five years. Evidently Turner had decided to try to comply with the requirements of the Mortmain Act, which made it illegal to give land in a will only for charitable purposes. Unfortunately the indenture or deed of agreement was not legally implemented. Did some of the trustees refuse the task? Did Turner have second thoughts? Whatever the reasons, it meant that eventually his cherished scheme unravelled. A great muddle ensued.

Other worries overtook him at different hours of day and night. He was not happy about some of his bequests, and in 1846, 1848 and 1849 he added various codicils to his will, leaving £1000 for a monument 'for me and my memory' in St Paul's Cathedral, appointing Hannah and Sophia his residuary legatees, with annuities of £150 each, and revoking his previous bequests to his Turner uncles and cousins and to Sarah Danby, Evelina and Georgiana. He left his 'finished pictures' to the National Gallery as long as it provided a room or rooms called 'Turner's Gallery', giving it ten years to do so. Until then the pictures were to stay at Queen Anne Street with Hannah as custodian. He appointed as trustees and executors Thomas Griffith, John Ruskin, Philip Hardwick, his solicitor Henry Harpur, W. T. Wells, Henry Trimmer, Samuel Rogers, George Jones and Charles Turner. (Wells, he seems to have forgotten, had died in 1836.) For this service they were to get £19 19s each 'for a Ring' – a sum that cannily just escaped legacy duty.

In a fifth and final codicil of 1849 he left £100 each to Clara Wheeler and her sisters Emma and Laura. If the National Gallery ultimately did not want his pictures they were to be sold, after the lease of his gallery ran out. Out of the money received, he wanted £1000 to go to the RA pension fund, £500 to the AGBI, £500 to the Foundling Hospital in Lamb's Conduit Street, £500 to the London Orphan Fund, and the residue to his intended Artists' Charity. He had various other testamentary thoughts in these years, and made rough drafts for codicils, but none of them seems to have been legally drawn up; and so scattered notions about female servants to help the gallery custodian, copyright proceeds from copying fees, a change of mind about giving his *Carthage* rise and fall paintings to the nation and donating his 'funded property' to the RA or Dulwich College were not given legal effect.

Late in the day, he began to have new ideas about the sale of his work. Despite his deep-seated dislike of dealers, he took on Thomas Griffith in that capacity in this decade. Griffith not only introduced John Ruskin to Turner but took the American James Lenox to Queen Anne Street in 1848, when Lenox vainly tried to buy the *Temeraire*. Griffith ran a gallery close to the Athenaeum in Pall Mall. In 1842 Turner seems to have decided that he was short of commissions and needed cash to pay for five costly plates he was having engraved – Edward Goodall being paid £700 for one. So he took to Griffith some 'sample studies' of mostly Alpine subjects. Griffith was meant to find customers for a number of finished watercolours – Turner first proposed twenty, but revised this to ten. Turner made four of these in advance, as Ruskin wrote later, to '"show his hand" … whether it shook or not, or had otherwise lost its cunning'. In Griffith's gallery Turner took out the four drawings and the roll of what Ruskin remembered as fifteen sketches and (in Ruskin's account) asked Griffith:

'What do you think you can get for such things as these?'

Says Mr Griffith to Mr Turner: 'Well, perhaps commission included, eighty guineas each.'

Says Mr Turner to Mr Griffith: 'Ain't they worth more?'

Says Mr Griffith to Mr Turner: (after looking curiously into the execution which, you will please note, is what some people might call hazy) 'They're a little different from your usual style' – (Turner silent, Griffith does not push the point) – 'but – but – yes, they are *worth* more, but I could not *get* more.'[31]

Griffith managed to sell nine: Ruskin, Hugh Munro and Bicknell came through. But the once staunch Windus was not enthusiastic enough to buy, and in the following year another set for Griffith found only two patrons – Munro and Ruskin – for six watercolours. Whether Turner was beginning to falter, as Ruskin in spite of his support believed, or the Taste and he were drifting further apart, is a moot point. Many of these watercolours could be called 'hazy'. Many – with their quick dashes of paint and hatched strokes of colour – could (with our hindsight) be described as vital precursors of Impressionism and Pointillism.

Turner's tightness about money did not relax with age. In June 1842, in a letter to the engraver William Miller, he asked what discount there would be per hundred for greater quantities of prints and payment in 'ready money'.[32] And he remained at cross-purposes with many printdealers. The dealer Dominic Colnaghi later told John Pye that Turner had over several years reduced his firm's trade discount on *Liber* prints from 20 per cent to 10. Then, around 1848, said Colnaghi,

> I received an order for a set of the work. As usual, I sent to his house for it with the money. He was not in London; but his housekeeper furnished my messenger with a copy, but had received orders from her master not to allow more than 5 per cent. The money (£14) was of course paid, and I thought no more about the transaction. But, some five or six weeks after, I received a visit from Mr. Turner, and in his rather uncourteous manner he said, 'You owe me fourteen shillings.' 'I was not aware of being indebted to you,' said I. He explained that before he left town, he had made up his mind not to make any allowance to the trade on sales. He acknowledged that he was not quite certain of having mentioned this determination of his to his housekeeper, but still he thought I owed him the money. I then took some silver out of my pocket, and, offering it to him, I said, 'if you really think I owe you the money, take it'; which he felt very much inclined to do, but I suppose an unusual fit of liberality

came across him, and he said, 'No, not this time – but recollect, in future, no discount to the trade.' 'But,' said I, 'in that case how are we to live?' 'That's no affair of mine,' said he. Upon which we shook hands and parted.[33]

His 'generosity' also continued to be of a circumscribed kind. In December 1844 the committee of a group of student artists purchased a set of the *Liber* from Turner, in person. The agreed price was fourteen guineas, but Turner, 'on hearing that the work was being bought by a society of students, returned one guinea as a donation to their funds'.[34]

Things might be tidy in Chelsea but at headquarters in Queen Anne Street they were running down – not fast, but with the inexorable accretion of soot and dust, damp and decay. Visitors rang the bell with foreboding. In 1844 the young artist and art teacher James Hammersley, to whom Turner had declined to give painting lessons as Hammersley's father had requested in 1838, called to see the gallery. As he waited for a short time in 'a cold and cheerless' room he supposed was the dining room, he heard a 'shambling, slippered footstep' on the stairs.

> When the door opened, I nobody, stood face to face with, to my thinking, the greatest man living ... I saw, felt (and still feel) his penetrating grey eye! ... At his request I followed him into his gallery ... The room was even less tidy than the one we had left ... most of the pictures, indeed all those resting against the wall, being covered with uncleanly sheets or cloths of a like size and character. Turner removed these protections to his pictures, and disclosed to my wondering and reverend observation many of those works which are now known so generally ... Turner and I walked many times from end to end of the apartment, he occasionally giving brief descriptions of the pictures, and asking after my proceedings at the institution with which I was connected. Generally ... he was taciturn, though still sufficiently chatty to remove all idea of inattention or discourtesy.[35]

At one point Turner suggested that, because the gallery was so cold, Hammersley should put his hat on. Hammersley replied that he could not think of doing so in Turner's presence. After a few seconds Turner said he would feel much more comfortable if Hammersley complied with his wishes. Hammersley put his hat on and thought thereafter of Turner's 'kindly and most considerate mind'.[36]

Elizabeth Rigby, soon to be Lady Eastlake, called with Hugh Munro at the gallery in May 1846. Hannah let them in.

> She showed us into a dining-room, which had penury and meanness written on every wall and article of furniture. Then up into the gallery; a fine room- indeed, one of the best in London, but in a dilapidated state; his pictures the same. The great *Rise of Carthage* all mildewed and flaking off; another with all the elements in an uproar, of which I incautiously said: 'The End of the World, Mr. Turner?' 'No, ma'am; *Hannibal crossing the Alps*' ... Then he uncovered a few matchless creatures, fresh and dewy, like pearls just set – the mere colours grateful to the eye without reference to the subjects. The *Temeraire* a grand sunset effect. The old gentleman was great fun: his splendid picture of *Walhalla* had been sent to Munich, there ridiculed as might be expected, and returned to him with £7 to pay, and sundry spots upon it: on these Turner laid his odd misshapen thumb in a pathetic way. Mr. Munro suggested they would rub out, and I offered my cambric handkerchief; but the old man edged us away, and stood before his picture like a hen in fury.[37]

He was funny about his works, caring for them deeply even if he didn't always look after them or even look at them. Ruskin's Cambridge friend, the Reverend William Kingsley ('a pale, thin man, who stammers', according to the future Lady Eastlake),[38] visited the gallery and saw that a piece of paint 'as large as a fourpenny piece' had fallen from the sky of *Crossing the Brook* and lay on the floor.

'How can you look at the picture and see it so injured?' asked Kingsley.

Turner said, 'What does it matter? The only use of the thing is to recall the impression.'[39]

On another occasion, Ruskin said, 'I have watched him sitting at dinner nearly opposite one of his chief pictures – his eyes never turned to it.' And further: 'Turner appears never to have desired, from any one, care in favour of his separate works. The only thing he would say sometimes was, "Keep them together."'[40] He was annoyed when a doctor called at the gallery, ostensibly to see his pictures, and proceeded to ask about an early painting of Rochester Castle, commissioned from Turner by the Reverend Douglas, which the doctor now owned. Did Turner remember painting it? A tortuous dialogue ensued, Turner refusing to authenticate the picture, the doctor saying he was not asking for this, Turner saying the doctor had no right to tax his memory of what he might have done *one hundred and fifty years ago*, the doctor apologizing, Turner growling, the doctor bowing his way out. Perhaps Turner was particularly grumpy because he had been interrupted while painting.

The gallery, despite its grimy reputation, was still on the list of places cultured people tried to visit when in London. Ralph Waldo Emerson and his friend George S. Hillard, a lawyer, were taken to Queen Anne Street on 28 June 1848 by the distinguished zoologist Richard Owen. Several days earlier Emerson had met Clarkson Stanfield at a dinner and been taken by him to Tottenham to see B. G. Windus's Turners. Stanfield told Emerson that Turner had confided that he would not 'suffer any portrait to be taken of him, for nobody would believe such an ugly fellow made such beautiful things'. Turner's face, Emerson learnt, 'resembles the heads of Punch'. In 1856 the American published his book *English Traits*, in which he considered the character of the English, their moroseness and taciturnity, their cheerfulness and mildness – in fact their great range of moods: 'They hide virtues under vices, or the semblence of them.' 'The Englishman is a churl with a soft place in his heart, whose speech is a brash of bitter waters, but who loves to help you at a pinch. He says no, and serves you, and your thanks disgust him.' And Emerson presents an example:

> Here was lately a cross-grained miser, odd and ugly, resembling in countenance the portrait of Punch, with the laugh left out; rich by his own industry; sulking in a lonely house; who never gave a dinner to any man, and disliked all courtesies; yet as true a worshipper of beauty in form and colour as ever existed, and profusely pouring over the cold mind of his countrymen creations of grace and truth, removing the reproach of sterility from English art, catching from their savage climate every fine hint, and importing into their galleries every tint and trait of sunnier cities and skies; making an era in painting; and, when he saw that the splendor of one of his pictures in the Exhibition dimmed his rival's that hung next to it, secretly took a brush and blackened his own.[41]

A younger visiting American who actually met the cross-grained miser was W. J. Stillman, who later became a correspondent for the London *Times*. In 1850 Stillman was twenty-two, an art student and a passionate admirer of Turner's work. He heard that Turner was ill and through Thomas Griffith offered to nurse him. Turner declined the offer, but, Griffith told Stillman, was not unmoved by it. One day, after he had recovered, Stillman heard from Griffith that Turner was coming to his gallery at a certain hour on a business appointment. If Stillman happened in just before the time fixed for it he might see him.

> At the appointed hour Turner came and found me in an earnest study of the pictures in the farther end of the gallery, where I remained, unnoticing and unnoticed, until a sign from Griffith called me up. He then introduced me as a young American artist who had a great admiration for his work, and who, being about to return home, would be glad to take him by the hand. It was difficult to reconcile my conception of the great artist with this little, and, to casual observation, insignificant old man with a nose like an eagle's beak, though a second sight showed that his eye, too, was like an eagle's, bright, restless, and penetrating. Half awed and half surprised, I held out my hand. He put his behind him, regarding me with a humorous, malicious look, saying nothing. Confused, and not a little mortified, I turned away, and, walking down the gallery, went to study the pictures again. When I looked his way again, a few minutes later, he held out his hand to me, and we entered into a conversation which lasted until Griffith gave me a hint that Turner had business to transact which I must leave him to. He gave me a hearty handshake, and in his oracular way said, 'H'mph – (nod) if you come to England again – h'mph (nod) – h'mph (nod)' and another handshake with more cordiality and a nod for good-bye. I never saw a keener eye than his, and the way that he held himself up, so straight that he seemed almost to lean backwards, with his forehead thrown forward, and the piercing eyes looking out from under their heavy brows, combined to make a very peculiar and vivid impression on me … In the conversation we had … I alluded to our good fortune in having already in America one of the pictures of his best period, a sea-coast sunset in the possession of Mr. Lenox, and Turner exclaimed, 'I wish they were all put in a blunderbuss and shot off!' But he looked pleased at the simultaneous outburst of protest on the part of Griffith and myself.[42]

Stillman apparently did not notice – or think worth mentioning – the decay or the cats. Hugh Munro, after a Sunday afternoon visit to Queen Anne Street, told Frith that 'the very look of the place was enough to give a man a cold. I found Turner an hour ago crouching over a morsel of fire in the gallery, with a dreadful cold upon him, muffled up and miserable.'

'Yes, here I am,' said Turner to Munro, 'with all these unsaleable things about me. I wish to Heaven I could get rid of them; I would sell them cheap to anybody who would take them where I couldn't see them any more.'

'Well,' said Munro, 'what will you take for the lot?'

'Oh, I don't know; you may make me an offer if you like.'

Munro did a quick calculation and offered to write a cheque for £25,000. This made Turner's eyes glitter for a moment. He looked at the fire, thought for a while, and then told Munro to take a walk and come back in an hour. Munro did so. He may not have known that Turner was said to have refused offers of £100,000 for the contents of Queen Anne Street and £5000 for his two Carthages. When Munro returned, he found that Turner seemed to have forgotten their conversation. His first words were: 'Hullo! what, you here again? I am very ill; my cold is very bad.'

'Well,' said Munro, 'have you decided; will you accept my offer?'

'No, I won't – I can't. I believe I'm going to die, and I intend to be buried in those two' – pointing to the *Carthage* and the *Sun rising through Vapour*. 'So I can't; besides, I can't be bothered – good evening.'[43]

Bad colds were the least of it. Ruskin believed that in 1845 Turner's mind failed 'suddenly with snap of some vital chord'.[44] His works towards the close of that year, Ruskin thought, 'showed a conclusive failure of power; and I saw that nothing remained for me to write, but his epitaph'.[45] That he had in fact gone mad would have been credible to the many critics who considered his work touched with insanity, or to those with long memories, who had heard talk of Turner's mother in an asylum. However, the Reverend Kingsley placed the failure of Turner's powers two years later. The cause, Kingsley said, was 'the loss of his teeth. Cartwright did his best to make him a set of false ones, but the tenderness of the gums did not allow him to make use of them; so his digestion gave way and he suffered much from this to the end of his life.'[46] Kingsley also wanted to care for Turner and invited him to stay with him in Cambridge. 'He told me he could not, because he "was so nasty in his eating, the only way in which he could live being, by sucking meat".'[47]

It was in December 1846 that Turner told Hawksworth that being deputy to the President of the Academy had destroyed his happiness and appetite. In the summer of 1847 he was seriously ill for six weeks and a Chelsea surgeon, Dr Frederick Gaskell, attended him in Davis Place; on the way to Margate by land to see Dr Price, he was seized by a fit at Rochester and fell down. Mrs Booth later complained that it was she who paid Dr Gaskell's bill and that she had not been reimbursed. But despite her claim to David Roberts that Turner had, with the exception of their first year together, never contributed one shilling to their mutual support, she later said he occasionally gave her small sums, though never more than two pounds, and never more than twenty pounds in a year. Turner, she said, never used to have any money with him, and when he came home in a cab, she paid the fare.[48] The next year, 1848, was not much better. In a midsummer-day's letter to Ruskin senior he said that he had been 'laid up with a broken knee-pan',[49] and in a note to Ruskin junior on 5 November 1848 'ill-health' was mentioned.[50]

This could have been the result of cholera. Around this time, so David Roberts believed after talking later with Dr Price of Margate, Turner had 'a most severe attack of cholera' while in Deal; and if 'he had not had the most extraordinary constitution, with his habits as he [Dr Price] termed it, he could never have got over it'.[51] (His habits, presumably, were drinking too much.) Cholera caused vomiting, diarrhoea, severe cramps of the stomach and limbs, and often death. The epidemic of 1847–9 in Britain killed 53,000 in England and Wales, 14,000 of these in London. Croydon was badly hit by the visitation in 1849, when the marine artist J. C. Schetky was struck by the illness, but recovered. On Christmas Eve 1849 Turner wrote to Hawksworth, with a typical misspelling: 'I am sorry to say my health is on the wain. I cannot bear the same fatigue, or have the same bearing against it I formerly had – but time and tide stop not.'[52]

Many friends let him know they were thinking of him. Those letters to 'Hawkey' often began with thanks for a care package from Farnley: goose pie, pheasants and hares in 1849, or in 1847 what he called the 'three PPP viz. Pie Phea[sant] and Pud'. The Ruskins sent eggs and pork ribs with 'Portugal onions for stuffing them included'.[53] Dawson Turner sent his customary barrel of herrings. And George Jones before the opening of the Academy exhibition in April 1850 wrote a kind letter:

I saw your pictures this morning for the first time, and more glorious effusions of mind have never appeared – *your* intellect defies time to injure it, and I really believe that you never conceived more beautiful, more graceful, or more enchanting compositions, than these you have sent for exhibition – God bless you & preserve you as you are for your affectionate and admiring Friends – [54]

There were fewer paintings now. Six at the RA in 1845, five in 1846, one in 1847, none in 1848, and only one again in 1849. Unlike Jones, Ruskin thought these late works were 'of wholly inferior value'[55] and he claimed (in a letter to George Richmond) that Turner burst into tears when his hands ceased to obey him.[56] There were also fewer watercolours, though he made two for Ruskin in late 1847, *The Brunig Pass* and *Descent of the St. Gothard*. The other collectors who had supported him seemed to be dropping away. His reputation was unstable. Not only had his *Opening of the Wallhala* been knocked about during its return to him from a Congress of European Art in Munich in 1845, with payment due, but its reception had been unpleasant. His large celebration in oil of Ludwig of Bavaria's new Doric 'Temple of Fame' was taken by Bavarian viewers as a lampoon or satire and its artist as a 'dauber', whose talent had degenerated, and whose works were now 'seen only as curiosities of the art of painting'.[57] Perhaps some *were* curiosities; perhaps some were magnificent. Some undoubtedly were sad, like the drawing he had done of a drowned girl whose body was brought ashore at Chelsea near his cottage,[58] or like *The Wreck Buoy*, an old painting of his that he reworked for the exhibition in 1849. Despite the rainbow that arches over the sailing craft, the effect was – once more – of an approaching and perhaps final deluge, in which the sailors (and the oarsmen in several rowing boats) are going to go full fathom five, joining whatever is below the strange little bomb-shaped buoy marked WRECK.

Out of nostalgia or need, he was looking through old pictures. His sole 1847 exhibit was another reworking: *The Hero of a Hundred Fights*. This was the year, so George Jones reported, that one of their colleagues approached Turner on a varnishing day and said, 'Why, Turner, you have but one picture here this year.' And Turner replied, 'Yes, you will have less next year.'[59] Like *The Wreck Buoy*, *The Hero of a Hundred Fights* had originally been painted some forty years before – in the first decade of the century when he was about thirty. It began apparently as a picture of a forge or factory.

Now, it seems on varnishing days, he turned it into a revelation scene: an equestrian statue of the Duke of Wellington appearing in the mouth of a blazing furnace. (Such a statue had been cast in 1845, and the sculptor Wyatt had invited a group of artists to watch the process.) Turner had as a hanging neighbour Maclise's *Sacrifice of Noah*, and having helped Maclise with the rainbow in that picture, he decided to paint up 'such a blaze as to extinguish Noah's rainbow' – thus the *Literary Gazette*, a rare admirer, on 8 May 1847. The paper continued, 'It is a marvellous piece of colouring. If Turner had been Phaeton, he must have succeeded in driving out the chariot of the sun.'

The darker the days, the more he craved brightness. In Davis Place, he got up to watch from his roof-top balcony the sun rise downriver, a blanket or dressing gown over his shoulders. There was an early-morning sun in *Norham Castle, Sunrise*, painted during the mid-1840s, an oil painting that looked in many ways like a watercolour. In this he returned to one of his lucky places: the castle on the Tweed that he had first sketched and done in watercolour in the late 1790s. Norham had thereafter figured in the *Liber* and in numerous engravings, watercolours and colour studies. In the late painting, a solitary cow, standing shin-deep in the calm waters of the Tweed, is an almost calligraphically rendered survivor of several cattle in the *Liber* engraving. As noted previously, Turner had doffed his hat to Norham when he was there in 1831, and had explained to a companion that drawing and painting Norham Castle had set him on the road to being a successful artist. In this last painting on the subject, 'the powerful King of Day' – the sun celebrated in the Thomson lines he used with his Norham watercolour in 1798 – has risen just above the castle. Light penetrates the pale colours which form the misty structures of everything: hill, castle, riverbanks, cow, river. The castle and its hill are done with continuous strokes of cobalt blue on top of a warmer ground, producing a surprising cornflower colour. Substances are gossamer-light. One feels that the sunlight itself is a blessing that can suddenly fade or be withdrawn.

The painter for the Sun Fire Office (Chantrey's joke) was no closet sun-worshipper. In various poetic borrowings and quotations he had called the sun 'Prime Cheerer' and 'Fairest of Beings'. The Divine Light was of course the Fount of all Colour. He had tried to sketch an eclipse of the sun around 1804;[60] he had noted in a sketchbook of 1809–10 the presumed distance of the sun from the earth.[61] Apollo – the God of Light – confronted darkness in his *Apollo and Python* of 1811. Viewers of his paintings were forced to use words such as blazing, fiery and resplendent. Ruskin called him 'a Sun-worshipper of the old breed', a veritable Zoroastrian in his solar enthusiasm.[62] And in 1843 Ruskin saw that Turner's works were distinguished from those of other colourists

> by the dazzling intensity … of the light which he sheds through every hue, and which, far more than their brilliant colour, is the real source of their overpowering effect upon the eye, an effect so *reasonably* made the subject of perpetual animadversion; as if the sun which they represent were a quiet, and subdued, and gentle, and manageable luminary and never dazzled anybody, under any circumstances whatsoever. I am fond of standing by a bright Turner in the Academy, to listen to the unintentional compliments of the crowd – 'What a glaring thing!' 'I declare I can't look at it!' 'Don't it hurt your eyes?' – expressed as if they were in the constant habit of looking the sun full in the face with the most perfect comfort and entire facility of vision.[63]

Once, like Ariel in *The Tempest*, Turner had 'flamed amazement'.[64] Now his yellows were becoming white, as in white-hot. He wanted to paint pure light, the ultimate measurement and the final unity. The sun had given and the sun would take away. The sun, in seven billion years or so, will burn us up, we now know; man and his achievements, including all his art, will have been consumed and our earth will be a dead cinder. It is as if Turner already felt dread and despair from this: the horrible pointlessness that formed the backdrop to human striving and to his own compulsions and hard work. And yet he also felt a common gratitude for existence. He continued to get up early to watch the sun rise, making use of the light of every day he had. W. J. Stillman recorded an occasion in these closing years when 'Callow, the water-colour artist, happening to be in the early morning train with him, and seeing him at sunrise look at the full risen sun unflinchingly, expressed his wonder. Turner said, "It hurts my eyes no more than it would hurt yours to look at a candle."'[65] Despite that boast, one wonders, thinking of Regulus: were his eyes injured by so much looking at the sun? Or did his presumed cataracts protect them?

In 1846 one of his Academy exhibits was a painting called *The Angel Standing in the Sun*. This was a harder subject than Norham Castle. It seemed to be an attempt to paint the unpaintable. The Angel of the Apocalypse stood with uplifted sword in a vortex of light, with birds flying in the upper left and a serpent and various human beings below, among them Adam and Eve, alive, and Abel and Holofernes, dead. Turner found this passage for the Academy catalogue in the Book of Revelation:

> And I saw an angel standing in the sun; and he cried with a loud voice, saying to all the fowls that fly in the midst of heaven, Come and gather yourselves together unto the supper of the great God; That ye may eat the flesh of kings, and the flesh of captains and the flesh of mighty men, and the flesh of horses, and of them that sit on them, both free and bond, both small and great.[66]

To reinforce the note of voracious doom, he added two lines from Samuel Rogers' *Voyage of Columbus*:

> The morning march that flashes to the sun;
> The feast of vultures when the day is done.

And perhaps he also had in his well-stocked mind Byron's poem *Cain*, which concluded with the appearance of the Angel of the Lord.

The painting got a mixed response. Ruskin thought it 'indicative of mental disease'.[67] The press wavered between those who – like the *Athenaeum* – considered it an aberration of talent (9 May 1846) and those who approved it, like the *Times*, which (6 May) called it 'a truly gorgeous creation … It is all very well to treat Turner's pictures as jests; but things like these are too magnificent for jokes.'

What Ruskin called Turner's 'infidelity'[68] was his despair. He saw mankind ending in an all-consuming fire. It is the merciless light of this solar furnace that blazes behind the Angel.

But he kept going nevertheless. At least he did not have the ill fortune that drove Haydon to kill himself in June 1846, and he found shreds of hope as well as of despair in the Bible. Around this time he painted a watercolour that has since been given the title *The Angel Troubling the Pool*. His underlying text was from the Gospel of St John, where an angel stirred the waters of a pool near Jerusalem and sick people who stepped into it were cured. Turner took a watercolour he had done of Alpine landscape and added the helpful angel and the sick; one man supports himself on a stick. The Holy Land comes to Switzerland!

His 'range of mind' continued to intrigue those who encountered him. The anthologist F. T. Palgrave met him at a party and was impressed by his 'eminent sense and shrewdness', talking-once he warmed up – 'of the mysteries of bibliography and the tangle of politics'. Palgrave asked Turner about a star in a *Liber* print called *From Spenser's Fairy Queen* – a star that had disappeared from later states of the print – and Turner said, with an ironic laugh, that the stars and their ways were beyond his control. When he left, Palgrave helped Turner into his 'rough and old-fashioned great coat'. Turner must have felt he had been too abrupt with Palgrave before, because 'he pointed to Jupiter keenly shining in the cold upper sky and gaily said I might ask that star why it pleased to shine'.[69]

He took an interest in novel ways of representing nature. The young American daguerrotypist J. J. E. Mayall had a studio in the Strand. On several occasions between 1847 and 1849 a small, elderly, dark-suited man visited Mayall's establishment, and the pioneer photographer got the impression that his visitor, a Mr Turner, had to do with the law – was possibly a Master in Chancery; and Turner did not dissuade him from this idea. Mayall's visitor was inquisitive about the way light worked on iodized silver plates, and he got Mayall to explain how images were copied. They talked about magnetism and about light. Mayall made several daguerrotype portraits of Turner and was paid for them; one of these Turner 'presented to a lady who accompanied him' – presumably Mrs Booth. Turner was particularly interested in Mayall's views of Niagara and the rainbow that spanned the great falls. 'He told me he should like to see Niagara, as it was the greatest wonder in Nature.'[70]

One evening in May 1849 Mayall met his Master in Chancery at a soirée of the Royal Society:

> He shook me by the hand very cordially, and fell into his old topic of the spectrum. Some one came up to me and asked if I knew Mr. Turner; I answered I had had that pleasure some time. 'Yes,' said my informant, rather significantly; 'but do you know that he is *the* Turner?' I was rather surprised, I must confess; and later on in the evening I encountered him again, and fell into conversation on our old topic. I ventured to suggest to him the value of such studies for

his own pursuits, and at once offered to conduct any experiments for him he might require, and, in fact, to give up some time to work out his ideas about the treatment of light and shade. I parted with him on the understanding that he would call on me; however, he never did call again.[71]

Mayall, to begin with gloomy about prospects in London, was grateful to Turner for his support. Turner once said to him, 'You are sure to succeed; only wait. You are a young man yet. I began life with little, and you see I am now very comfortable.'

'Yes,' Mayall replied, 'and if I were on the same side of Chancery you are, perhaps I might be comfortable also.'[72]

Mayall said later that at one stage in this period he was having money problems because of litigation over patent rights. Turner, 'unasked, brought him a roll of bank notes, to the amount of £300, and gave it to him on the understanding that he was to repay him if he could. This, Mr Mayall was able to do very soon.'[73]

As for the spectrum, one recalls that Turner had been reading Eastlake's translation of Goethe on the theory of colours and making crabbed, often inscrutable notes in the margins. Some of those that are legible suggest that he differed with Goethe, who was not sufficiently practical for him: how a writer *thought* painting was done could be different from how it *was* done.

The sketchbooks tail off. What Ruskin called Turner's 'Actually Last Sketchbook' is from 1847 or thereabouts and has few drawings in it. In one sketchbook from the mid-1840s, children play on a seashore, perhaps at Margate, and there is a little note in Turner's hand: 'The lost vessel'. In the same sketchbook he wrote: 'May 30 – Margate. A small opening along the horizon marked the approach of the sun by its getting yellow.'[74] And the poetic urge still seized him; there are in this sketchbook some late attempts at verse, partly illegible:

> Then on the lonely shore the bold wave
> ... who crowd the many hills
> ... by love

And even some nature notes, in a terrible hand:

> May. Blossoms. Apple Cherry Lilac
> Small white flowers in the Hedges

in Clusters, D. Blue Bells,
Buttercups and daisies in the fields
Oak. Warm. Elm. G. Ash yellow.[75]

He and Mrs Booth continued to go down to the Kent coast after the Academy exhibition had opened or if he was feeling particularly run down. From Deal he looked out to the Goodwin Sands, scene of many a wreck. He made a few watercolours now of these shallow waters. The sun set. He added a word or two: 'Lost to all Hope'.[76] His depression pervades these studies of often peopleless beaches, the waves rolling in and withdrawing again and again, the high skies. But for him these Thanet skies were still the loveliest and many of his late informal coastal studies – of the sand, the sea, the sunsets and storm clouds – done with bold sweeps of watercolour, are stunningly beautiful.

Some of his sketches were done on the beaches of the North Foreland and around on the Channel coast at Folkestone. He took a few jaunts afloat and sketched from offshore. Some studies, in watercolours or oil, were perhaps painted in the front room of Mrs Booth's house, looking out to sea. A few have fishy creatures or sea monsters lurking within them. A stranded whale is certainly real and the scene is inscribed by Turner, 'I shall use this.'[77] He was in Folkestone in 1845 and entitled his roll sketchbook 'Ideas of Folkestone'.[78] Twenty-three out of the twenty-four drawings in it are watercolour studies of clouds, cliffs, waves, boats and the harbour. Although his health had been bad this year, after his deputy presidential duties, it is not evident from this sketchbook: there is rather a sense of an artist moving his brush across the paper with untrammelled freedom and panache. While he worked, the impending conclusion – the loss of all hope – was wonderfully held at bay.

21: World's End

From January to April 1850 Turner worked on four three-foot-by-four-foot paintings for the Academy exhibition – his fifty-seventh, sixty years after he had first shown there. He worked at Davis Place, in his small painting room facing the river, sometimes concentrating on one, sometimes retouching one after another. He had always liked series, and this was a modest sequence; the theme was Carthage once again and Aeneas' sojourn there, with the Trojan hero ensnared (almost) by Dido to the point of giving up his search for a new homeland in Italy. The *Aeneid* had been a favourite source of picture matter for Claude in his later years. It had been Turner's own longest-running subject: Aeneas had made his first appearance in his work in 1798 with the Cumaean sibyl at Lake Avernus. And here he was again, though in a less definite, even less physical form; all was haze and suggestion, glow and iridescence.

The titles of these paintings were *Mercury sent to admonish Aeneas, Aeneas relating his Story to Dido, The Visit to the Tomb* and *The Departure of the Fleet.* That resourceful manuscript 'The Fallacies of Hope' provided short tags for each painting. His musings in the *Aeneid*, perhaps his bedside reading, gave him three of the subjects, while that of *The Visit to the Tomb* seems to have been an idea or dream of his own. He interpolated in Virgil's scenario an excursion by the lovers to the mausoleum of Dido's late husband Sychaeus – by remembering him, the Carthaginian Queen had attempted to diminish her passion for Aeneas. Did the Dido story still have for Turner reverberations of Sarah Danby, or did Sophia sometimes give him cause for jealousy by regretting the loss of Messrs Pound and Booth? Sychaeus' point of view seems inherent in Turner's 'Fallacies' line for this picture: 'The sun went down in wrath at such deceit.'[1]

He let Mrs Booth look at the paintings before he sent them up to the Academy; but she later recalled that he told her she was not to comment on them.

Despite George Jones's friendly letter about Turner's 'glorious effusions of mind', these pictures had an uneasy reception at the exhibition. Some critics wanted to be kind but could not follow the artist in his deviations from nature, his carelessness with form and his eccentricities of manner, though they acknowledged the brilliant light and suggestive power. Possibly beyond the radiance there were hints of irradiation: the sunlight had become fatal. None was sold.

He was seventy-five in April 1850. He was still going out to dinner, for instance to Roberts's in Fitzroy Square, where a young artist who was a fellow guest found him very agreeable: 'his quick bright eye sparkled, and his whole countenance expressed a desire to please'.[2] He continued to make short trips on the river. A local boatman named Greaves rowed him up- and downstream and across to Battersea. If the weather was poor, he would say, 'Well, Mrs Booth, we won't go far.'[3] But his health was shaky. At the end of the year he wrote to Hawksworth thanking him for an excellent pie, recalled days at Farnley, and went on: 'Old Time has made sad work with me since I saw you in Town. I always dreaded it with horror now I feel it acutely now whatever – Gout or nervousness – it having fallen into my Pedestals – and bid adieu to the Marrow bone stage.'[4]

He was 'too unwell' to attend the David Roberts party on New Year's Day 1851, to go to the Eastlakes on 8 January, or to be with the Ruskins at Denmark Hill on 8 February for the birthday 'of the talented Mr. J. Ruskin'.[5] Ruskin at this point did not know about Turner's Chelsea ménage. For a time in 1846 there had been some sort of disagreement between artist and writer, possibly to do with Turner's objection to Ruskin's Switzerland trip in 1845 or because Ruskin was offended that same year when Turner thought of raising the prices of his Swiss watercolours from 80 guineas to £100. Perhaps, too, Turner may have sensed that Ruskin thought his hero's mind was failing. Turner's interest in what was going on in the world seemed undiminished. The same end-of-1850 letter to 'Hawkey' told him about the Crystal Palace going up in Hyde Park for the Great Exhibition, and in another letter at the end of January, thanking Hawksworth this time for a brace of Longtails and a brace of hares, Turner described the huge glass cathedral, looking 'very well in front because the transept takes a centre like a dome, but sideways ribs of Glass frame work only Towering over the Galleries like a Giant'.[6] It was the year in which this 'worlds fair' – as he parenthetically complained to Griffith in May – appeared to be taking all the attention, to the detriment of the sales of Turner prints.[7]

He had nothing he wanted to offer the RA exhibition this spring. But he called in during the varnishing days and stopped to chat with Maclise about his painting *Caxton's Printing Press*. Jones saw him call for a chair and sit for a while there, 'expressing his pleasure by his odd and jocose remarks'.[8] Maclise no doubt was relieved that the great man this year refrained from competing rainbow with rainbow. Turner also attended the Private View, though he looked frail; the writer Peter Cunningham thought Turner was 'breaking up fast' and 'would hardly live the year out'.[9] The *Times* wrote on 3 May, 'We miss those works of inspiration.' This led Ruskin to write:

> *We* miss! Who misses? The populace of England rolls by to weary itself in the great bazaar of Kensington, little thinking that a day will come when those veiled vestals and prancing amazons, and goodly merchandize of precious stones and gold, will all be forgotten as though they had not been, but that the light which has faded from the walls of the Academy is one which a million Koh-i-Noors could not rekindle, and that the year 1851 will, in the far future, be remembered less for what it has displayed than what it has withdrawn.[10]

Prince Albert, chief promoter of the Great Exhibition, was the principal guest at the Academy's annual banquet. The painter T. Sidney Cooper was about to leave when he saw Turner sitting by himself near the door:

> He called out to me and said: 'Come and sit down, Cooper, and have a glass of wine with me.'
> I replied that I had taken as much as I required, and that I was anxious to get away, as I was going elsewhere; but he pressed me, and I agreed to stay with him for a short time. He soon wished to leave himself, and asked me to give him my arm down the stairs, which I willingly did. Sir Edwin Landseer and Lord John Russell, then Prime Minister, were in conversation together near the entrance, and I heard the former say to Lord John, as we passed:

'There is Cooper, leading out the "Nestor" of the Royal Academy.'

'Never mind them,' said Turner to me – 'Never mind them. They shan't lead me out.'[11]

He had not been a regular at the Academy Club for some time. His fraternal feelings were at the mercy of his age and health. But in early May Solomon Hart – on his way to a Club dinner at the Thatched House tavern – met Turner, who quizzed him and found out his destination. Hart thought Turner seemed depressed. Turner said he was sorry that he wasn't going too. So Hart took him along and, leaving him for a moment outside the room where the Club members had assembled, told them he wanted to bring in a stranger. 'They all objected, as it was against the rule to admit any one save the members. I replied that they on that occasion would gladly break the rule, if I produced my friend. Turner was cordially welcomed. He was placed on the right of the chairman, and was the hero of the evening.'[12]

On this occasion, Turner had apparently been up in town on art business, hoping to see Griffith about drawings and watercolours that might be sold. But Griffith was away. Turner dropped him a note from the Athenaeum to ask 'How shall we meet? I am yet very unwell and unable to walk much.'[13] He was up from Chelsea again a few weeks later and called on his long-time engraver Charles Turner, who recorded in his diary for 28 May: 'Mr Wm. Turner. The last time I ever saw him.'[14] He was too ill to attend the 'soirée' held when the Academy exhibition closed at the end of July, and some of his friends now began to worry in earnest. Roberts knew that

it was no use calling at Queen Anne Street as he was seldom there. I had long observed that he had become very infirm. I therefore thought that I might, from the friendly terms we were on, aske to call upon him. I therefore wrote a letter something to the following effect: Dear Turner / I rarely even see you now. I hope you are not ill; I should like to see you as formerly. If unwell will you let me call upon you? I promise no one shall know it but myself if such be your wish – & I think your experience of me is such that you may depend on my honour in this matter. I should like to tell you what is going on in the Academy as I am sure you would also wish to know. There are many things that they (The Council of which I am one) would like to consult you about & have the benefit of your experience. Take this as it is ment, honestly & sincerely. I am the very last man who has a wish or desire to pry into the affairs of other people. God knows I have quite enough of my own to care for but should [you] deem this an intrusion upon your privacy, put it in the fire, & think no more about it

ever yours David Roberts

Roberts noted that Turner rarely answered a letter, and there was no reply now. However, sometime after this, Turner called, and, thanking Roberts, said

you must not press me on the matter *it cannot be*. But I will do what will be the same thing – I will never come to town without calling upon you. *He keept his word.* I think he called once or twice after that time. The last time he stood by my table where I usually write and putting his hand upon his breast, he said, there is something wrong here: it is no use hiding it but I feel something here is all wrong. I looked steadfastly at him and could not but remark that, although all the once burly figure had now *Shrunk* up, the little dark piercing eye seemed as brilliant as that of a child. I had been accustomed to look on the Vacant eye of those suffering with Opthalma in Egypt and the bleared pupil or orbit, but here all was clear & lucid as youth.

This was about the beginning or end of August. His cabman was a little bandy legged dwarf about two heads shorter than himself, with whom he seemed to be on intimate terms & spoke of putting him in a livery. I thought him in better Spirits than usual.

I never saw him again.[15]

Roberts learnt that Turner had also called on George Jones that day. Jones was working on a very large canvas, *The Battle of Hyderabad*, seven feet long, in an upstairs room. Jones recalled: 'Turner was too infirm to get up the stairs to see it, and [although] he never before appeared vexed with me, yet on this occasion he did so; but at that time it was almost impossible to move the canvas, and I hoped to see him again. My hope was fallacious' – Turner's terminology was catching – 'and I lost his invaluable advice.'[16]

Ruskin, whose own psychological problems may have coloured his view of Turner, was convinced that Turner's last days were unhappy and 'very sorrowful'.[17] He wrote to Elizabeth Barrett Browning in 1858 to say that, while going through Turner's later drawings, he had concluded that 'the old man's soul had been gradually crushed within him, leaving him at the close of his life weak, sinful, desolate

– nothing but his generosity and kindness of heart left'.[18] It could be said, somewhat to the contrary, that if some of these later drawings were erotic enough to disturb Ruskin they were evidence that Turner's sexual energies were still pulsing. Moreover, Ruskin, still relatively young, may not have taken account of the effects of illness and pain – the loss of 'marrow-bone' strength, the failing connections and falterings of nerves, the trembling of limbs – and their effects on morale. Weak in body, it is a rare man who is not also weak in spirits. Hazlitt wrote, in an unpublished final paragraph for his essay *On the Fear of Death*: 'Time has already anticipated the work of Death, and left him but half his spoils; for we die every moment of our lives …'[19]

Turner and Mrs Booth managed a trip to Margate, no doubt hoping for 'revival'. Frith said: 'A slight change for the better took place, owing, as Turner thought, to the skill of a local doctor, and the sick man went back to his lodgings in Chelsea, where his illness returned upon him with great virulence.'[20] With his bad teeth, he was having trouble eating solid food. Mr Bartlett, the Chelsea 'Surgeon Dentist and Cupper' who had made a set of false teeth for the patient he knew as Mr Booth, now called often at 6 Davis Place. From what he saw, he later told Ruskin, 'There was nothing about the house at all to indicate the abode of an artist,' though he noticed the *Art Journal* and the *Illustrated London News* lying on a table. As for his patient, 'he was very fond of smoking and yet had a great objection to any one knowing of it. His diet was principally at that time rum and milk. He would take sometimes two quarts of milk per day and rum in proportion, very frequently to excess.'[21] Turner had been missing his summer tours; he told Mr Bartlett that, should he recover, he would take him on the Continent and show him all the places he had visited. He obviously did not mind being saddled with a companion so long as he could go on a sketching tour again.

In the autumn and early winter of 1851, while the crowds continued to visit the exposition in Hyde Park, he declined. He stayed in bed from the beginning of October. He tried to draw in bed. Mrs Booth told John Pye that some of his last work was inspired by his dreams. Pye recorded: 'One night he was disturbed, and called out excitedly. She brought him drawing materials, with which he made some notes afterwards used for a picture.'[22] What did he dream about?

Castles – mountains – seashores – shipwrecks – his boat – riverbanks – fishing at Petworth – a woman's body pressed against his?

Into his residence at World's End – 'the world well lost', as Roberts called it – none of his friends could intrude, not knowing where he was living. Even the faithful Hannah didn't know how to find him. Roberts believed, with little evidence, that this 'poor old deseased wretched creature … [had] served all the purposes of a wife in her time and had still some afection for this Don Juan'.[23] Turner's instructions to her that summer, during the Great Exhibition, had been to admit no visitors to his gallery. However, Turner had arranged for money to reach her; he wrote to Charles Stokes on 1 August, saying his limbs were 'so weak' and he feared the worst, and asking Stokes to call – presumably at Queen Anne Street – so that Hannah could 'take what may be wanted of the Exchequer Bill'.[24] But as the autumn passed Hannah became worried, not seeing him in Queen Anne Street or hearing from him. As Roberts told the story, she found a note in one of his coat pockets, giving Mrs Booth's name and the address in Chelsea. With an elderly woman friend she made her way out to that suburb:

> They seem to have been afraid to go to the house itself, but in the house adjoining is a little shop where they sell Ginger beer; here they went in & had a bottle, asking at the same time whether they knew anything of a Mrs Booth next door. The answer was that two very quiet *respectable* people of that name had lived for years next door, but that the old gentleman had been very ill & in fact was supposed to be dying. The description left no doubt in this poor creature's mind that Mr Booth and Mr Turner were the same. She gave the information to Mr Harper [Harpur, Turner's solicitor and cousin] who at once went to see & ascertain the truth; with defuctulty got acces, & found the great painter in the last stage of illness.[25]

In an earlier journal entry Roberts said that Harpur knew of Turner's whereabouts as of the end of November, when Hardwick had made enquiries of the solicitor, and Harpur told the Academy Treasurer that Turner would not be able to dine with him on Christmas Day 'as was his custom' because he was 'confined to bed and had been since the commencement of October'. In 1853, Mrs Booth said that 'Mrs Harpur called with Mr Harpur to see Mr Turner many times during his illness.'[26]

At some point in mid-December Turner managed to write a note to his stockbroker and moneyman, Charles Stokes:

> Dear Stokes
>   Enclosed is a wish for Mr F. Marsh to advance on my account £100
>   I do not like the debts of Mr Woods – not paid. Have the goodness to do it
>   yours truly
>   J. M. W. Turner[27]

So what was apparently his last letter was about money.

He was well – even lovingly – cared for at the end. Mr Bartlett dropped in several times a day to see 'Mr Booth'. Dr David Price came up from Margate to be with him. Accounts vary slightly about his final days. Roberts heard from Harpur that Turner was 'speechless two days at the end'.[28] Frith and several others, probably from hearsay, have him talking on his last day alive. Mrs Booth said later that two days before the end, 'he suddenly looked steadily and said he saw Lady Eastlake' – the very bright woman he had always admired.[29] The December weather at the time was dull and cloudy, and Archer was told by Mrs Booth that Turner often said, restlessly, 'I should like to see the sun again.'[30] Ruskin seems to have been responsible for turning this into the magniloquent: '"The Sun is God," said Turner, a few weeks before he died, with the setting rays of it on his face.'[31] (Ruskin was not there.) Archer learnt from Mrs Booth that not long before Turner died 'he was found prostrate on the floor, having tried to creep to the window, but in his feeble state had fallen in the attempt'. His bedroom window faced the river.[32]

Finally, Dr Price was with him and told him that his life was ebbing; he should prepare for the worst. Turner said: 'So I am to become a nonentity then?'

Price, evidently not a man for long words, said he was not sure what Turner meant by this, but yes, his days were numbered. Turner said: 'Go downstairs and have a glass of sherry.'

Perhaps he wanted Price to have some Dutch courage to help him through this ordeal. Perhaps he thought some brown sherry might improve the doctor's diagnosis. In any event, the suggestion about sherry seems to have formed his last recorded words.[33]

The accounts concur that on the morning of 19 December, the clouds parted slightly and the sun broke through, filling his room with brilliant light.[34] It was ten o'clock when he breathed his last, 'without a groan'.[35] The vortex had ceased to whirl. All was calm; the roar of the world had ended; and all his contradictions were resolved in silence.

Next day Mr Bartlett informed the Parish Registrar of St Luke's, Chelsea, of Turner's death. The entry in the parish book of deaths gave his age as eighty-one – wrong if he was born in 1775 – and his rank or profession as 'Artist. Royal Academician'. The cause of death was said to be 'Natural Decay'.[36] Henry Harpur told Turner's executors. Philip Hardwick wrote to Charles Stokes, 'I thought you should be informed that we have lost him.'[37] The landlord of the King's Arms, the pub next to Cremorne Wharf, now learnt the identity of Mr Booth. The undertaker's men came in for a drink after their labours. The stairs of 6 Davis Place were too narrow for them to be able to get a coffin up to the body, and they had had to carry the body down to the coffin – a satin-lined model, fit for a lord, they said. Then the neighbours came into the pub after the hearse had left, and talked of how it had gone to Queen Anne Street. Mr Booth was Turner, the great painter.

There, arrangements were made for a death mask to be cast. Thomas Woolner, a twenty-six-year-old sculptor who admired Turner greatly, made the mask: Turner's eyes closed, his lips sunken in because of his missing teeth, his beak of a nose. Turner's body in its open coffin was placed in his gallery. His colleagues and acquaintances came to pay their respects. George Jones paid his tribute by sketching the scene and painting an oil: friends around the coffin; the crowded pictures seeming to lean from the walls in a sort of blessing.

The funeral took place on Monday, 30 December. More people wanted to attend than the executors had provided carriages for. Richard Redgrave – who had had Turner's help on varnishing days, had been elected a full Academician in February 1851 and was now one of the mourners – thought it 'curious that he, who had seemed all his life to despise appearances, whose dress and personal arrangements were of the most homely kind, should desire to leave the world and to be carried to his last rest with so much pomp! The whole affair, however, was strongly characteristic of the man.'[38]

The undertaker had invited the mourners to arrive at Queen Anne Street at 9 a.m. Redgrave rose and shaved by candlelight, had a quick cup of coffee and, unable to find a cab, set off on foot across the park from his house in Hyde Park Gate, Kensington, hoping he was going to get breakfast at Turner's house. He and the other mourners were shown into the gallery – as dusty and dirty as ever, he noted, with the plaster broken and the pictures dropping from their canvases, the gold on the frames gone and bare wood showing. *The Bay of Baiae* was bulging at the bottom; Redgrave and Maclise saw that this was caused by fallen plaster, piled up between the stretcher and the canvas. The funeral arrangements had been made by Henry Harpur, the chief mourner, who wore a crepe hatband. George Jones, Philip Hardwick, Hugh Munro, Thomas Griffith, Charles Eastlake, Clarkson Stanfield, David Roberts and Charles Leslie were there, along with many other Academicians: among them Chalon, Baily, Mulready, Pickersgill, Westmacott and Creswick. Godfrey Windus and William Kingsley, two of his patrons, were on hand. Mr Bartlett and Dr Price had come, as had his business advisers Stokes and Marsh. Young Daniel John Pound was there, though not, it seems, his mother; she still honoured his secretiveness.[39] Absentees included Charles Turner, who wrote in his diary 'I did not go' but gave no reason,[40] and John Ruskin, who was abroad. Roberts recognized the undertaker as the same man who had buried the impoverished Scots painter Patrick Nasmyth nineteen years before in Lambeth, an undertaker he hadn't seen since.

The mourners chatted quietly about the departed. Roberts conversed with Dr Price about Turner's health. Redgrave and the others talked about his eccentricities, his glorious pictures, his proposed charity for distressed artists, and eventually, their stomachs grumbling, about the early start they had made that morning. Would there be any breakfast here? 'But it seemed as if Turner, who was never known to feast or feed any one in his own house when alive, was determined that no one should brag of having feasted there when he was gone.'[41]

The mourners were called to the small ground-floor parlour where the coffin now reposed. Redgrave noted the silver plaque on it which gave Turner's age, inaccurately, as seventy-nine. At ten they set off. Eleven coaches had been hired, and eight private carriages had come. Hannah Danby was assisted by the undertaker into one of the coaches. Redgrave found himself in one with Edwin Landseer, C. A. Cockerell and Patrick MacDowell (who was to sculpt a statue of Turner for St Paul's). Landseer told some funny stories – they had to sit well back in their seats so that they didn't show faces that would have been deemed improper for mourners – and Redgrave reflected that if Turner had been with them, 'instead of somewhat ahead', he would have enjoyed himself in this company; his eye would have sparkled. The solemn convoy moved slowly through the streets, gaped at by the weekday throngs, threading its way among the carts and cabs and omnibuses. It went via Cavendish Square, Regent Street and Trafalgar Square – past the Royal Academy – and then the Strand, a hundred yards from Maiden Lane, past Somerset House and along Fleet Street and up Ludgate Hill. Thus Turner arrived at the great domed cathedral, where he had wanted to be buried alongside his peers. His worries at the time of Lawrence's funeral – 'Who will do the like for me?' – proved groundless. There Hannah, sobbing and weeping, was helped in.

The native Londoner got the full grand treatment from his city's cathedral. The coffin, carried by pallbearers, was ceremonially received by the clergy. It proceeded up the aisle followed by choristers, vicars choral, vergers, minor canons. The choristers chanted the Dead March from Handel's *Saul*, 'with the full blast of the organ, and the voices of the boys which rose to join it, and the basses coming in with a solemnity of effect which was almost startling' – so Thomas Griffith thought.[42] The noble service for the dead was conducted by the Dean, the Very Reverend Henry Milman, a fellow member of the Athenaeum, who as a boy had witnessed the burial here of Lord Nelson. Milman had apparently heard Chantrey's story about Turner making him promise he would ensure that he was rolled up for burial in his *Carthage*. On hearing of Turner's death and wish to be buried in St Paul's, the Dean said, 'I will not read the service over him if he is wrapped up in that picture.'[43] But Chantrey had predeceased him and had no promise to keep. Dean Milman's clear, melodious voice touched the congregation. Five hundred were on hand, many in tears. One wonders if Evelina was present, or Sarah Danby. The organ boomed again as the coffin was carried down into the crypt, far from the sunlight. The committal service was read as the coffin was deposited in a vault near the tombs of Reynolds,

Lawrence, West, Opie, Barry and Fuseli, and the choristers, now unaccompanied by the organ, 'put out their full force'.

Back at Queen Anne Street – it was now 2 p.m. – the famished mourners reassembled in the gallery and removed their black sashes. Were they about to be ushered in to the funeral feast? Redgrave hoped so.

> But no, nothing came of it; until at last one of the undertaker's men entered with a black bottle of port, and another of sherry, which, with a dozen or two of glasses, he had procured from a neighbouring public-house, together with a sixpenny bag of mixed biscuits from a baker's, and this finished the ceremony. At about three o'clock we were turned out, all but fasting, to reach home as best we could ... I came home to a sick headache and a sad evening, and this was the last of him whose works will long enchant mankind.[44]

The executors stayed on for a while to hear Mr Harpur read the will.

In 1807, aged thirty-two, Turner had copied in his 'Spithead' sketchbook these lines from some verses addressed to Time:

> For thou hast made me gaily tough
> Inured me to each day thats rough
> In hopes of calm tomorrow
> When Old Mower of us all
> Beneath thy sweeping Sythe I fall
> Some few dear friends will sorrow
> Then though my idle prose or rhime
> Should half an hour outlive me time
> Pray bid the Stone ingravers
> Where'er my bones find church-yard rooms
> Simply to chisel on my tomb
> Thank Time for all his favours.[45]

22: Turner's Gift

'It is a very stupid will.' That was Elizabeth Eastlake's opinion and apparently that of the people she talked to at the Academy dinner on the first night of the New Year.[1] A good deal of legal wisdom later concluded that Turner's intentions had been evident enough in his will, stupid or not, and could have been given effect to with strong enough backing from those in whose hands he left his estate; but the volition of the executors he had chosen turned out to be shaky. Although they turned up for frequent meetings at 47 Queen Anne Street, their attention to the task was not rigorous. Opposition soon appeared, and, though one might think it would have caused them to gird their loins, it failed to elicit much determination. The result was serious change and compromise. True, Turner had not – in his thriftiness – allowed them much in the way of expenses for their labours: just under twenty pounds each. The frail or uncertain dropped out. Griffith resigned apparently because of a conflict of interest with his art dealing. Ruskin did not get on very well with Charles Turner, whom he called 'the old lying rascal' in a letter to his father of 17 February 1852,[2] and he was fearful of becoming enmeshed in legal and financial hassle. Samuel Rogers was eighty-nine, 'utterly white in hair, skin and eyes', said Lady Eastlake,[3] and he also dropped out. This left Henry Harpur, who had retired as a solicitor in 1849, and the Academy treasurer Philip Hardwick, to handle money matters; and Hugh Munro, Charles Turner, George Jones and the Reverend Henry Scott Trimmer to organize the fate of the pictures and drawings. It would have helped if Turner had earlier sat down with his executors and had several long conversations with them to clarify his purposes; but he does not seem to have done this. The executors gave the impression that they had been landed in a muddle and were trying to make the best of a bad job. One major problem arose from the failure of Turner and his legal advisers,

Cobb and Harpur, to ensure that the three-quarters of an acre of land at Twickenham, on which the almshouses for distressed artists – 'Turner's Gift' – were to be built, was transferred to the trustees of the charity at some time between July 1844 and December 1850, at least a year before his death. This transfer did not take place.

Turner died wealthy, though inevitable mystery shrouds some of the particulars. For a start there were over 100 'finished' paintings, over 200 unfinished paintings, and more than 19,000 sketches, drawings and watercolours. There was his property: little bits of land in Twickenham, Barking and Great Missenden; the run-down Ship and Bladebone in Wapping, although it was soon to be demolished; and his leasehold houses in Harley Street and Queen Anne Street, valued for legacy duty for a total of £900. There was 'cash in the house' amounting to £605 – a great deal to have lying around, but burglars wouldn't have thought 47 Queen Anne Street a promising target. There were his savings in Government Funds. Charles Eastlake told Samuel Rogers that Turner 'had not more than £80,000 in the Funds',[4] though the actual amount, in Consols and Three Per Cent stocks seems to have been just under £70,000. Charles Turner wrote in his diary for 11 September 1852 that Turner's will was proved for £140,000, not including the pictures, drawings and so on, but in fact the executors declared to the probate court 'that the whole of the goods chattels and credits of the Deceased do not amount or value to [more than] the sum of One hundred and forty thousand pounds'.[5] This 'whole' would seem to incorporate his art work – and that included about £5000 worth of engravings and plates. One hundred and forty thousand pounds then was worth, at a rough estimate, about five-and-a-half million today.

It was enough to excite many of his relatives. His first cousins may have been chatting, hopefully, for several years. Now, as news circulated of his death, the first cousins were pestered by second cousins, asking why they shouldn't receive some of the benefits. Jabez Tepper, son of Turner's South Molton, Devon, cousin Mary Turner Tepper (1770–1855) and providentially (for her and the other next-of-kin) a London solicitor, fired an opening shot five days after Turner's death. He wrote a letter to the *Times*, which had announced that Turner was not known to have had any relatives, that 'Mr Turner had five first cousins at his decease; one of them is my mother.'[6] When it became evident that Turner's will and codicils gave these cousins absolutely nothing, Mr Tepper went into action. Hannah Danby and Sophia Booth were made parties to the cousins' case.

The group of claimants represented by Tepper first of all tried to stop probate being granted to the executors on the ground that Turner had been of unsound mind and incapable of making a valid will. They failed in this. Then, when the executors asked the Court of Chancery to let them administer the estate, the next of kin asserted that the will could not be 'construed'; and – their second line of attack – that, even if it could be, the Mortmain Statutes made void its chief provision for the decayed artists' charity, 'Turner's Gift'. It was nearly four years later, on 19 March 1856, that the Court gave its approval to a settlement that the executors and the claimant group had finally reached. Harpur and Tepper had been talking and arguing with each other. As members of the legal profession they knew that a case of *Jarndyce* v. *Jarndyce* length could benefit only lawyers, and presumably the next of kin and other executors had been putting pressure on them to find a solution that did not exhaust Turner's wealth. At this point the claimants no longer included Hannah Danby, for she had died in December 1853, but did include *her* heirs, the three surviving daughters of John and Sarah Danby. The settlement resulted in the abandonment of 'Turner's Gift', his primary dream. George Jones was upset, though he evidently gave his agreement as executor. It was the most inequitable act he had ever heard of, 'considering that no human being doubts Turner's intentions declared in his will'.[7] The relatives got the money, the property, the engravings and any works of art not by Turner. Some uncontroversial bequests had already been ordered by the Court, including the legacies to Clara Wheeler and her sisters, and by the March 1856 agreement the annuities to Hannah Danby and Mrs Booth were ordered to be paid; that owed to Hannah before her death was divided between Marcella, Caroline and Theresa Danby. Their half-sister and Turner's daughter Evelina Dupuis was to receive an annuity of £100. This was a decision made despite the fact that in 1848 Turner had revoked any bequest to her in his third codicil; the decision was an act of generosity for which the disputing parties and Court of Chancery could take more credit than he.

The legal arrangement honoured his bequests to the Artists General Benevolent Institution, the Foundling Hospital and the London Orphan Fund. The Royal Academy did particularly well, since instead of the £1000 he had bequeathed it for its pension fund it received £20,000; some of this was set aside for the relief of distressed artists, some eventually for the Academy schools. His legacy of £1000 for erecting a monument to himself in St Paul's Cathedral was declared 'good and valid'.

The nation also came out ahead. Once again, there was a fudge about fulfilling his intentions in regard to his art – but, here too, it would be possible to say that those intentions had varied from time to time, now clear, now hazy, now requesting this, now that. His executors in this respect seem to have done their best, although the institutions they had to deal with were often dilatory. The National Gallery in the first instance acted promptly about the two paintings he had wanted to hang alongside Claude: *Dido building Carthage* and *Sun rising through Vapour* were whisked off to Trafalgar Square eleven months into the year after his death that he had specified as a time limit, and this precluded them going elsewhere. According to Thomas Uwins, the Keeper (from 1848 to 1855), the *Carthage* was particularly dirty and neglected, with its paint flaking off in large pieces. Uwins was in charge of its removal from Queen Anne Street, along with *Sun rising through Vapour*, and had it dusted down before it was put in the movers' van. He said, 'The pavement in front of the door looked afterwards almost as if a chimney had been swept upon it.'[8]

Turner had changed his mind several times about the nature and location of a Turner gallery to preserve a collection of his pictures after his death, but in the codicils of 1848 he gave his 'finished pictures' to the Trustees of the National Gallery – provided that a room or rooms called Turner's Gallery was provided. Until then the pictures were to stay at Queen Anne Street. Moreover, if the National Gallery failed to accept the pictures or house them properly, they were to remain at Queen Anne Street as long as the lease of his house could be renewed; if it could not be, the pictures were to be sold. As it happened, the oil paintings, watercolours, drawings and sketchbooks were sent – apparently for reasons of 'safety' – to some empty rooms at the National Gallery before the Chancery settlement was reached.

In 1856 and 1857 Ruskin and two assistants sorted the sketchbooks and drawings that were in seven tin boxes in one of the basement rooms. Ruskin used such words as rot, damp, dust, soot, mildew and mouse-eaten to describe their condition.[9] It was during this period of sorting sketches that, by the account of one of his helpers, W. M. Rossetti, Ruskin found some 'which from the nature of their subjects it seemed undesirable to preserve'.[10] According to Frank Harris, Ruskin some years later determined that these 'shameful' works were the product of Turner's weekends in Wapping living with 'sailors' women'. For some weeks Ruskin hesitated over what to do, 'till suddenly it flashed on me that perhaps I had been selected as the one man capable of coming in this matter to a great decision'.[11] Ruskin decided to destroy these offending items. Several years later, in 1862, Ruskin was worried about having an accident during a Continental tour, and before going wrote to Ralph Wornum, Keeper of the National Gallery from 1855 to his death in 1877, to take the credit or blame for the act of destruction: 'As the authorities have not thought proper to register the reserved parcel of Turner's sketchbooks, and have given no directions about them, and as the grossly obscene drawings contained in them could not be lawfully in any one's possession, I am satisfied that you had no other course than to burn them, both for the sake of Turner's reputation, (they having been assuredly drawn under a certain condition of insanity) and for your own peace. And I am glad to be able to bear witness to their destruction; and I hereby declare that the parcel of them was undone by me, and all the obscene drawings it contained burnt in my presence in the month of December, 1858.'[12] Despite this cull, Ruskin remained disturbed by items he continued to turn up. In his diary for 5 June 1867, he wrote: 'At National Gallery; worked over Turners – felt element of vice in them.'[13] In 1860, in the last volume of *Modern Painters*, he had confessed about his old hero: 'I find myself more and more helpless to explain his errors and his sins.'[14]

Much of Turner's work remained unsorted. Some 185 of the 285 oils in the Bequest, still uncatalogued and unnumbered, had perhaps bewildered their new guardians; they were found in the cellars of the National Gallery at the start of the Second World War, thick with dust, and were thought by Kenneth Clark at first sight to be 'old tarpaulins'[15] Turner might have felt that the Queen Anne Street tradition was being maintained. His works were being kept together *and* neglected.

Nevertheless, it was a benefaction. The British nation got the work from the old Aladdin's Cave, finished and unfinished oils, watercolours and drawings – a Bequest that made up for the failure to implement what Jones called his 'great object',[16] the Gift. But the gift horse had stabling problems. Because of lack of room at the National Gallery, some of the paintings and watercolours were shown first at Marlborough House, next to St James's Palace at the west end of Pall Mall.[17] There some people became acquainted with Turner for the first time. The American consul in Liverpool, Nathaniel Hawthorne, felt the Turners were 'tantalizing' and 'full of imaginative beauty', but found himself in a world that made him grope around: 'There was a mist over it; or it was like a tract of beautiful dream-land, seen dimly through sleep …'[18] The selected Turners then moved to the South Kensington Museum for a time before coming back to the National Gallery. In October 1861, the West Room, the Gallery's largest, was crammed with eighty-two paintings and renamed Turner's Gallery in a last-minute attempt to meet Turner's ten-year deadline for their acceptance.[19] In the following years the pressure was relieved a little by lending some to provincial museums. From 1905 many were housed in the new Tate Gallery of British Art at Millbank, and since 1987 in the Tate's Clore wing, specially built for the Turner collection – a tardy, welcome, but not entirely satisfactory fulfilment of his wishes. The pictures of his Bequest are not, as he had wanted, all together, and not all can be seen at any one time. But they are better looked after than they have ever been.[20]

In the last two years of Hannah's life, 47 Queen Anne Street slowly shed its air of gloom. The house was busy with executors' meetings. John James Ruskin, John's father, brought gifts of food – newly laid eggs, for example – to the housekeeper-custodian. After a visit in February 1852 he wrote to his son: 'Nothing since Pompeii so impressed me as the interior of Turner's house – some of the dust of 40 years had been cleared away and windows opened to let in the light.'[21] Henry Syer Trimmer called, presumably accompanying his father the Reverend Trimmer, an executor, and made a melancholy tour of inspection. His reflections were mundane but some of the things he remarked were of interest. Let in by Hannah, he found all silent: 'The master mind was gone; the mainspring had snapped.' The younger Trimmer looked around the house, at the sombre-coloured walls, the deserted studio, the jars of colours, brushes and travelling paint-box, the books (Young's *Night Thoughts*, Isaak Walton and Horace), and the pictures, many of which did not appeal to him. In the studio, on a side table, he saw a small wooden box in which, covered by a glass pane, lay the death mask:

> Dear old Turner! … He reminded me strongly of his old father, whom long years before I had seen trudging to Brentford market from Sandicomb Lodge, to lay in his weekly supplies. Alas for humanity! This was the man whom in my childhood I had attended with my father, and been driven by on the banks of the Thames; whom I had seen sketching with such glee on the river's banks, as I gathered wild flowers in my earliest years; who had stuffed my pockets with sweetmeats, had loaded me with fish, and made me feel as happy as a prince.[22]

After Hannah's death, the executors had an inventory drawn up of Turner's possessions in the house; this was done in November 1854 by an appraiser, Mr Elgood from nearby Wimpole Street; and it made sad reading. The ship models, three small telescopes and sea chest; the rugs, iron stoves and dressing tables; the palettes, drawing boards and sketchbooks, and – not your usual studio necessity – a gun in its case, maybe a shotgun for the Farnley moors or a souvenir of his days in brigand-infested Italy. In the 'West Room' on the second floor were six pairs of trousers, two waistcoats and three 'Shirts Cravat'. (Presumably he had other clothes and sets of underclothes at Chelsea.) His library contained much Scott, Byron and Milton, maps of Scotland and *Antiquities of Italy*, and many volumes of his own *Annual Tours*. There was a stuffed bird and, in the back kitchen, six beer barrels. Among the 'Plate', little silver cutlery to speak of, but the appraiser for some reason noted a 'pair of Sugar Tongs (broken)'.[23] In a separate schedule of his estate, mention is made of engraving plates, sundry proofs and 'A Quantity of Old Pictures all in very bad condition'.[24] Roughly twenty-five paintings were actually hanging in the Queen Anne Street gallery at his death, among them such wonders as *London from Greenwich*, *Fishing upon the Blythe-Sand*, *Frosty Morning*, the two *Carthages*, *Bay of Baiae* and *Snow Storm – Steam-Boat off a Harbour's Mouth*. The *Temeraire* and *Polyphemus* must have been in the dining room or amid the paintings stacked against the gallery walls. Going through Turner's accounts, the executors discovered (so George Jones reported) 'that the rents for houses in Harley Street had not been paid during some years; in application to the lawyer, the answer was that "Mr Turner would not allow him to distrain."'[25]

Turner occasioned some postmortem scurrying around by memento gatherers, bargain hunters and recorders of recent history. The teapot and sherry bottle at 6 Davis Place were kept busy as John Archer, John Pye, John Ruskin and David Roberts called on Mrs Booth. She was in deep mourning when Roberts paid a visit; the cottage was 'clean to a nicety, and the walls covered with pictures, principally Engravings from his works'. This was when she told Roberts that Turner had never given her money – not a farthing – towards their common living expenses or the cost of the cottage. She assured Roberts that the only money she had had from him in eighteen years was 'three half crowns she found in his pocket after death, black, She says with being so long in his pocket & which She keeps as a souvenir'.[26] In October 1851 she had given Turner £59 19s 9d to invest for her in Government Funds; she never heard any more about it. But she kept the three half-crowns 'together with numerous *scraps of his poetry* – not the fallacys of hope (*for I put the question*) but Verses in honour of herself & her personal charms ... What simpletons the greatest become when a woman's in the case.'[27]

Sophia Booth also told Roberts that she was going to claim expenses from the executors for six years' board and washing – a claim that Roberts thought well founded. (The executors apparently allowed her only five years.) As well as the poems in her honour, she had a number of coastal pictures and drawings done, it seems, at her Margate house, that Turner had given her. (Her son Daniel Pound organized a sale at Christie's in March 1865 where some of these were sold, bringing nearly £4000.) She kept Turner's fishing rod until 1864, when she gave it to the art dealer William Vokins, who greatly admired Turner. She presented a late watercolour study of a sunset to Bartlett, the doctor. On the back of its mount he had inscribed 'Given to me by Mrs Booth August 1855 W. Bartlett M.P.S. 1 Bretton Terrace, Chelsea who attended Mr B [that is, Mr T] during the last six months of his existence.'[28] Her tending of the flame was not impeccable. Bartlett wrote to Ruskin in 1857: 'I was grieved after [Turner's] death to find Mrs Booth burning a clothes' basket full of letters from him received, many of them poetical effusions.'[29]

Charles Turner called at Chelsea twice, on 23 March and 6 September 1852. Mrs Booth struck him as ill-educated, 'exactly like a Fat Cook', but she may have disappointed him in his hunt for Turner bargains.[30] However, two years later he noted with self-satisfaction that she called on him and offered him 'a small case with 4 sketches by Mr. J. W. M. Turner *which I refused*'.[31] John Pye also visited Mrs Booth that 23 March 1852, got on well with her and liked the little house, with its flowers, creepers and bird singing in its cage. J. W. Archer went to Chelsea hoping to draw the room in which Turner died. Mrs Booth would not let him do this, but she did allow him to draw the exterior of the house, and then – telling him that Turner used to call her a handmaid of Art – gave him a sandwich and some sherry. Ruskin by now had at last made her acquaintance, and became a long-term friend. She gave him one of Turner's last sketchbooks, a travelling colour box and a small watercolour palette. Ruskin wrote to her on her birthday, 9 January 1862 (Thornbury's biography, the first large-scale attempt to deal with Turner's life, had just been published):

> I caught cold the first thing on coming home, or I should have come to see you today. I will come some day next week early if I hear you can receive me; and indeed I wish you many happy returns still of the day; at least as happy as they can be. I have been sad and very sad myself about many things. Not least about the wretched 'Life', which I hope you have cast aside with contempt and carelessness. A better one will be done some day; be assured of that; but never I fear by me ...[32]

Ruskin had been of some help to Thornbury but now wished he hadn't. It was clearly embarrassing and aggravating for him to think of Mrs Booth reading Thornbury's comment that Turner 'died unmarried, with no hands but those of mercenary love to close his eyes and smooth his dying pillow'.[33] When George Jones came on this he underlined 'mercenary love' and wrote in the margin: 'Mercenary love burnt all his letters that they should not be criticised by the public – was that mercenary?'[34] Ruskin may have felt that he had been responsible for steering Thornbury into nooks and crannies that he now wished had been avoided. According to Thornbury, Ruskin had admonished him thus:

Fix at the beginning the following main characteristics of Turner in
your mind, as the keys to the secret of all he said and did: –

> *Uprightness.*
> *Generosity.*
> *Tenderness* of heart (extreme)
> *Sensuality.*
> *Obstinacy.* (extreme)
> *Irritability.*
> *Infidelity.*

And be sure he knew his own power, and felt himself utterly alone
in the world from its not being understood. Don't try to mask the
dark side ...[35]

In 1863, also in January, Ruskin wrote to Mrs Booth from
Mornex, in the Haute Savoie: 'Every year that passes brings with it
to me a deeper sense of the loss of my dear and honoured friend, and
therefore a deeper sense of gratitude to the only person who cared
for him and helped him during his life.'[36]

Mrs Booth continued to live at 6 Davis Place until her twenty-
one-year lease ran out in 1867. Then, perhaps helped by the
profits from the Christie's sale, she moved to Haddenham Hall,
Haddenham, on the Oxfordshire–Buckinghamshire border, where
she lived another eleven years. She died on 25 June 1878, aged eighty,
and was buried close to her second husband's grave in St John's
churchyard, Margate. Since St Paul's was not on offer, at the last she
had to be with the real Mr Booth.

The enterprising Charles Turner also tracked down Sarah Danby.
Perhaps he had got the information about where she was living from
Hannah. He called on Sarah on Saturday, 9 September 1854, at 29
William Street, off the Hampstead Road in St Pancras, where she
had been living for over twenty years with her unmarried daughter
Marcella, a music teacher, and still collecting her thirteen shillings
a week pension from the Royal Society of Musicians. In December
1852 she had to write to the Society to say that there was no truth in
a report that Mr Turner had left her an annuity or legacy. According
to what he recorded in his diary, Charles Turner softened up the
now very elderly lady (she was about eighty-eight) by asking her
about JMWT. Could she tell him where he was born? Hand Court,
Maiden Lane, she said – the Maiden Lane part of her answer
correct; Turner had been living at Hand Court when she first met

him. He then got her to sell him seventeen drawings and two small oil sketches 'of trees' for three guineas.[37] He went back to William Street on 13 November and bought two further drawings by Turner that she told him she had had for nearly fifty years. This time he gave her a sovereign for both. 'She was delighted,' he noted. And a little over two weeks later he took her a brace of partridge 'for her civility'.[38] Three years after this he sold the seventeen 'small drawings' at Christie's for ten guineas each – a total of £177 17s. Charles Turner may have felt that he was finally getting his own back on JMWT for the poor rates of pay he had received for engraving *Liber* plates. Sarah Danby lived nearly ten years after the death of her former lover. She died, aged about ninety-five, on 16 February 1861 at 34 George Street, off Euston Square, where she had moved with Marcella. Sarah was buried in the Catholic cemetery at Kensal Green in a common grave; her estate was less than £200.

Hannah died at Queen Anne Street on 11 December 1853, aged sixty-seven. She was described in the death certificate as 'Housekeeper to a gentleman'. ('My Damsel' was the way Turner had once referred to her, in a letter to William Wethered, a Norfolk collector who had sent a turkey, no doubt appreciated by Hannah.) The cause of death was given as '*Eczema exedens* for many years'. The eldest Trimmer son told Thornbury, 'She had some fearful cancerous malady which obliged her to conceal her face, which did not add to the charms of his [T's] domicile.'[39] Hannah may not have kept a spotless house but her loyalty to her employer was exemplary. She left £600, with £50 to Evelina and a painting of Turner as a youth, that he had given her, to John Ruskin.

And thus to Evelina. In 1853 she was living with her husband Joseph Dupuis in Covent Garden, at 2 Tavistock Street, a few yards from the eastern end of Maiden Lane. Four days after Hannah's death, Dupuis, the ex-consular official, wrote to the solicitor Jabez Tepper. The office of custodian of Turner's Gallery at Queen Anne Street was now vacant. Dupuis (severely in debt, it seems) put himself forward for that job. He wrote:

> I am the husband of the Evelina Danby mentioned in Mr. Turner's Will. My wife is a natural daughter of Mr. Turner. She was for

several years recognised as his daughter, and was, till the age of womanhood, brought up in the expectation of always enjoying a respectable function in Society, and was married to me when I was about leaving England to fill a consular situation abroad with Mr. Turner's consent and approbation. We have been married now upwards of thirty-six years and have brought up a family of four children, of whom two are daughters.

Dupuis goes on to mention their 'state of absolute want' and asks Tepper's help to save them 'from absolute destitution'.[40]

Dupuis did not get the job; no one did. The £50 Hannah had left Evelina was given specifically *not* to be used to pay her husband's debts. A further request for Tepper's help came from Mr Hutton, at the Rectory, Covent Garden, on 20 November 1856, and referred to the very needy circumstances of the Dupuis family 'at present located in this Parish'. Hutton asked for a small annuity out of Turner's property to be made over to them.[41] As we have seen, the Chancery settlement indeed gave Evelina such an annuity, recognizing that she was Turner's child, despite his revocation of a bequest to her in the first codicil of 1832. But this annuity of £100, not quite £2 a week, paid from December 1856 onwards, did not enable Mr and Mrs Dupuis to live well. At least for a time it went to pay off a loan of £100 plus interest that they owed a solicitor. Evelina wrote to Tepper on 14 November 1865, from 18 Great Ormond Street. She mentioned their 'narrowed circumstances', the annuity being 'encumbered', and 'the past, so fraught with adverse destiny'. She asked Tepper for his help to 'alleviate the sorrows which oppress the last lineal descendant of the race of Turner, the surviving daughter of an artist of such repute. Thus afflicted, E. Dupuis.'[42]

Joseph Dupuis – by then living with his wife south of the river, in Kennington Lane, Lambeth, not far from the Henry Harpurs – died on St Valentine's Day, 1874. He was evidently a difficult man, but for Evelina that was nothing new; as she had pointed out, she had been burdened with adverse destiny. The high point of Joseph's career seems to have been the publication in 1824 of his *Journal of a Residence in Ashantee*, which was reviewed in many of the weighty periodicals. Evelina died six months after her husband, still in Lambeth. She was seventy-three and had had a heart attack. Her two surviving sons must have given her pleasure. Joseph and Hanmer served long careers in the Consular Service, more successfully than their father.

One daughter, Rosalie, never married, taught music. Of the other daughter, another Evelina, little is known. These were Turner's four grandchildren.

Turner's death made a vacancy in the ranks of the Academicians. William Frith was elected to fill it. The commission to sculpt Turner's monument, for which he had left £1000, was given to Patrick MacDowell RA; the full-length statue was set on a pedestal on the south side of St Paul's, below the dome, and showed Turner in middle age, his head turned in profile, with the bold nose and sideburns, and in his right hand what looks like a compass for scribing circles. He had not asked for a statue, simply a monument, but the sum he had left ensured that his fame would be solidly commemorated. Along with his ambition to be a great artist, he had had an almost archaic hunger to be recognized as such; he wanted his name remembered, as in 'Turner's Gift'. Of course, if he had thought about all the possible ramifications, and considered that a marble portrait of himself might ensue, he might have stipulated that the monument should not take the form of a statue or bust.

His 'afterlife' has had (at least) one bizarre episode. A few years on, William Stillman, back in the USA, became interested in spiritualism. Although he believed most professional mediums were fakes, he thought a few were not. Stillman met a fourteen-year-old New York girl, 'Miss A', the daughter of an ironworks foreman, who heard 'rappings', went into trances, made involuntary gestures and wrote messages in handwriting that resembled that of dead people – or so relatives of the deceased were convinced. On these occasions her eyes were closed or bandaged. Questions to her were not spoken aloud but were simply framed in the questioner's head. In one session with Miss A, Stillman silently put the question to her, or through her, whether his dead cousin Harvey had encountered someone called Turner, who had died not long before. 'The reply was "Yes," and I then asked what he was doing, the reply being a pantomime of painting.' Shortly after this Miss A said 'I don't like it,' and then

> sat up in her chair with a most extraordinary personation of the old
> painter in manner, in the look out from under the brow and the

pose of the head. It was as if the ghost of Turner, as I had seen him at Griffith's, sat in the chair, and it made my flesh creep to the very tips of my fingers, as if a spirit sat before me. Miss A. exclaimed, 'This influence has taken complete possession of me, as none of the others did. I am obliged to do what it wants me to.'

I asked if Turner would write his name for me, to which she replied by a sharp, decided negative sign. I then asked if he would give me some advice about my painting ... This proposition was met by the same decided negative, accompanied by the fixed and sardonic stare which the girl had put on at the coming of the new influence.

Presently Miss A said she had to get up. She crossed the room 'with the feeble step of an old man'. She took down from a wall a coloured French lithograph and placed it before Stillman. She went through the motions of stretching a piece of paper on a drawing board, sharpening a pencil and tracing the outlines of the lithograph. Then, still in pantomime, she chose a brush and made some broad strokes, washing in the drawing. The next step was with brush and handkerchief to rub out the lights. Stillman mentally questioned whether Turner worked in this manner and Miss A gave an affirmative sign. He wondered about Turner's *Llanthony Abbey*, and its central passage of sunlight and shadow: was it done that way? Again, this time emphatically, she gave an affirmative sign. Stillman left convinced he had been humbugged, although he was sure the girl knew nothing of drawing or Turner.

Nearly two months later, again in England, he went to see Ruskin and told him the story. 'He declared the contrariness manifested by the medium to be entirely characteristic of Turner and had the drawing in question down for examination. We scrutinised it closely, and both recognised beyond dispute that the drawing had been executed in the way that Miss A. indicated. Ruskin advised me to send an account of the affair to the *Cornhill*, which I did; but it was rejected ... and I can easily imagine Thackeray putting it into the basket in a rage.'[43] Either Turner was functioning as ever on the astral plane, or his fame had spread to circles in New York well beyond James Lenox, and the empathetic daughter of the iron-works foreman had somehow cottoned on to who Stillman's hero was.

The verger of St Mary's, Battersea, shows visitors the chair under the west window where the artist from Chelsea is said to have sat and drawn. In the Yorkshire Dales, a tourist brochure notes picturesque spots where he sketched the hillsides and valleys. Bits of the *Temeraire* were saved: her timbers provided material for an altar table, altar rails and two sanctuary chairs for a Rotherhithe church. An old people's home in Margate has been named after Turner, as has an annual prize given to a modern British artist. Turner's work generally fetches large prices but is occasionally 'bought in' (too bewildering, too weird ...) and once in a while – an accolade – is stolen. His houses have had varying fates: 47 Queen Anne Street was demolished in the late nineteenth century, as were the two houses – 21 and 26 – in which he had lived in Maiden Lane. The site of 21 Maiden Lane has recently been occupied by an American-style 'diner', sheathed in cream-and-blue aluminium, called 'Fat Boys', but is now being redeveloped. (No plaque for Turner is apparent.) Sandycombe Lodge survives, well cared for, with some additions to its wings, and so does 6 Davis Place, incorporated with two of its neighbours in a large house, 118–119 Cheyne Walk, that Mrs Eve Fleming, a First World War widow, created in the 1920s. There she brought up her four sons, two of whom – Peter and Ian – became writers. She called it 'Turner's House'. Turner might have enjoyed knowing that his Carthaginian harbourscapes had an impact in the 1890s at the Chicago World's Fair, where the critic Montgomery Schuyler saw Turner's 'dreams of classic architecture' made real. The designers of the temporary exposition buildings had provided, Schuyler thought, 'a stage setting ... They have realized in plaster that gives us the illusion of monumental masonry a painter's dream of Roman architecture. In Turner's fantasias we have its prototype much more nearly than in any actual erection that has ever been seen in the world before. It is the province and privilege of the painter to see visions ...'[44]

At the last, we accept the extravagance of his contradictions; the determination which did not resolve those contradictions but defined him as a person; the discontent that kept driving him to attempt the impossible and make his dreams real; the 'dark side' but also that which was sun-lit.

Appendix
47 Queen Ann (or Anne) Street

Although Turner (and subsequently many writers) refer to it as number 47, his property seems to have been given other numbers by various authorities. For a while in the early nineteenth century, it was considered part of 44 Queen Anne Street and later was one of several properties included in number 47. Turner's first use of '47' occurs in a note to T. J. Pettigrew, watermarked 1824. Turner mostly favoured the then common spelling 'Ann' but sometimes used 'Anne', which is the way the Queen herself spelt it, and the way it is spelt now.

In Richard Horwood's map of the 1790s, the site where he built his Queen Anne Street house and gallery is shown as part of a gap between 44 Queen Ann Street and 64 Harley Street.

In the St Marylebone parish rate books for 1811–12, Wimpole Ward, 44 Queen Ann Street is an address shared by five different tenants and/or ratepayers: the Earl of Effington, rent £260; William Brown, £14; Robert Bennett, £45; John Jones, £20; and Joseph William Turner, Esq., £20. Turner's section of the property seems to have been a mews building which had a door giving access to his first gallery running back over the garden behind his house at 64 Harley Street; '47 Queen Anne Street' is in quite different hands at this date.

In Peter Potter's map of 1832, Turner's Queen Anne Street property is shown without a number between 47 Queen Ann Street and 64 Harley Street, facing north, near the south-west corner of Queen Anne and Harley Street.

In the 1841 census, Hannah Danby is listed as the only inhabitant present on the night preceding 6 June at one entry for 47 Queen Anne Street. In another entry, on a different page, for presumably another house named 47 Queen Anne Street, many people in another household are listed.

In the 1850 rate books for St Marylebone parish, Turner's property is called '44c Queen Anne Street'.

name of occupier	Josh Mallard William Turner
name of owner	Duke of Portland
description of property	house
gross estimated rental	72
rateable value	65
poor rate	6.10.
rate for repairing, cleaning, and lighting streets	2.16.10

In the 1851 census (30–31 March), the only inhabitant listed at '47a Queen Ann St.' is Hannah Danby, serv. age sixty-four. At '47 Queen Ann St.' are Edward Bullen, married, age fifty, magistrate, his wife Mary Ann, forty-eight, two daughters and nine servants. At '64 Harley St.' are Edward Harran, forty-six, inn-keeper, his wife Sarah, daughter Sarah (age ten), three servants and two lodgers. One wonders what Magistrate and Mrs Bullen thought of their neighbours the artist and his solitary servant. In several legal papers in the Turner family dossier 47 Queen Anne Street is also referred to as 46a. It is described as 'a messuage or tenement, gallery, outbuildings, and other erections on the south side of Queen Ann St. West'. The papers concern 'the residue of a 60 year lease from April 1822 at a yearly rent of £60'.

The house was thirty-five feet wide but had only five windows at the front, presumably to avoid window tax. It was built of the yellow-brown bricks known as London Stock and (unfashionably) was not stucco covered. In 1859, when the street was renumbered, it became number 23 Queen Anne Street. Jabez Tepper, the lawyer for the relatives in the Chancery case, lived in the house some of the time between 1868 and 1871. The house was demolished in 1882.

Notes

Abbreviations	(see Select Bibliography for full details)
AR	C. R. Leslie, *Autobiographical Reflections*
B&J	Martin Butlin and Evelyn Joll, *The Paintings of J. M. W. Turner*
Century	Richard and Samuel Redgrave, *A Century of British Painters*
Dossier	a collection of MS material kept by Turner descendants
Finberg	A. J. Finberg, *The Life of J. M. W. Turner*
Geese	Selby Whittingham, *Of Geese, Mallards and Drakes*
IGI	International Genealogical Index
Letters	John Gage, ed., *Collected Correspondence of J. M. W. Turner*
Lindsay	Jack Lindsay, *J. M. W. Turner: his Life and Work*
Monkhouse	W. Cosmo Monkhouse, *Turner*
Powell	Cecilia Powell, *Turner in the South*
Pye-Roget	John Lewis Roget, ed., *Notes and Memoranda*
TB	Turner Bequest
Th.	Walter Thornbury, *The Life of J. M. W. Turner, R.A.*
TS	*Turner Studies*
TSN	*Turner Society News*
Watts	Alaric Watts, biographical sketch in Leitch Ritchie, *Liber Fluviorum*
Will	Selby Whittingham, *An Historical Account of the Will of J. M. W. Turner, R.A.*
Wilton	Andrew Wilton, *Turner in his Time*

Preface

1 *AR*, i, p.205.
2 Ruskin, *Praeterita*, p.544.
3 Gowing, introduction to Finberg, *Turner's Sketches and Drawings*, p.xxi.
4 Th. 1877, p.286.
5 Letter to Jacques Durand, March 1908, Debussy, *Letters*.
6 Sickert, *A Free House!*, p.200.

1: Mere Beginnings

1 Redding, *Fifty Years' Recollections*, i, p.198.
2 *St Erasmus and Bishop Islip's Chapels*, illus. Wilton, p.9. He also signed a tombstone with his name, and inscribed his date of birth in a watercolour of Petworth Church, 1792–4.
3 *Will*, 2, p.29.
4 St Paul's, Covent Garden, parish registers, Westminster Library.
5 Henry Syer Trimmer, quoted in Th. 1877, p.5.
6 Finberg, p.10; Lindsay, p.12.
7 *The Survey of London*, xxxvi, p.83.
8 George, *London Life*, p.92.
9 Ibid., p.50.
10 Hampden, ed., *An Eighteenth Century Journal*, p.334.
11 George, *London Life*, p.267.
12 Woodforde, *Diary*, p.105.
13 Th. 1877, p.16.
14 St Paul's, Covent Garden, parish register, Westminster Library.
15 Previous biographers have been led astray about the date of Mary Ann's death. After Turner's death, when lawyers were seeking to establish whether he had living siblings, the parish clerk at St Paul's, John Spreck, looked through the registers, missed the 8 August 1783 entry for Mary Ann and found another 'Mary Ann Turner from St Martin in the Fields' who was buried at St Paul's on 20 March 1786 and has since been assumed to be JMWT's sister. St Paul's, Covent Garden, parish register, Westminster Library; Dossier.
16 Th. 1877, p.4.
17 Monkhouse, p.13.
18 *Notes and Queries*, 2nd series, cxxviii (1858), p.475; and 5th series, viii, (1877), p.114.
19 Th. 1877, p.11.
20 Henry Scott Trimmer's son told Thornbury that Turner and his father first met in Hammersmith c. 1807 (Th. 1877, p.116), but Henry Scott Trimmer's knowledge of Turner's doings in Brentford seems to

predate this.

21 Ibid., pp.10, 12.
22 The book was given to Brentford Library by Miss E. Lees in the 1920s and is now in Chiswick Library.
23 Marryat, pp.21–2.
24 Edward Bell, engraver, quoted in Th. 1877, pp.12–13.
25 TB CXXIII.
26 TB CII, f.4v.
27 Feret, *Bygone Thanet*, pp.56–7, says it was another brother. Whittingham, *Geese* III, p.12, says it was more likely a Marshall, uncle or cousin.
28 Bretherton, *Methodism in Margate*, pp.13–15.
29 Watts, p.ix.
30 Ibid., p.x.

2: Up and Coming

1 TB I A and I B.
2 Th. 1877, p.236.
3 Ibid., p.26.
4 Ibid., pp.28–9.
5 Ibid., pp.27–8.
6 Watts, p.xiii.
7 *Century*, p.252.
8 Farington, *Diary*, 20 January 1799.
9 Twenty-six of the thirty-two drawings exhibited by Turner from 1790 to 1796 feature buildings such as abbeys and cathedrals: see C. F. Bell, *A List of the Works Contributed to Public Exhibitions by J. M. W. Turner*, 1901.
10 Gage, *Wonderful Range*, p.24.
11 Th. 1877, p.29.
12 Shanes, *Human Landscape*, p.256.
13 Th. 1877, p.27.
14 Finberg, p.17.
15 Th. 1877, p.2.
16 Hutchison, 'R.A. Schools', *Walpole Society*, xxxviii, pp.123–81.
17 Whitley, *1800–20*, p.262.
18 Whitley, *Artists and Friends*, p.287.
19 TB XXXVIII, f.19.
20 Farington, *Diary*, 22 December 1796; 31 December 1795.
21 Whitley, *1800–20*, p.82.
22 Farington, *Diary*, 15 January 1798.
23 Reynolds, *Discourses*, pp.323–37.

24 Ibid., Rogers' introduction, p.2.
25 Th. 1877, p.37.
26 TB V D.
27 Ruskin, *Modern Painters*, iii, pp.327–8.
28 Monkhouse, p.39.
29 Hamerton, *Turner*, p.25.
30 Th. 1877, p.36.
31 *AR*, i, p.145.
32 Whitley, *Artists and Friends*, p.334.
33 TB II.
34 TB III A.
35 Watts, pp.xlii–xliii.
36 Th. 1877, p.39.
37 Robin Hamlyn, 'An Early Sketchbook by J. M. W. Turner', *Record of the Art Museum*, Princeton University, vol.44, no.2, 1985, p.7.
38 Ruskin, *Works*, xiii, p.473; Finberg, pp.27, 50.
39 Finberg, pp.27, 50, 28.
40 TB XIII H.
41 TB XIX f.35. Turner's 'E.P.B.' may stand for 'E.P.B.', possibly meaning 'Ephesian Base'.
42 TB XXVI p.5 itinerary. 'Mr Landseer' was presumably the engraver John Landseer.
43 TB XX.
44 TB XXVI p.3 itinerary.
45 TB XX, f.35.
46 Lindsay, p.22.
47 Th. 1877, p.8.
48 Finberg, p.19.
49 Farington, *Diary*, 30 December 1794.
50 Ibid., 11 November 1798.
51 Roget, *'Old Water-Colour' Society*, i, p.83.
52 Ziff, *TS*, 6, 1, pp.18–24.
53 Roget, *'Old Water-Colour' Society*, i, p.122, 122n.
54 Finberg, p.39.
55 Ibid., p.40.
56 Gage, *Colour*, p.26.
57 Sickert, *A Free House!*, pp.201–2.
58 Th. 1877, p.38.
59 *Century*, p.155.
60 Th. 1877, p.98. 'Hand Court' now appears as part of his address for these years in the RA catalogues.
61 *Walpole Society*, 1, pp.105–6.

62 TB XXV; written in pencil inside cover.
63 Tate Gallery, 941.
64 *Century*, p.252; Wilton, p.46.
65 TB XX, f.17.
66 TB XXV, f.1.
67 Th. 1877, pp.77–8.
68 Farington, *Diary*, 12 October 1799.
69 TB CXCV, 156. See C. Price, 'Turner as Scene Painter', *TSN*, no.50, pp.7–9 and *TS* 7, 2, pp.2–8.
70 TB IX A.
71 Th. 1877, p.115.
72 *Century*, p.161.
73 Finberg, *Sketches and Drawings*, p.20.
74 TB XXX.
75 Finberg, p.35.
76 TB XXXVII.
77 Finberg, p.35.
78 Th. 1877, pp.41–3.
79 Ruskin, *Dilecta*, in *Praeterita*, pp.539–40.

3: Rising Star

1   Lindsay, p.172.
2   Ibid., p.31.
3   Redding, *Past Celebrities*, p.57.
4   Delacroix, *Journal*, quoted in Lindsay, p.174.
5   *Century*, p.264.
6   Th. 1877, p.39.
7   *AR*, i, p.205.
8   Gowing, *Imagination and Reality*, p.42.
9   TB XLVI, f.120.
10 TB XLIII, ff.3a, 5. See Tate catalogue, *Turner and the Human Figure*.
11 Whitley, *Artists and Friends*, p.211.
12 Farington, *Diary*, 24 October 1798. See TB XXXV, 1797.
13 Finberg, p.41.
14 Timbs, *Anecdote Lives*, p.326; Finberg, p.42.
15 Lord Harewood bought two local landscapes in oil from Turner in 1798. D. Hill, *TS* 5, 1, p.31.
16 Jones, 'Recollections', in Letters, p.4.
17 Monkhouse, pp.44–5.
18 Farington, *Diary*, April–May 1798, quoted in Lindsay, p.36.
19 Finberg, *Sketches and Drawings*, pp.32, 31.
20 Turner's only known comment on the 'Sublime' occurs in an 1809

sketchbook (TB CX), where he quotes the radical writer Tom Paine to the effect that 'the sublime and the ridiculous are often so nearly related that it is difficult to class them separately. One step above the sublime becomes ridiculous and one step above the ridiculous makes the sublime again.'

21 Lindsay, p.44.
22 Th. 1877, pp.234–6.
23 Finberg, p.69. RA Catalogue 1801 (Wells was an exhibitor).
24 Th. 1877, pp.234–6.
25 Ibid., p.4.
26 Lindsay, p.72.
27 Powell, *TSN*, no.62, p.11.
28 Farington, *Diary*, 2 April 1804.
29 Powell, *TSN*, no.62, p.11.
30 Powell, *TSN*, no.62, p.12.
31 Th. 1877, pp.4, 319.
32 TB CVI, f.67a.
33 Finberg, p.27.
34 TB CIV; Ann Livermore, *TS* 3, 1, pp.44–8. She also points out that six books of music were found in Turner's effects after his death.
35 Finberg, p.155.
36 Golt, *TS* 9, 2, pp.4–10.
37 IGI; *Geese*, p.107.
38 Dossier.
39 Farington, *Diary*, 22 March 1804. The RA catalogue for 1804 also gives 64 Harley Street as his address once again.
40 Th. 1877, p.122.
41 TB XLIII.
42 TB LXIX.
43 TB XLIX. Although some words of Turner's lament are hard to decipher, I have for the most part followed the reading in Hill, *Turner on the Thames*, p.60.
44 Whitley, *1800–20*, p.28.
45 Watts, p.xvi.
46 Whitley, *1800–20*, pp.6–7.
47 Ibid., p.19.
48 *TS*, 1, 1, p.6; cited *Monthly Mirror*, June 1801.
49 Farington, *Diary*, 26 April 1801.
50 Finberg, p.71.
51 TB LXIX.
52 Ibid., f.116.

4: Fair Winds and Foul

1. Farington, *Diary*, 30 August 1802.
2. Smollett, vol.viii, pp.3–4.
3. Hibbert, *Grand Tour*, p.41.
4. Finberg, *Sketches and Drawings*, pp.47–8.
5. TB LXXV.
6. TB LXXVIII, f.1.
7. Haydon, *Autobiography and Journals*, pp.207–8, 216.
8. TB LXXII, f.51.
9. Ibid., f.28.
10. Farington, *Diary*, 2 May 1803.
11. Lindsay, p.79; Finberg, pp.89–90.
12. Farington, *Diary*, 12 December 1802.
13. Finberg, p.92.
14. Farington, *Diary*, 26 January 1803.
15. Th. 1877, pp.71, 222.
16. Ibid., p.222.
17. Farington, *Diary*, 10 December 1802.
18. Whitley, *1800–20*, pp.150–1.
19. Farington, *Diary*, 24 December 1803.
20. Ibid., 11 May 1804.
21. Farington, *Diary*, 29 April 1803. In this and other quotations from Farington, I have for clarity sometimes altered punctuation, spelling and emphases.
22. Finberg, p.99.
23. A. P. Oppe, quoted in Lindsay, p.83.
24. Constable's letter to Dunthorne, May 1803, quoted in ibid.
25. Finberg, p.100.
26. See Ziff, *TS*, 8, p.13

5: Aladdin's Cave

1. Farington, *Diary*, 22 March 1804.
2. The 'e' on Anne was sometimes used by Turner and sometimes not. Thornbury spells it with the 'e' and Finberg does without it. I have followed present usage.
3. Farington, *Diary*, 19 April 1804.
4. Ibid., 11–13 May 1805.
5. Letters, p.107.
6. Farington, *Diary*, 8 June 1811.
7. Letters, p.43.
8. Lindsay, p.115; Letters, p.49.
9. Letters, p.82.

10   Finberg, p.268.
11   Ibid., p.186.
12   TB CV, f.67a and 68.
13   R. S. Owen, cited Butlin with Wilton, p.186.
14   Letters, p.235.
15   1811: Redding, *Past Celebrities*, p.45; 1813: Wilton, p.125.
16   Redding, *Past Celebrities*, pp.51–2.
17   William Leighton Leitch, quoted in Wilton, pp.221–2.
18   Both G. D. Leslie, in *Inner Life*, p.143.
19   Eastlake, *Journals*, p.188.
20   Letter to Thomas Griffith, 1844, in Letters, p.196.
21   Eastlake, *Journals*, p.188.
22   *TS*, 1, 1, p.34.
23   Ruskin, quoted in *TSN*, no.46, p.8.
24   Wilton, pp.221–2.I have abbreviated some sentences and altered
      punctuation here and there.
25   Th. 1877, p.244.
26   Ibid., p.317.
27   *TSN*, no.42, pp.8–12.
28   Mary Ann Widgery, Chancery affidavit, 24 January 1854, Dossier, f.72.
29   Gage, *Colour*, p.166.
30   Frith, *Autobiography*, i, pp.141–2.
31   Ruskin, *Dilecta*, in *Praeterita*, p.540. Captain Elisha Morgan
      commanded a Black X Line sailing packet.
32   Ibid., p.543.
33   Th. 1877, p.235.
34   Leslie, *Inner Life*, p.143.
35   Th. 1877, p.317.
36   Ibid., p.321.
37   Monkbouse, p.87; Th. 1877, pp.363 ff.

6: Gold Apples, Silver Thames

1   Greig, *Diary*, i, p.284n.; Haydon, *Autobiography and Journals*, pp.78–9.
2   Letters, p.31.
3   Hill, *Turner on the Thames*, p.59.
4   TB XC, f.58a.
5   TB XCIII.
6   TB XCIV.
7   Hill, *Turner on the Thames*, pp.60–2.
8   TB XCVI.
9   Wilton, *Painting and Poetry*, pp.40, 149–50.
10   TB XC.

11 Ibid., f.16.
12 TB LXXXIV.
13 TB CVIII.
14 TB XCIX, f.86.
15 Poem in TB XLIX, 1799.
16 TB XCVIII, f.8a.
17 Th. i, p.343.
18 Ibid.
19 Th. 1877, p.456.
20 TB CVIII.
21 TBXCV.
22 *Barge on the River, Sunset*, 1805, oil on canvas, Tate no.2707; Hill, *Turner on the Thames*, pp.98–100.
23 TB XCIII, f.12.
24 TB XCIII.
25 Haydon, *Autobiography and Journals*, p.36.
26 TB LXXXVII, TB LXXXIX.
27 TB CXXI s.
28 TB CXX c.
29 TB LXXXIX f.14.
30 Kennedy, *Nelson and his Captains*, pp.331–2. First published as *Nelson's Band of Brothers*, 1951.
31 Haydon, *Autobiography and Journals*, p.36.
32 B&J, no.58.
33 Finberg, p.142.
34 TB CXVIII c.
35 TB CXII.
36 TB CI.
37 TB CIV.
38 TB CI f.88a.
39 TB CV.
40 TB CV, flyleaf; Th. 1877, p.486, and Finberg, p.152, misread Turner's handwriting here as 'painting art'. Turner was talking about the laborious and thus breathtaking attempt of the artist to capture the 'truth' (see Hill, *TSN*, no.67, pp.11–16).
41 Th. 1877, p.116.
42 Whitley, *1800–20*, p.195.
43 Th. 1877, p.116.
44 TB CI.
45 TB XCVI, f.74v.
46 TB XCVIII.
47 Gage, *Colour*, p.260n.

48 Lloyd, *Sunny Memories*, pp.31 f., 36.
49 Ruskin, *Modern Painters*, v, pp.345, 392.

7: Boxing Harry
1   Farington, *Diary*, 22 May 1804.
2   Ibid., 8 September 1804.
3   Finberg, p.119.
4   Letters, p.293.
5   Ibid., p.36.
6   Farington, *Diary*, 8 June 1811.
7   Finberg, p.243.
8   TB CXXII.
9   Th. i, p.74.
10 Rosalind Turner brought this to my attention.
11 Chancery affidavit, Dossier.
12 TB CX.
13 Townsend, p.48.
14 MS note in Haskell copy of Th. ii, p.146.
15 *Athenaeum*, no.178 (14 December 1861), p.808.
16 Whitley, *1821–37*, pp.135–6.
17 Watts, p.xxiv.
18 Gage, '*Wonderful Range*', p.65.
19 Ibid., p.xxxix.
20 Letters, p.9.
21 Smith, *Nollekens*, pp.75, 302.
22 Letters, pp.2–3.
23 Finberg, p.391.
24 Letters, pp.8, 2, 4.
25 Archer, *TS*, 1, 1, p.32.
26 Hamlyn, *Record of the Art Museum, P.U.*, p.5 citing J. B. Atkinson, *Portfolio*, ed. Hamerton, 1880, p.71.
27 Letters, pp.3, 10.
28 *TS*, 3, 1, p.26.
29 Redding, *Fraser's Magazine*, February 1852; *Fifty Years' Recollections*, p.204.
30 Letters, p.10.
31 Th. 1877, p.245.
32 Finberg, p.46.
33 Th. 1877, p.235.
34 Ruskin, *Modern Painters*, v, p.374.
35 Frith, *Autobiography*, i, pp.126–7.
36 Hamerton, *Turner*, p.373.

37 Archer, *TS*, 1, 1, p.34.
38 Watts, p.xxiv.
39 Archer, *TS*, 1, 1, pp.32,37 n.4.
40 Th. i, p.172; see also 1877, pp.223–4.
41 *Century*, p.356; Falk, *Turner*, pp.88–9.
42 Haydon, *Autobiography and Journals*, p.200.
43 Th. 1877, p.235.
44 Finberg, p.257.
45 Th. 1877, p.236.
46 TB XCV Fa.
47 Lindsay, p.100.
48 TB CXI.
49 *Geese* I, p.115.
50 TB CXIII.
51 Golt, *TS*, 9, 2, p.4.
52 TB CXIII, f.59.

8: The Bite of the Print

1   Finberg, 1924, p.lxxxiv. See also Forrester, *Turner's 'Drawing Book'*.
2   Th. 1877, p.491.
3   Ibid.
4   Wilkinson, *Turner on Landscape*, p.18.
5   Letters, pp.50–1.
6   TB CXI.
7   Pye-Roget, p.82.
8   Wilkinson, *Turner on Landscape*, p.21.
9   Pye-Roget, p.22.
10 Numbers 28, 35, 39, 44, 50, 55, 58, 60, 64, 66, 70. See Forrester, op.cit.
11 TB XCI, ff.96a, 97a.
12 Finberg, p.150.
13 Wilton, p.59.
14 Quoted by Rogers in Reynolds, *Discourses*, p.399 n.28.
15 Ibid., p.322.
16 Ruskin, *Modern Painters*, i, p.170.
17 Letters, p.276.
18 Pye-Roget, pp.18, 96.
19 Wilkinson, *Turner on Landscape*, p.42.
20 Pye-Roget, p.31.
21 Ibid., pp.12–13.
22 Letters, pp.33–4. Finberg, 1924, p.1, takes Turner's side against the 'rapacious' Lewis.
23 Pye-Roget, pp.60–1.

24 Letters, pp.43–4.
25 Ibid., pp.121–2.
26 Pye-Roget, p.61.
27 Ibid., pp.79–80.
28 Ibid., pp.78–9.
29 TB CLXVIII C.
30 Letters, pp.104–6.
31 Th. 1877, p.316n. See also Goodall, *Reminiscences*, pp.161–2.
32 Letters, pp.187, 255.
33 Peter Cunningham, quoted in Watts, p.xxxix. A guinea is £1.1s.
34 Miller, quoted in Shanes, *Turner's England*, p.12.
35 Th. 1877, p.299. Lindsay, p.261, cites p.xxii of an unidentified work by 'E. Bell', and says this story is 'incorrect'.
36 Th. 1877, pp.343–4.
37 Frith, *Autobiography*, i, pp.133–4.
38 Huish, *TS*, 5, 2, p.27.
39 Finberg, pp.285–6.
40 Th. 1877, pp.195–6.
41 Huish, *TS*, 5, 2, p.26. For J. C. Allen, see Letters, pp.76–7.
42 Th. 1877, p.183.
43 Ibid., pp.192–3.
44 Jones, 'Recollections', in Letters, p.2.
45 Whitman, *Charles Turner*, p.18; Letters, p.159.
46 Redgrave, *Memoir*, pp.341–2.
47 Th. 1877, p.342; Letters, pp.86–8.
48 Watts, p.xxix.
49 Finberg, p.327.
50 Th. 1877, p.495.
51 Wilkinson, p.113.
52 Ruskin, *Harbours of England*, p.xix.
53 Ibid., p.102; Lyles and Perkins, p.63.

9: Deep Puzzles

1 Davies, *Turner as Professor*, p.21. Since this is more or less what Turner's audience heard, I have corrected several misspellings in Turner's draft for this lecture.
2 Whitley, *1800–20*, pp.180 ff.
3 Farington, *Diary*, 28 January 1811.
4 *Century*, p.257.
5 Letters, p.35.
6 Davies, *Turner as Professor*, p.15.
7 Letters, pp.29–30.

8   Finberg, p.154.
9   *Encyclopaedia Britannica*, 11th edition.
10 Davies, *Turner as Professor*, p.43.
11 Ibid., pp.82–3.
12 Leslie, *Inner Life*, p.20.
13 TB CXXXIV, f.81.
14 Venning, *TS*, 3, 1, p.39.
15 *TS*, 1, 2, p.30.
16 Leslie, *Constable*, p.44.
17 *Century*, p.258.
18 Ibid.
19 TB CVIII.
20 British Library Add. MS 46151, N, p.22, cited by Shanes, *Turner's Human Landscape*, pp.255 and 370 n.28.
21 Whitley, *1800–20*, p.184.
22 Ibid., p.204.
23 Ibid., pp.265–6.
24 Letters, pp.46–7.
25 Ibid., pp.48–9 n.3.
26 Whitley, *Burlington Magazine*, xxii (1912–13), pp.202, 255.
27 Whitley, *1800–20*, p.266.
28 Finberg, p.369.
29 Ballantine, *Roberts*, p.238.
30 Whitley, *1800–20*, p.184.
31 *Century*, p.257.
32 Wilton, *Painting and Poetry*, p.143.
33 TB CVIII, f.31r.
34 TB CXII, f.88r.
35 Wilton, *Painting and Poetry*, pp.180–1.
36 Timbs, *Anecdote Lives*, p.340.
37 Finberg, pp.408–9.
38 Lindsay, *Sunset Ship*, pp.53–4.
39 Richardson, *Works*, pp.249, 37.
40 Reynolds, *Discourses*, p.112.
41 Ziff, *TS*, 4, 1, p.51.
42 *British Itinerary*, f.80v; Wilton, *Painting and Poetry*, p.172.
43 TB CXI
44 Stokes, *Painting and the Inner World*, p.77.
45 Jones, 'Recollections', in Letters, p.7.
46 *TS*, 9, 1, p.4.
47 Letters, p.57.
48 Finberg, p.230. Finberg improves Turner's punctuation.

49 TB CX.
50 As suggested by Wilton, *Painting and Poetry*, p.14.
51 TB CXXII.
52 TB CVI, f.68.
53 Letters, p.55 n.3.
54 TB CXIX Y.
55 Letters, pp.50–1.
56 Ibid., pp.51–2.
57 Hazlitt, *Collected Works*, 'Conversations of Northcote', 6, p.416.
58 Ruskin, *Modern Painters*, iii, p.94.

10: Crossing the Brook

1   Leslie, *Inner Life*, p.144.
2   Redding, *Past Celebrities*, p.66.
3   Redding, *Fifty Years' Recollections*, i, p.198.
4   Ibid., p.200.
5   *Fraser's Magazine*, February 1852, cited Finberg, pp.199–200.
6   Redding, *Fifty Years' Recollections*, i, pp.204–5.
7   *Fraser's Magazine*, February 1852, cited Finberg, pp.200–1.
8   Ibid., pp.202, 203.
9   Th. 1877, p.153.
10 Gage, *Colour*, p.32.
11 TB CXCVI E.
12 Redding, *Fifty Years' Recollections*, pp.201–2.
13 Th. 1877, p.152.
14 Letters, p.207.
15 Letter to Holworthy, 21 November 1817, Letters, pp.71–2.
16 Letter to Ruskin, quoted in Letters, p.280.
17 Schetky, *Ninety Years*, pp.108–9.
18 Ibid.
19 Ibid., pp.127, 129.
20 TB CXCIX.
21 TB CXXXVI.
22 TB CXXXIII.
23 TB CXXXVII.
24 TB CXLII.
25 Farington, *Diary*, 11 February 1809.
26 Th. 1877, p.281.
27 Ibid., p.120.
28 Ibid. p.242.
29 Ruskin, *Dilecta*, in *Praeterita*, pp.533–5, 537. On p.533 Leslie gives the date of this incident as 1832, and on p.536 as 1834. The observant

young Leslie nonetheless lets us know that Turner smoked. Note, too, how it is Charles Leslie, not Turner, who tips the boatman.

30 Wilton, *Painting and Poetry*, p.163.
31 TB CXII.
32 Letters, p.96.
33 Ibid., p.102.
34 Th. 1877, p.228. Abbreviated, and punctuation altered.
35 TB CCLXIII 339.
36 Th. 1877, p.242.
37 Letters, p.240.
38 Ibid., p.205.
39 Walton, *Compleat Angler*, pp.30–2.
40 Letters, pp.108–10.
41 TB CCXXVI f.64.
42 B&J, no.127.

11: Sir George Thinks Otherwise

1 Finberg, p.218. The picture is *Distraining for Rent*.
2 Hazlitt, 'On Imitation', *Works*, i, p.76n.
3 Farington, *Diary*, 5 June 1815.
4 *TS*, i, i, p.31.
5 Farington, *Diary*, 26 April 1799.
6 *Century*, p.4.
7 Farington, *Diary*, 3 May 1803.
8 Ibid., 1 April 1804.
9 Ibid., 26 April 1806.
10 Ibid., 3 June 1806.
11 Ibid., 8 June 1811.
12 Ibid., 21 October 1812.
13 Th. 1877, p.432. Thornbury calls the baronet Sir John Beaumont.
14 Farington, *Diary*, 8 April 1813.
15 Ibid., 4 June 1815.
16 Figures collated from provenances listed in B&J.
17 Farington, *Diary*, 9 October 1809.
18 Greaves, *Regency Patron*, p.99.
19 Haydon, *Autobiography and Journals*, p.49.
20 *AR*, i, p.157
21 Farington, *Diary*, 25 May 1806.
22 Greaves, *Regency Patron*, p.114.
23 Haydon, *Autobiography and Journals*, p.421.
24 Greaves, *Regency Patron*, pp.154–5.
25 Ibid., pp.121–3.

26   Ibid., p.100.
27   Finberg, p.248.
28   Lindsay, p.96.
29   Farington, *Diary*, 5 July 1809.
30   Lindsay, pp.130–1.
31   Ziff, *TS*, 8, 2, p.18.
32   Finberg, p.208.
33   Farington, *Diary*, 12 June 1815.
34   Ibid., 6 May 1806.
35   Brown, *Callcott*, p.22.
36   Th. 1877, p.353.
37   TB CXXXV.
38   Finberg, pp.246–7.
39   Gage, *Colour*, pp.19, 226.
40   Haydon, *Autobiography and Journals*, p.200.
41   Ibid., p.265.
42   Whitley, *1800–20*, pp.150–1.
43   Finberg, p.143.
44   Burnet, *Turner and his Works*, p.61.
45   *Century*, p.262.
46   Swinburne, *Turner*, p.204.
47   Finberg, p.142.
48   Farington, *Diary*, 3 June 1806.
49   TB CXIII.
50   TB CXL.
51   TB XXX, f.96v.
52   *Century*, pp.254–5.
53   Finberg, p.109.
54   Gage, *Rain, Steam and Speed*, p.89.
55   Ruskin, *Modern Painters*, i, p.201.

12: Dear Fawkes
1   Hill, *In Turner's Footsteps*, p.17. Newby Lowson, Turner's travelling companion on that tour, may have brought Turner and Fawkes together.
2   Farington, *Diary*, 4 November 1812.
3   Hill, *In Turner's Footsteps*, pp.17, 126n.
4   Leitch/Huish, *TS*, 5, 2, p.26.
5   Letters, p.227.
6   Ibid., p.203.
7   Th. 1877, p.237.
8   Ibid., p.239.

9   Edith Fawkes, typescript in National Gallery, cited by Wilton, p.114.
     Th. 1877, p.239, has Turner 'tearing up the sea with his eagle-claw of
     a thumb-nail'; Hill, *Turner's Birds*, p.20, suggests that Turner kept
     his left thumb-nail long in order 'to scratch at the paper on which he
     was painting'.
10   Harper, 'Memoirs', *Walker's Monthly*, no.10 (October 1928), p.2.
11   Ian Warrell, *Turner in the North of England, 1797*.
12   Th. 1877, p.139.
13   Farington, *Diary*, 20 December 1817.
14   Finberg, p.242.
15   Ibid., p.243.
16   Letters, pp.67, 70.
17   TB CXLVIII.
18   Finberg, p.244.
19   TB CXXVIII, TB CXLIX.
20   Finberg, p.244.
21   Letters, p.68.
22   TB CLII.
23   Letters, pp.68–70.
24   Th. 1877, p.191.
25   Harper, 'Memoirs', *Walker's Monthly*, no.10 (October 1928), p.2. See
     also Th. 1877, p.238, which – inaccurately – has Turner landing at
     Hull from his Rhenish tour and going straight to Farnley. Powell,
     Turner's Rivers of Europe, p.26.
26   Letters, p.71.
27   Finberg, p.253; Forrester, pp.136–7.
28   Ibid., pp.274, 288.
29   TB CLIII.
30   TB CXXII f.4.
31   Finberg, p.292.
32   *TS*, 5, 2, p.26.
33   Farington, *Diary*, 29 April 1818.
34   Whitley, *1800–20*, pp.294–5.
35   Finberg, p.258.
36   Carey, *Memoirs*, p.147.
37   Farington, *Diary*, 10 July 1796.
38   Lindsay, pp.138–9, 239 n.12.
39   TB CXX Z.
40   Byron, *Childe Harold's Pilgrimage*, canto 3, XXVIII.
41   Th. 1877, p.292.
42   Shanes, *Turner's Human Landscape*, pp.17, 347.
43   Lindsay, p.141.

44 Ibid.
45 TB CXXIII.
46 TB CLIV: 'Farnley' sheets, 1816 and later.
47 Hill, *Turner's Birds*, pp.12, 26 n.16. Finberg, p.287, says that Turner was not at Farnley in 1823; evidently a mistake.
48 Finberg, p.291.
49 Letters, pp.96–8.
50 TB CXCVI Y.
51 Perkins, *Third Decade*, p.29.

13: The Squire of Sandycombe

1   Letters, p.60.
2   TB CXIV.
3   Gage, *Colour*, p.22.
4   TB CXX.
5   TB CXL.
6   Livermore, *Country Life*, 6 July 1951.
7   Youngblood, *TS*, 2, 1, pp.21, 34.
8   Th. 1877, p.120.
9   Ibid., p.118.
10 Letters, p.294.
11 Ibid.
12 Ibid., p.61.
13 Smith, *Nollekens*, pp.199–200.
14 Farington, *Diary*, 7 July 1819.
15 Letters, p.86.
16 Th. 1877, p.226.
17 Ibid., p.224.
18 Monkhouse, p.89.
19 Ibid.
20 Th. 1877, p.124.
21 Ibid., p.121.
22 Ibid., p.122.
23 Watts, p.xxvii.
24 Ibid.
25 TB CXXVII.
26 Th. i, pp.6–7.
27 Ibid.
28 Th. 1877, p.117.
29 Monkhouse, p.85.
30 Finberg, p.196.
31 Dossier.

32 Letters, p.89.
33 TB XLII.
34 TB CXXXV.
35 TB CXXIX.
36 Th. 1877, p.127; Letters, p.84.
37 Letters, p.61.
38 Th. 1877, p.392.
39 Powell, *TSN*, no.62, p.14.
40 Letters, p.103.
41 Ibid., p.107.
42 Farington, *Diary*, 6 April 1821.
43 B&J, no.140.
44 Hill, *Turner on the Thames*, p.152.
45 Th. 1877, p.117.
46 Haydon, *Autobiography and Journals*, 27 May 1824.
47 Finberg, p.283.
48 Th. 1877, p.429.
49 Wyllie, *Turner*, p.44.
50 B&J, no.252.
51 Munro MS note in G. Jones's copy of Th. i, pp.292–3.
52 Finberg, p.253.
53 Letters, pp.7, 10.
54 Youngblood, *TS*, 2, 1, pp.22, 34 n.43.
55 Watts, p.xxv.
56 TB CCV.
57 Ruskin, quoted in Harris, *Life and Adventures*, pp.288–9.
58 Falk, *Turner*, p.173.
59 TB CCV.
60 Chancery affidavit, Dossier.
61 Archer, *TS*, 1, 1, pp.35–6.
62 Letters, p.109.
63 Ibid., p.181.
64 TB CXXIX.
65 Letters, p.101.
66 Th. 1877, p.116.
67 Letters, p.96.
68 TB CXII. The house at Twickenham still stands.

14: Southern Light

1   Letters, p.70
2   Powell, p.19.
3   TB CLXXIII.

4   Byron, *Childe Harold's Pilgrimage*, canto 3, LXII.
5   Powell, p.31.
6   TB CLXXXVIII, f.26; *Apollo*, Oct 1996, pp.25–32.
7   *Letters*, p.81n. 1; Finberg, p.261; *Apollo*, op.cit.
8   Finberg, p.262.
9   Hazlitt, *Collected Works*, ix, p.367.
10   Letters, p.263.
11   Ibid., p.97.
12   Ibid., p.82.
13   Ruskin, *Ruskin Today*, p.220.
14   Wilton, p.131.
15   Th. 1877, p.103.
16   B&J, no.233.
17   See TB CXXXV with its five pages of formulations for yellow
     pig ments. He used chrome yellow in 1814, the year it was first
     manufactured; Townsend, 1993, p.41.
18   Finberg, pp.295–6.
19   B&J, no.232.
20   Letters, p.108.
21   B&J, no.239.
22   Letters, p.100.
23   Ibid., p.103 n.2.
24   Ibid., p.138.
25   Th. 1877, p.294.
26   *Dictionary of Artists*, p.437.
27   *TSN*, no.53, p.5.
28   B&J, no.230.
29   Finberg, pp.279–80.
30   Ibid., p.273.
31   Letters, pp.119–20.
32   Ibid., p.135 n.2.
33   Gotch, *Lady Callcott*, p.118.
34   Finberg, p.311.
35   Gotch, *Lady Callcott*, p.279; Letters, p.118.
36   Letters, p.120.
37   Whitley, *1821–37*, p.159.
38   Broughton, *Recollections*, iii, pp.294–5.
39   Uwins, *Memoir*, ii, pp.239–41.
40   Powell, p.142.
41   Letters, p.127.
42   Powell, pp.158–9.
43   TB CCXXXVII, ff.8a, 9.

44 Uwins, *Memoir*, ii, pp.239–41.
45 Letters, pp.125–6.
46 Ibid., p.126.
47 *Odyssey*, book IX (trans. Fitzgerald, p.172).
48 B&J, no.330.
49 *Odyssey*, book IX (trans. Fitzgerald, p.162).
50 Th. 1877, p.446.
51 Shelley, 'Julian and Maddalo', ll.70–4.
52 Letters, p.132 n.9.
53 Finberg, p.249.
54 *Will*, 1, p.2.
55 Dossier.
56 Letters, p.135.
57 Ibid., p.137.
58 Th. i, p.177.
59 B&J, no.342.
60 Byron, *Childe Harold's Pilgrimage*, canto 4, XXVI.
61 Hamerton, *Turner*, p.260.
62 B&J, no.355.
63 Powell, 1995, p.44.
64 Ruskin, *Modern Painters*, i, p.140.
65 *TSN*, no.3, p.53.
66 B&J, no.365.
67 Ruskin, *Works*, iii, pp.635–40.
68 Letters, pp.160–1.
69 Brown, *Turner and Byron*, p.96.

15: Figures on the Shore

1   Th. i, p.223.
2   Watts, p.xxxii.
3   Falk, *Turner*, p.195, gives the year 1827, but no authority; Wilton, p.163, suggests 1829.
4   Census, Parish of St John the Baptist, p.15, Margate Public Library.
5   Falk, p.238; Walbrook; *Geese* III, p.37.
6   Charles Turner, *Diary*, 8 September 1852.
7   Roberts, *TS*, 9, 1, p.6.
8   Ibid., p.3.
9   Letters, p.199.
10 G. Jones's copy of Th. ii, p.232.
11 Th. 1877, p.243.
12 W. Sandby, *The History of the Royal Academy of Arts*, 2 vols, London, 1862. i, pp.281–2; ii, p.36.

13   *Century*, p.269.
14   Ruskin, 1856, quoted in Shanes, *Turner's Human Landscape*, p.339.
15   Archer, *TS* 1, 1, p.34.
16   Ruskin, *Praeterita*, pp.434–5.
17   Yale, Mellon Collection, no.151.
18   Finberg, p.327.
19   Letters, pp.143–4.
20   Ibid., pp.209–10.
21   Th. 1877, p.337; B&J, pp.180–1.
22   Yale, Mellon Collection, no.144.
23   Ruskin, *Notes by Mr. Ruskin*.
24   My thanks to Fred Bachrach for this observation.
25   Ruskin, *Diaries*, 29 April 1844; *TSN*, no.42, p.10.
26   B&J, no.398.
27   Ruskin, *Works*, xiii, p.161.
28   TB CCXLI.
29   B&J, no.320.
30   Miller, *Picturesque Views*, p.xxxix.
31   Letters, p.83.
32   Ibid., p.163.
33   Th. 1877, p.236.
34   Ibid., pp.624–8.
35   TB CCCLXIII. C. J. Feret, p.59; *Geese* III, pp.59, 116; Watts, p.xxxiii.
36   Lindsay, p.172.
37   Falk, *Turner*, p.198.
38   Wilton, *Life and Work*, p.468.
39   TB CCXCI b.
40   Wilton, *Life and Work*, p.928; TB CCCLXIV f.269; B&J, p.453.

16: Varnishing Days

1   Whitley, *1800–20*, pp.148–9.
2   Turner's first actual completion of a painting at the RA, 'adding glazes and toning' to transform it from a sketch into a finished picture, may have been in 1818. Townsend, p.58.
3   Jones, 'Recollections', in Letters, pp.1–2.
4   Frith, *Autobiography*, i, p.139.
5   Whitley, *1821–37*, p.319.
6   Farington, *Diary*, 13 May 1803.
7   B&J, no.131.
8   Ruskin, *Dilecta*, in *Praeterita*, pp.535–9.
9   Ibid.
10   Finberg, pp.351–2.

11   *Century*, p.255.

12   Ibid., pp.263–4.

13   Ibid., p.265.

14   Shanes, *Turner's Human Landscape*, pp.22–3.

15   Jones, 'Recollections', in Letters, p.8.

16   Ibid., p.9; Cooper, *My Life*, ii, pp.9–10.

17   Cooper, *My Life*, ii, pp.2–3.

18   Stillman, *TS*, 9, 2, p.49.

19   Ruskin, *Dilecta*, in *Praeterita*, p.537.

20   Leslie, *Inner Life*, p.144.

21   Ibid., p.145.

22   *AR*, i, p.201.

23   Frith, *Autobiography*, i, pp.129–30.

24   Archer, *TS*, 1, 1, p.36.

25   Leslie, *Inner Life*, p.145.

26   Jones, *Chantrey*, p.126.

27   Leslie, *Inner Life*, p.148.

28   Frith, *Autobiography*, i, pp.132–3. *Masaniello* is now in the Tate.

29   Jones, 'Recollections', in Letters, pp.5–6.

30   *AR*, i, pp.202–3.

31   Th. i, p.305.

32   Whitley, *1821–37*, p.282. Shanes, *TS* 3, 1, pp.49–50.

33   Hilda Finberg, *Burlington Magazine*, xcix (1957), p.48.

34   B&J, no.238.

35   Leslie, *Inner Life*, p.75.

36   Whitley, *1800–20*, p.187.

37   *AR*, ii, p.12.

38   Th. 1877, p.295.

39   Jones, 'Recollections', in Letters, p.5.

40   Ibid., p.6.

41   Roberts, *TS*, 9, 1, p.4.

42   Monkhouse, p.101.

43   Frith, *Autobiography*, i, p.131.

44   *Century*, pp.255, 343.

45   Falk, *Turner*, p.161.

46   Leslie, *Inner Life*, pp.146–7.

47   Ruskin, *Modern Painters*, i, pp.144–5.

48   Whitley, *1821–37*, pp.211–12.

49   B&J, no.294.

50   See e.g. Gage, *Colour*, p.143.

51   Ibid., p.167.

52   *AR*, i, p.201.

53   *TS*, 9, 1, p.3.

17: Liberty Hall

1   Cobbett, *Rural Rides*, i, pp.215–22.
2   Ibid., ii, pp.13–20.
3   Creevey, *Papers*, pp.505–6.
4   Ibid., p.506.
5   Whitley, *1821–37*, p.344.
6   Farington, *Diary*, 9 October 1803.
7   Falk, *Turner*, p.90.
8   Ibid., p.89.
9   Wyndham, *Wyndham and Children First*, p.29.
10   *AR*, i, p.102.
11   Ibid., p.103.
12   Butlin, *Turner*, p.192.
13   Haydon, *Autobiography and Journals*, 15 November 1826.
14   Youngblood, *TS*, 2, 2, p.18.
15   *AR*, ii, p.220.
16   Ibid., p.237.
17   Ibid., i, p.103.
18   Gore and Joll, *Picture Collection at Petworth*, p.18.
19   B&J, no.333.
20   R. C. Leslie, p.57. Ruskin, *Praeterita*, p.536.
21   Jones, *Chantrey*, p.122.
22   Th. 1877, p.306.
23   Jones, 'Recollections', in Letters, p.2.
24   Ibid., p.3.
25   Letters, p.278.
26   TB CCXLIV. See Butlin et al, *Turner at Petworth*.
27   Wyndham, *Wyndham and Children First*, p.37.
28   TB CCXLV, f.54v.
29   TB CCXLIV f.102.
30   Wyndham, *Wyndham and Children First*, pp.38–9. See also *AR*, i,
     pp.128–9.
31   *TS*, 2, 2, pp.30–2.
32   Ibid., p.33.
33   Letters, p.168.
34   Ibid., p.169.
35   B&J no.449; Andrew Wilton in *TS* 9, 2, pp.26–7 believes the picture is
     c.1830 and does not show a Petworth interior, though it may contain
     Petworth references. The Tate now calls it *Sack of a Great House*. Partly
     because of the dogs, I prefer the earlier, Egremont-connected theory.

18: Home and Away

1 Letters, pp.174, 275.

2 Ibid., p.152.

3 Dates given to some sketchbooks of this period by Finberg in his Inventory are very approximate. Tours listed in some chronologies – e.g. in Wilton's *Turner Abroad* and *Turner in his Time* – should be checked against more recent studies, especially Powell's illuminating *Turner's Rivers of Europe* and *Turner in Germany*.

4 Redding, *Fifty Years' Recollections*, i, p.296.

5 Lindsay, p.174. Several years after this, Delacroix wrote to Theophile Silvestre: 'Constable, an admirable man, is one of England's glories … He and Turner were real reformers. They broke out of the rut of traditional landscape painting. Our school, which today abounds with men of talent in this field, profited greatly by their example.' Paris, 31 Dec 1858. Eugene Delacroix, *Selected Letters 1813–63*, ed. J. Stewart, London, 1971.

6 TB CCL f.10.

7 TB CCVIII o; Warrell, *Turner: The Fourth Decade*, pp.30–1.

8 TB CCXLVIII.

9 Van der Merwe, *TSN*, no.57, pp.11–13.

10 Egerton, *Fighting Temeraire*, p.68.

11 TB CCLIX f.104.

12 TB CCXI.

13 Watts, p.xxxv.

14 Ibid.

15 TB CCXLIX.

16 Th. 1877, pp.102–3.

17 Ibid., p.99.

18 Watts, p.xxx.

19 MS note on stationery in G. Jones's copy of Th. ii, p.148. Turner's interest in his own work was also evident in July 1833, when Dr Monro's collection of drawings was sold at Christie's. He bought thirteen lots containing drawings attributed to him, as well as two drawings attributed to Rembrandt, and some studies by Hoppner (Finberg, p.342).

20 Letters, p.141.

21 4 December 1826, Letters, p.103.

22 Th. 1877, pp.103–4.

23 Finberg, p.360.

24 Ibid.

25 MS note in G. Jones's copy of Th. i, p.230.

26 Ruskin, Works, vii, p.446n.

27 Powell, *Turner in Germany*: 1833, 1835, 1839 and 1840 tours.
28 Wilton, p.177.
29 Powell, *Turner in Germany*, p.66; TB CCCX f.68.
30 Wilton, p.207, says that Turner was in Paris and visited Versailles; Powell, Turner's *Rivers of Europe*, pp.61–2 n.18, says nothing is known of this tour.
31 See Powell, *Turner's Rivers of Europe*, pp.14, 18, 48.
32 Letters, p.174.
33 Finberg, p.332.
34 TB CCLXXX 78.
35 Solender, *Dreadful Fire!*, p.42.
36 TB CCCLXIV 373.
37 Finberg, p.352.
38 Solender, *Dreadful Fire!*, p.61.
39 Ibid., p.62.
40 Finberg, p.343.
41 Ibid., p.363.
42 Jones, 'Recollections', in Letters, p.5.
43 B&J, no.376.
44 Letters, pp.192–3.
45 Finberg, p.369.
46 Letters, p.154.
47 Jones, 'Recollections', in ibid., p.7.
48 *Will*, 1, pp.28–9.
49 Finberg, p.280.
50 Ibid., p.284.
51 Th. 1877, pp.353–4.
52 Farington, *Diary*, 4 July 1811.
53 Th. 1877, p.355.
54 Letters, p.134.
55 Jones, 'Recollections', in ibid., p.8.
56 Emerson, *Collected Writings*, v, pp.169, 21–2, 141.
57 Ruskin, Journal, 22 June 1840.
58 Letters, pp.163–4.
59 Ibid.
60 Finberg, p.213.
61 Egerton, *Fighting Temeraire*, pp.88–90.
62 Th. 1877, p.458.
63 MS note by Munro in G. Jones's copy of Th. i, p.335.
64 B&J, no.377.
65 Wilton, p.176.
66 Ruskin, *Modern Painters*, i, pp.162–3.

67 Letters, pp.172–3.
68 Ibid., p.211.

19: The Rigours of Winter

1   Ruskin, *Praeterita*, p.276. Ian Warrell points out that this as-it-were immediate record written in the 1880s is much fuller than that actually in Ruskin's diary. There the meeting is written about on 23 June, concerning 'yesterday'. The *Praeterita* entry also seems to include some of Ruskin's diary entry for 5 July 1841. Warrell, *Through Switzerland with Turner*, p.29 n.12.
2   Ruskin, ibid., p.234.
3   Ruskin, *Ruskin Today*, p.206n.
4   Hunt, *The Wider Sea*, p.138.
5   Finberg, p.395.
6   Ibid., p.403.
7   Roberts, *TS*, 9, 1, p.6.
8   Lloyd, *Sunny Memories*, p.34.
9   Fawkes: Gage, *Colour*, p.225; Kingsley: Ruskin, *Works*, xiii, p.536.
10 Ruskin, *Modern Painters*, v, p.252.
11 Ruskin, *Elements of Drawing*, p.132n.
12 Stillman, *Autobiography*, i, p.108.
13 Finberg, p.400.
14 B&J, no.402.
15 Letters, pp.202–3.
16 B&J, p.392
17 Whitley, *1821–37*, p.213.
18 B&J, no.371.
19 TB CXXIX.
20 One pair of his spectacles, saved by Ruskin, is now in the Ashmolean Museum, Oxford. Another is in the Tate.
21 Th. 1877, p.292.
22 Gage, *Colour*, p.40.
23 Falk, p.208, suggests that this was said about *Slavers*.
24 Trevor-Roper, *Blunted Sight*, pp.87–90.
25 Monkhouse, p.122.
26 Smith, *Nollekens*, p.365.
27 Th. 1877, p.246.
28 TB CXI.
29 TB CCXCI a; TB CCLXV; TB CCLXXIX.
30 Letters, pp.147–8.
31 Ibid., p.197.
32 Ibid., p.203.

33   Ibid., p.206.
34   Leslie, *Inner Life*, p.143.
35   Th. 1877, p.120.
36   TB CCXCI.
37   Roberts, *TS*, 9, 1, p.6.
38   Th. 1877, p.310.
39   Ibid., pp.243–4.
40   Letters, p.235.
41   Th. 1877, p.326.
42   Ibid., p.313.
43   MS note in G. Jones's copy of Th. ii, p.168.
44   Th. 1877, p.314.
45   Ibid., p.352.
46   Trevor-Roper, *Blunted Sight*, p.120.
47   Jones, 'Recollections', in Letters, p.3.
48   Letters, p.186.
49   Th. 1877, pp.323–4.
50   Ibid., pp.279–80.
51   Letters, p.201.
52   Roberts, *TS*, 11, 1, p.61.
53   IGI; *Geese* I, pp.10, 115–6.
54   Ruskin, *Dilecta*, in *Praeterita*, pp.542–3.
55   Finberg, p.399.
56   Forster, *Dickens*, ii, p.86.
57   Bicknell, *TS*, 9, 1, p.3.
58   *AR*, i, p.201.
59   *TS*, 9, 1, p.2.
60   Ibid.
61   Ibid., p.3.
62   Ibid., pp.3–4.
63   Ibid., p.3.
64   *TSN*, no.33, p.6.
65   Letters, p.82.
66   *TS*, 9, 1, p.3.
67   Disraeli, *Sybil*, pp.245–7.
68   Graves, *Leather Armchairs*, p.46.
69   Th. 1877, p.352.
70   Frith, i, p.333.
71   Frith, i, p.333; Th. 1877, p.265, has Maclise calling at Turner's
     house to tell him of Haydon's death. George Jones noted in his
     copy of Thornbury that Maclise 'utterly denies telling Turner
     that Haydon had destroyed himself'. But someone evidently did

tell Turner, and his response seems in character.

72 B&J, no.415.
73 Wilton, *Painting and Poetry*, p.180.
74 B&J, no.385. Ruskin, *Modern Painters*, I, p.404.
75 Letters, p.190.
76 Gage, *Rain, Steam and Speed*, p.14.
77 Ibid., p.16.
78 Ruskin, *Dilecta*, in *Praeterita*, pp.576–8. The GWR train shown by Turner seems to have open-topped carriages. Third-class GWR passengers were carried in open wagons until 1844. If he was with Lady Simon, Turner, presumably, was travelling first-class.

20: Chelsea Harbour

1   Roberts, *TS*, 9, 1, p.3.
2   *Century*, p.253.
3   Ibid., pp.253–4.
4   Lindsay, p.197.
5   Falk, *Turner*, p.204.
6   Roberts, *TS*, 9, 1, p.7.
7   Armstrong, *Turner*, p.179.
8   Roberts, *TS*, 9, 1, p.7.
9   Ibid., pp.3, 6.
10 Th. ii, p.46.
11 Roberts, *TS*, 9, 1, p.7. Here and elsewhere, Roberts's spelling and punctuation retained.
12 Th. 1877, p.360.
13 Ibid., p.361.
14 Ibid.
15 Falk, *Turner*, p.204.
16 Armstrong, *Turner*, p.182.
17 Finberg, p.376.
18 Armstrong, *Turner*, pp.181–2.
19 Letters, pp.195–6.
20 Feret, *Isle of Thanet Gazette*, 23 September 1916.
21 Letters, pp.217–18.
22 Ibid., p.221.
23 Ruskin, *Praeterita*, p.310.
24 NPG archive; *TS*, 3, 1, pp.29–30.
25 Frith, *Autobiography*, i, p.137.
26 Redgrave, *Memoir*, p.58.
27 Roberts, *TS*, 9, 1, p.3.
28 Letters, p.216.

29 *AR*, i, p.199.
30 Leslie, *Inner Life*, p.144.
31 Ruskin, *Works*, xiii, pp.478–80. Ian Warrell points out that Ruskin wrote this account when suffering one of his nervous breakdowns. Warrell, *Through Switzerland*, p.149.
32 Letters, p.187.
33 Pye-Roget, pp.73–4.
34 Ibid., p.97.
35 Th. 1877, pp.278–9.
36 Ibid.
37 Eastlake, *Journals*, i, p.189.
38 Ibid., p.322.
39 Ruskin, quoted in B&J text, p.83, letter to Charles Eliot Norton, 7 August 1870. The painting, restored, is now in quite good condition.
40 Ruskin, *Modern Painters*, v, p.366n.
41 Emerson, *Collected Works*, v, pp.75–6,260 n.75.
42 Stillman, *Autobiography*, i, pp.113, 115.
43 Frith, *Autobiography*, i, pp.134–6.
44 Ruskin, *Notes*, p.10.
45 Ruskin, *Modern Painters*, iii, p.v.
46 Finberg, p.416.
47 Ibid., pp.437–8.
48 *Geese* I, p.34; *Will* 2, p.13; *Geese* III, pp.115–21 and 127.
49 Letters, p.220.
50 Ibid.
51 Roberts, *TS*, 9, 1, p.6.
52 Letters, pp.222–3.
53 Ibid., p.205.
54 Ibid., p.223.
55 Ruskin, *Works*, xiii, p.99.
56 Ibid., xxxvi, p.595.
57 B&J, no.401.
58 Pye, quoted in Falk, *Turner*, p.220.
59 Jones, 'Recollections', in Letters, p.8.
60 TB LXXXV.
61 TB CXIII.
62 Ruskin, *Works*, xxii, p.490.
63 Ruskin, *Modern Painters*, i, pp.174–5.
64 *The Tempest*, I, ii, line 198.
65 *TS*, 9, 2, p.49.
66 Revelation, xix: 17–18.
67 Ruskin, *Works*, xiii, p.167.

68 Th. 1877, p.xi.
69 Finberg, p.434.
70 Th. 1877, pp.349–51.
71 Ibid., p.350. MS note on Haskell copy of Th. ii, pp.259–62: Hugh Munro doubted this story because of Turner's dislike of being portrayed; but it seems more likely than not, if one discounts a few of Thornbury's embellishments.
72 Th. 1877, pp.350–1.
73 Monkhouse, p.132.
74 TB CCCLXIII, ff.2, 6.
75 Ibid., f.41.
76 Wilton, *Life and Works*, nos.1425, 1426.
77 Brown, *Turner and the Channel*, p.12.
78 TB CCCLVI.

21: World's End

1 Turner's tag for *The Departure of the Fleet* gives the impression that Dido killed herself by drinking poison, but in the *Aeneid* she used a Trojan sword.
2 Roberts, *TS*, 9, 1, p.2.
3 Lindsay, p.248 n.33.
4 Letters, p.224.
5 Ibid., pp.225–6.
6 Ibid., p.227.
7 Ibid., p.228.
8 Jones, 'Recollections', in ibid., p.9.
9 Wilton, p.238.
10 Ruskin, *Modern Painters*, i, June 1851 postscript (1897 edn, p.454).
11 Cooper, *My Life*, ii, pp.10–11. Cooper's anecdote is nice; but his statements on Turner's death and funeral on p.11 are untrue.
12 Finberg, p.432.
13 Letters, p.228.
14 Whitman, *Charles Turner*, p.20.
15 Roberts, *TS*, 9, 1, p.6.
16 Jones, 'Recollections', in Letters, p.9.
17 Ruskin, *Works*, xxii, p.512.
18 Ibid., xxxvi, p.292.
19 Hazlitt, *Selected Writings*, p.509.
20 Frith, *Autobiography*, p.139.
21 Finberg, p.437.
22 Armstrong, *Turner*, p.181.
23 Roberts, *TS*, 9, 1, p.6.

24 Letters, p.229.
25 Roberts, *TS*, 9, 1, p.7.
26 Ibid., p.6. *Geese* III, p.66.
27 Letters, p.230.
28 Roberts, *TS*, 9, 1, p.6.
29 Eastlake, *Journals*, i, p.273. She was forty-two in 1851.
30 Archer, *TS*, 1, 1, p.36.
31 Ruskin, *Works*, xxii, p.49; xxviii, p.147.
32 Archer, *TS*, 1, 1, p.36.
33 Roberts, *TS*, 9, 1, p.6.
34 Archer, *TS*, 1, 1, p.36; Jones, 'Recollections', in Letters, p.4; Finberg, p.438.
35 Whitman, *Charles Turner*, p.20.
36 Dossier: certified copy of death entry.
37 Letters, p.230 n.1.
38 Redgrave, *Memoir*, pp.80–1.
39 If Mrs Booth had attended, David Roberts would have known her when he met her, apparently for the first time, in Chelsea the following summer: *TS* 9, 1, p.7.
40 Whitman, *Charles Turner*, p.20.
41 Redgrave, *Memoir*, p.82.
42 Finberg, p.439.
43 *AR*, i, pp.207–8.
44 Redgrave, *Memoir*, pp.83–4.
45 TB C. Jan Piggott in *TSN* no.74, pp.12–13, identifies Turner's source as a poem by the dramatist George Colman Jr., first published c.1808–9.

22: Turner's Gift

1 Eastlake, *Journals*, i, p.273.
2 Whittingham, *Ruskin as Turner's Executor*, p.7.
3 Eastlake, *Journals*, i, p.235.
4 *Will*, 2, p.27.
5 Ibid., p.32.
6 *Times*, 24 December 1851.
7 Jones, 'Recollections', in Letters, p.10.
8 Whitley, *1821–37*, pp.282–3.
9 Ruskin, *Modern Painters*, v, pp.v-vii.
10 W. M. Rossetti, *Rossetti Papers*, 1903, p.383; Falk, p.233.
11 Harris, *Life and Adventures*, pp.288–9.
12 Robertson, *Sir Charles Eastlake*, p.303, citing letter of Ruskin to Wornum, 3 May 1862, in National Gallery archives.

13 Ruskin, *Diaries*, II, p.619.
14 Ruskin, *Modern Painters*, v, p.372.
15 Gowing, introduction to Finberg, *Sketches and Drawings*, p.xx.
16 Jones, 'Recollections', in Letters, p.10.
17 The huge collection of watercolours presented a separate problem
   of selection. A committee met at the National Gallery in December
   1856 to choose 102 items for display at Marlborough House. Warrell,
   Through Switzerland, p.148.
18 Hawthorne, *English Notebooks*, ii, pp.382–9.
19 Finberg, p.450.
20 The first codicil, 1832, refers to 'the object of keeping my works
   together.' *Will*, 1, p.29. One cannot help but think that Somerset
   House would have made the best home for Turner.
21 Whittingham, *Ruskin as Turner's Executor*, p.27.
22 Th. 1877, pp.362–5.
23 Wilton, p.248.
24 Dossier.
25 Jones, 'Recollections', in Letters, p.3.
26 Roberts, *TS*, 9, 1, p.7.
27 Ibid.
28 Wilton, *Life and Work*, p.470.
29 Letters, p.xxvi n.2.
30 *Will*, 2, p.20.
31 Ibid., p.21.
32 Walbrook, 'Light on an Old Mystery', *Daily Telegraph*, 27 June 1924.
33 Th. i, p.40.
34 G. Jones's copy of Th. i.
35 Th. i, preface.
36 Walbrook, 'Light on an Old Mystery', *Daily Telegraph*, 27 June 1924.
37 *Will*, 2, p.21.
38 Ibid., p.22.
39 Th. 1877, p.127.
40 Dossier.
41 Ibid.
42 Ibid.
43 Stillman, *Autobiography*, i, pp.162–5.
44 Schuyler, *American Architecture*, pp.289–90.

Selected Bibliography

All titles published in London except where cited.

General

Armstrong, Sir Walter, *Turner*, London and New York, 1902
Ballantine, James, *Life of David Roberts*, 1866
Bayes, Walter, *Turner, a Speculative Portrait*, 1931
Berger, John, *About Looking*, London and New York, 1980
Boswell, James, *London Journal*, 1950
Bretherton, F. F., *The Origins and Progress of Methodism in Margate*,
    Margate 1908
Broughton, Lord (J. C. Hobhouse), *Recollections of a Long Life* vol. iii,
    1910
Bryant, Arthur, *The Age of Elegance*, 1954
Burnet, John, *Turner and His Works* (incl. memoir by Peter Cunningham),
    1852
Butlin, Martin and Joll, Evelyn, *The Paintings of J. M. W. Turner*, 2 vols,
    1977, rev. edn 1984
Butlin, Martin with Mollie Luther and Ian Warrell, *Turner at Petworth*,
    1986
Carey, William, *Some Memoirs of the Patronage and Progress of the Fine
    Arts*, 1819
Cobbett, William, *Rural Rides*, 1830, repr. 2 vols, 1908
Colvin, Howard, *Biographical Dictionary of British Architects 1600–1840*,
    1978
Cooper, T. Sidney, R. A., *My Life*, 2 vols, 1890
Creevey, Thomas, *The Creevey Papers*, ed. H. Maxwell, 2 vols, 1904
Cunningham, Peter: *see* Burnet
Disraeli, Benjamin, *Sybil*, 1845, rep. 1954
Eastlake, Lady, *Journals and Correspondence*, 2 vols, 1895
Emerson, Ralph Waldo, *English Traits*, 1856 (in *Collected Writings*, vol. 5,

Cambridge, Mass., 1994)

Falk, Bernard, *Turner the Painter*, 1938

Farington, Joseph *see* Grieg; and Garlick, Macintyre and Cave

Finberg, A. J., *A Complete Inventory of the Drawings of the Turner Bequest*,
 2 vols, 1909

  The History of Turner's Liber Studiorum, 1924

  In Venice with Turner, 1930

  Turner's Sketches and Drawings, 1910, repr., New York, 1960

  The Life of J. M. W. Turner, 2nd edn, Oxford, 1961

  Turner's Watercolours at Farnley Hall, n.d.

Finley, Gerald, *Turner and George IV in Edinburgh*, 1981

Forster, John, *Life of Dickens*, 3 vols, 1873

Frith, William Powell, *My Autobiography*, 3 vols, 1887

Gage, John, *Colour in Turner: Poetry and Truth*, 1969

  J. M. W. Turner: 'A Wonderful Range of Mind', 1987, New Haven,
 Conn. and London

  Turner: Rain, Steam and Speed, 1972

  ed., *Collected Correspondence of J. M. W. Turner*, Oxford, 1980

Garlick, K., Macintyre, A. and Cave, K., eds, *The Diary of Joseph
 Farington*, 16 vols, New Haven, Conn. and London 1978–84

George, M. Dorothy, *London Life in the Eighteenth Century*, 1925, repr.
 1966

Goodall, Frederick, *Reminiscences*, 1902

Gotch, Rosamund, *Maria, Lady Callcott*, 1937

Gowing, Lawrence, *Turner: Imagination and Reality*, NY, 1966

Graves, Charles, *Leather Armchairs*, 1963

Greaves, Margaret, *Regency Patron: Sir George Beaumont*, 1966

Greig, J., ed., *The Diary of Joseph Farington*, 8 vols, 1922–8

Hamerton, Philip Gilbert, *The Life of J. M. W. Turner R.A.*, 1879

Hampden, John, ed., *An Eighteenth Century Journal 1774–76*, 1940

Harris, Frank, *His Life and Adventures*, 1947

Hawthorne, Nathaniel, *Passages from the English Notebooks*, Boston, 1870

Haydon, Benjamin Robert, *Autobiography and Journals*, 1853, ed.
 M. Elwin, 1950

Hazlitt, William, *Selected Writings*, ed. R. Blythe, 1970

  Collected Works, 1903

Herrmann, Luke, *Ruskin and Turner*, 1968

Hibbert, Christopher, *The Grand Tour*, 1987

Hill, David, *In Turner's Footsteps through the Hills and Dales of Northern
 England*, Oxford 1984

  Turner in the Alps, 1992

  Turner on the Thames, New Haven, Conn. and London, 1993

Turner's Birds, Oxford, 1988

Homer, *The Odyssey*, trans. R. Fitzgerald, New York, 1961

Hunt, J. D., *The Wider Sea: a Life of John Ruskin*, 1982

Hutchison, Sidney, *The History of the Royal Academy 1768–1968*, 1968

Jones, George, MS 'Recollections of J. M. W. Turner', in Gage, *Collected Correspondence of J. M. W. Turner*, pp.1–10
  Sir Francis Chantrey R.A., 1849

Kennedy, Ludovic, *Nelson and his Captains*, 1975 (first published as *Nelson's Band of Brothers*, 1951)

Kitson, Michael, *Turner*, 1964

Leslie, Charles Robert, *Memoirs of the Life of John Constable, R.A.*, 1845
  Autobiographical Reflections, 2 vols, 1860

Leslie, George D., *The Inner Life of the Royal Academy*, 1914

Leslie, Robert C., *A Waterbiography*, 1894, repr. Southampton 1985

Lesure, F. and Nichols, R. eds, *Letters of Claude Debussy*, 1987

Lindsay, Jack, *The Sunset Ship: The Poems of J. M. W. Turner*, 1966
  J. M. W. Turner: his Life and Work, London and Greenwich, Conn., 1966

Lloyd, Mary, *Sunny Memories*, privately printed, 1880 (pp.31–8 repr. *TS* 4, 1, p.22)

Marryat, Captain Frederick, *Jacob Faithful*, 1929

Marsden, Christopher, *The English at the Seaside*, 1947

Mayhew, Henry, *London Labour and the London Poor*, 4 vols, vols i–iii 1851, vol. iv 1862

Miller, Thomas, *Turner and Girtin's Picturesque Views*, 1854

Monkhouse, W. Cosmo, *Turner*, 1879

Moore, Thomas, *Memoirs*, vol. iii 1853

Nevill, Ralph, *London Clubs*, 1911

Nicholson, Kathleen, *Turner's Classical Landscapes*, Princeton, 1990

Owen, Felicity and Brown, David Blaney, *Collector of Genius*, New Haven, Conn. and London, 1988

Powell, Cecilia, *Turner in the South*, New Haven, Conn. and London, 1987

Raistrick, Arthur, *The Pennine Dales*, 1968

Rasmussen, Steen Eiler, *London: The Unique City*, 1934, repr. 1961

Rawlinson, W. G., *Turner's Liber Studiorum*, 1878, 2nd edn 1906

Redding, Cyrus, *Fifty Years' Recollections, Literary and Personal*, 2 vols, 1858
  Past Celebrities Whom I Have Known, 1866

Redgrave, Richard, *A Memoir*, ed. F. M. Redgrave, 1891

Redgrave, Richard and Samuel, *A Century of British Painters*, 2 vols, 1866, 2nd edn 1890, repr. 1947

Reynolds, Sir Joshua, *Discourses*, ed. P. Rogers, 1992

Richardson, Jonathan, *Works*, ed. J. Richardson Jr, 1773

Ritchie, Leitch, *Liber Fluviorum*, 1853

Robertson, David, *Sir Charles Eastlake and the Victorian Art World*, Princeton, 1978

Rogers, Samuel, *Table Talk*, 1856

Roget, John Lewis, *A History of the 'Old Water-Colour' Society*, 2 vols, 1891
    ed., *Notes and Memoranda respecting the Liber Studorium* by John Pye, 1879

Ruskin, John, *Praeterita* (including *Dilecta*), 1885–9
        Elements of Drawing, 1857
        Notes by Mr. Ruskin on his Drawings by Turner, 1878
        Modern Painters, 6 vols, 1897–8 edn
        The Works of John Ruskin, Sir E. T. Cook and A. Wedderburn, eds, 39 vols, 1903–12
        The Harbours of England, repr. 1907
        Diaries, J. Evans and J. H. Whitehouse, eds, 3 vols, Oxford, 1956–9
        Ruskin Today, K Clark, ed., 1964

Sandby, W., *The History of the Royal Academy of Arts*, 2 vols, 1862

Schetky, S. F. L., *Ninety Years of Work and Play, sketches from the career of John Christian Schetky*, Edinburgh, 1877

Schuyler, Montgomery, *American Architecture and Other Writings*, Cambridge, Mass. 1961

Shanes, Eric, *Turner's Picturesque Views in England and Wales*, 1979
        Turner's England 1810–38, 1990
        Turner's Human Landscape, 1990

Sickert, Walter, *A Free House!*, ed. O. Sitwell, 1947

Simond, L., *Journal of a Tour and Residence in Great Britain during the years 1810 and 1811*, 1815

Smith, J. T., *A Book for a Rainy Day*, 1845, repr. 1906
        Nollekens and his Times, 1829, repr. 1920

Smith, Sydney, *Selected Writings*, ed. W. H. Auden, 1956

Smollett, Tobias, *Travels through France and Italy* (1766), *Works*, 1872

Stainton, Lindsay, *Turner's Venice*, 1985

Stillman, W. J., *Autobiography of a Journalist*, 2 vols, 1901

Stokes, Adrian, *Painting and the Inner World*, 1963

Summerson, John, *Georgian London*, 1962

Swinburne, C. A., *Life and Works of J. M. W. Turner R.A.*, 1902

Thomson, David, *England in the Nineteenth Century*, 1950

Thornbury, Walter, *The Life of J. M. W. Turner, R.A.*, 2 vols, 1862, one-vol. rev. edn 1877, repr. 1904

Timbs, John, *Lives of the Wits and Humourists*, vol. ii, 1862
        Anecdote Lives, 1872

Trevor-Roper, Patrick, *The World through Blunted Sight*, 1970

Trimmer, Sarah, *Some Account of the Life and Writings of Mrs Trimmer*, 2 vols, 1814

Turner, Charles, Diary, MS in Osborn Collection, Beineke Library, Yale University; repr. Whitman 1907 and *Will*, 2, 1995

Uwins, Thomas Mrs, *Memoir of Thomas Uwins*, 2 vols, 1858

Virgil, *The Aeneid*, trans. R. Fitzgerald, 1983, repr. 1993

Walden, Sarah, *The Ravished Image*, 1985

Walton, lzaak, *The Compleat Angler*, 1653, repr. 1962

Whitley, W. T., *Art in England 1800–20*, Cambridge, 1928
    Art in England 1821–37, Cambridge 1930
    Artists and their Friends in England 1700–1799, vol. ii 1928

Whitman, Alfred, *Charles Turner*, 1907

Whittingham, Selby, *Ruskin as Turner's Executor*, 1995
    Of Geese, Mallards and Drakes, 3 vols, 1993–6
    An Historical Account of the Will of J. M. W. Turner, R.A., 5 parts, 2nd edn, 1996

Wilkinson, Gerald, *Turner on Landscape*, 1982
    Turner's Early Sketchbooks, 1972

Wilton, Andrew, *The Life and Work of J. M. W. Turner* (with catalogue of watercolours), 1979
    Turner Abroad, 1982
    Turner in his Time, 1987

Woodforde, James, *Diary of a Country Parson*, ed. J. Beresford, 1935, repr. Oxford 1978

Wornum, Ralph, *The Turner Gallery*, 1875

Wyllie, W. L., *J. M. W. Turner*, 1905

Wyndham, John, *Wyndham and Children First*, 1968

Reference Works

Dictionary of National Biography
A Dictionary of Artists, by Samuel Redgrave, 2nd edn, 1878
Encyclopaedia Britannica, 11th edn, 1910
International Genealogical Index
The London Encyclopaedia, ed. Ben Weinreb and Christopher Hibbert, 1992
The Survey of London, esp. vols xviii 1937 and xxxvi 1970

Exhibition Catalogues

All catalogues are from the Tate Gallery except where cited.

Bachrach, A. G. E., *Turner's Holland*, 1994
Bower, Peter, *Turner's Papers*, 1990
Brown, David Blaney, *Augustus Wall Callcott*, 1981
    Turner and Byron, 1992
    Turner and the Channel, 1987
Butlin, Martin, with Andrew Wilton, *Turner 1775–1851*, 1974
Chumbley, Ann, and Ian Warrell, *Turner and the Human Figure*, 1989
Davies, Maurice, *Turner as Professor*, 1992
Egerton, Judy, *Turner: The Fighting Temeraire*, 1995, National Gallery, London
Forrester, Gillian, *Turner's 'Drawing Book': The Liber Studiorum*, 1996
Gore, St John, and Evelyn Joll, *The Picture Collection at Petworth House*, Petworth, Sussex, n.d.
Lyles, Anne, *Turner and Natural History: The Farnley Project*, 1988
    Turner: The Fifth Decade, 1992
    Young Turner: Early Work to 1800, 1989
Lyles, Anne and Diane Perkins, *Colour into Line: Turner and the Art of Engraving*, 1989
Merwe, Pieter van der (with Roger Took), *The Spectacular Career of Clarkson Stanfield*, Newcastle, 1979
Perkins, Diane, *Turner: The Third Decade*, 1990
Powell, Cecilia, *Turner in Germany*, 1995
    Turner's Rivers of Europe, 1991
Solender, Katherine, *Dreadful Fire! Burning of the Houses of Parliament*, Cleveland, Ohio, 1984
Townsend, Joyce, *Turner's Painting Techniques*, 1993
Upstone, Robert, *Turner: The Final Years*, 1993
    Turner: The Second Decade, 1989
Warrell, Ian, *Turner: The Fourth Decade*, 1991
    Turner in the North of England, 1797, 1996
    Through Switzerland with Turner: Ruskin's First Selection from the Turner Bequest, 1995
White, Christopher, *English Landscape 1630–1850* (drawings, prints and books from the Paul Mellon Collection, New Haven), 1977
Wilton, Andrew, with Rosalind Mallard Turner, *Painting and Poetry*, 1990
Wilton, Andrew, *Turner in the British Museum*, British Museum, 1975

Periodicals and Newspapers

Apollo, Oct. 1985, pp.280–7, R. Walker on Lord Egremont. Oct. 1996,
    pp.25–32, H. George on Turner, Lawrence and Canova.
Athenaeum, 1852: 3 Jan; 28 Feb.; 24 Apr.; 10 Jul.
        1861: 16 Nov.; 23 Nov.; 14 Dec.
        1862: 4 Jan.; 11 Jan.; 22 Feb.; 1 Mar.; 8 Mar.; 15 Mar.
        1878: 23 Feb.
Burlington Magazine: vol. xxi, 1912, Lionel Cust on Turner in early life
        vol. xxii, 1912–13, W. T. Whitley on Turner as lecturer
        vol. xcv, 1953, Hilda F. Finberg on Turner's Gallery in 1810
        vol. xcix, 1957, Hilda F. Finberg on Turner as a teacher
Catholic Ancestor, 5, 1994, S. Whittingham on the Danbys
Cobbett's Political Register 1802–35, various issues
Country Life, 6 Jul. 1951, Ann Livermore on Sandycombe Lodge
Daily Telegraph, 27 Jun. 1924, 'Light on an Old Mystery', by H. M.
    Walbrook
Fraser's Magazine, vol. xlv, Feb. 1852
Isle of Thanet Gazette, 1914–19, articles by C. J. Feret, 'Bygone Thanet', as
    collected in scrapbook in Margate Local History Library
J. M. W. Turner R.A., no. 1, 1988; no. 2, 1993
New Yorker, 16 March 1987, Calvin Tompkins on the restorer John Brealey
Notes & Queries, 29 Jan. 1853; 12 Jun. 1858; 21 Jun. 1862; 28 Jul. 1877
Brighton *Patriot*, 28 Nov. 1837, Lord Egremont's funeral
Record of the Art Museum, Princeton University, vol. 44, no. 2, 1985
Turner Society News, 1977–97
Turner Studies, vols i–xi, 1981–91
Walker's Monthly, no. 10, Oct. 1928
Walpole Society, vol. xxxviii, pp.123–81, Sidney Hutchison on the Royal
    Academy Schools 1768–1830

Index

Abbotsford, near Galashiels 276, 333
Academy of St Luke, Rome 246, 248
Ackermann, Rudolf 123
Adam, James 31
Adam, Robert 31, 225
Addison, Joseph 91
Adelphi, London 10, 31
Adelphi Terrace, London 46; No.6 31
Admiralty 51, 100, 239, 345
The Aeneid (Virgil) 58–9, 91–2, 261, 392
Aeschylus 90
AGBI *see* Artists' General Benevolent Institution
Aire, River 326
Akenside, Mark xvii, 92, 149, 158, 159
Albano 248
Albemarle Street, London 358
Albert, Prince Consort 279, 351, 363, 368, 394
Aldeburgh, Suffolk 268
Alexander I, Tsar of Russia 245
All Saints Church, Isleworth 93
Allason, Thomas 242
Allen, J. C. 138
Almanack of the Month 252
Alps 205, 223, 245, 266, 331, 351, 354
Althorp, Lord 221
Alum Bay, Isle of Wight 30
Ambleteuse 367
Ancona 245
Anderson, Robert 91, 196
Angerstein, John Julius 46, 47, 287
Annals of Fine Arts 23
Anti-Slavery League 362
Antiquities of England and Wales, The (Boswell) 11–12, 122
Antiquities of Italy 408
Antwerp 364
Aosta 66, 222, 331

Apennines 244
Apollonius Rhodius 91
aquatints 128–9
Arch, J. and A. 137
Arch of Titus, Rome 248
Archer, John W. 117, 240–41, 293, 368, 397, 409, 410
Argonautica (Apollonius Rhodius) 91
Argyll, Duke of 107
Ariel (ship) 277, 278
Arnold, General Benedict 369
Arnold's Magazine of the Fine Arts 335–6
Arras 330
Ars Poetica (Horace) 90–91
Art Journal 395
The Art of Painting (Fresnoy) 146
Art-Union 198, 278, 362
Artists' Conversazione 133
Artists' General Benevolent Institution (AGBI) 113, 238, 261, 340–42, 376, 404–5
Arun, River 325
Ashmole, Elias 182
Athenaeum Club 342, 360–61, 362, 372, 376, 400
Athenaeum magazine 278, 314, 350, 363, 386
Athens 46
Atkinson, Mr (master of the *Victory*) 99
Atlas Fire Office 109
Auckland, Lord 77
Audubon, James 110
Aulnoye, Mme d' 249
Austen, Jane 18, 66, 267
Auxerre 244
Avignon 253
Avon gorge 28
Avon, River 94, 325

Babbage, Charles 174
Backhuysen, Ludolf 61
Baiae 246, 248
Bailey's Alley, London 9

Baily, Edward Hodges 399
'The Baite' (Donne) 179
Banks, Sir Joseph 276
Barbers and Surgeons Guild 7
'The Bard' (Gray) 49, 350
Barker, Henry Aston 24
Barker, Robert 24
Barking, Essex 240, 403
Barnard, Thomas 106
Barnes 229
Barnes, Thomas 337
Barnstaple, Devon 1, 3, 166, 170
Barry, James 24, 25, 106, 215, 400
Bartlett, Mr (surgeon dentist) 395, 397, 399, 409–10
Bath 27
Battersea, London 95, 181, 391
Battersea Bridge 95, 367, 369–70
Bay of Naples 246, 252, 258
Beagle, HMS 328
Beale, Benjamin 267
Beamsley Beacon, Yorkshire 212
Beatson's yard, Rotherhithe 344
Beaugency 327
Beaumont, Sir George, accuses T of 'misleading the Taste' 198; battle against the White Painters 200; Claude as his hero 188; and Claude's influence on T 69; Constable as his protege 61, 191; and *Crossing the Brook* 173, 190; death (1827) 192, 280; and *Dido building Carthage* 188; as a director of the British Institution 196; dislikes Turner's imprecision 193; and *Dutch Boats in a Gale* 61, 188–9; and *Fishing upon the Blythe-Sand* 84, 189; as part of the old order 203; as a patron 188, 191; Scott on 192; taste in art 191; and T's 'blots' 74, 189; and T's clientele 190; on T's colouring 193, 199; and T's gallery at Harley Street 77;

T's reaction to his criticisms 195

Beaumont, Lady Margaret 191–2
Beaumont sur Oise 244
Beckford, William 32, 46, 49, 60
Bedford, Earl of 4
Bedford Street, London 9, 52
Beechey, Sir William 46, 71, 310, 315; *Mrs Hasler as Flora* 319
Belgium 322, 328
Belgravia, London 367
Bell, Edward 95, 123
Bell inn, Margate 267
Bell Tavern, Exeter Street, London 48
Bell's Weekly Messenger 235
Bennet, Julia *see* Gordon, Lady Julia
Bennett, Robert 417
Berlin 331
Bernini, Gian Lorenzo 247
Berry Pomeroy, Devon 171
Berwick-on-Tweed 209
Bethlehem Hospital for the insane (Bedlam), Finsbury Circus, London (later Lambeth) 31, 51–2, 63, 75, 194–5, 339
Beverley, Humberside 209
Bible, the 92, 363, 387
Bicknell, Christine (nee Roberts) 302–3, 357, 358, 360
Bicknell, Elhanan 181, 265, 361, 376
Bicknell family 356, 357, 358
Billingsgate, London 14, 97
Bird, Edward 298
The Black Dwarf (newspaper) 249
The Black Dwarf (Scott) 249
Blackfriars Bridge, London 10
Blackheath, London 251, 329, 330
Blackwall, London 114
Blackwall Point 14
Blackwood's Magazine 265, 266, 336, 347, 350–51
Blair, Hugh 162
Blake, Catherine 269
Blake, William 157, 202, 369
Blake, William (a gifted amateur) 37
Blessington, Lady 306–7
Bloomsbury, London 14
Blythe Sand 14, 98
Boaden, James 194
Board of Ordnance 228
Boccaccio, Giovanni 184
Bohn, H. G. 135–6, 336
Bologna 244, 256

Bolton Abbey, Wharfedale 147, 207, 212
Bolton Castle, near Aysgarth, Yorkshire 12
Bond Street, London 136–7
Bonington, Richard Parkes 265
Bonneville 66, 330
Bonomi, Joseph 17–18, 55, 59
Book of Revelation 386
Boore and Bannister's, Messrs 150
Booth, John 269, 270, 273, 411
Booth, John Pound 269
Booth, Sophia Caroline (previously Pound; nee Nolt) 282, 310, 359, 366, 392, 397; and 'Colour Studies' 283–4; death 411; marriage to Henry Pound 269; marriage to John Booth 269; moves to Haddenham Hall 411; property in Margate 268–9; Pye on 370–71; Ruskin becomes a long-term friend 410; T becomes a new 'Mr Booth' 270; T lodges with in Margate 268, 269, 270; T moves her to Chelsea 270, 283, 367–9; T writes poetry for 270, 409–10; T's choice of an 'unladylike' friend 272–3; and T's lack of financial contribution 368, 382, 409; T's secretiveness about 270–72, 273; and T's will 356, 375, 404; visits to Kent continue 389
Boringdon, Lord 168
Bosch, Hieronymus 202
Boswell, Henry 11, 12, 122
Boswell, James 5, 24, 114
Boucher, Francois 127
Boulogne 64, 327–8, 366
Bourdon, Sébastien 188
Bourgeois, Sir Francis 73
Boydell, John 122, 140
Brasbridge, J. 6
Brent, River 13
Brentford, Middlesex 19; Grand Junction canal 89; as a historic spot 13; Joseph Marshall as a butcher in 3; market 231, 236, 408; Sunday school 11; T at John White's school 11, 12; T lives as a child with the Marshalls 10–13, 89, 110, 176, 226, 230; T works for John Lees 11–12, 17, 122
Bridgewater, Francis Egerton, Duke of 61, 98, 110
Brienne 324

Brighton 40, 94, 201, 267, 307
Brighton Patriot 320
Brighton Pavilion 18
Bril, Paul 311
Bristol 27, 29
British Empire 362
British Institution for Promoting the Fine Arts 106, 107, 190; Beaumont as a director 196; prizes 196, 312; as a rival to the Royal Academy 77; T exhibits 92, 107, 288, 301, 334, 335
The British Itinerary 155, 221
British Museum 23
British Press 340
Brittany 353
Britton, John 163, 188
Broadhurst, John 183, 323
Broadmead, Bristol 28
Broderip, W.J. 117
Brook Street, London 357
Brown, Lancelot 'Capability' 304
Brown, Robert 52
Brown, William 417
Browning, Elizabeth Barrett 394
Browsholme, near Clitheroe 210
Bruce, James 162
Buckingham Palace, London 182, 215
Buckingham Street, London 367
Bugsbys Reach, London 97
Bullen, Edward 418
Burdett, Sir Francis 218
Burgh Island, Bigbury Bay 166–7
Burke, Edmund 24, 48
Burnet, John 200
Burney, Dr Charles 24, 25
Burney, Fanny 24, 25, 26, 267
Burton, Decimus 360
Byron, George Gordon, 6th Baron Byron of Rochdale 221, 262–3, 265, 267, 386; and the Alps 244; T illustrates 219, 262; T reads 158, 243, 246, 262; and T's library 408

Cadell, Robert 140–41, 275, 324, 332, 336, 352
Caernarvon Castle 12, 46
Caesar, Julius 13
Cain (Byron) 386
Calais 15, 63, 64, 65, 69, 243, 279, 325, 330
The Caledonian Comet (Taylor) 152
Callcott, Sir Augustus Wall, RA, 288, 310; in the

Academy Council 286; and
Beaumont 189, 190, 191;
and the *Catalogue* backing
T 197; death (1844) 355; on
the hanging committee 297;
Knight buys his works 198;
knighthood 337; marries
Maria Graham 250, 253; and
Sarah Danby 54, 56, 57, 119;
and T's fishing 177; as T's
friend and follower 55; and
T's pricing of his pictures 77;
*Dutch Fishing-Boats running
foul, in the endeavour to board,
and missing the painter-rope*
294; *Mouth of the Tyne* 297;
The Pool of London 217
Callcott, John Wall 55
Callow, William 264–5, 349, 386
Calstock, Cornwall 170
Calstock Bridge 173
Camac, Colonel245
Cambrensis, Giraldus 161
Campbell, Thomas 113–14, 116,
142, 344
Canaletto 265
Canning, George 117
Canova, Antonio 199, 245
Canterbury 268
Canterbury Cathedral 31
Canvey Island 98
Capitol, Rome 245
Carew, J. E. 180, 310, 320
Carisbrooke Castle, Isle of
Wight 12
Carlini, Agostino 21–2, 23
Carlisle, Sir Anthony 145, 146,
320, 351–2
Carlisle, Earl of 107
Carlton House, Pall Mall 360
Carr, John 206, 207
Carr, Reverend W. Holwell
190, 197
Carrara 253
Carrick Moore, James 357
Carrick Moore, Mrs 271, 354, 357
Carrick Moore family 104
Carthage 194, 329, 390
Cassiobury Park, Watford,
Hertfordshire 165, 195
Cassivellaunus 13
Castel Gandolfo 252
Castle Street, London 24
Catalani, Madame 168
*Catalogue Raisonni of the Pictures
now Exhibiting at the British
Institution* 197
Cato, Mrs (*née* White) 41, 273

Caversham, Berkshire 97
Cerceau, Jacques de 146
Chalon, John James, RA 334, 399
Chamberlaine, John 129
Chambers, Sir William 19, 21
Chambery 66, 244
Chamonix 66
Champion (magazine) 187
Change Court, Covent Garden
5
Chantrey, Sir Francis 250, 253,
358, 386; on the Academy
Council 338; at Blackwall 114;
death 354; and the farewell
dinner at Somerset House
286; jokes about T's colours
293, 386; marries his cousin
227; *Paul at Iconium* 226; at
Petworth 178–9, 310, 315,
316, 319; in Rome 244–5; at
Sandycombe 227; T gives
practical help 117; T paints a
Venice picture for 272; on T's
financial circumstances 235;
and T's wish to be wrapped
in *Carthage* for burial400;
and varnishing days 296
Charing Cross, London 15, 364
Charles II, King 103
Charlotte, Queen 24
Chelsea 10, 328, 367–70, 384, 395;
T moves Mrs Booth to 270,
283, *see also* Davis Place
Chelsea Hospital 339
Cherry Garden Pier,
Bermondsey 345
Cheyne Walk, Chelsea 368; Nos
118–19 416
Chicago World's Fair 416
Chichester 307
Childe Harold (Byron) 246, 262–3
Childe Harold's Pilgrimage
(Byron) 266
Chillon 66
Chiltem Hundreds 109
Chinnery, George 23
Chittenden, Mr (undertaker) 139
Choat, Mr (lessee) 240
cholera 382–3
Christ Church college, Oxford
97
Christchurch Abbey, Hampshire
176
Christie's 312, 329, 409, 411, 412
*Chronology of the History of
Modern Europe* (Fawkes) 205
Churchill, Charles 145
Cibber, Colley 52
Cibber, Gabriel 52

Cicero 338
Cider Cellar tavern, Maiden
Lane 6
City of Canterbury (steamer) 268
Civita di Bagnoregio 255
Clarence, Duke of (later King
William IV) 237–8, 332
Clark, Sir Kenneth, Baron 406
Clarkson, Thomas 361
Claude Lorrain 60, 96, 146, 193,
197, 226, 244, 265; and the
Aeneid 390; in Baiae 248; in
the Royal Collection 129; T
influenced by 69, 122, 171, 173,
185, 188, 196, 202, 208, 236,
243, 255, 256, 263, 301, 318, 348,
364; T sketches Claudes in
the Louvre 323; *Hagar and the
Angel* 188, 191, 192; *Landscape
with Jacob with Laban and
his Daughters* 196, 253, 255,
311–12, 313; *Liber Veritatis* 122;
Mill 261, 282; *Seaport with the
Embarkation of the Queen of
Sheba* 46, 261, 282
Clein, Francis 4
Clerkenwell sessions house 241
Cliffe Marshes 98
Clint, George 132
Cliveden Reach 97
Clyde River 67
Coates, Miss 212
Cobb, George 240, 241, 281,
312, 403
Cobbett, William 48–9, 61,
304–5, 307
Cobbett's Political Register 49
Coburg, Bavaria 350
Cockerell, Charles R., RA 20,
175, 341, 399
Cockenmouth Castle,
Cumberland 165, 311
Col de Ia Seigne 66
Col du Bonhom.me 66
Cold Harbour, Margate 269,
273, 367
Coleman, Thomas 14–15, 49, 213,
218, 267
Coleorton, Leicestershire 191
Coleridge, Samuel Taylor 48, 158,
191, 192, 193
Collier, John, MP 166, 167
Collins, Wilkie 353–4
Collins, William, RA 135, 175,
354
Colnaghi, Dominic 126, 131, 377
The Compleat Angler (Walton)
179

Complete Poets (Anderson) 197
Congress of European Art
  (Munich, 1845) 385
Constable, John 186, 249, 252,
  263; admires T 201; and
  Beaumont 61, 192; conceit
  300; death (1837) 321, 333;
  elected ARA 74, 148, 248;
  elected RA 300; exhibits
  his first picture at the RA
  (1802) 74; and the light key
  201; never travels abroad 323;
  and painting in the open air
  96; at Petworth 311, 315; and
  Shee's attempts to reduce
  varnishing days 302; on T 148;
  and T's *Liber* 126; visits T's
  exhibition at Queen Anne
  Street (1813) 233; *Opening of
  Waterloo Bridge* 296; *Salisbury
  Cathedral from the Meadows*
  300
Cook (an artist, later stonemason) 28
Cooke, George 133, 134, 137, 166,
  172, 175, 222
Cooke, Mrs 133
Cooke, W. B. 138, 166, 172, 175,
  213, 227, 235, 326; and Coombe
  163; exhibition in Soho
  Square (1822) 251; and T's
  property at Wapping 241; T's
  relations with 132–3, 135
Coombe, William 163
Cooper, Abraham, RA 230
Cooper, Samuel 4
Cooper, T. Sidney 292–3, 374,
  394–5
Cope, Charles 114
Copenhagen 332
Copper-plate Magazine 30,
  122–3, 227
Cordell, Mr (of the Royal
  Society of Musicians) 120
Corfe Castle 166
Cornhill Magazine 417
Cornwall 80, 166
Corporation of London 340
Correggio (Antonio Allegri) (St
  Jerome) 69
Cotman, John Sell 85, 117–18, 151
Cottenham, Lord Chancellor 358
Courmayeur 66
Court of Chancery 406, 407,
  415, 420
Coutances, Normandy 326
Covent Garden, London 220,
  226; notoriety 4–5; T's parents
  set up home in 3

Covent Garden Market 4, 9,
  77, 123
Covent Garden Theatre 9, 20,
  38, 145
Cowes Castle 37
Cowes, Isle of Wight 202
Cowes Regatta 183, 252
Cowes Roads 183
Cowley Hall, Uxbridge xviii, 84,
  115, 177, 272, 354
Cowper family 309
Cox, David 126, 218
Cozens, Alexander 74, 192
Cozens, John Robert 32, 54, 192,
  247; *Hannibal, in his march
  over the Alps, showing to his
  Army the Fertile Plains of
  Italy* 32
Creevey, Thomas 306, 307, 310,
  313–4
Cremorne Pier, Chelsea 368, 371
Cremorne Pleasure Gardens,
  Chelsea 368
Cremorne Wharf, Chelsea 400
Creswick, Thomas 295, 401;
  Squally Day 293
Cribb, Mr (churchwarden) 281
Cristall, Joshua 23, 218
Croker, John Wilson 361
Cromarty Firth 334
Cromwell, Oliver 207, 222
Crown and Anchor Tavern,
  Strand 219, 341
Croydon, Surrey 384
Crystal Palace, Hyde Park 393
Cumberland, Duke of 51
Cunningham, Peter 394
Cuyp, Aelbert 218, 312; *The
  Rotterdam Ferry* 218; *View of
  Dordrecht* 218

daguerrotypes 389
Daily Advertiser 8
Danby, Caroline Melissa 56, 406
Danby, Hannah 84, 223, 254,
  274, 310, 323, 380, 409; and
  censuses 419, 420; death
  (1853) 414; Elizabeth Rigby
  on 81; finds T in Chelsea 398;
  her illness 82, 398; inventory
  taken of T's possessions
  after her death 410; leaves
  money to Evelina 414, 415;
  and Mrs Booth 368; and
  the Reverend Trimmer 360;
  Roberts on 396; Sarah's
  widow's allowance 119, 120;
  starts work for T as a servant
  (1809) 56; suggestions that T

was her lover 56, 57; treatment
  of visitors 81, 82–3; and T's
  funeral 402; and T's palette
  87, 88; and T's wills 262, 283,
  340, 357, 376, 406
Danby, John 55, 56, 57, 119, 120,
  283, 406
Danby, Louisa Mary 56
Danby, Marcella 56, 119, 406,
  413, 414
Danby, Sarah (*née* Goose) 58,
  63, 77, 81, 91, 148, 226, 271, 272,
  392; breaks up with T 120,
  206; Callcott and 54, 56, 57,
  199; death 414; at Evelina's
  wedding 215; her children
  54, 55, 56, 118, 119, 120, 406;
  marries John Danby 55; sells
  paintings to Charles Turner
  413–14; Sophia financially
  better off than 270; starts
  living with T 54; and T's wills
  56, 262, 283, 376; as the widow
  of a musician 54; widow's
  pension 56, 119, 342
Danby, Teresa 56, 120, 406
Danby family xviii, 59
Dance, George, RA 43, 145, 299
Dance, Nathaniel 235
Daniell, Reverend Edward
  357, 359
Daniell, William 73, 106, 199
Danube, River 326, 333
Darlington, Earl of 64, 174
Dart, Ann 29, 55, 114
Dart River 326
Darwin, Charles 329
David, Jacques-Louis 70
David Copperfield (Dickens) 279
Davies, Tom 5
Davis, Mr, of Lewisham 37
Davis Place (No.6), Cremorne
  New Road, Chelsea 384, 392;
  as an extension of Cheyne
  Walk 368–9; Archer draws
  the exterior 412; Daniel
  Pound stays at the cottage
  370; described 369–70; Dr
  Gaskell attends T 384; and
  the drowned girl 385; Hannah
  finds the address 398;
  incorporated in a large house
  418; Mr Bartlett attends T
  397, 411; Mrs Booth's lease
  expires (1867) 413; Pye and
  369, 371–2; T and Sophia
  move in 369; T's death
  399–400
Dawe, George 262

Dayes, Edward 31, 32, 35, 42
de Loutherbourg, Mrs 39, 103
de Loutherbourg, Philippe-
    Jacques 31, 35, 39, 44, 46, 103,
    238, 239; *Glorious First of
    June* 331
De Maria, James 167, 168
de Piles, Roger 148
de Robespierre, Maximilien 245
de Tabley, Lord (*previously* Sir
    John Leicester) 111, 312, 313
De Wint, Peter 218
del Monte, Guidobaldo 146
Deal, Kent 1, 41, 176, 182, 274,
    284, 384, 391
Debussy, Claude xviii
The Decameron (Boccaccio) 184
Dee, River 102, 179
Delacroix, Eugene 42, 325–6, 332
Delamotte, William 96
Denmark, Princess of 246
Denmark Hill, London 393
Deptford, Kent 14, 97
*Designs for Parsonage Houses,
    Alms Houses, etc.* (Hunt) 340
Devon 3, 80, 115, 166, 205, 226,
    268
Devonshire, Duchess of 244
Devonshire, Duke of 122
Dibdin, Tom 260
Dickens, Charles 86, 358
Didsbury, near Manchester 240
Dieppe 324, 367
Dijon 331
Discourses (Reynolds) 24–5,
    144, 157
Disraeli, Benjamin 361
Dixon, William 22, 38
Dobson (architect) 17, 18–19
Dodbrooke, Devon 167
Dolbadern Castle 49–50, 60
Dole 331
Domenichino 69
Don Quixote (Cervantes) 28
Donaldson, T. L. 112
Doncaster 108, 211
Donne, John 179
Dorchester 97
Dordrecht 218
Dorset 166
Douglas, Reverend J. 35, 380
Dove inn, Hammersmith
    Terrace 103
Dover 63, 64, 244, 270, 274, 279,
    326, 331, 367
Dover Castle 12
Dow, Alexander 162
Doyle, Dicky 252
Dresden 332

Dryden, John 91
Dubois, Edward 112
Dudley 185, 329
Dulwich College 377
Dunkirk 64
Dupuis, Evelina (T's daughter)
    see Turner, Evelina
Dupuis, Evelina (T's
    granddaughter) 415
Dupuis, Hanmer (T's grandson)
    415
Dupuis, Joseph, junior (T's
    grandson) 415
Dupuis, Joseph, senior 215, 357,
    414–15
Dupuis, Rosalie (T's
    granddaughter) 416
Dupuis, William (T's grandson)
    357
Dürer, Albrecht 149
Durham 45, 174, 215

Eagle Court, Covent Garden 5
Eagles, Reverend John 267, 337
Earlom, Richard 122
East Cowes, Isle of Wight 243
East Cowes Castle 182, 183, 184,
    251, 314
Eastern Dock, London 241
Eastlake, Sir Charles 173,
    301, 322; and Calstock 170,
    173; elected President and
    knighted 376; features
    brigands in his paintings 247,
    253; on Hannah Danby 81;
    marries Elizabeth Rigby 358;
    as a perceptive colleague 256;
    and reform of the Academy
    304, 361; in Rome 247, 255,
    256, 257, 260; translates
    Farbenlehre 364, 390; at T's
    funeral 401; and T's savings in
    Government Funds 405; and
    varnishing days 304
Eastlake, Lady *see* Rigby,
    Elizabeth
Eastlake family 284, 393
Eaton, Nottinghamshire 108
Eclogues (Virgil) 91, 149
Edinburgh 66, 174, 175, 202
Edinburgh Castle 66
Edinburgh Review 194, 362
Edridge, Henry 106, 110, 190,
    196
Edward I, King 49
Edwards, Edward 144
Edwards, Thomas 211
Eel Pie House, Twickenham 230
Effington, Earl of 419

Egremont, Elizabeth Iliffe,
    Countess of 307
Egremont, George O'Brien
    Wyndham, 3rd Earl of 275;
    apparent loss of interest in
    T's work (1812–25) 312–13;
    buys the *Confluence of the
    Thames and Medway* 101;
    buys a Dionysus 257; buys
    Ships bearing up for anchorage
    62, 95; and Carew 180; and
    Chantrey 178–9; death 321;
    feast for his tenants 320; gets
    on well with T 316; Greville
    on 309–10; his Claude 197,
    255, 312; his informal court
    339; as Lady Melbourne's
    lover 307; liberality 308, 309,
    310–11; owns Cockermouth
    Castle 165; and Petworth
    165, 305–22; purchase of oils
    from T (1806–12) 191; and T's
    gallery 107; and white ground
    paintings 199; his will 321–22
Egremont family 315
Egremont House, Piccadilly 307
Eidophusikon, Spring Gardens
    39
Elbe River 326
Elements of Architecture
    (Wooton) 20
Elements of Art (Shee) 158, 196–7
Elgin, Lady 46
Elgin, Lord 46, 90
Elgin marbles 83, 90, 91
Elgood, Mr (an appraiser) 410
Elliott, H. 228, 229
Emerson, Ralph Waldo 343, 381
English Channel 101, 174, 185,
    205, 277, 280, 323, 324, 330, 344
English Traits (Emerson) 381
engraving 123, 125
Essex 97
Essex, Earl of 107, 165, 196
Eton, Berkshire 96, 216
Etty, William 116, 266, 289, 368
Eu 367, 368
Euclid 146
Eustace, Reverend J. J. 244
Examiner 100, 101, 145, 163, 188,
    194, 201, 253
Exeter 171, 366
Exeter Street, London 5, 6

Fables (Northcote) 164
Fairfax, General Thomas 207,
    208, 221, 222
Fairy (government survey vessel)
    279

Falk, Bernard xvii
Farbenlehre (Goethe) 364, 390
Farington, Joseph 67, 75, 102,
    106–7, 233, 236, 244; the
    Academy Club on the river
    230; and the AGBI 341; and
    Beaumont 61, 189–92, 194;
    and Callcott's comment on
    Sarah Danby 54–5, 56, 57;
    and Callcott's complaint in
    the Academy Council 297;
    and Carlisle's charges 353;
    death 240; deplores student
    behaviour 23; his diary 23,
    65; and the Egremonts 307;
    in France 63–4, 66, 69; and
    Fuseli 61, 63–4, 70, 90; on the
    hanging committee 298–9;
    and the Incorporated Society
    of Artists 6, 31; and the
    Louvre 68, 70; and Monro's
    patronage of the arts 31–2;
    and politics 49; in Scotland
    66; and Serres 50; supports
    West 72; T offers to draw
    for 44–5; T tells of his 1819
    Italian tour 248; and T's
    argument with Bourgeois
    73; and T's *Battle of Trafalgar*
    100, 201; and T's behaviour
    73–4; and T's concern for
    his reputation 196; and T's
    dealings with Longman's 211;
    and T's election as ARA 47;
    and T's election as RA 59;
    and T's health 205–6, 225;
    and T's lecturing 144; and T's
    practical helping of students
    37; and T's treatment of Mrs
    Richards 342; and T's wish to
    help artists in distress 239–40;
    and varnishing days 288
Farnley Hall, Yorkshire 95,
    117, 181, 205–23, 225, 229,
    256, 277, 354; care packages
    from Hawksworth 384,
    393; described 206–7; *Dort,
    or Dortrecht* hangs at 325;
    evolution of *The First Rate
    taking in Stores* 209–10; fatal
    shooting accident 213, 214;
    and *Hannibal crossing the Alps*
    209; private museum in 207;
    the sketchbook from T's
    last visit (1824) 332; T brought
    out of his shell by Fawkes
    206; T capsizes a tandem
    carriage 208, 231; T combines
    a working trip and a holiday

205; T never visits again after
    Fawkes' death 223, 322
Farnley Moor 208, 410
Farrell, Thomas 241
Fatboys Diner, 21–2 Maiden
    Lane, London 418
Fawkes, Amelia 211
Fawkes, Anne (later
    Wentworth) 216
Fawkes, Ayscough 211
Fawkes, Edith Mary 209–10
Fawkes, Guy 219, 335
Fawkes, Hawksworth 208–9,
    216–18, 223, 249, 351, 354, 375,
    383, 384, 393
Fawkes, Jane 349
Fawkes, Maria 211
Fawkes, Miss 82
Fawkes, Mrs 207, 211–13, 215, 216,
    218, 222
Fawkes, Major Richard 208, 211
Fawkes, Richard Hawksworth
    (Walter's brother) 213
Fawkes, Walter 82, 95, 109, 117,
    191, 198, 199, 205–23, 239, 240,
    244, 254, 308, 312, 322, 335, 341
Fawkes family 174, 205, 211–14,
    216, 223, 248, 307, 313
Fenning's timberyard 334
Fetcham, Surrey 225
Fielding, Henry 4
Fielding, Sir John 4–5
Finberg, A. J. xvii, 40, 56
Finch, Robert 228, 254, 261
Finden brothers 134, 323, 337
Fingal's Cave, Staffa 12, 277
Firenzola 258
Fisher, Archdeacon John 187, 188
Fitzherbert, Mrs Maria 18, 90
Fitzroy Square, London 359, 393
Flaxman, John 90, 145; *St
    Michael and Satan* 318
Fleet Street, London 130, 402
Fleming, Mrs Eve 418
Fleming, Ian 418
Fleming, Peter 418
Florence 247
Foligno 258
Folkestone, Kent 274, 391
Fontana di Trevi, Rome 245
Fonthill Abbey, Wiltshire 46, 61
Foots Cray, Kent 20, 36, 37
Forster, John 358
Foundling Hospital, Lamb's
    Conduit Street 377, 406
Fox, George 221
Fra Diavolo (Michele Pezza) 247
Fragonard, Jean-Honoré 70
France 34, 63–5, 68–70, 89, 94,

165, 244, 247–8, 253–4, 260,
    287, 324, 331, 367–8
Fraser's Magazine 156, 345, 365
Frazer, Major 37
Free Society of Artists 6
Freemasons' Hall, Great Queen
    Street 341
Freemasons' Tavern, Great
    Queen Street 133, 230
French National Assembly 48
French Revolution 19
Fresnoy, Charles du 146
Friar Bacon's Study, Oxford
    12, 27
Frith, William Powell 85, 116,
    136, 293–5, 301, 362, 374, 382,
    397, 399, 416
Fuller, John, MP ('Mad Jack')
    109, 176, 218
Fuseli, Henry 44, 52, 61–3, 70,
    74–6, 90, 151, 158, 196, 240,
    298, 336, 358, 403

Gage, John xvi
Gainsborough, Thomas 11, 17, 31,
    61, 126, 197, 201, 231, 312
Galileo Galilei 291
Gallions Reach, London 97
Garrick, David 31
Gaskell, Dr Frederick 384
Gazzetta Privilegiata di Venezia
    265
Geneva 66
Genoa 254
George II, King 90, 282
George III, King 31, 44, 50, 51, 53,
    60, 70, 72, 73, 89–90, 93
George IV, King (*previously*
    Prince of Wales, *then* Prince
    Regent) 18, 23, 35, 45, 72, 90,
    107, 145, 151, 166, 175, 183, 200,
    236, 238, 345
George Street (No.34), London
    414
Georgics (Virgil) 91
Gérard, Baron François 69–70
Gérard, Marguerite 69
Germany 261, 370
The Ghost (Churchill) 145
The Giaour (Byron) 220
Gibbons, Grinling 306, 313
Gibraltar 101
Gilbert, John 303
Gillott, Joseph 293, 351
Gillray, James 46
Gilpin, Sawrey 48
Gilpin, Reverend William
    28, 198
Giorgione 69

Girtin, Thomas 31–4, 44, 46,
70–71, 111–12, 135, 192, 210, 333;
White House 71
Glastonbury 162
Glorious Revolution (1688) 221
Goethe, Johann Wolfgang von
364, 390
Gold Coast 215
Goldsmith, Oliver 197
Golt, Jean 56, 57
Goodall, Edward 133, 134,
139–40, 377
Goodall, Frederick, RA 297
Goodwin Sands 280, 391
Goold, Mr 37
Gordale Waterfall 212
Gordon, Sir J. Willoughby
37, 184
Gordon, Lady Julia (*née* Bennet)
37, 184
Görgei (Hungarian leader) 221
Goring, Oxfordshire 97
Gowing, Lawrence xvii
Gracechurch Street, London 353
Graham, James 31
Graham, Maria (*later* Callcott)
251, 255, 256
Graham, Captain Thomas 255
Grand Canal, Venice 349–50
Grand Chartreuse 66
Grand Fleet 24
Grand Junction Canal 89
Grantham, Lincolnshire 108,
210, 211
Granville, Earl 308
Gravesend, Kent 10, 97
Gray, Thomas 49, 351
Great Exhibition (1851) 393,
394, 398
Great Missenden,
Buckinghamshire 405
Great Ormond Street (No.18)
415
Great St Bernard Pass 66
Great Western Railway (GWR)
186, 365, 366
Greaves (boatman) 393
'Greek Craze' 90
Greek independence 220
Greek Street, Soho 139
Green, John 330
Green, Thomas 45
Greenwich 10, 97, 191, 205, 216,
230, 239, 331, 346, 358, 359
Greenwich Naval Hospital 14,
239, 331, 340
Grenoble 66
Greville, Charles 309–10, 320–21
Grey, Earl 107, 221

Griffith, Thomas 107, 376, 348,
350, 361, 372, 377, 378, 382, 394,
395, 401, 404, 417
Grindelwald 66
Grosvenor Place, Belgravia 307;
No.45 216, 218, 223
Guercino, 11 69
Guérin, Pierre-Narcisse (*Return
of Marcus Sextus*) 69–70
Guernsey 325
Guestling church, Sussex 57, 119
Guildford, Surrey 96
Gwynne, Nell 103
Gyfford, Edward 22

Haddenham Hall,
Buckinghamshire 413
Hadley, Surrey 35
Hakewill, James 133, 244, 254
Hall, Chambers 71, 336
Halstead (printdealer) 137
Ham Meadows, Surrey 228
Hamerton, Philip 26
Hammersley, James 356, 379–80
Hammersmith 102, 103, 104
Hammersmith Terrace 103
Hampstead 51
Hampstead Heath 127
Hampton Court, Herefordshire
30
Hampton Court, Middlesex
96, 104
Hand Court, Covent Garden 21,
35, 48, 413
*Handbuch den Englischen
Umgangssprache* 324
Hanover Terrace, London 358
Hansard, Thomas Carson 108
Hardcastle, Reverend W. 50
Hardwick, Philip, RA 341, 375,
377, 398, 400, 401, 404
Hardwick, Thomas, junior 17, 19,
20, 208, 375
Hardwick, Thomas, senior 19
Hardy, Captain Thomas 99, 239
Harewood House 210
Harewood, Lord 46
Harley Street, London 51, 78,
109, 411, 419; No.64 50, 57, 59,
76–9, 166, 224, 242, 312, 313,
405, 419, 420
Harper, Robert 50, 79, 361, 398
Harpur, Reverend Henry 3
Harpur, Henry 241, 377, 398–401,
403–5, 415
Harran, Edward 420
Harran, Sarah, junior 420
Harran, Sarah, senior 420
Harris, Frank 408

Hart, Solomon 291–2, 395
Harwich, Essex 279
Haskell, Professor Francis xvi
Hasler, Julia 319
Hastings, Sussex 119, 135, 176,
181, 333
Hathersage, Derbyshire 180
Havell, William 33, 96, 107, 174,
199, 227
Hawkins, Miss 37
Hawksmoor, Nicholas 20
Hawksworth Moor, Yorkshire
208
Hawthorne, Nathaniel 409
Haydon, Benjamin 32, 68, 70,
72, 76, 90, 99, 106, 114, 118,
170, 192, 193, 235, 238, 310–11,
362, 388; *Alexander the Great
taming Bucephalus and Eucles*
311; *Judgement of Solomon*
118, 200
Haymarket, London 24
Hazlitt, William 146, 164, 188–9,
194, 197, 200, 246, 397
Hearne, Thomas 32, 35, 106,
107, 196
Heath, Charles 134, 135, 138, 163,
172, 253, 254, 337
Heath, Vernon 264
Hegel, Georg Wilhelm
Friedrich xvii
Henley-on-Thames 97
Henrietta Street, London 5, 9,
355; No.26 55
Herbert, J. R. 374
Herbst family 228
Hereford 30
Herne Hill 350, 358, 361
Heston, Middlesex 230, 231, 261
Heston church, Middlesex 231
Hill, David xv
Hillard, George S. 381
Hilton, William 292, 339
Hindhead Hill, Surrey 124
*History of the Abolition of the
Slave Trade* (Clarkson) 363
History of Hindoostan (Dow) 162
History of Yorkshire (Whitaker)
(incomplete project) 211, 214
Hoare, Sir Richard Colt 30,
46, 247
Hobhouse, John Cam (*later*
Lord Broughton) 222, 256
Hodges, William 38
Hodgson, Isaac 241
Hofland, T. C. 197
Hogarth, J. 347
Hogarth, William 4, 6, 21, 103
Holborn, London 14

Hollam, Judith 270
Holland 278, 324
Holland, Lady 309
Holland, Lord 158
Hollond, Robert 344
Holmes, Hannah 2078
Holworthy, James 77, 180, 212, 214, 216, 223, 224, 234, 236, 239, 242–3, 244, 248, 251, 261, 331, 355
Holy Island 12
Homer 90, 216, 259, 260
Hooper's windmill, Margate 268
Hope, Thomas 162
Hoppner, John 45, 48, 71, 74, 77
Horace 90–91, 410
Horwood, Richard 419
Hoskins, John 4
Hotel Europa, Venice 265, 350
House of Hanover 175
Houses of Parliament, London 219, 334–5
Howard, Henrietta (*later* Countess of Suffolk) 90
Howard, Henry, RA 117, 148, 231–2, 291
Huggins, William John (painter of ships) 239
Huish, Marcus 217
Hull *Advertiser* 234
Humphrey, Ozias 6
Hungarian independence 221
Hungerford, Berkshire 10
Hunt, Leigh 352
Hunt, Robert 194, 253
Hunt, T. F. 340
Hurst and Robinson 134, 140, 180
Hurstmonceux 57
Hutton, Mr (of the Rectory, Covent Garden) 415
Hyde Park, London 14, 393, 397
Hyde Park Gate, Kensington 401

Iliad (Homer) 91
Ilkley, Yorkshire 207
Illustrated London News 397
Impregnable, HMS 176
Impressionism 378
Incorporated Society of Artists 6
Iona 277
Ireland 338
Ireland, John 6
Isle of Dogs, London 346
Isle of Wight 27, 30, 39, 100, 182–4, 198
Isleworth, Middlesex 89–93, 96, 102–4, 124, 227, 228, 230
Islington, London 3, 14

Italy 34, 68, 94, 173, 237, 268, 296, 410; Dickens in 358; keeps surfacing in T's work 263; T in northern Italy (1843) 351; T visits the Italian Alps with Munro (1836) 266; T's first tour(1819) 113, 244–8, 251–3, 313, 324; T's second tour (1828–29) 253–8, 325; and T's technique 252

Jackson, John 192, 246
Jacobin Clubs 48
Jarndyce v. *Jarndyce* 406
Jaubert, Roch 57
Jaullie, Mademoiselle 70
Jerdan, William 111
Jersey 353
Johns, Ambrose 160, 170, 227
Johnson, Dr Samuel 5, 15, 27, 114, 336
Jones, George 130, 221, 251–2, 254, 298, 311, 319, 343, 358, 384, 393; and *The Battle of Trafalgar* 239–9; and *Bay of Baiae* 249; friendly rivalry with T 296, 300, 334, 355–6; and the Harley Street houses' rents 410–11; and organizing the fate of T's pictures and drawings 404; at Petworth 177; and the prices of T's pictures 337; in Rome 263; and Thornbury xvi, 110, 412; and T's admiration for Claude 46; and T's attitude to money 110–15; T's death and funeral 400, 401; and T's engravers 138–9; and T's involve ment in the RA 286–7; on T's love of mystery 272; and T's project for artists in distress 240; and T's sole 1847 exhibit 385; on T's tenderness towards his friends 316–17; and T's thought-processes 160; and T's will 282, 377, 406; and 'Turner's Gift' 340, 406, 409; *The Battle of Hyderabad* 396
Jones, Inigo 2, 4, 19, 21, 152
Jones, John 419
Jones, Mr, of Lewisham 37
Jones, Sir William 162
Journal of a Residence in Ashantee (Dupuis) 215, 415
Judkin, Reverend T. J. 111, 260, 269, 328
Junius, Franciscus 146
Jura 332

Kauffmann, Angelica 168
Keats, John 159, 256, 268
The Keepsake annual 138, 253
Kemble, John Philip 63, 72
Kendal, Cumbria 212
Kennington Lane, Lambeth 415
Kensal Green cemetery 414
Kensington, London 255
Kent 1, 27, 35, 47, 97, 123, 176, 274, 330, 343, 391
Kent Road, London 14
Kew, Surrey 13, 95, 96, 236
Kew Palace 89, 92, 93
King Lear (Shakespeare) 79
King Street, London 5, 10, 17, 32
King William (steamer) 269
King's Arms pub, Cremorne Wharf 400
King's Arms pub, Hounslow 234
King's College School 118
King's New Road, London 368
Kingsbridge, Devon 167
Kingsley, Mrs 278–9
Kingsley, Reverend William 81, 278–9, 349, 380, 383, 401
Kingston-upon-Thames, Surrey 96
Kirby, John Joshua 146, 231
Kneller, Sir Godfrey 4
Knight, Richard Payne 147, 198, 199
Knockholt, Kent 51, 54, 118, 121, 165
Koninck, Philips de 238

Lahee, James 125
Lairesse, Gérard de 146
Lake Avernus 247, 264, 392
Lake Como 245, 253
Lake District 48, 210, 2121
Lambert, Daniel 107
Lambert, General John 222
Lambeth 10, 401, 415
Lambeth Palace 12, 19, 26
Lamy, Bernard 146
Lancashire 211
Lancaster 210
Lance, George 81, 114, 116, 192, 273
Landseer, Sir Edwin 297, 339, 394, 402
Landseer, John 30, 86, 141, 144, 201
Lanslebourg 245, 248
Lascelles, Edward 46, 70–1, 206, 210
Lascelles family 210
Launceston Castle 221
Launceston, Cornwall 221

Lausanne 331, 334
Lawrence, Sir Thomas 44, 47,
60, 71, 72, 75, 87, 110, 130, 135,
139, 175, 188, 194, 200–1, 238,
244–6, 251, 263, 266, 298, 303,
311, 402
Lear, Charles Hutton 373–4
Leçons de perspective positive
(Cerceau) 146
Lectures on Painting (Opie) 144,
160–61
*Lectures on Rhetoric and Belles-
Lettres* (Blair) 162
Lee Common,
Buckinghamshire 109, 242
Leeds 108, 174, 185, 210, 211
Leemput, Remigius van 4
Lees, John 11–12, 17, 122
Leicester, Sir John (*later* Lord
de Tabley) 78, 102, 106, 107,
109, 111, 163, 165, 172, 190–91,
192, 218
Leicester Fields (Reynolds'
house at 47 Leicester Square)
26
Leitch, William Leighton 82–3,
138, 171, 217
Leith, Edinburgh 175
Lely, Sir Peter 4
Lenox, Colonel James 278, 347,
377, 382, 417
Leslie, Charles R. 201, 252, 303;
on Beaumont 192; describes
T's appearance xv, 42–3; and
Hannibal 299; and Lenox 278;
at Petworth 178, 308, 309, 311,
313, 316; on the RA Council
339; on Reynolds 26; and
the *Temeraire* 347; and T's
competitiveness 296–7; at T's
funeral 401; and T's method
of preparing works for future
exhibition 301; and T's social
nature 294, 359; and T's
unsuitability to be President
of the RA 375; and varnishing
days 288, 290; visits T's
gallery 80, 85
Leslie, George D. 86, 147, 165,
288, 289, 293–5, 301, 354,
365, 375
Leslie, Robert C. xvi, 41, 43,
85–6, 101, 177–80, 274, 288–9,
293, 315–16, 357; *A Sailor's
Yarn* 293
Leslie family 311, 357
Lewes, Sussex 57
Lewis, F. C. 128, 129
Lewisham 36, 37

Liège 329
Lincoln's Inn Fields, London
226, 250
Lincolnshire 46, 55
Lindsay, Jack xvi, xvii
Linnell, John 35, 148, 237
Lisle Street, Soho 119
Literary Gazette 250, 348, 386
Little Catherine Street, Covent
Garden 5
Little Clarendon Street, London
242
Liverpool, Lord 341
Lives (Plutarch) 91
Livy 216
Llangollen Bridge 37
Lloyd, Mary 104, 349
Loch Ulver 277
Lockhart, J. G. 358
Loire River 324, 326, 328
London, financial collapse of
the City 180; omnibuses in
343; route io Dover 64, *see also*
under individual streets and
districts
London Apprentice pub,
Isleworth 93
London Bridge 10, 97, 240
London Corresponding Society
48, 220
London Orphan Fund 377, 406
Long Acre, London 5
Longman & Co, Messrs 211,
212, 214
Lord Melville (paddle-steamer)
326
Louis-Philippe, King of the
French 70, 325, 367–8
Louvre, Paris 66, 68, 69, 70,
89, 324
Love Lane, Margate 15
Low Countries 223, 261, 275, 365
Lowe, Mauritius 27
Lowson, Newbey 64, 65, 66
Lucerne 351
Luddite movement 219
Ludwig of Bavaria 385
Lulworth Cove 166
Lupton, Thomas 132, 138, 142
Lyceum, Wellington Street,
London 24
Lyell, Sir Charles 329
Lying-In Hospital, Lambeth 357
Lyon, Emma (*later* Lady
Hamilton) 31
Lyon 66, 245

McConnel, Henry 110–11, 266,
338

MacDowell, Patrick, RA 402, 416
Macerata 257
Maclise, Daniel 290, 292, 362,
401; *Caxton's Printing Press*
394; *Sacrifice of Noah after the
Deluge* 292, 386
Mâcon 66, 69, 75
Macpherson, James 277
Macready, William 260
Magna Carta 222
Magnet (steamer) 269
Maid of Morvern (steamboat)
277, 333
Maiden Lane, Covent Garden
6, 9, 55, 123, 189, 261, 368, 402,
413; No.21 3, 4, 6–7, 13, 14, 17,
31, 203, 372, 418; No.20 6, 31;
No.26 3, 4, 7, 21, 30, 44–5, 51,
59, 418
Maidenhead Bridge 365
Malden, Viscount 30
Mallord, Joseph (T's maternal
great-grandfather) 3, 241
Malton, Thomas 18, 20, 26, 32,
38, 47, 60, 146, 208
Malton, Thomas, senior 146, 152
Manby, George 276
Marble Hill House,
Twickenham 90
Margate 62, 94, 117, 182, 255,
279–81, 284, 290, 323, 326–7,
333, 339, 345, 346, 367, 384,
390, 397; described 274–5, 268;
Mrs Booth buried at 413; Mrs
Booth's property at 269–70;
T at Coleman's school 14–15,
220; T incognito in 272, 371–2;
T lodges with Mrs Booth
269–70; T very attracted to
1, 176–7; T visits when very
ill 399; and T's Brighton
sketchbook 40; and T's health
41; T's pictures and drawings
house 411
Margate Sands 96
Marlborough House, Pall Mall
409
Marlow, Buckinghamshire 97
Marryat, Frederick 12
Mars (an East Indiaman) 96
Marseilles 254
Marsh, William 108, 243, 262,
282, 401
Marshall, James Garth 336
Marshall, Joseph Mallord
William (T's uncle) 3, 10, 19,
27, 177, 240
Marshall, William (T's maternal
grandfather) 3

Marshall family xviii, 3, 14, 54, 110
Martigny 66
Martin, John, RA 371
Martin, Leopold 371
Marvell, Andrew 6
Marylebone, London 14, 89, 355
Marylebone Fields, London 181
Marylebone Street, London 331
Mason, Monck 344
Massa 254
Mathews, Dr 30
Maw, John H. 321, 333, 339
Mayall, J. J. E. 389–90
M'Connell, Henry see McConnel, Henry
Medina River 183
Mediterranean 254
Medway River 97, 175, 274, 325, 345
Medway valley 1
Melbourne, Lady 307
Melbourne, William Lamb, Lord 308
Menai Strait 46
Menston Hall, Yorkshire 207
Merton College, Oxford 333
Metamorphoses (Ovid) 91, 92
Methodism 14–15
Meuse River 324, 326, 333
Michelangelo 25, 249
Middleton, Lord 30
Milan 245
Mill Gill falls, near Askrigg 212
Miller, Thomas 135
Miller, William 138, 221, 378
Milman, Very Reverend Henry 402
Milton, John 92, 142, 149, 291, 334, 410
Missolonghi 263
Mitcham, Surrey 78, 263, 282
Modern Painters (Ruskin) xvii, 348–9, 350, 408
Moitte, Jean-Guillaume 70
Monkhouse, Cosmo xvii, 26, 301, 352
Monro, Dr Thomas 39, 192; cottage at Fetcham 225; death 282; owns T's works 31, 34; patronizes the arts 31–2; as principal physician at Bethlehem Hospital 31, 53, 54; sale of his art collection 103; T works for 32–5, 36, 71
Mont Blanc 65, 66
Mont Cenis pass 245, 248, 253, 258
Mont Tarate 258

Montanvert 66
Monthly Magazine 61, 203
Moore, Harriet 372
Moore, Thomas 246, 247, 266, 338
Morecambe Bay 210, 212
Morgan, Captain Elisha 86
Morland, George 106, 196
Morlent, M. J. 326
Mornex, Haute Savoie 413
Morning Chronicle 61, 150, 151, 264, 302, 315
Morning Herald 259, 335
Morning Post 45, 151, 250, 251
Mornington, Lord 116
Mortlake 251
Mortmain Act 282, 376, 406
Mosel, River 324, 326, 328, 333
Mount Edgcumbe, near Plymouth 115, 170, 171
Mount Street, London 51, 300
Mulready, William 116, 401
Munich 380, 385
Munro, Hugh A. J., laird of Novar xvi, 138, 223, 239, 266, 267, 287, 330–32, 334, 336, 338, 352, 362, 376, 378, 380, 382–3, 401, 404
Murray, John 358, 361
Murwith, Mr 36

Naiae 246
Naples 246, 247, 253, 256
Napoleon I (Bonaparte) 68, 70, 73, 89, 98–9, 154, 166, 187, 198, 264, 325, 364
Narraway, John 28, 29, 114
Narraway, Miss 235
Narraway family 28, 29, 55, 117, 326
Nash, John 182, 183–4, 216, 251
Nash, Mrs 185, 202
Nasmyth, Patrick 401
National Debt 341
National Gallery, London 141, 296; Beaumont and 193; built in Trafalgar Square 287; lack of room at 409; much of T's work found at the start of the Second World War 408; in Pall Mall 262, 287–8; Royal Academy shares the Trafalgar Square building 287, 287–8, 339; some of T's work housed in empty rooms before a settlement reached 407; and T's will 283, 376–7, 407; William IV opens 333
Naval Academy, Portsmouth 175

Needles, Isle of Wight 39, 181, 259
Nelson, Horatio, Viscount 99, 100, 156, 238, 346, 402
Nemi 248
New Bridge, Tamar River 173
New Gravel Lane, Wapping 241
New Monthly Magazine 151, 152
A New Picture of Paris, or, the Stranger's Guide to the French Metropolis (Planta) 325
Newington, Kent 14
Newman, James 183–4
Newton, Sir W. J. 339
Niagara 389
Nice 254
Nichols, Captain 167
Nicolson, William 175
Night Thoughts (Young) 410
Nimes (spelled 'Nismes' by T) 254
Niton, Isle of Wight 184
Nixon, Reverend Robert 20, 35–7, 231
Nollekens, Joseph 113, 229, 353; Seated Venus 320
Nore, the 97, 99
Norfolk, Duke of 72
Norham Castle, Northumberland 37, 211, 326, 386, 388
Normandy 324, 325
North Audley Street chapel, London 357
North Downs, Kent 51
North Foreland, Margate 274, 391
North Sea 275–6, 278
Northanger Abbey (Austen) 37
Northcote, James 23, 44, 71, 76, 164, 192, 199
Northcourt, Shorwell, Isle of Wight 184
Northumberland 48
Northumberland, Duke of 12, 19, 89, 90, 240, 347
Norton Street (No.75), London 57, 59, 63, 77
Novar 330, 334
Nuneham Courtenay House, Oxfordshire 27
Nuneham Harcourt, Oxfordshire 27

Observations relative chiefly to Picturesque Beauty (Gilpin) 198
Observer 112
'Ode to the West Wind' (Shelley) 247

Odyssey (Homer) 91, 259, 260
Offley's, Henrietta Street 355
On the Costume of the Ancients
(Hope) 162
On the Fear of Death (Hazlitt)
397
Opie, John 44, 75, 106, 144,
160–61, 403
Oracle (newspaper) 195
Orléans, Duke of 70
Orvieto 257
Ossian 277
Ostend 15, 180, 234, 324
Osterley House, Middlesex 231
Othello (Shakespeare) 266
Otley, Yorkshire 207, 211
Ottoman Empire 46
Ovid 91, 92, 197
Owain ap Gruffydd 50
Owen, Professor Richard 273,
381
Owen, William, RA 218
Oxford 20, 28, 97, 333
Oxford Almanack 97, 122–3
Oxford Street, London 14

Paestum 247
Paganini, Niccolo 264
Paine, Thomas 48, 161
Palace of Westminster, London
334
Palazzo Poli, Rome 245
Palgrave, F. T. 389
Palin, Miss 37
Pall Mall, London 262, 343, 409
Pangbourne, Berkshire 97
Pantheon, Oxford Street,
London 38, 55, 99, 335
Paris 63, 64, 66, 68, 245, 255, 324,
325, 332
Park Lane, London 90
Park Street, Mayfair, London 331
Park Street, Southwark 357
Parker, John 212, 213
Parker, Thomas Lister 199,
211, 218
Parliamentary Reform Bill
(1832) 221
Parsons, William 120
Parthenon, Athens 90
Pasquin, Anthony 45
Peacock (dealer) 331
Peel, Mrs 135
Pembroke Castle 162
Penn, Buckinghamshire 231
Pennines 211
Penrice, Thomas (a Yarmouth
collector) 72, 200–1
Percy family 307

Perks, Miss 228
perspective 146–7
Peter Court, London 21
Petrie, Harriet 183
Pettigrew, T. J. 419
Petworth, Sussex 312
Petworth House, Sussex 62, 101,
165, 177, 180, 183, 257, 261, 275,
305–22, 330, 333, 339
Petworth parish church 319
Pevensey 57
Phillips, Thomas, RA 191, 251,
311, 312, 318, 321, 356
Phipps, General 300, 359
Piazza, Covent Garden 1, 3,
4, 9, 10
Picardy 367
Pickersgill, Henry, RA 323,
355, 401
Pimlico, London 368
'Pindar, Peter' (Dr John Wolcot)
167
Piranesi, Giovanni Battista 247,
250, 263
Pitt, William, the younger
58, 245
Placentia 258
Planta, Edward 325
The Pleasures of Hope (Campbell)
116
The Pleasures of the Imagination
(Akenside) 149
Pliny the Younger 146
Plutarch 91
Plym River 168
Plymouth 166, 168, 169, 227
Plympton, Devon 170
Pocket Magazine (Harrison) 30
Poetical Works (Milton) 334
Pointillism 378
Pompeii 247
Pool of London 10, 97
Poor Rate Collector's Books (St
Paul's parish) 3, 4, 21
Pope, Alexander 90, 91, 92, 104,
227, 260
Pope's Villa, Twickenham 90,
227
Porcupine (newspaper) 49, 61
Porden, William 17, 18
Porson, Richard 6
Porter, Robert Ker 23–4; *Battle of
Agincourt* 24
Portland, Duke of 78, 79, 420
Portland Place, London 37
Portsmouth 124, 175, 368
Potter, Peter 419
Pound, Daniel John 270, 284,
370, 401, 411

Pound, Henry 270
Poussin, Nicolas 60, 92, 96,
189, 194, 197; *Deluge* 69; *The
Israelites gather manna* 69
Powell, Cecilia xv, 53
Prague 332
Price, Dr David 271, 354, 370,
384, 399, 401
Price, Ellis 2
Price, Martha 2
Principles of Geology (Lyell) 329
Prout, Samuel 266, 349
Provis, Mary Ann 46
Punch 156–7, 297
Pye, John xvi, 124–5, 127–9, 130–1,
140, 163, 181, 220, 228, 369,
371–2, 378, 411, 412
Pyne, William. Henry 33
Pyrenees 354

Quakers 221
Quarterly Review 357
Quattro Fontane, Rome 255
Queen Anne Street, London 50,
77, 109, 216, 345, 419; No.44
419; No.44c 420; No.46a 420;
No.47 91, 125, 140, 171, 181,
206, 226, 242, 257, 258, 322, 323,
339, 395, 418–20; American
visitors 381; Bohn's offer 136;
and Callcott's death 356;
censuses 419, 420; Cockerell's
visit 342; demolished 418;
dilapidated and dusty 81,
83, 379–80, 408; Dupuis
asks to be custodian 414–15;
engravings in 141; the gallery
opens (1822) 80; Hannah
Danby as house-keeper/
custodian 81, 82–3, 254, 274,
283, 310, 340–1, 377, 398, 419,
420; and Harper's school 50,
361; Henry Syer Trimmer
looks around 409–10; Lenox
tries to buy the *Temeraire* 377;
and Manx cats 81, 83–4, 186,
274; Marshall buys a House
of Parliament painting 336;
Mortlake Terrace finished
in 265; parish rate books
419, 420; rateable value 369;
Reverend Trimmer visits
58; Ruskin often visits 350;
the stock of 84; T ejects
a dealer 85; T encourages
artist-colleagues to visit 80;
T moves to Chelsea 368, 370;
T's father looks after the
house 183, 233, 247, 254; and

T's funeral 400, 401–3; T's hospitality towards Christine Bicknell 361; T's studio 79, 80, 84, 86–7, 88; and T's will 377, 404, 405, 407; work on T's second gallery 78–80, 235, 248; No.47a 420
Queen's Arms inn, Margate 269

Raby Castle 64, 174, 215
Radley Hall, Oxfordshire 20, 27
Raeburn, Henry 175
Ramsgate, Kent 176, 274
Rance, Reverend Ezekiel 2
Rance River 354
Raphael (Raffaello Sanzio) 129, 143, 149, 248; *Infant Jesus caressing St John* 68
Rathbone Place, London 136
Ratisbon 333
Reading, Berkshire 97
Rectory, Covent Garden 415
Redding, Cyrus 1, 64–5, 80, 114, 115, 165–70, 173, 233
Redgrave, Richard 139, 144, 149, 153, 252, 290–1, 374, 400–3; *The Castle Builder* 291
Redgrave, Samuel 252
Redgrave family 42, 202–3, 273, 301, 304, 367
Reeve, Lovell 27, 42–3
Reformation 220
Regensburg 333
Regent's Park, London 183
Reichenbach Falls 66
Reinagle, R. R. 294, 374
Rembrandt (Harmensz van Rijn) 61, 62, 189, 266, 275, 334, 364; *Lady with a Fan* 314; *Het Ledekant* 204; *A Philosopher* 314; *Susannah* 69
Report on the Mode of Preventing the Forgery of Bank Notes (Hansard et al) 108
Repton, Humphrey 17
Resolution and Independence (Wordsworth) 193
Retz, Gilles de Laval, Baron de (Bluebeard) 327–8
Review of Publications in Art 124, 201
Reynolds, Sir Joshua RA 17, 22, 24–6, 46, 90, 127, 144, 146, 148, 157, 198, 216, 227, 235, 312, 355, 402
Rheims 331
Rhine, River 174, 215, 324, 326, 332, 333, 350, 351, 354
Rhône, River 66, 326

Rhymes on Art (Shee) 93, 158
Richards, John, RA 73, 342
Richards, Mrs 342
Richardson, Sir John 329
Richardson, Jonathan 146, 157
Richmond, Duke of 310
Richmond, George 366, 385
Richmond, Surrey 69, 95, 96, 154, 227, 240; Old Deer Park 89
Richmond, Yorkshire 212
Richmond Bridge, Surrey 109, 224, 226, 227, 230
Richmond Hill, Surrey 90, 236
Ridsdale (a parson) 309
Rigaud, John Francis 20, 35–6, 288
Rigaud, Stephen 35, 36, 114, 115
Rigby, Elizabeth (*later* Lady Eastlake) 81, 352, 358, 380, 390, 399, 404
Rimini 245
Rippingille, E. V. 289–90
Ritchie, Leitch 327
Rob Roy (steam packet) 326
Roberts, David xvi, 284, 331, 349, 367, 393, 395, 401; first meets T 341; and Hannah Danby 398; and Ruskin's reviews 349; sees T for the last time 396; T becomes estranged from the RA 375; T influences 199; T makes a 'Mistery' of his life 271–2; on T and Mrs Booth passing as man and wife 284; and T's antipathy towards RA innovations 304; and T's competitiveness 295–6; and T's conversation 160; and T's lack of financial support of Mrs Booth 369, 411; and T's lectures 153; T's modesty v. Constable's 'conceit' 300; and T's possible cholera 384; on T's secretiveness 360–2; T's sociability *chez* Roberts 359–60; unaware of the location of T's other home 370; *A View of Edinburgh* 295
Robertson, Andrew 342, 343
Robinson, Mr (Leeds printdealer) 214–15
Rochester 384
Rochester Castle 12, 35, 380
Rogers, Samuel 63, 113, 142, 174, 247, 253, 282, 311, 317, 338, 348, 349, 356, 358, 376, 388, 404, 405
Rogers, Sarah 317, 358
Roget, John Lewis 128
Rokeby, Lord 7

Rolls, W. 147
Roman History (Goldsmith) 197
Rome 112, 244–8, 253, 254–5, 257, 260, 263, 302–3, 313, 325
Romeo and Juliet (Shakespeare) 266, 267
Romney, George 6, 17
Romney, Lady E. 309
Rooker, Michael Angelo 31
Roper, W. L. 342
Rose, Mrs Thomas 83, 272, 353
Rose, Thomas xiv, 83–4, 115, 177, 272, 354
Rosehill Park, Sussex 176
Rosetti, J. Baptista 22
Rossetti, W. M. 408
Rossi, Charles 47, 73, 144, 229
Rossini, Gioacchino 366
Rotherhithe 345, 355, 418
Rotterdam 350
Rouen 324, 326
Rowlandson, Thomas 203
Royal Academy, xv, 21, 92, 169, 343, 402; Academy Club 229, 240, 248, 252, 341, 359, 395; Academy Council 22, 47, 72, 73–4, 78, 144, 145, 150, 151, 153, 199, 205, 248, 264, 287, 288, 339, 373, 395; and the *Athenaeum* 361; and the British Institution 197, 198; Charles Turner elected an Associate Engraver 130; as a club and a trade union 71; Council Room 294; dinners 61, 72, 199, 286, 287, 3734, 404; Eastlake becomes President (1850) 375; factions within 71–2; first exhibition at Trafalgar Square (1837) 287–8, 339; free training of artists 21; General Assembly 72, 286–7, 339; gives financial relief to elderly artists 72; last exhibition at Somerset House (1836) 287, 331; Lawrence succeeds West as President 200; move from Somerset House (1836) 287–8; and poetry 154, 156; Professorship of Landscape Painting 262, 283; Reynolds gives the last of his series of Discourses 24–5; royal patronage 72–3; rules 47, 273; T as Auditor 286, 375; T as Deputy President 375, 384, 391; T elected ARA (1799) 47; T elected Professor of Perspective 143; T elected

RA (1802) 59–60; T exhibits watercolour of Canterbury Cathedral (1794) 32; T on the hanging committee for the firsttllne(1803) 73; T lectures on perspective 122, 143–53, 156, 179, 206, 225, 339; T resigns his professorship 153, 339, 344; T sketches pictures in the Exhibitions 31; T unwilling to take payment for his duties 114; and T's business acumen 112; and T's death 416; T's first exhibited oil (1796) 39; T's first watercolour exhibited (1790) 19, 26; and T's gallery sales 107; T's increasing antipathy to innovations 304; T's involvement with 43–4, 75, 286, 287, 339, 373; T's last exhibits (1850) 392; and T's will 2, 262, 283, 377, 406–7; Turner Gold Medal 262, 283; varnishing days 286, 288–304, 365, 385; and the Vatican marbles 22–3; William IV opens the new buildings 333
Royal Academy Schools 19, 20, 407; Antique School 90; Life School 22, 23, 43, 153, 202, 265, 339; Plaister Academy 22; rules 22, 23; School of Painting 199; T at 21–6; T as a Visitor 38, 71, 153, 199, 202, 286, 339, 373
Royal Collection 129
Royal George (royal yacht) 175
Royal Navy 345
Royal Society 389
Royal Society of Musicians 56, 119, 120, 342, 413
Royal Yacht Squadron, Cowes 183
Rubens, Peter Paul 189, 194; *Landscape with a Rainbow* 69
Rural Rides (Cobbett) 305
Ruskin, Effie 104, 373
Ruskin, John 25–8, 54, 105, 125, 128, 273, 297, 323, 330, 331, 358, 365, 375–7, 387, 392, 395, 397, 415; abroad at time of T's funeral 401; ardent advocacy of T 26, 362; and *Blackwood's Magazine* 267, 337; and Charles Turner 404; and the deterioration of T's paintings 302; encourages Thornbury xvi; and the *Fighting Temeraire* 346;

Griffith introduces to T 377; and Hannah Danby 414; and *Modern Painters* xvii, 349–50, 408; and Mrs Booth 270, 411–13; and the plates for *The Harbours of England* 142; and RA Schools 26; and *Slavers* 363; sorts T's sketchbooks and drawings 407–9; T as 'English-minded' 343; T on Ruskin's writings xviii; T worries about Ruskin 373, 393; and T's ability to 'think in light and shade' 127; and T's attitude towards other artists 116; and T's caring deeply for his own pictures 380; and T's 'dislike to appear kind' 332; and T's 'erotic' drawings 203–4, 241; and T's gallery 80; and T's last days 398, 399; and T's light 387; and T's mental health 383–4, 388; T's reaction to criticism of *Snow Storm* 279–80; and T's response to criticism 195; and T's visit to Rome 249; and T's will 377; visits Venice 267
Ruskin, John James (Ruskin's father) 348, 349, 354, 363, 409
Ruskin, Mrs 366
Ruskin family 278, 350, 384, 393
Russell, Lord John 394
Russell Street, London 5
Ruysdael, Salomon van 276; *A Storm off the dikes of Holland* 69
Ryman, James 333

Sadler's Wells, Islington 14
St Albans, Hertfordshire 71
St Anselm's Chapel, Canterbury Cathedral 32
St Bertin abbey 331
St Catherine's Point, Isle of Wight 185
St David's, Dyfed 30
St Dunstan's in the West, Fleet Street 20
St German's river 1, 166
St Giles's Cathedral, Edinburgh 175
St Gothard Pass, Switzerland 65
St James's Chronicle 203
St James's church, Piccadilly 215
St James's Palace, London 175, 238, 239, 409
St James's Park 180, 183

St James's Place, London 338, 358
St John-in-Thanet church, Margate 270, 413
St Luke's Church, Chelsea 400
St Mark's, Venice 266
St Mark's Place, Venice 267
St Martin-in-the-Fields, London 4
St Martin's bridge, near Salanches 332
St Martin's Lane, London 5
St Mary Magdalene Church, Bermondsey 357
St Mary the Virgin Church, Wanstead 19
St Mary's Church, Battersea 370, 418
St Marylebone parish rate books 419, 420
St Michael's Mount, Cornwall 12, 166
St Orner 331
St Paul's Cathedral, London 12, 51, 100, 216, 263, 371, 376, 402, 407, 416
St Paul's Church, Covent Garden, London 1, 2, 9, 19, 71, 112, 261, 281
SS Giovanni and Paolo church, Venice 68
Salanches 332
Salisbury 58
Salisbury Stairs, London 10
Salisbury Street, London 129
Saltash, Cornwall 168
Saltram 168
San Giorgio, Venice 266
Sand Pit Close, Twickenham 224
Sandby, Paul 31
Sandwich 284
Sandycombe Lodge (previously 'Solus Lodge'), Twickenham 78, 236, 254, 268, 313, 354, 410; described 226; fishpond 179, 225, 232, 243; life at 227–8; members of the Academy Club entertained 229–30; name changed to 226–7; survival of 418; T builds 109, 198, 206, 224–6; T sells 243, 360; T's father and *see under* Turner, William
Santissima Trinidad (ship) 99
Saône River 66, 69
Sarre-valli 258
Savoy 198, 247
Savoy Palace 35

Sawyer, Mr (Hammersmith boatmaster) 103
Schaffhausen fall 66–7
Schetky, Alick 174
Schetky, Jane 174, 175
Schetky, John Christian 175, 238, 345, 384
Schuyler, Montgomery 418
Scotland 66, 94, 165, 174–5, 276–7, 333–4, 354, 410
Scott, David 85
Scott, Samuel 4
Scott, Sir Walter 118, 140, 142, 152, 174, 175, 193, 250, 276, 277, 325, 333, 337, 358, 410
Sea Reach 98
Seasons (Thomson) 103, 237
Sefton, Countess of 306, 307
Sefton, Earl of 306, 307
Seguier, F. P. 301
Seine, River 94, 324, 325, 326, 327–8, 330
Sens 245
Sense and Sensibility (Austen) 18
Serpentine, Hyde Park 180
Serres, Dominic 50
Serres, John Thomas 50, 51
Serres, Olivia 51
Severn, Joseph 256
Severn, River 28, 94
Sfax, Tunisia 357
Shakespeare, William 2, 12–13, 72, 203, 251, 260, 267
Shanes, Eric xvi
Shaw, Dr 54
Shee, Sir Martin Archer 23, 47, 63, 75, 93, 152–3, 158, 162, 196–7, 286, 298, 303–4, 375, 376
Sheepshanks, John 252, 266, 338
Sheerness, Kent 14, 97, 99, 345, 346
Shelley, Percy Bysshe 159, 247, 260
Sheppey 14, 99
Sherrell, Francis 372
Sherridan, J. 22
Shillingford, Oxfordshire 97
Ship and Bladebone inn, Wapping 241–2, 405
Ship inn, Margate 269
Shippen, Peggy 370
Shoeburyness, Essex 97
Sickert, Walter xviii, 34
Sidmouth, Devon 268
Simon, Lady 366
Simplon pass 244, 258
Sir John Soane's Museum, Lincoln's Inn Fields 340
Skipton 211

slavery 363
Smirke, Robert 63, 73, 145, 198, 299
Smith, John Raphael 5, 17, 32, 71, 123
Smith, Sydney 329
Smith (tenant) 243
Smollett, Tobias 64
Soane, Sir John 19, 22, 73, 77–8, 145, 149, 225, 226, 246, 250, 287, 321, 333, 336, 340, 341
Soane, Mrs 78
Society for the Betterment of the Conditions of the Poor 308
Sockett, Reverend Thomas 319, 321
Soho Square, London 183, 253
Solent 183, 184, 185
Solus Lodge see Sandycombe Lodge
Somers Town, London 242
Somerset House, London 5, 19, 20, 21, 100, 150–51, 402; Great Room 143, 146, 148, 151, 287, 297, 298, see also under Royal Academy
South Foreland lighthouse 344
South of France 254
South Kensington Museum 409
South Molton, Devon 2–3, 405
South Western Railway Company 240
Southampton Street, London 6, 7, 9, 21, 49
Southend, Essex 97
Southwold, Suffolk 229, 268
Spanish Chapel, Manchester Square, London 55
Spanish Steps, Rome 255
'Spectacle Mecanique', King Street 10, 39
Spectator 335
Spenser, Lady 308
Spezzia 254
Spithead 24, 176, 345
Spread Eagle inn, Strand, London 5
Staffa 277, 333
Stanfield, Clarkson 80, 199, 266, 288, 292, 293, 295, 301, 334, 346, 356, 358–9, 381, 401; Throwing the Painter 295
Stanfield, Rebecca 359
Steers, Dr 32
Stephens, Frederick George 103
Stillman, William J. 293, 349, 381–2, 387, 416–17
Stoke Point 167

Stokes, Charles 398, 399, 400, 401
Stonehenge 12, 186
Stothard, Thomas 16, 60, 107, 144, 148
Stourhead, Wiltshire 46
Straits of Dover 344
Strand, London 5, 7, 9, 10, 19, 21, 35, 123, 166, 177, 389, 402
Strawberry Hill, Twickenham, Middlesex 90
Strong, Wally 243
Strowger, Sam 23
Stubbs, George (Phaeton and the horses of the sun) 168
Summer (Pope) 92
'Summer' (Thomson) 363
Sun 74, 75, 126, 143, 195, 341
Sunningwell, Oxfordshire 27, 240
Sunningwell Church, Oxfordshire 27
Sunny Memories (Lloyd) 104
Surrey 27, 335
Sussex 176, 307, 308
Sutherland, Lady 70–1
Swan inn, Lambeth 19
Swan inn, Walton 96
Swift, Dean (Jonathan) 228
Swinburne, Edward 216
Swinburne, Sir John 199
Switzerland 34, 268, 373, 389, 393; T in 65–8, 165, 205, 244, 287, 332, 334, 351, 352
Syon Ferry 89
Syon Ferry House, Isleworth 90, 91, 93
Syon House, Isleworth 12, 19, 89

Tabley Hall, Cheshire 79, 102, 111, 165, 177, 179, 181, 205
Talbot (paddle-steamer) 326
Tamar, River 80, 166, 168, 169, 170, 172, 173
'The Taste' 190, 198, 199, 378
Tate Gallery of British Art, Millbank, Clore wing 409
Tatler 352
Tattersall, Reverend James 2
Tavistock 169
Tavistock Place, London 163
Tavistock Street, London 5
Tavistock Street, London. No.2 414
Taylor, Dr Brook 146
Taylor, John 143, 152, 195
Taylor, Tom 297
Teddington, Middlesex 93
Tees, River 210, 212

Teesdale 212, 220
Temeraire (ship) 175, 186, 344–7, 418
The Tempest (Shakespeare) 279, 387
Teniers, David, the younger 203, 312
Tepper, Jabez 405–6, 414, 415, 420
Tepper, Mary Turner (T's cousin) 405–6
Terni 248
Thackeray, William Makepeace 156, 345–6, 365, 417
Thames Ditton, Surrey 104
Thames, River 10, 14, 34–5, 92–8, 102–5, 122, 227–8, 243, 254–5, 257, 331, 334, 354, 357, 410; at Brentford 13, 177, 227; at Chelsea 340, 368, 385; and Eastern Dock 241; the frozen 104, 180; and Greenwich 331, 340, 346; at Hammersmith 102; and the Houses of Parliament fire 335; at Isleworth 89, 93, 96, 227; at Mortlake 251; and *Rain, Steam, and Speed* 365; at Richmond 69, 95, 109, 154, 224, 236; Syon Ferry House and 90; and T's fishing 177; T's preoccupation with 165
Thames Estuary 275
Thanet coast 1, 15, 274–5, 284, 391
Thatch'd House Alley, London 9
Thatched House club, St James's Street 359, 395
Thompson, Thomas James 357
Thompson, Thomas William (T's grandson) 357
Thomson, Henry, RA 177, 218; *Crossing the Brook* (1803) 172
Thomson, James xvii, 92, 103, 104, 106, 154, 159, 237, 363, 386
Thornbury, Walter xvi–xviii, 7, 8, 18, 20, 21, 28, 37, 39, 41, 40, 56, 84, 87, 95, 110, 111, 117, 133, 135, 136, 138, 141, 190, 214, 231, 241, 269, 278, 328, 342, 354, 355, 362, 370, 371, 412
Thornhill, Sir James 4
Three Pigeons inn, Brentford 11
Thurlestone, Devon 259
Tilbury, London 14, 97
Times 151, 259, 338, 351, 381, 388, 394, 405
Tintoretto, Jacopo Robusti 246, 266

Titian 46, 246, 312; *Christ crowned with Thorns* 68; *Death of St Peter Martyr* 68; *The Entombment* 68
Tivoli 248
Tobermory 277
Todd, Joseph 243
Tomkison, Humphrey 9, 16, 18
Tomkison, Thomas 9
Tooke, Horne 220
Torbay, Devon 221
Tothill Fields, London 14
Tour through Italy (Eustace) 244
Tower of London 14, 326, 336
Tradescant, John 182
Trafalgar, Battle of 70, 99, 100, 344
Trafalgar Square, London 183, 287, 343, 346, 402
'The Transformation of Appullus' (Ovid) 197
Trarbach 324
Travels (Bruce) 162
Tredcroft, Mrs 309
Tremlouw, Richard 52
Tréport 367
Trevelyan, Lady Pauline 84
Trevor-Roper, Patrick 352
Trimmer, Reverend Henry Scott 8, 31, 71, 87, 146, 194, 206, 235; becomes a close friend of T's 11; death 60; and *Frosty Morning* 186; at Hammersmith 103; ordained in the Church of England 11; at Sandycombe Lodge 227–8; in Southwold 229, 268; and T's boat 95; and T's favourite colour 200; and T's kindness 116; and T's response to criticism 195; and T's will 282, 377, 404, 409; as the Vicar of Heston 195, 230, 231; visits T in Queen Anne Street 58
Trimmer, Henry Syer 8, 87–8, 95, 102, 103, 117, 118, 177, 187, 227–8, 230–1, 243, 354, 409–10, 414
Trimmer, James 11
Trimmer, Mrs 231
Trimmer, Sarah (*née* Kirby) 11, 268
Trimmer family 230, 231, 232, 261, 360
True Briton 74, 208
Turin 66, 247, 332
Turk's Head inn, Strand, London 5
Turner, Charles 43, 107, 121, 126,

129–31, 139, 271, 282, 376, 377, 395, 401, 404, 405, 412–14
Turner, Dawson 173–4, 322, 339, 356, 364, 384
Turner, Evelina (T's daughter; *later* Dupuis) 56–7, 63, 119, 120, 173, 215, 262, 283, 314, 357, 376, 406, 414, 415
Turner, Georgiana (T's daughter; *later* Thompson) 56, 119, 120, 173, 262, 283, 314, 357, 376
Turner, Joseph Mallard William, RA, accent 143–4, 152; affair with Sarah Danby see Danby, Sarah; amasses property 239–42; appearance xv, 28, 29, 34, 42–3, 140, 143, 165, 209, 266, 284, 289, 290, 308, 326, 342, 366, 373, 375–6, 381, 382, 400; and architecture 17–20, 27, 36, 147, 149, 209, 224–5, 253, 326, 418; in the Artists General Benevolent Institution 341–3; Beaumont's criticisms 189, 191, 194, 196, 199, 200; birth of Evelina 56; birth of Georgiana 119; boating 94–8, 103, 104; christened 2; claims to have been born in the country 1; Claude influences 69, 121–2, 171, 173, 185, 189, 197, 203, 209, 237, 244, 256, 257, 264, 303, 319, 349, 365; copying 17, 26, 27, 30–31, 32, 34–5, 68, 91; and daguerrotypes 389; daughter Evelina marries 215; death and funeral (December 1851) 2, 399–403; death of Georgiana 357; death of his little sister xvii, 8, 54; death of his mother (1804) 54; devoted to his art 29, 36; dislike of dealers 76, 85, 125; drinking 354–5, 360, 362, 384; Dutch painters' influence 39; Dutch themes in his paintings 275–6; early drawing 8–9, 11, 13, 15–16, 17; education 11–13, 14, 15, 90, 161; elected ARA (1799) 47, 59; elected Professor of Perspective 144; elected RA (1802) 59–60; and engravings 121–42; eyesight 352–3, 387; first attempt to become an Associate (1798) 47, 48; first exhibited oil (1796) 38–9; first Italian tour (1819) 112; first signed drawings 17; first

watercolour exhibited at the RA (1790) 19, 26; fishing 97, 176–82, 208, 280, 317, 327; founds 'the White Painters' 198; his galleries 57, 59, 75–86, 100, 107, 109, 123–4, 154, 165–6, 173, 174, 184, 187, 188, 191, 200, 233, 235, 242, 248, 278, 283, 312, 340, 343, 350, 356, 368, 377, 379–82, 398, 400, 403, 410, 414, 419; as a good salesman for his work 107; grasp of naval detail admired 101; health 40, 41, 150, 205–6, 225, 234–5, 254, 276–7, 321, 322, 351–54, 370, 376, 381–4, 391, 393–9, 401; helps other painters 291–3, 297–8, 300–301, 374, 386; and his father's death 260–63; and his mother's admission to Bethlehem Hospital 51–2, 53–4; and his mother's death 54, 75, 77; inventory of his possessions (1854) 410; jilted in Margate 41, 54; last exhibits at the RA (1850) 392; lectures on perspective (1811–28) 122, 143–53, 156, 179, 206, 225, 339; looks after his father 59; Loutherbourg influences 39; Low Countries tours 223, 261; Malton influences 20, 26, 38; in Margate as a child 14–15; and marriage 235; mental health 54, 85, 161, 195–6, 383–4, 388, 406; moves to Chelsea (1846) 368–70; moves to Hand Court 35; moves to Harley Street 50; and music 55; and Nelson 99–100; and painting in the open air 96, 102–3; Petworth's role 312; and politics 49, 219–22, 329; his reading 162; and Rembrandt 61, 62, 266, 314, 334; resigns his professorship (1838) 153, 339, 344; and the Royal Academy see Royal Academy; Royal Academy Schools; in Scotland 66, 165, 174–5, 276–7, 333–4, 354; and Sophia Booth see Booth, Sophia; spelling and syntax problems 2, 13, 49, 107, 163, 364; statue in St Paul's 402, 416; and the status of landscape painting 126–7, 197; stays with his uncle in Brentford 10–13, 89, 110, 177, 227, 231; 'stolen proofs' drama

130, 131; tablet to his parents 112, 281; as a teacher 36–7; tours see individual countries; his travelling paint-box 87, 88, 96, 170; and varnishing days 286, 288–304, 365, 386; visits Delacroix 42, 325–6, 332; wills and testaments xviii, 2, 56, 57, 76, 262, 282–3, 340, 357, 376–7, 403, 404–7, 414–5; works for Dr Monro 32–5, 36, 71; works for John Lees 11–12, 17, 122; works for John Raphael Smith 17, 32, 71, 123;
personality: attracted to water 30, 89, 102, 104, 105; churlishness xv, 279; competitiveness 196, 294–300, 317, 356; fondness of children 118; gregariousness xv, 294, 359; interest in theatre 38–9, 260; as a keen observer xi, 65, 66–7, 297–8; need for mystery 271–73, 359–60, 371–2; non-conformism 15; Ruskin on 412–13; solitary nature xi, 26, 245, 286, 387, 338, 350; thought processes 159–61
style: artistic freedom xv, 391; breadth and harmony 33; brushes 88, 289, 293, 303, 365, 372; careful detail/precision xv, 33, 137; chiaroscuro 127, 253, 314; cloud study 104, 238; colour 38, 39, 45, 48, 50, 74, 75, 86, 87, 88, 128, 171, 186, 189, 190, 194, 199–200, 218, 219, 245, 249–52, 255, 259, 275, 288–90, 295, 301, 302, 315, 322, 329, 344–5, 352, 352, 355, 386, 390; use of coloured paper or paper stained with dark washes 40; dramatic compositions 75, 98; figure-drawing criticised 201–204; finishing skills judged 106–7; uses gouache 40; impasto 301; indistinctness becomes his forte 194, 278; and Italy's impact 252; lack of longevity of his paintings 301–2; layers of wash 40; light 39, 40, 171, 252, 295; light and shade 127, 201, 250; line 171, 186; makes drawing after drawing before painting xv; palettes 87–8, 303, 372, 412; use of pasted cut-out figures 33, 264, 297; preoccupation with fire 334–6; preserves areas of

white 33–4, 40; reflections and refraction 102, 147, 149, 179, 253; secretive about his work 33, 66, 170, 209, 232, 316; shadows 37, 40, 149, 417; short-cuts 40; swirling effect 209, 223; vortex effect 209, 280; watercolour methods 171–2; white grounds 198, 199
drawings and sketchbooks: 'Actually Last Sketchbook' (c. 1847) 390; Attalus declaring the Greek States to be free 220; boat sketching 93–8, 149, 176, 183–4, 280; Brighton sketchbook (1796) 40; 'Brown Eyes' 320; 'Chemistry & Apuleia' sketchbook 200, 235; 'Cockermouth' sketchbook 109, 161; 'Colour Studies' 284–5; 'Death of Achelous' 92; 'Death of Liseus' 92; 'Death of Nessus' 92; 'Derbyshire' sketchbook 162; 'Devon Rivers' sketchbooks 176; 'Dogs and Cats' 324; 'Dolbadarn' sketchbook 63; 'Eneas and Evander' 91; 'Farnley' sketchbook 217; 'Finance' sketchbook 162; 'Frittlewell' sketchbook 158; 'Girl breaking off sticks and putting them on the grate' 104; 'Girl filling the tin kettle out of a large brown jug' 104; 'Hastings' sketchbook 119, 159, 353; 'Hastings to Margate' sketchbook 202; 'Ideas of Folkestone' sketchbook 391; 'Lowther' sketchbook 202; 'Marford Mill' sketchbook (1794) 37; Neptune's Trident 132; The North-West View of Friar Bacon's Study and Folly Bridge, Oxford 17, 27; organises his sketchbooks 240; 'Oxford' sketchbook 27; 'Perspective sketchbook 149, 157; printmaking sketches 123; Ruskin culls sketchbooks after T's death 408; 'St Gothard and Mont Blanc' sketchbook 65; sketches of Petworth 318–20; 'Smaller South Wales' sketchbook (1795) 37; 'South Wales' sketchbook (1795) 30; Spilt milk 319; 'Spithead' sketchbook 403; 'Studies

for Pictures, Isleworth'
sketchbook 91, 93; 'Studies for
Pictures' sketchbook (1800–
1802) 62; 'Studies in the
Louvre' sketchbook 68, 69;
Sussex sketchbook 57; 'Tabley
Hall' sketchbook 80, 156;
'Tabley no. 3' sketchbook 162;
'Ulysses and Poly' 104; *View
of Nuneham Courtenay from
the Thames* 17, 27; 'Wilson'
sketchbook 40; 'Woodcock
Shooting' sketchbook 233
illustrations: 29; *Aesacus and
Hesperie* 142; *Annual Tours*
327, 410; *Childe Harold's
Pilgrimage* 264; *The
Epicurean* (Moore) 338;
Friendship's Offering 348;
From Spenser's Fairy Queen
389; *The Harbours of England*
(previously *The Ports of
England*) 142; *A History of
Richmondshire* (Whitaker)
174, 211, 220; *Hythe* 137; *Italy*
(Rogers) 113, 317, 348; *Lake
Albano* 253; *Lake of Thun* 126;
*Landscape Illustrations of the
Bible* (Finden brothers) 337;
*Liber Fluvorium or River
Scenery of France* (Ritchie)
327; *Liber Studiorum* 19–20,
121–32, 134, 136, 141, 162, 171,
174, 181, 198, 209, 214, 216,
231, 280, 349, 379, 386, 389,
414; *Life of Napoleon* (Scott)
325; *Light Towers of the Heve*
328; 'Little *Liber*' 125, 127, 142;
Mer de Glace 142; Milton's
Poetical Works 334; *Moonlight
at Sea* 142; *Norham Castle on
the Tweed* 130; *Picturesque
Tour of Italy* (Hakewill) 244;
*Picturesque Views in England
and Wales* (Heath) 134,
135–6, 221, 337, 338; *Pleasures of
Memory* (Rogers) 113; *Poetical
Works* (Scott) 141, 276, 277,
333, 337, 338; *Pope's Villa* 127,
163, 202, 228; *Portsmouth*
142; *Provincial Antiquities
of Scotland* (Scott) 174, 175;
The Rivers of Devon (Cooke;
unpublished) 172; *The Rivers
of England* (Cooke) 135, 175,
326; *Sandbank with Gypsies*
142; *Severn and Wye* 349;
The Shipwreck 121, 129, 130,
131, 191, 217; *The Southern*

Coast (Cooke) 132, 133, 134,
137, 163, 166, 171, 172, 338;
Stonehenge at Daybreak 142;
The Stork and the Aqueduct
214; *Thames Scenery* (Cooke)
227; *Turner's Annual Tour:
Wanderings by the Loire* 327;
*Tyre at Sunset, with the Rape
of Europa* 127; *View of Oxford
from the Abingdon Road* 163;
Wanderings by the Seine 327,
328; *Windsor Castle from
Salt Hill* 216; *Works of Lord
Byron* 263, 338, 338; *The Young
Anglers* 181
paintings and watercolours:
*Admiral van Tromp's Barge at
the Entrance of the Texel, 1645*
275, 336; *Aeneas relating his
Story to Dido* 157, 196, 392;
*Aeneas and the Sibyl, Lake
Avernus* 91; *Ancient
History – Ovid Banished from
Rome* 339; *Angel Standing in
the Sun* 388; *The Angel
Troubling the Pool* 388–9;
Apollo and Python 387; *Apullia
in Search of Appullus vide
Ovid* 191, 197, 313; *The Army of
the Medes destroyed in the
Desart by a Whirlwind* 61, 70;
*The Battle of Fort Rock, Val
d'ouste, Piedmont, 1796* 70, 81;
Battle of Trafalgar (1823–4)
169, 175, 238, 331, 345; *Bay of
Baiae, with Apollo and the
Sibyl* 249, 252, 336, 401, 410;
*Between Quilleboeuf and
Villequier* 327; *Boats Carrying
Out Anchors and Cables to
Dutch Men of War, in 1665* 76,
203; *Boccaccio relating the Tale
of the Birdcage* 184; *Bonneville*
330; *Bridge of Sighs, Canaletti
Painting* 337, 338; *Brighton
from the Sea* 316; *The Brunig
Pass* 385; *Burning Fiery
Furnace* 334; *Burning of the
Houses of Parliament* paintings
289–90, 302, 334–6;
Caernarvon Castle 49; *Calais
Pier, with French Poissards
preparing for Sea, an English
Packet arriving* 65, 74, 75, 190;
*Calais Sands, Low Water,
Poissards collecting Bait* 280;
Caligula's Bridge 134; *Caligula's
Palace* 300; *Carthage*
paintings 156, 197, 199, 262,

383, 402, 410; *The Cathedral
Church at Lincoln* 40; *Cicero at
his Villa* 339; *Cologne, the
Arrival of a Packet Boat,
Evening* 250, 298, 324, 325;
The Colosseum 253; *Confluence
of the Thames and Medway*
101; *A Cottage destroyed by an
Avalanche* 84; *The Country
Blacksmith* 202; *A Country
Blacksmith disputing upon the
Price of Iron ...* 196; *Crossing
the Brook* 80, 172–4, 188, 189,
191, 336, 380; *The Death of
Nelson* (later *The Battle of
Trafalgar, as seen from the
Mizen Starboard Shrouds of
the Victory*) 84, 100, 201, 238;
Death on a Pale Horse 261; *The
Decline of the Carthaginian
Empire ...* 194–5, 377; *The
Departure of the Fleet* 392;
Descent of the St.Gothard 385;
Diana and Callisto 91, 244;
Dido and Aeneas 59, 191, 197;
Dido building Carthage 140,
188, 189, 191, 194, 195, 200, 201,
203, 283, 336, 407; *Dido
directing the equipment of the
Fleet, or The Morning of the
Carthaginian Empire* 184;
Dinner in a Great Room 314;
Dolbadern Castle 49–50, 60;
*Dort, or Dordrecht, the Dort
Packet Boat from Rotterdam
Becalmed* 218, 249, 298, 325;
*Ducal Palace, Dogano, with
part of San Giorgio,Venice* 273;
Dudley 247; *Dutch Boats in a
Gale: fishermen endeavouring
to put their fish on board* 61, 62,
98, 110, 189; *Ehrenbreitstein*
181; *England: Richmond Hill,
on the Prince Regent's Birthday*
236, 288; *Entrance of the
Meuse: Orange-Merchant on
the Bar going to Pieces; Brill
Church bearing S.E. by S.,
Masensluys E. by S.* 164, 237,
288; *The Evening Star* 281;
*The Festival upon the Opening
of the Vintage at Mâcon* 69,
106; *Field of Waterloo* 247; *The
Fifth Plague of Egypt* 60;
*Fighting Temeraire tugged to
her last berth to be broken up,
1838* 278, 344–7, 365, 371, 377,
380, 410; *Figures in a Building*
315; *Fire at Fenning's Wharf*

334; *Fire at Sea* 334; *The First Rate taking in Stores* 210, 223, 262; *Fishermen at Sea* 39, 182; *Fishermen coming ashore at Sunset previous to a Gale* 45; *Fishermen upon a Lee-Shore, in Squally Weather* 62; *Fishing upon the Blythe Sand, Tide setting in* 84, 98, 188, 190–91, 410; *Forum Romanum, for Mr. Soane's Museum* 249–50; *Fountain of Fallacy* 337; *The Fountain of Indolence* 181; *Frosty Morning* 173–4, 186–7, 191, 232, 410; *Funeral of Sir Thomas Lawrence, a sketch from memory* 263; *The Garreteer's Petition* 84; *The Goddess of Discord choosing the Apple of Contention in the Garden of the Hespericks* 92; *The Golden Bough* 156, 264, 297, 338; *Grouse-Shooting, Beamsley Beacon* 213; *Harbour of Dieppe (Changement de Domicile)* 324–5; *Harvest Dinner, Kingston Bank* 85; *Helvoetsluys; – the City of Utrecht*, 64, *going to Sea* 275, 296–7, 336; *The Hero of a Hundred Fights* 292, 385; *The Holy Family* 68–9, 203; *Hulks on the Tamar: Twilight* 172; *Interior at Petworth* 322; *The Interior of St Peter's* 253; *Jason* 91; *Jessica* 203, 314–15; *Juliet and her Nurse* (later *St Mark's Place, Venice (Moonlight)*) 266–7, 336, 337, 349; *Keelmen Heaving in Coals by Night* 338; *Kirkstall Abbey* 210; *Lake of Geneva from Montreux* 217; *Life-Boat and Manby Apparatus going off to a Stranded Vessel making Signal (blue lights) of Distress* 164, 276; *Light and Colour (Goethe's Theory) – The Morning after the Deluge -Moses writing the Book of Genesis* 364; *Lightermen heaving in Coals* 111; *Line-Fishing off Hastings* 338; *Llanthony Abbey* 417; *London from Greenwich, Kingston Bank* 84, 191, 205, 217, 410; *Looking east from the Giudecca, sunrise* 265; *Masaniello and the Fisherman's Ring* 295–6; *Mercury and*

Herse 107, 166; *Mercury sent to admonish Aeneas* 392; *Moonlight – a study at Millbank* 39; *Mortlake Terrace, the Seat of William Moffat, Esq. Summer's Evening* 251, 265, 297; *The Music Party* 184, 314; *Narcissus and Echo* 91, 95; *Neapolitan Fisher Girls* 338; *Near Northcourt in the Isle of Wight* 184; *Near the Thames Lock, Windsor* 201; *The New Moon: or, 'I've Lost My Boat, You shan't have Your Hoop'* 280; *Norham Castle, Sunrise* 386; *Norham Castle on the Tweed* 211; *Northampton* 221; *November: Flounder Fishing* 95; *'Now for the Painter', (Rope). Passengers going on Board* 295; *The Old Pier, Margate* 275; *The Opening of the Wallhalla* 302, 380, 385; *Ostend* 365; *Oxford pictures* 295; *Palestrina – Composition* 256, 263, 314, 336, 359; *Peace: Burial at Sea* 356; *Petworth from the Lake, Dewy Morning* 199; *Pilate Washing his Hands* 314; *Polyphemus* 410; *Pope's Villa During Its Delapidation* 227; *Port Ruysdael* paintings 276, 365; *The Prince of Orange, William III, embarked from Holland, and landed at Torbay, November 4th, 1688* 275; *Rain, Steam, and Speed – the Great Western Railway* 293–4, 365–6; *Regulus* 255, 256, 302–3, 387; *Rembrandt's Daughter* 298, 301, 314; *The Rise of Carthage* 83, 377, 380; *Rome from the Vatican …* 248; *Rosehill Park, Sussex* 110; *The Rotterdam Ferry Boat* 275, 336; *Saint Benedetto* 350; *St Erasmus and Bishop Islip's Chapels* 210; *St Michael's Mount* 338; *Satan Summoning his Legions* 334; *Schaffhausen* 195; *Schloss Rosenau, Seat of H. R. H. Prince Albert of Coburg* 351; *Shade and Darkness – The Evening of the Deluge* 364; *Sheerness and the Isle of Sheppey* 98; *Sheerness as seen from the Nore* 95; *Ships bearing up for Anchorage (the Egremont Seapiece)* 62, 95, 312;

The Shipwreck 78, 96, 107, 121; *Shoeburyness Fishermen* 217; *Shooting Party on the Moors* 213; *Slavers throwing overboard the Dead and Dying – Typhon coming on* 156, 182, 362–3; *Snow Storm: Hannibal and his Army crossing the Alps* 70, 154, 191, 209, 249, 299, 380; *Snow Storm – Steam-Boat off a Harbour's Mouth …* 278–80, 366, 410; *Snow Storm, Avalanche, and Inundation* 352; *Spithead* 124; *Staffa, Fingal's Cave* 277–8, 327, 336, 347; *Study of Sea and Sky, Isle of Wight* 185; *Sun rising through Vapour* 191, 283, 383, 407; *The Sun of Venice going to Sea (Sol di Venezia)* 350–51; *Sunrise with Sea Monsters* 182; *Tabley House and Lake – Calm Morning* 312; *Temple of Jupiter Restored* 140; *The Tenth Plague of Egypt* 60, 84; *The Thames at Weybridge* 209; *Thomson's Aeolian Harp* 154; *Tivoli – Temple of the Sibyl and the Roman Campagna* 91; *Tivoli and the Roman Campagna, after Wilson* 244; *The Tower of London* 326; *Trout Fishing in the Dee* 181; *Ulysses deriding Polyphemus* 259–60, 318, 336; *Van Goyen, looking out for a Subject* 275; *Van Tromp, going about to please his masters, ships a sea, getting a good wetting* 164, 275; *Van Tromp returning after the Battle of the Dogger Bank* 275; *Van Tromp's Shallop, at the Entrance of the Scheidt* 275; *Venice* 111, 338; *Venice: A Storm on the Lagoon* 265; *Venice, from the Canale della Guidecca* 338; *Venus and Adonis* 330; *Vesuvius Angry* 348; *The Victory returning from Trafalgar* 100–101; *View from the Terrace of a Villa at Niton, Isle of Wight, from Sketches by a Lady* 184; *View of Orvieto* 255, 263; *The Vision of Medea* 255, 256; *The Visit to the Tomb* 392; *War. The Exile and the Rock Limpet* 70, 364; *Watteau study by Fresnoy's rules* 316; *Whalers* pictures 359, 362; *What You Will!* 203; *The Wreck*

Buoy 385; *Wycliffe, near Rokeby* 220

writings: xvii, 49, 58, 92–3, 101, 109, 153–9, 160–64, 179, 213, 266, 389; *Argo* poem 95, 97; *British Itinerary* poem (1811) 155–6, 222; 'Dear Molly' 155, 159; 'Fallacies of Hope' 154, 156, 264, 351, 362, 364, 392; 'Ode to Discord' 155; 'On Thomson's Tomb' 155; writes poetry for Sophia Booth 271, 411

Turner, John (T's uncle) 3, 57

Turner, Jonathan (T's uncle) 3, 59, 234

Turner, Joshua (T's uncle) 52, 234

Turner, Mary (*née* Marshall; T's mother) 7, 44, 59, 120, 224, 241, 362; appearance 8; in Bethlehem Hospital 51–4, 63, 75, 340, 383; death (1804) 54, 75, 77, 340; marries William 2, 261; mental health 8, 11, 14, 35, 85, 161, 235; sets up home in Maiden Lane 3, 32; tablet in St Paul's, Covent Garden 112, 281

Turner, Mary (T's aunt) 59

Turner, Mary Ann (Ts sister) xvii, 8, 11, 54

Turner, Mrs (T's paternal grandmother) 57, 59, 112

Turner, Price (T's uncle) 57, 171, 234

Turner, Thomas Price (T's cousin) 171

Turner, William (T's father) 18, 44, 57, 96, 246, 254, 312; appearance 3, 233; attends several of T's lectures 148; as a barber 3–9, 15–16, 20, 35, 53, 58–9, 224, 234; collects Sarah Danby's widow's allowance 119, 120; and *Cologne* 298; complains about T working for Monro 34; death (1829) 260–63, 281, 341; Devon origins 2–3, 226; encourages T 15–16, 59, 224; health 235, 254; his estate 261; his mother's will 57, 59; Linnell draws 148, 237; loquacity 161, 233; marries Mary Marshall 2, 261; and Mary's admission to Bethlehem Hospital 51–4; and nephew Thomas 171; and Sandycombe Lodge 224, 226, 228, 229, 232–3, 235, 243; sets

up home in Maiden Lane 3, 31; starts to live with T 59; on T 85; tablet in St Paul's, Covent Garden 112, 281; thrifty nature 8, 108, 233; and T's Isle of Wight visit 183

Turner Bequest 283, 376, 408–9

Turner family xvii, 3, 21, 59, 171, 420

Turner in his Time (Wilton) xix

Turner Prize 418

Turner Society News (periodical) xvi

Turner in the South (Powell) xv

Turner on the Thames (Hill) xv

Turner Studies (periodical) xvi

Turner the Painter: His Hidden Life (Falk) xvii

Turner's Gift 262, 282, 283, 340, 342–3, 376, 377, 404, 405, 406, 416

Twain, Mark 352

Tweed, River 48, 94, 210, 326, 386

Twelfth Night (Shakespeare) 203, 251

Twickenham, Middlesex 79, 187, 230, 233, 236, 242, 248, 325, 376, 405; Louis-Philippe in exile 70; T acquires more land 239; T sells some land to a railway company 240; T's house in *see* Sandycombe Lodge; and T's will 2 61

Twickenham Little Common 239, 242

Tyburn Lane, London 13–14

Tyne, River 326

Tyrol 351

Upper Harley Street, London 216, 223

Upper John Street (No.46), London 56, 57

Uwins, Thomas, RA 188, 217, 256, 257, 407

Van Dyck, Sir Anthony 309, 312

Vanbrugh, Sir John 20

Varley, Cornelius 33

Varley, John 107, 126, 206, 218

Vauxhall 10

Vega Carpio, Lope Felix de 158

Velde, Willem van de, the younger 31, 61, 276

Venetian Academy of Painting, Rome 246

Venice 84, 111, 245, 253, 265–7, 273, 276, 317, 330, 332–4, 343, 350, 351, 359, 364

Vere (engraver) 123

Vernon, Robert 264, 266, 337, 338, 362

Verona 245

Veronese 246

Vesuvius, Mount 112, 244, 246, 247, 253

Vevey 66

Via Sacra 250

Victoria, Queen 333, 338, 351, 368

Victory, HMS 99, 100–101, 169, 175, 201, 205, 238

Virgil 91–2, 149, 197, 247, 392

Vokins, William 411

Voltaire 6, 295

Voyage of Columbus (Rogers) 388

Voyage sur la Seine, en bateau a vapeur (Morlent) 326

Walcot, near Bath 59

Waldegrave, Lady Maria 307

Wales 27, 29, 30, 47, 48, 49, 61, 94

Walker 30

Waller, John 334

Wallingford, Oxfordshire 97

Walpole, Horace 90, 307

Walton, Henry 6

Walton, Izaak 179, 182, 410

Walton Bridges 102

Wapping 10, 14, 241–2, 313, 329, 355, 362, 408

Ward, James 199

Warren Street, London 126

Warwick Road (No.10), London 120

Watercolour Society 76, 77

Waterloo 174, 324

Waterloo, Battle of 70, 220

Waterloo Bridge 335

Waterloo Place, London 343, 361

Watteau, Antoine 184, 203, 236

Watts, Alaric 18, 111–12, 140, 240, 269, 284, 300, 327, 330

Weir Head 80

Wellington, Duke of 292, 336, 386

Wells, Clara (*later* Wheeler) 17, 51, 54, 86, 107, 115–16, 118, 121, 134, 223, 228–9, 254, 258, 261, 262–3, 265, 282, 353, 360, 361, 377, 406

Wells, Emma 377

Wells, Harriet 262

Wells, Laura 377

Wells, Mrs 51, 54

Wells, William Frederick 17, 50, 76, 206, 234–5, 262, 361; death 282, 377; founds the Watercolour Society 76; and

Liber Studorium 121; lives in Mitcham 79; T's relationship with 51
Wells family 51, 54, 118, 121, 165, 223, 228, 360
Wensleydale, Yorkshire 212
Wentworth, Godfrey 216
Wesley, John 15
West, Benjamin 44, 46, 47, 63, 72, 73, 76, 90, 127, 143, 195, 298
West Country 27, 80, 94, 166–73
West End, Upper Mall, Hammersmith 102–4, 119, 125, 166, 224
Westall, William 200
Western Isles 277
Westmacott, Sir Richard 230, 252, 302, 311, 339, 401
Westminster, London 5, 14, 334
Westminster Abbey 2, 4, 216
Westminster Bridge, London 10, 104, 230, 335
Westminster Hall, London 334, 335
Westminster Sessions 4
Wethered, William 414
Wey, River 96
Whalley parish 47, 211
Wharfe, River 207, 208
Wharfedale, Yorkshire 209, 218, 249
Wheatley, Francis 6
Wheeler, Charles 228
Wheeler, Clare *see* Wells
Wheeler, James 228, 360
Wheeler, Maria 360
Wheeler, Thomas 229, 282, 360
Wheeler family 223
Whitaker, Dr Thomas Dunham 47, 211, 214
White, John 11, 12
White Horse inn, Brentford 11
White Lion inn, Guildford 96
'White Painters' 198, 200, 201
White Peruke lodging house, Maiden Lane 6
Whitehall, London 183
Whitfield's Methodist Chapel, Tottenham Court Road 56
Whitstable, Kent 274
Whittingham, Selby xvi, xviii
Wick House, Richmond Hill 90
Wickham, Miss 184
Widgery, Mary Ann (T's cousin) 85
Wilberforce, William 363
Wilkie, Sir David 68, 263, 311, 339, 355–6, 358; *The Blind Fiddler* 196; *Distraining for*

Rent 188; *Village Politicians* 196
William IV, King *see* Clarence, Duke of
William of Nassau, Prince of Orange (*later* King William III) 221
William Street (No.29), St Pancras 413
Williams, Hugh 138
Williams, John 240
Willmore, J. T. 235
Wilson, Andrew 1
Wilson, Richard 4, 40, 88, 91, 126, 140, 189, 190, 197, 201, 244, 245, 249, 266, 312
Wilton, Andrew xvi, xix
Wilton, Joseph 23, 24, 73
Wilton Place, London 82
Wimereux 367
Wimpole Street, London 410; No.81 51
Winchelsea 56
Windsor, Berkshire 93, 96, 240
Windsor Castle 73, 92, 93, 177
Windus, Benjamin Godfrey 266, 338, 349, 362, 378, 381, 401
Wingrave, Francis Charles 22
Winsor, Mr (paint supplier) 252
Witherington, W. F. 292
Wolcot, Dr John ('Peter Pindar') 167
Wollaton Hall 30
Woodfield (engraver) 123
Woodforde, Reverend James 5
Woodington, W. R. 346
Wooley Park, Yorkshire 216
Woollett, William 140
Woolner, Thomas 400
Wordsworth, Dorothy 192–3
Wordsworth, William 48, 159, 192, 193–4, 203, 315, 333
Works of the British Poets (ed. Anderson) 91
World's End, Chelsea 368, 398
Wornum, Ralph 408
Wotton, Sir Henry 20
Wren, Sir Christopher 340
Wyatt, James (architect) 18, 19, 46
Wyatt, James (Oxford printseller) 78, 107, 163, 288, 299, 333
Wyatt, Matthew Cotes 386
Wyatt, Mrs (Catholic school for girls) 119
Wyattville, Sir J. 177
Wycliffe, John 220
Wycliffe Hall, near Rokeby 220

Wyndham, Charles 307
Wyndham, Colonel 319
Wyndham, Miss (daughter of William Wyndham) 306
Wyndham, William 307
Wynne (at Petworth) 309

Yantlet Spit 98
Yarborough, Earl of 46, 64, 106, 107
Yarmouth 276
'Ye Mariners of England' (Campbell) 345
Yeats, W. B. 155
The Yellow Dwarf (d'Aulnoye) 250
Yonne, valley of the 245
York 210, 368
York Buildings Stairs, London 10
York inn, Margate 269
Yorkshire 47, 137, 176, 186, 199, 205–6, 220, 244, 268
Yorkshire Dales 205, 418
Yorkshire Stingo, Lisson Grove, Marylebone 355
Young, Arthur 319
Young, Benjamin 242
Young, Edward 92, 410

Zong (sailing ship) 363
Zoology of the Voyage of HMS Erebus and Terror (Richardson) 329
Zuccarelli, Francesco 168